W9-CGM-100

# TWENTIETH-CENTURY **type**

# TWENTIETH

**LEWIS BLACKWELL**

---

# CENTURY
# type

RIZZOLI
NEW YORK

First published in the United States of America in 1992 by
Rizzoli International Publications, Inc.
300 Park Avenue South, New York, NY 10010



Library of Congress Cataloging-in-Publication Data

Blackwell, Lewis 1958–
Twentieth-century type / Lewis Blackwell.
p. cm.
Includes bibliographical references and index.
ISBN 0-8478-1596-X
1. Type and type-founding—History—20th century. 2. Printing–History—20th century. I. Title.
Z250.A2B57 1992
686.2′24—dc20 92-7527
CIP

Picture research by Susan Bolsom-Morris
Designed by Mikhail Anikst
Typeset on a Linotronic 300 by
Wyvern Typesetting Limited, Bristol
Printed in Singapore by Toppan

## Acknowledgements

This book is set in Gill Sans, originally designed by Eric Gill in the 1920s for Monotype, and used here in a digital format on the Linotype-Hell Imagesetting system. The text is in Gill Sans Light, 12 on 14 point for the main text and 8½ on 10½ point for the captions; quotations within the text are displayed in Bold Italic.

The acknowledgements for this book are many – not least to the countless designers and their clients, living and dead, who gave birth to the history I have tried to outline. A more particular attribution of credit is due to the following who helped with text and picture research: Neville Brody, London; David Barr of FontWorks, London, and Jurgen Siebert of Fontshop International, Berlin; Rudy VanderLans of Emigre Graphics, Berkeley, California; Annely Juda Fine Art, London; Laurie Burns of the International Typeface Corporation, New York; Ellen Lupton of the Herb Lubalin Archive, New York; Alexander Steiner of DDB Needham Worldwide, New York; Catherine Burer of the Museum für Gestaltung, Zürich; Carol Wahler of the Type Directors Club, New York; David Saunders and René Kerfante at Monotype Typography.

The greatest single debt is to James Mosley and Nigel Roach at the St Bride Printing Library, London, without whose assistance many of the most interesting illustrations in the book would not have been discovered or made available.

I would also like to acknowledge the extensive advice and protracted work of the book's designer, Mikhail Anikst; the editor Jane Havell, the picture researcher Susan Bolsom-Morris and the production consultant Geoff Barlow.

Lewis Blackwell
London 1992

**Introduction**

The guiding ideas behind *Twentieth-Century Type:* the aim, scope and drawbacks of this survey. The "Holy Grail" of type design and other unanswered questions. The shift in typographic emphasis over the century.

**Page 8**

# Contents


## 1890

The development of mechanised typesetting. The growth of demand for print and the implications for type and typography. William Morris and the private press movement. Art Nouveau and the freedom of lithography.

**People**
Beggarstaff Brothers, Linn Boyd Benton, Tolbert Lanston, Ottmar Mergenthaler, William Morris.

**Typefaces**
Akzidenz Grotesk, Cheltenham, Golden, Grasset.

**Page 12**

## 1900

Art and design movements question nineteenth-century values, with new ideas spreading into typography. Art Nouveau and Jugendstil. Arts and Crafts and Wiener Werkstätte.

**People**
Peter Behrens, Morris Fuller Benton, Otto Eckmann, Koloman Moser.

**Typefaces**
Auriol, Doves, Eckmann, Franklin Gothic.

**Page 30**

## 1910

The impact of Cubism and Futurism. Marinetti's "typographic revolution". The Russian Futurists and Suprematists. The beginnings of De Stijl and Dada. Continuing mechanical advances in the speed, size and sophistication of setting possible with hot metal.

**People**
Guillaume Apollinaire, Frederic Goudy, Edward Johnston, Rudolf Koch, F. T. Marinetti, Bruce Rogers.

**Typefaces**
Centaur, Imprint, Johnston Railway Type, Kennerley, revivals.

**Page 42**

## 1920

Modernism and Revivalism both forge ahead. The importance of typographic study at the Bauhaus, explored as abstraction, implementation and constituent of art and architectural thought. The quest for simpler, purer type and layout through reductive geometrics. The beginnings of the grid. Asymmetry, sans serif and Tschichold's "new typography" commandments. In contrast, the principles laid down by Morison and others connected with *The Fleuron*. The advance of revival designs. Art Deco and the French poster artists.

**People**
Herbert Bayer, Eric Gill, El Lissitsky, Lászlo Moholy-Nagy, Stanley Morison, Aleksandr Rodchenko, Kurt Schwitters, Jan Tschichold, Hendrik Werkman, Piet Zwart.

**Typefaces**
Baskerville, Bembo, Bifur, Broadway, Cable, Gill, Futura.

**Page 62**

# 1930

Doubt and the new typography. The impact of the Great Depression in the United States and growing political repression in Europe on the climate for new ideas in art and design. Commerce, compromise and emigration for the apostles of Modernism. Keller, Williman, Ballmer, Bill and the origins of Swiss Style. Surrealism and the typographic pun. Early attempts at photosetting.

**People**
Theo Ballmer, Max Bill, Alexey Brodovitch, A. M. Cassandre, Herbert Matter, Albert Tolmer.

**Typefaces**
Beton, Peignot, Times New Roman.

**Page 98**

# 1940

War breaks the advance of ideas in Europe, cuts off investment and materials for new typefaces, but gives impetus to the adoption of exiled Modernists in the United States. War poster work draws together the disparate directions of twentieth-century graphics. Paul Rand indicates a direction for the look of post-war advertising. Tschichold's apostasy as he rejects the New Typography and embraces classicism.

**People**
Paul Rand, Bradbury Thompson, Jan Tschichold.

**Page 122**

# 1950

The revolutionary principles of the 1920s typographers and artists are now part of the establishment and, embodied in Swiss Style, are propagated as a comprehensive and reductive solution. Meanwhile, Tschichold and others build the case for a new classicism, and commercial growth demands new choices in display typography. Corporate design programmes become more sophisticated and stimulate typographic thought. Investment in type technology lifts off and the first commercially viable photosetting systems are launched. Television graphics begin to take their own form.

**People**
Roger Excoffon, Adrian Frutiger, Josef Müller-Brockmann, Hermann Zapf.

**Typefaces**
Banco, Helvetica, Optima, Palatino, Univers.

**Page 132**

# 1960

The arrival of "cold type", transfer lettering, more media and the attack on professionalism and traditional craft. The golden age of American advertising and the typographic pun: the spread of American "conceptual" graphics into Europe. Pop Art, psychedelia and communication design. Readability becomes more complex.

**People**
Willi Fleckhaus, Adrian Frutiger, Herb Lubalin, Victor Moscoso.

**Typefaces**
Antique Olive, Eurostile, OCR-A, Sabon.

**Page 152**

# 1970

The decline of metal setting and concern at lowering of standards. The proliferation of typographic routes, as electronic setting begins to appear. The explosion of information leads to a wide range of attempts to improve communication across different media: typography is now being clearly seen as a discipline that extends beyond print into television and other graphic communication, such as pictograms. International Typeface Corporation puts down a marker for the type designer's rights. Wolfgang Weingart and the New Wave provide a new perspective on the conventions of readability, as does Punk.

**People**
Otl Aicher, Herb Lubalin, Wolfgang Weingart.

**Typefaces**
American Typewriter, Bell Centennial, Frutiger, Galliard.

**Page 170**

# 1980

Digital typesetting takes over and with it come new powers in type design and manufacturing. The significance of PostScript as a language that unites different systems. Low-cost computer technology takes control out of the hands of the specialist typesetter. From Matthew Carter and the rapid growth of the Bitstream library, to the "school" of self-conscious typography projected by (among others) Neville Brody in London, Rudy VanderLans and Zuzana Licko in California, Tibor Kalman in New York. A rich vein of nostalgia is present in a wide range of commercial work, taken to sophisticated heights in *Rolling Stone*, while minimalism is refined by a few, such as Peter Saville.

**People**
Neville Brody, Matthew Carter, Gert Dumbar, Zuzana Licko, Katherine McCoy, Peter Saville, Rudy VanderLans.

**Page 186**

# 1990

The ever-changing conception of type – from cold metal to hot metal to film to digital information and several thousand faces on a compact disc. The demand for old standards in the new technology while the potential of digital information opens up new possibilities. Type design becomes a cottage industry. Questioning and experimentation continue around the concept of readability. The potential shift of typography from a specialist craft to a common area of knowledge embraced as part of computer literacy.

**People and typefaces**
All those previous, some present, many future . . .

**Page 212**

Analysis of characters and measurements
**Page 230**

Type description and classification
**Page 232**

Glossary
**Page 248**

Notes
**Page 250**

Further reading
**Page 251**

Picture credits
**Page 252**

Index
**Page 254**

# Introduction

The dramatic changes currently taking place in the way text is generated and designed, and the impact this has upon the opportunities for communication, make this an apposite time to endeavour to give some order to the quantity of data involved in considering the development of typography. Although there are many volumes available concerning methods of working with type, or giving the background to a particular facet of type history, and many more on related histories in art, design, technology and other studies that all affect type, there is a dearth of material that assembles all the information in an approachable way. This is an attempt to do just that, concentrating on the past century's revolution in typographic form.

But a warning note: type, for all its apparent physicality, is a very elusive subject when it comes to being specific. Consider how many thousands upon thousands of faces there are, some with scarcely any perceptible differences at first or even second look. Then take account of the many different cuts from different manufacturers there may be of supposedly the same face, which nevertheless often look remarkably unalike. Imagine the effect of different weights and sizes, spaces and leading on the visual appearance of that face. Explore the typographic context – the layout that the type appears within. And finally, notice that the method used for printing can alter the effect. All this makes for an infinity of variables floating around a craft that is associated with precision and detail. And for all such unavoidable variety, the quest continues for adding new faces and theories to the roll of typographic honour, all in pursuit of ideas about improving on the forms already available.

Our story in *Twentieth-Century Type* starts just before the century began. In a number of ways, the most significant changes for more than 400 years took place in the last decade or so of the nineteenth century. A discussion of the consequent innovations, both technical and creative, supported by many illustrated examples of typefaces, constitutes that story. To pare the subject of typography down to manageable proportions the method of analysis has been to cover the principal movements, people and creative work – judging these largely on their influence on others and popularity. This does not mean that only overnight successes get recognition; in some cases the best part of a century may have passed before fuller recognition is afforded a face or a movement. By concentrating on the roots and branches of the modern typographic story in the main text, and presenting some flowers in the extensive illustrations, the basis is laid for further research of particular areas.

Attention has necessarily been restricted to the typeforms that have emerged in relation to the European languages: the Latin forms. Others, such as those connected with the Cyrillic, Arabic and Kanji alphabets, are of course no less important, but before entering upon comparative commentaries it is necessary to have some depth of understanding of a subject, and in this case our focus must be on the development of the Latin face, with regard principally to work in Europe and the United States, though also referring occasionally to other cultures.

Type is not designed to exist alone. It has an essential relationship with the other elements on a page or a poster or on the screen, formally and in its colour. For this reason, as many works as possible are printed here in their original form. It is a serious error to see type as something inherently monochromatic.

While typography at its broadest embraces everything from art to architecture in its influences and impact, and its scientific learning and borrowings pull together psychology, material science and electronics and much more besides, the space of this volume inevitably limits the field of exploration to the development of the printed, and latterly, projected alphabet. Typography is the design and production of printed matter, whereas type design is the creation of a printed character or set of characters, or imitations of them, as in computer representation. This book is concerned with both: they are inseparable in any discussion of the significance of either. Nor is this a do-it-yourself manual. Instead the aim is to explore the key issues that lie behind the explosion of typeforms and expressions in the past century. And it is quite a neat and logical period: it was only in 1886 that the first successful mechanical setter for movable type was developed, beginning by far the most dramatic change in the manner of creating the printed word since Gutenberg was credited with creating movable type around 1440. For 450 years hand-setting prevailed. Even the coming of the mechanical press in the early nineteenth century could only multiply the numbers of such work printed – it could not change the nature of the means of production of all printed communication: its dependence on the speed of a man's hand in and out of a tray of characters of type. Mechanised setting broke radically with this tradition; it also symbolised the introduction of printed communication into the mainstream of the industrial age.

As the story of modern typography unfolds, certain regular themes become apparent: key issues and seminal figures, whose presence provokes major questions. Why are there so many typefaces? Is there really an infinite number of forms? Is there a Holy Grail for type design? A one-type-fits-all? Many notable designers have made their contribution to that pursuit. Does the move from paper to screen graphics as the primary source of information in society demand radically different type designs? Is legibility – the distinction of design between letterforms in a particular font – the key judge to the quality of a typeface? Is there more to "readability" than the ease with which type can be read? How far can one go in the expressive, *art* statement of type and typography? These questions, and many more, will be treated in the course of the book, in such a way that the reader may come to a conclusion as well.

A few comments here are necessary on the problems of describing and classifying type. There are several current forms of description of typefaces, based around the historical associations and/or the visual connections between designs, and they have points in common. But to use such classifications presupposes some advanced typographic knowledge on the part of the reader, which is not assumed here. Instead, the connections will be explained in the course of the text, referring in part to the kind of groupings being developed among typefaces. Pages 230–45 illustrate the different groupings of type, based on the most widely accepted scheme, that set out by the French typographer Maximilien Vox in the 1950s and adopted or adapted by many bodies. Intended simply to show the kind of groupings that can be formed out of the mass of faces created, it is the beginning of further research for those readers particularly interested in looking at or using a certain kind of type, and it can be used for finding alternative ways around the material in this book if cross-referenced with the index. Typeface classifications are to be viewed with care: while several faces quite clearly fall under one or other category, many also display characteristics that require them to be considered in relation to another grouping as well. Types were never designed to flesh out classification tables, so they should be seen merely as a map grid laid over a terrain in which many other connections and routes are worth plotting.

Because of the vast number of faces, and the many odd avenues of highly specialised, sometimes bizarre oddities, novelty typefaces have been avoided, except as indicators of certain spirits of the time. Attention is devoted to giving a broad picture covering the significant contributors to ideas on typographic communication, as representatives of aesthetic merit, technological change, new ideas from art, or commercial demand. As a result, the range of script faces to be seen in this book is small; likewise other variations on basic text and display faces, such as shadow outlines.

The development of a new face is affected both by its application and by its typographic arrangement. Within this book there is a move from fine printing to printing on an industrial scale, and other forms of mass communication in which fine design has found a place. In line with this is the emergence of the designer/art director as a separate and powerful figure within the typographic domain, sometimes directly feeding ideas back into type design, sometimes creating the demand or conditions for new faces. Innovative art directors in the fields of poster design, brochures, magazines, newspapers, television titles and other areas became increasingly empowered, over the century, to have a direct influence on the type they used (if they had the time, money or inclination to take that control). New print and composition technologies also had a major effect on the creation of new faces. This shifting emphasis in the media that prompted typographic innovation means that some areas of typography are not covered by this book; for example, the fine book printing of today is given sparse attention as this is a small and highly selective, mostly revivalist, market that – unlike the work of William Morris, which could be similarly described – does not promise a wider impact in its ideas. Today the opportunity for a Morris-like revival of standards has to be found in television, not books.

The book is arranged chronologically. The reason behind this approach to history is to avoid over-dramatising the significance of certain themes, and to leave it to the reader to make connections. Of course, there are problems with such a linear approach: the relationship between one designer's examples of work is perhaps more powerful across a career than in one particular place; it may be difficult to assess the significance of something as becoming immediately obvious during the decade it was created; some decades are crammed full of typographic activity, others appear relatively lightweight, and yet they are both given structurally the same emphasis, if not space; and often a movement or the launch of a new face straddles different decades. The subjectivity and the selectivity of the research behind the text may also be masked: instead of treating a subject thematically in the way that the writer may have examined it, it is passed off under a seemingly objective structure that suggests some inevitable flow and connection to the facts relayed.

However, these disadvantages are outweighed by one very positive advantage: presenting the subject under the "time-line" frame locates it within the context of other histories instead of imposing a thematic structure that would distort or even ignore whole areas of discussion. The story of type started before these pages and will continue after, and did not always proceed in an orderly fashion but reflected at times a number of currents in art and related movements. This book can be viewed as presenting many openings to an appreciation of modern typography, suggesting new questions and new ideas as to what lies behind the many faces of twentieth-century type.

# 1890...

## Cheltenham
## Clarendon
## Century

## Akzidenz Grotesk

Incipit carmen secundum ordinem literarum Alphabeti.

This was a decade of different directions. "1890" is set in Antique Number Seven, a new cut of 1899 of a woodtype face first issued in the 1870s in the USA. New technology and increased demand for print required the development of robust, legible faces such as Cheltenham and Century, encouraged the continuing use of Clarendon and spawned new display lineales, such as Akzidenz Grotesk – a face that acquired a symbolic status over the following sixty years. Meanwhile, William Morris, through the Kelmscott Press and such publications as *The Works of Geoffrey Chaucer*, rejected the promise of new technology and sought to restore lost values in print and its typography (left).

Most printed communication during the last hundred years has been produced by machines that owed much to key printing inventions of the late nineteenth century. It is due to the development in the 1880s and 1890s of equipment that could mechanically create and set type, along with the advancement of print technology, that the emergence of the art and craft of typography as something separated from the print shop became possible. Technical advances were crucial in order to cope with the rapid growth in the demand for printed work at the turn of the century. For the consumers of the product, increased breadth of choice was welcome and necessary; the greater pooling of knowledge and stimulation of ideas rapidly became essential. These somewhat arcane industrial developments would in time affect everybody who came in contact with printed materials.

At the heart of this change was a trio of inventions: the pantographic punch-cutter of 1884; the Linotype linecasting machine of 1886; and the Monotype character caster of 1893. For the world of print, this period of technological discovery was the equivalent of certain other key advances of the time – such as Benz's first motor car of the 1880s, the adoption of the electric light bulb, or the experiments of early broadcasting. The advances in printing never attract the same attention as these technological innovations, partly because their impact is not direct, but indirect: the general public experiences the car or the radio, but consumes the product of the printer. Another development of the period, the widespread use of the typewriter in office life, also fails to appeal as a major advance, for the same reason. Indirectly, the sudden advances in typesetting of the 1890s were an indispensable part of the communication revolution that followed in the path of the Industrial Revolution and the political and social reforms of the developed countries. The background to this breakthrough in the generation of type was the arrival of the technological means, coupled with a pressing demand for much greater speed and quantity in creating the printed word for a much larger market than before.

The early and middle nineteenth century had brought substantial change to printing processes with the development and refinement of the lithographic process, and the building first of powered flat-bed presses and then rotary presses. The discovery and development of photography would also in time come to have major implications, as would cinematography – which made the leap from experimentation to early commercial application in the 1890s. All these made an important impact on the potential and the context for reproducing the printed word and image, and helped to serve the demand for dramatically increased amounts of information in line with the growth of literacy and the emergence of a new educated middle class in Europe and the United States.

Yet from the point of view of the creation of type and typography little had changed in the physical process of designing, making and setting type since the invention of movable type by Gutenberg more than 400 years earlier. The production or "composition" of a page of type ready for printing was usually an intensely manually skilled industry, in which each character of type, each space and each piece of leading between lines was taken by hand out of a case of type, placed in the compositor's "stick", and the operation repeated hundreds and possibly many thousands of times until the text was set. Where once this type would have been used to print from, after the lines had been locked up in a steel frame called the "chase", in the nineteenth century printers increasingly used the stereotype plate, which enabled copies of the complete type page to be cast, dramatically increasing the potential for printing large quantities of a publication and reducing the amount of type that needed to be carried.

Not all setting was done by hand, however. Although hand-setting did continue well into the twentieth century (and still survives in a very few printworks), the nineteenth century had seen a number of half-successful forays into mechanising the process. Throughout the 1800s, attempts were made to devise a form of machine composition, which led to many patents being taken out. The main difference between these inventions and the Linotype machine of 1886 was their use of cold-metal setting rather than hot. With the older machines, an operator using a keyboard would assemble already-cast (therefore "cold metal") type into lines, but this type had to be justified manually, involving the spacing of words and characters to make each line start and finish at the same points. And after platemaking, when the complete page was cast to provide the printing surface, the type had to be redistributed by hand for re-use. The improved speed of setting made it desirable for some newspapers and magazines, but there were not the savings nor the improved productivity to make it desirable for most printers. While the machinery did become more sophisticated in the late nineteenth century, with attempts at mechanised re-sorting of type and justification, the process was still deeply flawed in its requirement for a degree of manual work that slowed the whole operation down and increased the costs. There was also understandable opposition from hand-compositors. Furthermore, the machines appear to have been highly unreliable (*The Times* is said to have had a number of discarded models in its cellars in the 1870s). But that there was a pressing demand awaiting satisfaction is evidenced by the decision of New York newspapers to club together and offer a huge cash prize in 1880 for an invention that would substantially cut the composition time.

The breakthrough known as hot-metal setting, using molten metal to cast fresh type from matrices (moulds) stored in the typesetting machine, came in the 1880s. However, it did require another innovation first – a means of generating or "punching" the numerous matrices to cast the type. Conventional punchcutting was a highly skilled job that went hand-in-hand with the design of the type. First, the design of a type character was incised on to metal such as brass or steel. The "punch" thus created would be used as a mould or matrix to receive molten metal, thus creating an individual letterform. To have issued large numbers of typesetting machines relying on such traditional methods

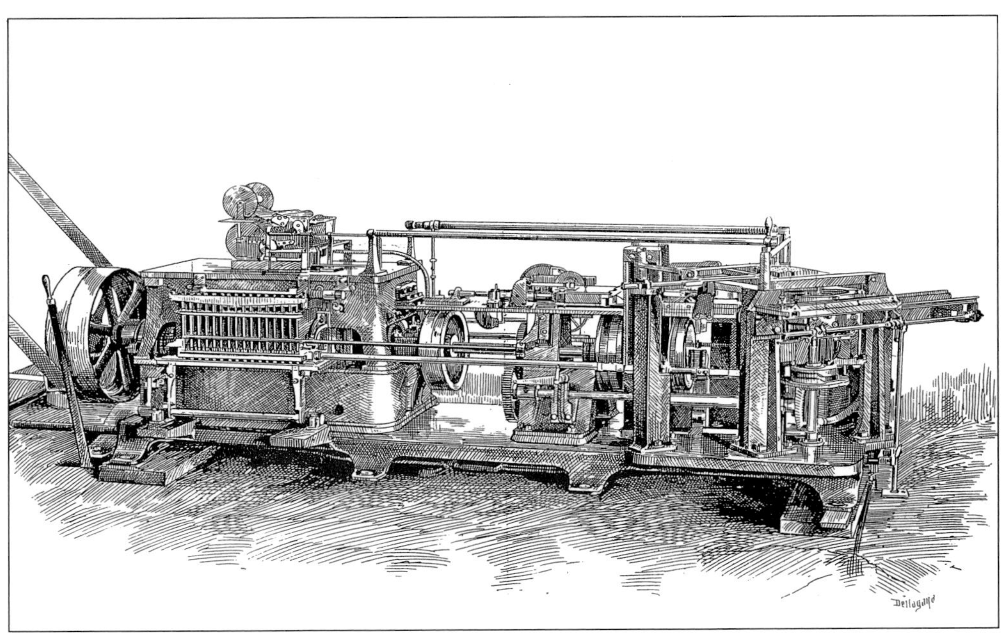



Below: the pantographic punchcutter invented by Linn Boyd Benton in 1884. A pattern plate at the bottom of the machine was traced, and controlled the movement of a tool at the top that engraved the matrix of the letter. Benton's invention changed the processes of type design, mechanising the craft of the punchcutter and effectively ending his role in the creative development of letters.

Below left: the "Lanston" automatic typesetter as illustrated on the front page of *The British & Colonial Printer & Stationer*, 7 January 1892. This was an early version of the Monotype system developed by the American Tolbert Lanston; not until the end of the century was he able to offer a reliable version, which centred on casting and setting individual characters by machine. In effect he was directly automating the hand-setting process, unlike the Linotype which set and cast whole lines ("slugs") of type. Lanston's system required two machines: a keyboard produced a coded, punched tape, which was then

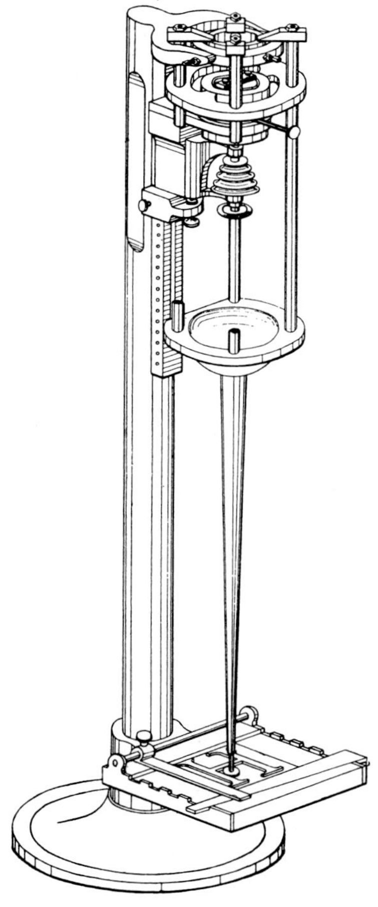

mounted on top of the typesetter (illustrated) and read by having air blown through the holes. The tape was run through the machine backwards, so that the spacing information, keyboarded last, instructed the machine from the outset of setting each line.

Left: the process of setting type changed little from Johannes Gutenberg's invention of printing with movable metal type at Mainz in the mid-fifteenth century until the twentieth century. Despite the invention of machine setters, hand-setting continued to dominate for some years after the 1890s. This view of a composing room at Vacher & Sons, circa 1910, shows how the compositors sat with the upper and lower cases of type before them, from which we derive our terminology for the two forms of the alphabet.

Below: the Linotype composing machine, 1889, and a page from an 1893 manual for the machine explaining the process.

# THE LINOTYPE:

## *ITS CONSTRUCTION AND OPERATION.*

### MECHANICAL DESCRIPTION.

The Linotype machine is not a type-setting machine in the ordinary sense of the word. On the contrary, it is a machine which, being operated by finger-keys like a type-writer, creates, or produces, type matter ready for use on the press or stereotyping table.

The machine shown as Fig. 1 on cover marks a wide departure from the ordinary method of using single letter type. It produces and assembles, side by side, metal bars or slugs, Fig. 2, each of the length and width of a line of type, and having on the upper edge the type characters to print an entire line. These bars, having the appearance of solid lines of type, and answering the same purpose, are called "linotypes." When assembled side by side, as shown in Fig. 3, they constitute jointly a "forme," presenting on its surface the same appearance as a "forme" composed of ordinary type, and adapted to be used in the same manner. After being used, the linotypes are returned to the melting-pot to be recast into other lines, thus doing away entirely with distribution.

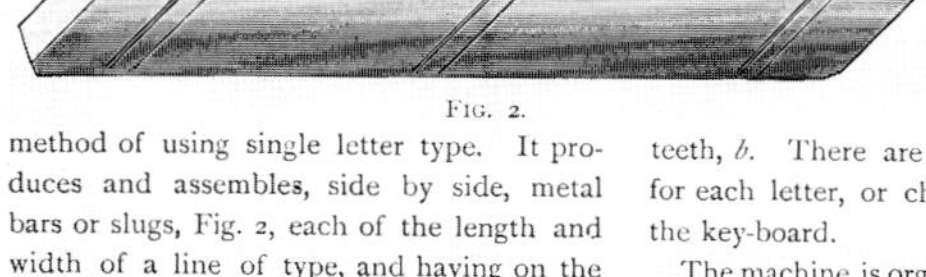

Fig. 2.

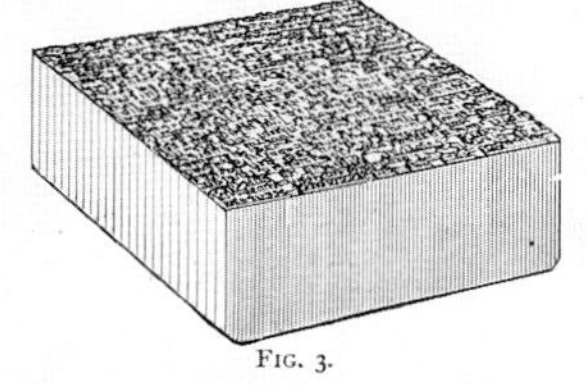

Fig. 3.

The production of linotypes is effected as follows :—

The machine contains, as its leading members, a large number of small brass matrices, such as shown in Fig. 4, consisting each of a flat plate, having in its vertical edge a female letter or matrix proper, *a*, and in the upper end a series of teeth, *b*. There are a number of matrices for each letter, or character, represented on the key-board.

The machine is organised to select matrices bearing the required characters, and set them up in line side by side with intervening spaces, in the order in which they are to appear in print, as shown in Fig. 6, and thereafter to present the line to a mould so that the linotypes or slugs may be cast against and into the entire line of matrices at one operation.

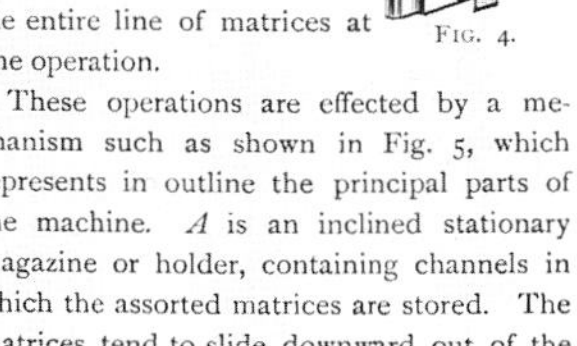

Fig. 4.

These operations are effected by a mechanism such as shown in Fig. 5, which represents in outline the principal parts of the machine. *A* is an inclined stationary magazine or holder, containing channels in which the assorted matrices are stored. The matrices tend to slide downward out of the magazine by reason of their gravity, but they would have called for armies of punchcutters. A means of mechanising the whole process and maintaining standards was bound in with the aim of mechanised typesetting.

Opportunely, these developments came about within a couple of years of each other in the 1880s in the United States. An engineer in Milwaukee called Linn Boyd Benton had been investigating means of cutting master type (not for a typesetting machine, but to assist improvements in the electrotype plate process). In 1884 his improvements on the pantographic wood-letter cutting method produced a machine capable not only of cutting the matrices that he needed but also of cutting steel punches. This advance was picked up by Ottmar Mergenthaler, a German immigrant in Baltimore who had been labouring hard to perfect a mechanised typesetter with a group of associates. He had already lodged a number of less notable patents when he devised his Blower Linotype and demonstrated it at the *New York Tribune* office in July 1886. It was immediately acclaimed, and was soon in use. But it was only after his company acquired Benton's punchcutting method and incorporated it in their machine that the Linotype was able to go into commercial production, large-scale series output beginning in 1890.

The Linotype worked by holding individual matrices for each character, which were released by keyboard strokes. These matrices were assembled together into the lines of type, with spacing wedges between words. When the measure of a line was nearly full the compositor would end a word (if necessary breaking it over to the next line), and press a lever that would push down the spacing wedges, equalling out the inter-word measurements and justifying the line of matrices, which would then be cast in hot metal as a line-length slug of type – hence the name, a contraction of "line of type". This would automatically be trimmed and dropped down into place next to previous lines while the matrices were returned to the storage magazine above the machine by means of a coded key notched into them (compressed air was the power forcing them

Right and far right: examples of the output of the Kelmscott Press. Troy type is shown in use (far right) in *The Tale Of Beowulf*, 1895, translated from Anglo-Saxon by William Morris and A. J. Wyatt, while Golden type (right) is seen in a page from *A note by William Morris on his aims in founding the Kelmscott Press and an annotated list of the books printed thereat by S. C. Cockerell*, 1898. Morris looked to fifteenth-century Venetian printers for the model for Golden, cut in 1890, rejecting the "excessive" thick and thin strokes of modern faces. Troy, 1892, looks to fifteenth-century German printers to create a black-letter that tends towards a roman. Chaucer is a smaller version of Troy.

Below right: pages from a brochure on the Lanston Monotype typesetter, 1903. By this time Lanston, with John Sellers Bancroft, had overcome most of the technical difficulties in the system. The setting up of a European manufacturing base at Salfords, Surrey in 1899 opened up an important market.

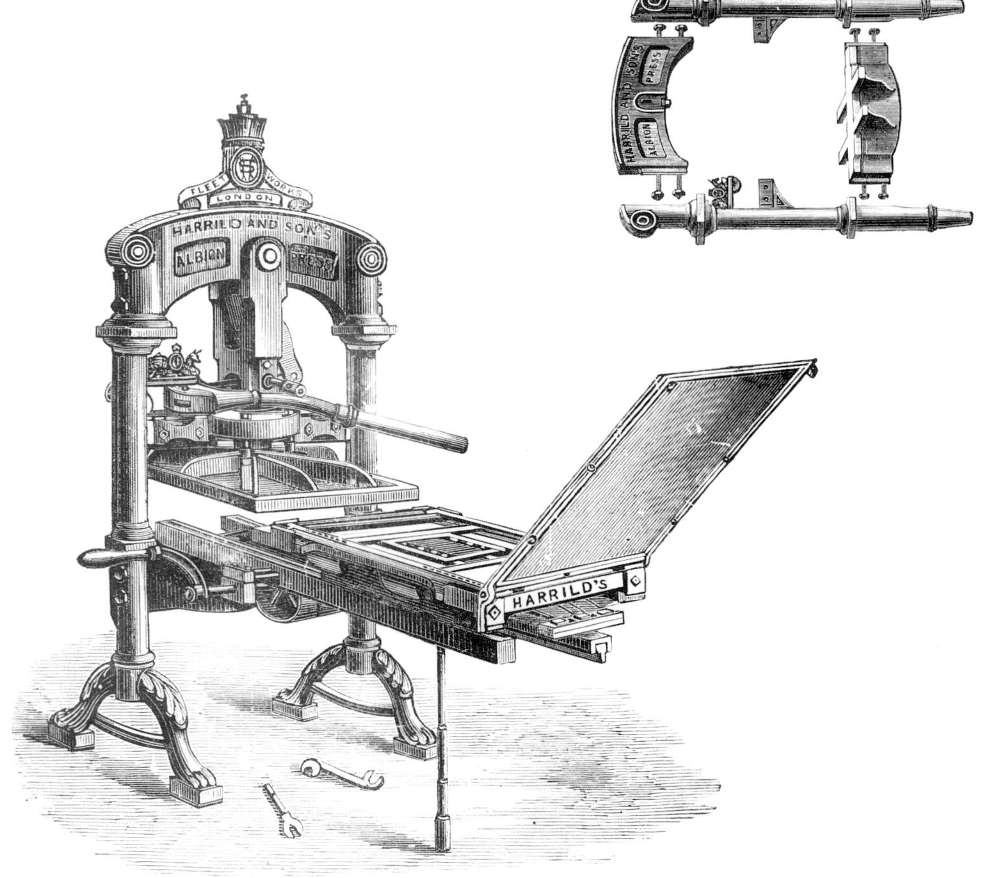


Right: the Portable Overland Albion Press, a version of a popular iron hand-press of the late nineteenth century (the detail shows how this model could be taken apart in manageable pieces for easy transport). The iron hand-press first came into being at the beginning of the nineteenth century; it was superseded both by cylindrical platen presses (the platen being the surface that presses on to the type and enables the paper to take the impression in letterpress printing) and machine presses, but Albions and other hand-presses have continued to be used for some proofing, specialist print and small-run work throughout the twentieth century.

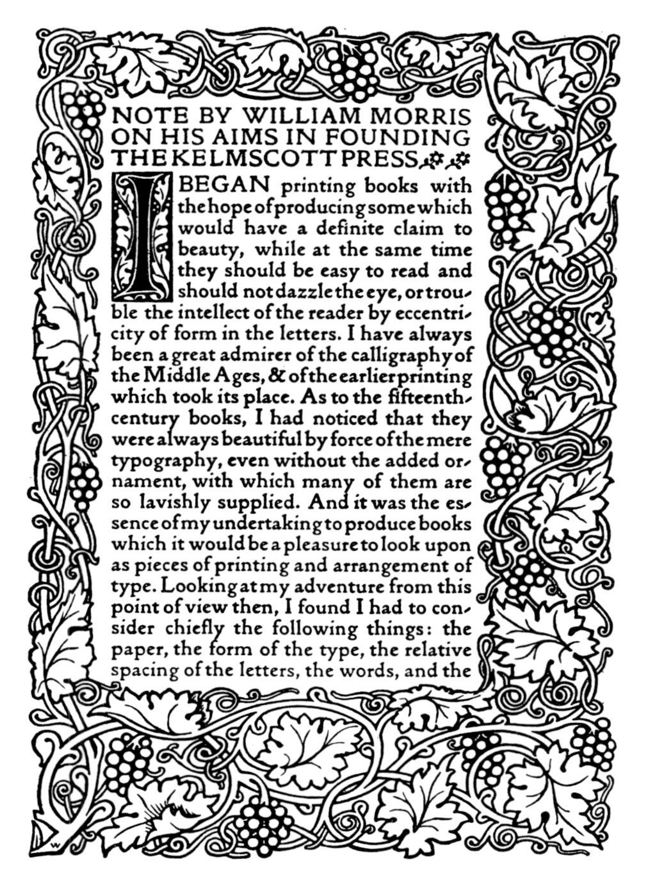

NOTE BY WILLIAM MORRIS ON HIS AIMS IN FOUNDING THE KELMSCOTT PRESS.

I BEGAN printing books with the hope of producing some which would have a definite claim to beauty, while at the same time they should be easy to read and should not dazzle the eye, or trouble the intellect of the reader by eccentricity of form in the letters. I have always been a great admirer of the calligraphy of the Middle Ages, & of the earlier printing which took its place. As to the fifteenth-century books, I had noticed that they were always beautiful by force of the mere typography, even without the added ornament, with which many of them are so lavishly supplied. And it was the essence of my undertaking to produce books which it would be a pleasure to look upon as pieces of printing and arrangement of type. Looking at my adventure from this point of view then, I found I had to consider chiefly the following things: the paper, the form of the type, the relative spacing of the letters, the words, and the

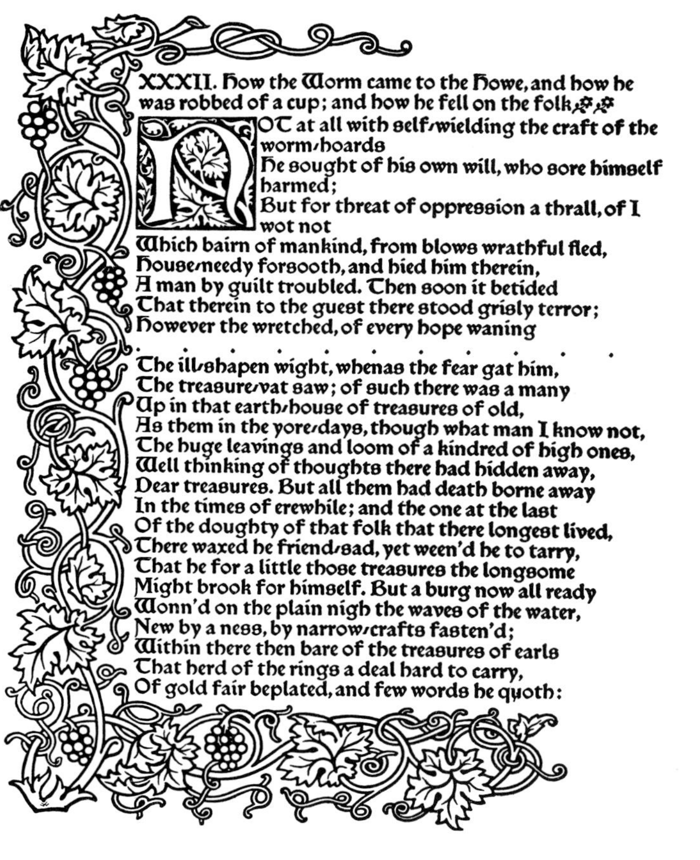

XXXII. How the Worm came to the Howe, and how he was robbed of a cup; and how he fell on the folk.

NOT at all with self-wielding the craft of the worm-hoards
He sought of his own will, who sore himself harmed;
But for threat of oppression a thrall, of I wot not
Which bairn of mankind, from blows wrathful fled,
House-needy forsooth, and hied him therein,
A man by guilt troubled. Then soon it betided
That therein to the guest there stood grisly terror;
However the wretched, of every hope waning
. . . . . . . . . . . . .
The ill-shapen wight, whenas the fear gat him,
The treasure-vat saw; of such there was a many
Up in that earth-house of treasures of old,
As them in the yore-days, though what man I know not,
The huge leavings and loom of a kindred of high ones,
Well thinking of thoughts there had hidden away,
Dear treasures. But all them had death borne away
In the times of erewhile; and the one at the last
Of the doughty of that folk that there longest lived,
There waxed he friend-sad, yet ween'd he to tarry,
That he for a little those treasures the longsome
Might brook for himself. But a burg now all ready
Wonn'd on the plain nigh the waves of the water,
New by a ness, by narrow-crafts fasten'd;
Within there then bare of the treasures of earls
That herd of the rings a deal hard to carry,
Of gold fair beplated, and few words he quoth:

4

THE MONOTYPE.

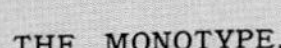

THE MONOTYPE is the only book and job type-making and composing machine upon the market. Working automatically, it casts and finishes foundry type, sets, justifies, and delivers it on the galley ready for proving.

Its speed is as great as that of any other machine, whilst its range is phenomenal; it passes with ease from straight composition, which it sets as cheaply as any other machine, to tabular and other intricate work—work of a class which *no other machine can pretend to do.*

It carries at one time 220 characters, comprising, in the case of a jobbing board :—

Upper and Lower Roman.

Sanserif caps.

Upper and lower Clarendon, or other jobbing face.

Two sets of figures.

Three sets of punctuation marks, and a selection of sorts, including accents, diphthongs, ligature letters, reference signs, etc., etc.

The price of a complete Monotype single equipment is £600, free on rail, London. It includes the keyboard, casting machine, air compressor, and two founts, to be selected by the buyer from an ever increasing list, the bodies being of any two sizes, from Pearl to Pica.

5

The Lanston Monotype Corporation, Ltd., will supply a competent instructor to superintend installation of plants in the United Kingdom and to instruct printers' operators in the use of the machine—the purchaser being only called upon to pay the railway fares and 30s. per week for the instructor's boarding expenses.

Extra founts, complete, in any body size from Pearl to Pica (220 characters) .. £32 10s.

Extra faces and accessories, without mould (where the mould necessary for casting the required body size is already in the printer's possession) .. .. £12 10s.

Jobbing sets of matrices (generally comprising upper and lower case and figures, say 81 matrices) .. .. .. 1s. each.

Three-step cone pulleys, one attachable to the casting machine and one to be fitted to the printer's countershaft to run at 300 revolutions per minute, will be furnished if required at .. £4 the set—fitted.

THE MONOTYPE CASTER.

through these movements, hence the term "blower"). The compositor would already be setting the next line.

The Linotype machine was capable of doing the work of seven or eight hand-compositors. Its take-up was swift: by the time Mergenthaler died in 1899 his machine had revolutionised the production and cost structure of many printers, particularly on newspapers. While the main business was in the US, the machines were also soon being built under licence in Britain and Germany. By the turn of the century 6,000 of the machines were in use, establishing a basic technology for much print production that did not start to change until the 1960s.

But the Linotype was not the only hot-metal machine to be launched during this period, nor was it the automatic choice or a necessity for all printers. Machines involving precast type continued to be developed. In Europe, particularly, the results from the Linotype were found unsatisfactory for higher-quality printing such as books. Serious capital investment was also a consideration, though some smaller printers availed themselves of the economies of a Linotype by first having copy set out of house by a larger firm which owned the machine, and then making up the pages and printing the work themselves. During the decade of the launch of the Linotype, though, a hot-metal competitor began to appear in the form of the Monotype, another American invention, attributed chiefly to Tolbert Lanston. The Monotype system differed significantly in that the keystrokes did not directly select the matrices, but instead produced a spool of coded punched tape. This was then taken to a separate machine, the caster, which held the matrix cases, each containing all the different characters. The instructions for both spacing and individual characters were incorporated in the coded holes on the tape. In response to this tape, the matrix case moved into position to receive the hot metal to cast the correct individual character. The end result had more in common with a galley of hand-set founder's type than the slugs of a Linotype. Monotype setting had the advantage of being easier to correct, with single letters easily replaceable, and found its earliest success in Europe, where printers had been unable to achieve the desired quality with the Linotype. Book printers especially were interested in the Monotype, attracted to its ability to handle and print its type in the same way as if hand-set. However, acceptance of the machine was slower than that of the Linotype. Substantial refinements continued to be made to both, so that they stood out as the two pre-eminent typesetting systems, even though other machines were still being launched. Hand-setting continued to be preferred for many jobs where high quality was required, or simply because that was the established practice and skill-base among the workforce, and the cost of adopting machine-setting was unattractive.

Among certain influential figures, albeit not in the commercial mainstream, there was serious concern at typographic standards in the 1890s. These critics argued that the pressures of commercialism, the undermining of earlier craft practices and their partial replacement by less tried and tested methods of casting machines and power presses, had brought printing standards to a low point. One important manifestation of this opposition was the work of the small independent specialist quality presses in Europe and the United States. In Britain this was most noticeable in two areas: the work and proselytising of William Morris, and the private-press movement. Morris (1834–96), who had inspired the Arts and Crafts Movement chiefly through other aspects of design and the decorative arts until this last decade of his life, led the way with the founding of

Right and far right: the 1890s urn for Coca-Cola is one of the earliest examples of the famous logotype in use; the calendar shows one of the variants that had preceded it. The drink was first advertised in 1886 (coincidentally the year the Linotype was launched) and since then the Coca-Cola Company of Atlanta, Georgia, has established its premier product as perhaps the most ubiquitous in the world. Central to its success has been that logotype, which has now survived a century. With careful tweakings and precisely controlled applications and copyright, it is the paragon of corporate identity, instantly recognisable and now timeless. And yet the lettering puts overall readability over the legibility of each character.
Far right: *L'Etendard Français* poster by Jules Chéret, 1895. Powerful lettering and dynamic contrasts in characters and the arrangement of words were integral to Chéret's effective lithography, which used comparatively few stones (in other words, separate colour printings) to create effects that were rich, not gaudy.

Coca-Cola

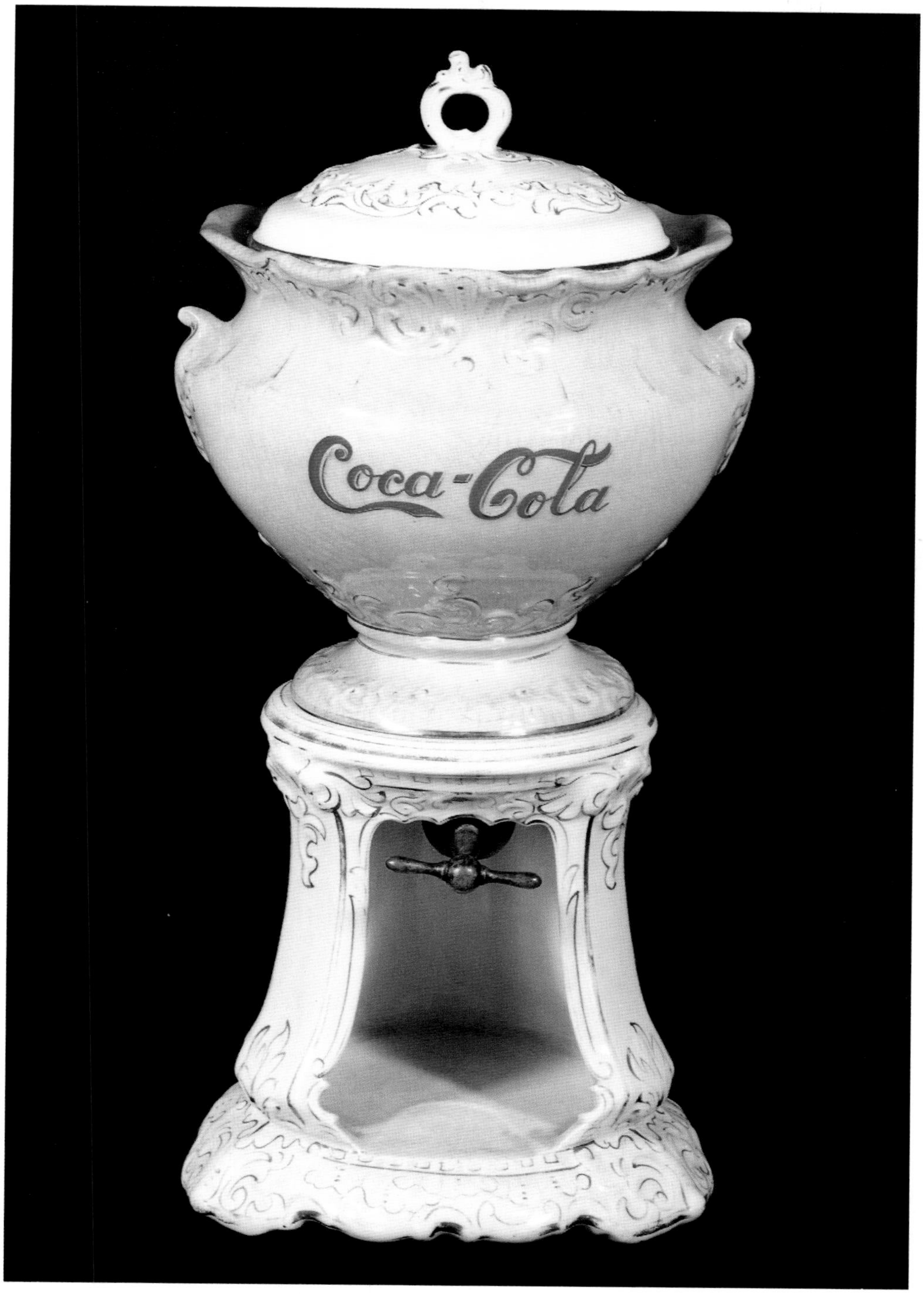

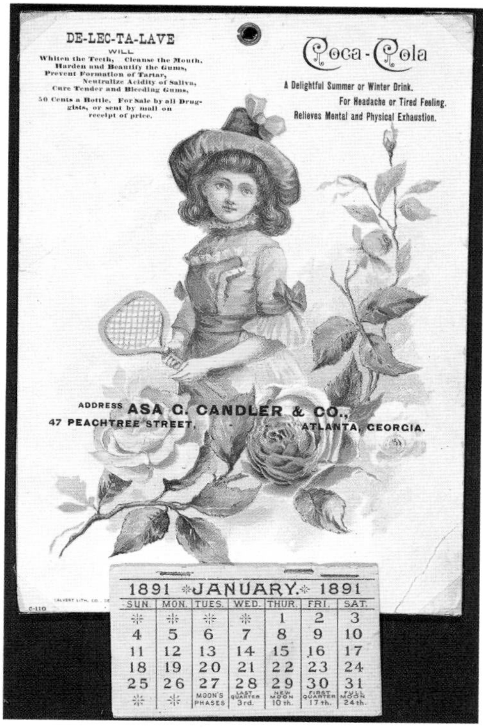

DE-LEC-TA-LAVE
WILL
Whiten the Teeth, Cleanse the Mouth,
Harden and Beautify the Gums,
Prevent Formation of Tartar,
Neutralize Acidity of Saliva,
Cure Tender and Bleeding Gums,
50 Cents a Bottle. For Sale by all Druggists, or sent by mail on receipt of price.
Coca-Cola
A Delightful Summer or Winter Drink.
For Headache or Tired Feeling.
Relieves Mental and Physical Exhaustion.
ADDRESS ASA G. CANDLER & CO.,
47 PEACHTREE STREET, ATLANTA, GEORGIA.
1891 JANUARY 1891
SUN. MON. TUES. WED. THUR. FRI. SAT.
1 2 3
4 5 6 7 8 9 10
11 12 13 14 15 16 17
18 19 20 21 22 23 24
25 26 27 28 29 30 31

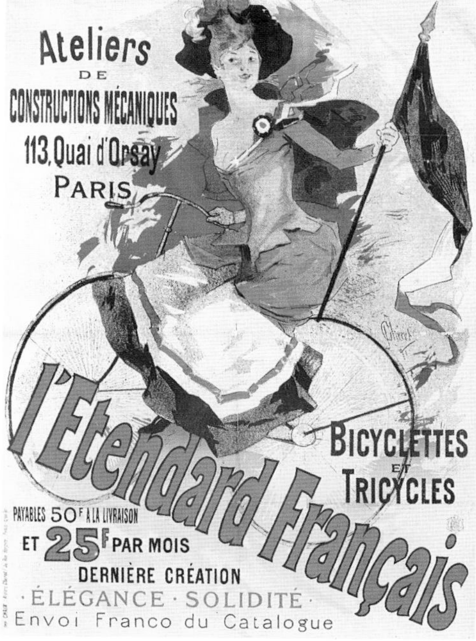

Ateliers
DE
CONSTRUCTIONS MÉCANIQUES
113, Quai d'Orsay
PARIS
l'Etendard Français
BICYCLETTES
ET
TRICYCLES
PAYABLES 50F À LA LIVRAISON
ET 25F PAR MOIS
DERNIÈRE CRÉATION
·ÉLÉGANCE·SOLIDITÉ·
Envoi Franco du Catalogue

the Kelmscott Press and his designs for new, revivalist, typefaces for the books that it produced.

The output of the Kelmscott Press, and of other private presses such as the Vale, Eragny, Essex House and Doves presses, was an invisible fraction of the growth of publishing. But while none of them gave direct examples of methods of improving printing – they were all too costly in their execution, backward-looking in their use of technology, and arcane in their styling – they held up a beautiful mirror to the less than perfect image of mass printing: they showed the standard of the finest craft work towards which design and execution had to aspire if the advances of printing were truly to be considered progress.

Integral to Morris's ideals was the creation of new typefaces. Kelmscott faces were inspired by the idea that type can be beautiful, and they carried a political statement instead of being dependent on the commercially motivated, popular, chunky and showy Victorian faces (for example, the square seriffed group known as Clarendon). Morris designed three faces that aimed to combine ideas of clarity and utility with a personal character which embodied his opposition to industrialisation and his celebration of high craft skills. Working with the engraver and printer Emery Walker (who later co-founded the Doves Press) and the punchcutter Edward Prince (who cut faces for several of the renowned private presses of this time), Morris produced Golden (1890), Troy (1892) and Chaucer (1893), a smaller size of Troy. Morris turned to the manuscripts of the late Middle Ages where he found what he saw as a relatively pure form of page layout, untainted by the manufacturing processes and crude commercial pressures of the Industrial Revolution, which had called for increasingly coarse designs to cope with greater-quantity, lower-quality mass printing. In his designs Morris was also rejecting the "modern" style of typeface, exemplified by Bodoni, where there is great contrast between thick and thin strokes. His faces were characterised by details such as the oblique cross stroke of the lower case "e", bracketed serifs and oblique serifs on lower case ascenders, and curves whose axis inclines to the left (showing oblique stress) – all points that reflect the pen or brushstroke reference. Morris also avoided any squashing of the design of letters (known as condensed forms), a popular choice for print in this period as a way of setting more words in less space, often at the cost of legibility and attractiveness.



Right: page 223 of *The Works of Geoffrey Chaucer*, published by the Kelmscott Press in 1896. This masterpiece of the press and of William Morris, published in the year of his death, is a folio edition of 556 pages, set in a double-column page of Chaucer type (a new, smaller cut of Troy) for the text and Troy type for the headings. Morris drew the various levels of ornament – numerous initial letters, initial words, page borders and picture borders – and 87 woodcuts after designs by Burne-Jones were also cut. This volume was the ultimate statement of Morris's commitment to reviving print values and celebrating the finest traditions of the graphic arts. Below: an adjustable composing stick as commonly used to hand-set type at the end of the nineteenth century. Despite various attempts at mechanically setting cold-metal type (precast pieces of type as normally assembled by hand), only with the advent of effective hot-metal systems from Linotype and Monotype was the shift from hand- to machine-setting made possible.

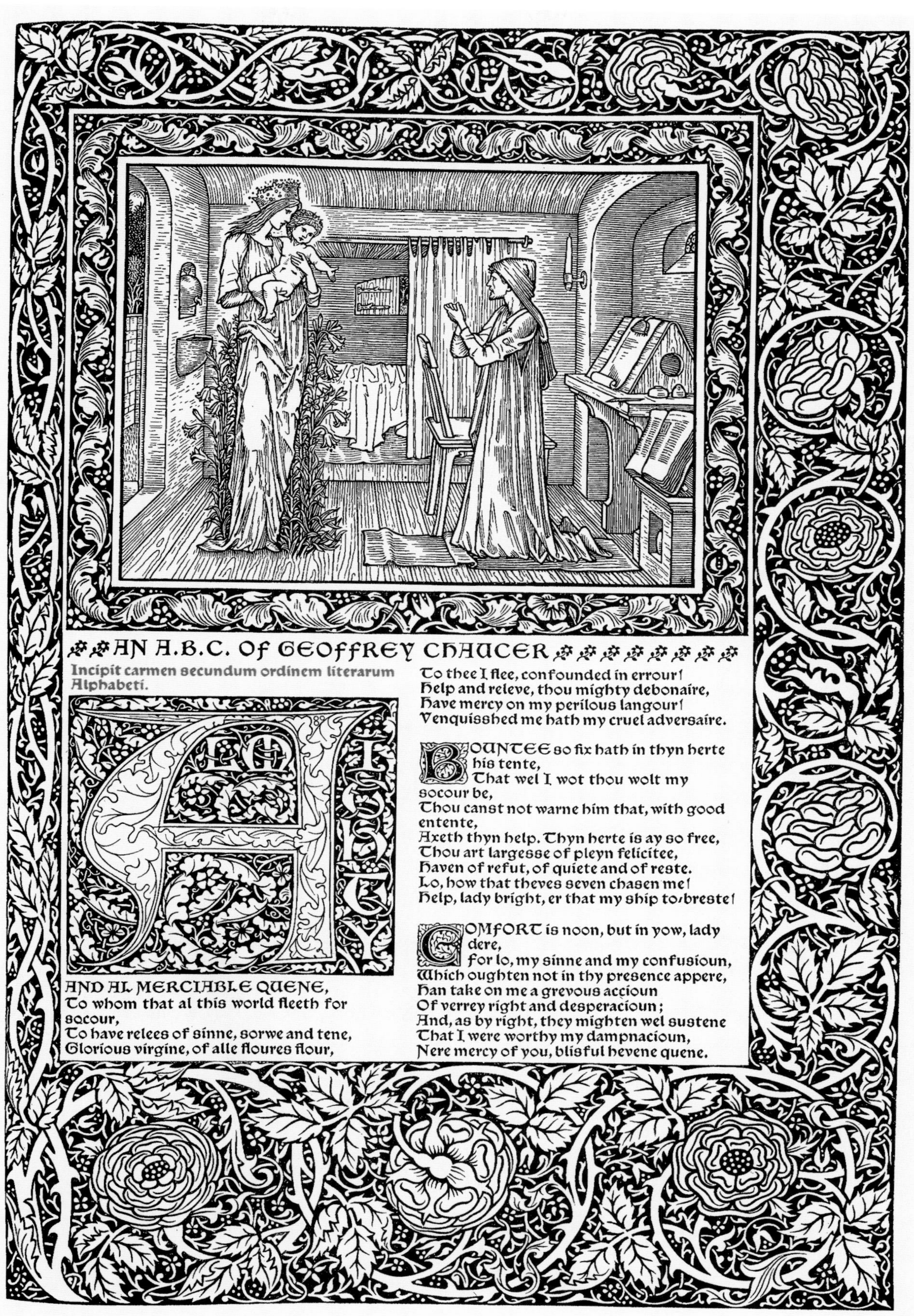

AN A.B.C. OF GEOFFREY CHAUCER

Incipit carmen secundum ordinem literarum Alphabeti.

ALMIGHTY AND AL MERCIABLE QUENE,
To whom that al this world fleeth for socour,
To have relees of sinne, sorwe and tene,
Glorious virgine, of alle floures flour,
To thee I flee, confounded in errour!
Help and releve, thou mighty debonaire,
Have mercy on my perilous langour!
Venquisshed me hath my cruel adversaire.

BOUNTEE so fix hath in thyn herte his tente,
That wel I wot thou wolt my socour be,
Thou canst not warne him that, with good entente,
Axeth thyn help. Thyn herte is ay so free,
Thou art largesse of pleyn felicitee,
Haven of refut, of quiete and of reste.
Lo, how that theves seven chasen me!
Help, lady bright, er that my ship to-breste!

COMFORT is noon, but in yow, lady dere,
for lo, my sinne and my confusioun,
Which oughten not in thy presence appere,
Han take on me a grevous accioun
Of verrey right and desperacioun;
And, as by right, they mighten wel sustene
That I were worthy my dampnacioun,
Nere mercy of you, blisful hevene quene.

Kelmscott's finest books displayed what would appear to be a welter of illustration on the page, almost burying the type. At first appearance this may belie the fact that Morris and his colleagues strongly opposed what they saw as an excess of idle decoration in books. Their concern, though, was for a dedicated relationship of all the parts – text, illustration, paper, binding and so on, all hand-set and hand-printed – in order to create a book that could be set alongside the early books they so admired. The excellence of the Kelmscott books' craftsmanship, like so much of the Arts and Crafts Movement output, can be seen as ironic in that it sought to raise by fine example the supposedly debased conditions of labour endured by the working classes. The same policy stimulated some of the other private presses. Doves, Eragny and others took inspiration, like Morris had done, from earlier sources – in their case the "humanist" faces of the fifteenth-century Venetian printers such as Nicolas Jenson. Of course, the idealism of these presses was lost on the general public, and certainly the books were out of reach of all but the wealthy. Yet Kelmscott was highly influential: other printers were stirred by the medieval/Venetian revival, and set about cutting their own faces. These stood out simply for having a design philosophy and being so exactingly produced in small batches, when the graphic sensibilities of the period seemed surrounded by a mass of fairly incoherent approaches, thoroughly debased and derivative, which celebrated the technology but was urged on almost exclusively by commercial imperatives.

One notable copy of Morris's work was produced by the new foundry American Typefounders (ATF), with its Jenson face. This company was established from the union of several existing US type foundries in 1892 as a defensive measure against the growth of the Linotype business. It supplied precast type and was active in the commissioning of new faces and copies of old faces to meet the growing demand for a wider choice. Piracy of designs was rampant at the time, printers being quickly able to pass off a new design as their



Below and right: Cheltenham. Below centre and below right: Clarendon. Bottom and far right: Century. Bertram Goodhue created Cheltenham in 1896. With legibility in text his overriding concern, he shortened the descenders while lengthening the ascenders, reasoning that the top half of letters is more important for recognition. However, Cheltenham became most commonly used as a display type. Century was cut in 1894 by Linn Boyd Benton working with Theodore de Vinne in order to create a stronger, more readable face for use in the *Century* magazine. Although classified as a "didone" face, with an upright stress, the contrast between thick and thin strokes is not pronounced: it was designed as a functional face, slightly condensed for economy of space. Clarendon, originally presented in 1845 by Robert Besley & Company, London, was an immensely popular square serif face used in display, signage and text typography when emphasis was required (the sample here is from Besley's catalogue).

abcdefghijklmnopqrstuvwxyz
ABCDEFGHIJKLMNOPQRSTUVWXYZ
1234567890

**abcdefghijklmnopqrstuvwxyz**
**ABCDEFGHIJKLMNOPQRSTUVWXYZ**
**1234567890**

abcdefghijklmnopqrstuvwxyz
ABCDEFGHIJKLMNOPQRSTUVWXYZ
1234567890

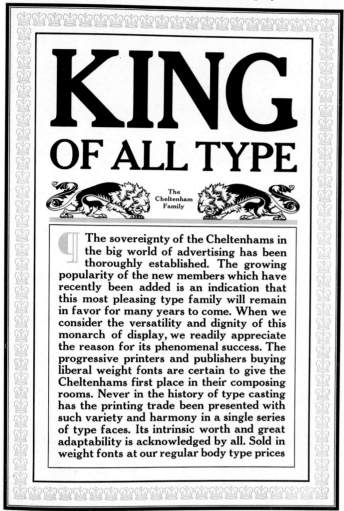

Cheltenham Bold in Practical Display

# KING
## OF ALL TYPE

The Cheltenham Family

The sovereignty of the Cheltenhams in the big world of advertising has been thoroughly established. The growing popularity of the new members which have recently been added is an indication that this most pleasing type family will remain in favor for many years to come. When we consider the versatility and dignity of this monarch of display, we readily appreciate the reason for its phenomenal success. The progressive printers and publishers buying liberal weight fonts are certain to give the Cheltenhams first place in their composing rooms. Never in the history of type casting has the printing trade been presented with such variety and harmony in a single series of type faces. Its intrinsic worth and great adaptability is acknowledged by all. Sold in weight fonts at our regular body type prices

Chap-Book Border Twentieth Century Ornaments 179 Cheltenham Paragraph Mark

## The Century Family

*AN EXCEEDINGLY DIGNIFIED TYPE FAMILY*

Century Expanded
*Century Expanded Italic*
**Century Bold**
***Century Bold Italic***
**Century Bold Condensed**
**Century Bold Extended**
Century Oldstyle
*Century Oldstyle Italic*
**Century Oldstyle Bold**
***Century Oldstyle Bold Italic***

**American Type Founders Co.**

*ORIGINATOR OF THE FAMILY IDEA IN TYPES*

---

SMALL PICA CLARENDON ON PICA BODY.

*Cast to range with ordinary Pica, the Figures to En Quadrats.*

**PIRACY** is the great sin of all **manufacturing communities**:—there is scarcely any Trade in which it prevails so generally as among **Type Founders. Messrs. BESLEY & COMPANY** originally introduced the **Clarendon Character,** which they registered under the **Copyright of Designs' Act,** but no sooner was the time of Copyright allowed by that Act **expired,** than the **Trade was inundated** with all sorts of **Piracies** and **Imitations,** some of them **mere effigies of letters.** Notwithstanding this, nearly all the **respectable Printers in Town and Country** who claim to have either **taste** or **judgment,** have adopted the original Founts, and treated the **Imitations** with the contempt they deserve.

---

own by producing a copy of the new face by electrotype (a kind of plate), casting from this and then selling the resulting slightly degraded type as their own (a move that has parallels with the present-day problem of software-copying). While ATF was not averse to learning from somebody else's ideas, such as Morris's, it did have standards it needed to protect in order to compete with machine-setting. ATF's position was partly one of strength through unity for the threatened small foundries, who were also aware that clubbing together would bring them economies of scale and the opportunity to market a wide range of faces to the burgeoning advertising market, whose display typesetting was still entirely in the world of the hand-set, precast type. ATF, under its general manager and subsequent president Robert Nelson, pioneered the idea of extensive type families, across different sizes and in different weights: in the Victorian period faces were often cut in a highly restricted range – sometimes just one size, one weight. Linn Boyd Benton and his son Morris Fuller Benton (1872–1948) were key designers for ATF during its first decade, implementing ideas of revised and copied faces, along with cutting extended families. Morris Benton went on to become one of the most prolific of all type designers, drawing around 180 faces during a long career at ATF. This figure needs to be qualified: his reputation rests not so much on being an innovator, as on being a highly skilled technician who could revive old faces or produce ATF variants of new ideas coming into the type market from other foundries.

The creation of a new face for the *Century* magazine in 1894 by Linn Boyd Benton, with Theodore de Vinne, is an example of one of the better faces that betray the characteristics of the period: Century was required to be blacker and more readable, and to be slightly condensed to fit the double-column setting of the magazine, in which it was first seen in 1895. These specifications are typical of the often seemingly contradictory demands placed upon a type designer – at one and the same time requiring the type to be condensed and yet more legible. Several versions of Century were subsequently cut by Morris Benton, and its popularity can be judged by the fact that other major type suppliers moved in time to cutting their own versions. The face was specially cut to cope with the problems of magazine-quality print, with its large runs and poor-quality paper, factors which had mitigated against the finer points of a typeface surviving into print. It is perhaps this practical application that explains why the face was so successful and indeed it still has its adherents.

Another early major commercial success for Morris Benton and ATF was Cloister Old Style, which was first made available in 1897. Here ATF can be seen to be responding to the aesthetic merit of the Kelmscott Golden type by producing an Old Style Venetian face, drawing on the sample of Jenson's roman. Other foundries followed ATF in providing further variants of the face. Jenson never produced an italic, or indeed a "w" in his face, so there is considerable creative development in Benton's work. He also provided a set of swash capitals – italic capitals with a calligraphic flourish.

The most popular face to emerge during the mid-1890s, subsequently notorious, was Cheltenham. In its origins and its take-up it says much about the impact on type design of new attitudes and methods. Although loathed almost from the outset by those with refined type tastes, the face displays a character that has come to be seen as distinctly American, thanks to its wide application by jobbing printers and its common use, at times to the point of being a first and obvious choice. It became a kind of "one size fits all" face for advertising, display

Right: title and inside page from *Histoire des Quatre Fils Aymon*, 1883, designed and illustrated by Eugène Grasset. This book (which repackages a popular story about Charlemagne and his barons) linked the typographic and illustrative elements of the page in an unprecedented way and was highly influential. Grasset appreciated the potential of the developing chromolithographic process for more easily facilitating the complex interplay of picture and colour than was possible with letterpress. His visual references integrate the look of mediaeval manuscripts with the stylisation that came to be seen as Art Nouveau. With Alfonse Mucha and Jules Chéret, Grasset was one of the most popular artists during the 1890s heyday of poster art in Paris.

Below right: page from "Some Specimens of Letterpress Printing" by printers Raithby & Lawrence, 1886, showing examples of the ornate styles of display typeface and type furniture on offer from printers at the turn of the century. This was the vernacular for display advertising in the emerging popular press.

Généreux Chevalier, je vous donne ma sœur en mariage. — Sire, dit Regnaut, je vous remercie de ce présent; il n'appartient pas à un Chevalier tel que moi. Regnaut cependant prit la Dame par la main et la conduisit à l'Église, où l'Évêque de Bordeaux leur donna la bénédiction nuptiale.

Quand ils furent mariés, Regnaut manda ses frères, qui étoient à Montauban. Ils arrivèrent et assistèrent aux fêtes, qui durèrent huit jours. Le Roi Yon fut bien charmé du mariage de Regnaut, car il pensoit bien que ce vaillant Chevalier le défendroit de tout son pouvoir.

IX

Comme Charlemagne ayant appris que Regnaut et ses frères étoient au fort de Montauban, somma le Roi Yon de lui rendre ses ennemis, savoir Regnaut et ses frères, sous peine d'être assiégé. Le Roi répondit qu'il n'en feroit rien.

Le Roi Charlemagne étant à Paris, eut un jour envie d'aller en pèlerinage à Saint-Jacques en Galice. Il partit de Paris, et mena avec lui Oger le Danois, Naimes de Bavière, et plusieurs autres Seigneurs. Après plusieurs journées de marche, ils arrivèrent à Saint-Jacques. Quand ils y furent, le Roi entra dans l'Église et offrit dix marcs d'or sur l'autel. Après avoir fait sa dévotion, il se mit en marche pour passer à Bordeaux. Comme il étoit en chemin, il aperçut le Château de Montauban au delà de la Gironde. Il dit alors : Seigneurs, voici une forteresse considérable ; je sais que le

75

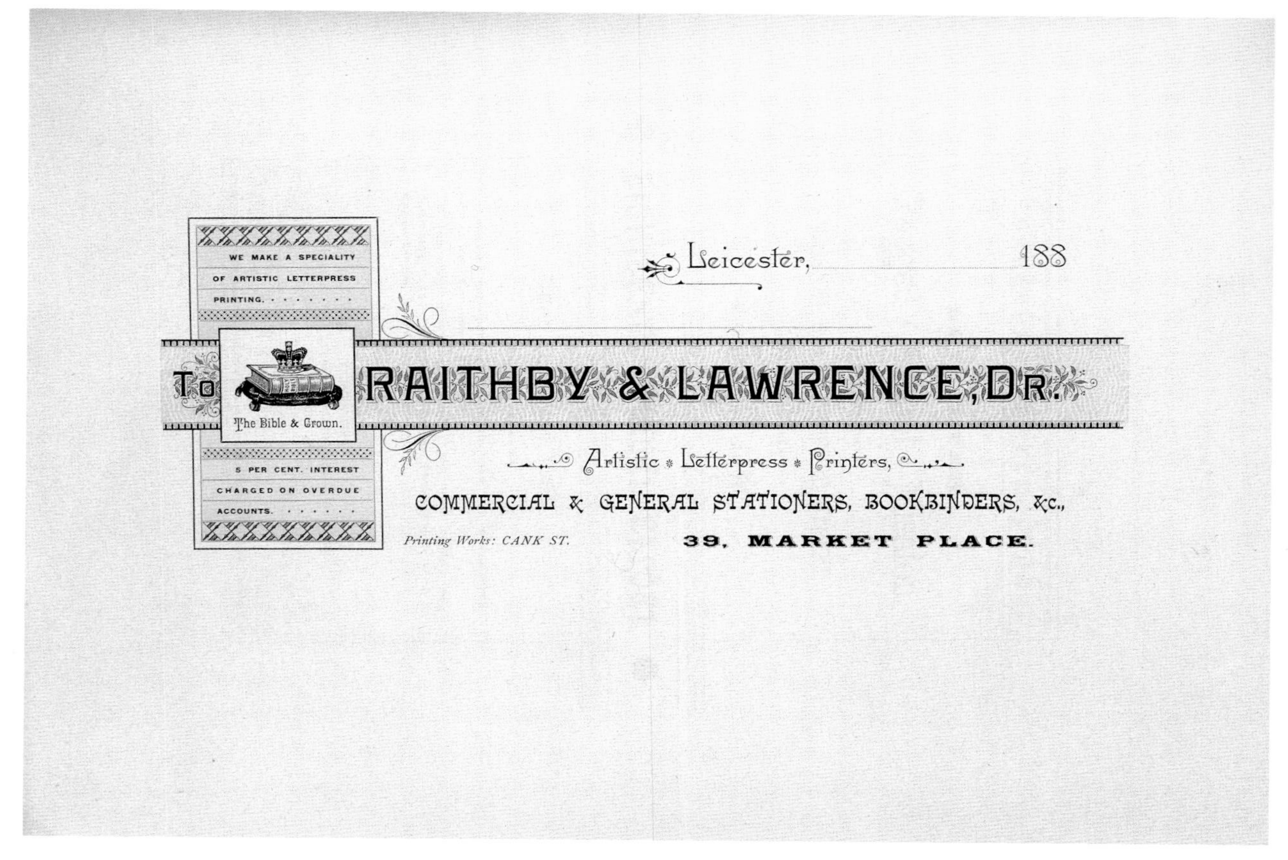

and text. Its solid soft forms – rounded terminals to some of the letters and stubby serifs, short descenders, thickened strokes – have little appeal for the purist, but perform reliably under various different conditions. They never look elegant but are distinctly practical and perhaps genuinely popular for being rugged and legible. The typeface was designed by Bertram Goodhue (1869–1924), an architect who was also interested in the graphic arts. Specially designed for the Cheltenham Press of New York, the face was first seen around 1896. Goodhue's prime concern was to create a highly legible book type and he set out to do this by pursuing the idea that the upper half of a letter is more significant in recognition than the lower, so he lengthened the ascenders and shortened the descenders. This theoretical basis appears to be sound, according to more recent research into legibility. Ironically, though, the face did not find great popularity for book setting, but its strong recognition factor, and its supply in many sizes and from many different foundries over the next two decades, pushed it to the fore as a possible option for advertising purposes. It did not become commercially available, however, for almost a decade (through ATF and Linotype, then other imitations).

Advertising, meanwhile, was becoming the most active and demanding area of typographic experimentation in the late nineteenth century. Many distinctive designs for display faces were never cut as steel types, but existed only in wood letter, an easier and cheaper way of cutting larger types as they were cut straight from a drawn trace of the character, with no need for punches. There were many wood-letter shops supplying to printers, cutting familiar designs, and specials to order.

The more extreme invention in lettering art in this period occurred in lithographic design, where there was no material technology affecting wood or steel to inhibit the forms. But neither is this strictly typographic design, in that the letters in a one-off image cannot be taken out and re-used elsewhere: they are unique and need to be redrawn (or copied) for each use. Instead of requiring typesetting and illustration, a lithograph could reproduce the one drawn image, combining text and image in complicated formal and colour arrangements. The basic technology dated back to the end of the eighteenth century, but the chromolithographic process was developed and reached a peak in the late nineteenth century. The improvement of photogravure methods (the etching of a photographic image on a plate through an arrangement of dots produced by screening) challenged lithography and led to a decline in its use from the 1890s.

During the decade, poster advertising reached a peak, combining the increased information needs of industry and other cultures with lithography or early photogravure. French poster art led the way, particularly in propagating the ideas of Art Nouveau and Post-Impressionism. Bound in with the often highly artistic images, which were even then collected as art, was innovative lettering that would become copied and introduced as a "type style" for posters, although not necessarily cut by a foundry as a metal face. Jules Chéret (1836–1932) is generally considered to be the father of the French poster cult, which became internationally acclaimed at the turn of the century, and was a focus of expression for Art Nouveau and related art movements. The son of a typographer (a craftsman whose work differed greatly from the modern designer-typographer), Chéret's integration of images with equivalent lettering, fluctuating from extremes of florid brush-work lettering to refined and formal letters, was highly influential. The typographic content of this heyday of French

Right: two posters by Will Bradley, both 1895: one advertising the Springfield Bicycle Club Tournament and the other *The Chap Book* printing journal. As with French posters of the same period, the development of Art Nouveau in the United States was realised through bold print effects that took advantage of advances in lithography. Bradley integrated type and image, and adapted and twisted characters to suit his designs, moving from the decorative Art Nouveau style seen here to an almost crude, wood-cut technique by the end of the decade. He became a consultant to American Type Founders in 1900. Below right: Le Grasset, a typeface designed by Eugène Grasset in 1898 for the Peignot foundry in Paris (later known as Deberny & Peignot). Though roman, it carries a strong sense of script, with its splayed forms and blunt serifs placed on one side or on the outside of letters.

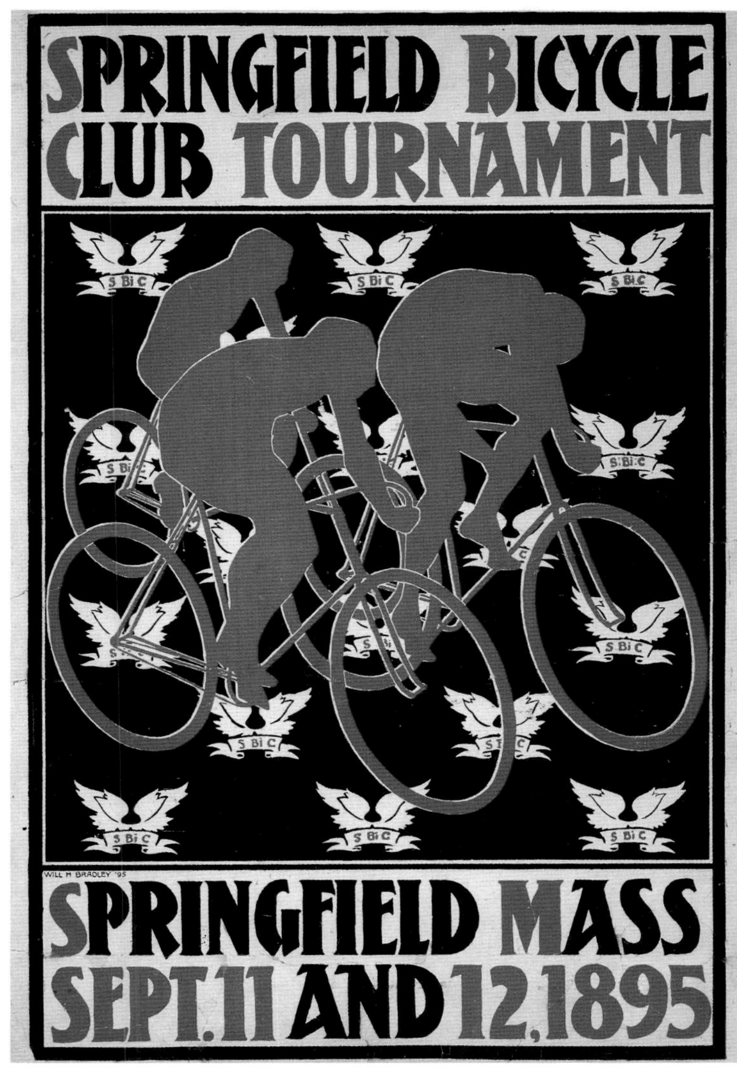


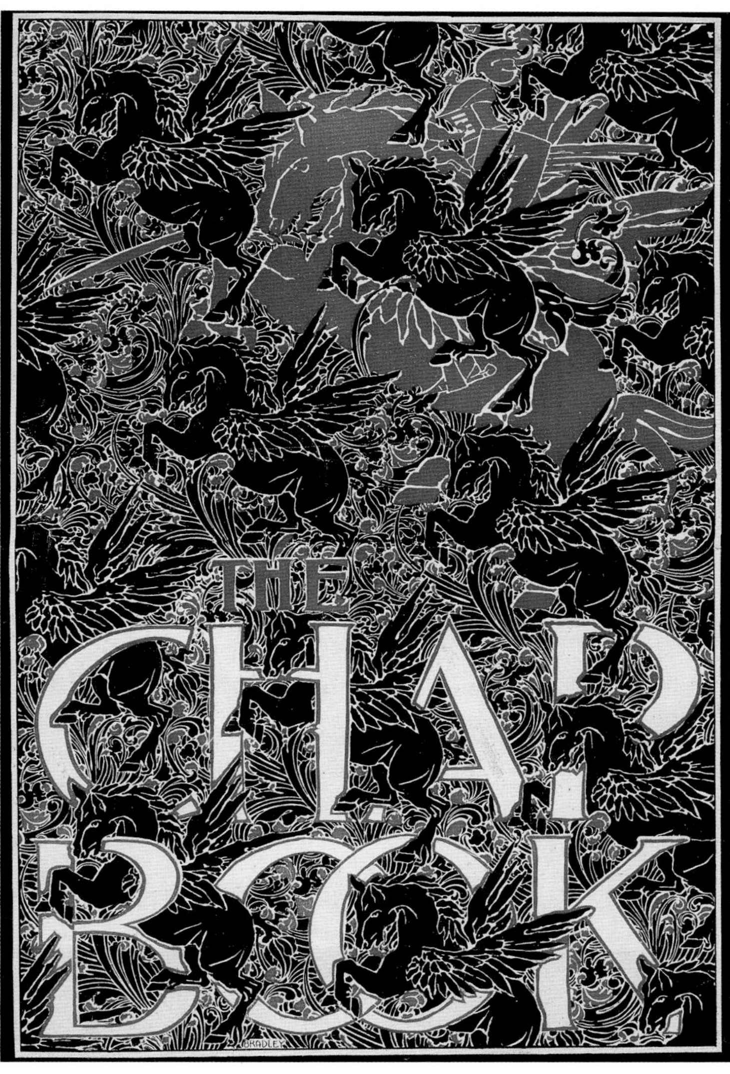


Le caractère dominant
de l'art français, c'est
ce souci de la clarté, de
*Il faudrait n'avoir pas*
12345 *67890*
SAISON *CLIMAT*

poster art was perhaps taken furthest by Eugène Grasset (1841–1917) and Georges Auriol (1863–1938), both of whom designed typefaces. Grasset's eponymous face of 1898 can be seen to have connections with the old-style revivals of Morris, and in turn influenced the Auriol face of 1901 (both were from the Deberny & Peignot foundry). Auriol was a much more calligraphic face, with pen-drawn associations accentuated by the odd white gaps in many strokes, as if the pen had just lifted off the page for an instant. The effect was in keeping with the organic imagery of Art Nouveau, thus making it the most appropriate face for use in this context, but of little appeal once the prevailing fashion had declined.

Besides the more florid aspects of Art Nouveau typography displayed by many of the French and certain other European and American artists, the 1890s also saw poster artists who combined the decorative aspects of the poster with a search for simpler, less cluttered and perhaps more elegant design. The work of the Beggarstaff Brothers in Britain, Van de Velde in Belgium and Will Bradley (1868–1962) on *The Chap Book* magazine in the United States can be seen as expressing the emergence of the art director, a figure whose major concerns are the relationships between typeface detail, the nature of the medium and the supporting images. Although Bradley did design type (his face of 1890 was later bought and named after him by ATF), his typographic sensibility was displayed to a greater degree by his appreciation of varied lettering and type styles, and his advancement of ideas relating to layout. He revived appreciation of earlier American print work, celebrating the charm of "colonial typography" and carrying as a motto for handling type "do with me as little as you can, not as much".

These artists' commercial works contain the seeds of examination of those formal issues and ways of seeing connections that were soon to explode in the fuller explorations of abstract art, which in turn would feed back into commercial art design, and type and typography, for years to come.

The presaging of twentieth-century type developments in the work of the late Victorian era can be illustrated finally in this chapter by the launch of Akzidenz Grotesk from the German foundry of Stempel in 1898. This face, which went on to be known by other names (as with many type designs), notably Standard in America, can be seen as polishing up the sans serif faces dating from the early nineteenth century. These faces are also known as "gothic", but as this term is sometimes used to describe the typeface based on broad-nib script entitled "black-letter", its use can be misleading. The sans serif Akzidenz Grotesk, in its heavy, rather monotonous qualities, suited prevalent German taste, but would seem to have had little relevance to wider movements of the time, being more an astute revival. Its importance lies in the fact that it forms the foundation of one of the most popular faces, and groups of faces, of today – those based around Helvetica.

Right: Rowntree's Elect Cocoa poster by the Beggarstaff Brothers (William Nicholson and James Pryde), 1895, London. This lithograph is an example of the Beggarstaffs' bold, and commercially unsuccessful, departure from the rich and cluttered typography and lettering of contemporary advertising. They simplified the relationship of colour, image and message in a way that presages the quest of twentieth-century advertising art direction.
Far right: Victor Cycles poster, 1898, designer unknown. Type merges into illustration, foreground into background, the abstract into the figurative in this image that comes out of Art Nouveau poster style and yet is not simply decorative but suggests the conceptual strengths of later advertising. The web of interlaced ovals visually connects with the letterform "O" and can also represent the bicycle wheel and the pattern of tyres on the ground.
Below right: Auriol, by the poster artist Georges Auriol, issued by Deberny & Peignot, 1901. The extreme calligraphic Art Nouveau style of this face has made it popular every time Art Nouveau is revived. Designed with a suggestion of thick-nibbed pen-drawn strokes, it was a source for the lettering used on the Paris Métro signage by Hector Guimard. It was commissioned by Georges Peignot, following the success of Le Grasset (see page 27).
Far right: Akzidenz Grotesk, bold and semi-bold, was first issued by the Berthold foundry in Berlin in 1896; as with many nineteenth-century sans serifs, its designer is unknown. Also known as Standard, it attracted a growing following and became a statement of principle for Swiss typography during the 1950s. The evenness of the design and its legibility over more geometric sans serifs are its chief qualities.

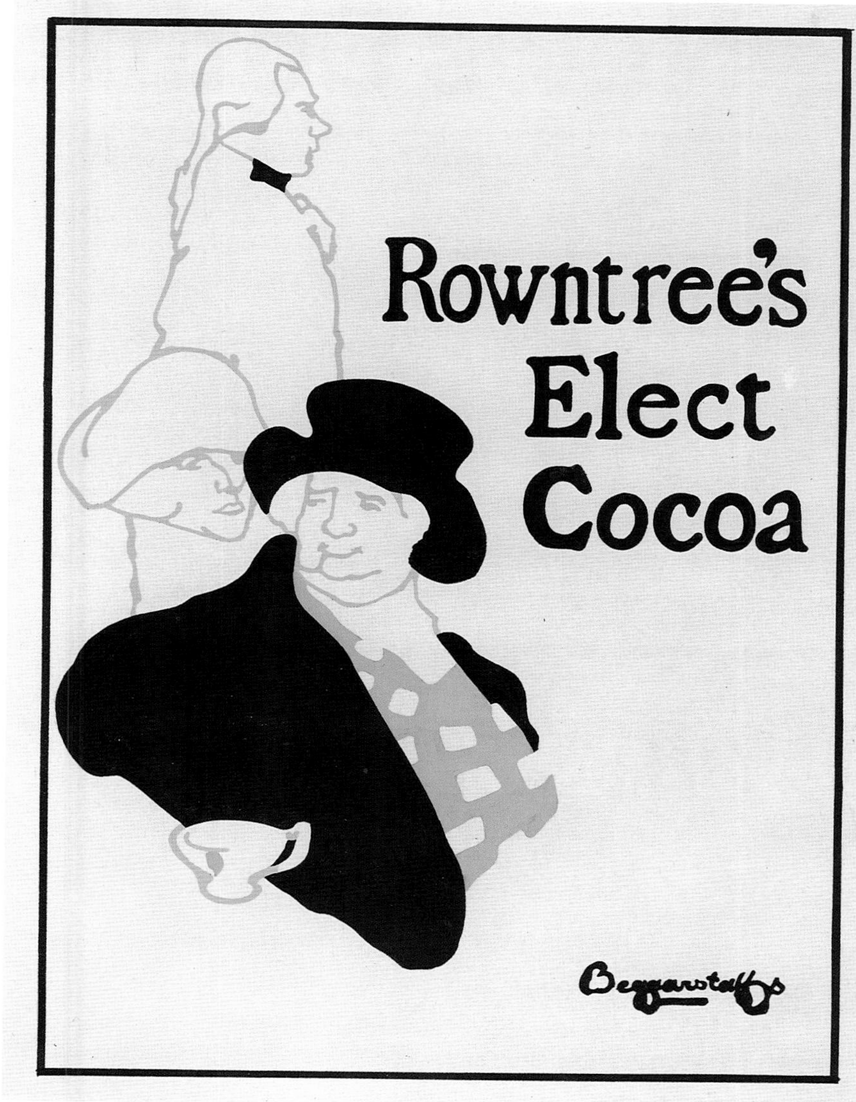

Un parfait mélange d'Auteurs littéraires.
ABCDEFGH

Oft ist das Leben nur ein Traum
Manchmal ist im menschlichen
Leben der Zufall entscheidend

GRAPHISCHE KUNSTANSTALT

Rausch
NATUR

ECKMANN

# News Gothic

# 1900...

Below: the exaggerated size of Frederic Goudy's Copperplate Gothic of 1901 shows the minute serifs on the figures "1" and "9" which give sharpness to the face when printed small. It has continued to be popular for announcement cards. News Gothic was one of a series of highly successful sans serifs that Morris Fuller Benton cut for American Type Founders during this decade. By contrast, Eckmann, by Otto Eckmann for Klingspor in 1900, is a period-specific face, an extreme reworking of black-letter redolent of Art Nouveau.

Above: taking a different direction in organic expression in art, *Ver Sacrum*, designed by Koloman Moser, led to the setting up of the Wiener Werkstätte and its quest for basic principles in design.

In Europe and the United States, 1900 and the years just before and after saw a wave of artists and movements that questioned the values of modern society, particularly criticising the effect of commercial pressures on craft standards. This tension between old and new technology took a number of different forms. Sometimes there was a suggestion of looking back at lost values and modes of expression, particularly apparent in the work of the small presses in Britain and the United States and the artist-craft groups such as the Secession movements in Austria and Germany. But there were also new practices derived from the pressures of changing technologies and mass production; this search for the new was evident within these groups and was part of the attitude behind such movements as the Neue Sachlichkeit, or "new objectivity", a radical rethinking of two- and three-dimensional design including typography.

The emergence of the type designer and the art director as distinct from the printer was a result of the massively increasing volumes of printed material, and the results were soon apparent in the work of certain typographers of this period. While the boom in print gave rise to a great deal of poor work, it also presented opportunities for new forms of excellence. At the same time came the beginnings of a sensibility derived from fine art and literary movements, foreshadowing the shattering impact of Cubist and Futurist thought and images.

The Arts and Crafts Movement in Britain was one of the first manifestations of the concern for craft revival, attacking the low standards of print and the aesthetic that seemed to go hand in hand with modern industrial culture. William Morris's work at Kelmscott, already mentioned, had a wide influence. His colleague in that enterprise, Emery Walker, went on to found the Doves Press in 1900 with Thomas Cobden-Sanderson. It seems that together they designed the one type that the press held, called Doves, a roman cut in one size only by Edward Prince (another Kelmscott link), based, like Morris's Golden type, on a fifteenth-century model from Jenson. But it is lighter and nearer the original than Morris's – the result being a face with a less medieval look: more legible, more elegant, and apparently more modern. Cobden-Sanderson's axiom on typography displays this quest for a functional but interpretive form for the characters and their disposition, pointing the way towards future Modernist thought. The only duty of typography, he claimed, was "to communicate to the imagination, without loss by the way, the thought or image intended to be communicated by the author". Doves had a brief, if glorious life: it was used by the Doves Press for some of the finest of private-press books (which were also beautifully bound), peaking with the Doves' Bible, but the type matrices came to a violent end when Cobden-Sanderson smashed them and threw the lot in the River Thames after a row with Walker – reputedly over who had the better claim to having created the face.

The manner in which the private-press books conceived of the various elements of a page as combining to form the whole artwork finds a strong echo in the work of the group of artists and designers in Vienna who first formed the Secession group in 1897, some of whom later went on to set up the Wiener Werkstätte in 1903. They ranged from architects to fine artists and, as the Wiener Werkstätte, produced finely crafted modern artefacts for sale until 1932. In the movement's early years, however, when the artists were at their most propagandist and innovative, influential lettering and typographic work was produced that gave a highly distinctive character – part Art Nouveau, part Arts and Crafts.

This idiosyncracy can be seen particularly in the work of Koloman Moser (1868–1918). His illustrative calligraphy for the Secession magazine *Ver Sacrum*, and his logotype identity marks (possibly that of the Wiener Werkstätte, and certainly his own) show a questioning of letterforms and a search for new ways of carrying the typographic message beyond the rigidity of established foundry faces. Initially his work was quite florid, organic, Art-Nouveau-influenced, but it became increasingly geometric. Although his designs appear highly decorative to modern eyes, the theory behind the work was to limit decoration to that which came out of the nature of the medium. The masterpiece of the Secession/ Wiener Werkstätte's print output is often seen as the luxurious commemorative book for the Austro-Hungarian royal printworks, produced in 1904, featuring a specially cut typeface by Rudolf von Larisch, a title page and initial letters by Moser, and woodcuts by Czeschka. The similarities with Kelmscott and other British private-press work are apparent: the typeface is again drawn from fifteenth-century Venetian precedents, and the text is set into wide margins of heavy but sympathetic decoration.

In Germany a similar mix of ideas between notions initially connected with the Art Nouveau style (the Jugendstil) and less decorative, more fundamentally questioning, design was apparent among designers. The most distinctive of Art Nouveau typefaces came out of Germany. Designed by Otto Eckmann for the Klingspor foundry in 1900, Eckmann was available in two weights, both relatively heavy. It can be seen to mix the organic requirements of the Jugendstil with the black-letter tradition of Germany, reflecting the medieval pen in the open bowls of letters. A highly distinctive face, perhaps good for display when character is desired, it is low on legibility thanks in part to the poor letterforms derived from the overwhelming styling. It is nevertheless remarkably original, a forerunner of the free expression of exotic display faces cut since the lower

Below: the centenary book for the Austro-Hungarian royal print works in Vienna, produced by the Wiener Werkstätte in 1904. The Vienna Staatsdruckerei book, the first official contract given to the Werkstätte, features a typeface designed and cut by Rudolf von Larisch, with ornament and production by Koloman Moser and woodcuts by Carl Otto Czeschka.
Below left: Endeavour type by C. R. Ashbee, 1901, as seen in the Essex House Press edition of a letter from Percy Bysshe Shelley to Thomas Love Peacock, 1901. Ashbee's celebration of hand craft skills was displayed in inconsistencies between forms of the same letter, plus shortened ascenders and descenders contrasting with the flourished and truncated rounding of letters.
Right: a section from the Doves' Bible, shown actual size, set in the only typeface The Doves Press possessed.

this glacier we saw as we sat on a rock close to one of the streams of the Arveiron, masses of ice detach themselves from on high, and fall with a loud dull noise into the vale. The violence of their fall turned them into powder which flowed over the rocks in imitation of the waterfalls whose ravines they usurped and filled. In the evening Mary and Clara remained at home and I went with Ducrèe my guide the only tolerable person I have seen in this country, to visit the glacier of Boisson. This glacier like that of Montanvert comes close to the vale, overhanging the green meadows and the dark woods with the dazzling whiteness of its precipices and pinnacles. These glaciers flow perpetually into the valley ravaging in their slow but irresistible progress the pastures and the forests which surround them, and performing a work of desolation in ages which a river of lava might accomplish in an hour, but far more irretrievably—for where the ice has once been the hardiest plant refuses to grow—if even, as in some extraordinary instances, it should recede after its progression has once commenced. The glaciers perpetually move onwards at the rate of a foot each day with a motion which commences at the spot where on the boundaries of perpetual congelation they are produced by the freezing of the waters which arise from the partial melting of the eternal snows. They drag with them from the regions whence they derive their origin all the ruins of the mountain, enormous rocks, and immense accumulations of sand & stones. These are driven onwards by the irresistible progress of the stream

8

ROTATIONS-MASCHINEN F·Ü·R·E·I·N· UND·ZWEI· F·A·R·B·E·N· D·R·U·C·K

Bei einer Beurteilung der graphisch-technischen Leistungen der Staatsdruckerei ist es nur natürlich, wenn dem Buchdruck der breiteste Raum zugewiesen wird. Nicht allein seine kulturelle Bedeutung, welche den Charakter der von uns „Neuzeit" genannten geschichtlichen Epoche weitaus mehr zu beeinflussen bestimmt war, als es die Entdeckung Amerikas vermochte, ist hiefür maßgebend, sondern auch der Umstand, daß der Buchdruck als die Mutterkunst aller übrigen graphischen Fächer anzusehen ist, und endlich die Tatsache, daß ihm vor allem andern der größte Anteil an der Beschaffung der für die verschiedensten Bedürfnisse auf allen Gebieten des staatlichen, gesellschaftlichen und geschäftlichen Lebens notwendigen Druckwerke zukommt. Die außerordentlichen Verdienste, welche sich unser Staatsinstitut vornehmlich in der Sphäre des Buchdrucks erworben hat, sind von weit über die heimischen Grenzen ragender Bedeutung. Die Anstalt beschränkte sich nicht allein darauf, dem

47

son, & the people that were present with them, abode in Gibeah of Benjamin:
but the Philistines encamped in Michmash. And the spoilers came out of the
camp of the Philistines in three companies: one company turned unto the way
that leadeth to Ophrah, unto the land of Shual: & another company turned
the way to Beth-horon: & another company turned to the way of the border
that looketh to the valley of Zeboim toward the wilderness. Now there was
no smith found throughout all the land of Israel: for the Philistines said, Lest
the Hebrews make them swords or spears: but all the Israelites went down to
the Philistines, to sharpen every man his share, & his coulter, & his axe, & his
mattock. Yet they had a file for the mattocks, and for the coulters, and for the
forks, and for the axes, & to sharpen the goads. So it came to pass in the day of
battle, that there was neither sword nor spear found in the hand of any of the
people that were with Saul and Jonathan: but with Saul and with Jonathan
his son was there found. And the garrison of the Philistines went out to the
passage of Michmash. ¶ Now it came to pass upon a day, that Jonathan the 14
son of Saul said unto the young man that bare his armour, Come, & let us go
over to the Philistines' garrison, that is on the other side. But he told not his
father. And Saul tarried in the uttermost part of Gibeah under a pomegranate
tree which is in Migron: and the people that were with him were about six
hundred men; and Ahiah, the son of Ahitub, I-chabod's brother, the son of
Phinehas, the son of Eli, the Lord's priest in Shiloh, wearing an ephod. And
the people knew not that Jonathan was gone. And between the passages, by
which Jonathan sought to go over unto the Philistines' garrison, there was a
sharp rock on the one side, & a sharp rock on the other side: and the name of
the one was Bozez, & the name of the other Seneh. The forefront of the one
was situate northward over against Michmash, & the other southward over
against Gibeah. And Jonathan said to the young man that bare his armour,
Come, & let us go over unto the garrison of these uncircumcised: it may be that
the Lord will work for us: for there is no restraint to the Lord to save by many
or by few. And his armourbearer said unto him, Do all that is in thine heart:
turn thee; behold, I am with thee according to thy heart. Then said Jonathan,
Behold, we will pass over unto these men, & we will discover ourselves unto
them. If they say thus unto us, Tarry until we come to you; then we will stand
still in our place, and will not go up unto them. But if they say thus, Come up
unto us; then we will go up: for the Lord hath delivered them into our hand: &
this shall be a sign unto us. And both of them discovered themselves unto the
garrison of the Philistines: & the Philistines said, Behold, the Hebrews come
forth out of the holes where they had hid themselves. And the men of the garrison answered Jonathan & his armourbearer, & said, Come up to us, & we will
shew you a thing. And Jonathan said unto his armourbearer, Come up after
me: for the Lord hath delivered them into the hand of Israel. And Jonathan
climbed up upon his hands and upon his feet, and his armourbearer after him:

Right: typographic design by Adalb Carl Fischl, 1900, predating the formation of the Werkstätte. It attempts to rationalise the letterforms within a set of angles and curves, creating a coherent design, but it lacks sufficient distinction between the characters for legibility.

Below right: page from *Schriften und Ornamente*, issued by the Klingspor foundry in 1900 to show Otto Eckmann's typeface. One of the best known of the Art Nouveau faces, its soft forms are stylised in a way that makes any clear relationship with hand-written lettering impossible, yet suggests the natural movement of a single pen or brush-stroke within the characters. Eckmann ranged across the applied arts after starting as a painter.

Opposite: the Wiener Werkstätte logo, probably designed by Koloman Moser, together with various monograms by artists of the group, including Moser, 1902. These reductive typographic marks explored the potential of letterforms as branding devices, individual yet forming a distinct family. Reading top to bottom and left to right, they belong to Leopold Bauer, Friedrich König, Gustav Klimt, Koloman Moser, Josef Hoffmann, Adolf Böhm, Richard Luksch, Alfred Roller and Ernst Stöhr.

Eckmann
Initialen · u · Vignetten

Rudhard'sche Gießerei
in Offenbach am Main

WIE
NER
WERK
STÄTTE

production costs of dry transfer lettering and, now, digital technology. Producing such sports in metal required considerable investment in time and money, which presumably proved worthwhile for Klingspor as Eckmann became almost the definitive Art Nouveau face. Unfortunately, Eckmann himself died of tuberculosis in 1902, aged 37.

Peter Behrens (1869–1940) is the German designer whose ideas travelled the furthest during this decade. His interests ranged from architecture through to type design and in the latter, as well as in the field of corporate identity, he can claim credit as a founding force. His reputation rests mainly on his stature as an architect, but his positive attitude to industrialisation was equally evident in the field of typography. From mixing traditional German black-letter (or *textur*) type with Jugendstil illustrative work, he underwent a deeper questioning of the ornamental, stripping away many preconceptions about form until he began creating work whose logic derived from his appreciation of modern industrial methods. Around 1900 his typographic ideas can be seen in the face he designed for Klingspor, Behrens Roman. Like Eckmann, this was a pen-drawn roman face, but less florid and more seriously trying to evolve from the German black-letter tradition. At about the same time he designed a book set entirely in sans serif, *Feste des Lebens*, an abrupt break with the expected black-letter of the *textur* variety, but now seen as a precursor of the German evolution from black-letter to a heavy reliance on bold sans serifs. Behrens's

Behrens' contribution to the Jugendstil is suggested by the initial letters he designed in 1900 (below), yet his most significant impact came in the development of more functionalist design. The logo for AEG (far right) was a branding symbol developed by Behrens' team with basic type elements configured in a visual pun suggestive of the electricity turbine; a simpler version is below, and remains similar today (the two logos below this are earlier versions). The turbine hall he designed in 1909 (below right) became a touchstone for modernist architects, while the poster for lights of 1910 (right) finds a form for the arrangement of type that relates well to the picture.

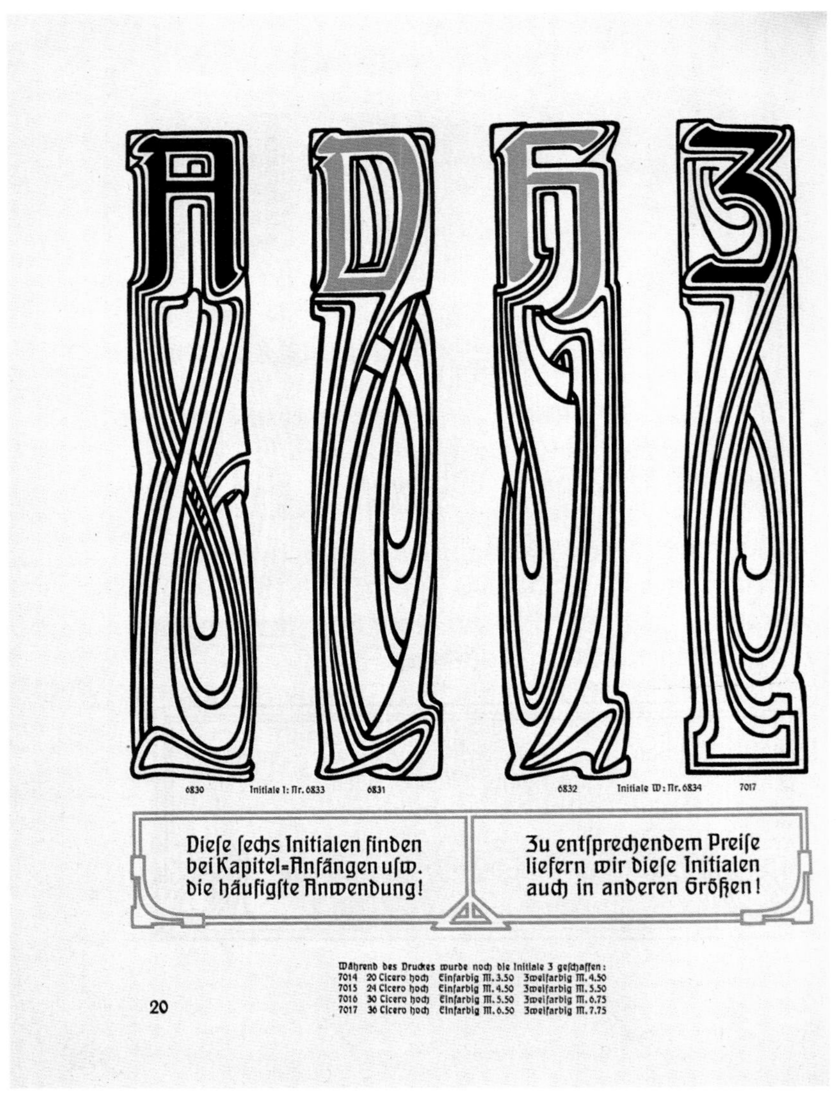

ALLGEMEINE
ELEKTRICITÆTS
GESELLSCHAFT
A·E·G-METALLFADENLAMPE
ZIRKA EIN WATT PRO KERZE

A
E G

AEG

AEG

TURBINENFABRIK

most famous work came in 1907 when he received the commission to review the entire visual identity of AEG, even then one of the world's largest manufacturers of electrical products. It is a large multinational today, and it still has basically the same typographic logo that Behrens gave it. His designs covered not only graphic identity and its application but also the products themselves, and culminated in the AEG building in which products were manufactured – the turbine factory of 1909 became a seminal point in the evolution of Modern architecture for its extensive use of glass. This appreciation of the relationship between typographic detail and the wider nature of a company's environmental concerns sounds a note of maturity in the development of type as well as architecture. It gives a function to type beyond the concern about legibility: it makes meaningful the concept of character in typefaces.

The German interest in sans serif, as a modern development departing from the usual heavy black-letter faces, was reflected elsewhere in the search for a sans face of the era, in preference to the numerous and apparently undistinguished cuts that had been amassed during the nineteenth century. The American Typefounders amalgamation of firms had about fifty "gothics" (sans serifs) in its early specimen book, covering everything from extra-condensed to extra-expanded. Yet one of the first faces Morris Benton was asked to develop as their chief designer was a new sans, presumably an attempt to improve the choice and launch a face targeted at the burgeoning advertising requirements. Benton's drawings in 1902 were of a face that did indeed amalgamate the qualities of the early nineteenth-century models: Franklin Gothic stands out in contrast to Stempel's Akzidenz, released just a few years earlier, by having odd characterful features, rather than a dourly regular line. Details such as the thinning of strokes where curves join stems give a life to the face that distinguishes it from other heavy sans. It was released in 1905 and proved popular, with Benton going on to cut other weights besides this initial extra bold. ATF's

Prominent faces promoted by American Type Founders in the early 1900s.
Below: one of Morris Fuller Benton's most successful faces, Franklin Gothic of 1905, takes the model of earlier, heavy sans serifs and is related to the lively range of wood-letter extra bold display types that proliferated throughout the nineteenth century. Franklin Gothic has remained in popular use up to the present and is offered by all major manufactures of type.
Right: Morris Benton's News Gothic and below it another page from the same ATF catalogue of 1912 with a specimen of Clearface, a Benton design of 1907 that proved immensely popular and was widely copied. Its condensed design remains clearly legible, with a high x-height which partly compensates for the horizontal squashing.
Below far right: Copperplate Gothic, 1901, was one of the first faces to come from Frederic Goudy; it exists only in upper case and is distinguished by its minute serifs.

**ASTRONOMER WROTE**
**Prominent Incorporator**
**Linguist Bought Stone's**

**SPEAKER REFORMS GUIDE**
**Great Entertainer Preparing**
**Englishman Leaving Gotham**

**HUSKY SAILOR DROPS ANCHOR**
**Considered Beautiful Decorations**
**Nervous Printer Became Alarmed**

Clearface in Practical Display

INTERESTING HINTS IN REGARD TO THE ROLL-FRONT

Case Rack

MANY printers have often desired to abandon the regular case racks and substitute a cabinet, thus increasing the life of the type by having it free from dust

The new Roll-Front Case Racks solve the problem, as they are equal to cabinets in every way. They are made of ash, finished in bright antique oak

The Roll-Front Case Racks are fitted with steel runs and are thoroughly manufactured in every way. Have a fine brass desk lock in center and a single key secures the entire tier of cases. For further information write to nearest House of the American Type Founders Co., Selling Agent

Century Border     Strathmore Ornament

Time wasted in hunting sorts constitutes one of the greatest losses encountered in a composing room. The way to obviate such a condition is to buy Job Type in Weight Fonts at Body Type prices and fair discounts.

Clearface

A new and very beautiful book and job letter with distinctive characteristics, making it very desirable where a stylish and easily read type is required. Unsurpassed for all-round work.

American
Type Founders Co.

FOURTEEN EVENLY GRADUATED SIZES, RANGING FROM FIVE POINT TO SEVENTY-TWO POINT, FORMING A USEFUL SERIES

Versatile Ornament     Cast Squares

286

MODERN SHORTHAND
RENUMBERING FURNITURE
HONEST MERCHANTS RETURN
MAGNIFICENT REPORTS PRESENTED

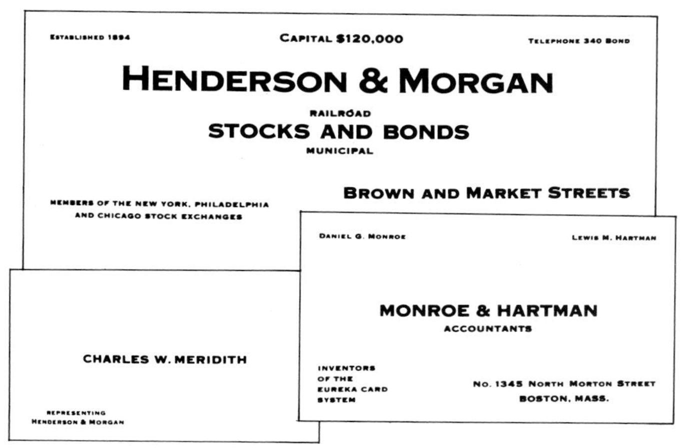
ESTABLISHED 1894
CAPITAL $120,000
TELEPHONE 340 BOND
HENDERSON & MORGAN
RAILROAD
STOCKS AND BONDS
MUNICIPAL
MEMBERS OF THE NEW YORK, PHILADELPHIA AND CHICAGO STOCK EXCHANGES
BROWN AND MARKET STREETS

CHARLES W. MERIDITH
REPRESENTING HENDERSON & MORGAN

DANIEL G. MONROE
LEWIS M. HARTMAN
MONROE & HARTMAN
ACCOUNTANTS
INVENTORS OF THE EUREKA CARD SYSTEM
NO. 1345 NORTH MORTON STREET
BOSTON, MASS.

production of a whole family of gothic faces (Alternate Gothic and News Gothic being just two of the other weight variants) was an early example of the type foundries' gradual comprehension of the printer's requirement for a full range of weights and sizes in one face, rather than odd sizes and weights of dramatically different cuts. But Franklin Gothic is the most distinctive of Benton's sans serif faces, giving full expression to the characteristics. The face has stayed in extensive use ever since, despite the explosion of more geometric sans faces that are distinctly "twentieth-century". Indeed, perhaps that indefinable lack of overt modernity has given Franklin Gothic the basis for a long life.

A different kind of so-called gothic was being drawn by the other highly prolific type designer of the period, Frederic Goudy (1865–1947). His Copperplate Gothic, also for ATF, is not, in fact, "gothic" in the sense of being either a bold sans face, or a black-letter face, but owes its origins to the forms of letters chiselled in stone, more accurately described as "glyphic". But Copperplate Gothic does cross boundaries: the serifs are so tiny as to be almost invisible in small sizes, converting the appearance to that of a sans serif, and the subtlety of the chiselled effect could easily be overlooked. The appearance is stylised and the face was intended for – and is still used for – titling and card work as well as packaging, combining a crisp legibility with strong display. There is a subtle inflection on the weight of strokes – evident, for example, in the capital "C" – giving a dynamic missing with constant-line sans serifs.

The type design and typographic development of this period took place against the gradual acceptance of the crucial role hot-metal setting would come to play. While the Linotype had been enthusiastically received for the mass printing of newspapers and magazines, it was at this point that the slow-developing Monotype machine began to appear as a genuine rival. In 1905 the Monotype caster was improved to cope with larger sizes, casting up to 24 point although it was only able to compose up to 12 point and needed hand-composition for the larger sizes. In 1907 the Monotype was further developed with a keyboard that was faster to use, copying the layout of the typewriter. Refinements continued, as they did for the Linotype machine. As an aside to this progression in technology, a consistent measurement for typefounding sizes became established in America and Britain, with agreed practices concerning the point system. Continental Europe, however, still worked to a different measurement, which made for difficulties at times in the compatibility of foundry faces and equipment. The points system had first been proposed by Fournier in Paris in 1737, and was later amended by Didot so that the measurement of one point equalled 0.3759mm, but in 1886 American foundries settled on a point size of 0.3513mm. Despite its lack of decimal logic, the system generally still applies, overlapping with metric and imperial measurements.

The search for a new and international order was not only to be found in the realm of typography. Although still to have an impact on design, the revolutionary ideas put forward by early Cubist and then Futurist art formed a background to the graphic arts of the period. Both radically questioned the assumptions behind the workings of two- and three-dimensional space, and both soon gave new impetus to the conception of typographic forms, exploding the fairly respectful investigations of type design and layout seen until now.

Right: *Catalunya Artistica*, cover by Joaquim Renart, Barcelona, 1904. An example of the bold lettering and flowery imagery of Modernisme, a Spanish variant of Art Nouveau, which spawned various publications that demonstrated a freer and more decorative approach to graphic design. By the end of this decade there was a move back towards more classic layouts and Roman faces, often of German origin (several German type foundries had set up in Barcelona).
Far right: cover of *Revista Musical Catalana*, designer unknown, Barcelona, 1909. This cover suggests the transition between Modernisme and the more restrained Noucentisme style that followed.
Below right: spread from the influential German arts magazine *Jugend*, design and illustration by E. Volbeht. The classic regimented columns of magazines of the period are here disrupted; type hung from the top of the page challenges the reader to consider the relationship between type and illustration in a way that the conventional, separated layout does not.

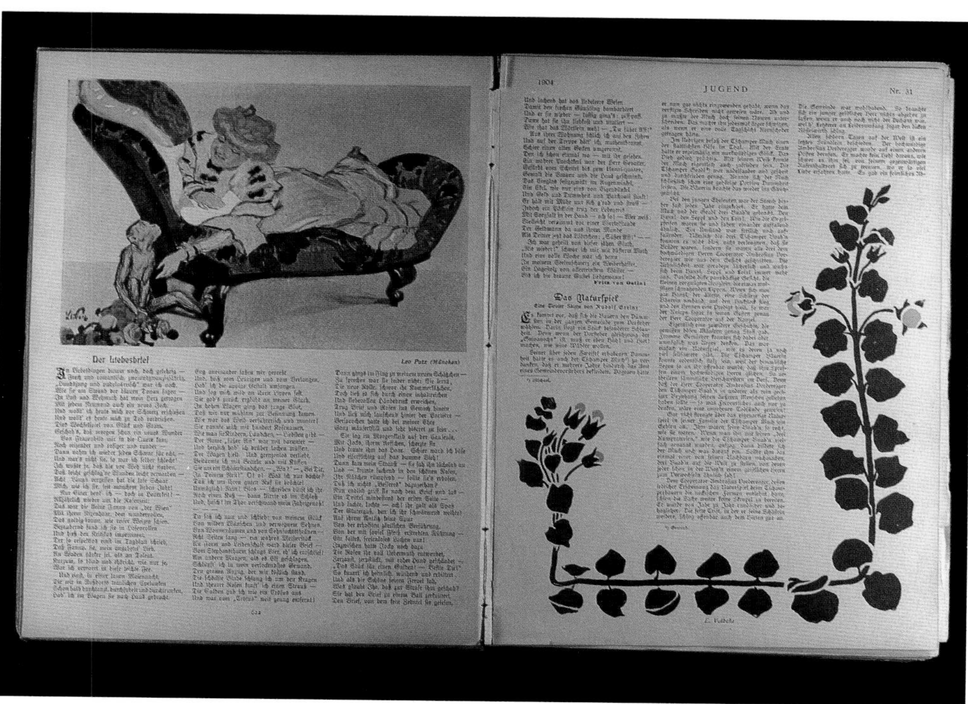
1904 JUGEND Nr. 31

# IMPRINT
# GOUDY OLD STYLE
# CENTAUR

# 1910...

Imprint (1913), Centaur (1914) and Goudy Old Style (1915) looked back to much earlier types to find a standard, while the Futurists and De Stijl artists sought revolutionary new ways of expression. Illustrated are Theo van Doesburg's alphabet of 1919 (right) and a detail by Ardengo Soffici from a page of *BIF & ZF+18* of 1915 (below).

Around 1910, new ideas in art emerged that disrupted and reconstructed the representative agenda of the arts. In time these would have a major impact on typography, as they would on virtually every aspect of Western art. Where painting and sculpture had been concerned with obeying, or at least examining, the requirements of realism – centred around the rules of perspective and the depiction of observable life – there was now a dramatic revision of the potential and purpose of graphic representation. Several complementary movements were involved in this revolt against the orthodox: although they had different motivations, they combined to relocate the leading edge of the graphic arts. Across Europe, from Russia to Spain, artists and writers were questioning assumptions about vision and language, and attacking existing values and projecting new ones.

The debate was particularly active in the work of those connected with Futurism. Their radical shift in approaching the elements of visual form came from exposure to the Cubist ideas of Picasso and Braque who, from 1907 onwards, began compressing the differing planes of three-dimensional forms, viewed simultaneously from more than one angle within the single picture plane. It was particularly after Braque's and Picasso's experiments with *papiers collés* montage constructions in 1911 and 1912 that the Futurist art of Balla, Carra and Severini began to incorporate intriguing forms that had a typographic resonance, picking up on the Cubists' incorporation of letterforms such as newspaper and other printed materials in their collages. The Italian Futurist philosophy called for the expression of the dynamic forces at work in modern society, while rejecting – aggressively – the established forms of art and communication. They set out to shock, particularly in the manifestos written by their propagandist leader, Filippo Tommaso Marinetti (1876–1944).

Marinetti advocated the principle of "words-in-freedom" as a way of communicating, doing away with the orthodox rules of language, both verbal and visual. In his 1914 book *Zang Tumb Tumb* this idea took on a dramatic expression through typography. It did with type what the Futurist artists were attempting with painting and sculpture, applying ideas of "dynamic force" and "lines of force" to visual representation.

The concept of a "typographical revolution" was clearly set down by Marinetti in his 1913 manifesto *Destruction of Syntax – Imagination without Strings – Words – Freedom*:

***I initiate a typographical revolution aimed at the bestial, nauseating idea of the book of passéist and D'Annunzian verse, on seventeenth-century handmade paper bordered with helmets, Minervas, Apollos, elaborate red initials, vegetables, mythological missal ribbons, epigraphs, and Roman numerals. The book must be the Futurist expression of our Futurist thought. Not only that. My revolution is aimed at the so-called typographical harmony of the page, which is contrary to the ebb and flow, the leaps and bursts of style that run through the page. On the same page, therefore, we will use three or four colours of ink, or even twenty different typefaces if necessary. For example: italics for a series of similar or swift sensations, bold face for the violent onomatopoeias, and so on. With this typographical revolution and this multicoloured variety in the letters I mean to redouble the expressive force of words.*** [1]

Marinetti also wrote of the role of typography in Futurist cinema, setting down (in a different manifesto) its place in a formula for the new film-making. Point number 14 was:

***Filmed words-in-freedom in movement (synoptic tables of lyric values – dramas of humanised or animated letters – orthographic dramas – typographical dramas – geometric dramas – numeric sensibility, etc.).***

***Painting + sculpture + plastic dynamism + composed noises + architecture + synthetic theatre = Futurist cinema.***[2]

Such clattering of words together is the equivalent of the conflicting, disintegrated elements within Futurist paintings, or the discordant "music" performed by their noise machines, and is echoed too in the anarchic typography produced by Marinetti, Soffici and Carlo Carra (1881–1966). The magazine *Lacerba* published a series of Carra's free-word experiments in 1914, "Tipografia in libertà", and was an important propagator of the Futurist idea of print.

The concept of "dynamism" was bound up with finding a mode of expression for the new industrial age, particularly represented through mechanical forms and, above all else, the sense of motion and speed. Both Cubism and Futurism were searching for a way of expressing the fourth dimension of time within the two or three dimensions of painting and sculpture. Futurist ideas naturally spread into photography and film, where the images and sense of movement could be depicted by the very industrial processes they sought to embrace. The Futurists also mounted performances that were so confrontational and anarchic in their unharmonious music or hectoring monologues and impenetrable dramas that they drew an aggressively negative response from the audience. This interaction was welcomed, being a mark of successfully breaking through the complacency in society. The explosive, unreadable but emotive quality of

Below: cover and an inside page of the novel *Zang Tumb Tumb*, 1914, by F. T. Marinetti, telling a true story from the Balkan war of 1912 between the Bulgarians and the Turks. In it, the Futurist leader explores theories of "words-in-freedom" and a typographical revolution, in which language – freed from the chains of orthodox literary and typographic composition – could take on much greater power and a new range of meanings.
Right: *Manifestazione interventista* by Carlo Carra, 1914, a collage of paper and paint by one of the leading Futurist painters. As it celebrates the Futurist principles of dynamism, speed and conflict, it also explores the potential for communication through a range of innovative techniques: the layering of planes within a picture; the rotation of elements; the contrast of light and shade; the unpredictable juxtaposition of word and image.

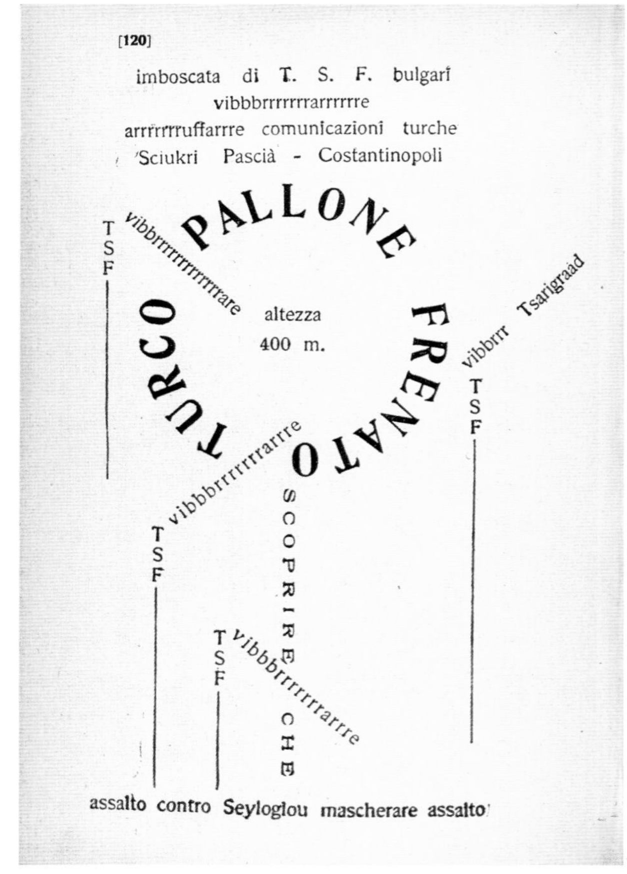

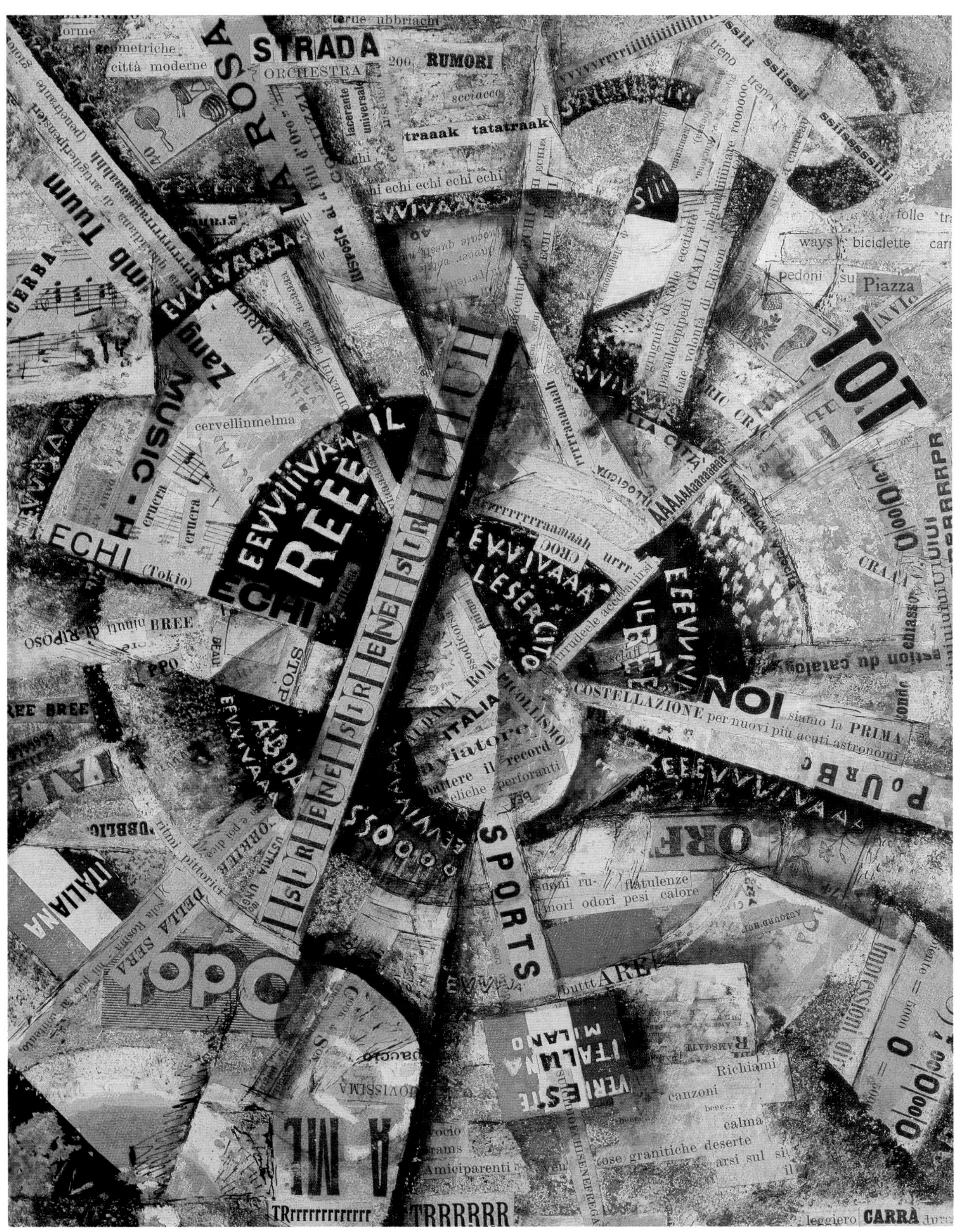
STRADA
ORCHESTRA
RUMORI
città moderne
geometriche
LA ROSA
traaak tatatraak
echi echi echi echi
EVVIVA
MUSIC - H
cervellinmelma
ECHI
(Tokio)
EEVVIIIVAAA IL
RÉÉÉ
EVVIVAAA
L'ESERCITO
ways biciclette
pedoni
Piazza
TOT
NOI
COSTELLAZIONE per nuovi più acuti astronomi
siamo la PRIMA
EEEVVVIVAAA
SPORTS
suoni ru- flatulenze
mori odori pesi calore
ITALIANA
ITALIA
MILANO
Richiami
canzoni
calma
cose granitiche deserte
Amiciparenti
TRrrrrrrrrrrr
TRRRRRR
leggiero
CARRÀ

Marinetti's and others' experiments with typography has to be seen partly as seeking for a similar reaction, although it was also freeing the potential of the printed page in a way that in time would have more positive results. By the 1920s, the second wave of Italian Futurists were taking on advertising and other commercial commissions, proof of the revolutionary effect of these works.

Of the post-Cubist movements breaking across Europe almost simultaneously, it was the Russian that gave the strongest expression through graphic design. The Russian Futurists, or Cubo-Futurists as they sometimes called themselves, were substantially different from the Italians, taking inspiration from the Cubist break with representational traditions, but remaining unconnected with the Italian manifestos. They had their own reaction, against Russian symbolist art and in favour of reviving more primitive forms as a rejection of Czarist culture, and they published their own agendas, for there were a number of different movements lumped together under the Futurist tag. Between 1912 and 1916, though, they combined to produce a range of work which included many books and other printed artefacts.[3]

The books are distinguished by their absence of typography. Lithography was the means of production, and the artists' handwriting was the method of communication, using the same hand as the drawings. As publications they were influential on the Russian painting of the time and perhaps could be seen as rather remote from any direct typographical input. However, in showing the freedom of the printed page and the dynamic forms possible for the relationship between words, images and page layout, they are significant to typographic development. The 1912 *Worldbackwards* and 1913 *Explodity* by Kruchenykh used techniques such as rubber stamp blocks to imprint poems, accompanied by stencilled or potato-print key letters. These innovations, however, came from the opposite direction from that of the Italian Futurists: instead of singing the praises of the industrial age, theirs was a deliberate rejection of modern processes.

But one book did contain intriguing use of type, and this was the most influential in graphic design terms. Vladimir Mayakovsky's *A Tragedy* uses different weights of type, odd capitals and white space to give an original texture to the printed page, constructing a visual metaphor for the emotive response sought from Mayakovsky's play. It was designed by Vladimir and David Burliuk, and includes their drawings. Thought to have been admired by Aleksandr Rodchenko and El Lissitsky, the book can be seen as a direct influence on post-war, post-Revolution graphic design.

The Russian Futurists made a short-lived group, but out of it evolved other movements that also created an impact on typography. Kasimir Malevich's Suprematist paintings from 1916 onwards, boldly non-figurative and geometric, exploring the relationship of simple forms and colours, suggested a new concept of the two-dimensional plane and its formal relationships that was to affect typography in the years ahead. El Lissitsky developed the connection between Suprematist ideas and typographic communication; his early Constructivist painting of 1919, *Beat the whites with the red wedge*, can be seen in direct connection with his children's story-book of 1922 (conceived in 1920), *Of Two Squares*.

A key starting point for El Lissitsky's typographic journey was the English Vorticist movement, another Cubist/Futurist-related group. The propagandist periodical *Blast*, launched and designed in 1914 by the Vorticist leader Percy Wyndham Lewis (1882–1957), was credited by El Lissitsky as being an import-

Right: "Il Pleut" by Guillaume Apollinaire, from *Calligrammes 1913–16*, 1918. Apollinaire found reference for his style of graphic poems in ancient texts, but the work is also in a symbiotic relationship with the art movements of the time. The fractured, multiple readings opened up by the layout of such verse relate to the fragmentation in Cubism and the typographical statements and experiments of the Futurists.
Far right: page from *BIF & ZF+18* by Ardengo Soffici, 1915, a book of typographical experiments and montages using found and constructed imagery to find a new manner of literary communication. Soffici (1879–1964), a painter and writer, had broken with the main Italian Futurist group by the time he came to publish this, following a period spent in Paris where he had associated with Apollinaire.
Below right: calligram by J. M. Junoy on the cover of a Miró exhibition catalogue, Barcelona, 1917. The typographical pun of the poem running through the painter's name is coupled with an appreciation of the expressive quality of dramatic contrasts in type size. The Futurist notion was spreading that new visual and verbal ideas called for a radically new use of the page rejecting classical formats, but Junoy seems to have difficulty in wholly rejecting the impact of a centred title.

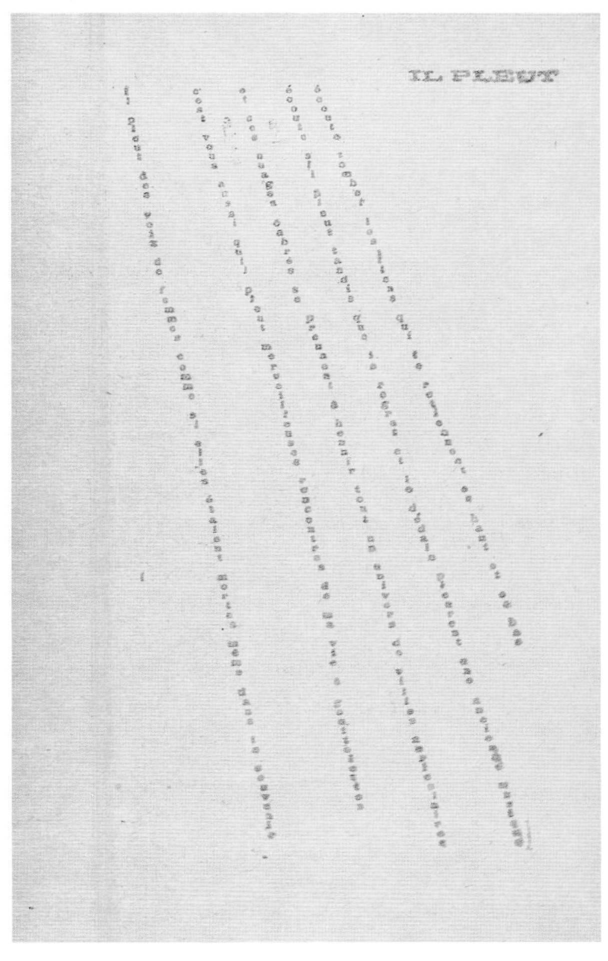
IL PLEUT

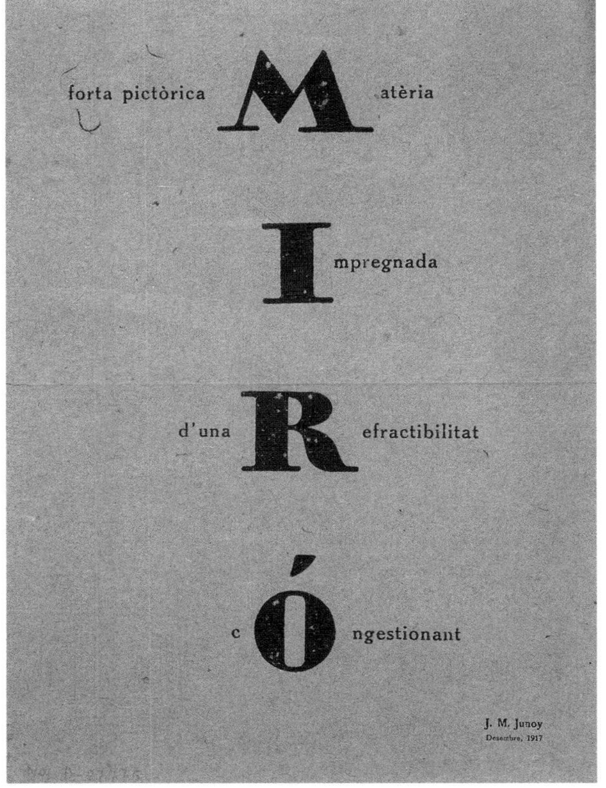
forta pictòrica
M
atèria
I
mpregnada
d'una
R
efractibilitat
c
Ó
ngestionant
J. M. Junoy
Desembre, 1917

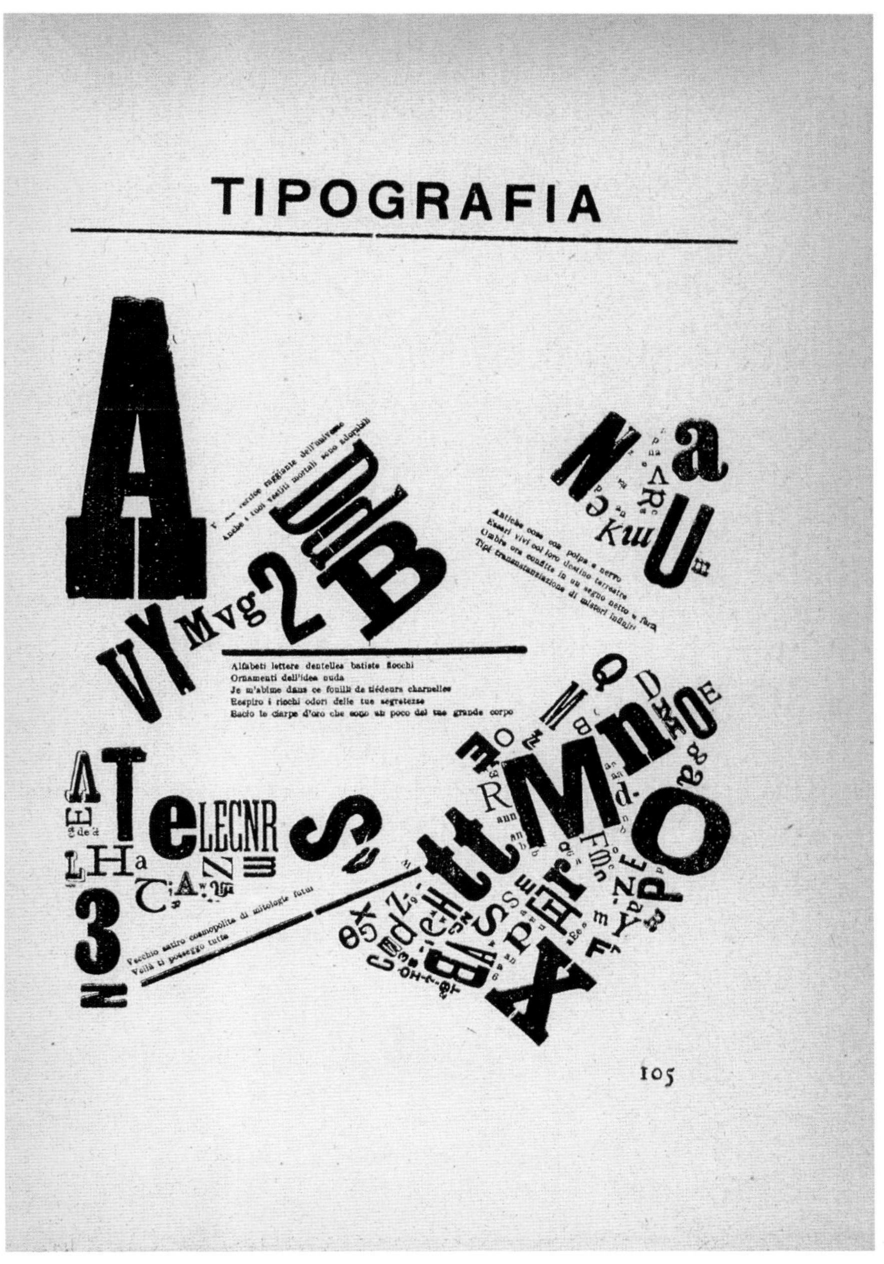
TIPOGRAFIA
Alfabeti lettere dentelles batiste fiocchi
Ornamenti dell'idea nuda
Je m'abime dans ce fouillis de tiédeurs charnelles
Respiro i ricchi odori delle tue segretezze
Bacio le ciarpe d'oro che sono un poco del tuo grande corpo
105

ant inspiration for Burliuk and Mayakovsky's 1915 publication *Vzyal: baraban futuristov* [*Took: a futurist's drum*] which used a similar device: a large, declamatory, single-word title on the cover. *Blast* was provocative in its design, with crude block lettering and coloured paper, but otherwise had little to say in typographic terms, and was out of key with other activity in Britain and the US, which at this point centred on the revival of traditional typographic values.

Another Russian Futurist whose work was later to be influential in its use of type was the writer Ilya Zdanevitch, whose experiments in Paris in the 1920s are highly inventive. They should perhaps, however, be more closely identified with the Dada movement, which first manifested itself around the middle of the First World War in Zürich and soon spread to several German cities, Moscow and Paris. Initially literary and firmly anti-war, anti-art and anti-establishment, Dada's early graphic ideas can be seen in the poetry of Hugo Ball, which mixed different typefaces in a deliberately illogical, nonsensical manner that parodies poetic form. His statement that "the word and the image are one" shows the determination to integrate the verbal and visual meaning of words and pages as one coherent – or incoherent – whole. Another key Dadaist, Kurt Schwitters, used printed ephemera as early as 1919 in his series of works entitled *Merz*, which presented an art culled from random typographic communication in a way that went beyond the Cubists' montages. In 1919 Raoul Hausmann edited the first number of the periodical *Der Dada*, which had a typographically expressive cover that built on Futurist ideas. Hausmann's, Hannah Hoech's and, particularly, John Heartfield's work in photomontage from 1917 were distinctive and lasting Dadaist contributions that re-presented the relationship of two-

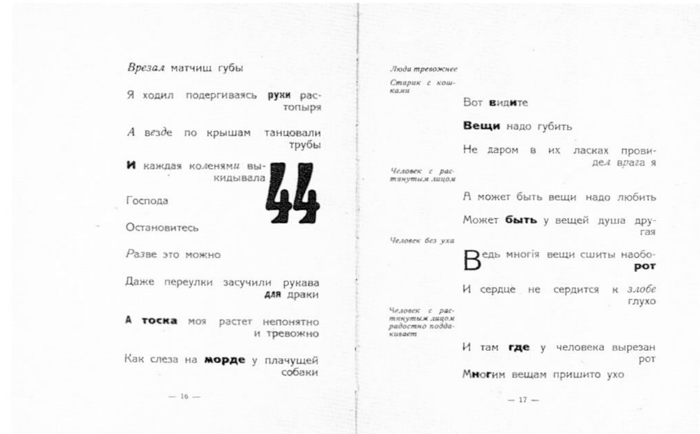

*Врезал* матчиш губы

Я ходил подергиваясь **руки** растопыря

*А везде* по крышам танцовали трубы

**И** каждая коленям*и* выкидывала **44**

Господа

Остановитесь

*Р*азве это можно

Даже переулки засучили рукава **для** драки

**А тоска** моя растет непонятно и тревожно

Как слеза на **морде** у плачущей собаки

— 16 —

*Люди тревожнее*

*Старик с кошками*

Вот **вид**и**те**

**Вещи** надо губить

Не даром в их ласках провидел врага я

*Человек с растянутым лицом*

А может быть вещи надо любить

Может **быть** у вещей душа другая

*Человек без уха*

Ведь многія вещи сшиты наоборот

И сердце не сердится к *злобе* глухо

*Человек с растянутым лицом радостно поддакивает*

И там **где** у человека вырезан рот

Многим вещам пришито ухо

— 17 —

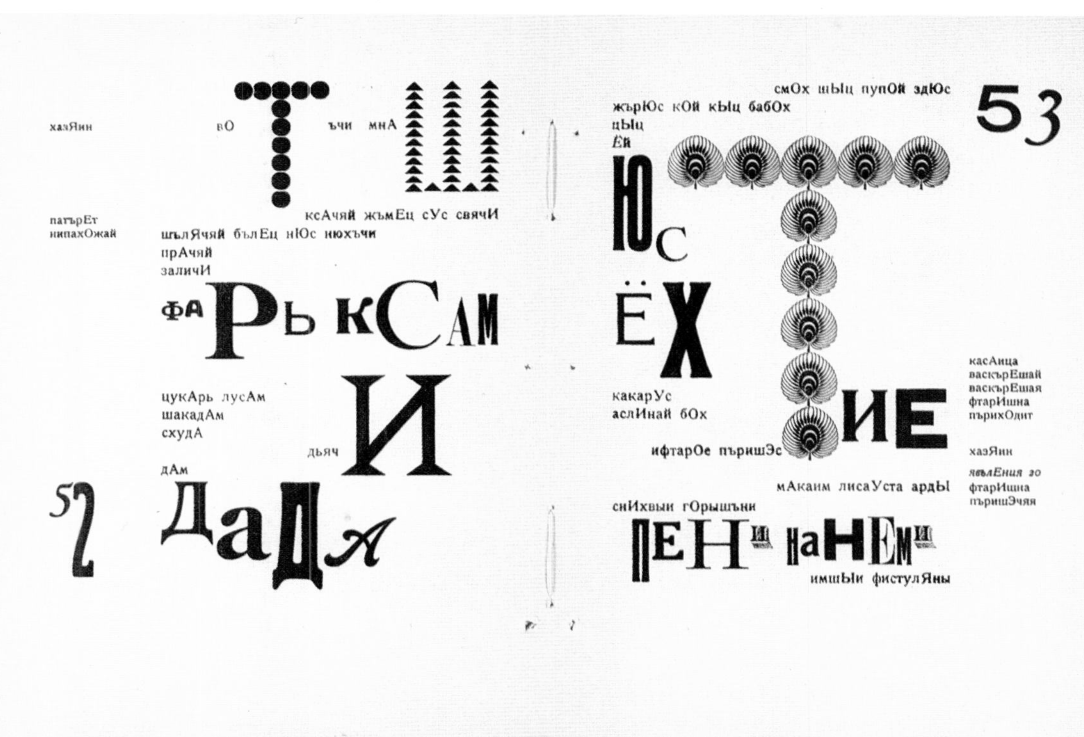

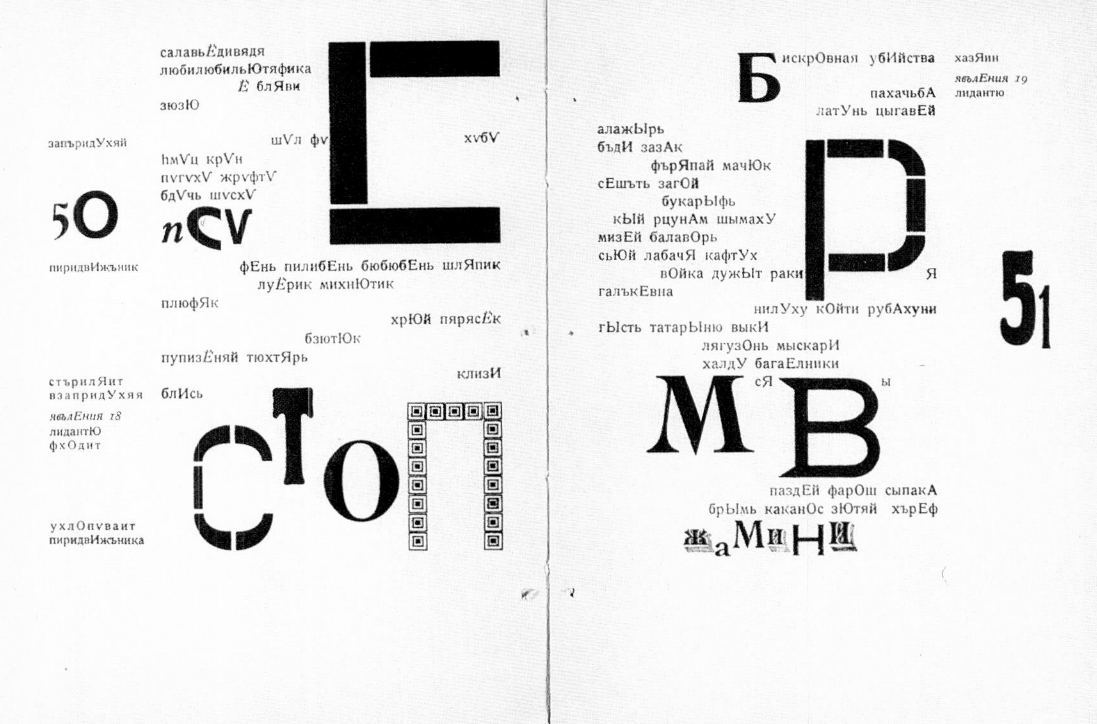

Opposite page, far left: spread from *A Tragedy* by Vladimir Mayakovsky, designed by David and Vladimir Burliuk, 1914. The expressive staggering of the lines as bold type moving across and down the page, the names of characters in italics in the margin, with unexpected elements such as capitals and numbers introduced in stark contrast, made this book an influential departure from convention and a forerunner of later Constructivist work. It has interesting similarities to the contemporary publication, in England, of the Vorticist *Blast* (see page 59).
Opposite page, right: title page of *Studiya* [*Impressionists' Studio*], a journal of Russian Futurist work edited by N. I. Kulbin, 1910. Designed by A. A. Andreev (Dunichev), it features lettering for the word *studiya* composed of cut-out human figures in mediaeval costumes, which relates to the experimental theatre of Nikolai Evreinov, while the triangle suggests the title of an exhibition by Kulbin. While the centred layout is orthodox, the typographic pun and the abstract symbolism within the design break with convention.
This page: two consecutive spreads from *Le-Dantyu as a Beacon* by Ilia Zdanevich, Paris, 1923, the fifth volume of a drama, the first four parts of which were published in Tbilisi, Georgia. Zdanevich (1894–1975) was a Russian Futurist who helped develop from 1910 onwards the idea of *zaum* – a theory of a "transrational language" that takes words and other forms of artistic expression beyond their utilitarian role. In the play as printed, this takes the form of typography that puts words and pages together to have a content beyond the usual function of printed language: each spread is a composition in which there are often different possible readings. The use of typographic ornament to construct letterforms and create visual/verbal choices of meaning disregarding most layout conventions pushed the expressive potential of the page to new heights. Marking the end of Russian Futurism, this book prefigures Surrealist ideas and also shows signs of influence from De Stijl and Dada.

and three-dimensional representation and gave a new vitality to the connections between type and its context.

Typography in Spain followed two divergent routes. A clean classicism characterised the typography created by the Noucentistes art movement, making refined use of roman types, usually from German foundries, with a sobriety that was in itself a reaction against the Spanish Art Nouveau variation, Modernisme (most definitely not to be confused with Modernism) around 1900 and just after. By contrast, a distinctly Spanish contribution to the Dada movement appeared in the form of Francis Picabia's magazine *391*, of which four issues were produced in 1917 before Picabia left Barcelona for Zürich. Rather than beginning a movement in its own right, *391* issued a warning shot of the international changes that would affect Spanish design over the next few years. It promoted the challenge to reason expressed in other Dadaist publications, but did not carry this far into the typographic detail. However, in the requirement that type and image were essentially bound together, with puns demanding a close picture/word relationship that rejected traditional illustrative practice, Picabia's work was promoting the avant-garde in art direction.

Holland, remaining relatively untouched by Dadaism, was the birthplace of the De Stijl movement, a Modernist group which formed around the magazine *De Stijl*, founded in 1917 by the painter, designer and writer Theo van Doesburg (1883–1931) and edited by him until his death. The first cover displayed a logotype based on a painting by Vilmos Huszár (1884–1960), drawing the words as a series of rectangles, arranging the type in rectangular straitjackets as well, and indicating some of the principles of using primary elements in non-decorative ways that typified De Stijl and van Doesburg's work in the coming years, but lacked the contact with Dadaism that developed in his work in the 1920s.

In France there was limited but significant post-Cubist experimentation with the presentation of the printed word. Although the Cubist painters did not reach out into this area, other than to incorporate printed text into paintings

Below left: experimental alphabet by Theo van Doesburg, 1919. Abolishing all curved and diagonal lines, he created a geometric face that presages the Bauhaus and other work of the 1920s and onwards in its search for the fundamentals of the alphabet. While the legibility of the face is clearly compromised (the degree of differentiation between letters and the ease of their conjunction into recognisable words are both inadequate), the face does have considerable harmony.

Below: cover of the first issue of Theo van Doesburg's *De Stijl* magazine, 1917, featuring a geometric masthead by van Doesburg and an illustration by Vilmos Huszár, projecting the rectangle as the basic unit of composition. The magazine was concerned with revealing the essential nature of forms and with integrating fine art with applied art, and thus took an active interest in typography.

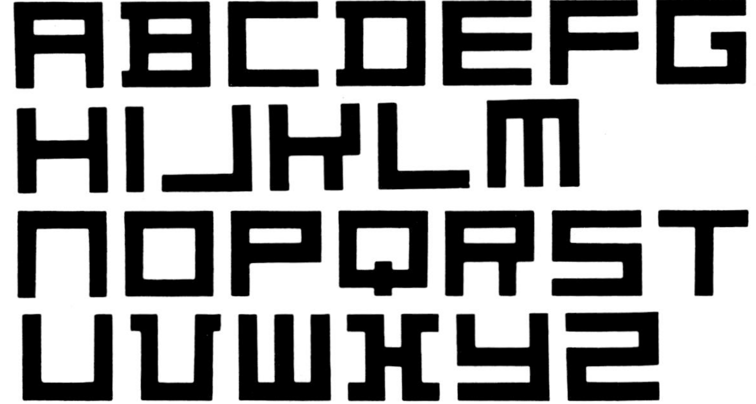

IM JUNI 1917

# NEUE JUGEND

PREIS 20 PF.

PROSPEKT
zur Kleinen Grosz Mappe.

Prospekt zur Kleinen Grosz Mappe. — Der Malik-Verlag, Berlin-Südende — 34, Steglitzer Strasse, Südende.

**CHRONIK** Friedrich Adler ist zum Tode verurteilt, Stockholm-Getöne gegen internationale Teuerung - das Leben weiterhin billiger, Lebensmittel bleiben in Cornerstimmung. Nach Reuter verhungern in Ovamboland die Ovambos, keine Kaffern - in den European Dominions niemand! Verhungert doch - Steigerung!! Spinoza ist eingestampft für Bedarf diplomatischer Sendschreiben - Liberia, Pseudoliberia - Molière verrieselt in Sternheim (Zukunft vom 26. 5. 1917), Umfassungsmanöver gegen Wallner in Wien, Durst! - das Aktionsbuch ist erschienen. Frühlingswende fiebert Sexualität, Heufieber. Liebeloh la l'au! Sich hinzu-schmeissen! Lichtmord!! — unsere Seelen sind so wund. **Amokläufer . . . . . . .** Die Messer raus!!!

## Man muß Kautschukmann sein!

Ja, Kautschukmann sein — eventuell den Kopf zwischen die Beine stecken oder durchs Faß springen — und spiralig in die Luft schnellen! sieh, ein Paragraph rempelt Dich an,
eine Affiche,
ein Flohzirkus . . .
. . . . . . . . . . . . . .
(sämtliche Flöhe liegen an Schlingen — desertieren ausgeschlossen — Springen von Flöhen auf Kommando, Parademarsch der Flöhe . . . . . . . . . . . . . .)

Immerhin wichtig ist, das Gleichgewichtzu behalten!
Wo vordem die gotische Kirche,
messelt sich heute das Warenhaus hoch — !

EIN „MARSIAS" INTERESSENT

— Die Fahrstühle sausen . . . Eisenbahnunglücks, Explosionskatastrophen . . . .
— quer durchrast der Balkanzug Mitteleuropa,
doch gibts auch Baumblüte und Edelmarmeladenrationierung . . . .
Wie gesagt, Kautschukmann sein
beweglich in allen Knochen
nicht blos im Dichter-Sessel dösen
oder vor der Staffelei schön getönte Bildchen pinseln.

Den Bequemen gilts zu stören
beim Verdauungsschläfchen
ihm den pazifistischen Popo zu kitzeln,
rumort! explodiert! zerplatzt! — oder hängt euch ans Fensterkreuz . . . . . . . . . . . .
Laßt euren Kadaver in die Branntweingasse baumeln!
Ja! Wieder elastisch werden, nach allen Seiten höchst federnd — sich verbiegen — anboxen! Kinn- oder Herzgrubenhieb!

### Ladies and gentlemen!!
jeder hat Zutritt!

Nur nähertreten!! . . . nur nähertreten!! . . .
Schon beulen sie den Weihrauchkessel ein.
Nervös rutscht das weiche Gesäß hin und her!
. . . . . . . . . . . . . . . . . . . . . . . . . .
Ja! Wenn nicht sämtliche Flöhe an Schlingen lägen! . . . . . . . . . . . .

Dieses Blatt ist der

## Die Sekte 1917

**Die Sekte Neunzehn Siebzehn** wächst aus dem Intellekt der umstehenden Zuhörer empor und zwingt ihre Mitglieder gegen den Block der Überzeugten. Die ohnmächtige Wut unserer Leser verpflichtet, einen bereits in Schwingung umgesetzten Glauben wieder zu fixieren, um mit den Gläubigen von neuem dagegen loszugehen. Die Leute wollen halt nichts alleine tun.

Sekten. Mehr Sekten. Noch mehr Sekten.

Das Wunder der Christian Science ist über unseren kürzlich veranstalteten Werbe Abend gerauscht und schüttet Glück aus über diejenigen, die uns lieben, um uns hinterrücks zu erdolchen.

Darum muss Einer seine Stimme erheben: Nicht mehr glauben, überhaupt nicht glauben. Sich selbst. (Sich und selbst) Beten.

Wenngleich jeder schuldig ist an der Unfähigkeit der andern, Feind zu sein, sondern schlotternder Neidhammel, soll keiner an dieser Schuld sich selbst beruhigt genug sein lassen. Nicht das Peinliche dieser Schuld schmatzend zu fressen, soll es ankommen, sondern Genuss auch noch auszukotzen — und wiederum zu fressen und wiederum!

Es ist in jeder Sekunde, die ein hundertmalverfluchtes Leben schenkt (unsägliche Wonne durstend das galizische Petroleumgebiet zu durchfahren, die Gestänge der Bohrtürme verrusst!) so unendlich vieles zu tun.

### Betet mit dem Schädel gegen die Wand!!

Wir — aha! — wir treten gegen die Menschen nicht auf. Wir treten geduldig noch mit den Menschen auf. Die Sekte Neunzehn Siebzehn schlägt gegeneinander, Sturmflut aus unseren Gebeten, die aus der Ohnmacht der Gläubigen emporgewachsen sind. Unsere Mitglieder verrecken, weil die Sekte sie nicht mehr locker lässt. Betet aus unseren Gebeten zu diesem Ende. Damit ihr endlich in die Schlinge kommt. Es ist ein so ungleiches Spiel mit diesen Sanften, Zappelnden. Der Magen der **Neunzehn Siebzehn** will das alles nicht mehr verdauen, immer wieder dasselbe, die Ohnmacht der Gläubigen, der Block der Ueberzeugten, das Einfangen, Verarbeiten, Auskotzen, Fressen,

98 Tempelh.
TELEPHON

REKLAMEBERATUNG

das Ich triumphierend über Puntas Arenas, Michigan See, Sachalin bis Sorau. Dort wurde der Dichter Heinrich Steinhausen geboren, steht in der Zeitung.

Halt dich, Junge.

Die Frist ist um. Her die neue Ladung. Sektierer, los! Wieviel zappeln schon wieder?

Die Arbeit Arbeit Arbeit Arbeit: Triumph der Christian Science.

**Das Wunder der Sekte Neunzehn Siebzehn.**

1917.

SCHREIT!!

## Kannst du radfahren ?

Zu den reinsten unverbildeten Erklärungen und Dokumenten unseres Lebens gehören jene Bilder auf den Rückfronten der Häuser, diese Erlasse des Kaufmanns (des wahren Herrn dieser Zeit) — von unerhörter Sachlichkeit vorgetragen, gigantisch eingeätzt wie auf alten Pyramiden, pressen sie das psychologische und formale Erleben des in knallendem Stadtbahnzug Dahinrollenden. Fabelhaft bunt und klar, wie nie ein Tafelbildchen, — von kosmischer Komik, brutal, materiell, bleichsüchtig, verwaschen — drohend und mahnend gleich Ragtimestepptanzmelodie immer wieder sich ins Gehirn bohrend —

Das gröhlt in einem fort!

Zwingt uns zum prallenden Marineblau, zu Grellrots (ganze Straßen Buchstaben), Varietégrün, Spezialitätengelb, Wollwarengraus, und fistelndes Rosa —

Moziationen tauchen auf . . . . . . . . .

Champagner-Flasche — der Korken knallt davon, ho! ho!

Sekt Schloss Vaux.

Ich, Dannemann-Zigarre schief im Maul, Zeitung — vor mir knerzen die Knattermotore — hart überholt nach Backbord der rote Autobus!

Ho! ho! schon wieder brüllen die Häuserwände:

Regie-Zigaretten, *Satrap*, Palast-Hotel, Teppich-Thomas, **bade zu Hause**, Steiners Paradiesbett . . . . . ho! . . . . . *Sarg's Kalodont* . . . . .
Passage-Cafe . . . . . . **AEG** . . . . . Ceresit.

z. B., vom Training kommend, am Punching Ball . . . . Den Joe hiebst Du nieder.

**z. B.**, Du segeltest fabelhaft in die Chausseen, eben noch flog Dir der Fußball an die klemmerlose Nase, Du hingst oben im Aeroplan unter der Bergsonne — zwischen den Stämmen knallte Deine Winchesterbüchse (Gott ließ ja Eisen wachsen, bravo)

Abends in deu Asphaltbrüchen, in Geldsack-Hills, zwischen Porter-Bierplakaten, oder an der Bar bei Kantorowicz, in Zooquellen oder piklein mit steifem Hemd aalglatt bei Adlon, strömendes **Pils Coctails Ersatz** und Agoston, **Apollotheater** und Kinohäuser . . . . . . . . . . . und dem Treiben der beiden Herzfelder! . . . . . . . . . . .

Sag mal? — . . . . . . **graults Dir** da **nicht** in den Kunstsalons? in den Ölgemäldegalerien . . . . . . . ?
in den literarische Soiréen . . . . . ?

Lieber Leser! Ein guter Fußballspieler enthält immerhin eine ganze Menge Wert — obwohl er nicht dichtet, malt und Töne setzt!

Bleibt die Frage?

Kennst Du Schiller und Goethe — ? — ja!

**Aber kannst Du radfahren?**

*Weitere Marsyas-Interessenten wollen sich noch melden!*

Top: advertisement for war loans by Lucien Bernhard, 1915. The German Plakatstijl simplified the idea of the advertising poster to a single image in flat colour, with a copyline reduced either to the advertiser's name or else a short, powerful exhortation as here. Bernhard (1883–1972) was one of the leading developers of this style, which generated its own forms of display lettering as a result of the cleaner, more open layout and the brief, powerful statements. In the 1920s he went to the United States and from 1928 designed fonts for American Type Founders.

Above left: German poster advising returning prisoners of war where they could go to for help, designed by Louis Oppenheim, 1919. The convention of words in black-letter centred under an illustration of the target reader would have added to the soldiers' sense of coming home. The poster does not have a radical layout, but is designed to communicate security; at the same time, it has the simplicity of the Plakatstijl.

Above: cover of the journal *Neue Jugend* by John Heartfield, 1917. A pioneer of photomontage, Heartfield (1891–1968, born Helmut Herzfelde) was associated with the Dadaists, with anti-war constructions in the First World War and with anti-Nazi images later. He also explored the visual potential of typographic collage, often with photography. He founded, with his brother Wieland, the Malik publishing company in Berlin and they brought out the newspaper *Neue Jugend*, publishing Dadaist writings against art. He played with mixing fonts and breaking the rules of orthodox newspaper layout, but did not become so disruptive as to obscure the writings. His illustrations mix found materials with different faces; different sizes of type sometimes appear within one word, letters do not range to any discernible baseline but are laid down often to contrast and conflict with each other.

and assemblages, the poet and critic Guillaume Apollinaire (1880–1918), an important champion of Picasso and Braque, did make the connection between the new approach to art and the visual potential of writing. He wrote calligrams – poems that used the page in their layout to express the subject matter. There are earlier references for this approach, notably Lewis Carroll's mouse's tale/tail as a sentence and typographic joke in *Alice's Adventures in Wonderland* (1865), or Stéphane Mallarmé's expressive layouts in *Un Coup de Des* (1897), but these are one-off efforts, and, although significant, formed part of a literary tradition of early self-consciousness (Laurence Sterne's *Tristram Shandy* of 1760 being an even earlier and more remote example). Apollinaire's close connections with the Cubists and his contact with the Futurists (about whom he was not particularly flattering) make his literary experiments more significant, since they approach the idea of a new kind of graphic design from the writer's viewpoint. A collection of his calligrams was published in 1917. Blaise Cendrars, another French writer, also showed the writer/designer/typographer at work in 1913 in his "simultaneous" book, *La Prose du Transsiberien et de la petite Jehanne de France*. This was a two-metre-long poem in different colours and sizes of letters, which dispensed with the concept of the neutral page background in having the poem superimposed on an abstract painting, specially designed by Sonia Delaunay. Although no typefaces in the orthodox sense resulted from these experiments, they were the prefiguring of more fully resolved ideas for revolutionising graphic design and typography, which were to come into full flower during the 1920s.

The typographic implications of Futurism and the related early Modernist movements were recognisable in the introduction of new ideas that conveyed the dynamic of composition and the awareness that legibility involved more than simple, orthodox typographic layout. The eye can glide smoothly over a collection of words on a page with a centred piece of text, set in a frame of white space, but this is only one way of seeing – and a static, unquestioning one at that. The Futurists, taking on board first Cubism, then Suprematism and Dadaism and finally the Bauhaus, forced through the case for new modes of expression to encapsulate contemporary forces at work in twentieth-century life; these ideals would flourish in typography and type design during the decade following these first explosive signals of the Modernist sensibility.

While these revolutionary ideas were filtering through, the world of commercial typography was seeing the influence of a concerted effort to revive the classic faces and to cut modern variants of these. In its way this revivalism is just as vital to understanding the basis for present-day typographic art and industry as the dramatic new vision of the artists and designers grouped under early Modernism. Both drew inspiration from the craft movements, particularly the work of William Morris, but each took different paths of reaction or revival.

During this decade the pace of technological change continued to accelerate, its impact on design and printing practice growing with the refinement of typesetting machines. In 1911 the Linotype's efficiency was improved by carrying three magazines of matrices at one time on a machine – different founts being available at the press of a lever. Later in the same year this was increased to four magazines, and further major refinements continued to be announced almost annually.

The problem of being unable to set large sizes of type by machine was also being tackled. Until now wood-block letters were still in use for headline setting

Right: cover of *Almanach dels Noucentistes* designed by Josep Aragay, 1911. This luxurious publication was central to projecting the values of the Barcelona artistic movement Noucentisme. Classical roman typography and orthodox order sit oddly with the shifted focus of the layout: not only is the illustration cropped in by the border, but the headline is also set as if it is too large for the page.

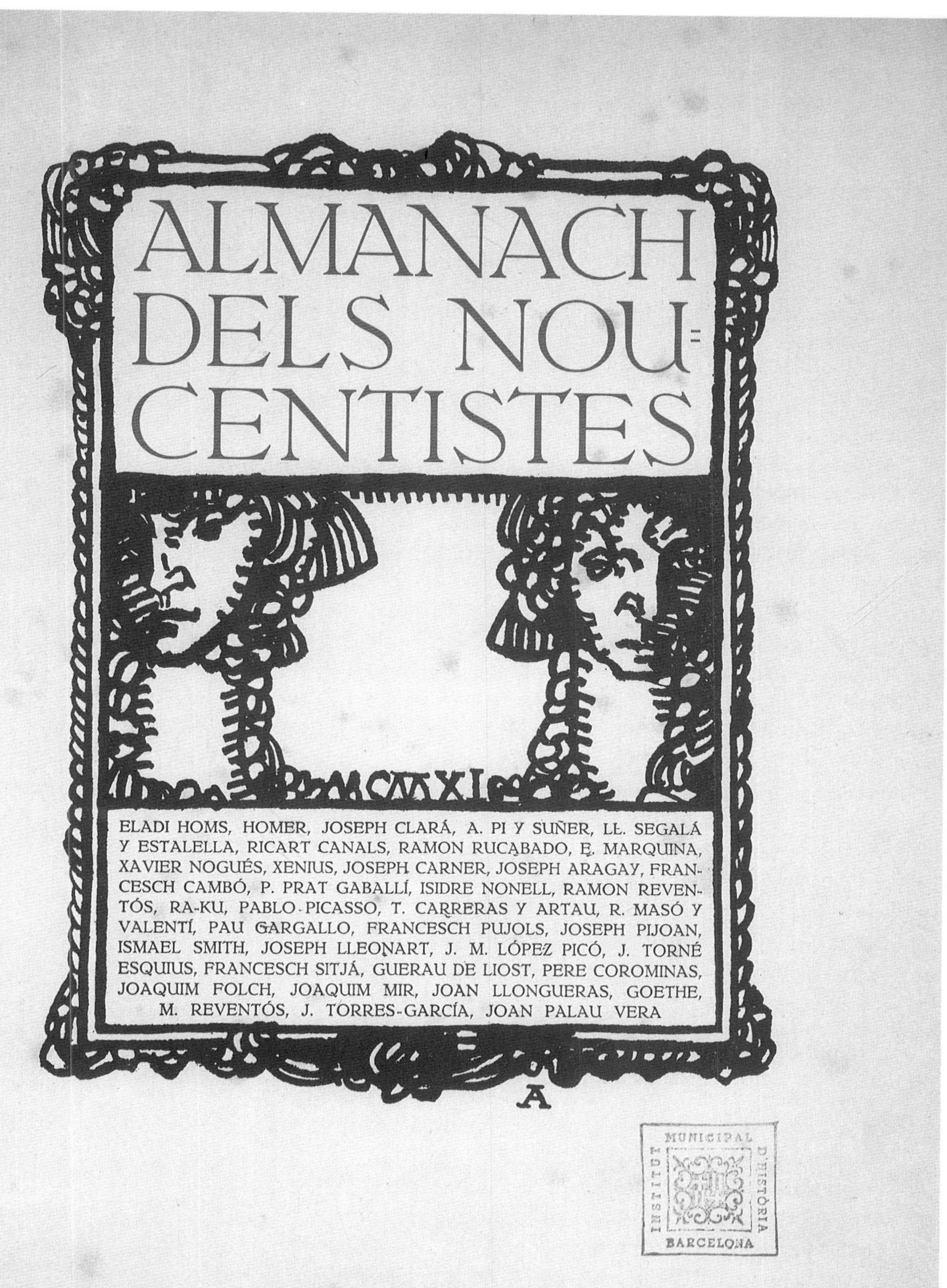
ALMANACH DELS NOU=CENTISTES

MCMXI

ELADI HOMS, HOMER, JOSEPH CLARÁ, A. PI Y SUÑER, LL. SEGALÁ Y ESTALELLA, RICART CANALS, RAMON RUCABADO, E. MARQUINA, XAVIER NOGUÉS, XENIUS, JOSEPH CARNER, JOSEPH ARAGAY, FRANCESCH CAMBÓ, P. PRAT GABALLÍ, ISIDRE NONELL, RAMON REVENTÓS, RA-KU, PABLO-PICASSO, T. CARRERAS Y ARTAU, R. MASÓ Y VALENTÍ, PAU GARGALLO, FRANCESCH PUJOLS, JOSEPH PIJOAN, ISMAEL SMITH, JOSEPH LLEONART, J. M. LÓPEZ PICÓ, J. TORNÉ ESQUIUS, FRANCESCH SITJÁ, GUERAU DE LIOST, PERE COROMINAS, JOAQUIM FOLCH, JOAQUIM MIR, JOAN LLONGUERAS, GOETHE, M. REVENTÓS, J. TORRES-GARCÍA, JOAN PALAU VERA

A

and advertising, being relatively easily made, cheap and not as heavy to store as metal. But the Ludlow Typograph Company's launch of its machine for casting type from hand-assembled large-character matrices showed a way forward for the production of slugs of display type that would lead to the decline of the wood-letter industry.

In 1912 Linotype's first direct rival to provide a linecasting system came on to the horizon when the Intertype machine was demonstrated. This followed the expiry of Mergenthaler's patent on the basic linecasting concept. In 1918 the *New York Times* placed a substantial order for the Intertype machine that firmly established the company as a serious competitor.

Monotype's advances in this decade were directly aimed at holding the leading edge in the field of fine typesetting, and it was becoming seen as the credible new technology for book production, while the Linotype was considered more suited to newspaper work. The Monotype's handling of kerned letters was perfected and the size of type it could set was gradually increased (up to 24 point in 1914).

The most significant development supported by the Monotype Corporation from the creative point of view was its cutting of the first original face designed for mechanical typesetting. Imprint was cut in 1913 especially for a new magazine of that name dedicated to typography. The founders and editors of the magazine, Gerard Meynell and J. H. Mason, with F. Ernest Jackson and Edward Johnston, originated the design, which was loosely based on Caslon but is distinctive in having a large x-height (aiding legibility in small sizes) and a thickened and very regular italic. When issued by Monotype for wider use, the face proved popular and many sets of matrices were sold. *Imprint*, although short-lived and ceasing after nine issues, was a determined effort to encourage higher standards in printing and typography. It was notable in clearly projecting the concept of the role of the typographer as designer rather than craftsman, and expressed concern for the idea of a professional who sought to control typographic quality.

In 1914 the American Institute of Graphic Arts was founded, another signal of the new status of the graphic designer. It was during this period that certain key type designers built their reputations: Frederic Goudy and Bruce Rogers in America, Rudolf Koch and Edward Johnston in Europe.

Goudy's prolific credits for typeface design rest on his reputation as the creator of a number of beautiful faces, often built on revived forms but given a unique character by the designer. Goudy came to his main calling relatively late in his career. He was born in 1865, became a designer during the 1890s and had his first face accepted by ATF late in the decade (an undistinguished period piece called Camelot). It was not until he set up as a freelance lettering artist and then established his Village Press in 1903 that he became more set upon the path that was to see him become a full-time type designer in a career that continued until his death in 1947.

Goudy's first major face was Kennerley, designed for the publishing company Mitchell Kennerley in 1911. He had been invited to design an edition of H. G. Wells's stories, but decided that the eighteenth-century Caslon they had in mind was not to his liking. Kennerley is another old-style face (like Morris's and Benton's Cloister) but has its own distinct manner. The spur on the "G", the high bar of the "H", the fancy tails of the "Q" and "R" (with suggestions of swash letters) all show Goudy's flourish. Various ancient sources have been found for

Right and far right: Kennerley, designed by Frederic Goudy in 1911, is one of this prolific designer's most respected faces. The italic demonstrates the pen qualities evident in much of his work, where the individual character of the face begins to edge in on the straight readability.
Below right: the Ludlow typecasting machine and matrix cabinets, successfully produced from 1911. This equipment was the first effective way of setting slugs of type from hand-assembled matrices and was an important addition to the potential of the new technology – notably for headline setting in newspapers, where sufficiently large sizes of type were not available through the Linotype or Monotype. The operator would assemble the matrices and cast the slug of type to fit the page forme by hand.

KENNERLEY OLD STYLE

THIS FACE was designed in 1911 for use in a sumptuous presentation of ten short stories by H. G. WELLS published by MITCHELL KENNERLEY & was afterward offered to printers generally. A modest showing in *Typographica No.* 1 of the two sizes then available brought response at once from printers, and the demand, in spite of its piration by certain unscrupulous machine men, today is as great as ever. It is an original face; that is to say, its essential characteristics are not drawn from existing sources. One writer says "Kennerley besides being beautiful in detail, is beautiful in mass; and the letters set into words seem to lock into one another which is common in the letter of early printers, but is rare in modern type."

Eleven sizes in the roman, 10 to 72 point; eight sizes in the italic, 10 to 36 point,

KENNERLEY OPEN CAPS

A B C D E F G H
I J K L M N O P Q
R S T U V W
X Y Z &

[36 PT. (48 PT. FACE) SINGLE LETTERS 5 CTS. 3A $4.00 PER SET]

[ 6 ]

ABCDEFGHIJKL
MNOPQRSTUV
WXYZabcdefghijk
lmnopqrstuvwxyz
1234567890

*ABCDEFGHIJKL*
*MNOPQRSTUV*
*WXYZabcdefghijklm*
*nopqrstuvwxyz*
*1234567890*

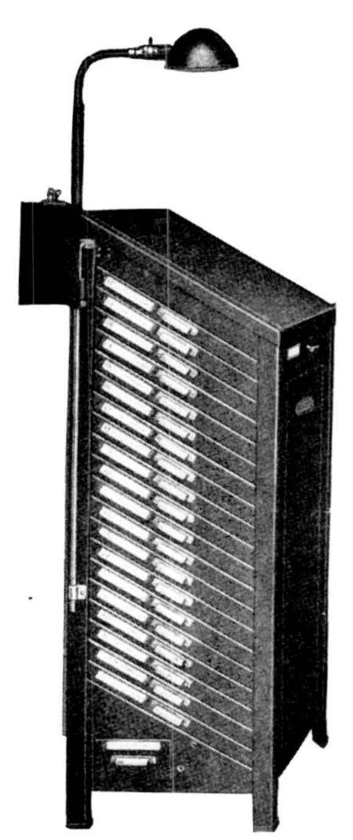

Goudy's ideas, but what is remarkable is the quality of the revival and the originality it has in that context. Although it was produced only for Mitchell Kennerley and for Goudy's Village Press, the rights were sold to Monotype, who issued the face in 1920. In the same year Goudy also drew a tilting face of capitals, called Forum, the first of his faces inspired by classical precedents.

The building of a reputation on the back of these faces earned Goudy a commission from ATF to design a new face in 1914: from this came one of his most notable and lastingly popular, Goudy Old Style. Here, according to Goudy, the reference was Renaissance lettering, drawn from letters in a painting (possibly a Holbein). The letters are more rounded than Kennerley, and this face also owes much to Jenson. The short ascenders were a feature that Goudy was persuaded by ATF to incorporate against his better judgement. The italic, drawn before the Kennerley italic, was to make an influential contribution to the italic tradition, being closer to the roman than normal – indeed it is only slightly inclined, with the "m" and the "n" actually upright, albeit with splayed legs. Overall, the face was much appreciated by typographers, including such authorities as D. B. Updike, the printer and type historian, for its qualities as a book face: it fulfils admirably the criteria of knitting letters together to work as words, and of having lightness on the page.

While Goudy was designing this key face, Bruce Rogers was also building a reputation as a brilliant type designer. Rogers (1870–1957) had a career that spanned a vast tract of the American modern design tradition; he began professional work in the 1890s and continued working into the 1950s. However, his reputation rests on his being one of the finest of fine book designers, and at the core of this achievement is his creation of the typeface Centaur in 1914. It was originally designed for the Metropolitan Museum of Art in New York for use in their ephemeral printing, basically as a titling fount, but Rogers had it for his own use as well and in 1915 it first appeared on the book *The Centaur* by

Below: Imprint (top), Plantin (centre) and Goudy Old Style (bottom). Goudy Old Style, designed by Frederic Goudy in 1915, is basically a revival form, belonging to the garalde group, along with Plantin, created for Monotype by Frank Hinman Pierpont (1860–1937) and issued in 1913.
Right: Centaur, designed by Bruce Rogers in 1915 for the Metropolitan Museum in New York, took its name from the setting used in Maurice de Guérin's *The Centaur*, Montague Press, 1915 (far right). This face, a strikingly elegant revival of the fifteenth-century Jenson, was produced by Monotype with an accompanying italic in 1929, and was used for the Oxford University Press lectern bible of 1935 (right).
Below right: Imprint, as seen in *The Imprint*, volume one, number one, June 1913. This old-face revival has a design pedigree associated with Gerard Meynell, J. H. Mason, Ernest Jackson and Edward Johnston. It drew on Caslon in its styling (itself a Jenson-influenced design), but with a larger x-height.

abcdefghijklmnopqrstuvwxyz
ABCDEFGHIJKLMNOPQRSTUVWXYZ
1234567890

**abcdefghijklmnopqrstuvwxyz**
**ABCDEFGHIJKLMNOPQRSTUVWXYZ**
**1234567890**

abcdefghijklmnopqrstuvwxyz
ABCDEFGHIJKLMNOPQRSTUVWXYZ
1234567890

# I Chronicles Chapter I

the armies, they and their men, heard that the king of Babylon had made Gedaliah governor, there came to Gedaliah to Mizpah, even Ishmael the son of Nethaniah, and Johanan the son of Careah, and Seraiah the son of Tanhumeth the Netophathite, and Jaazaniah the son of a Maachathite, they and their men. ❡24 And Gedaliah sware to them, and to their men, and said unto them, Fear not to be the servants of the Chaldees: dwell in the land, and serve the king of Babylon; and it shall be well with you. ❡25 But it came to pass in the seventh month, that Ishmael the son of Nethaniah, the son of Elishama, of the seed royal, came, and ten men with him, and smote Gedaliah, that he died, and the Jews and the Chaldees that were with him at Mizpah. ❡26 And all the people, both small and great, and the captains of the armies, arose, and came to Egypt: for they were afraid of the Chaldees.

❡27 And it came to pass in the seven and thirtieth year of the captivity of Jehoiachin king of Judah, in the twelfth month, on the seven and twentieth day of the month, that Evil-merodach king of Babylon in the year that he began to reign did lift up the head of Jehoiachin king of Judah out of prison; ❡28 And he spake kindly to him, and set his throne above the throne of the kings that were with him in Babylon; ❡29 And changed his prison garments: and he did eat bread continually before him all the days of his life. ❡30 And his allowance was a continual allowance given him of the king, a daily rate for every day, all the days of his life.

# The First Book of the CHRONICLES

## CHAPTER I

ADAM, Sheth, Enosh, ❡2 Kenan, Mahalaleel, Jered, ❡3 Henoch, Methuselah, Lamech, ❡4 Noah, Shem, Ham, and Japheth.

❡5 The sons of Japheth; Gomer, and Magog, and Madai, and Javan, and Tubal, and Meshech, and Tiras. ❡6 And the sons of Gomer; Ashchenaz, and Riphath, and Togarmah. ❡7 And the sons of Javan; Elishah, and Tarshish, Kittim, and Dodanim.

❡8 The sons of Ham; Cush, and Mizraim, Put, and Canaan. ❡9 And the sons of Cush; Seba, and Havilah, and Sabta, and Raamah, and Sabtecha. And the sons of Raamah; Sheba, and Dedan. ❡10 And Cush begat Nimrod: he began to be mighty upon the earth. ❡11 And Mizraim begat Ludim, and Anamim, and Lehabim, and Naphtuhim, ❡12 And Pathrusim, and Casluhim, (of whom came the Philistines,) and Caphthorim. ❡13 And Canaan begat Zidon his firstborn, and Heth, ❡14 The Jebusite also, and the Amorite, and the Girgashite, ❡15 And the Hivite, and the Arkite, and the Sinite, ❡16 And the Arvadite, and the Zemarite, and the Hamathite.

❡17 The sons of Shem; Elam, and Asshur, and Arphaxad, and Lud, and Aram, and Uz, and Hul, and Gether, and Meshech. ❡18 And Arphaxad begat Shelah, and Shelah begat Eber. ❡19 And unto Eber were born two sons: the name of the one was Peleg; because in his days the earth was divided: and his brother's name was Joktan. ❡20 And Joktan begat Almodad, and Sheleph, and Hazarmaveth, and Jerah, ❡21 Hadoram also, and Uzal, and Diklah, ❡22 And Ebal, and Abimael, and Sheba, ❡23 And Ophir, and Havilah, and Jobab. All these were the sons of Joktan.

❡24 Shem, Arphaxad, Shelah, ❡25 Eber, Peleg, Reu, ❡26 Serug, Nahor, Terah, ❡27 Abram;

Zz 353

THE CENTAUR. A TRANSLATION BY GEORGE B. IVES FROM THE FRENCH OF MAURICE DE GUÉRIN

MDCCCCXV

of them—will find it bear any comparison. Mr. Duncan has indeed added a fine feather to his cap in producing it. Though cut for The Imprint, it is on sale to the general public ; we have made no attempt to tie it up ; for our policy is sincerely to improve the craft of which we are so proud. The type has been christened IMPRINT OLD FACE.

The Imprint Old Face type was produced in an incredibly short space of time, and accents have not yet been made. Will readers kindly insert them for themselves, if they find their omission harsh ? For ourselves we rather like the fine careless flavour, which their omission gives, after we have recovered from the first shock inevitable to us typographical precisians.

We hereby promise bookbinders that they too shall find their account with us ; and only regret that limitations of space preclude their delightful craft from finding place in this number.

Maurice de Guérin. Here again Jenson was the basis, as a designer looked once more back to the Venetian printers as the foundation for excellence in form. Rogers's achievement is in having the imagination and skill to find new details of beauty in the original and to come up with a face that is more elegant than the rival derivations of Jenson. Though widely admired, the face is rarely used. It was not until 1929 that Monotype cut a version under Rogers's instruction, and this was subsequently used to set the Oxford Lectern Bible in 1935, Rogers's masterpiece as a type and book designer.

The work of the German designer Rudolf Koch (1876–1934) for the Klingspor foundry in Offenbach from 1906 onwards is the story of a craftsman dedicated to his art, definitely outside fashion and yet making some valuable contributions to the development of type forms. His first faces were black-letter, almost the only kind of face in use in Germany at the time. His calligraphic skills can be seen as fundamental to his art, as revealed by two of the faces he designed in this decade, Frühling and Maximilian (both developed from 1914). The first is a lightweight version of the kind of black-letter known as fraktur, and is extremely elegant. The second is a black-letter distinctive in having a set of matching roman capitals, inlined. This is not a decorative trick, but reveals his concern at bringing greater legibility to the use of black-letter, doing away with the exotic capitals for a simpler, but still coloured, letterform. The capitals had the quality of interesting display lettering for advertising, and found some favour outside Germany. But Koch's main achievements in mixing the German tradition with more modern forms was to come in the 1920s.

A similar mix of the brilliant calligraphic hand and the typographer's brain was to be found in Edward Johnston (1872–1944), a leading authority on fine writing, illuminating and lettering from soon after the turn of the century. His influence was international – his lettering skills inspired the young Jan Tschichold to pursue the career that would make him one of the great twentieth-century typographers. The "foundation hand" he developed, based on tenth-century manuscripts, was for many years held as the basis for good writing style. Despite this apparent rooting in antiquity, Johnston had the sensibility to produce one of the most avant-garde of designs when he was commissioned to produce a face for the exclusive use of London Underground in 1916. He drew on his know-

Below: Maximilian Antiqua, designed by Rudolf Koch for Klingspor in 1914. This early face from a master calligrapher combines a sense of the freehand-drawn roman, seen in the inlined capitals, with black-letter lower case. The stress is remarkably low down on the rounded letters (note the "O" and the "C").
Right: the first issue of *Blast*, 1914, manifesto of the Vorticist movement, edited by Percy Wyndham Lewis, painter and writer. Lewis was also behind the design, which combines bold, explosive layouts, echoing the Futurists, with a sense of order projecting texts that are still largely readable in a conventional, narrative manner. Nineteenth-century wood-letter sans serif provides a reference to advertising conventions, which colours the tone of this declamatory, propagandist work.

ALL IS WELL THAT ENDS WELL

MERCHANTS SOCIETY

REO MOTOR CAR

SAINT LOUIS

**1**

# BLAST First (from politeness) ENGLAND

CURSE ITS CLIMATE FOR ITS SINS AND INFECTIONS

DISMAL SYMBOL, SET round our bodies,
of effeminate lout within.

VICTORIAN VAMPIRE, the LONDON cloud sucks
the TOWN'S heart.

## A 1000 MILE LONG, 2 KILOMETER Deep

BODY OF WATER even, is pushed against us
from the Floridas, TO MAKE US MILD.

OFFICIOUS MOUNTAINS keep back DRASTIC WINDS

## SO MUCH VAST MACHINERY TO PRODUCE

THE CURATE of "Eltham"
BRITANNIC ÆSTHETE
WILD NATURE CRANK
DOMESTICATED
POLICEMAN
LONDON COLISEUM
SOCIALIST-PLAYWRIGHT
DALY'S MUSICAL COMEDY
GAIETY CHORUS GIRL
TONKS

11

ledge of classical forms to create a pioneering sans serif face; it broke with sans serif Victorian precedents by applying a rigorous idea of geometric simplicity to the letters, creating a face that anticipated the wave of Modernist design of the 1920s. The face was an instant classic, quickly absorbed into the identity of the Underground, whose image was being expertly and innovatively developed by its design manager Frank Pick. Johnston, now in a revised digital form known as New Johnston, is still used throughout the Underground system. This face was a major contribution to a new way of thinking in type design – its inspiration being most apparent in seminal faces such as Futura and Gill.

Such innovation took place against a background of growing awareness of the need to revive the typographic heritage, partly motivated by those concerned at the perceived decline in printing standards due to mass production, and partly in response to the increased demand for more choice of type. One of the more important revivals of this period was the beginning of the reworking of Garamond – first, from 1912, at Deberny & Peignot in Paris, and then followed by all the other major foundries who looked to produce their own versions in the years after. The variety of choice in the cuts illustrates the problem of crystallising the essence of the character of a particular face – analysed separately the key points can seem similar, but put next to each other, the difference in form and colour is quickly apparent. This struggle to achieve the look of fine printing seen in key early sources was to occupy much time in the major type design and typesetting companies – and still does as the digital revolution continues.



Underground sans serif by Edward Johnston, 1916, the first truly twentieth-century sans serif. It was deeply influential on the development of Gill (Eric Gill had worked with Johnston), and became an essential part of the London Underground corporate identity (it survives today as New Johnston, a version redrawn by Banks and Miles in the 1980s to meet the range of applications now demanded). The drawing by Johnston of 1916 with explanatory notes (below) is in his customary beautiful hand. In the full font as drawn by Johnston (right), note the monotone width of the stroke offset by the character of certain forms, such as the diamond dot over the "i" and "j" and the uneven bar on the "t". The typical application is shown in a station sign (above right), the name sitting within the London Underground logo, the roundel.

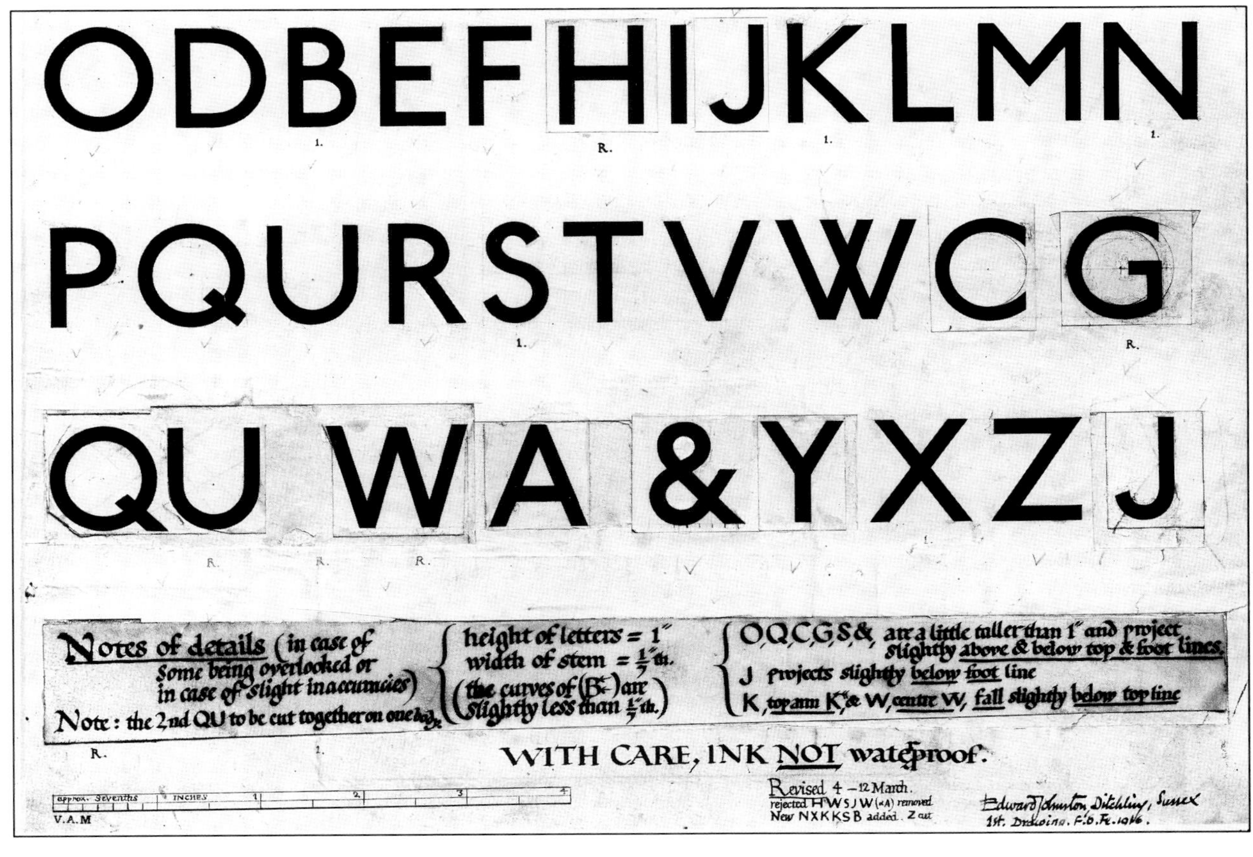

ABCDEFGHIJKLMN
OPQRSTUVWXYZ
abcdefghijklmnopq
rstuvwxyz 123456
7890 (&£.,:;’!?-*“”)

**ABCDEFGHIJKLMN**
**OPQRSTUVWXYZ**
**1234567890**

This was a decade of experimentation and expression for new typography: from the central influence of El Lissitsky (one of his settings of Mayakovsky's poetry is shown below right) through the years of the Bauhaus, to the emergence of lasting typefaces such as Futura and Gill, and the distinctive style of Cassandre, as seen in the Bifur face used for "1920".

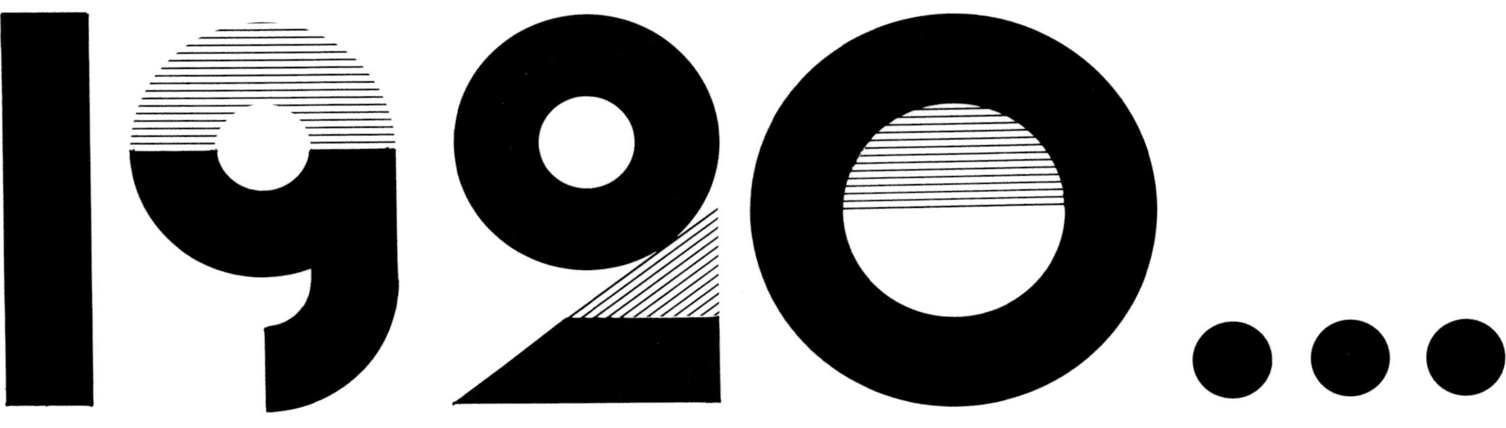

Futura

The manifestos that engendered much of the activity in graphic design during this century were written and visualised in the 1920s. The decade saw a foment of both radical and conservative thought as to the proper path for typographic development. While the experimental was encouraged, it was also laying down the basis for a new dogma of what constituted the Modern, which was soon to filter into advertising; meanwhile, the clarification of what constituted good typographic practice for the traditionalists involved a critique of the status quo, rather than a respect for current practices. For typographers, the activities of these years revealed the emerging significance of their craft, its relationship in the flux of creativity between fine art and architecture, and its value as a crucial political and commercial tool.

At the centre of the emergence of a new typography was the Bauhaus. The work produced by its teachers and students, and by others associated with them or influenced by them, came out of a synthesis of the new ideas in art. This radically new kind of school, which taught architecture and the applied arts as interdisciplinary subjects, mixing fine art and sculpture with practical studies, and splitting teaching between artists and craftspeople, was founded in Weimar in 1919. Das Staatliches Bauhaus emerged from an earlier, pre-war Weimar school that had been run by the Belgian architect and designer Henry Van de Velde, renowned for his influential contribution to Art Nouveau. But the agenda of the new school's director, the architect Walter Gropius, a former assistant of Peter Behrens, projected a philosophy that sought to express and expand the emerging Modernist sensibility, in which the integration of art and technology and the development of a mass-production aesthetic were vital. Its innovation and its problems reflect the difficulties of the time, with its lifespan of 1919 to 1933 mirroring that of the Weimar Republic. It struggled for funds, moved three times in fourteen years and was regularly attacked for its socialism.

At first typography was not officially a part of the Bauhaus programme. The first leader of the Bauhaus's preliminary course, Johannes Itten, included lettering skills and produced some Dada-influenced typographic art of his own, but it was with the arrival in 1923 of László Moholy-Nagy (1895–1946) to run the preliminary course that the Bauhaus really began to make a significant statement in graphic design. His five years at the college produced a remarkable body of work and publicatons that set down ideas that spread out around the world. This period also saw graphic design, photography and film take a more prominent role in the output of the Bauhaus than they had before or would afterwards, a direct result of Moholy-Nagy's teaching. Gropius had set up the school's teaching structure from the viewpoint that architecture was the ultimate objective, thus building was the final course of study, following on from the other applied arts. His successors in the role of director, first Hannes Meyer in 1928 and then Mies van der Rohe in 1930, further emphasised the architectural content of the school's programme. Gropius, however, reached out from his own architectural background to create a school that made a major contribution to the development of graphics, products, furniture and fine art as well as architecture. Teachers such as Klee, Kandinsky and Feininger at the school itself, and other artists such as van Doesburg and El Lissitsky as outside influences who had some impact on the school, ensured a dramatic and eclectic contribution to new ideas in two-dimensional art. Moholy-Nagy was a key contributor, issuing, as soon as he arrived, a manifesto in which new ideas in typography played a crucial part. In 1923 he declared:

***Typography must be clear communication in its most vivid form.***

***Clarity must be especially stressed, for clarity is the essence of modern printing in contrast to ancient picture writing.***

***Therefore, first of all: absolute clarity in all typographical work. Communication ought not to labour under preconceived aesthetic notions. Letters should never be squeezed into an arbitrary shape – like a square.***

***A new typographic language must be created, combining elasticity, variety and a fresh approach to the materials of printing, a language whose logic depends on the appropriate application of the processes of printing.***[1]

Moholy-Nagy's artistic development before joining the Bauhaus shows a merging of different influences into a strong personal approach. From his Hungarian origins he had connections with the Activist movement, which itself was an intriguing synthesis of differing art ideas of the war and post-war period located around a central concern for social issues. The Activists' periodical *MA* put across the commitment to using art as a way of propagating its social "morality" – part socialist, part anarchist – and saw Cubism, Futurism, Expressionism "or any other 'ism'" as being usable towards these ends. Moholy-Nagy wrote in a letter in 1924 that this group was highly influential in the evolution of his art and intellectual development until around 1920.[2] His work at that point can be seen to draw inspiration from Dada before taking on a character that draws on the pure geometry of Malevich's Suprematist ideas and El Lissitsky's closely related non-objective Constructivism. The paintings and sculptures he produced during the twenties saw him exploring the relationship of the circle, rectangle and square, along with a fresh approach to colour, depth, layering and perspective. His examining of the potential of the canvas in this way is clearly related to the bold, elemental qualities of the typographic arrangements produced by and under him. His three-dimensional work (he was actually appointed to direct the metalwork course, but made his biggest impact through the teaching of the preliminary course) connects with the exploration of light and texture, as seen in his two- and three-dimensional photography.

Moholy-Nagy was not the only artist pursuing this quest for taking typographic communication into a new sphere along with fine arts, applied arts and

DER OFFSET-VERLAG G.M.B.H. LEIPZIG
OFFSET
BUCH UND WERBEKUNST
HEFT 7
1926
ENTWURF: JOOST SCHMIDT · BAUHAUS IN DESSAU
BAUHAUS-HEFT
HOFBUCHDRUCKEREI VON C. DÜNNHAUPT G.M.B.H. DESSAU


Opposite page: poster designed by Herbert Bayer announcing an architecture lecture with slides to be given by Hans Poelzig at the Bauhaus in 1926. Under Bayer, students in the printing and advertising workshop applied and developed modernist theories to real commissions. Bayer refined further the simplified approach of strict geometric design, minimal change of type size and form (here it is all upper case) and the use of red and black. He was fascinated by the psychology of visual communication and its application through advertising: here, the reductive layout draws attention to the date and the use of red to the idea of the lecture, while the red circle also symbolises the lens through which the slides will be projected.
Left: cover of issue number seven of *Offset Buch und Werbekunst*, 1926, designed by Herbert Bayer. The rapid growth of interest in the work of the Bauhaus was confirmed by this printing industry magazine devoting a special number to it.

abcdefghi
jklmnopqr
stuvwxyz

**HERBERT BAYER: Abb. 1. Alfabet**
**„g" und „k" sind noch als**
**unfertig zu betrachten**

d

**Beispiel eines Zeichens**
**in größerem Maßstab**
**Präzise optische Wirkung**

sturm blond

**Abb. 2. Anwendung**

399

1000000
EINE MILLION MARK
WEIMAR, DEN 9. AUGUST 1923
DIE LANDESREGIERUNG
1000000 Mark zahlt die Kasse der Thüringischen Staatsbank dem Einlieferer dieses Notgeldscheines. Vom 1. September 1923 ab kann dieses Notgeld aufgerufen und gegen Umtausch in Reichsbanknoten eingezogen werden.
Wer Banknoten nachmacht oder verfälscht oder nachgemachte oder verfälschte sich verschafft und in den Verkehr bringt, wird mit Zuchthaus nicht unter zwei Jahren bestraft.
Serie C
№ 091809
BAUHAUS-ARCHIV
1000000 MARK. EINE MILLION MARK
NOTGELD DES LANDES THÜRINGEN

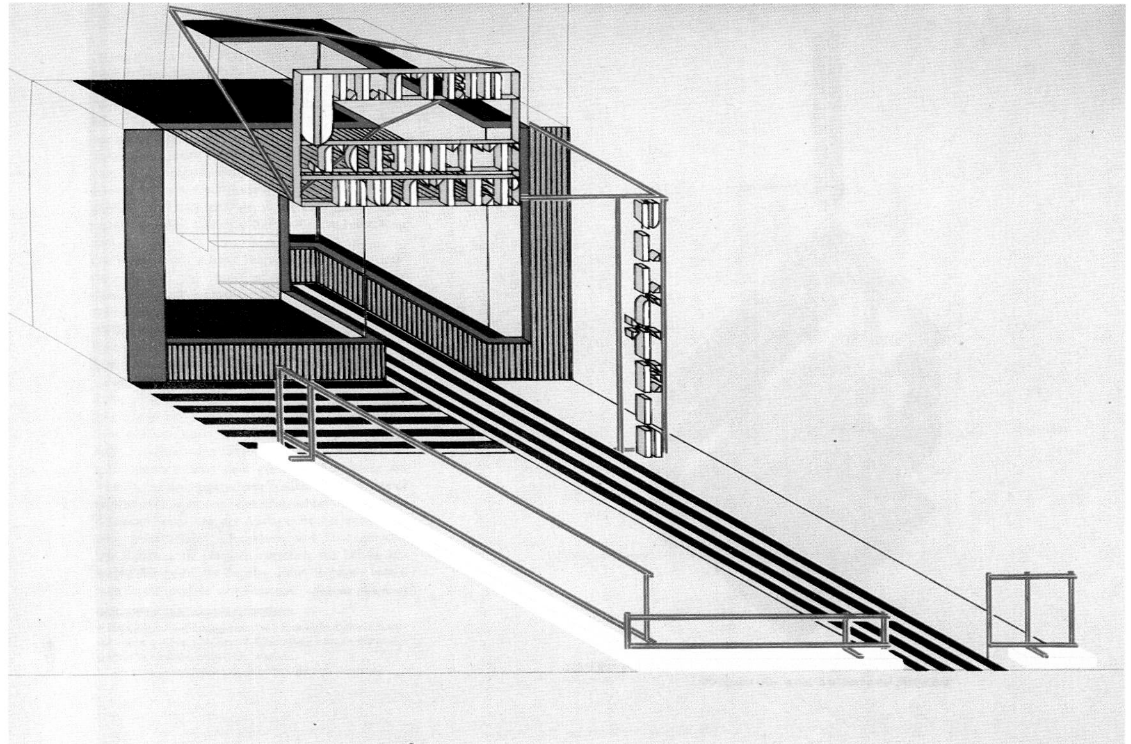

Far left: design for a single alphabet by Herbert Bayer, 1925. Pure geometric reduction of letterforms governs this face, which rejects capitals as an unnecessary complication. Note the consistency of the arc (as highlighted in the "g" and "k"), the loss of clear character distinction ("i" and "j") and the ingenious reflection or inversion of forms ("h" and "y", and "x").

Below far left: two of a series of emergency banknotes for the State Bank of Thuringia designed in 1923, during the inflation of the Weimar republic, while Bayer was still a student at the Bauhaus. Throwing out the convention of intricate design and fine type on banknotes, he used a bold sans serif with large numbers and blocks of colour to distinguish the notes.

Left: design for stencil lettering by Josef Albers at the Bauhaus, 1925. Like Bayer, Albers sought to reduce type to a combination of geometric shapes, aiming to create characters with strong legibility for use in posters. The square, the triangle and a segment of the circle were his units, with certain exceptions such as double line crosses on the "f", "F", "H" and "S". Each element remains separate, creating letters that are distinct and yet always have a relationship to a whole. Albers (1888–1976) taught at the Bauhaus from 1923 until it closed in 1933, making a major contribution to the preliminary course.

Left: project for the rebuilding of a shopfront by Josef Albers, 1926, showing his stencil face in its intended use in a bold display. In keeping with the Bauhaus approach of reducing design to its essential components, Albers designed the signage as a separate layer of the building.

architecture, but his role as a prime teacher at the Bauhaus in its most productive period gave him a special prominence. At the forefront of his graphics output was the Bauhaus books series dating from 1923. His advertising for the books can be seen to incorporate Constructivist and De Stijl ideas: elements of the page such as rules, full points and blocks of text, colour and white space are organised asymmetrically on modular grids (as opposed to traditional centring on linear grids) and are suggestive of the paintings of van Doesburg and Mondrian. The covers, which worked as a series but had different arrangements, stripped down the design constituents to those that were purely typographic, and arranged these so boldly as to be a statement at least as strong as the meaning of the words displayed. The typography has a self-consciousness about it – the principles being expressed unmistakably as unifying the whole visual effect, without any other illustrative statement of the subject matter. This is clearly appropriate for a series of books relating to art and design.

For all its self-consciousness and relationship with ideas seen in related art movements, this work is among the first examples of a commercially relevant new typography, showing a move away from the more strident art statements of Futurist, and then Dada, De Stijl and Constructivist typography. More than being idealistic manifestos, the Bauhaus books and subsequent work from the printshop and advertising course were a stepping stone relating these ideas to the concept of mass communication.

The eighth book in the series was Moholy-Nagy's own *Malerei, Photographie, Film* [*Painting, Photography, Film*], published in 1925 and putting the case for the central role of photography in new representation that the artist/teacher advocated. For Moholy-Nagy photography had its own laws giving it expressive potential beyond painting, a view not shared by Malevich, but close to the thought of Russian photomontage pioneers such as Rodchenko whose search for expressive media of communication ranged across many creative



Below: *Die Neue Typographie*, written and designed by Jan Tschichold, 1928. Set entirely in sans serif, with large blocks of text occasionally punctuated by heavy bold headlines, the whole effect might have been brutal, were it not for Tschichold's sense of rhythm and "colour" in typographic form, which shows that he had absorbed many of the traditional rules of typography although he calls for a rejection of much that is traditional.

Below right: single alphabet of "universal" type, designed by Jan Tschichold, 1929. As with the single alphabets designed by Albers and Bayer, there is a quest for clear character forms created from the minimum geometry.

Right: spread from *Malerei, Photographie, Film [Painting, Photography, Film]*, written and designed by Lászlo Moholy-Nagy, 1925. Its avant-garde approach to the subject matter is reflected in the typography: rigid control and reduction of the elements, with distinctive use of white space.

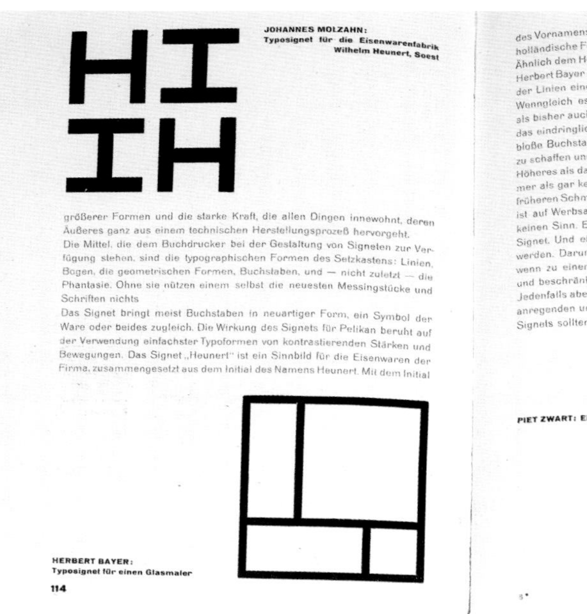

**JOHANNES MOLZAHN:**
**Typosignet für die Eisenwarenfabrik Wilhelm Heunert, Soest**

größerer Formen und die starke Kraft, die allen Dingen innewohnt, deren Äußeres ganz aus einem technischen Herstellungsprozeß hervorgeht.
Die Mittel, die dem Buchdrucker bei der Gestaltung von Signeten zur Verfügung stehen, sind die typographischen Formen des Setzkastens: Linien, Bogen, die geometrischen Formen, Buchstaben, und — nicht zuletzt — die Phantasie. Ohne sie nützen einem selbst die neuesten Messingstücke und Schriften nichts
Das Signet bringt meist Buchstaben in neuartiger Form, ein Symbol der Ware oder beides zugleich. Die Wirkung des Signets für Pelikan beruht auf der Verwendung einfachster Typoformen von kontrastierenden Stärken und Bewegungen. Das Signet „Heunert" ist ein Sinnbild für die Eisenwaren der Firma, zusammengesetzt aus dem Initial des Namens Heunert. Mit dem Initial

**HERBERT BAYER:**
**Typosignet für einen Glasmaler**

114

des Vornamens Piet zusammen wird das schwarze Quadrat („zwart" ist die holländische Form des deutschen „schwarz") zu einer unvergeßlichen Marke. Ähnlich dem Heunertsignet gibt auch das Typosignet für einen Glasmaler von Herbert Bayer ein zusammengedrängtes Sinnbild des Berufs: die Abstraktion der Linien eines Glasfensters.
Wenngleich es sehr zu begrüßen wäre, wenn sich der Buchdrucker mehr als bisher auch der Gestaltung von Signeten zuwenden würde, muß aber auf das eindringlichste davor gewarnt werden, mit dem Setzkasten hergestellte bloße Buchstabenverbindungen (Monogramme) als Signete anzusehen, sie zu schaffen und sie gar zu verwenden. Ein Signet ist etwas durchaus anderes, Höheres als das bloße Monogramm, und ein mangelhaftes Signet viel schlimmer als gar keines. Der Buchdrucker ist heute oft verführt, an die Stelle des früheren Schmuckstücks ein Typomonogramm zu setzen. Aber nur das Signet ist auf Werbsachen berechtigt; Monogramme haben dort in unserer Zeit keinen Sinn. Ein Monogramm als Warenmarke ist stets schlechter als ein Signet. Und ein schlechtes Signet kann zum Grundfehler einer Werbung werden. Darum verzichte man lieber auf das Monogramm als Signetersatz, wenn zu einem Typosignet die Zeit, die man dazu unbedingt braucht, fehlt, und beschränke sich auf die bloße Schrift.
Jedenfalls aber bietet das Typosignet dem Buchdrucker die Möglichkeit einer anregenden und dankbaren Betätigung, und die Schwierigkeiten eines guten Signets sollten nur ein Ansporn zu ihrer Bewältigung sein.

**PIET ZWART: Eigenmarke (Typosignet)**

115

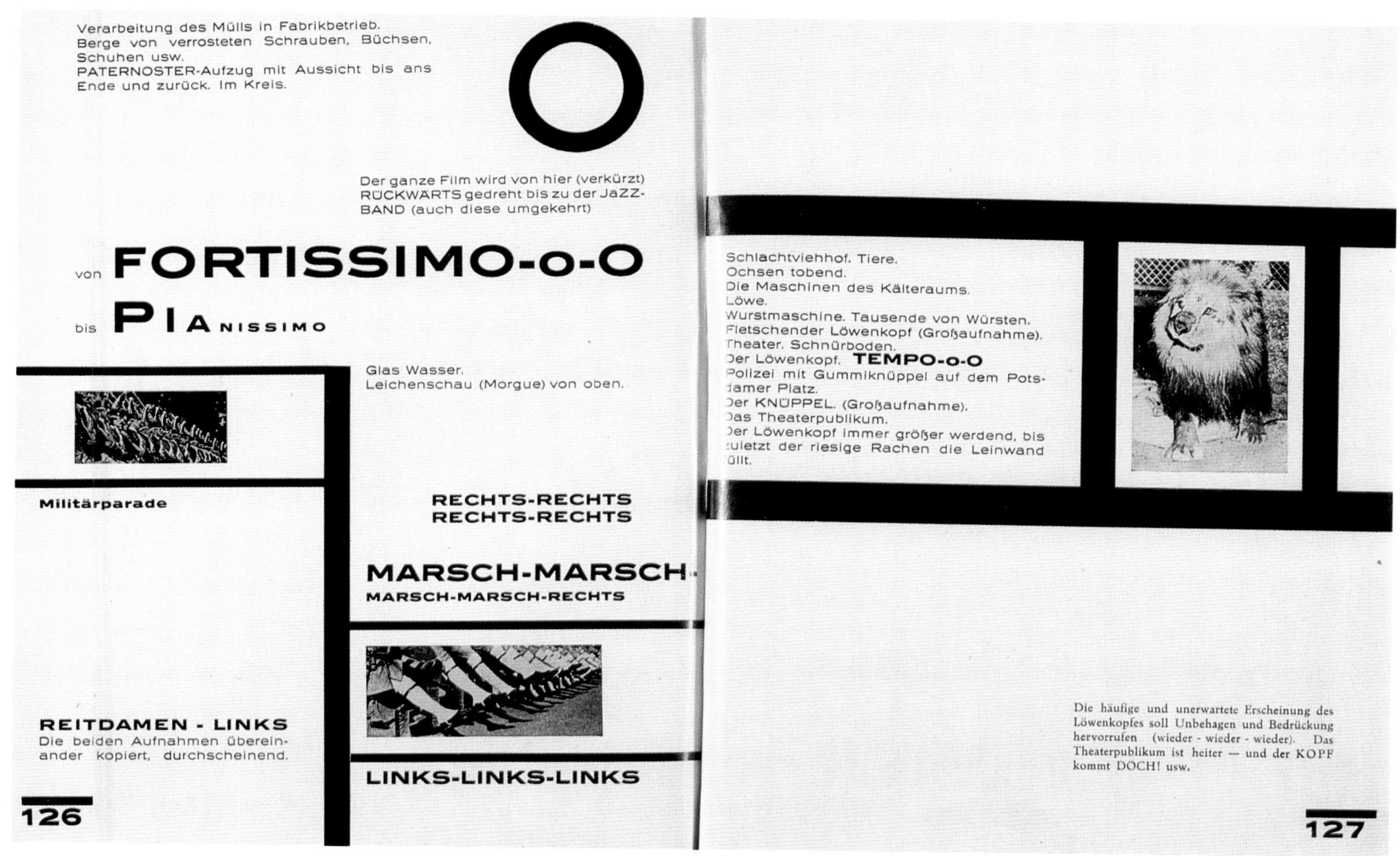

Verarbeitung des Mülls in Fabrikbetrieb.
Berge von verrosteten Schrauben, Büchsen, Schuhen usw.
PATERNOSTER-Aufzug mit Aussicht bis ans Ende und zurück. Im Kreis.

O

Der ganze Film wird von hier (verkürzt) RÜCKWÄRTS gedreht bis zu der JaZZ-BAND (auch diese umgekehrt)

von **FORTISSIMO-o-O**

bis **P I A** N I S S I M O

Glas Wasser.
Leichenschau (Morgue) von oben.

**Militärparade**

**RECHTS-RECHTS**
**RECHTS-RECHTS**

**MARSCH-MARSCH**
**MARSCH-MARSCH-RECHTS**

**REITDAMEN - LINKS**
Die beiden Aufnahmen übereinander kopiert, durchscheinend.

**LINKS-LINKS-LINKS**

**126**

Schlachtviehhof. Tiere.
Ochsen tobend.
Die Maschinen des Kälteraums.
Löwe.
Wurstmaschine. Tausende von Würsten.
Fletschender Löwenkopf (Großaufnahme).
Theater. Schnürboden.
Der Löwenkopf. **TEMPO-o-O**
Polizei mit Gummiknüppel auf dem Potsdamer Platz.
Der KNÜPPEL. (Großaufnahme).
Das Theaterpublikum.
Der Löwenkopf immer größer werdend, bis zuletzt der riesige Rachen die Leinwand füllt.

Die häufige und unerwartete Erscheinung des Löwenkopfes soll Unbehagen und Bedrückung hervorrufen (wieder - wieder - wieder). Das Theaterpublikum ist heiter — und der KOPF kommt DOCH! usw.

**127**

fur den noien menʃen eksistirt nur das glaihgeviht tsviʃen natur unt gaist· tsu jedem tsaitpuŋkt der fergaŋenhait varen ale variatsjonen des alten ›noi‹· aber es var niht ›das‹ noie· vir dürfen niht fergesen· das vir an ainer vende der kultur ʃtehen· am ende ales alten·

disciplines, including typography. Rodchenko's experiments and his proselytising of the power of the photograph – and the "photogram", the word he coined for the photographs similar to Man Ray's "rayographs" that he produced without a camera – were a major initiative in the move to link photography directly to graphic design, and conversely to include graphic design in the language of photography and film.

In his 1925 essay "Contemporary Typography – Aims, Practice, Criticism"[3] Moholy-Nagy anticipated the replacement of much typographic communication by sound recordings and film images. In response, he advocated that typography needed to raise itself to a new level of expressive power and effectiveness. This involved embracing and developing the machine age in print production, and moving on from the period when experimental typography used old technology to express new ideas (a jibe possibly directed at the Futurists and De Stijl artists) to a more serious grasping of new technology and the new visual experiences of the age. He looked forward to the pages of grey text being transformed into colourful narratives, being conceived of as a dramatic whole, individual pages working in sequence in much the same way as film frames.

In the essay, Moholy-Nagy went on to outline certain principles of new typographic practice. Sharp tension was to be introduced into layouts by contrasting visual elements – such as empty/full, light/dark, multicoloured/grey, vertical/horizontal, upright/oblique – and these were to be achieved chiefly through the disposition of type. Typographic signs were also an element, but not the ornamental borders and the like beloved of the traditional printshop and typical of the vernacular ephemera. He concluded that "... it will be clear to everybody that typography is not an end in itself, that typographical communication has its

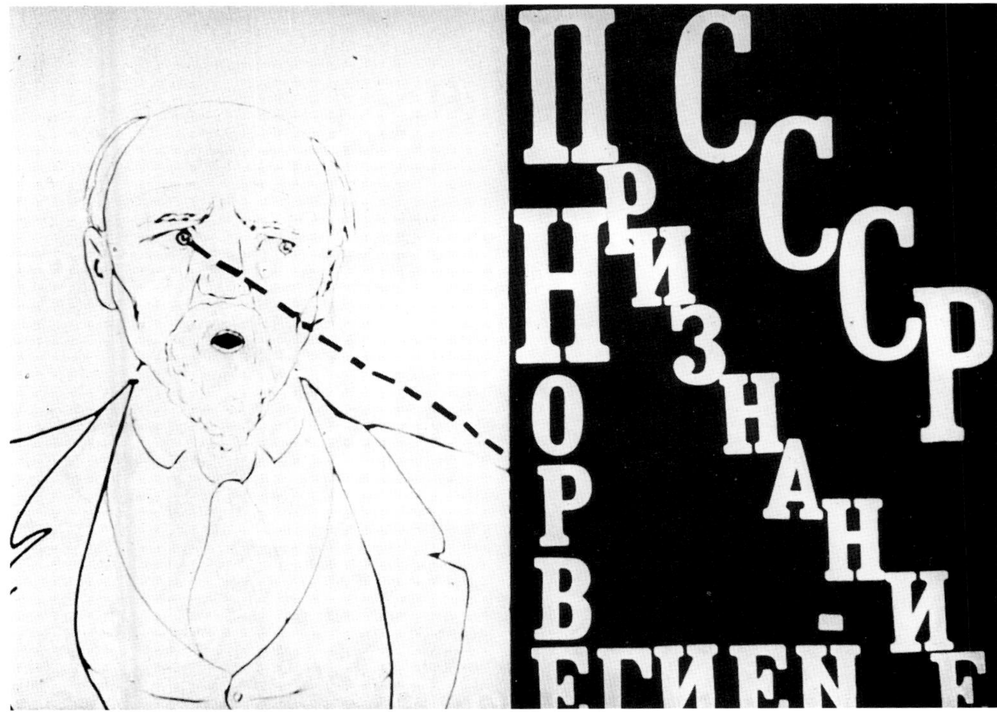


Opposite page, far left: advertisement for GUM, Moscow's state department store, designed by Aleksandr Rodchenko with text by Vladimir Mayakovsky, 1923. This Constructivist advertisement is formed from blocks of expressive type and product shots; the message is that watches are essential, the only ones worth having are Mozer, and they are available only at GUM.
Opposite page, right: film poster for *Man With Movie Camera* by the Stenberg brothers, 1928. The partnership of Vladimir (1899–1982) and Georgy (1900–1933) was prolific throughout the Twenties. Here, type is integrated with illustration by an exploration of genuine links in form and perspective: the lettering suggests both the motion of the girl and of the film, and accentuates the perspective of the towering buildings.
This page: stills from the documentary film *Kino Pravda* by Vertov, 1922, designed by Aleksandr Rodchenko.
Top announces details of the health of Lenin, who had recently suffered a stroke. Bottom proclaims the diplomatic recognition of the new Soviet state by Norway. Film was a new medium of dramatic mass communication potential; the absence of sound created a strong case for expressive typography, but few designers took the opportunity.

own specific forms determined psycho-physically and by its content, and it must never be subordinate to some speculative aesthetics".

One point raised in passing was the need for a standard form of writing, without the two sets of letters involved in lower case and capitals. Moholy-Nagy lamented the lack of a typeface that had correct proportions, that had stripped away individual flourishes and was based on the bare functional compositions of each letter and no more. Just such a face was drawn in 1925 by a Bauhaus colleague and former student, Herbert Bayer (1900–85), whose work over the next thirty years continued to make valuable contributions to the evolution of modern typography.

Bayer was the first head of a new typography workshop at the Bauhaus, established in 1925 when the school moved to Dessau. He held the post until 1928, when he resigned along with Gropius and Moholy-Nagy. As a student he had already displayed a bold clarity in his work and integration of the ideas of De Stijl and Constructivist thought. His banknotes for the State of Thuringia produced in 1923 were an early signpost of the distinctive Bauhaus look that was to emerge in graphics. Such a notion of a "style" dismayed Gropius, who rejected as superficial the idea of a group of works linked by appearance, rather than by principles. Being seen to have a style, however, was inevitable, due to the ruthless radicalism of Bauhaus thought when set against so many of the traditions of typographic form, and particularly the conservatism of German printing with its emphasis on dense black-letter faces.

Asymmetry, rectangular fluid grids, bold abstract forms and absence of decoration marked out a specific Bauhaus look (regardless of the individual thought built into each piece of work). The search for a fitness of form to function was a philosophical quest underlying all the studies at the Bauhaus and the work that resulted. While there may have been concern not about a style but about a way of thinking, the freshness and coherence of Bauhaus teaching was so distinct as to be always recognisable through visual characteristics.

Bayer's minimalist sans serif face was one of a number of proposals for such a reductive typeface – others included van Doesburg's alphabet of 1919, or Tschichold's universal lettering a few years later – but had the benefit of being preached through the Bauhaus course. The case for a single alphabet, a popular issue with the Modernist pioneers, and returned to later, was based on the fact that the upper case is not pronounced verbally and can be seen as causing a substantial waste of time (in setting or typing), and a waste of money and other resources in the amount of type that needs to be carried. In that it also adds to the general complexity of written language, and further complicates typographic communication, it has often been seen as unnecessary by experimental typographers. Bauhaus publications began dropping the use of capitals from this time and Bayer was still exploring such an approach (albeit less didactically) when he came to design the 1938 Museum of Modern Art Bauhaus exhibition catalogue. Bayer's single-alphabet proposal is distinctive for generating its forms from a declared reductive range of a few angles, arcs and selected lines, resulting in a simplicity in which the "m" and "w" are the same inverted, and the "x" is little more than an "o" cut in half and turned inside-out. Bayer developed a number of experimental typefaces in the period from 1925 to 1927, mostly of interest only for display purposes – such as a semi-abstract shadow typeface in which the shadow was all that was left, the original outline being removed as unnecessary. His type design ideas took root as a commercially available face, Bayer



Right: cover of *Die Kunstismen [The Isms of Art]* by El Lissitsky and Hans Arp, 1925. This attempt to summarise the numerous art movements of the period 1914–24 is an interesting graphic work in its own right. Designed by Lissitsky, the pages display a ferocious grid structure, ordering the different "isms" within three columns of the page, each given to a different language (German, French, English). Akzidenz Grotesk bold, with few changes of size or weight, points the way towards the principles of the Swiss school decades later.

Far right and below right: cover and inside page from *Of Two Squares* by El Lissitsky, created in 1920 at the Vitebsk art school and printed in Berlin in 1922. The "total concept" of the book is explored in this work, which takes Malevich's idea of the square as a generator of form and develops a child's story around a black and red square. Language and layout (the elements behind typographic constructions) are presented in a way that examines space and time – a kind of four-dimensional graphics. By using various sizes, weights and fonts and dramatically exploring the angles between the format of the page and the elements placed upon it Lissitsky gave great impact to the few words of his story, themselves at one with the illustration. They tell a tale of two squares crashing to earth to bring dynamic life, and are another expression of the radical statement seen in the design.

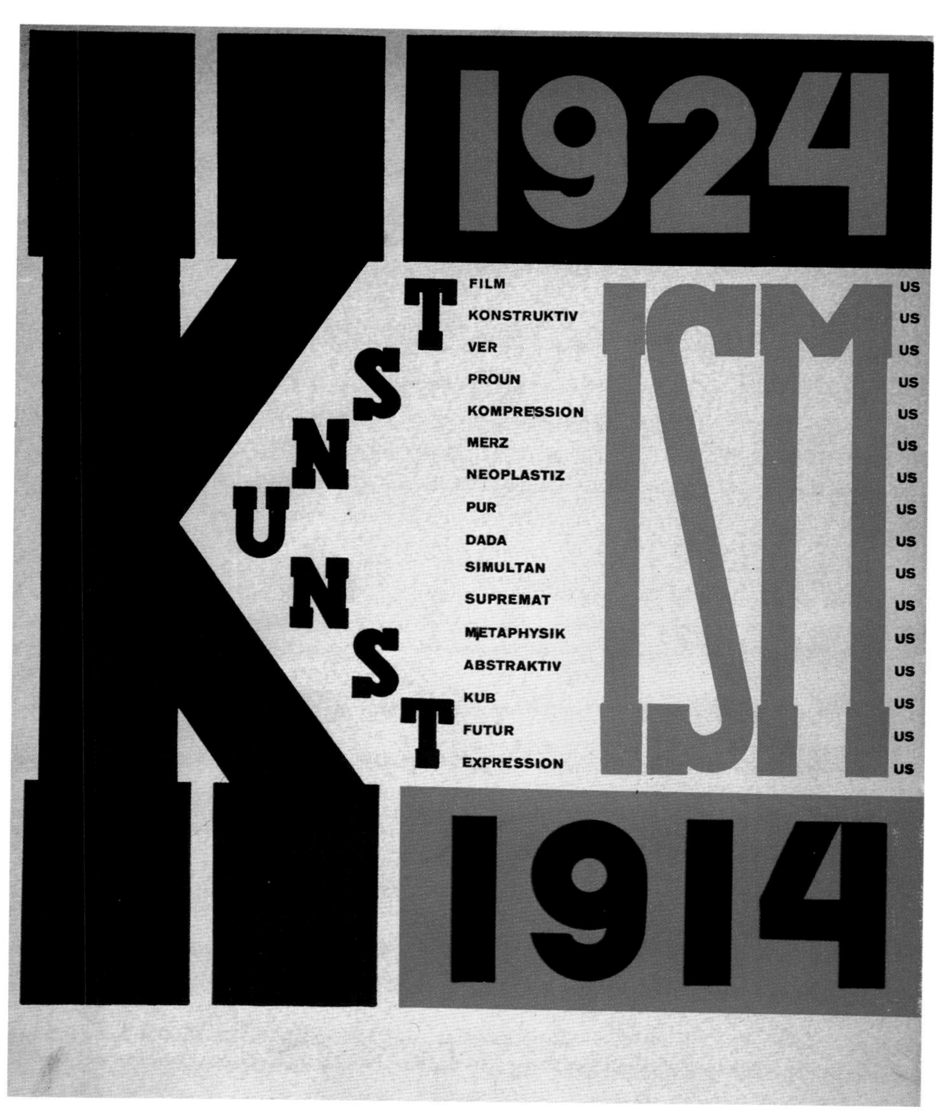
1924
KUNST
KUNST
FILM US
KONSTRUKTIV US
VER US
PROUN US
KOMPRESSION US
MERZ US
NEOPLASTIZ US
PUR US
DADA US
SIMULTAN US
SUPREMAT US
METAPHYSIK US
ABSTRAKTIV US
KUB US
FUTUR US
EXPRESSION US
ISM
1914

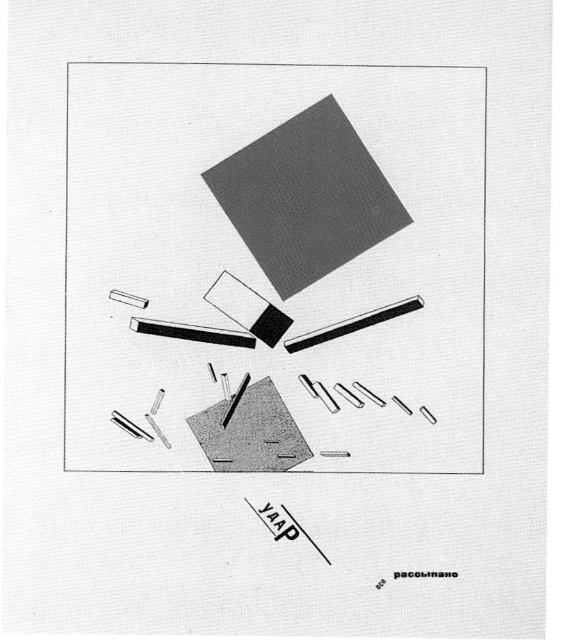
удар
все рассыпано

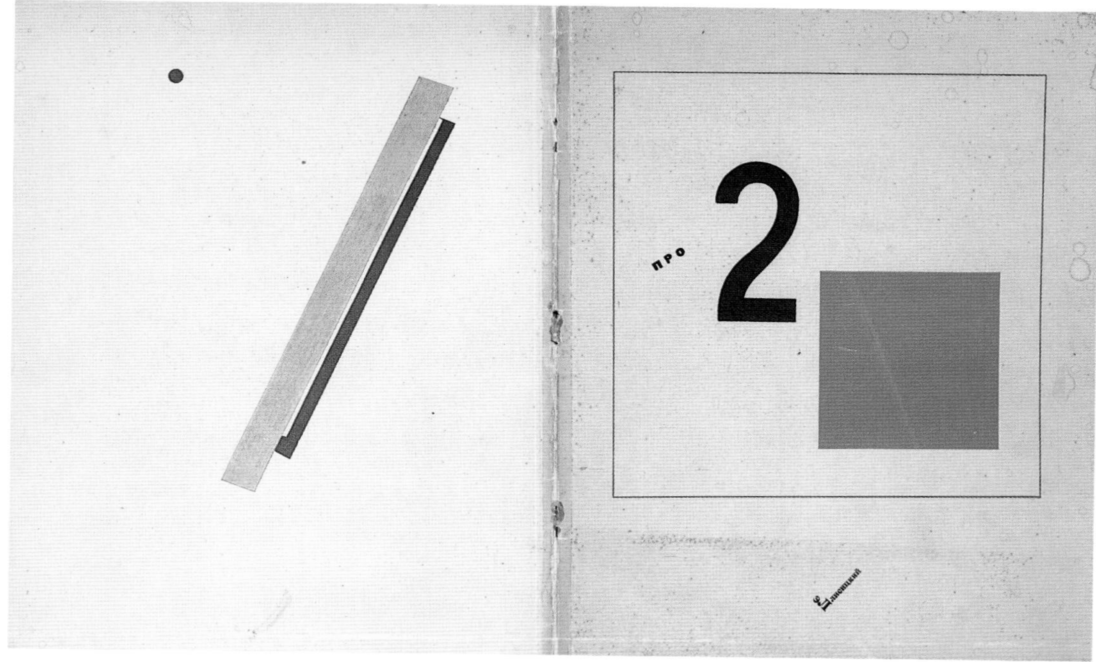
про
2

Type, for Berthold in 1935 – but this was a condensed didone, with short descenders and a rather fussy character, very distant from the Bauhaus ideas.

Ironically, for all the Bauhaus aspirations for a machine-age approach to communication, the printing workshop under Bayer was generally restricted to the earlier technology of manual work, a neat paradigm to the work of Modernist architects of the period who in their buildings sometimes simulated the plasticity of concrete, steel and glass forms by rendering over brick or stone. A sans serif face existed in a number of sizes for hand-setting, which could be printed on a platen (flat-bed) press or a rotary proof press. All the printed materials needed by the college – forms, brochures and posters – emanated from the print department, produced to designs by Bayer or students.

Bayer's teaching was not formal; instead he monitored and directed the work of students on real commissions that were handled by the department. Advertising was a particular interest of Bayer's and he researched and promoted ideas on the psychology of advertising and its relationship to consciousness; such an approach generated an awareness of modern communications, in which the concern at understanding subconscious motivations is at least as important as rational argument. The value of placing arresting and symbolic components within a typographic format was made apparent. The primacy of red and black in two-colour printing, the power of dynamic white space (rather than static borders), the use of highly contrasted sizes of type to express the relative values of information and the growing use of photomontage and collage were all quickly recognised as being key concepts. In line with Bayer's determination that work should contribute to a mass-production age, all commissions were carried out to standard DIN sizes (A0, A1, A2, A3, A4, A5 etc.).

Bayer was succeeded in 1928 by Joost Schmidt (1893–1948), under whom the printing workshop changed its name to the advertising workshop, revealing how significant this new discipline was to the Bauhaus, when elsewhere it was not possible to train in this subject. There was even more emphasis on bringing in outside projects, and Schmidt favoured certain of Bayer's and Moholy-Nagy's traits – such as ideas incorporating photography, or the high-contrast elements in form and colour. On the other hand, he dropped some of the more reductive (perhaps Constructivist) aspects of the earlier work: he encouraged a slightly wider range of typefaces, and evolved grids that moved away from the strictly modular, experimenting more with overlaying one simple pattern on another to create dynamic complexities. In Schmidt's time typography became even more strongly a part of the Bauhaus core curriculum, being taught over two terms of the preliminary course.

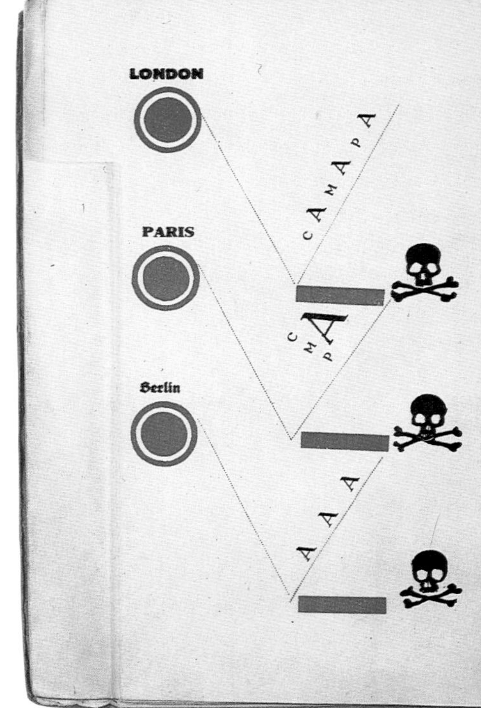


Besides those who taught at the Bauhaus, there were many typographic pioneers associated with or influential upon it, or in contact with the ideas coming out of the school. Prior to the Bauhaus becoming typographically energetic, and during its period of main activity in this area (1923–30), there were significant contributions to Modernist graphic communication in the Soviet Union, Holland, elsewhere in Germany, in Poland, Czechoslovakia and Hungary. In the recently established Soviet Union, a whole cluster of artists were exploring new ideas about photomontage and type elements in the cause of political and commercial design in the 1920s. Chief among them were El Lissitsky (1890–1947) and Aleksandr Rodchenko (1891–1956).

Lissitsky produced a tremendous amount of work during the 1920s, and was influential on others, such as Moholy-Nagy and van Doesburg, whom he met

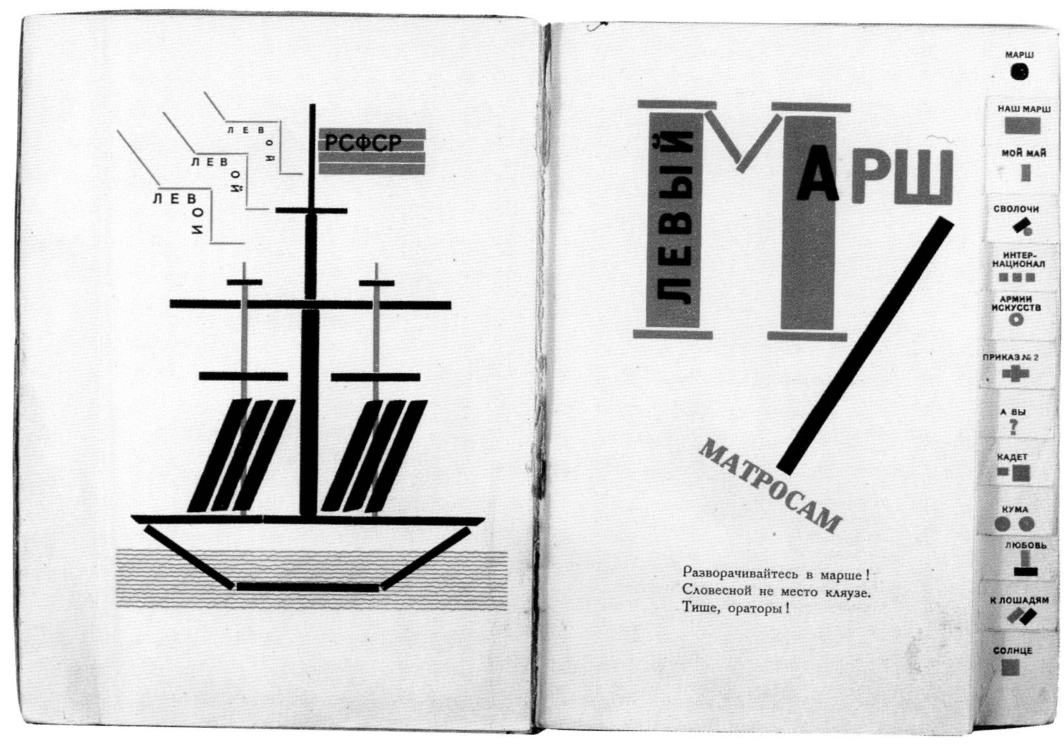


Three spreads from *For Reading Out Loud*, a collection of poems by Mayakovsky, designed by El Lissitsky, published in Berlin, 1923. Each spread is a poem, and the tabs on the right-hand side of the page are die-cut steps to help the reader find each one as quickly as possible; they are in alphabetical order, with symbolic codes linking through to the relevant pages. Only materials already available to the typesetter were used in the design: the depiction of a boat, the allusion to a map and indeed the shaping of some of the large characters are all created from utilitarian rules, bars and other devices used to lock up pages, along with vernacular printers' symbols such as engraved hand blocks to suggest page turns, often used ironically by modernist typographers to draw attention. The completeness of this book, which applied Lissitsky's Constructivist ideas without compromise, ensured that it was highly influential: it sought to maximise the potential of the page and the series of pages as well as that of the word. The dynamic properties of white space are one of its most dramatic aspects, controlling the balance of the elements.

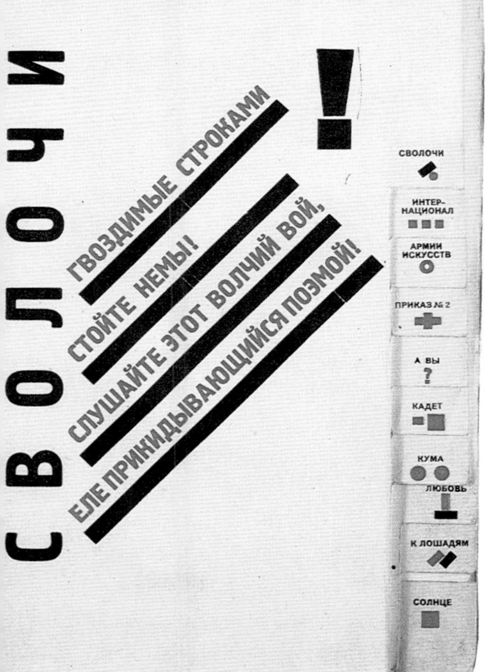


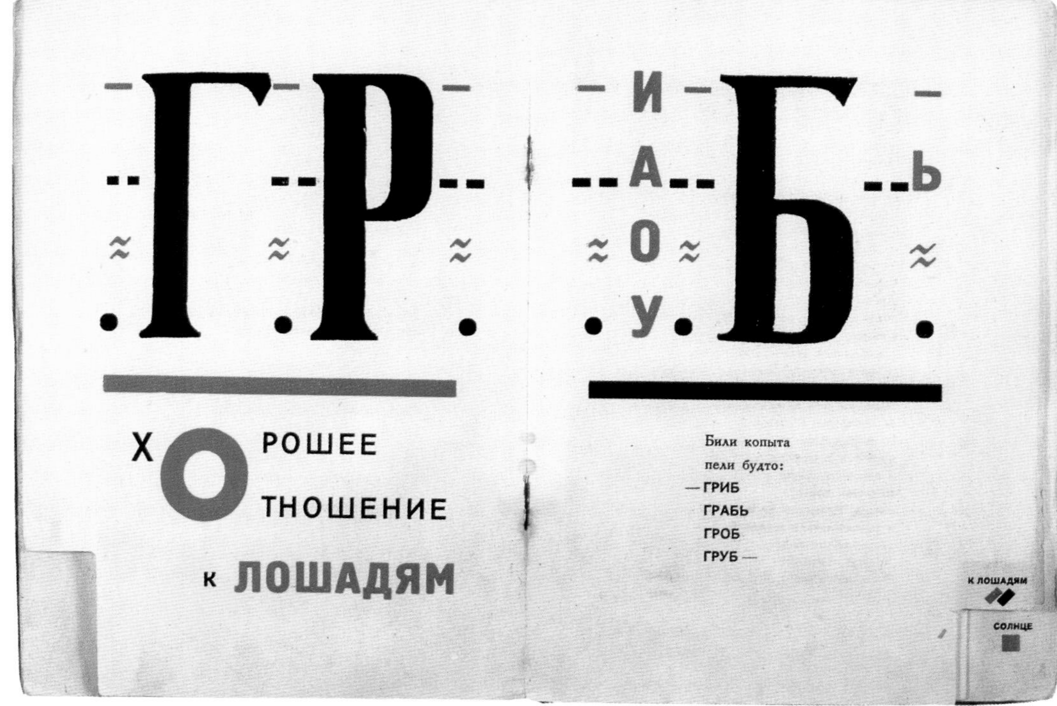

regularly early in the decade. His work varies between the ferociously restricted elements packed into the pages of *The Isms of Art* of 1925 and the light, spare statements of his design for Mayakovsky's poems *For Reading Out Loud* in 1923 or Lissitsky's own earlier *Of Two Squares*, his Suprematist children's story book that explores the relationship between the fourth dimension – time – and the three dimensions of the book and the two dimensions of the page. Lissitsky's ideas partly evolved and were propagated through innovative Soviet art movements (the Vkhutemas group in Moscow and the art school in Vitebsk) where he was brought in by Kandinsky and Chagall. Here the crossover between innovative ideas in graphic design and the fine art world was at its most fluid, with questions relating to colour, abstraction, form and space being relevant to both, as was the discussion of the social relevance of such debate. The new typographic and illustrative forms that were derived from this teaching can be seen in the strong poster culture centred on Moscow in the 1920s.

Aleksandr Rodchenko pushed ideas about integrating photography and type into new areas, also questioning form and spatial understanding: his posters emanate a directness and distortion of reality for propagandist purposes that are still powerful. His originality in photography was combined with a sensitivity to the point of focus on type: confrontational slabs of type, with colour integrating word and image, challenge the viewer to find connections and interpret documentary stories between pictures or typographic elements. At times there are traces of the ephemeral, found imagery of Dada – but Rodchenko uses it not for absurdist melodrama, but as part of an effort to present the message directly, speaking with the elements of mass communication.

The De Stijl and Dada movements also continued to evolve in the 1920s. Theo van Doesburg, a seminal figure in both, had an interesting relationship with the Bauhaus. Between 1921 and 1923 he lived in Weimar and conducted lectures attended mostly by Bauhaus students. He saw his lectures as a directly subversive element intended to infiltrate student ideas and take root within Gropius's system. In 1922 he published the first issue of *Mecano*, a Dadaist journal. Its eclectic mix of elements contrasts with the purer form of the *De Stijl* magazine that he brought out and which can be seen, along with Lissitsky's work, as the clearest influence on Moholy-Nagy's ideas at the Bauhaus. Like Lissitsky and then Moholy-Nagy, van Doesburg was among the first to be concerned with exploring a new plasticity in the nature of print – a response both to the swirling mass of information and to new ideas that needed to be communicated. All three men also sensed the potential of new technology and the significance of film and broadcast communication.

Kurt Schwitters (1887–1948) was close to Lissitsky and van Doesburg in the early 1920s, his work presenting a different synthesis of Dada, De Stijl and Constructivism. His assemblages from 1919 – which he titled *Merz* – evolved into a journal of the same name from 1923 until 1932, with many influential figures from these movements contributing. An edition in 1924 was jointly edited with Lissitsky, and a later edition was devoted to advertising typography. There is more of the humorous, ironic juxtaposition of elements in Schwitters's output than in his contemporaries'; form and spatial ideas characteristic of Lissitsky are mixed with the Dadaist sense of experimentation for disruption's sake. Underlying Schwitters's work seems to be a sense of the dislocation required in effective poster and cover art, akin to the "defamiliarisation" espoused by the Formalist literary theoretician Viktor Shklovsky in Russia as a

Right: wrapping paper by Piet Zwart for Vetpot, 1924. Zwart knew the De Stijl designers and, although not part of the group, responded to their ideas in making his own contribution to the new typography, independent of any group or school. His work displays a bold use of the diagonal and a control over the copy that was undoubtedly helped by his writing the words as well as doing the art direction. See also his work for NCW (page 81).
Below right: back and front cover of *Merz 8/9*, edited by Kurt Schwitters and El Lissitsky, and designed by Schwitters, 1924. The type is ranged left and right, justified and centred: it is run every way round except upside down. But the strong modular nature of the layout, with different areas of information contained within firmly delineated blocks (similar to Lissitsky's work on *The Isms of Art*) ensures that the whole is firmly controlled and balanced. The use of the red against the blue works to express the message, but is also aesthetically pleasing. In 1927 Schwitters founded the Ring neuer Werbegestalter (the Circle of New Advertising Artists), whose members included Piet Zwart and Jan Tschichold.

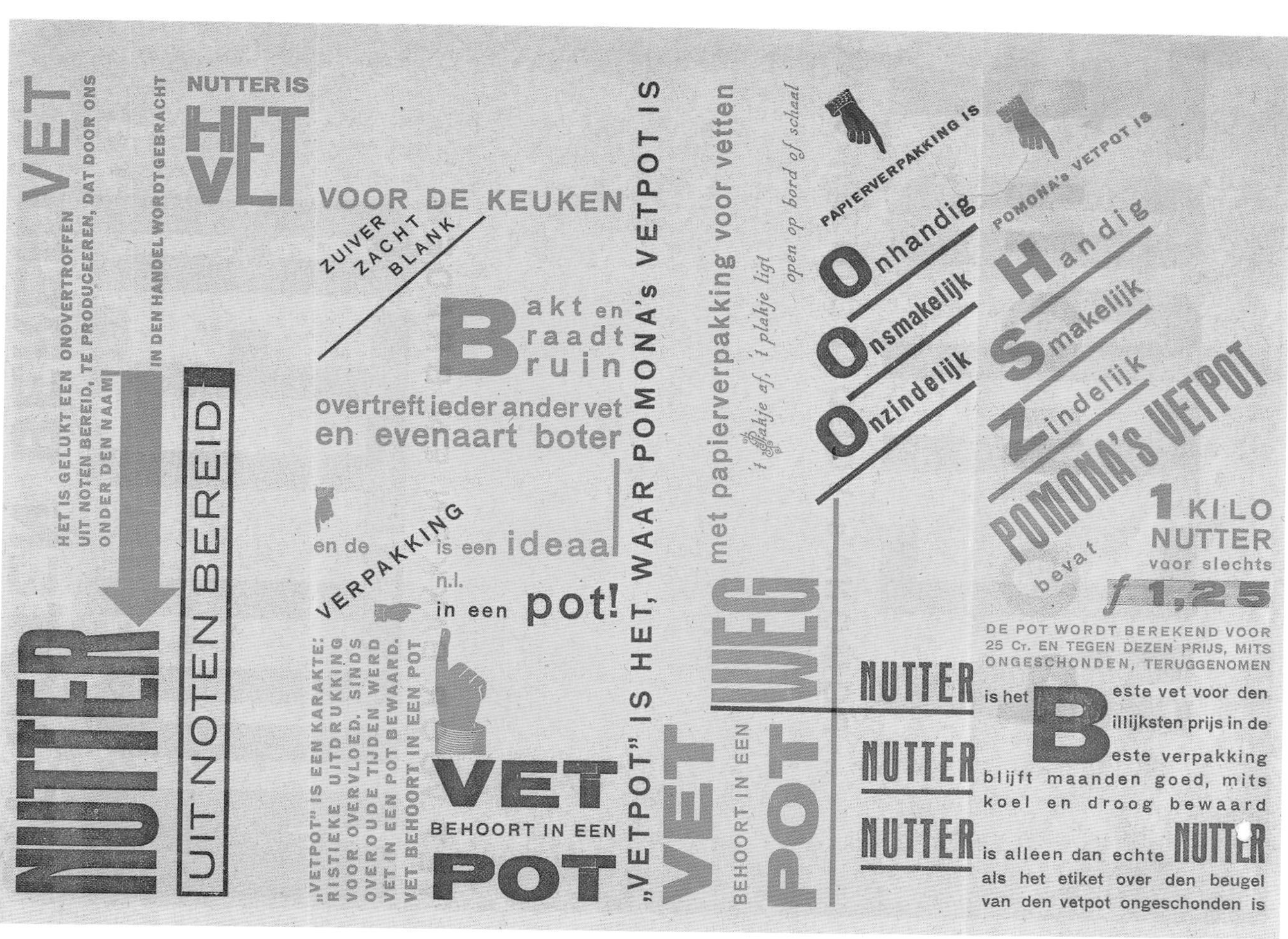
NUTTER
HET IS GELUKT EEN ONOVERTROFFEN VET
UIT NOTEN BEREID, TE PRODUCEEREN, DAT DOOR ONS
ONDER DEN NAAM
IN DEN HANDEL WORDT GEBRACHT
UIT NOTEN BEREID
NUTTER IS HET VET
VOOR DE KEUKEN
ZUIVER ZACHT BLANK
Bakt en Braadt Bruin
overtreft ieder ander vet en evenaart boter
en de VERPAKKING is een ideaal n.l. in een pot!
„VETPOT" IS EEN KARAKTERISTIEKE UITDRUKKING VOOR OVERVLOED. SINDS OVEROUDE TIJDEN WERD VET IN EEN POT BEWAARD. VET BEHOORT IN EEN POT
VET BEHOORT IN EEN POT
„VETPOT" IS HET, WAAR POMONA's VETPOT IS
VET BEHOORT IN EEN POT
WEG met papierverpakking voor vetten
't plakje af, 't plakje ligt open op bord of schaal
PAPIERVERPAKKING IS
Onhandig Onsmakelijk Onzindelijk
POMONA's VETPOT IS
Handig Smakelijk Zindelijk
POMONA'S VETPOT
bevat 1 KILO NUTTER voor slechts f 1,25
DE POT WORDT BEREKEND VOOR 25 Ct. EN TEGEN DEZEN PRIJS, MITS ONGESCHONDEN, TERUGGENOMEN
NUTTER is het Beste vet voor den Billijksten prijs in de Beste verpakking
NUTTER blijft maanden goed, mits koel en droog bewaard
NUTTER is alleen dan echte NUTTER als het etiket over den beugel van den vetpot ongeschonden is

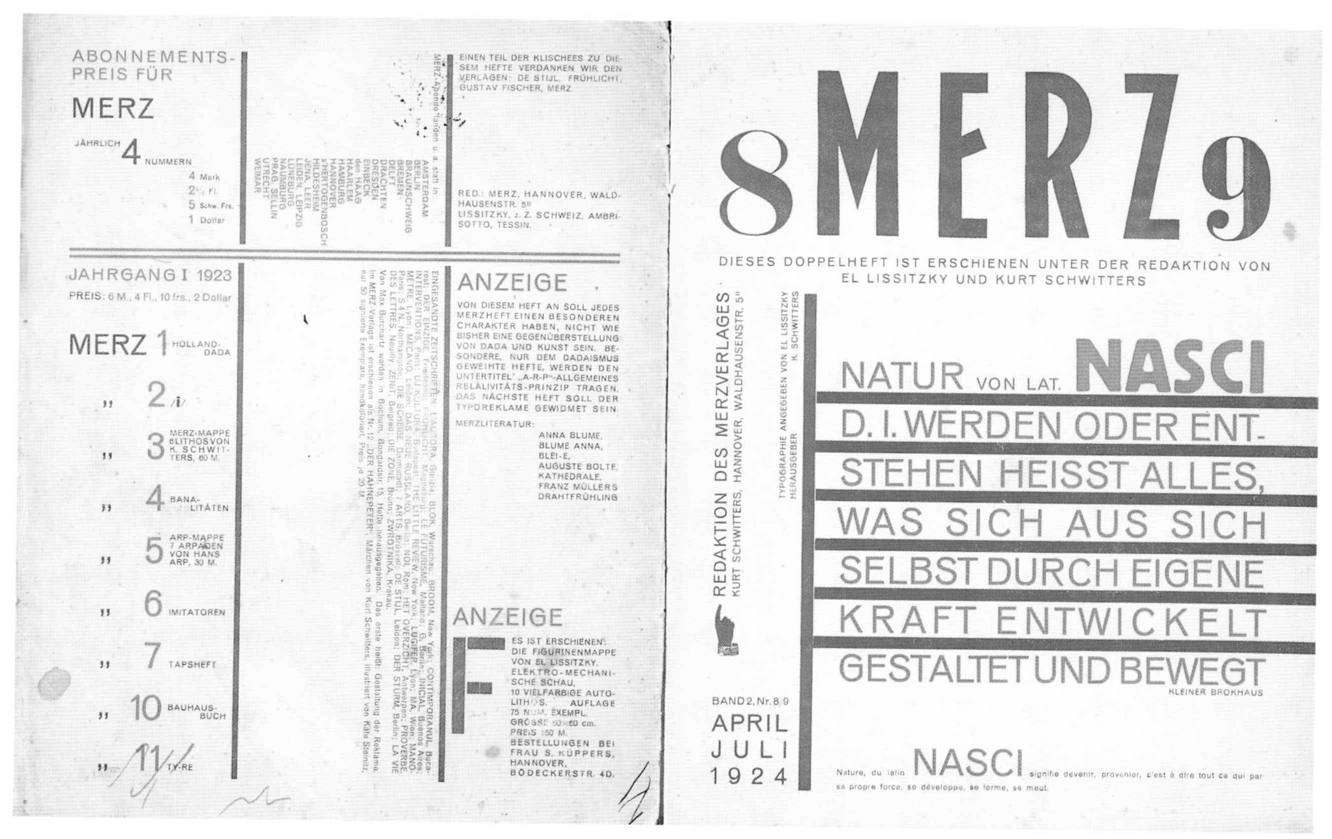
ABONNEMENTS-PREIS FÜR MERZ
JÄHRLICH 4 NUMMERN
4 Mark
5 Schw. Frs.
1 Dollar
JAHRGANG I 1923
MERZ 1 HOLLAND-DADA
„ 2
„ 3 MERZ-MAPPE
„ 4 BANALITÄTEN
„ 5 ARP-MAPPE
„ 6 IMITATOREN
„ 7 TAPSHEFT
„ 10 BAUHAUS-BUCH
„ 11
EINEN TEIL DER KLISCHEES ZU DIESEM HEFTE VERDANKEN WIR DEN VERLAGEN: DE STIJL, FRÜHLICHT, GUSTAV FISCHER, MERZ
RED.: MERZ, HANNOVER, WALDHAUSENSTR. 5II
LISSITZKY, z. Z. SCHWEIZ, AMBRI-SOTTO, TESSIN.
ANZEIGE
VON DIESEM HEFT AN SOLL JEDES MERZHEFT EINEN BESONDEREN CHARAKTER HABEN, NICHT WIE BISHER EINE GEGENÜBERSTELLUNG VON DADA UND KUNST SEIN. BESONDERE, NUR DEM DADAISMUS GEWEIHTE HEFTE, WERDEN DEN UNTERTITEL „A-R-P" ALLGEMEINES RELAIVITÄTS-PRINZIP TRAGEN. DAS NÄCHSTE HEFT SOLL DER TYPOREKLAME GEWIDMET SEIN.
MERZLITERATUR:
ANNA BLUME, BLUME ANNA, BLEI-E, AUGUSTE BOLTE, KATHEDRALE, FRANZ MÜLLERS DRAHTFRÜHLING
ANZEIGE
ES IST ERSCHIENEN: DIE FIGURINENMAPPE VON EL LISSITZKY, ELEKTRO-MECHANISCHE SCHAU, 10 VIELFARBIGE AUTOLITHOS. AUFLAGE 75 NUM. EXEMPL. GRÖSSE 50×60 cm. PREIS 150 M. BESTELLUNGEN BEI FRAU S. KÜPPERS, HANNOVER, BÖDECKERSTR. 4D.
8 MERZ 9
DIESES DOPPELHEFT IST ERSCHIENEN UNTER DER REDAKTION VON EL LISSITZKY UND KURT SCHWITTERS
REDAKTION DES MERZVERLAGES
KURT SCHWITTERS, HANNOVER, WALDHAUSENSTR. 5II
TYPOGRAPHIE ANGEGEBEN VON EL LISSITZKY
HERAUSGEBER K. SCHWITTERS
NATUR VON LAT. NASCI
D. I. WERDEN ODER ENTSTEHEN HEISST ALLES, WAS SICH AUS SICH SELBST DURCH EIGENE KRAFT ENTWICKELT GESTALTET UND BEWEGT
KLEINER BROKHAUS
BAND 2, Nr. 8/9
APRIL JULI 1924
Nature, du latin NASCI signifie devenir, provenir, c'est à dire tout ce qui par sa propre force, se développe, se forme, se meut.

central element of the emerging Modernist consciousness of art. Schwitters's laying of type over the bold rules that establish the grid, interruption of blocks with other lines, and insertion of pictures in seemingly unbalanced asymmetrical layouts all relate to ideas of a new typography and begin to subvert them in a way similar to earlier disruption of the traditional forms.

Another even more isolated innovator was the Dutch printer-typographer Hendrik Werkman (1882–1945). After becoming aware of the new art of the early 1920s, he began to channel his ideas into print, producing from 1923 his own magazine, *The Next Call*. By 1926 there were nine issues of the magazine, which became increasingly experimental in their investigation of the nature of the printing task. Elements of the printing process – the ink, the paper, the pressure, the wooden or metal types and the pieces of page furniture inserted to hold a chase together, along with colour and form – were all revealed in different ways. Random elements crept into the designs that reflected aspects of the materials and construction of the page. The first issue, for example, included an apparently abstract image that was actually part of a lock that had been incorporated into the design. While considered extreme at the time, Werkman's self-conscious style, with its suggestion of a conceptual weight to characters, can be seen as a forerunner of many later referential and reverential displays of communication.

Piet Zwart (1885–1977) was another Dutchman who found a way of adding a distinctive personal stamp to the emerging Modernist typography. From an architectural background, his first typographic exercises around 1920 and 1921 were influenced by the De Stijl group, but by 1925 typography was his main occupation and he had evolved a strong individualism. He was highly prolific in producing advertising and other promotional literature, his designs displaying some of the most dramatic contrasts in type size possible within the confines of a poster. Characters were used so large as to become abstract forms on the page, as well as existing within words. He often wrote his own copy, to enhance the clever playing with words and image, and frequently used the primary colours red, blue and yellow, beloved also by the Bauhaus. In the late 1920s he incorporated more photography, exploring negative images, overprinting and sharp cropping in highly formalised shapes (often a circle, as if a telescopic



Right: *Small Dada Evening*, poster by Theo van Doesburg and Kurt Schwitters, 1922. The breaking away from the horizontal axis and the confusion aroused by the layering of type (albeit still highly readable and with key words prominent) show the graphic anarchy that typified Dada work, which contributed ideas and forms to new rules – notably, the value of the diagonal as a dynamic device, the effect of layering letters over each other, and the combination of different fonts and hand-lettering to disrupt reading and emphasise a message.
Below: *Die Scheuche Marchen* (The Scarecrow) by Kurt Schwitters, Kathe Steinitz and Theo van Doesburg, 1925. Schwitters and Steinitz had collaborated on two earlier children's books when, according to Steinitz, van Doesburg suggested that a "more radical" picture book could be created by using just typographical elements. Van Doesburg seems to have been the lead figure in the design of this book, which deconstructs type to tell a story; his inspiration was Lissitsky (see *Of Two Squares* and *For Reading Out Loud*, pages 73–5).

Below: single alphabet proposal by Kurt Schwitters, 1927. Unlike the universal alphabets of Bayer, Albers and Tschichold, this "Systemschrift" does not have a balanced, geometric order. Although it is constructed from a limited series of elements, the results are deliberately not harmonious. Instead, Schwitters sought to draw an alphabet that could express related sounds with related forms, with the possibility of having vowels in heavier types. He devised different versions, the most extreme being an almost unrecognisable divergence from Latin character forms.

**meister preise**

**müsik im leben der völker am 2. jüli**
**20 ühr dirigiert im opernhaus**
**warschaus berühmter dirigent werke**
**polnischer meister preise 1–5 Mk.**

Right: poster for an exhibition of contemporary industrial arts by Vilmos Huszár, 1929. Huszár contributed to the first issue of *De Stijl* but left the group in 1923. Here, he creates a coherent illustrative work based solely around typographic and geometric forms, which utilises a whole range of disruptive techniques (juxtaposition of diagonal against the right angle, layering of letters over each other, reversing out, breaking the frame) and yet assimilates them in a way that suggests the smooth style of Art Deco as much as the hard line of early De Stijl.
Far right: spread from a catalogue for the Netherlands Cable Works, designed by Piet Zwart, 1927–8. From 1925 onwards, Zwart produced hundreds of designs for this client, forging his own contribution to the new typography. Dramatic use of white space, contrasts of scale and deployment of the diagonal typify his work.
Below far right: on the left, cover of the first issue of *The Next Call*, 1923, and on the right "The Cylinder Press", 1925, both by Hendrik Werkman, whose typographic compositions were works of art not of mass production, produced laboriously by hand with individual variations across the small editions. The unusual shape on the cover of *The First Call* (which reappeared on some subsequent covers) is part of a lock, used as if it is a piece of type, its forms suggesting bold, heavy faces as well as causing a tension between the floating letters in the construction of the pages on which it appears. Werkman reversed the normal process of printing, placing the paper on the bed of the press and then pressing the type and other objects on to it; each page displays the effect of the hand behind it, in the precise points of the composition and the depth of the impressions, exploring the detail in the relationship of ink, paper and the wood, metal or other forms used to make the impression. His so-called "druksels", such as "The Cylinder Press", composed found elements from the printshop and elsewhere to produce abstract images.

HOW CABLE-HAVOC BEGINS
AT LAST: HOT SPOTS
H T
SP TS
50
AND BREAK DOWN
WHY RISK BREAK DOWN
WHILST THERE ARE
N.C.W.-CABLES
WITH HIGH
IONISATION
VOLTAGE
?
if you like to make money
by saving it
buy N.C.W. products
51
power cables
telephone cables
copper wire
solid and stranded
compounds

image). According to Zwart, the simpler and more geometric the character, the more useful he found it – as witnessed by his frequent use of chunky sans serif and capitals.

All these various experiments and implementations of a new sensibility in graphic communication found their chronicler and apostle in the seminal book *Die Neue Typographie* [*The New Typography*]. Its author, Jan Tschichold (1902–74), was a young Austrian who was teaching typography and lettering in Munich, and who had been a close observer of the work of Lissitsky, those at the Bauhaus and others, as well as being an uncompromising modern designer in his own right. In 1925 he had published his first writings on the subject in a special issue of the printing journal *Typographische Mitteilungen*, which was given over to his essay "Elementare Typographie". In this essay (a remarkable achievement for such a young designer) Tschichold introduced Lissitsky's work to the audience of practising printers for the first time. The ideas behind asymmetric typography, sans serif typefaces and limited choice of faces, plus the relationship of type and white space, were put in terms aimed at providing new rules for the printer. His was the familiar attack on the supposedly debased standards of nineteenth-century printing, expressing contempt for the grey nature of standardised blocks of text with little to excite the eye, and berating the clutter of advertising typography. While criticising traditions, he also eschewed some of the print-form variations that derived from more exotic typefaces and typographic arrangements, chosen by printers in the 1920s as they aimed for new decorative qualities.

Tschichold's key points were all directed at creating a purer, elementary functionalism in typography. The thesis could be summarised as: asymmetry, sans serif. Certain more naive aspects of the book were later renounced by Tschichold, but in its clarification of some of the coherent themes in the work of the Modernist typographers this publication was most important. It was also in many ways the first book to concentrate on the idea of typography as the graphic arrangement of type and choice of type, rather than being concerned with other more practical aspects of printing.

Tschichold's own design work made a notable contribution to the spread of his ideas in both commercial and experimental form. The design of his book and its promotional material rigorously laid down ideas about the grid that would form a basis for the Swiss designers of almost twenty years later. His film posters for the Phoebus Palast cinema merged certain concepts of the German movement Plakatstijl – simplicity of wording, strong colouring and a key image – with the asymmetry, photography and exploration of the dynamic of the diagonal that identify the graphic style of the Bauhaus. His 1929 design of a universal alphabet also showed him following in the path of Bayer's quest for total reductivity in the typographic elements.

But it was the man who gave Tschichold his teaching job in Munich who created the most emblematic face of the 1920s: Futura was the face (its name was an inspired piece of identity) and Paul Renner the designer. Designed for the Bauer foundry and issued from 1927, Futura can be seen to have antecedents in the Erbar sans serif released only a few years before and also highly popular. It is distinguished from Erbar by aspects such as the upper case "Q" with its tail beginning inside the bowl, and the lack of a tail on the lower case "j". Renner first designed an even more elemental face, almost abstract in parts (with an "r" consisting of a simple stem and an unattached point floating where

Right and page 85: promotional material for Futura Schmuck (ornament), issued by the Bauer foundry after the launch of the seminal sans serif face Futura in 1927. Designed by Paul Renner, Futura quickly became highly popular, meeting the desire of the new typography for geometric faces; its appearance from a commercial foundry ensured its rapid spread. The ornaments that were made available (far right and page 85) show the idea of a perfect geometry being employed: the suggestion was that the components in the face were the basic building elements of design. This brochure carries on its back cover (below far right) an advertisement for Venus, another Bauer sans serif issued from 1907–27 the design of which dates back essentially to the nineteenth century. Venus has none of the distinctive geometry and features of Futura, such as the splayed "M", the narrow, tail-less "t" and "j", the single-storey "a" and the "u" that follows the upper case. It is ironic that Moholy-Nagy, so much an advocate of the geometric qualities in Futura, should be persuaded by Bauer to endorse Venus.

# FUTURA Figuren-Verzeichnis

A B C D E F G H I J K L M N O
P Q R S T U V W X Y Z Ä Ö Ü
a b c d e f g h i j k l m n o p q r ſ s t
u v w x y z ä ö ü ch ck ff fi fl ft ſſ ſi ſt ß
mager 1 2 3 4 5 6 7 8 9 0 & . , - : ; · ! ? ' ( * † « » §
Auf Wunsch liefern wir Mediäval-Ziffern 1 2 3 4 5 6 7 8 9 0

A B C D E F G H I J K L M N O
P Q R S T U V W X Y Z Ä Ö Ü
a b c d e f g h i j k l m n o p q r ſ s t
u v w x y z ä ö ü ch ck ff fi fl ft ſſ ſi ſt ß
halbfett 1 2 3 4 5 6 7 8 9 0 & . , - : ; · ! ? ' ( * † « » §
Auf Wunsch liefern wir Mediäval-Ziffern 1 2 3 4 5 6 7 8 9 0

**A B C D E F G H I J K L M N O**
**P Q R S T U V W X Y Z Ä Ö Ü**
**a b c d e f g h i j k l m n o p q**
**r ſ s t u v w x y z ä ö ü ch ck**
**ff fi fl ft ſſ ſi ſt ß**
**1 2 3 4 5 6 7 8 9 0**
fett **& . , - : ; · ! ? ' ( * † « » §**

FUTURA
SCHMUCK
LEIPZIG BERLIN BARCELONA MADRID BILBAO SEVILLA
BAUERSCHE
GIESSEREI
FRANKFURT-M

FÜR DIE
ELEMENTARE
TYPO-
GRAPHIE
ist nach Aussagen ihrer
vielen Anhänger unsere
VENUS
die geeignetste Schrift
Der bekannte und be-
rühmte Bauhausmeister
L. MOHOLY-NAGY
urteilt in „Offset-, Buch-
und Werbekunst" Nr. 7:
Als Auszeichnungs-
und Titelschrift besitzen
wir dagegen annähernd
brauchbare, gute Schrif-
ten, deren geometrische
und fonetische Urform,
wie Quadrat oder Kreis,
ohne Verzerrungen zur
Geltung kommt. Das ist
die Venus-Grotesk
BAUERSCHE GIESSEREI
FRANKFURT A. MAIN W 13

the spur should be). In comparison with earlier sans faces, Futura's main features are the clear geometric forms, the single storey "a" and the open-tail "g". For twenty-five years Futura would be the leading sans serif face, taking a prominent role in advertising in its many variations (such as an inlined form, or Futura Black, a stencil cut that is quite distinct from the main family).

Some of the ornaments made available for Futura, showing Renner's conception of the face's geometry (see also page 83).

One of the first strong implementations of these ideas of a new typography in commercial practice took place in Czechoslovakia, where the group of artists and designers who went under the group banner Devetsil included two influential typographers, Karel Teige and Ladislav Sutnar. The poet and artist Teige (1900–51) wrote his own version of typography principles in an essay, "Moderní typo [Modern Type]" (1927). Its call for dynamic forms that rejected the traditional was embraced by Sutnar (1897–1976) who was a design teacher as well as being art director for a publisher. His work in the late 1920s and early 1930s contained yet another original mixture of the ideas of De Stijl, Constructivism and that of Bauhaus teachers. Bold photomontage is placed with pared-down type, and with demonstrations of the play possible with perspective and the use of colour for depth and bringing elements to the fore. Sutnar was to exert further influence after emigrating to the United States in 1939.

In Poland, the work of Henryk Berlewi (1894–1967) followed a different route from the Constructivist ideas spread by Lissitsky. His approach to a new functional communication was to create a "Mechano Faktur" [mechanical art], a systemised idea of creativity that sought to reduce typographic work (amongst other things) to a range of functional elements that could be combined as building elements. It was a bold rejection of individualism as well as of the traditional forms associated with a past age. Berlewi went on to apply his ideas through his own advertising agency as well as by promoting them in other areas of the applied arts. A strong sense of the link between expressive typography and abstract forms is apparent in Berlewi's work, where the message of the words is subsumed within the whole composition.

For all this revolution in the creation of a new typography reflecting Modernist sensibility, most printed communication continued to conform to traditional values, for good or for bad. A number of people were concerned at the bad: they sought not to effect a revolution in the principles underlying typographic form in its grander scheme, but to restore the values they felt had been debased in much of the material that mass communication had brought.

Publication of the seventh and final issue of the typographic journal *The Fleuron* by the University Press, Cambridge, in 1930 is a seminal point in the recording and exploration of traditional typographic values. Over its seven issues, 1,500 pages and eight years, *The Fleuron* set out to cover the concerns arising from the search for the highest typographic standards in Europe and the USA, its contributors and article subjects spanning many of the key figures in typographic history in Western culture, both recent and historic. A noticeable gap was caused by the lack of any reference to anything "Modernist". In the final issue, the editor Stanley Morison (1889–1967) set out to state the basis of the principles behind the tradition explored in the journal. His "First Principles of Typography" addressed the craft of book design in particular, but his comments clearly applied more broadly to continuous text and he took the opportunity to imply what he thought of innovative work in other areas. In his postscript to the final issue he fired a direct attack on those who sought to remain outside the rules advocated in his essay and in the magazine:

GROSSER
UMSATZ!

Dieses Geschäfts-Prinzip versetzt mich in die Lage, meiner Kundschaft vorteilhafte Angebote zu machen. Ganz besonders weise ich hierbei auf die reiche Auswahl in Rohseide, Crêpe de Chine und Waschseide hin

SEIDENHAUS
WEINBERGER

KLEINER
NUTZEN!

WIR
KAUEN
WRIGLEY

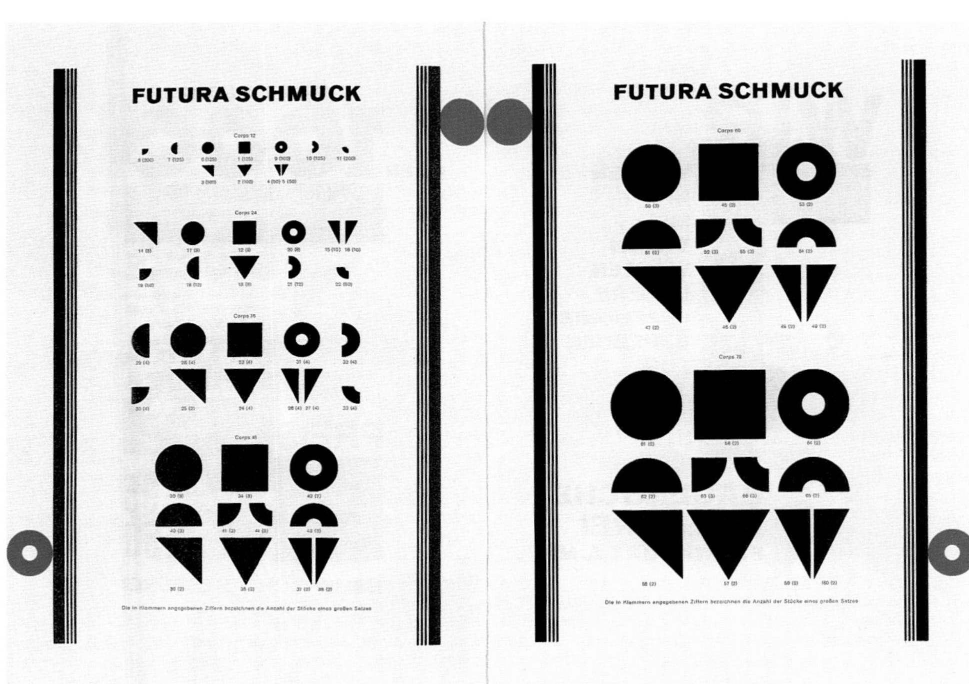
FUTURA SCHMUCK
FUTURA SCHMUCK

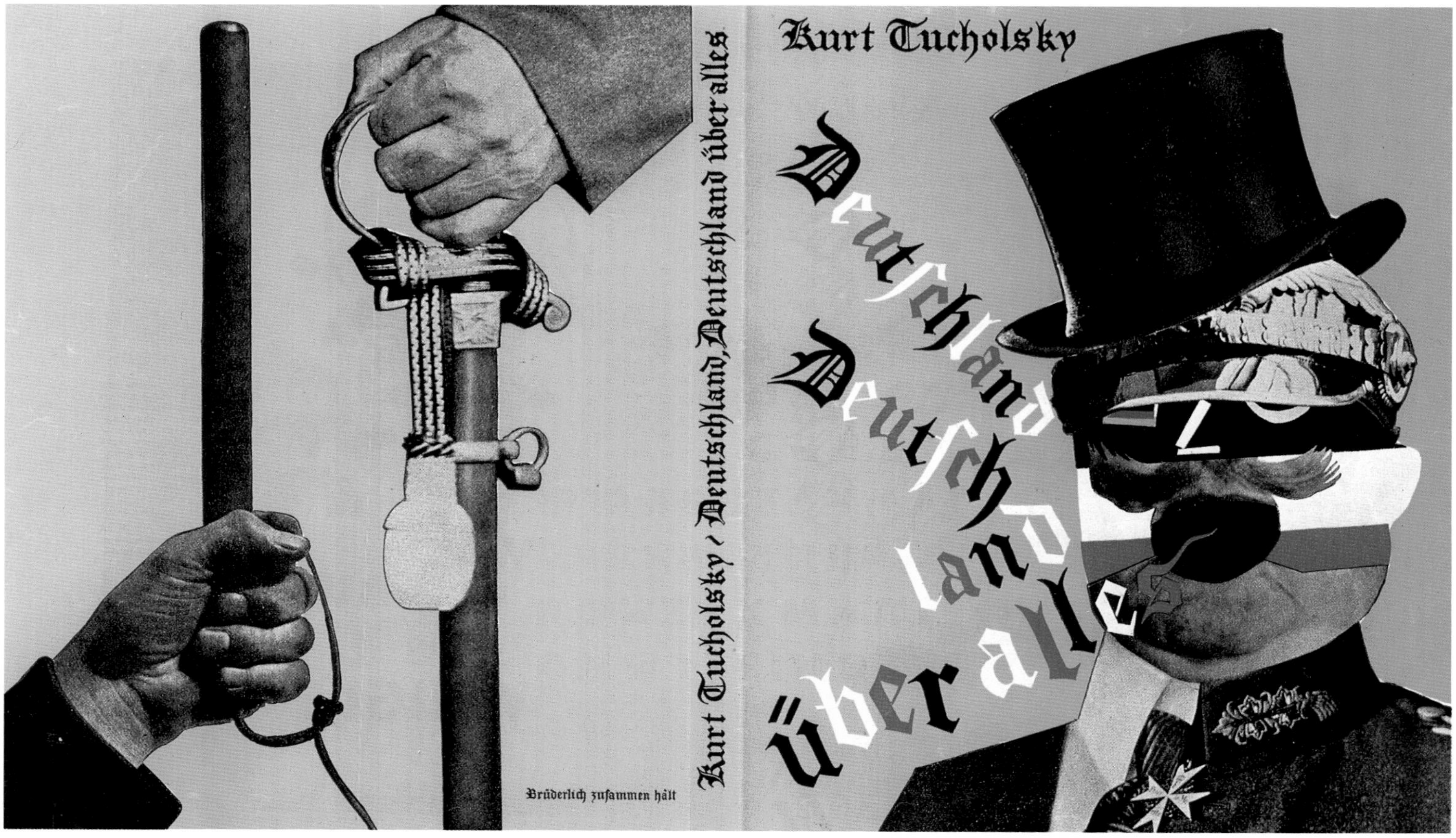

Kurt Tucholsky
Deutschland Deutschland über alles
Kurt Tucholsky / Deutschland, Deutschland über alles
Brüderlich zusammen hält

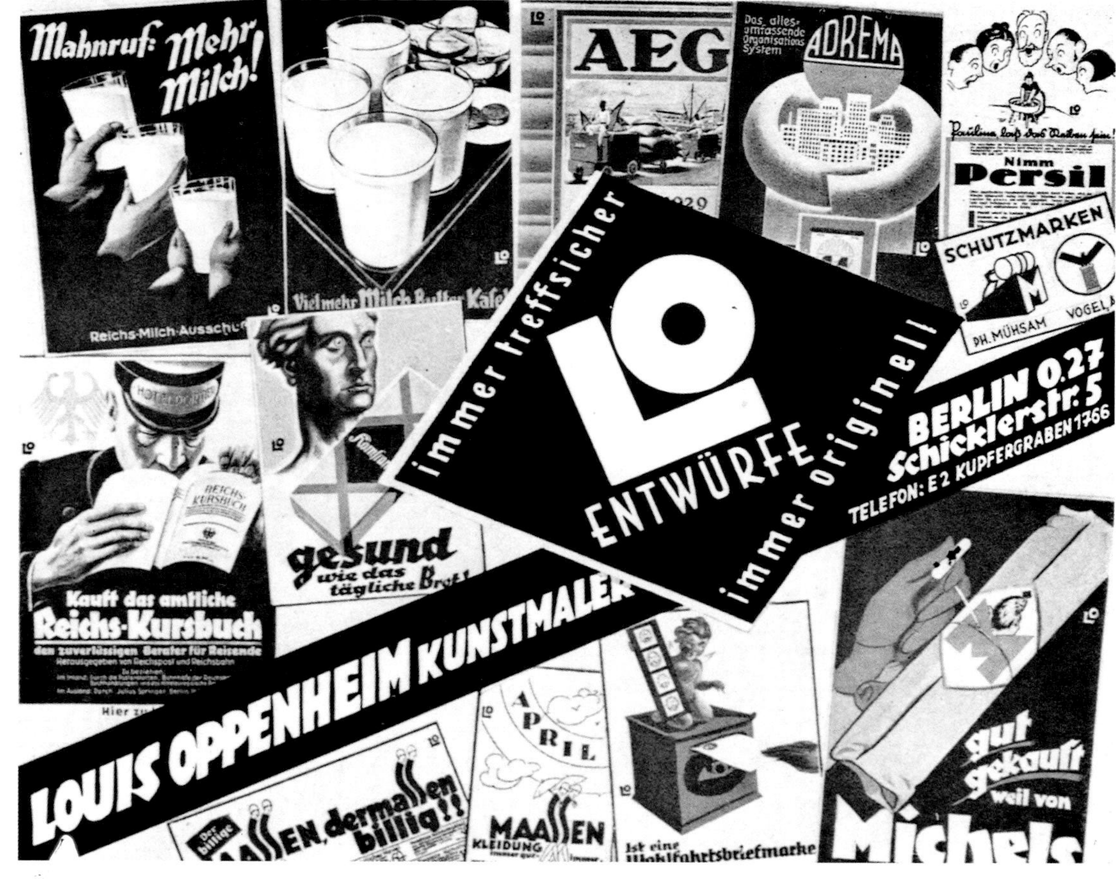

Mahnruf: Mehr Milch!
Reichs-Milch-Ausschu
Viel mehr Milch Butter Käse
AEG
Das alles-umfassende Organisations System
ADREMA
Nimm Persil
SCHUTZMARKEN
PH. MÜHSAM
immer treffsicher
LO
ENTWÜRFE
immer originell
BERLIN O.27
Schicklerstr. 5
TELEFON: E 2 KUPFERGRABEN 1766
Reichs-Kursbuch
Kauft das amtliche
Reichs-Kursbuch
den zuverlässigen Berater für Reisende
gesund
wie das tägliche Brot!
LOUIS OPPENHEIM KUNSTMALER
APRIL
MAASSEN, dermaassen billig!!
MAASSEN
KLEIDUNG
Ist eine Wohlfahrtsbriefmarke
gut gekauft weil von
Michels

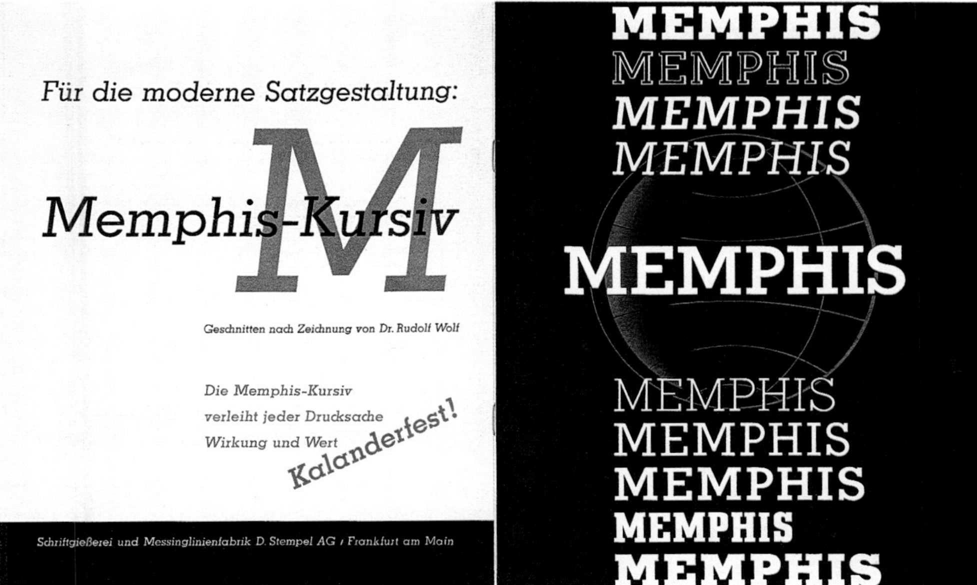


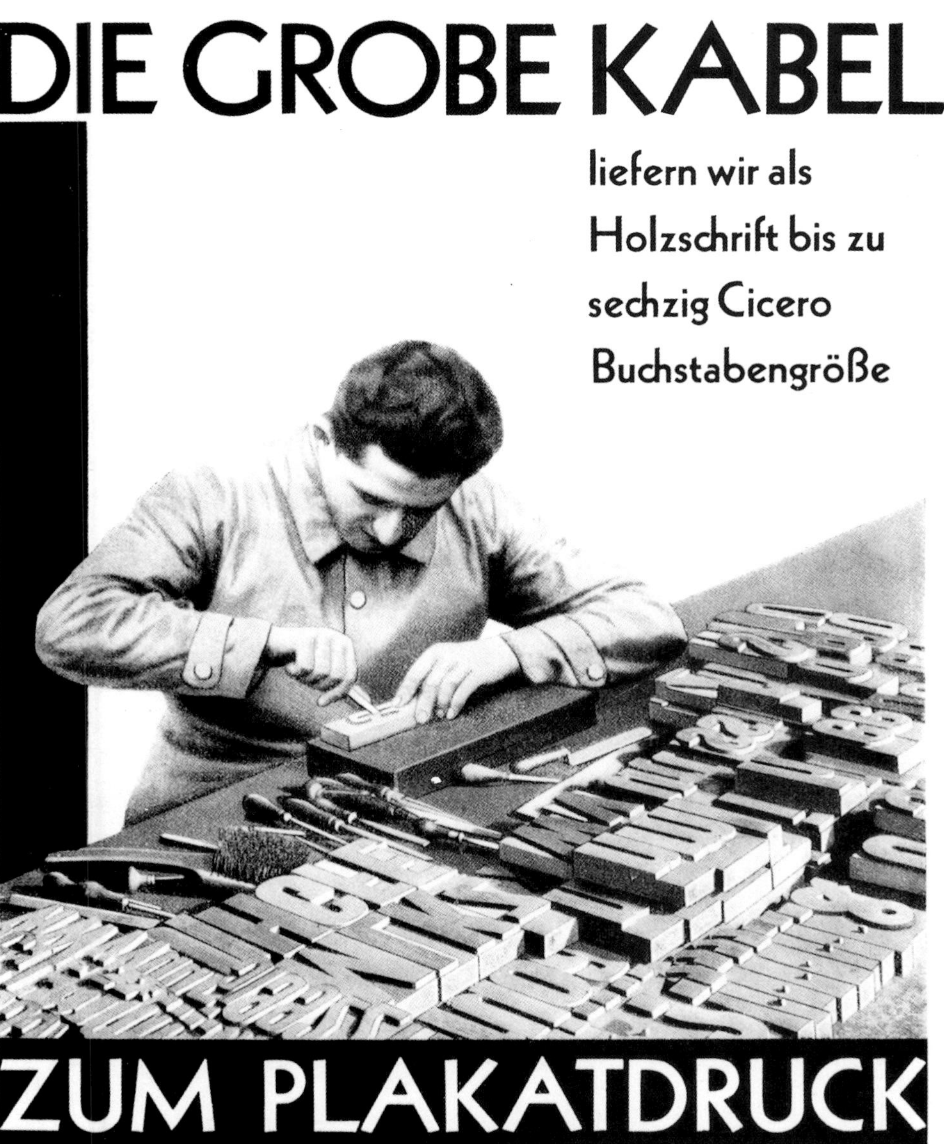


Far left: cover for *Deutschland Deutschland über alles* by Kurt Tucholsky, designed by John Heartfield, 1929. The strength of this photomontage depends not only on the quality of Heartfield's manipulation of the various elements but on new ideas of layout: the back cover, for example, has a sharp crop on the picture, with both the vertical and diagonal strongly emphasised. On the front, type on the diagonal is set against the vertical, while the black-letter face, printed in the colours of the German flag and picking up the face of a businessman/militarist, uses nationalistic associations in an ironic and satirical manner.

Below far left: self-promotional advertisement by the designer Louis Oppenheim, *Gebrauchsgraphik*, 1929. This Berlin-based designer, who a decade before had been involved in Plakatstijl, offered his talents across a range of styles, a mark of the explosion in ideas and demand during the middle and late 1920s, when earlier styles and new ideas from the various art movements filtered into the commercial arena.

Above left: promotional material for Memphis, designed by Rudolf Weiss (1875–1943) and released in 1929 by the Stempel foundry. This was the first face to revive the square serif form (also known as Egyptian or slab serif), which had fallen into virtual disuse since the turn of the century. Other German foundries quickly followed the lead: Bauer produced Beton and Berthold City, and the style then spread further afield with Monotype's Rockwell, among others. In the US, ATF launched Stymie, but Linotype imported Memphis and made it the first choice in this area.

Left: promotional material for Kabel, designed by Rudolf Koch (1876–1934) and issued by the Klingspor foundry, 1928. Named after the laying of the telephone cable under the Atlantic, Kabel met the demand for a sans serif face that would display some of the characteristics of the hand. Monotype produced a version of Kabel, but it never obtained the blanket application of its near-contemporary, Futura.

***The apostles of the "machine age" will be wise to address their disciples in a standard old face – they can flourish their concrete banner in sans serif on title pages and perhaps in a running headline. For the rest, deliberate experiments aside, we are all, whether we like it or not, in absolute dependence upon ocular law and national custom.***

His opening paragraph to "First Principles of Typography" preaches this orthodoxy from a platform tied to the very definition of the craft:

***Typography may be defined as the craft of rightly disposing printing material in accordance with specific purpose; of so arranging the letters, distributing the space and controlling the type as to aid to the maximum the reader's comprehension of the text. Typography is the efficient means to an essentially utilitarian and only accidentally aesthetic end, for enjoyment of patterns is rarely the reader's chief aim. Therefore, any disposition of printing material which, whatever the intention, has the effect of coming between author and reader is wrong. It follows that in the printing of books meant to be read there is little room for "bright" typography. Even dullness and monotony in the type-setting are far less vicious to a reader than typographical eccentricity or pleasantry. Cunning of this sort is desirable, even essential in the typography of propaganda, whether for commerce, politics, or religion, because in such printing only the freshest survives inattention. But the typography of books, apart from the category of narrowly limited editions, requires an obedience to convention which is almost absolute, – and with reason.***

For Morison, that "reason" is the need for a printed object to meet a common purpose, to fit into recognisable, highly familiar common archetypes of letter- and wordforms, traditions that the common reader can interpret. At the same time, of course, he did not desire it to be so recognisably average that it did not

Below: Bembo (top), Baskerville (centre) and Bodoni (bottom) were all revived by Monotype in the 1920s. Bembo (1929), like Monotype's Poliphilus (1923) before it, copies the work of the punchcutter Francesco Griffo for the Venetian printer Aldus Manutius (1450–1515). Its attraction lies in the refinement of the cut, which gives a "brightness" from the sharpness of the serif. Baskerville (1924) was a revival of the work of the eighteenth-century English printer and modern face designer John Baskerville. Monotype's Bodoni (1921) was another cleaning-up operation of revival: the "style of modern" face associated with Gianbattista Bodoni of Parma (1740–1813) had already been recut by the Italian foundry Nebiolo in 1901 and by ATF in 1911, but the quest to arrive at a definitive version of this seminal, high-contrast, unbracketed, serif face continued. Perhaps the most admired, although seen only in highly limited editions, were the Bodoni cuts created by Giovanni Mardersteig (1892–1977) for his private press, the Officina Bodoni, from the mid-1920s.

abcdefghijklmnopqrstuvwxyz
ABCDEFGHIJKLMNOPQRSTUVWXYZ
1234567890

abcdefghijklmnopqrstuvwxyz
ABCDEFGHIJKLMNOPQRSTUVWXYZ
1234567890

abcdefghijklmnopqrstuvwxyz
ABCDEFGHIJKLMNOPQRSTUVWXYZ
1234567890

# FIRST PRINCIPLES OF TYPOGRAPHY

by

STANLEY MORISON

Typography may be defined as the craft of rightly disposing printing material in accordance with specific purpose; of so arranging the letters, distributing the space and controlling the type as to aid to the maximum the reader's comprehension of the text. Typography is the efficient means to an essentially utilitarian and only accidentally aesthetic end, for enjoyment of patterns is rarely the reader's chief aim. Therefore, any disposition of printing material which, whatever the intention, has the effect of coming between author and reader is wrong. It follows that in the printing of books meant to be read there is little room for "bright" typography. Even dullness and monotony in the type-setting are far less vicious to a reader than typographical eccentricity or pleasantry. Cunning of this sort is desirable, even essential in the typography of propaganda, whether for commerce, politics, or religion, because in such printing only the freshest survives inattention. But the typography of books, apart from the category of narrowly limited editions, requires an obedience to convention which is almost absolute,—and with reason.

Since printing is essentially a means of multiplying, it must not only be good in itself—but good for a common purpose. The wider that purpose, the stricter are the limitations imposed upon the printer. He may try an experiment in a tract printed in an edition of 50 copies, but he shows little common sense if he experiments to the same degree in the tract having a run of 50,000. Again, a novelty, fitly introduced into a 16-page pamphlet, will be highly undesirable in a 160-page book. It is of the essence of typography and of the nature of the printed book *qua* book, that it perform a public service.

F VII 61 8

Left: Stanley Morison's "First Principles of Typography" was published in the seventh and final issue of *The Fleuron*, 1930. Setting out an alternative perspective to that of Tschichold's *Die Neue Typographie*, it called for designers to study and observe the lessons of tradition in order to extract from hot-metal technology a form of typographic excellence that could rival the standards of the past. Morison was concerned with issues of legibility, readability and good taste in typography – not for him the disruptive shock tactics of the Bauhaus and others. His ideas centred on the practice of fine book typography and *The Fleuron* was an example of the highest standards. Below left: cover detail from Monotype's specimen brochure launching Fournier in 1925, the first face that Stanley Morison, a typographic consultant to Monotype since 1922, clearly initiated unprompted by the revivals of others. His interest in the faces of the eighteenth-century French printer Pierre Simon Fournier underlies the design, a revival of a light roman and an italic form of transitional face.

have higher standards than mass-production "traditions" had hitherto projected. In one sense, Morison's aims relate to the Bauhaus search for simple, non-decorative forms of typography in which every element was significant to the message. But his methods of implementing such principles were quite different:

***No printer should say "I am an artist therefore I am not to be dictated to, I will create my own letter forms," for, in this humble job, individualism is not very helpful. It is no longer possible, as it was in the infancy of the craft, to persuade society into the acceptance of strongly marked and highly individualistic types – because literate society is so much greater in mass and correspondingly slow in movement. The good type designer knows that, for a new fount to be successful, it has to be so good that only very few recognise its novelty.***

Morison's principles would, if closely followed, deliver an accurate rendering of the classical, restrained pages that he himself designed. While such a regime might seem starkly conservative to all but the most leadenly orthodox of modern-day designers, Morison's words were a valuable contribution in print to what had existed as good practice and what underlay the finest achievements of the print revival projected by both industrial and private presses. For the young typographer-compositor in a printworks, this essay was a valuable marker. Morison's predecessor as editor of *The Fleuron*, Oliver Simon, was to add to this core of writing for book design with his *Introduction to Typography* in 1946. The comparison with today's information-laden age might be to consider the need for formalising good typographic practice in the office, where new word-processing technology has transformed the potential for producing bad typography, contrasting with the limitations of the typewriter. Morison saw his text as being addressed to the "amateur", even though by publishing it in *The Fleuron* it was going to reach an élite audience (a print run of just 1,000 copies on English made wove, and 210 on English handmade wove paper). In fact,

Right: design for a visiting card by Fortunato Depero, 1927. The early anarchism and explosiveness of Italian Futurism transformed itself in the 1920s. Here, Depero's layered and ordered type communicates the slick skill of the designer, with his name twisted into a neat pattern: an attractive adaptation of the once rebellious art movement to serve potential advertising clients.
Below left: poster by Theo Ballmer, 1928 (Museum of Modern Art, New York). The approach shown in Ballmer's work comes from his training at the Bauhaus; his commitment to the visible grid, however, comes from De Stijl and yet prefigures the Swiss-style designers of the 1950s in the restriction of type sizes and weights to one only for the headline, one for the supporting text.
Below: book jacket for *Růžové Viry* by Jiří Landa, designed by Hlavack, 1927, showing the Constructivist mode shading into Art Deco. Stylised, high-contrast sans serif lettering is combined with dynamic arrangement of abstract geometric forms that suggest a mechanical detail.

CREAZIONI
TIPOGRAFICHE
DEPERO

1927

however, its effects were widespread, and Morison's teaching remained influential in printworks across the land. In 1936, the essay was reprinted in British, American and Dutch editions, and after the war it was translated into German, Danish, Dutch and Spanish, and reprinted several times.

A glance through the index of *The Fleuron* shows that there was no room for Bauhaus artists or other Modernists such as Tschichold. Johnston and Gill appear, though, with a lengthy essay on Gill in the final issue. The narrowness of typographical study in this influential magazine is further proved by Morison's limitation of his own interests when presenting them in print. It is ironic that his definition of typography as a craft that "controls the composition, imposition, impression and paper" seems to exclude Gill's famous sans serif for Monotype, issued in 1928 under the authority of their typographic consultant – Morison. Because it originated as a piece of lettering painted on a fascia board, Gill Sans was not considered at all suitable for reproduction in *The Fleuron*; in the same way the journal avoided both the vernacular elsewhere and the widespread Modernist experiments.

Gill Sans was Eric Gill's first face for Monotype to be issued and quickly became highly popular, embracing the simple, geometric qualities advocated by the new typography while at the same time showing a liveliness that displays a sense of the hand behind it and gives some fluidity to the typeface when seen in continuous text. It was initially seen as very much a titling alphabet, a publicly available variation on Johnston's sans serif designed for use on the London Underground, from which it was partly derived (Gill had worked a little with Johnston on the earlier face). But it became more widely used thanks to its distinctive character, which prevents it from being a straightforward copy of

Opposite: Broadway, designed by Morris Fuller Benton for American Type Founders, 1929. This stylised type combines the characteristics of two kinds of sans serif, fat face and lineale, with the main stroke of most of the letters being the fat face and the rest line.
Below left: Bookman, also known as Antique Old Style, was a popular, rugged, commercial face in the US, notably in advertising in the 1920s. Its characteristics are its short descenders and ascenders and the liveliness of expression caused by the slight variations of stress.
Below: front page of *The New Yorker*, 1925, after its redesign with Irvin as a special headline face, styled around the logo. As with Broadway, its forms are styled to be showily elegant, especially the "E", "W" and the wide "O". The magazine retains elements of Irvin today.

Characters in Complete Font

A B C D E F G
H I J K L M N
O P Q R S T U
V W X Y Z & $
1 2 3 4 5 6 7 8 9 0
a b c d e f g h i
j k l m n o p q r
s t u v w x y z
ff fi ffi fl ffl
. : , ; - ' ! ? —

SPECIAL CHARACTERS
These special characters are available in all sizes and may be purchased with complete fonts, separately or by sets

The A M R

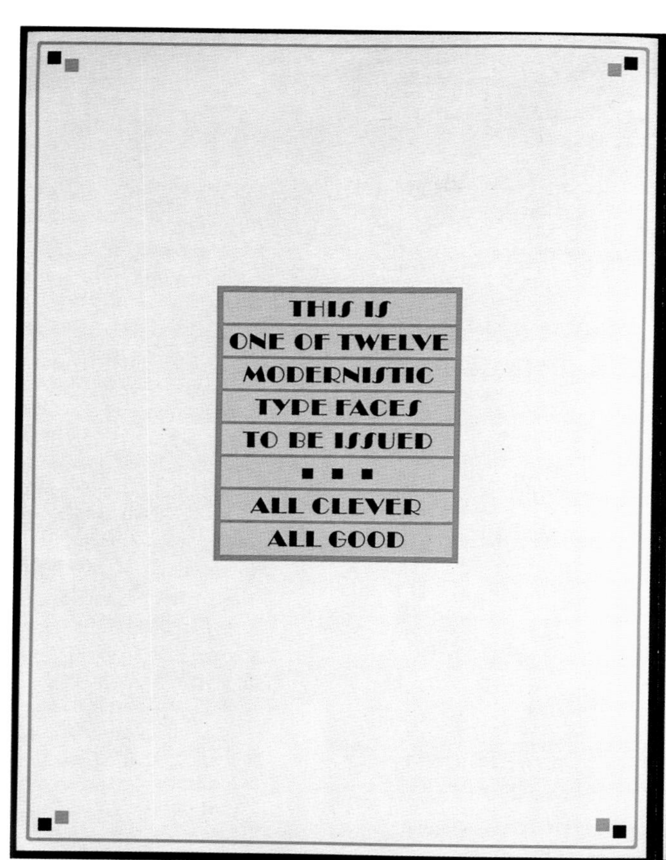
THIS IS
ONE OF TWELVE
MODERNISTIC
TYPE FACES
TO BE ISSUED
ALL CLEVER
ALL GOOD

THE
BROADWAY
SERIES
NOW READY FOR PRINTERS IN
SIZES FROM 12 TO 48 POINT
A
MODERNISTIC
TYPE
AMERICAN TYPE FOUNDERS
COMPANY

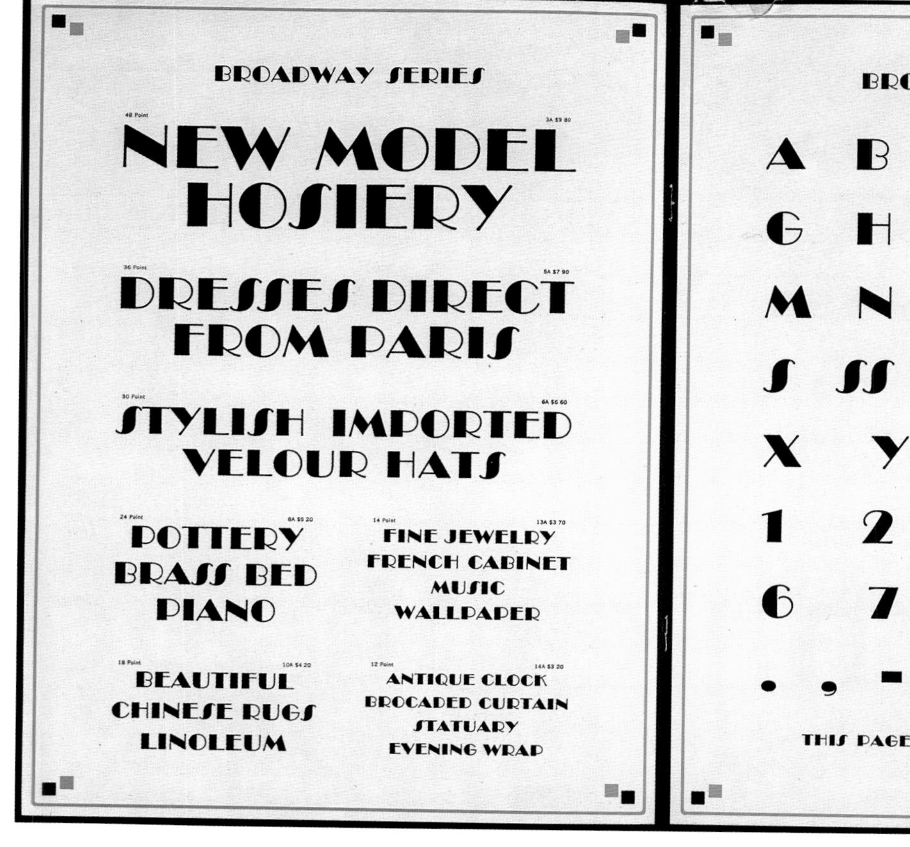
BROADWAY SERIES
NEW MODEL
HOSIERY
DRESSES DIRECT
FROM PARIS
STYLISH IMPORTED
VELOUR HATS
POTTERY
BRASS BED
PIANO
FINE JEWELRY
FRENCH CABINET
MUSIC
WALLPAPER
BEAUTIFUL
CHINESE RUGS
LINOLEUM
ANTIQUE CLOCK
BROCADED CURTAIN
STATUARY
EVENING WRAP

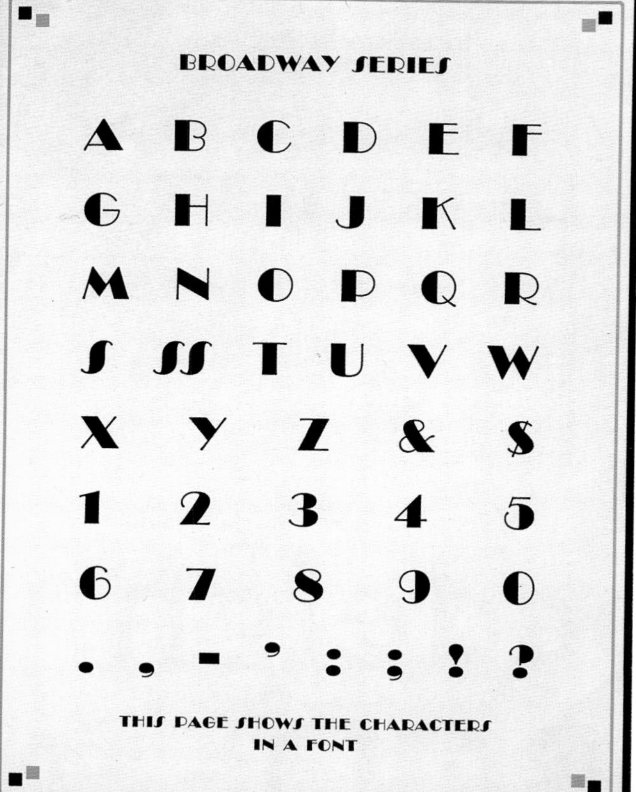
BROADWAY SERIES
A B C D E F
G H I J K L
M N O P Q R
S SS T U V W
X Y Z & $
1 2 3 4 5
6 7 8 9 0
. , - ' : ; ! ?
THIS PAGE SHOWS THE CHARACTERS
IN A FONT

Johnston's. Specific differences are the subtle down-curve of the "R", the half-height middle strokes of the "M" that avoid the optical shading noticeable in some heavy "M"s, and the dropping of the strictly monotone weight of stroke in the lower case.

Gill Sans was not the first typeface Monotype commissioned from the designer, although it was the first to be produced. Gill had begun work in 1925 on a face that drew on his lettercutting and signwriting skills to produce an elegant roman and italic in upper and lower case. This work produced Perpetua (with the italic being called Felicity), one of the most refined of modern old-face designs, distinguished by sharply cut serifs and other characteristics reminiscent of the designs Gill had been cutting in stone for some years. The face was introduced in 1929, being first fully seen in a Cambridge University Press edition of Gill's own writings, *Art-Nonsense and other essays*; in the same year a beautifully produced and appropriate setting of it was printed with woodcuts by Gill, *The Passion of SS. Perpetua and Felicity*. This was issued finally as a bound insert in the final issue of *The Fleuron* in 1930.

Work of a very different nature thrived during the 1920s under the classification of Art Deco. Certain typefaces and typographic or calligraphic practices gave a strong flavour to some of the print of the inter-war period, noticeably in stylish advertising applications of some posters and magazines. The Art Deco style formally centred on the 1925 Exposition Internationale des Arts Décoratifs et Industriels Modernes in Paris and its advocacy of a revival of decorative craft in modern production. In fact, however, the Deco label was applied in all creative areas from architecture to advertising. It had different inflections in different countries, being particularly strong initially in France and later on in America, and continued into the late 1930s, subject to Jazz Age modifications before adopting the streamlined look. Graphic artists working in this area mixed the new approaches of Cubism and post-Cubism with the bold illustrative traditions of Art Nouveau and the Plakatstijl's development of advertising language. Perhaps the most notable of all the poster artists of this period was A. M. Cassandre (the pseudonym of Adolphe Jean-Marie Mouron, 1901–68). His posters pared down the language both of pictorial images and typographic forms and then put these through the warp of perspectives drawn from the Modernist artists of Cubism and after. Out of this approach came his first face, the semi-abstract, highly stylised Bifur, issued in 1929 by Deberny & Peignot. He

Right: Perpetua, designed by Eric Gill for Monotype, 1925, a highly popular old-face roman, admired for its elegant line and serifs. It had an unusual process of generation. Gill's qualities as a lettercutter and signwriter attracted the interest of Stanley Morison, who invited him to design a face for Monotype around the forms he was using in his inscriptions. Gill supplied large-scale drawings of the letters, but Morison doubted that the Monotype drawing office would transfer them properly into the form for hot-metal matrices. Instead, he commissioned a Parisian punchcutter, Charles Malin, to create a trial font. A long gestation period followed, before Monotype brought it out from 1929. Below: Gill Sans, designed by Eric Gill for Monotype, 1928, a modern sans serif with letterforms based on geometric elements, but with quirks that gave it a different character from the contemporary new German sans faces. (It was modelled on Edward Johnston's Underground type.) There is greater uniformity in the width of letters than found in Futura, for example, and the "a", "g" and "t" followed the traditional roman forms rather than Futura's pared-down versions.

abcdefghijklmnopqrs

ABCDEFGHIJKLMN

1234567890

ABCDEFGHIJKLMN
OPQRSTUVWXYZ
abcdefghijklmnopqrst
uvwxyz 1234567890
&.,:;‘’“”-!?()—

tuvwxyzfi
OPQRSTUVWXYZ
&.,:;‘’-!?()—

explained that it was "designed for advertising ... designed for a word, a single word, a poster word". It was not ornamental, he stressed, but an attempt to get back to the essential characteristic of individual letters. "If Bifur looks unfamiliar and strange, it is not because I have dressed it up eccentrically but because, in the midst of a fully clothed crowd, it is naked."[4] The type specimen book issued had Cassandre demonstrating how the face could be used in different ways, such as having colour dropped in on the shadow part of the letter.

The Art Deco look spread rapidly in advertising communication, and a page of magazine small ads of the late 1920s and into the 1930s would often contain a variety of fancy Art Deco faces, now mostly long disused. One that was widely employed was Broadway, designed by Morris Benton, issued by both American Typefounders and Monotype at the end of the twenties. Its reductive, crude contrasting of thick and thin strokes, made even more extreme by an unlined version, reflects a concern with style, not content: Broadway does not work as a readable or flexible face in different uses. But, like many extreme faces, its built-in obsolescence makes it a characterful period piece.

Much of what is typographically interesting in Art Deco lettering and layout was not formalised as a foundry face or under any clear rules, such as those set out by Tschichold or Morison. But one influential Art Deco-related publication was A. Tolmer's *Mise en Page*, published in Paris, which set down principles for the advertising designer and printer and had a practical, commercial application that guaranteed greater success than the more substantial theoretical positions of Tschichold or the Bauhaus designers. It emphasised the need for a clarity and boldness in execution that would give maximum impact to an advertisement, and it expressed, through ideas for good practice in typography, notions concerning effective advertising.

The posters by Cassandre and Jean Carlu in France, E. McKnight Kauffer in Britain, Robert Bereny in Hungary and other key commercial artists of the period often display original hand-drawn variations of Deco type themes, and distinct decorative elements are often a part. Sans serif and slab serif (serifs drawn in "slabs", without curves or thick/thin variations, set at right-angles to the letter-stem) are common to the type groupings, but the integration of image, message and identity in this vital flowering of advertising art provoked many one-off letterforms to be drawn. In layout terms, the rules seemed to draw on Bauhaus ideas but also referred to the simplest of symmetrical arrangements, with upper-case headline blocks. Besides the sheer variety of attention-grabbing, deliberately pleasure-giving typographic tricks of this work, it is also one of the first indications of the exploding commercial demand for a seemingly infinite variety of faces, only today being readily answered through digital technology.

Right and below right: Bifur, designed by A.M. Cassandre for Deberny & Peignot, 1929. This was the first of Cassandre's typeface experiments, in which he drew on his skills as a poster artist in combining typographic material with a dynamic understanding of layout. Bifur, which drops away parts of letters to leave the distinctive parts of the different forms, was available in a range of options: with line shading; with block colour for printing in two or more colours, and with just the essential line.

Below far right: Nord Express poster for the French railways by A. M. Cassandre, 1927. The colouring, form and weight of lettering in this lithograph becomes a part of the whole illustration, in which the power of the diagonal (explored so overtly by the Constructivist artists and others) is the underlying structure of the picture, creating a compelling path across the image.

BIFUR THIS IS NOT
USE BIFUR THIS IS
TO USE BIFUR THIS
AY TO USE BIFUR
HE WAY TO USE BI
T THE WAY TO USE
NOT THE WAY TO
S IS NOT THE WAY
R THIS IS NOT THE
BIFUR THIS IS NOT

THE TIMES

The advance of modernism was partly as a philosophy, also as a style – both apparent in the cover of *Left Review*, 1935, London (opposite page). In contrast, Stanley Morison's work on a new face for *The Times*,

# 1930...

1932, never strayed beyond the boundaries of reviving and reworking traditional typographic approaches – also both a philosophy and a style. The decade saw a revival of slab serifs, such as Heinrich Jost's Beton of 1931 (right). Meanwhile, Peignot by Cassandre of 1937, as shown in "1930", was displaying the characteristics of the time in its experimental forms.

**DIE FORM**

**ist die Zeitschrift der neu-zeitlichen Bewegung auf**

The period of the Great Depression also saw consumer culture reach a new peak of activity and expression. The decade that ended in the Second World War was one during which there was more international communication and travel than in any previous era, and when the ideas of the time – be it through print, cinema or broadcast – moved ever faster and farther. Clearly this was a time of tension and these contradictions are connected. The nature of a world market, of huge forces at work in controlling demand and supply, meant that a collapse in the financial markets had immense impact far and wide. The international communications and culture were not only a threat to political accountability if left uncontrolled, but also the opportunity for mass propaganda.

These major themes had their bearing on typographic development, and nowhere more so than in the path taken by the seminal apostle, then apostate, of the new typography, Jan Tschichold. From 1926 until 1933 Tschichold taught and worked as a designer in Munich, while also writing and having published his influential *Die Neue Typographie*. In 1933, however, he was arrested and removed from his job by the new Nazi government: his ideas were considered *Kulturbolschevismus* [cultural bolshevism]. The attack on him was part of a clampdown against all manifestations of Modernism – it led to the closure of the Bauhaus in 1933, then the Degenerate Art exhibitions, and later the expropriation of modern works of art and their sale or destruction. Tschichold left Germany and went to live in Basel, Switzerland, where he taught, designed, and wrote *Typographische Gestaltung*, published in 1935. Here his philosophy for good use of type had evidently evolved from the protest and propaganda tenor of his earlier book. While still advocating many of the same ideas, Tschichold had clearly moved on to a broader appreciation of typographic art that included some of the finesse of classical typography. The title page, with its combination of swash italic for the author's name, block serif for the title and Bodoni bold for the printer's name, laid out in a finely balanced composition of symmetric and asymmetric elements, displays Tschichold's change of heart. The main text is also set in Bodoni, with block serif headings.

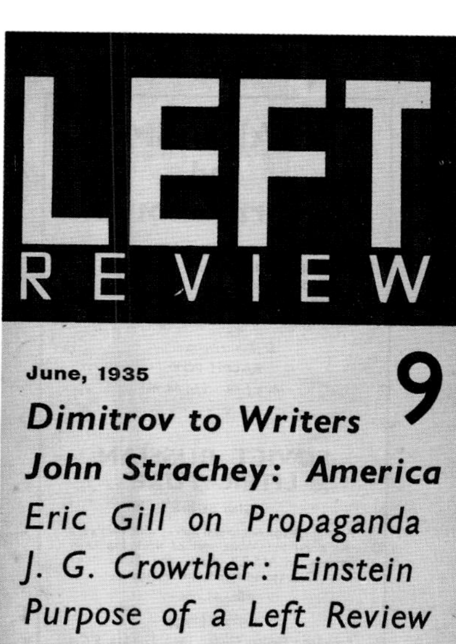


Tschichold later described *Typographische Gestaltung* as "more prudent" than the earlier book. Speaking at a Type Directors' Club seminar in 1959 he explained the transition of his thoughts from the hard line of his early writing to the embracing of traditionalism from the middle to late 1930s onwards:

***In time, typographical things, in my eyes, took on a very different aspect and to my astonishment I detected most shocking parallels between the teachings of "Die Neue Typographie" and National Socialism and fascism. Obvious similarities consist in the ruthless restriction of typefaces, a parallel to Goebbels's infamous "gleichschaltung" [political alignment], and the more-or-less militaristic arrangement of lines. Because I did not want to be guilty of spreading the very ideas which had compelled me to leave Germany, I thought over again what a typographer should do. Which typefaces are good and what typefaces are the most practicable? By guiding the compositors of a large Basel printing office, I learned a lot about practicability. Good typography has to be perfectly legible and, as such, the result of intelligent planning. The classical typefaces such as Garamond, Janson, Baskerville and Bell are undoubtedly the most legible. Sans serif is good for certain cases of emphasis, but is used to the point of abuse.***

An intriguing series of reactions and counter-reactions are bound up in these words: the Bauhaus-influenced *Die Neue Typographie*, its espousal of liberated ideas of form and space and its reaction against confused and confusing vernacular practices, is seen through the experience of Nazi repression and its advocacy of a ferociously Germanic tradition in the use of black-letter, emerging as an embrace of the strength of tradition. As a result, Tschichold rejected the values he had once espoused so fervently, a rejection matched by the Nazis. He welcomed traditionalism; not the same traditionalism as that admired by the Nazis, but certainly one respectful of some of the deeply conservative elements of typographic practice against which he had previously offered radical revision. Instead, he saw these recently revolutionary principles as a paradigm of the tyranny of the Nazis. The seeming confusion of this position is resolved not so much by considering the practice as by considering the stance of the man proposing it: he was effectively rejecting any overbearing philosophy that sought to prescribe a set of intolerant principles in place of the rich variety of human practices. From these first years in Switzerland (where he lived on and off until his death in 1974) Tschichold seems to have developed a much deeper appreciation of the craftsman's role in the printed artefact. The fury of the young designer – Tschichold was only twenty-three when he first espoused in print the case for Modernist practice – had been tamed, or at least informed, by political and technical feedback.

Tschichold's experience of the changed climate of 1930s Germany was, of course, one shared by all who had beliefs not countenanced by the Nazis. In 1933 the Bauhaus was shut down after struggling against its opponents for many years: the previous year it had been forced to move from Dessau to Berlin, but it was swiftly made impossible for it to continue there. First it was closed as a

Right and below: Deutschland Austellung prospectus, cover and inside spread, designed by Herbert Bayer, 1936. When the Bauhaus was closed in 1933 by the Nazis many of the leading designers associated with the modern movement left continental Europe for Britain and the United States, where they were to have a major effect. Bayer went to New York in 1938 to organise the Museum of Modern Art show of Bauhaus work, and stayed there. This promotional material for a Nazi-organised exhibition of German culture shows how he had had to compromise not only his beliefs, but his design. It displays the photographic montage pioneered in the 1920s, but there is no sign of sans serif or of the universal typeface (which he did use in the Bauhaus MOMA catalogue of 1938). Instead, he employs the condensed modern face he designed for Berthold in 1935, called Bayer type.

A B C D E F G H I J K L M N O P Q R S
T U V W X Y Z Ä Ö Ü
a b c d e f g h i j k l m n o p q r s ſ t u v w x y z
ä ö ü ch ſch ck ff fi fl ft ſſ ſi ſt ß tz &
1 2 3 4 5 6 7 8 9 0

**A B C D E F G H I J K L M N O P Q R S**
**T U V W X Y Z Ä Ö Ü**
**a b c d e f g h i j k l m n o p q r s ſ t u v w x y z**
**ä ö ü ch ſch ck ff fi fl ft ſſ ſi ſt ß tz &**
**1 2 3 4 5 6 7 8 9 0**

*A B C D E F G H I J K L M N O P Q R S*
*T U V W X Y Z Ä Ö Ü*
*a b c d e f g h i j k l m n o p q r s ſ t u v w x y z*
*ä ö ü ch ſch ck ff fi fl ft ſſ ſi ſt ß tz &*
*1 2 3 4 5 6 7 8 9 0*

A B C D E F G H I J K L M N O P Q R S
T U V W X Y Z Ä Ö Ü
a b c d e f g h i j k l m n o p q r s ſ t u v w x y z
ä ö ü ch ſch ck ff fi fl ft ſſ ſi ſt ß tz &
1 2 3 4 5 6 7 8 9 0

Above: Steel (Stahl) from the Klingspor foundry, the upper case designed by Rudolf Koch and the lower case by Hans Kuehne, 1939; the upper case derived its capitals from Offenbach, a black-letter designed by Koch, who had died in 1934. Steel attempted to unite the pen-drawn qualities of black-letter with sans serif, which ran counter to the notion that sans serifs were geometric forms associated with mechanised skills. Nevertheless, it scarcely fitted the mood of Germany in the late 1930s: when he came to power Hitler initially called for the black-letter form Fraktur to be the uniform German script, but changed his mind in 1940 since he thought that roman faces would be more easily understood across the countries he intended to dominate.

result of "Bolshevist" literature being planted on school property, and then the terms of reopening included a range of proposals that the director, Mies van der Rohe, and his staff decided were unacceptable – such as the removal of Jewish teachers (including Wassily Kandinsky) and the incorporation of Nazi propagandist elements in the timetable.

The wave of repressive activities that grew in Germany and later Austria, Holland and France under the Nazis had a major impact on the spread of the Modernist ideas pioneered in and around the Bauhaus group of artists and designers. In other parts of continental Europe, Britain and the United States, the development of the new approach to typography was spurred by the tyranny that made such progress largely impossible within the very countries that had spawned some of the most interesting ideas of the preceding years.

Tschichold's adopted homeland of Switzerland was a case in point, with the new principles quickly filtering through to young designers, and having an indelible effect on their imaginations. In the 1930s the first signs became visible of the approach to typography that was to influence a whole generation of post-war designers: the emerging stamp of what was later to be called International Style. From the teaching of Ernst Keller (1891–1968) and Alfred Williman at the School of Applied Art in Zürich after the First World War came a practical development of the new modular order that was being expressed in the work of the De Stijl artists and the Constructivists, as well as being applied through architects and three-dimensional designers. The establishment of a system for devising a flexible but firm underlying structure to typographic layouts complements the push to simplify and purify the form of that type, as seen in the promotion of new sans serif faces.

One student at the Zürich school was Theo Ballmer (1902–65), who went on to study at the Bauhaus and from the late 1920s used a grid to underpin the typographic order in a way that anticipated one of the most distinctive ideas associated with the Swiss school of the 1950s and 1960s. Ballmer's work of the late 1920s and 1930s perhaps exaggerates the grid for effect – it is quite self-consciously present in much of his work. But the design process of deriving the grid and then applying it to control the ordering of information was a major contribution to the structuring of a typographic designer's work and Ballmer was mapping out the way ahead.

Another Swiss student at the Bauhaus was Max Bill, who was also to become an influential teacher of the style that became the new orthodoxy of the post-war era among young designers. He combined a severity in type choice – Akzidenz Grotesk was popular (the foundation for Helvetica) – with a reductive approach to the elements within a communication, often ending up with posters that are almost entirely typographic, and consisting of few words at that; to some extent this followed the tradition extolled by the German Plakatstijl artists and their followers in the 1920s.

Among them was another leading Swiss designer, Herbert Matter (1907–84), whose posters for the clothing company NKZ (who commissioned a series of influential works) and then for Swiss tourism combined an appreciation of the art movements of the time with the development of the typographic craft. All the elements of the image were integrated in one powerful piece, sometimes with no distinct line of type but with the typographic elements worked into the picture. Exploration of the three-dimensional potential of combining photographic and typographic imagery is marked in his work. At the end of the

Right: Transito, designed by Jan Tschichold and manufactured by the Amsterdam Type Foundry, 1931. Tschichold applied his new typography ideas to stencil face, breaking down the characters into two or three components, and translating the immediacy of hoarding signs into typographic form for display application. However, Transito lacked the legibility and subsequent popularity of Paul Renner's stencil face Futura Black and Hunter Middleton's Stencil (see page 106).
Below right: back and front cover of S. I. Kirsanov's *The word belongs to Kirsanov*, designed by Solomon Telingater, 1930. This mix of Constructivist and Dadaist influences shows type ranging left and right; exploration of the diagonal and breaking loose from the line completely, and many changes of font, weight and size. The expressive possibilities of two-colour printing are tested by the type, and its forms and perspective are echoed in the angular, crude, cut-out portrait and its relationship to the drawn line illustration.
Below far right: advertising brochure from Waterlow & Sons promoting Uhertype photocomposition, 1939. The plasticity of form sought by the Constructivists and others found a technological echo in the early pioneering moves towards photosetting. From the late 1920s Edmund Uher explored various methods of exposing type on to light-sensitive material, involving both keyboard and manual processes; he commissioned Jan Tschichold, among others, to design new faces. In 1935 *The Penrose Annual*, for many years a bible of new printing developments, included a specimen page of early Uhertype hand-setting, suggesting its emerging commercial relevance.

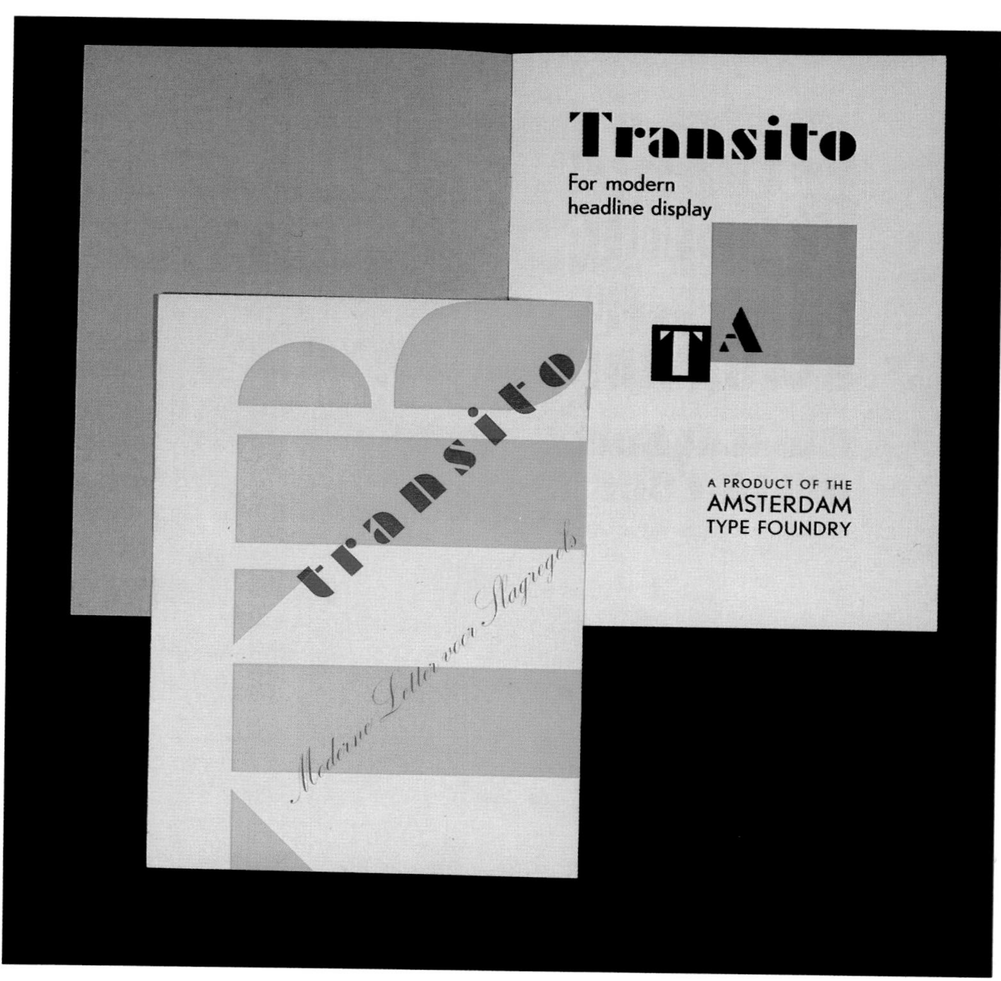
Transito
For modern
headline display
TA
A PRODUCT OF THE
AMSTERDAM
TYPE FOUNDRY
transito
Moderne Letter voor Slagregels

1 р. 50 к.
ЗИМНЯЯ
ВОСТОРЖЕННАЯ
РАЗГОВОР
ЖИЗНЬ
КАВКАЗ
ХОД
ЛЮБОВЬ
ТАМБОВ
БОЙ
АВТОМОБИЛЬНЫЙ
РОМАН
СЛОВО
предоставляется
КИРСАНОВУ
1930
К БАЛЛАДЕ О НЕИЗВЕСТНОМ СОЗДАТЕ
НАЩОТ ШУБЫ
с. б. телингатер

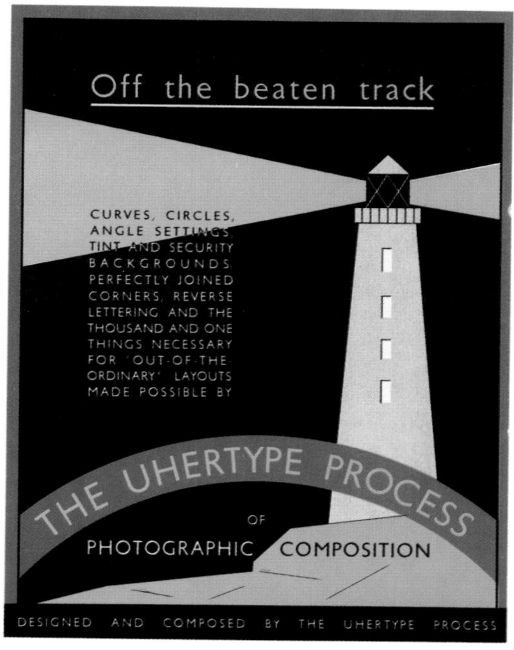
Off the beaten track
CURVES, CIRCLES, ANGLE SETTINGS, TINT AND SECURITY BACKGROUNDS, PERFECTLY JOINED CORNERS, REVERSE LETTERING AND THE THOUSAND AND ONE THINGS NECESSARY FOR 'OUT-OF-THE-ORDINARY' LAYOUTS MADE POSSIBLE BY
THE UHERTYPE PROCESS
OF
PHOTOGRAPHIC COMPOSITION
DESIGNED AND COMPOSED BY THE UHERTYPE PROCESS

decade he went to live in the United States, where his interest in photography developed further and became a crucial aspect of much of his output in the following decades.

Matter was one of many artists who emigrated to the United States when it became difficult to work in Europe. None was more under pressure to leave Germany than those associated with the Bauhaus – Gropius, Moholy-Nagy, Bayer and van der Rohe were among those who made the move. Two significant appointments were that of Mehemed Fehmy Agha (1898–1978) to art-direct *Vogue* in New York from 1929 until 1942, and Alexey Brodovitch (1898–1971) to the art directorship of *Harper's Bazaar* in 1934 (a post he held until 1958). Despite the ostensibly inhibiting economic backdrop of the Great Depression, the early work of these two, far from embodying a conservative approach, dramatically enlivened and accentuated the glamorous, fashionable qualities of the magazines. Each art director had worked in Paris and had brought with him an awareness of the work of the Bauhaus designers and their circle. They also had an appreciation of the new poster art and its emphasis on a strong visual and little type. Paris poster art helped feed their ideas on how to gain maximum impact and how to express the functional requirements of the page and reject the casually decorative. But both also developed something original in their roles as pioneers of magazine art direction. Neither was involved in designing type or following rigorous rules, but both were open to the novelty of Modernist ideas and drew these into their work, breaking the magazine page out of its former straitjacket, using bigger photographs and more white space, varying the typographic layout considerably to suit the material and also commissioning fresh kinds of fashion photography.

Brodovitch brought the work of photographers such as Brassai and Cartier-Bresson and artists such as Cassandre to *Harper's* readers in the 1930s. The relationship of the fresh work he commissioned to the typographic elements of the pages on which it lay demonstrated the holistic approach to the content of graphic design, the conceptual attitude that had distinguished the quest behind the Bauhaus studies. But Brodovitch was not so clearly motivated by the larger agenda of Bauhaus ideas in which the approach to design was part and parcel of a concept of society's needs and processes. He and Agha, and increasingly the other Europeans who arrived in the US, immersed their talents in communicating the needs of big business: selling whatever needed the new look, integrating the conceptual approach to design with an awareness of commercial design and advertising. Prior to working at *Harper's* Brodovitch had already notched up a string of medals from the Art Directors' Club through his illustration and art direction work freelancing for the advertising agency N. W. Ayer. He contributed work that was strategically close to that of the likes of Cassandre in Paris or E. McKnight Kauffer in London, mixing almost surreal elements which are symbolically associated with the advertiser, and projecting identity through short, bold, upper-case blocks of type.

A significant development in the notion of company identity was being demonstrated by Olivetti in Italy, which at this time was marking out the design-led policy that has continued to distinguish the company to the present day. Typography was allied with ideas of industrial design and exhibition display in the work of Giovanni Pintori, Xanti Schawinsky and Nivola, among those graphic designers who worked for Olivetti under its Development and Publicity Office, established in 1931.



Right: three versions of a poster for the Swiss tourist office designed by Herbert Matter, 1935. Growing international communications, commercial links and consumer travel led to pressures for international modes of typographic communication: different languages are reduced to a minimum, the visual is more important than the verbal, and the desired graphic forms are those that allow for a common identity to exist across language versions.
Below right: poster launching the first portable typewriter from Olivetti, by Xanti Schawinsky, 1934. Here, copy is dispensed with altogether, product and visual association being all that are required to put across the idea of portability and Olivetti. This radical departure was an intimation of a new emerging context for type in display applications: if it was to appear, it had to be integrated within the whole. Rather than meaning less type, this suggested a need for more: faces needed to be designed to express all manner of corporate communication needs, and companies increasingly demanded their own exclusive typography. Schawinsky's work for Olivetti in the 1930s demonstrated what he had learned at the Bauhaus: bold compositions for promotional brochures combined type and photography in dramatic ways, often with unexpected contrasts of scale. This poster takes it to an extreme, with the eye being drawn around the glamorous image before settling on the repeated statement of "Olivetti": it is a technique that has become the essence of most fashion and perfume advertising.
Far right: poster for an art exhibition in Zürich by Max Ernst, 1934. The Dadaist and Surrealist artist Ernst (1891–1976) played with typographic tradition in this poster, with an excess of pointing hands and the use of a shadowed florid wood-letter akin to a circus poster. The dynamic is not so much in the layout as in the associations of its play with the vernacular of the printer.

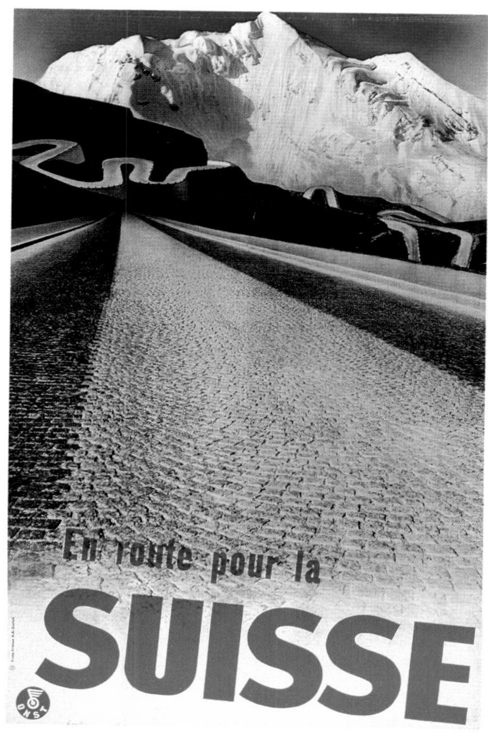
En route pour la
SUISSE

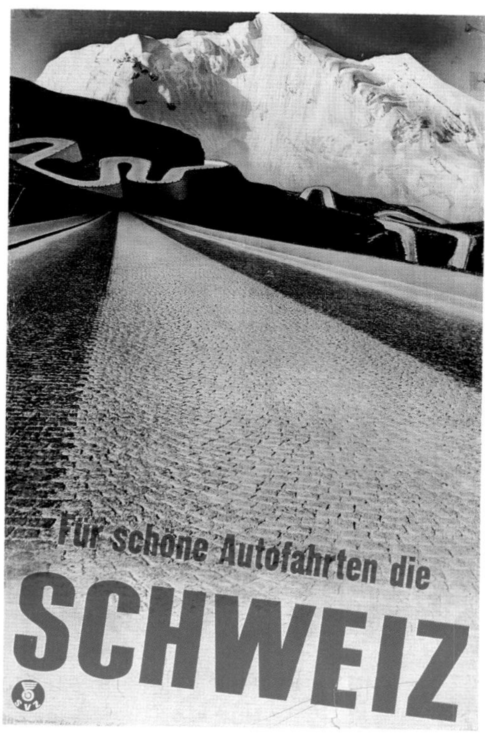
Für schöne Autofahrten die
SCHWEIZ

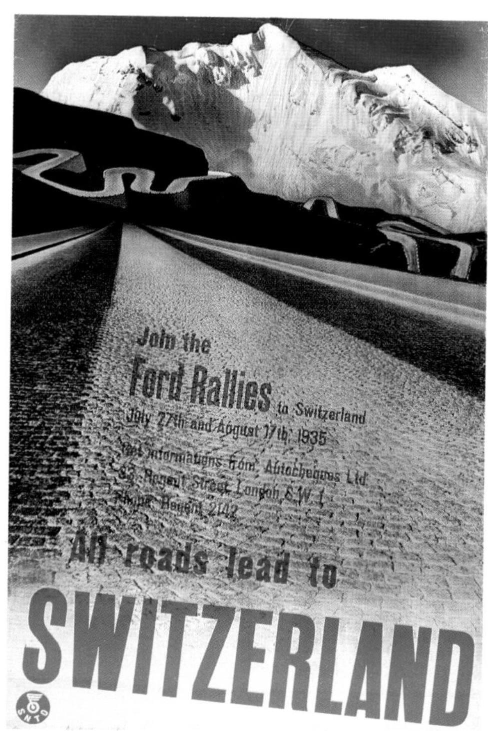
Join the
Ford Rallies to Switzerland
July 27th and August 17th, 1935
All roads lead to
SWITZERLAND

OLIVETTI
Ico
OLIVETTI

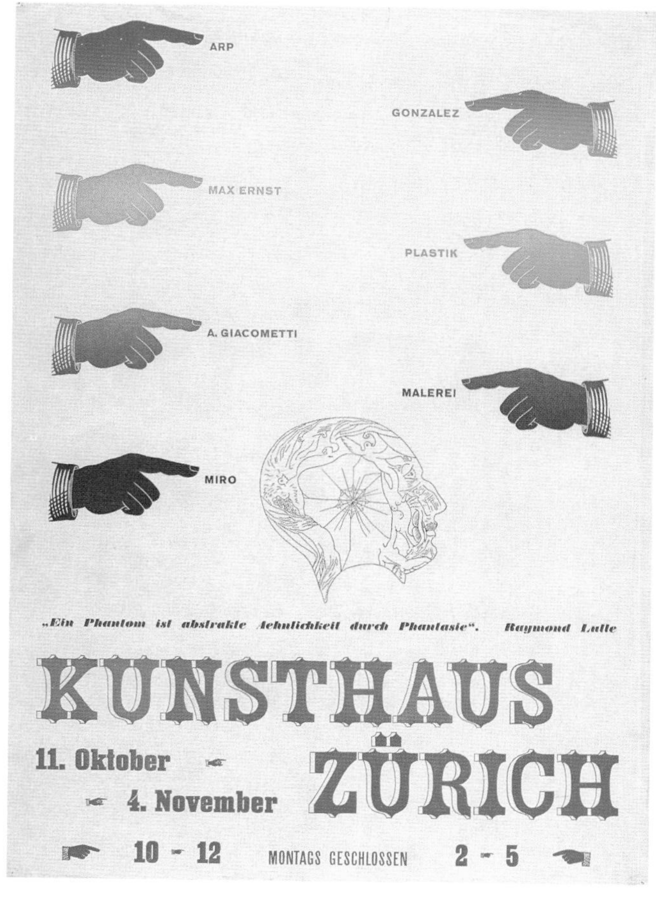
ARP
GONZALEZ
MAX ERNST
PLASTIK
A. GIACOMETTI
MALEREI
MIRO
„Ein Phantom ist abstrakte Aehnlichkeit durch Phantasie". Raymond Lulle
KUNSTHAUS
11. Oktober
4. November
ZÜRICH
10 - 12
MONTAGS GESCHLOSSEN
2 - 5

The relationship between the potential of type and the nature of typewriter print and how those words are produced (at some point, from the imagination) was explored in a 1934 folder designed by Schawinsky (a former Bauhaus student) and targeted at selling typewriters to doctors. It used layering of text over headline, type set flush against a curve, dramatically contrasting typographic and photographic elements, lines of type as pointers for the reader, and a host of other features. The brochure built on Bauhaus-derived ideas: it displayed flexibility, yet retained control in a way that leapt decades in both the technology of production and the reader context. In another Olivetti project, Schawinsky's fundamental questioning of typographic principles was flourished by the distinction of having a no-type design. He produced a promotional image that simply had a woman resting her hands on the petite form of a typewriter, the product's own branding (the Olivetti name being boldly displayed in two places) sufficing to make the advertising statement, the image bound together by the matching of the colour of the machine with that of her lipstick.

Schawinsky was one of a number of prominent designers who worked with Antonio Boggeri, whose Studio Boggeri opened in Milan in 1933 and became a highly influential focal point for graphic design in Italy. Boggeri's contact with many of the teachers and students of the Bauhaus led to the implementation of the new ideas into Italian commerce.

Such advertising and other promotions, and the commercial work by many of the former Bauhaus designers such as Bayer, Moholy-Nagy and Schmidt, were drawing in new influences from fine art alongside their earlier Modernist rationale. Surrealist touches are particularly noticeable, not by being formally derivative but in the integration of symbolic elements, the connections between typographic form and function being extended to embrace a sense of the wider emotive content of a design. Legibility and impact of type were discussed, and the desire for more precise ideas about advertising performance was emerging – these too would put new pressures and influences on typographic practice. The finer work of those artists who were most central to Art Deco graphics, such as Cassandre, often displays a preference for integrated typographic material, with a powerful image reduced to a simple, bold form. The merging of

Below: Stencil (top), designed by R. Hunter Middleton for Ludlow, 1938, drawing more on the vernacular than Tschichold's modernist reworking (see page 103). It is also more legible, featuring serifs and greater emphasis on the distinguishing characteristics of the letters.
Essential (bottom), an experimental design by Bruno Munari, 1935, was influenced by the concept underlying Cassandre's Bifur (see page 97), with characters consisting only of their one recognisable element.
Right and far right: Independent (Onafhankelijke), designed by G. Collette and J. Dufour, 1930. Another face from the Amsterdam Type Foundry (see Tschichold's Transito, page 103 top), this highly stylised design found some favour during the period, expressing the playful qualities of Deco.
Below right: Playbill, designed from drawings by Robert Harling, 1938, and issued by the foundry of Stephenson Blake (descendent of Caslon's foundry) in Birmingham, England. The idea was supplied by the type historian and journalist Robert Harling, drawing on a popular Victorian wood-letter form. The usual weights of the strokes and the serifs are reversed, giving a strong horizontal line.

ABCDEFGHIJKLM
NOPQRSTUVWXYZ
1234567890

ABCDEFGHIJKLM
NOPQRSTUVWXYZ

ABCD
EFGHIJKL
MNOPQRST
UVWXYZ&
abcdefghijkl
mnopqrstuv
wxyz.,;:'!?-)
1234567890

hotel
RITZ
WIJNEN

LL★PLAY
LAYBILL
LL★PLAY
Playbill: a prospectus

image and text takes place in ways that seek to express the message of the words – as words forming train lines in a railway poster, or a pool of oil in an oil company advertisement or, in a particularly famous example, the filling in of outline lettering to suggest the drinking of a glass of Dubonnet ("Dubo, Dubon, Dubonnet", punning not only visually but also verbally and aurally through the "du beau" and "du bon" suggestion).

On one level and as individual examples these might be seen as the graphic equivalent of the punning headline in a newspaper, a lightweight piece of humour. But *en masse* they suggest more. The many variations explored in the expressive content of type and typographic forms during these years, the flexibility of type displayed in advertising and other promotional art, show a commercial demand (where once it was an experimental desire, as with Futurists and Dadaists) for type to break loose from the constraints of its metal and wooden forms and to be as expressive as paint and other media.

The foundries' development of many sans serif and block serif faces on the Futura base from the late 1920s onward responded to the demand for a means of reproducing the Bauhaus look far and wide, but was also indicative of type designers working around the model of stripped-down Modernist forms, exploring them in all their inflections. Futura was not alone in influencing the vogue for a rational approach to type forms: Erbar was another popular geometric sans serif released during the 1920s and Rudolf Koch's distinctive Kabel face also had followers. Many major type designers added their contribution to the ranks of sans serif faces around this time, with foundries keen to take up the faces: Herbert Bayer (Bayer Type), Lucian Bernhard (Bernhard Gothic), William A. Dwiggins (Metro), Frederic Goudy (Goudy Sans) and R. Hunter Middleton (Stellar) were but a few of the designers and faces. The block serif revival followed, producing new forms of the traditional "Egyptian" face: Memphis, City, Beton, Cairo, Karnak, Rockwell (a revival), Pharaon and Scarab, to

Below: Libra, designed by S. H. de Roos for the Amsterdam Type Foundry, 1938, based on the mediaeval uncial script which had only a single alphabet. The foundry drew attention to its partial response to typographers' desire to use only the lower case, claiming that "balance" was the concept sought and that the uncial form projected this and maintained legibility.
Right: Motor and Dynamo, shaded and unshaded versions of a face designed by K. Sommer for Ludwig & Mayer, 1930. The embrace of technology and automisation found its reflection in gimmicky design.
Below right: Beton, designed for Heinrich Jost for Bauer, 1931. Following on from Memphis (see page 87), another square serif revival issued in a wide range of weights and forms, Beton was more quirky, with some contradictions in its inflections. The "A", for example, has a single backward sloping serif, the "y" has a foot serif going right and the "t" has a double foot serif; the "g" has a single-storey open tail, but the "a" has a two-storey one.

libra-medium

abcdefghij
klmnopqrs
tuvwxyz&
æ œ ch ij ß $ £
1234567890

Copyright by the Amsterdam Typefoundry, Amsterdam-Holland

libra a new typeface
presented by the amsterdam typefoundry

in recent years it has become evident that the fundamental differences in form between capitals and lower case letters does not give general satisfaction · typographers, in an endeavour to achieve freshness and better balance in general work have made many interesting experiments · for example the attempt to suggest harmony in type by using lower case exclusively has aroused much controversy · the device of using capitals alone is familiar but it is usually considered to fail from the standpoint of legibility, as well as harmony. it will be agreed that the lower case used exclusively, lacks distinction · in creating libra the guiding principle has been to secure the balance previously unattainable.
this new type is based on the same forms those of as the so-called 'uncials' which were used in the early middle-ages. 'libra', which means balance, is an epoch-making typeface which gives users extensive scope for the development of modern typographic styles · the handwritten form is one of its further characteristics which lends to 'libra' a vivacity and charm of its own.
in presenting our 'libra' we feel confident that it will meet with the approval of printers and general public alike.

amsterdam typefoundry
amsterdam-holland

MOTOR

Nr. 7147 36 Punkte
Min. 10 kg 14 A

KUPFERBERG GOLD

Nr. 7148 40 Punkte
Min. 12 kg 10 A

VOLKSBILDUNG

Nr. 7149 48 Punkte
Min. 16 10 A

OPERNHAUS

Nr. 7150 60 Punkte
Min. 20 kg 10 A

HAMBURG

Nr. 7151 72 Punkte
Min. 26 kg 8 A

STADION

Schriftgießerei Ludwig & Mayer Frankfurt am Main

DYNAMO

Nr. 7031a 10 Punkte
Min. 5 kg 80 a 32 A

Große Ausstellung von Meisterwerken der mohammedanischen Kunst
RECHENBUCH FÜR DIE KÖNIGSBERGER VOLKSSCHULEN 1234567890

Nr. 7032 12 Punkte
Min. 6 kg 70 a 28 A

Besichtigung des Städtischen Museums zu Ludwigshafen
ENTWICKLUNG DER BUCHDRUCKERKUNST 1234567890

Nr. 7032a 14 Punkte
Min. 8 kg 60 a 24 A

Internationale Einfuhr-Messe zu Frankfurt am Main
DEUTSCHE KUNST IM HAUSE WERKBUND 1234567890

Nr. 7033 16 Punkte
Min. 9 kg 50 a 20 A

Zeitschrift des Vereins deutscher Tiefbautechniker
DAS ZEITALTER DER RENAISSANCE 1234567890

Nr. 7034 20 Punkte
Min. 12 kg 40 a 16 A

Kieler Gesellschaft für Automobilbau
AMATEUR-RADRENNEN 1234567890

Schriftgießerei Ludwig & Mayer Frankfurt am Main

ZEITSCHRIFT
FÜR GESTALTENDE
ARBEIT

DIE
FORM

ist die Zeitschrift der neuzeitlichen Bewegung auf dem Gebiet der gestaltenden Arbeit. Sie unterrichtet am besten als einzige deutsche Zeitschrift in ihrem ganzen Umfang über das Gesamtgebiet des neuzeitlichen Formschaffens. Die Form stellt sich bewußt auf den Boden der neuen Zeit. Die Form bejaht die neuen Mächte der Technik, der Industrie, des Handwerks, der neuen wirtschaftlichen und sozialen Bindungen.

VERLAG HERM. RECKENDORF

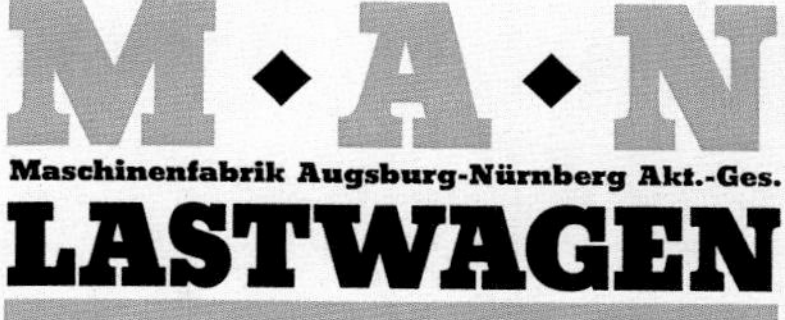


Maschinenfabrik Augsburg-Nürnberg Akt.-Ges.
LASTWAGEN

KOH-I-NOOR

der edelste
Bleistift

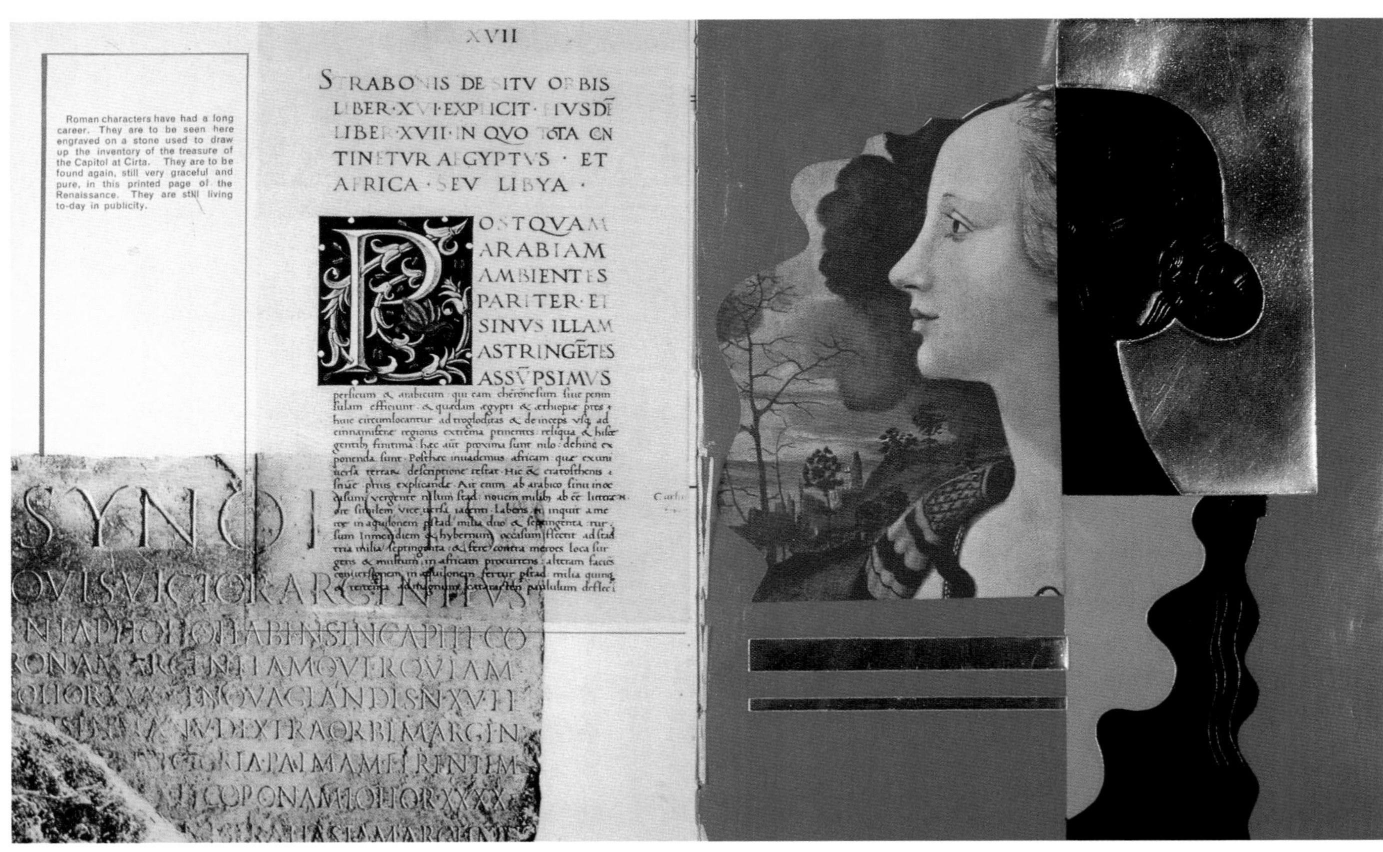
Roman characters have had a long career. They are to be seen here engraved on a stone used to draw up the inventory of the treasure of the Capitol at Cirta. They are to be found again, still very graceful and pure, in this printed page of the Renaissance. They are still living to-day in publicity.

WIRELESS

Before Picasso began to stick actual pieces of paper which he had cut out of newspapers on to his canvasses, we should never have had the courage to compose an advertisement page with such apparently unsuitable elements. Their diversity, however, is the only thing which could so vividly suggest the diversity of wireless announcements. There is no longer any excuse needed for rapid transition from one country to another, from politics to music or from boxing matches to stock exchange quotations. In this respect our ears have educated our eyes, and the art of lay-out has been quick to profit by this newly acquired adaptability.

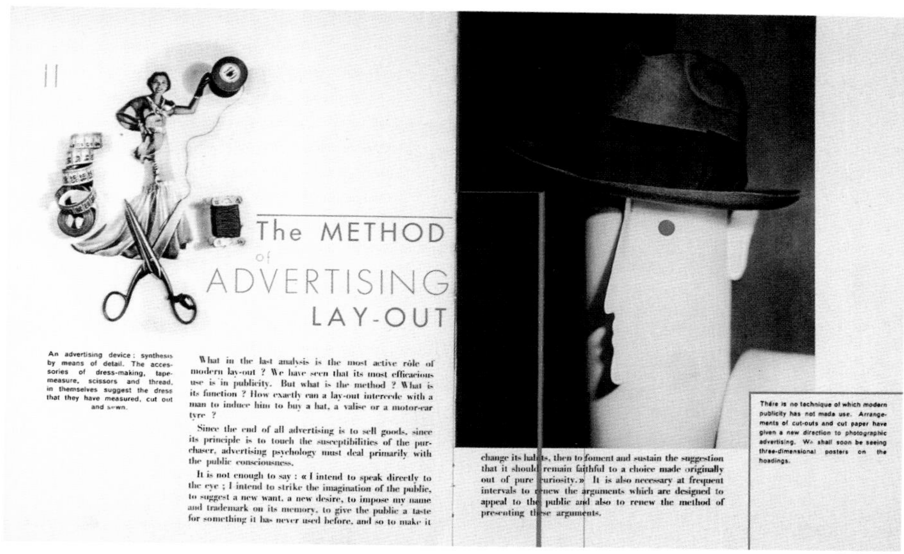

II

The METHOD of ADVERTISING LAY-OUT

An advertising device: synthesis by means of detail. The accessories of dress-making, tape-measure, scissors and thread, in themselves suggest the dress that they have measured, cut out and sewn.

What in the last analysis is the most active rôle of modern lay-out? We have seen that its most efficacious use is in publicity. But what is the method? What is its function? How exactly can a lay-out intercede with a man to induce him to buy a hat, a valise or a motor-car tyre?

Since the end of all advertising is to sell goods, since its principle is to touch the susceptibilities of the purchaser, advertising psychology must deal primarily with the public consciousness.

It is not enough to say: « I intend to speak directly to the eye; I intend to strike the imagination of the public, to suggest a new want, a new desire, to impose my name and trademark on its memory, to give the public a taste for something it has never used before, and so to make it change its habits, then to foment and sustain the suggestion that it should remain faithful to a choice made originally out of pure curiosity. » It is also necessary at frequent intervals to renew the arguments which are designed to appeal to the public and also to renew the method of presenting these arguments.

There is no technique of which modern publicity has not made use. Arrangements of cut-outs and cut paper have given a new direction to photographic advertising. We shall soon be seeing three-dimensional posters on the hoadings.

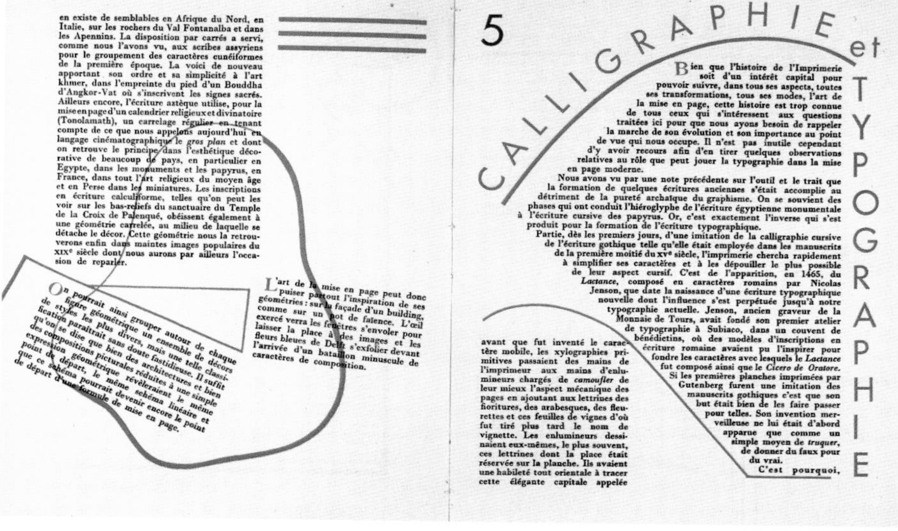

en existe de semblables en Afrique du Nord, en Italie, sur les rochers du Val Fontanalba et dans les Apennins. La disposition par carrés a servi, comme nous l'avons vu, aux scribes assyriens pour le groupement des caractères cunéiformes de la première époque. La voici de nouveau apportant son ordre et sa simplicité à l'art khmer, dans l'empreinte du pied d'un Bouddha d'Angkor-Vat où s'inscrivent les signes sacrés. Ailleurs encore, l'écriture aztèque utilise, pour la mise en page d'un calendrier religieux et divinatoire (Tonolamath), un carrelage régulier en tenant compte de ce que nous appelons aujourd'hui en langage cinématographique le *gros plan* et dont on retrouve le principe dans l'esthétique décorative de beaucoup de pays, en particulier en Egypte, dans les monuments et les papyrus, en France, dans tout l'art religieux du moyen âge et en Perse dans les miniatures. Les inscriptions en écriture calculiforme, telles qu'on peut les voir sur les bas-reliefs du sanctuaire du Temple de la Croix de Palenqué, obéissent également à une géométrie carrelée, au milieu de laquelle se détache le décor. Cette géométrie nous la retrouverons enfin dans maintes images populaires du XIXe siècle dont nous aurons par ailleurs l'occasion de reparler.

On pourrait ainsi grouper autour de chaque figure géométrique un ensemble de décors de styles les plus divers, mais une telle classification paraîtrait sans doute fastidieuse. Il suffit qu'on se dise que bien des architectures et bien des compositions picturales réduites à une simple expression géométrique révèleraient le même point de départ, le même schéma linéaire et que ce schéma pourrait devenir encore le point de départ d'une formule de mise en page.

L'art de la mise en page peut donc puiser partout l'inspiration de ses géométries : sur la façade d'un building, comme sur un pot de faïence. L'œil exercé verra les fenêtres s'envoler pour laisser la place à des images et les fleurs bleues de Delft s'exfolier devant l'arrivée d'un bataillon minuscule de caractères de composition.

5 CALLIGRAPHIE et TYPOGRAPHIE

Bien que l'histoire de l'Imprimerie soit d'un intérêt capital pour pouvoir suivre, dans tous ses aspects, toutes ses transformations, tous ses modes, l'art de la mise en page, cette histoire est trop connue de tous ceux qui s'intéressent aux questions traitées ici pour que nous ayons besoin de rappeler la marche de son évolution et son importance au point de vue qui nous occupe. Il n'est pas inutile cependant d'y avoir recours afin d'en tirer quelques observations relatives au rôle que peut jouer la typographie dans la mise en page moderne.

Nous avons vu par une note précédente sur l'outil et le trait que la formation de quelques écritures anciennes s'était accomplie au détriment de la pureté archaïque du graphisme. On se souvient des phases qui ont conduit l'hiéroglyphe de l'écriture égyptienne monumentale à l'écriture cursive des papyrus. Or, c'est exactement l'inverse qui s'est produit pour la formation de l'écriture typographique.

Partie, dès les premiers jours, d'une imitation de la calligraphie cursive de l'écriture gothique telle qu'elle était employée dans les manuscrits de la première moitié du XVe siècle, l'imprimerie chercha rapidement à simplifier ses caractères et à les dépouiller le plus possible de leur aspect cursif. C'est de l'apparition, en 1465, du *Lactance*, composé en caractères romains par Nicolas Jenson, que date la naissance d'une écriture typographique nouvelle dont l'influence s'est perpétuée jusqu'à notre typographie actuelle. Jenson, ancien graveur de la Monnaie de Tours, avait fondé son premier atelier de typographie à Subiaco, dans un couvent de bénédictins, où des modèles d'inscriptions en écriture romaine avaient pu l'inspirer pour fondre les caractères avec lesquels le *Lactance* fut composé ainsi que le *Cicero de Oratore*.

Si les premières planches imprimées par Gutenberg furent une imitation des manuscrits gothiques c'est que son but était bien de les faire passer pour telles. Son invention merveilleuse ne lui était d'abord apparue que comme un simple moyen de *truquer*, de donner du faux pour du vrai.

C'est pourquoi, avant que fut inventé le caractère mobile, les xylographies primitives passaient des mains de l'imprimeur aux mains d'enlumineurs chargés de *camoufler* de leur mieux l'aspect mécanique des pages en ajoutant aux lettrines des fioritures, des arabesques, des fleurettes et ces feuilles de vignes d'où fut tiré plus tard le nom de vignette. Les enlumineurs dessinaient eux-mêmes, le plus souvent, ces lettrines dont la place était réservée sur la planche. Ils avaient une habileté tout orientale à tracer cette élégante capitale appelée

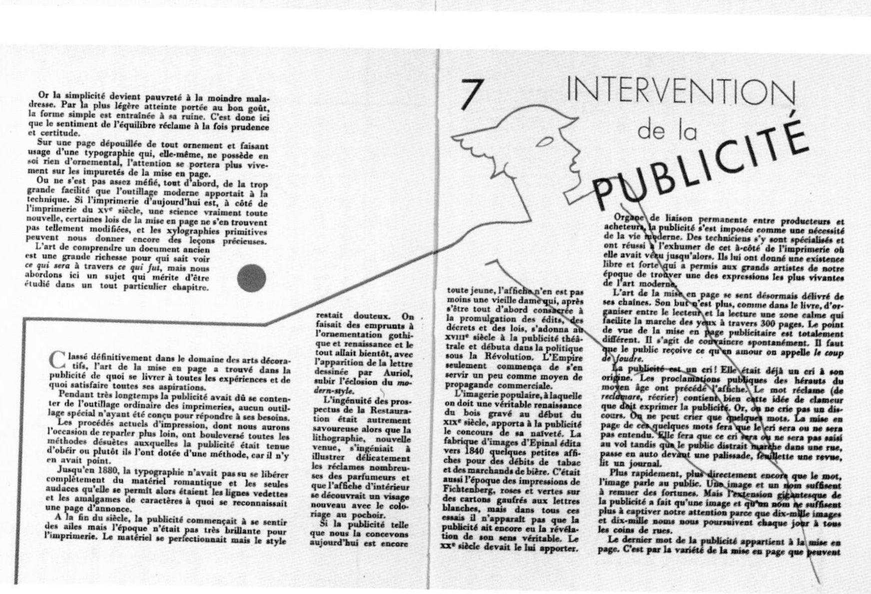

Or la simplicité devient pauvreté à la moindre maladresse. Par la plus légère atteinte portée au bon goût, la forme simple est entraînée à sa ruine. C'est donc ici que le sentiment de l'équilibre réclame à la fois prudence et certitude.

Sur une page dépouillée de tout ornement et faisant usage d'une typographie qui, elle-même, ne possède en soi rien d'ornemental, l'attention se portera plus vivement sur les impuretés de la mise en page.

On ne s'est pas assez méfié, tout d'abord, de la trop grande facilité que l'outillage moderne apportait à la technique. Si l'imprimerie d'aujourd'hui est, à côté de l'imprimerie du XVe siècle, une science vraiment toute nouvelle, certaines lois de la mise en page ne s'en trouvent pas tellement modifiées, et les xylographies primitives peuvent nous donner encore des leçons précieuses.

L'art de comprendre un document ancien est une grande richesse pour qui sait voir *ce qui sera* à travers *ce qui fut*, mais nous abordons ici un sujet qui mérite d'être étudié dans un tout particulier chapitre.

Classé définitivement dans le domaine des arts décoratifs, l'art de la mise en page a trouvé dans la publicité de quoi se livrer à toutes les expériences et de quoi satisfaire toutes ses aspirations.

Pendant très longtemps la publicité avait dû se contenter de l'outillage ordinaire des imprimeries, aucun outillage spécial n'ayant été conçu pour répondre à ses besoins.

Les procédés actuels d'impression, dont nous aurons l'occasion de reparler plus loin, ont bouleversé toutes les méthodes désuètes auxquelles la publicité était tenue d'obéir ou plutôt ils l'ont dotée d'une méthode, car il n'y en avait point.

Jusqu'en 1880, la typographie n'avait pas su se libérer complètement du matériel romantique et les seules audaces qu'elle se permit alors étaient les lignes vedettes et les amalgames de caractères à quoi se reconnaissait une page d'annonce.

A la fin du siècle, la publicité commençait à se sentir des ailes mais l'époque n'était pas très brillante pour l'imprimerie. Le matériel se perfectionnait mais le style restait douteux. On faisait des emprunts à l'ornementation gothique et renaissance et le tout allait bientôt, avec l'apparition de la lettre dessinée par Auriol, subir l'éclosion du *modern-style*.

L'ingénuité des prospectus de la Restauration était autrement savoureuse alors que la lithographie, nouvelle venue, s'ingéniait à illustrer délicatement les réclames nombreuses des parfumeurs et que l'affiche d'intérieur se découvrait un visage nouveau avec le coloriage au pochoir.

Si la publicité telle que nous la concevons aujourd'hui est encore toute jeune, l'affiche n'en est pas moins une vieille dame qui, après s'être tout d'abord consacrée à la promulgation des édits, des décrets et des lois, s'adonna au XVIIIe siècle à la publicité théâtrale et débuta dans la politique sous la Révolution. L'Empire seulement commença de s'en servir un peu comme moyen de propagande commerciale.

L'imagerie populaire, à laquelle on doit une véritable renaissance du bois gravé au début du XIXe siècle, apporta à la publicité le concours de sa naïveté. La fabrique d'images d'Epinal édita vers 1840 quelques petites affiches pour des débits de tabac et des marchands de bière. C'était aussi l'époque des impressions de Fichtenberg, roses et vertes sur des cartons gaufrés aux lettres blanches, mais dans tous ces essais il n'apparaît pas que la publicité ait encore eu la révélation de son sens véritable. Le XXe siècle devait le lui apporter.

7 INTERVENTION de la PUBLICITÉ

Organe de liaison permanente entre producteurs et acheteurs, la publicité s'est imposée comme une nécessité de la vie moderne. Des techniciens s'y sont spécialisés et ont réussi à l'exhumer de cet à-côté de l'imprimerie où elle avait vécu jusqu'alors. Ils lui ont donné une existence libre et forte qui a permis aux grands artistes de notre époque de trouver une des expressions les plus vivantes de l'art moderne.

L'art de la mise en page se sent désormais délivré de ses chaînes. Son but n'est plus, comme dans le livre, d'organiser entre le lecteur et la lecture une zone calme qui facilite la marche des yeux à travers 300 pages. Le point de vue de la mise en page publicitaire est totalement différent. Il s'agit de convaincre spontanément. Il faut que le public reçoive ce qu'en amour on appelle *le coup de foudre*.

La publicité est un cri ! Elle était déjà un cri à son origine. Les proclamations publiques des hérauts du moyen âge ont précédé l'affiche. Le mot réclame (de *reclamare*, récrier) contient bien cette idée de clameur que doit exprimer la publicité. Or, on ne crie pas un discours. On ne peut crier que quelques mots. La mise en page de ces quelques mots fera que le cri sera ou ne sera pas entendu. Elle fera que ce cri sera ou ne sera pas saisi au vol tandis que le public distrait marche dans une rue, passe en auto devant une palissade, feuillette une revue, lit un journal.

Plus rapidement, plus directement encore que le mot, l'image parle au public. Une image et un nom suffisent à remuer des fortunes. Mais l'extension gigantesque de la publicité a fait qu'une image et qu'un nom ne suffisent plus à captiver notre attention parce que dix-mille images et dix-mille noms nous poursuivent chaque jour à tous les coins de rues.

Le dernier mot de la publicité appartient à la mise en page. C'est par la variété de la mise en page que peuvent

Spreads from *Mise en Page* by Albert Tolmer, Studio Editions, 1931, a *tour-de-force* summary of layout techniques, principally aimed at the commercial designer of advertising and related literature. Written, designed and produced by the Parisian printer Albert Tolmer, it was published in London, with a main text in English and a French translation set in more condensed layouts at the end. In a clear appreciation of legibility and readability, Tolmer used letterspaced sans serif for headlines, playing around with their placement on the page and using diagonal and curved lines. The text is in a consistent roman, reading mostly on the strict vertical. A lavish range of print techniques are demonstrated here, including tip-ins and special treatments. Tolmer apparently absorbed the lessons of the Bauhaus and the new typography, merging them with a deep knowledge of fine printing traditions.

name those from the largest suppliers. Cutting these faces was part of the type foundries' response to the advertising typographers' search for a method imparting the spirit of the age to their clients' communications.

One of the most distinctive of sans faces, epitomising the character of the age, was Cassandre's Peignot for the foundry Deberny & Peignot. It was commissioned by Charles Peignot and named after him, a justified honour for a man who was a major promoter of innovation in type and typography, and who founded and edited the periodical *Arts et Métiers Graphiques* from 1927, employing Brodovitch for a while as an art director. Here Cassandre tackled the idea of a new kind of text face – he had already stripped down type to a highly stylised form for display work with his earlier design, Bifur. Peignot questions the whole premise for the existence of different forms for upper and lower case, seeking to do away with most of the different, supposedly corrupt, lower case forms. However, the face keeps, as an acknowledgement of reader expectations, the concept of ascenders and descenders and also has contrasted thick and thin strokes as a nod to ideas of legibility. Cassandre was insistent that this was not a decorative face, but a more pure form of the alphabet than tradition had led to thus far. The concept of the single alphabet was not carried through to its ultimate implication, however, as upper and lower case forms were cut.

Not all development was so fashionable or so dramatic. In the design of type for text, in particular, these years saw a pulling back from some of the radical proposals of the twenties and a search for revised standards in traditional faces,

AN original and interesting type face, "Peignot," designed by the famous French poster artist, A. M. Cassandre, and produced by Deberny et Peignot, Paris, has resulted in considerable discussion among typographic authorities. That the design is radical yet readable is indicated by the accompanying reproductions. "The Peignot type, intended for use in printing, is conceived as an engraved letter and not as a written letter," states the

LIGHT

AN original and interesting type face, "Peignot," designed by the famous French poster artist, A. M. Cassandre, and produced by Deberny et Peignot, Paris, has resulted in considerable discussion among typographic authorities. That the design is radical yet readable is indicated by the accompanying reproductions. "The Peignot type, intended for use in printing, is conceived as an engraved

MEDIUM

**AN original and interesting type face, "Peignot," designed by the famous French poster artist, A. M. Cassandre, and produced by Deberny et Peignot, Paris, has resulted in considerable discussion among typographic authorities. That the design is radical yet readable is indicated by the accompanying reproductions. "The Peignot type, intended for use in printing, is**

BOLD

ALPHABET
MEDIUM 72 POINT

Aa Bb Cc Dd Ee Ff Gg
Hh Ii Jj Kk Ll Mm Nn
Oo Pp Qq Rr Ss Tt Uu
Vv Ww Xx Yy Zz

1234567890
1234567890

Peignot, designed by A. M. Cassandre for Deberny & Peignot, Paris, 1937, is shown here in a sample, and in three different weights as published in a promotional leaflet by the English distributor Soldans in 1938. This unique sans serif aimed to dispense with distinct lower-case forms (except for "b", "d" and "f") and to create instead a new lower case by adding ascenders and descenders to capitals. Cassandre believed he had returned to a purer form of design, with letterforms bearing the "essential character" of the roman alphabet; he intended Peignot as a text face and was disappointed at its failure.

as well as the origination of faces that combined the best of the old with the ideas of the new. One prime example was the face that Stanley Morison designed for *The Times* in London, in 1932. Times New Roman went on to become one of the most popular romans available, a mainstay of the Monotype catalogue once it was released in 1933. Despite the necessity of coping with the particular problems the existing Times Roman had in relating to producing good type on newsprint, the new face emerged as a design suited to much of the print work of the time; two versions were cut, that as in the newspaper and a separate form for book production with longer descenders.

Morison's work for *The Times* was evidence of the emergent role of the typographic consultant to industry. Morison was brought in after having expressed (in an article in the paper) his dissatisfaction with the newspaper's setting. He was concerned by the general degradation of newspaper printing and included *The Times* in his criticism, despite its having comparatively high standards in this regard. Morison, however, saw a text face that was inadequate for the tasks placed upon it in the modern world and a generally sloppy sense of typographic discipline. Initially his consultancy honed down the area for improvement to a decision to go for a different but extant revival face: tests were carried out with some of Monotype's recent revivals and new faces, namely Plantin, Baskerville and Perpetua (Gill's new face). The niggling drawbacks of different aspects of these when used on newsprint helped Morison lead the management to the idea of having a face specially cut. It was decided this should be based on Plantin, whose main merit was that it was slightly more condensed than Baskerville and Perpetua. Morison drew up his new version, with finished drawings being prepared by Victor Lardent at *The Times* (Lardent later indicated that he felt he deserved more credit for refining the design than he had been afforded by history).

Although Times New Roman is ostensibly a loose revival, referring to the work of the sixteenth-century Amsterdam printer Christophe Plantin, it is a face that carries many key qualities of twentieth-century typeface design. Morison's aim was to improve newspaper type to a quality comparable with the average of book production; in this way he would bring the finer craft standards into the realm of mass production. Not only was he a firm traditionalist in many ways, but he was also an unassuming typographer and type designer who saw that anonymity in the design – the lack of any eyecatching individual quirks to a face – was an important quality in helping type fulfil the function of being read, not seen. That few lay people would spot his changes was a mark of success, not criticism. *The Times* is said to have received only one letter of complaint after the new face was introduced in the issue of 3 October 1932, which fits the stance outlined in Morison's "First Principles of Typography" essay: "For a new font to be successful, it has to be so good that only very few recognise its novelty." The face remained in use unchanged until 1972 when a revised form more suitable for phototypesetting came into use, Times Europa. In 1991 a further revision, Times Millenium, was introduced.

In fact, though much noted, the font was not such a success among other newspapers, as their paper rarely approached the quality of *The Times* and thus called for a type with less subtlety, less contrast of stroke and less fineness of serif. But Times New Roman raised a flag for the finer points of newspaper type, while also achieving admirable economy in space, both horizontally and vertically. The face was quickly adopted as a popular book face – indeed the

Right: Times New Roman, designed by Stanley Morison for *The Times* newspaper, London, 1931, and subsequently made widely available by Monotype, for whom Morison acted as a consultant and whose drawing office had helped to develop it. Later licensed to many other major type foundries, it is often said to be the most widely used text typeface in the world, for books, periodicals and jobbing printing. Deriving his design from Plantin, Morison went back to the original faces of Granjon used by the Dutch printer in the sixteenth century to find the old-face characteristics that would be most workmanlike. He was not driven by aesthetic considerations; in fact, he roundly condemned such an approach to text typography, insisting instead on a quest for a transparent typography that the reader would simply accept as clear communication. The sturdier characteristics of the old face combine with a more economic modern form, achieving a condensed character that does not look squashed nor lose its thin strokes under the duress of newspaper machine printing. There are short ascenders and descenders, and small, sharp serifs; the stress, combining the modern style of vertical contrast between thick and thin with the oblique accent of old face, tends in effect to be just off the vertical (this is especially noticeable on the "o"). The transition of the weight from thick to thin is not abrupt. Morison instigated the style, found the reference and made some preliminary drawings, and *The Times* draughtsman Victor Lardent produced the finished drawings of the characters. The face was introduced on 3 October 1932 (see pages 116–7).

abcdefghijklmnopqrst
uvwxyzABCDEFGH
IJKLMNOPQRSTU
VWXYZ1234567890

*abcdefghijklmnopqrst*
*uvwxyz ABCDEFGH*
*IJKLMNOPQRSTU*
*VWXYZ1234567890*

Right: the front page of *The Times* before Times New Roman was introduced.
Below: detail from the 29 September 1932 issue, which presented and explained the new face, masthead and design that was to appear the following week.
Opposite page: front page of the first issue of *The Times* to use Times New Roman. A year after its implementation in the newspaper, Monotype and Linotype made it more widely available. It quickly found popularity in book setting in Europe, but became successful in the United States only in the 1950s.

The Times

LONDON, WEDNESDAY, SEPTEMBER 28, 1932

DEATHS (continued) — PERSONAL — PERSONAL (continued) — PERSONAL (continued) — BUSINESS OFFERS — IN MEMORIAM — BUSINESSES FOR SALE

THE  TIMES

LONDON MONDAY OCTOBER 3 1932

The revived roman title-piece to be printed with the new text-types from October 3 next as the standard heading of *The Times*. The device is a re-engraving of the block of 1792 shown below.

THE TIMES OR DAILY UNIVERSAL REGISTER
PRINTED LOGOGRAPHICALLY
TUESDAY, JANUARY 1, 1788.
KING'S THEATRE, Haymarket.
By PARTICULAR DESIRE, on Thursday next, January 3, 1788.

The original roman heading of *The Times* of January 1, 1788. The paper was entitled the *Daily Universal Register* from 1785 to the end of 1787.

An early "gothic" title-piece to *The Times*, set with the device which has been revived for use with the roman title to be adopted from October 3.

An enlarged photograph made direct from cast type showing "*The Times* New Roman" to be adopted for the composition of the paper from October 3.

# THE  TIMES

LONDON MONDAY OCTOBER 3 1932


## DEATHS (continued)

**FISHER.**—On Sept. 29, 1932, ERNEST EDWARD FISHER, M.A., the dearly loved youngest son of the late Admiral and Mrs. Fisher, of Clifton, Bristol, aged 74. Funeral at Shirehampton Church, near Bristol, to-morrow (Tuesday), at 1.45 p.m.

**FLINT.**—On Oct. 1, 1932, at Bramshott, Oatlands Avenue, Weybridge, ALEXANDER FLINT, C.B., C.M.G., of the Admiralty, in his 56th year. Service on Wednesday, Oct. 5, at St. Mary's Church, Oatlands (Walton Station, S.R.), at 2.30. Interment at Weybridge Cemetery. No deep mourning.

**FOSTER.**—On Sept. 30, 1932, at 21, Lennox Gardens, London, S.W., EDWARD WILLIAM PERCEVAL FOSTER, C.M.G., late Inspector-General of Irrigation in Egypt, second son of the late Major-General Edward Horatio Foster. Funeral service, Holy Trinity Church, Brompton, 2.15 p.m., to-morrow (Tuesday). Interment afterwards at Putney Vale Cemetery. (Egyptian papers, please copy.)

**HAYNES.**—On Oct. 1, 1932, at The Cottage, Clifton, Nottingham, ANNIE MAY, widow of HENRY HAYNES, and fourth daughter of the late William Pilkington, of Roby Hall, Liverpool, aged 66. Funeral to-morrow (Tuesday) 3 p.m. at Clifton.

**HOLMES.**—On Sept. 27, 1932, at Ballyclare, Co. Antrim, the REV. ARCHIBALD HOLMES, Minister of the R.P. Church, Ballyclare, aged 70 years.

**HUTCHINSON.**—On Oct. 1, 1932, at 25, Dorset Square, N.W.1, ELLEN, widow of SIR CHARLES HUTCHINSON. Funeral at Mayfield Parish Church, Sussex, on Wednesday, Oct. 5, at 2.30 p.m. Flowers to 5, Baker Street W.1.

**JARMAY.**—On Oct. 2, 1932, suddenly, HILDA LESLEY, beloved wife of CAPTAIN J. B. JARMAY, Bulkeley Hall, Malpas, Cheshire. Funeral to-morrow (Tuesday), Bickerton Church, 2.30.

**LIVERSIDGE.**—On Oct. 1, 1932, at Oxley, Woodhouse, Huddersfield, NORMAN, eldest son of the late THOMAS LIVERSIDGE, of Brooklands, Selby, and loving husband of Margaret A. Liversidge, in his 63rd year. Interment at Woodhouse Churchyard, Huddersfield, to-morrow (Tuesday) at 3.30.

**LYELL.**—On Oct. 1, 1932, at 78, Woodstock Road, Oxford, CHRISTINA CLUNIE, the last surviving child of the late DR. JAMES LYELL, of Falkland, Fifeshire, in her 90th year.

**MARTIN.**—On Oct. 1, 1932, at Brendon, Limpsfield, Surrey, after a long illness, courageously borne, the REV. WILLIAM HOWARD MARTIN, eldest son of William Julius Martin, aged 31. Service at Oxted Church to-morrow (Tuesday) at 10.15 a.m., afterwards at West Norwood Crematorium at 11.45.

**MOORE.**—On Oct. 2, 1932, suddenly, of heart failure, at 7, Holmbush Road, Putney, LEWIS GRENVILLE MOORE, I.C.S. (retired), beloved husband of Ethel Moore, aged 60. Funeral at Putney Vale Cemetery to-morrow (Tuesday) at 2.30.

**MOREY.**—On Sept. 29, 1932, in London, CHARLOTTE HELEN, widow of JOHN MOREY, of Kensington. Requiem Mass and funeral to-day (Monday) at Our Lady of Victories, Kensington, and Requiem Oct. 10 in the Convent Chapel, Richmond, Yorks. R.I.P.

**NEWMAN.**—On Sept. 30, 1932, the result of a motor accident, the REV. WILLIAM ARTHUR NEWMAN, Rector of Upper Hardres and Stelling, aged 67. Funeral Broadway, Ilminster, Somerset, to-morrow (Tuesday), at 2.30. No flowers. Memorial service Upper Hardres Church the same day, at 2.30.

**PHIPPS.**—On Oct. 1, 1932, at Hampton Court Palace, CONSTANCE EMMA, wife of the late LORD WILLIAM PHIPPS, and daughter of the late Alfred Keyser.

**PORTER.**—On Oct. 1, 1932, at 55, Howards Lane, Putney, FLORENCE AMY (DAISY), the dearly loved wife of CHARLES PORTER, late of Sussex Place, South Kensington.

**RUBENS.**—On Oct. 1, 1932, at 10, Orme Court, W.2, JENNY, widow of VICTOR RUBENS, aged 80. Funeral service at Golders Green Crematorium to-morrow (Tuesday) at 12.30 p.m. No flowers.

**RUTHERFORD.**—On Oct. 1, 1932, in a London nursing home, EMILY GERTRUDE, widow of GEORGE RUTHERFORD, H.M. Patent Office, aged 75 years.

**SAMPSON.**—On Oct. 1, 1932, at a nursing home, Worthing, ETHEL LOUISE SAMPSON, daughter of the late James Sampson (of the Bank of England). Interment, Durrington Cemetery, Worthing, at 2.30, to-morrow (Tuesday).

**SOLDAN.**—On Oct. 2, 1932, suddenly, at a London nursing home, CHRISTIAN SOLDAN, of 3, Cambridge Road, Battersea Park, S.W.11. Flowers to Tookey, 51, High Street, Marylebone, W.1.

**STIRLING.**—On Oct. 1, 1932, at The Lindens, Victoria Park, Manchester, WILLIAM STIRLING, LL.D., D.Sc., M.D., late Brackenbury Professor of Physiology, Victoria University, Manchester, in his 82nd year. Funeral to-morrow (Tuesday). All inquiries to Messrs. Kendal, Milne, and Co., Manchester.

**TUCKER.**—On Sept. 30, 1932, at Sevenoaks, ROSA KATHARINE TUCKER, in her 72nd year.

**VIBART.**—MARIAN CHARLOTTE VIBART, eldest daughter of the late Captain Meredith Vibart, of the Indian Army. Funeral, Richmond Cemetery, Wednesday, Oct. 5, at 3.30.

**WALDRAM.**—On Oct. 1, 1932, at Robin's Croft, Whitchurch Gardens, Edgware, GEORGIANA ELLEN, the loving and greatly beloved wife of PERCY J. WALDRAM, and mother of J. M. and C. H. Waldram. Funeral at Edgware Parish Church to-morrow (Tuesday) at 3 p.m.

**WALKER.**—On Oct. 1, 1932, at 27, Stafford Terrace, Kensington, JAMES RONALD WALKER, Barrister, of Lincoln's Inn and Middle Temple, dearly loved husband of Frances Evelyn Walker, in his 60th year. No flowers, no mourning. Funeral private.

**WILLIAMS.**—On Oct. 1, 1932, at 111, Central Hill, Upper Norwood, KATHLEEN, widow of MAJOR HARRY PLUNKETT WILLIAMS, and last surviving child of the Rev. E. C. Ellis, Langham Rectory, Essex.

**WYTHE-TOMPSON.**—On Oct. 1, 1932, suddenly, at 2A, Marloes Road, ERNEST, the beloved husband of MARY TOMPSON, third son of the late George Edward Tompson, of Boxted House, Essex, aged 77. Funeral at Golders Green Crematorium, on Wednesday, Oct. 5, at 3 o'clock. (South African papers, please copy.)

## IN MEMORIAM

### ON ACTIVE SERVICE

**ALLEN.**—In ever-loving memory of LIEUT. ARCHIBALD STAFFORD ALLEN, 8th Batt. Royal Fusiliers, husband of Florence May Allen and only son of J. Archibald and Elizabeth Mary Allen, of "Wynnstow," Oxted, killed in action at Loos on Oct. 3, 1915.

**BENTALL.**—In ever-loving memory of ERNEST HAMMOND BENTALL, 2nd Lieut., 1st K.R.R., killed in action near Hulluch, Oct. 3, 1915.

**BLACKWOOD-PORTER.**—In loving and honoured memory of AUBREY BLACKWOOD-PORTER, Lieutenant, (4th) attached 2nd Highland Light Infantry, killed Battle of Loos, Oct. 3, 1915.

**BOILEAU.**—In memory of a most dearly loved son and brother, Lieut., 1st Dorset Regt., killed at Sequehart, Oct. 3, 1918, also of his devoted mother, Dec. 15, 1931.

**BRAIN.**—In ever-loving memory of FRANCIS SYDNEY BRAIN, Captain, Royal Berkshire Regt., attached 1st Dorset Regt., killed in action at Sequehart, Oct. 3, 1918, in his 25th year.

**CHANCE.**—In proud and loving memory of CAPTAIN ANDREW FERGUSON CHANCE, R.A., who died in action

## PERSONAL

THE same message for your happiness to-day and every day. Always the same.—M.

THE charge for announcements in the Personal Column is 10s. a line for two lines (minimum) and 5s. for each additional line. Trade announcements 25s. for two lines and 12s. 6d. for each additional line. Lost and Found notices 2s. 6d. per line (minimum two lines). A line comprises about six words. Private numbers, if added, form part of the advertisement and are charged for. Names and addresses of actual advertisers should accompany all advertisements, not for publication unless desired, but as a guarantee of good faith. For index to other classifications see column seven.

£40 REWARD.—LOST, on 22nd Sept., in or near Palace Theatre, DIAMOND BRACELET.—Summers, Henderson and Co., 48, Lime Street, E.C.3.

GUY'S IS ON THE DANGER LIST. Please help by sending a contribution to the Treasurer, Guy's Hospital, S.E.1.

ALCOHOLISM.—An interesting brochure on medical treatment free.—Secretary, 40, Marsham Street, S.W.1.

SUNNINGDALE, PRACTICALLY ADJOINING GOLF COURSE.—To be LET Unfurnished, self-contained ground-floor FLAT: four bed rooms, two sitting rooms, bath; South aspect; electric light, constant hot water; lock-up garage; delightful pleasure grounds, about three acres, tennis lawn, &c. Rent £156 p.a. inclusive; £125 asked for improvements, certain carpets, fittings, &c.—H. S., 20, St. James's Square, S.W.1.

"PRINTING THE TIMES."—The New Type and Heading are described, and the Reasons for the Change explained, in a Specially Written Booklet entitled "Printing The Times," which may be had free and post free on application to the Publisher, Printing House Square, E.C.4.

ALL ENGLISHMEN should join THE ROYAL SOCIETY OF ST. GEORGE.—Send for Booklet, 47, Victoria Street, London, S.W.1.

IN DESPERATION.—ERE WINTER will one influential person offer some JOB or otherwise temporarily help young Englishman? Married; educated, capable; genuine; investigations; interview.—Please write Box Y.1641, The Times, E.C.4.

GERMAN, excellent private LESSONS, colloquial; beginners taken.—Write Box J.4, The Times, E.C.4.

TO PARENTS, &c.—University Professor and Wife (trained Nurse) offer cultured home and education to two or three children (any age); own house; three acres; London suburb; references doctors, titled people. —Write Box M.77, The Times, E.C.4.

TO ADOPT a CHILD—apply through your vicar to The Adoption Society, Church House, Westminster.

WINTER SPORTS, ZERMATT.—Brilliant sunshine. Grand scenery. Inquire early.—C. T. U., 126, Baker Street, London, W.1. 'Phone, Welbeck 7088.

LADY will RECEIVE as Sole Guest FOREIGN or ENGLISH LADY in her well appointed flat, S.W.5 district; near Tube.—Write Box A.574, The Times, E.C.4.

MAJOR REDWAY Coaches for Promotion and Staff College Also prepares Candidates for Army Commissions.—87, Bishop's Mansions, S.W.6. Putney 7315.

A NEW IDEA.—TUDOR COURT EXTENSION (58, CROMWELL ROAD, SOUTH KENSINGTON.)—Specially designed and beautifully fitted Bed-Sitting Rooms at very moderate terms; breakfasts served in rooms, other meals at Tudor Court as required.—Call or 'phone Western 6393.

6D. a MILE, six-passenger SUNBEAM LIMOUSINE, or 50s. eight hours, 100 miles.—Sloane 5121.

ALCOHOLIC EXCESS and its Treatment. Treatise free.—Secretary, 14, Hanover Square. W. May. 3406.

DANCING.—GEM MOUFLET teaches, partners. (Near Ritz.)—11, Albemarle Street, PICCADILLY. Reg. 4629.

THE WEST END OFFICE of THE TIMES, at 72, Regent Street, W.1 (near Piccadilly Circus), contains a delightful period room, which readers will find restful and conducive to quiet thought. Assistance will gladly be given in the wording of advertisements and announcements so that they may be written to the best advantage. Remember the address: 72, Regent Street, W.1. Telephone numbers, Regent 2273, 2274, and 7400.

ARS VIVENDI BREATHING specific for ASTHMA. —Mr. Arthur Lovell, Wigmore Hall, W.1.

UNWANTED False Teeth urgently required for our Dental Aid Work.—Ivory Cross, 67A, Welbeck Street, W.1.

WANTED, West End London, three-four years from February next, partly or fully FURNISHED HOUSE or FLAT; two reception, six bed; maximum 6 guineas a week; no premium.—Reeve, Rougham Hall, Bury St. Edmund's.

WE only exist by gifts of jumble. Please send generously, otherwise clubs and treats will be no more. —Rev. S. Langton, Holy Redeemer, Clergy House, Exmouth Street, E.C.1.

A LADY resident 2½ years wishes to RECOMMEND cooking, service, and comfort offered at 122, SLOANE STREET, where large double room is vacant now.—'Phone Sloane 4761.

TUTOR WANTED for boy aged 4½; not governess; good salary, resident in country house, travelling expenses paid, and good honorarium on leaving to man who has done well.—Write, with testimonials, references, and stating experience, to Box K.1431, The Times, E.C.4.

6D. MILE LIMOUSINES.—99, Buckingham Palace Road. 'Phone, Vic. 1025 or Addiscombe 1000.

SPEECH!—Classes and private lessons in public speaking.—Garrett, Lombard House, Little Britain, E.C.1.

AT FIVE SHILLINGS a line it is impossible to describe my model DEVON COTTAGE. If you want the ideal and are prepared to pay £2,000 for it write Box W.962, The Times, E.C.4.

GENTLEWOMAN seeks POST, COMPANION-HOUSEKEEPER to another lady; gardening, animals; fond of country, literature, art.—Write Box W.967, The Times, E.C.4.

VERY grateful thanks to St. Philomena for wonderful favours received and to come.

FOR SALE, SHROPSHIRE, MODERN RESIDENCE, comprising three reception and five bed rooms, &c.; company's water, gas and electric light; also garages, stabling, cottage and paddock; vacant possession.—For further particulars and orders write Box Y.1649, The Times, E.C.4.

BIJOU COUNTRY RESIDENCE of character, four miles SUSSEX COAST, in 23 acres; every modern convenience; perfect order; seven bed, two bath, three reception, and delightful lounge; cottage and lodge; garages; most attractive grounds; well away from traffic. For SALE FREEHOLD.—Write Box Y.1652, The Times, E.C.4.

GENTLEMAN leaving Town compelled LET beautiful FLAT, Albert Court; Unfurnished; five bed, two baths, three reception; constant hot water, central heating; luxuriously appointed. Rent £425 p.a.—Write Box Y.1653, The Times, E.C.4.

DOCTOR and Wife would welcome child to share home and attend morning school with own girl of six; every care and comfort; large garden; Surrey.—Write Box Y.1661, The Times, E.C.4.

SOUTH DEVON, close to sea.—Roadside GUEST HOUSE, exceptionally well appointed, valuable furnishings; seven bed rooms, three reception rooms, two bath rooms; garage; charming gardens; most of the rooms face South and all have entrancing views; a remarkable opportunity to combine comfortable home with a lucrative and interesting business; excellent lease. PRICE £1,250. Strongly recommended.—Write Box Y.1646, The Times, E.C.4.

LADY, University Graduate, B.Sc., teachers' diploma, 25, seeks post.—Write Box Y.1642, The Times, E.C.4.

## PERSONAL

"WISDOM is the principal thing; therefore get wisdom: and with all thy getting get understanding. Exalt her, and she shall promote thee; she shall bring thee to honour, when thou dost embrace her."—Prov. iv., 7, 8.

£5 NOTE GRATEFULLY RECEIVED from an ANONYMOUS DONOR, who writes:—"May I ask you, in His Name, to accept this with the hope that it may be used in the good work you are endeavouring to do. . . . Trusting it may help yet another TIRED and NEEDY LIFE to have the PRIVILEGE and BENEFIT of a REST at 'THE RETREAT,' MALDON." FUNDS, VERY GREATLY NEEDED, will be thankfully acknowledged by the Secretary, ST. GILES' CHRISTIAN MISSION and WHEATLEY'S HOMES, 15, Gray's Inn Road, London, W.C.1.

BANK of ENGLAND.—RECLAIMED REDEMPTION MONEY and DIVIDENDS. No. 17043/4. —APPLICATION having been made to the Governor of the Bank of England to direct the PAYMENT of the REDEMPTION MONEY in respect of the sums of £50 Registered £5 per Cent. National War Bonds, 1927, and £50 Registered £5 per Cent. National War Bonds, 1928, Second Series, formerly in the name of MARIA ESTHER BADGER SIMPSON of Defford Road, Pershore, Worcestershire, Spinster, which Redemption Money was paid over to the Commissioners for the Reduction of the National Debt in consequence of having remained unreceived. Notice is hereby given that, on the expiration of three months from this date (October 3, 1932) the said Redemption Money and the unpaid dividends will be PAID to HERBERT BASIL HARRISON, Solicitor, and ARTHUR WILLIAM SMITH, Chemist, both of Pershore, Worcestershire, Administrators de bonis non of the estate of the said MARIA ESTHER BADGER SIMPSON, now deceased, they having claimed the same, unless some other claim thereto shall in the meantime be made and sustained.

SIR PHILIP BEN GREET can arrange performances of Shakespearean Plays and Old English Comedies at schools, &c., during autumn and winter. Pastoral Plays in the summer.—Address care of 40, Chandos Street, Strand, W.C.2.

"READING THE TIMES."—An Illustrated Guide to the Contents and Make-up of the Paper for those who are not yet regular readers free and post free on application to the Publisher, Printing House Square, E.C.4.

WHEN YOUR SON LEAVES SCHOOL send him out to South Africa without wasting time. Give him a fine, free life as a farmer. Three years' training given gratis; then moderate capital buys his own land.—Apply 1820 Memorial Settlers' Association, Dept. T.O.3, 199, Piccadilly, W.1.

DANCING SCHOOL.—Lady wishes to SELL her well-established SCHOOL of DANCING in a fashionable South Coast Town. Long lease, splendid ballroom, and spacious accommodation. Price £1,000 (part might remain).—Write Box "Principal," care of Davies and Co., 95, Bishopsgate, E.C.2.

C.H.W.—Patients and friends of the Chelsea Hospital for Women sometimes send Gifts in Kind. These are always very welcome, both at Arthur Street, S.W.3, and at the Convalescent Home, West Hill, St. Leonards-on-Sea.

VENETIAN GENTLEMAN, University Graduate, gives ITALIAN LESSONS.—Write Box M.138, The Times, E.C.4.

LEARN to WRITE ADVERTISEMENTS and earn from £5 to £20 per week. Unique offer open to those writing for our free book, "Advertising as a Career."—Dixon Institute of Advertising, Dept. 70, 195, Oxford Street, London, W.1.

HILLMAN WIZARD SALOON de LUXE, delivered July, 1932; mileage 2,000; perfect condition; £250. —Chauffeur, 83, Winchester Street, S.W.1.

PORTRAITS IN OIL from Life, Posthumous, or Photograph will be painted by well-known exhibitor R.A.—Write Box W.961, The Times, E.C.4.

GERMAN.—PRIVATE LESSONS by NATIVE UNIVERSITY GRADUATE.—Write Dr. H. W., 125, Westbourne Terrace, W.2.

RIDING GUESTS and PUPILS.—Moderate inclusive terms.—White Hill Riding School, Swanage.

GARAGE, Chauffeur's Flat, WANTED, near Portland Place.—Write Box G.1432, The Times, E.C.4.

MANNEQUINS.—LADIES trained to fill Posts.—London Mannequin School, 299, Oxford Street, W.1.

WELL FURNISHED FLAT, six bed, &c., overlooking Kensington Gardens. Rent 12gns., or offer.—'Phone Western 2840.

LADY wishes PUPILS, SPEAKING, READING, DECLAMATION.—Write Box Y.1630, The Times, E.C.4.

WANTED, two or three PAYING GUESTS for two or three months or longer; distinguished house West Sussex; every comfort; garage, stabling; 5 guineas a week each.—Write Box Y.1634, The Times, E.C.4.

EYE WORK.—Would retired doctor with knowledge eye work give honorary services old-established Eye Institution? Pleasant Western town.—Write, stating experience, Box Y.1650, The Times, E.C.4.

"ALL BRITISH CAMPAIGN." Established 1925.—43, Bedford Street, W.C.2. Founder George Ernest Osmond.

INDIVIDUAL TUITION for School Certificate, Matriculation and other examinations.—Redcliffe Tutorial, 50, Redcliffe Square, S.W.10. Flaxman 0452.

WIFE of RETIRED NAVAL OFFICER, devoted and experience children, wishes to take in one or two; happy, healthy home, Hants coast; every loving care; low terms; good day schools; not antagonistic; Christian Science preferred.—Write Box Y.1632, The Times, E.C.4.

AUTOGRAPH Letters and MSS.; modern authors and others; fine private collection; first reasonable offer; will appreciate.—Write Box Y.1623, The Times, E.C.4.

TRAINED NURSE, young, experienced voyager, like to TAKE INVALID or CHILDREN TRAVELLING.—F. C., 82, Gloucester Road, S.W.7.

WHAT AM I TO READ NEXT?—For valuable suggestions without obligation send your name on a postcard to Box Y.1636, The Times, E.C.4.

WHAT can RADIUM do for CANCER? Help our Cancer Research Department to answer this question.—The Middlesex Hospital, London, W.1.

"O GOD, BRING MY GEORGE BACK," is the nightly prayer of his aged mother; £35 will establish him in promised post; a great chance; full story on application. Please help.—Secretary, London Police Court Mission, 27, Gordon Square, W.C.1.

VALET REQUIRED by elderly gentleman; high wages; age 30-40; must be highly intelligent and have good memory; one who has had some nursing experience preferred, but not essential; good packer, used to travelling; physical fitness essential. Can any doctor or other person knowing such a valet personally recommend? Letter must give full particulars of experience, references, &c.—Write Box K.1428, The Times, E.C.4.

WRITE for PROFIT.—Send for free Booklet.—Regent Institute (77Q), Palace Gate, W.8.

OF course the children (9 and 7) don't know why their father takes their mother's place and keeps them clean and goes without that they may be fed. He, a boot repairer, is hindered by unemployment. Will you help father and children by your gift towards £10 to buy tools, leather, and pay rent to give him a start? Cheques, &c., Preb. Carlile, "Loving Father," Church Army, 55, Bryanston Street, W.1.

THE REVEREND H. R. L. SHEPPARD having been ordered abroad for health reasons wishes to LET for a nominal rent, November to May, his HOUSE on south side Hogs Back; three reception, seven bed, two bath; central heating; electric light; maids left by arrangement; five miles Guildford and Farnham, four Aldershot.—Apply Shoelands, Seale, Surrey.

## PERSONAL

HOME TIES, and many difficulties keep me. Can never forget.

TO LET or SELL.—Beautifully FURNISHED Country COTTAGE; 50 yards from lovely golf; private road. Five bed rooms, three reception, four lavatories, three bath rooms; radiators every room; lovely garden, views, veranda, lawn; 18 miles London, 60ft. above sea level.—Box A.580, The Times, E.C.4.

TO be LET, FURNISHED HOUSE, cosy, economical, newly decorated throughout; convenient for Charing Cross, &c. HAMPSTEAD GARDEN SUBURB, near Heath. Four bed, three sitting, good offices, bath room, two w.c.s, loggia, garden, garage, telephone. Electric light, power throughout; gas cooker, fires, and hot water; range and open fires available. Four guineas.—Write Box A.579, The Times, E.C.4.

THE VICAR of TEDDINGTON having to move wishes to SELL his HOUSE cheaply to a Catholic who would value. St. Albans, Teddington.

BEFORE SHOPPING READ the ADVERTISEMENTS of the following firms in to-day's issue:—Marshall and Snelgrove, page seven; Debenham and Freebody, pages 10 and 17; Selfridge's, page 10; Harvey Nichols, page 11; National Fur Company, page 12; Bradleys, page 13; Peter Robinson, page 17; Burberrys, page 18; Smartwear, page 18; Harrods, page 19; Dickins and Jones, page 21; Robinson and Cleaver, page 21.

COUNTESS RECEIVES GUESTS in VIENNA; central position; opportunity learning German; young society, music, skating, introduction society, dancing; moderate terms.—Write Box Y.1625, The Times, E.C.4.

INVALID LADY, unable to walk, would greatly APPRECIATE little HELP to purchase artificial leg, or gift of few books.—Write Box Y.1624, The Times, E.C.4.

MOULDS or MATRICES of Periodicals, Books, &c., required for Overseas printing; subjects must be non-dated.—Details or proofs to be sent to Box K.1435, The Times, E.C.4.

MENTALLY BACKWARD.—Few young gentlemen received.—Mr. and Mrs. Loveless, Woburn Sands, Bucks.

TOBACCO.—Nine years' administrative Manufacturing experience, Belgium, Denmark, Far East. Public School, age 28, desires position with good prospects; any branch tobacco business.—Write Box Y.1657, The Times, E.C.4.

HOLIDAYS are over. Make a Winter hobby of knowing London with the London Rambling Society. 'Phone 1733 Langham.

MAKE YOUR CHOICE OF A CAR from the selection offered under "Motor-cars," &c., on page two.

SIR REGINALD KENNEDY COX urgently APPEALS for JUMBLE badly needed by Dockland for winter work.—Do please send clothes, furniture, anything to 41A, Adams Mews, W.1. All gratefully received.

PROFESSIONAL man and wife require BED ROOM and SITTING ROOM, with breakfast, in modern private house or flat, other meals optional; W.1 or Knightsbridge.—Write Box 2377, The Times, 42, Wigmore Street, W.1.

## KENNEL FARM AND AVIARY

*3 lines 4s. 6d. (minimum)*

### DOGS

AIREDALES (Lt.-Col. Richardson's) world-known for protective purposes. Also first-class pedigree Fox, Cairn, Scotch Sealyhams, Cockers, Pups, Adults, Companions or Show. Export arranged.—Clock House, Byfleet, Surrey. Easy car drive or Green Line. Tele. 274.

A TREASURE from the LAND of SCOTT.—Nothing is so terrifying to burglars as the low growl and savage look of the DANDIE DINMONT, not half of the hold-ups would take place if a Dandie Dinmont was seen in the car. You can always get a good one from Ex-Provost Dalglish, Galashiels.

BAKER STREET DOG BUREAU, 10, Baker Street, W.1.—Charming Cairn Terriers, Golden Spaniels, Aberdeens, Sealyhams, and Wire-haired Terriers; beautiful selection always on show. Trimming and shampooing by animal expert. Telephone, Welbeck 9358.

CAIRNS, puppies and adults, gay and healthy, champion pedigrees; lovely colours.—Miss Haines, Cairn Halt, Crawley. 'Phone 227.

CHAMPION bred show bench and Field Trial Golden Retriever Puppies. Best 6gns. Others 4gns.—Hunt, Ottershaw, Chertsey. 'Phone, Ottershaw 12.

DACHSHUNDS.—Smooth red and black and tan. All ages; owner exhibiting Crystal Palace 5th and 6th.—Allan, Chipperfield, Herts. Kings Langley 7410.

GREAT DANES, 4 fawn bitch puppies, two 7 months black bitches; house trained; cheap to clear; lovely dog pups.—Parsons, Ferring, Worthing.

GREYHOUND, extra good, live or electric hare; great bargain to immediate purchaser, £12 12s.—Moseley, 60, Alma Street, Taunton.

GRIFFONS BRUXELLOIS.—The VULCAN KENNELS claim to have the largest selection in England of these charming puppies for sale—nearly 20 to choose from. Every type and colour.—Apply The Hon. Mrs. Ionides, Orleans House, Twickenham. (Popesgrove 2580.)

HIGH-CLASS SALUKIS; Ch. Sarona Kelb Strain; 18 months old; £10 each.—Miss Ridgway, Blythe Bridge, Stoke-on-Trent.

HOME wanted for house-trained Pedigree Dog, SEALYHAM; 16 months; 9 guineas.—Write Box M.146, The Times, E.C.4.

IRISH SETTER DOG, 2½ years, winner of several prizes, for sale cheap to good country home as pet; lovely head, beautiful coat and colour; house trained; over distemper.—Write Box Y.1663, The Times, E.C.4.

PEDIGREE COCKERS, reds and blacks, puppies and adults, both sexes. Some house-trained. From 4gns.—Hunt, Ottershaw 12.

PEDIGREE SMOOTH FOX TERRIER PUPPIES, fit for show or work, from game parents; from 3 guineas.—Harvey-Dixon, Tutnall, Bromsgrove.

PEDIGREE WIRE-HAIRED TERRIER PUPPIES for SALE; champion strain.—Apply Vivian, Luttrells Cottage, Fawley, Hants.

PEKINGESE.—Miss Frampton, world's record winning Puppies from 4gns.; miniatures and whites a speciality; 5 minutes from Olympia.—'Phone, Riverside 2757. 67, Hammersmith Bridge Road, W.6.

PEKINGESE.—The Ifield Pekingese Kennels have some lovely adults and puppies for sale at reasonable prices; all champion bred.—Apply Mrs. Whitehead, Ifield Hall, Crawley, Sussex. Tele., Crawley 73. Or 105, Piccadilly, W.1. Tele., Mayfair 2668.

PEKINGESE.—"The Fewling" pure white and coloured Puppies and Adults, champion bred.—Mrs. Elkan, 10, Hamilton Terrace, N.W.8. Cunningham 1980.

SMART WEST HIGHLAND WHITE TERRIER DOG, 14 months; house trained; good guard; 7gns.—Druce, Green Bank, Parkgate Road, Mollington, Chester.

THE VULCAN KENNELS have a large selection of Adorable CAIRN DOG PUPPIES for SALE at very reasonable prices.—Apply The Hon. Mrs. Ionides, Orleans House, Twickenham. (Popesgrove 2580.)

AMBROL is without doubt the best milk food for puppies and the cheapest. Obtainable at all Boots stores, and from many other chemists, or direct from Ambrosia, Lifton, Devon.

BELL MEAD KENNELS, Ltd, Haslemere. — The training School which is highly recommended by the

## BUSINESS OFFERS

*3 lines 15s. (minimum)*

FIFTY-FOUR YEARS IN FLEET STREET.—An unequalled series of advertising successes, including the development of many famous businesses from small beginnings to National status by sound economical advertising, continually adapted to ever-changing conditions. Proved experience combined with a modern outlook, the wisdom of age combined with the inspiration of youth. Full evidence willingly submitted at an interview, without obligation.—Apply Principal Director, Smiths' Advertising Agency, Ltd., 100, Fleet Street, London, E.C.4.

AN OPPORTUNITY to JOIN First-class BUSINESS is offered to gentleman of good education; exceptional prospects with salaried position and assured profits. Qualification £3,000 (secured and returnable). Full particulars at interview only to principals.—Write Box K.1411, The Times, E.C.4.

SUBSTANTIAL NET INCOMES up to and over £1,000 p.a. are being made by owners of a new and much-needed public utility service, the British BURTOL, requiring only ordinary business ability and a modest capital of about £1,000. This proposition is ideal either as an investment or as a business, and opportunities exist in all towns of 10,000 or over.—For full particulars and terms apply to James Armstrong and Co., Ltd., 151, Queen Victoria Street, London, E.C.4.

START A POSTAL BUSINESS of your own. Very profitable. Send 1½d. stamp for particulars. How £14 made £1,720 in one year.—(B) Hand and Co., 284, High Holborn, London, W.C.1.

A1 INVESTMENT OPPORTUNITY.—Sums up to £50,000 (with or without active participation) can be safely employed to acquire interests relative to an important industrial development and rationalization scheme. Unquestionably one of the finest opportunities for consistent profit-making and capital appreciation in England. Particulars sent on request and inspection invited.—Write Box W.928, The Times, E.C.4.

CONGENIAL HEALTHY OCCUPATION with assured future offered to several energetic YOUNG MEN able INVEST £2,500 and over by large British Farming Company of national importance now expanding to take full advantage of new tariffs; no special knowledge necessary provided willing work hard and progress.—Write Box A.410, The Times, E.C.4.

OPPORTUNITY for MANUFACTURERS.—Owing to business expansion firm desires to dispose of manufacturing rights and COMPLETE TOOLS for manufacture of ATTRACTIVE NOVELTY, made entirely of sheet metal stampings. Absolutely unique. Rapid seller at all stores and tobacconists at 17s. 6d. retail. Supplied to many foremost stores. Excellent line without competition. Tools complete ready for use only £475.—Write Box K.1434, The Times, E.C.4.

UNIQUE OPPORTUNITY for INVESTMENT occurs in sound county weekly newspapers paying 7½ to 10 per cent. Principals, accountants, or Solicitors only. —Write Box Y.1656, The Times, E.C.4.

OLD-ESTABLISHED LONDON LETTERPRESS PRINTERS propose forming Private Company and require GENTLEMAN to JOIN BOARD who controls substantial connexion and can make small investment. Investigation welcomed, but must produce proof of connexion first. Excellent opportunity for gentleman who is already on directorate of other companies.—Write Box M.140, The Times, E.C.4.

WOMAN PARTNER (over 30) WANTED in progressive Educational Bureau; must be interested in new ideas; good interviewer; ability to write an asset. Training given to suitable candidate. Investment.—Write Box Y.1647, The Times, E.C.4.

ARNOLD and Co., Southern House, Cannon Street Station, E.C., established 40 years, have BUYERS for sound Manufacturing and other Businesses.

TEA TRADE.—An excellent opportunity has occurred for retired Planters, Farmers, &c.; very little capital required.—Write Box Y.1648, The Times, E.C.4.

FOREIGN IMPORTERS REQUIRING BRITISH GOODS of every description will find this column an effective medium for securing contact with manufacturers able and willing to satisfy their requirements. Similarly those in a position to supply or specially manufacture goods for export may find this classification very successful in opening up new markets abroad. Orders are actually awaiting firms who are prepared to show initiative and enterprise, but prospective clients want their names and addresses and an indication of the goods which can be supplied.

WELL-CONNECTED PERSONS able to interest themselves actively and eventually with capital are invited to write for particulars of the formation of a Holding Syndicate to market an astonishing British-made instrument of the greatest importance to combat dangers of the roads and which instrument should be made compulsory on public service vehicles.—Write Box M.83, The Times, E.C.4.

GENTLEMAN aged 30, determined to succeed, REQUIRES POSITION in which common sense and perseverance are essential; considerable business experience.—Write Box A.570, The Times, E.C.4.

GENERAL, BONDED, SUFFERANCE WHARVES, WAREHOUSES, Thameside, City, old standing, high repute, ample finance, valuable Bonded Rights including Wines, Spirits, desire develop. Proposals considered on merits.—Write Box Y.1633, The Times, E.C.4.

COUNTRY FIRM of PRINTERS, one hour London, with daily delivery, are open to contract for the printing of a mid-weekly or weekly newspaper or magazine; very moderate charges; efficient service; up-to-date plant; good work.—Write Box 547, 8, Serle Street, London, W.C.2.

CITY RESTAURANT, close to the BANK, seating 150. Established over a century. Price £5,000, includes equipment, goodwill, and valuable ground lease. —WAY and WALLER, 7, Hanover Square, W.1. Mayfair 8022.

ACCOUNTANT, or other experienced man, REQUIRED for progressive business with excellent prospects. INVESTMENT £5,000. Directorship considered.—Write Box 0475, The Times, 72, Regent Street, W.1.

AN EXCEPTIONAL OPPORTUNITY for young man with £3,000-£5,000 to join Inventor Patentee and Manufacturer of a high-grade Automatic Machine in demand in all countries; one willing to take periodical trips to the Continent; a big income and share of the World's rights to suitable applicant. Fullest investigation invited and references exchanged.—Write Box M.142, The Times, E.C.4.

FILTRATION.—A Company having a new and proved method of filtration which is superior to known methods as regards capital cost, operating and maintenance costs, simplicity, efficiency, and space required is prepared at once to instal a few commercial units without cost or obligation to users. Principals only dealt with.—Reply with main particulars of material treated and daily tonnages handled (information will be regarded as confidential) to A.B.C., care of Walker, Rowe and Clark, Solicitors, 14, Union Court, Old Broad Street, E.C.2.

## BUSINESSES FOR SALE

*3 lines 7s. 6d. (minimum)*

A DELIGHTFUL RESIDENTIAL HOTEL (licensed), Sussex (main road); 22 bed rooms; handsome oak panelled public rooms; garages (with pumps), cottage; 8 acres; 3 tennis courts; takings (capable great improvement) £100 week. Price £5,000 (near offer).—HOLMES, 495, Oxford Street, Marble Arch.

A LUXURIOUS SMALL HOTEL, licensed, standing in 20 acres lovely grounds in Devon, for SALE at renowned American type historian and small-press printer D. B. Updike used it for the final book out of his Merrymount Press, *Some Aspects of Printing, Old and New*, in 1941 – quite an honour for a face that Morison would later ironically sum up as being "by the vice of Mammon and the misery of the machine ... bigoted and narrow, mean and puritan". In these words from 1953 he was reflecting on what William Morris might have thought, but at the same time revealing his own doubts about the standards brought by mass communication.

Morison's work is the most high-profile of all newspaper type-design projects of this period, but new faces of more widespread application in the press were also coming into use and deserve mention. Awareness of unsatisfactory standards in type in the 1920s had led newspaper proprietors in the US to call for the likes of Linotype and Intertype to improve what was available and workable on their high-speed letterpress machines. Ionic, cut in 1925, was a key development, being a throwback face that drew on the Victorian Clarendons for a rugged look distinguished by an almost even stroke line and a high x-height. It was swiftly adopted by newspapers internationally. In 1931 Linotype brought out Excelsior, a design specifically developed to overcome the ink-trap effect on counters of tighter characters; then came Paragon and Opticon, the latter opening out its characters even more to work with heavily inked newspapers. This series was part of Linotype's Legibility Group of new faces tackling the need for a type culture specifically suited to the special needs of newspapers and other large-run, low-cost text printing. The culmination of this period of development came in 1941 with the issue of Corona, a face that became immensely popular with American newspapers and is so still, even after transfer to modern technologies.

While the production of newspapers, magazines and other large-run items was now carried out entirely by mechanical typesetter, hand-setting was still widely practised by smaller printers and was a skill that continued to be taught. In the background, though, early phototypesetting systems were appearing, which would ultimately achieve the full break with Gutenberg's movable metal type. Edmund Uher took out international patents for his system during the

Below: book cover designed by Stanley Morison for Gollancz, early 1930s, one of many typographically adventurous covers by Morison for this publisher, making a virtue out of cheap, two-colour covers with no illustration. A consistent use of yellow paper with magenta and black printing developed into the Gollancz identity, while Morison's mixtures of fonts and exploration of decorative elements from the type case more than compensated for the absence of other expressive elements.

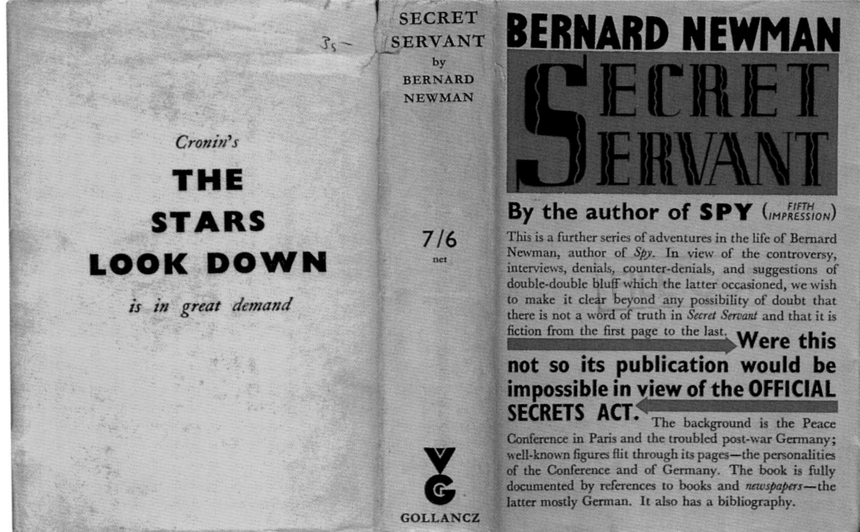

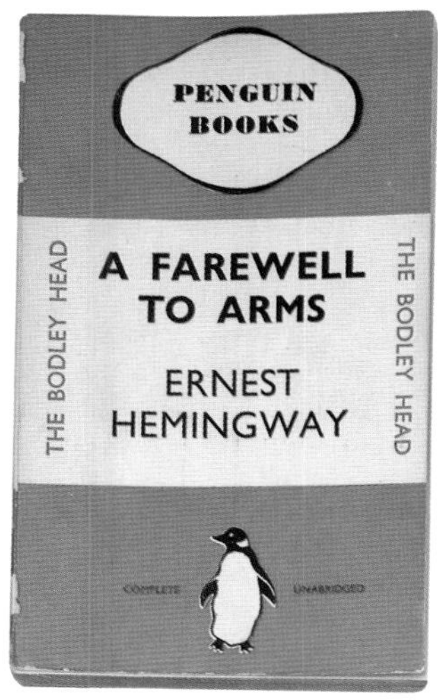


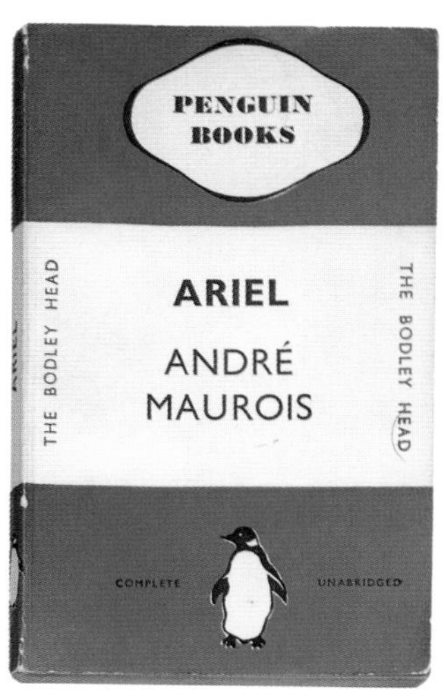


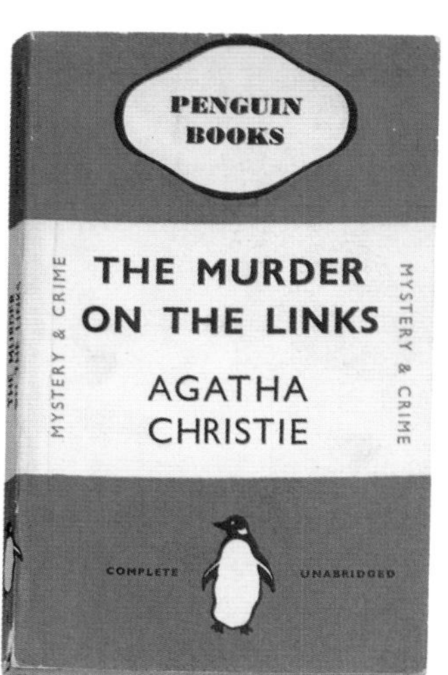

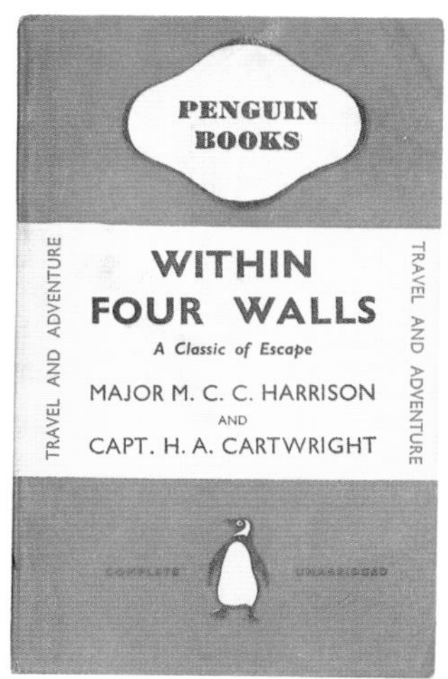

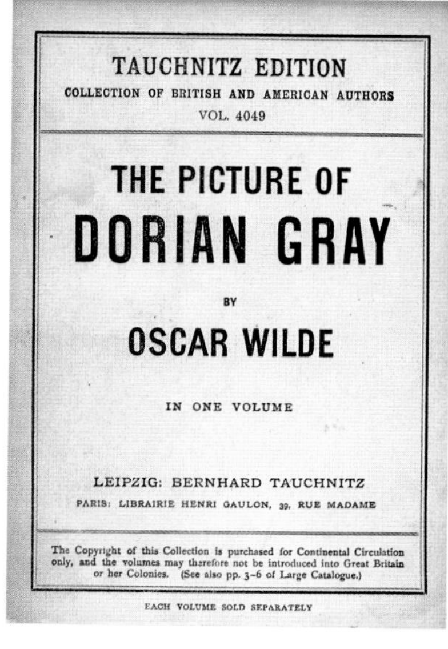

Left: early Penguin book covers from 1935 onwards. This London publishing house was to the fore in taking the cheap paperback format and using it for more upmarket books, which required a new graphic language. Gill Sans was used for the covers and Times New Roman for the text, both recently designed faces. The publisher Allen Lane and designer Edward Young drew on the example of the Hamburg-based Albatross editions (below), designed by Giovanni Mardersteig, which combined clean typography with strong, simple, colour-coded covers. These in turn had developed from the Tauchnitz paperbacks (below left).

Below far left: *AC 2* was the second issue of a short-lived Barcelona periodical espousing the modern movement in architecture. Its exploration of a square format, and a grid layout derived from the square, with Futura as the sole typeface, demonstrates the spread into Spain of northern European ideas.

1930s; his proposals involved both a keyboard and a manually set method of instructing the exposure of type design carried on a glass cylinder on to photosensitive paper. Jan Tschichold was commissioned by Uher while he was still in Munich to design promotional material and also to develop new typefaces. He is said to have designed around ten faces for the company in 1933, but unfortunately none of the drawings appears to have survived a change of policy at the company. In 1935 a specimen book of Uhertype hand-settings was released, designed by Imre Reiner to show how flexible the new process could be for innovative typography. Uher's was not the only phototypesetting development – other patents were lodged, other companies founded to offer services. In New York, Photo-Lettering Inc. offered a service of photocomposed display lettering using the Rutherford Photo-Letter Composing Machine, launched in 1933. This machine had similar features to the Uher invention in that it carried the character images on a glass slide, which was moved in front of the light source to expose various letters, the images passing through a focusing lens on to photosensitive paper. The method and control was crude; there was still plenty of development to be done, but the basis for a new understanding of type and print production was being established. Almost twenty years would pass, however, before the new phototypesetting technology became established in commercial use.



Below left: a spread from *An Essay on Typography* by Eric Gill, published by Hague & Gill, 1931. Here Gill set forward his typographic philosophy and he practised what he preached: the main text is in his recently cut Joanna face, in unjustified ranged left setting, twelve points with four points of leading.

Below and right: drawings made by Eric Gill for the first version of his sans serif type, produced for the London & North Eastern Railway. One shows the "g" (1928); the other combines "B", "P", "R" and "S" (1932). The LNER adopted Gill Sans for all advertising, signage applications and timetables.

48

It is clear that for any letter there is some sort of norm. To discover this norm is obviously the first thing to be done.

¶ The first notable attempt to work out the norm for plain letters was made by Mr. Edward Johnston when he designed the sans-serif letter for the London Underground Railways. Some of these letters are not entirely satisfactory, especially when it is remembered that, for such a purpose, an alphabet should be as near as possible 'fool-proof', i.e. the forms should be measurable, patient of dialectical exposition, as the philosophers would say—nothing should be left to the imagination of the signwriter or the enamel plate maker. In this quality of 'fool-proofness' the Monotype sans-serif face (figure 15)

ABCDEFGHIJKL
MNOPQRSTUV
WXYZÆ&Œ
1234567890

Figure 15: Monotype Sans-serif

49

is perhaps an improvement. The letters are more strictly normal—freer from forms depending upon appreciation and critical ability in the workman who has to reproduce them.

¶ But, as there is a norm of letter form—the bare body, so to say, of letters—there is also a norm of letter clothes; or rather there are many norms according as letters are used for this place or purpose or that. Between the occasion wherein the pure sans-serif or mono-line (block) letter is appropriate & that in which nothing is more appropriate than pure fancifulness (see fig. 17; 9–13, 15 &16), there are innumerable occasions.

¶ A typically moral and conscientious Englishman finds it exceedingly difficult to keep morals out of art talk; he finds himself inclined to think, e.g. that R ought to have a bow more or less semi-circular and of a diameter about half the height of the stem, & a strongly outstanding tail; that an R with a very large bow and hardly any tail at all is wrong. But such moral notions as the word 'ought' implies, & such words as 'right' & 'wrong'—taken as having a moral connotation—are obviously absurd in such a discussion, and we should be ready to admit that any old shape will do to make a letter with. Never-

d

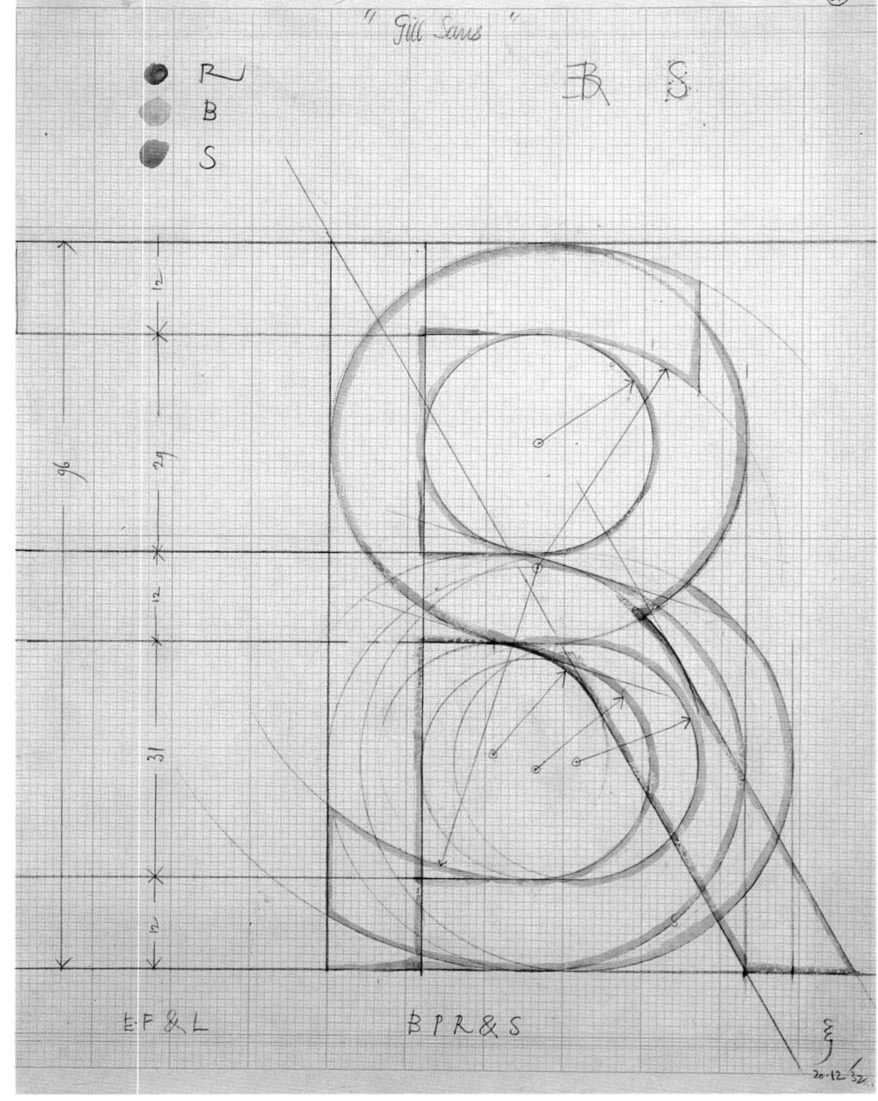

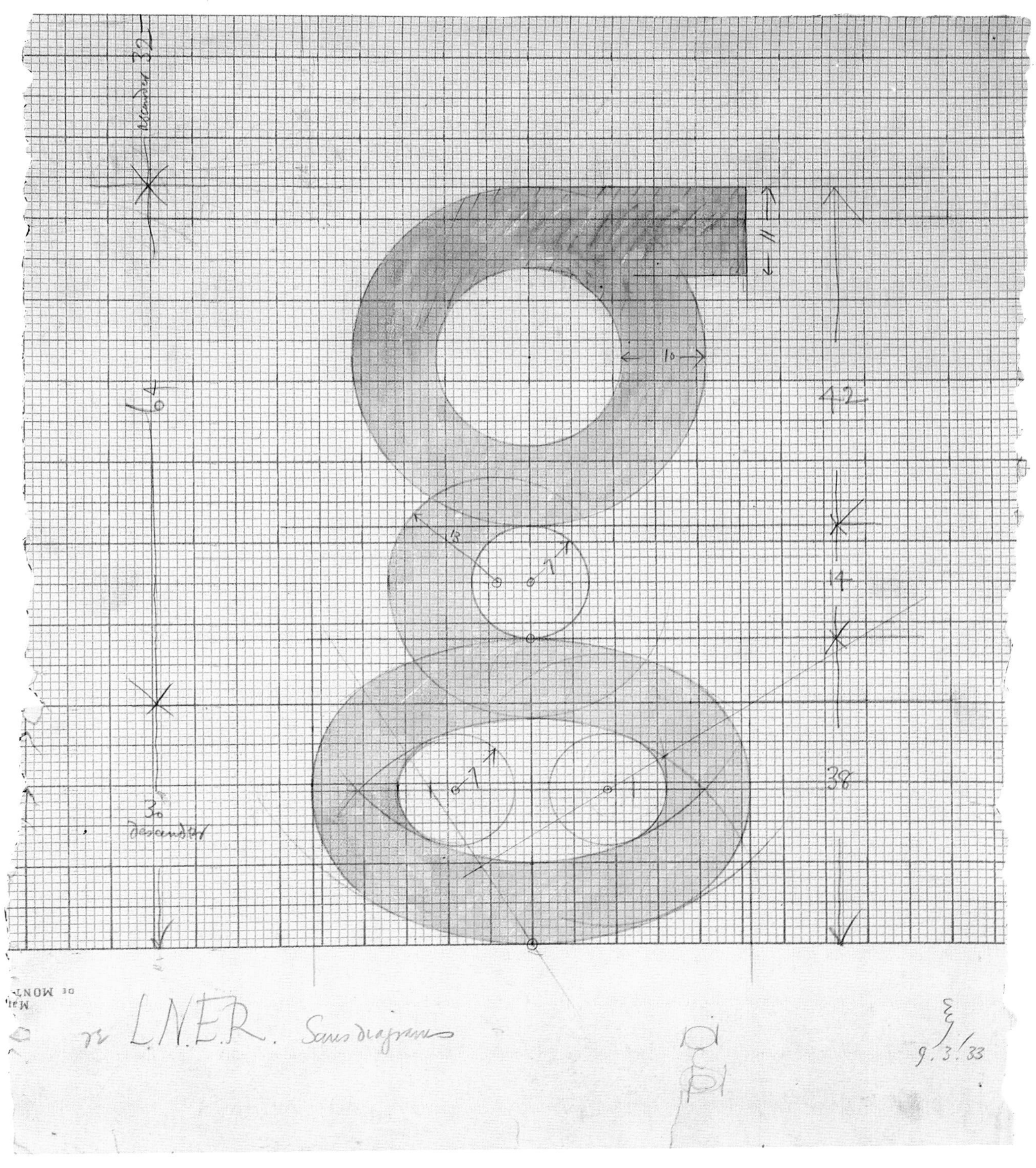
ascender 32
64
42
11
10
13
7
14
38
30
descender
L.N.E.R. Sans diagrams
9.3.33

1940...

The Second World War delayed the technological and commercial advance of many of the new ideas that had been vaunted in the years before 1939. It was a while after 1945 before the investment and development of many foundries, publishing companies and the wider communication and industrial context for typography such as television rose to levels that supported the cutting of new faces or spawned interesting new opportunities.

But war generates its own distinct demand for graphic design in the form of government information, particularly the powerful propaganda statement of the poster. In the US and Britain at least there were posters that drew on the more experimental output of the preceding years to give a new punch to their messages, and they were often the work of the leading European designers of the pre-war era. The US effort in this regard combined young American Modernists with European exiles: the Office of War Information commissioned such prominent designers as the Austrian Joseph Binder, the Italian Leo Lionni and the Frenchman Jean Carlu to create posters. The exiles' effort was also being mounted by Bayer, Matter and others for the Container Corporation of America's innovative series of promotions. These were more in the nature of art works than advertising; during the war they focused on helping the cause, and the most prominent contribution to advertising was their appropriation of key philosophical tracts, partly reworked into ads as a pitching of sponsored values. Typographic form had an important role to play in avoiding the crass language of advertising while remaining approachable and being bold.

Profil, designed by Eugen and Max Lenz for Haas, 1946. The exaggerated three-dimensional effect of a drop shadow and outline around the inclined bold figures creates a powerful, if crude, display face.

The immigrant designers clearly arrived with a ready-made approach, which had an immediate impact on the American scene. With Brodovitch and Agha art-directing the leading fashion magazines as well, the accession of a new typography to power at the heart of the world's most effective commercial force was achieved. At the same time, these designers took on board some new influences, evolving around the key Modernist principles of concentrating on the representation of a core message with a pared-down range of typefaces and stripped-away ornament.

New York was the centre of graphic design activity and was the proving ground for the interplay of the new ideas with the vernacular. The results are apparent in the work of what is sometimes called the "New York School" of American designers – Lester Beall (1903–69), Paul Rand (born 1914) and Bradbury Thompson (born 1911) being among the best known. Rand's prominent working life stretches across fifty years, from art-directing *Apparel Arts*, *Direction* and then *Esquire* magazines in the late 1930s to doing corporate consultancy work for IBM and writing in the 1980s. In the 1940s his work as an advertising art director at the Weintraub agency saw him encouraging higher standards for advertising layouts. Today's concept of the art director and copywriter team is in part based on his work with Bill Bernbach. Until much later in many agencies, the copywriter was king and the art director was a designer down the corridor, required to create something around a given idea rather than to contribute to an advertisement that had its elements integrated, a method which enables a much more expressive approach to be taken to typography as it can contain the idea, instead of simply carrying it. Rand and Bernbach's work for Ohrbach's department store is an example of this integration in action: logo, type, handwritten elements and illustration might all be mixed together, laid down without recourse to justified or centred type, perhaps using lines of type running at an angle – and the result would be entirely controlled, almost orderly, yet dynamic. Rand was aware of the new typography and some of his work of this era shows its influence strongly. But the freedom of his layouts and choice of type and mixing of faces had a sense of gaiety and a feel for the American commercial vernacular. In 1946 he wrote *Thoughts On Design*, an influential statement of his principles which laid down a marker in the coming of age of American graphics as a powerful theoretical force, rather than one always to be a recipient of ideas. Rand's career is characterised by a bringing together of larger visual ideas from fine art, recognising at the same time the case for an almost scientific approach to the issue of legibility with type. In *Thoughts On Design* he wrote of the need for typographic and visual communications to display "the integration of the beautiful and the useful". These two aspects were, ideally, linked; they would be arrived at together, with the right methodology and talent in a designer.

From the typographer's perspective the high points in Bradbury Thompson's long career centre on the years during which he was designer and editor of the promotional publication *Westvaco Inspirations*, between 1939 and 1961. His adventurous experiments with layouts that explored the processes of print and punned on the potential of type and image were more than just fun: they sought out a deep appropriateness of form for the subject. Thompson also designed *Mademoiselle* magazine from 1945 to 1959, art-directed *Art News* for twenty-seven years and, later in his career, became a prolific designer of fine books. But perhaps his most provocative contribution was his development of the single alphabet idea of Bayer and others when in 1946 he published his "mono alphabet". Like Bayer, Thompson proposed that the lower case alphabet only should be used. Experimenting with Futura, he developed a set of notions for making this proposal work, including beginning sentences with a full stop, or using a bolder weight of letter in replacement of the capital letter. In 1950 he presented a further refinement on the simplified alphabet idea, called Alphabet 26. Instead of the 45 different characters that exist in the upper and lower case



Right: "This is Nazi Brutality", poster for the US Office of War Information by Ben Shahn, 1943. The tension of the subject matter is brought out by the tension in the layout: the vertical stress of the figure is contrasted with the diagonals of the walls closing in around the prisoner, while the slapped-down, telegram-style message appropriates a familiar typographic image to suggest urgency. Sans serif is the almost automatic choice for a headline. Below: recently arrived US resident Herbert Bayer added the Bauhaus training to the war effort, with a minimal statement expressed in apparently naive terms which involves considerable control. The shift of colours and their application to the lettering, combined with the stark upper-case presentation with the quality of a stamped-out block, then the subtlety of the smaller but attention-drawing diagonally ranged line "your farm can help", all make for a bold and original piece of propaganda that draws on the psychology of typographic associations in the reader's mind.

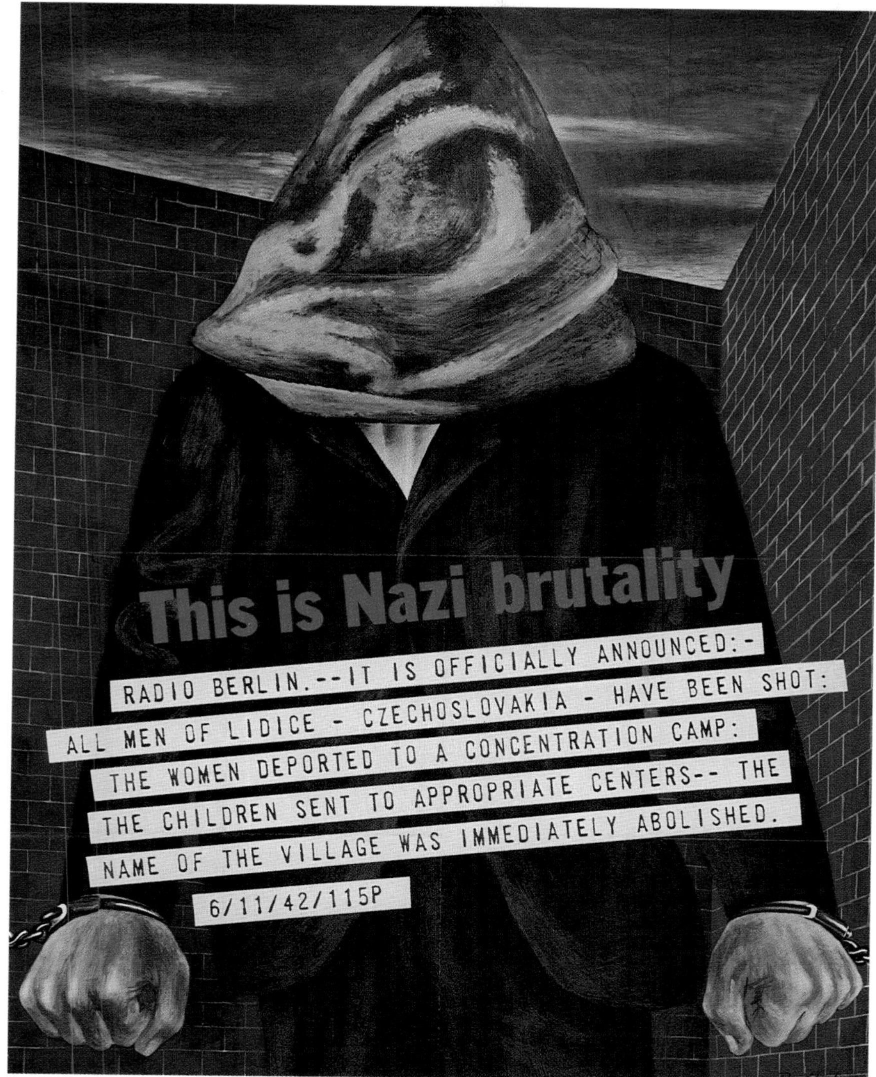


Below: front cover of *Scope* magazine, March 1948, designed by Lester Beall for the Upjohn Corporation. Beall was a master of tints and layering to create three-dimensional effects: here he plays with the sense of depth on the page, shifting impressions of the crab, placing it against the globe drawing, and floating a letterspaced italic across it. This illustrative technique is extended into the masthead, with the contrast of outline lettering with solid, heavy colours against light, and the shifting off from a baseline.

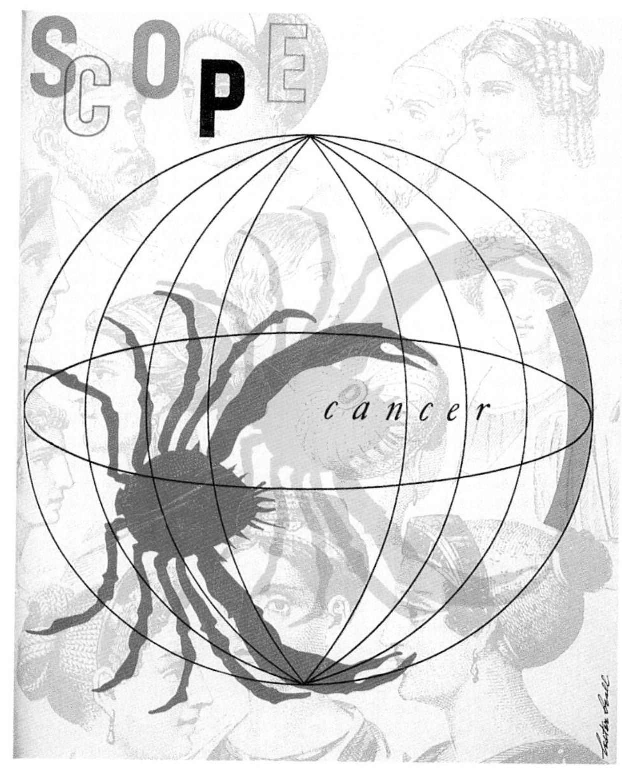


Left: spread from *Scope* magazine, June 1944, designed by Lester Beall. Beall managed to give a powerful drama even to something as technical and unglamorous as the life cycle of the malaria parasite. The egg-shaped copy block gives a dramatic, diagonal quartering of the spread, and controls the size of the pictures in a way that expresses the stages of evolution. Despite a mass of different data, only two sizes of type are used.

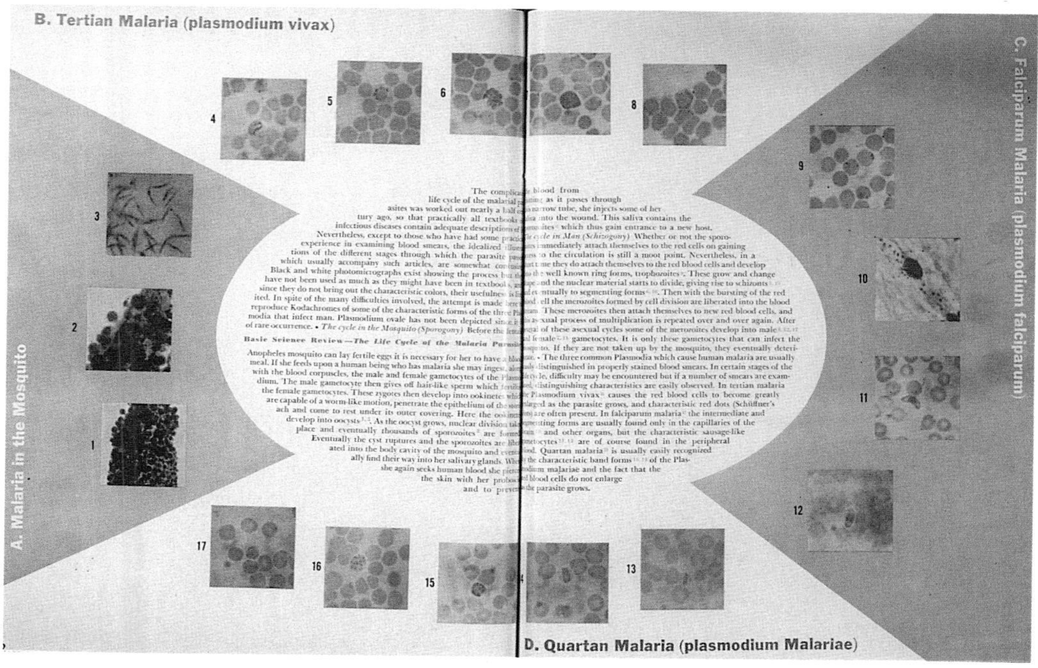

alphabets, Thompson took those that he saw as the most distinctive symbols for each letter. He did not design a new face for this exercise, but took an existing one – Baskerville. The use of a traditional face rather than a more modern one such as Futura was deliberate and related to the intention that the face should be more recognisable, not a radical innovation but a concentration on what is at the heart of familiar type forms. Later Thompson drew a refined version of the characters so that the large and small versions worked elegantly together. Although the idea is still entirely experimental, it also has points to commend it – particularly for the teaching of reading and writing.

Lester Beall's first flush of fame predated both Rand and Thompson, arising in the 1930s from his poster work for the Rural Electrification Administration. Against a background of the Depression, Beall produced images that were stark and unglamorous, yet promoted the message that attempts were being made to solve America's problems. The type has the warmth and crudeness of the wood-letter tradition of the local printer knocking out a poster and this element – usually for a simple phrase – is set with a bold, indeed raw illustration or

Designs by Paul Rand. Below and right: spread and cover for *Mechanized Mules Of Victory*, 1942, a book recording the Autocar Corporation's production of vehicles for the war effort. The stencil stamp of the title on the cover opens on to a dramatic series of spreads that set the text in a typewriter face, full out without margins across the bottom third of the page, with sharply contrasting crops and sizes of images placed above. There is a textural quality to the type: Rand

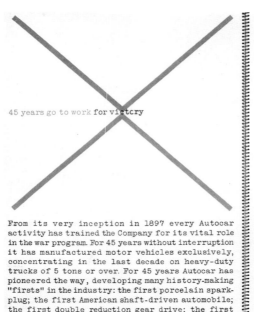

45 years go to work for victory

From its very inception in 1897 every Autocar activity has trained the Company for its vital role in the war program. For 45 years without interruption it has manufactured motor vehicles exclusively, concentrating in the last decade on heavy-duty trucks of 5 tons or over. For 45 years Autocar has pioneered the way, developing many history-making "firsts" in the industry: the first porcelain spark-plug; the first American shaft-driven automobile; the first double reduction gear drive; the first circulating oil system. For 45 years Autocar insistence on mechanical perfection has wrought a tradition of precision that is honored by every one of its master workers. These are achievements that only time can win. The harvest of these years, of this vast experience, is at the service of our government. Autocar is meeting its tremendous responsibility to national defense by putting its 45 years' experience to work in helping to build for America a motorized armada such as the world has never seen.

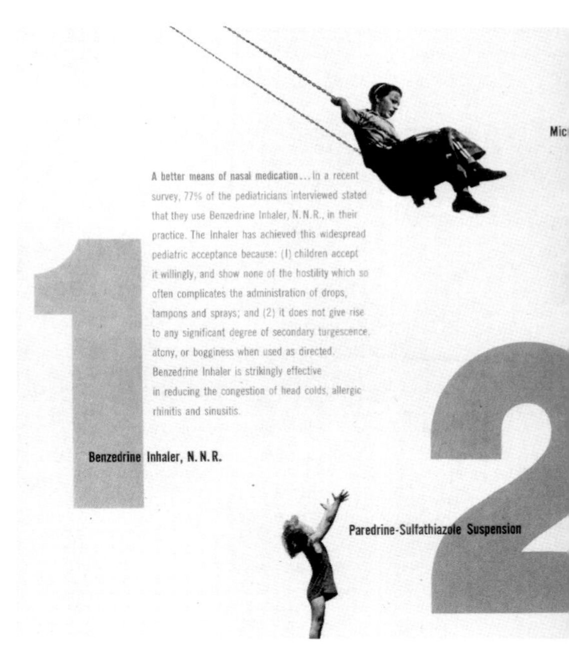
A better means of nasal medication... In a recent survey, 77% of the pediatricians interviewed stated that they use Benzedrine Inhaler, N.N.R., in their practice. The Inhaler has achieved this widespread pediatric acceptance because: (I) children accept it willingly, and show none of the hostility which so often complicates the administration of drops, tampons and sprays; and (2) it does not give rise to any significant degree of secondary turgescence, atony, or bogginess when used as directed. Benzedrine Inhaler is strikingly effective in reducing the congestion of head colds, allergic rhinitis and sinusitis.
1
Benzedrine Inhaler, N. N. R.
2
Paredrine-Sulfathiazole Suspension

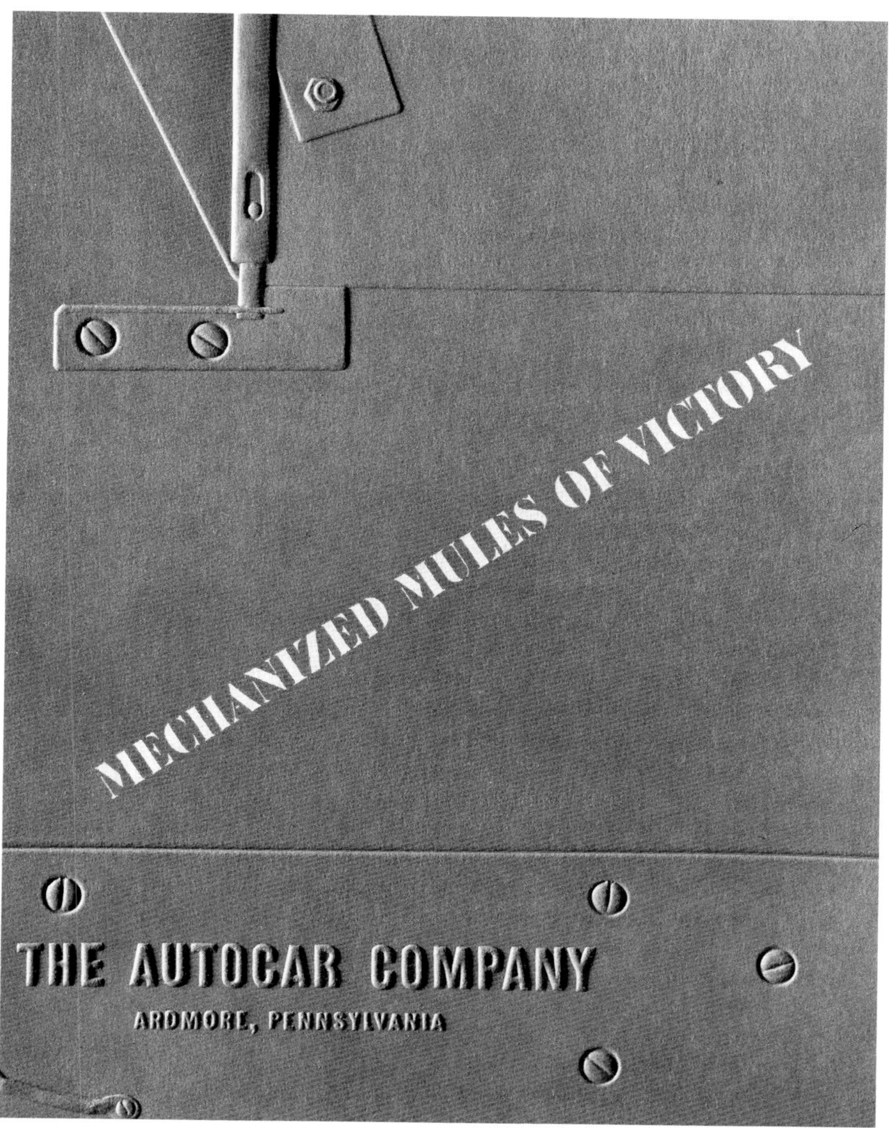


said he was aiming for the reader to sense the metal type. Stencil and typewriter suggest a basic functionality and are also highly recognisable and therefore readable. The book was spiral-bound, adding to its manual-like appearance. Below: spread from a prospectus for Smith Kline & French, 1945, a mass of data controlled and made dynamic by typographic devices. Rand used numbers to give rhythm and immediacy and described their power on the page as being "the visual equivalent of time, space, position and quantity". They stagger the reader's progress across the page, giving a sense of positioning, location and awareness of the three key points being made. A light, condensed sans serif, opened up with heavy leading, enables a large amount of information to be placed on the page without overwhelming the imagery. Below left: film poster, 1950. White space, a bold visual pun, and a clear ordering of the typographic elements drawing the eye from the title to the top corner and then the cast list provide a dramatic contrast with the prevailing vernacular on a London street corner.

3

Suspension, 20%

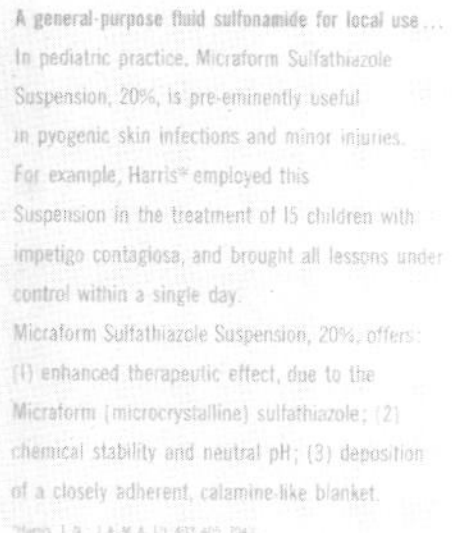
A general-purpose fluid sulfonamide for local use…
In pediatric practice, Micraform Sulfathiazole
Suspension, 20%, is pre-eminently useful
in pyogenic skin infections and minor injuries.
For example, Harris* employed this
Suspension in the treatment of 15 children with
impetigo contagiosa, and brought all lessons under
control within a single day.
Micraform Sulfathiazole Suspension, 20%, offers:
(1) enhanced therapeutic effect, due to the
Micraform (microcrystalline) sulfathiazole; (2)
chemical stability and neutral pH; (3) deposition
of a closely adherent, calamine-like blanket.

ary advance in intranasal sulfonamide
ecause it provides vasoconstriction
and bacteriostasis for hours, Paredrine
Suspension is prescribed by many
. Of this outstanding vasoconstrictor
, Livingston* in the "Proceedings"
h annual meeting of the American
Pediatrics, states:
nsion…may shorten the course of the
d and tend to prevent complications."
have noted the "absence of clumping
tion, and negligible absorption into
eam. They…obtained excellent results."

photomontage. Old-fashioned sans serifs or stencil cuts, often in upper case, reinforced this exploitation of the vernacular. In the 1940s the self-taught Beall moved on with further commercial commissions that drew afresh on the asymmetric and layering techniques of Modernist typographers. In his art direction of the Upjohn Company's *Scope* magazine (a scientific periodical) Beall produced layouts of a fine sophistication, combining hints of classicism and the new typography on one layout without seeming chaotic.

While the emigré Europeans and emerging school of home-grown talents fed on the still-active commercial scene of the US, along with occasional war effort pieces, there is comparatively little to show for those who remained in Europe. Rationed paper, conscripted troops and the removal of other resources for print and design work brought development to a virtual halt. But, as in the US, there was some poster art of note: in Britain Modernist design was promoted as the official line when the Ministry of Information asked Tom Eckersley, Abram Games and F. H. K. Henrion to produce posters. Their work displays an illustrative style drawing on art movements from Cubism to Surrealism, but in the type there is a fresh voice: as with the American designers of the same period, a reference to the vernacular appears in the lettering. Stencil cuts and Victorian-style playbill lettering found new uses, along with older sans faces and a few others. In other words, these desginers were breaking loose from the recent orthodoxy that had been settling in – the new typography was expanding to embrace the old, but keeping the flexibility that determined a functional form.

There was little incorporation of the new with the old for Jan Tschichold, however. As mentioned in the previous chapter, his role as high priest of the new typography had changed to that of apostle of the classical revival. During the war years he designed a series of book covers for the publisher Birkhauser as well as carrying out researches into type and calligraphic areas, the results of which appeared in his own books and articles. The Birkhauser books are the blueprint for the work Tschichold was to do when he was invited in 1946 to come and develop the design of the fast-growing paperback publisher Penguin. He arrived in London in 1947 and began what he saw as a massive task: essentially the provision of a new corporate identity for the whole range of existing Penguin products, as well as the design of new books.

Tschichold's impact can easily be seen by contrasting the earlier Penguins with the later ones: new type, new spacing, even a new penguin. The neatly centred, generously spaced, almost understated covers are unassuming from the designer's ego perspective – the effect is the assertion of many classic values of book design. As said above, there are similarities with Tschichold's earlier work and a strong reference must be seen in the work of the fine typographer and printer Giovanni Mardersteig (1892–1977) on the Albatross books in the 1930s. Tschichold realised that the clue to the typography of mass-production books was to devise an approach to communication and design *and implementation* that was rigorously applied. The Penguin Composition Rules were the result of Tschichold's concern to ensure that the various printers and typesetters who took on Penguin work would understand the requirements and work to them. Grids were produced for the different series, an innovation for the publisher. No hard and fast rules were set for typefaces: each book was tackled on its own merits, albeit jacket design elements fitted in with the identities for the various series. But every cover, title page and run of body text was deemed to be part of an individual work that had to have its own coherence, as indeed it

Right: poster for motor racing at Monza, Italy, by Max Huber, 1948. Tricks with perspective here give a great sense of movement to the page: the type is disappearing into the distance, while the arrows give a forward motion. Different sizes of lettering and different inks laid over each other give further depth to the image. The potential for distorted type to integrate dramatically with an image and yet remain readable prefigures the flexibility of photocomposition, digital composition and computerised type handling. Huber (born 1919) studied in Zürich and worked with the Studio Boggeri designers in Milan.

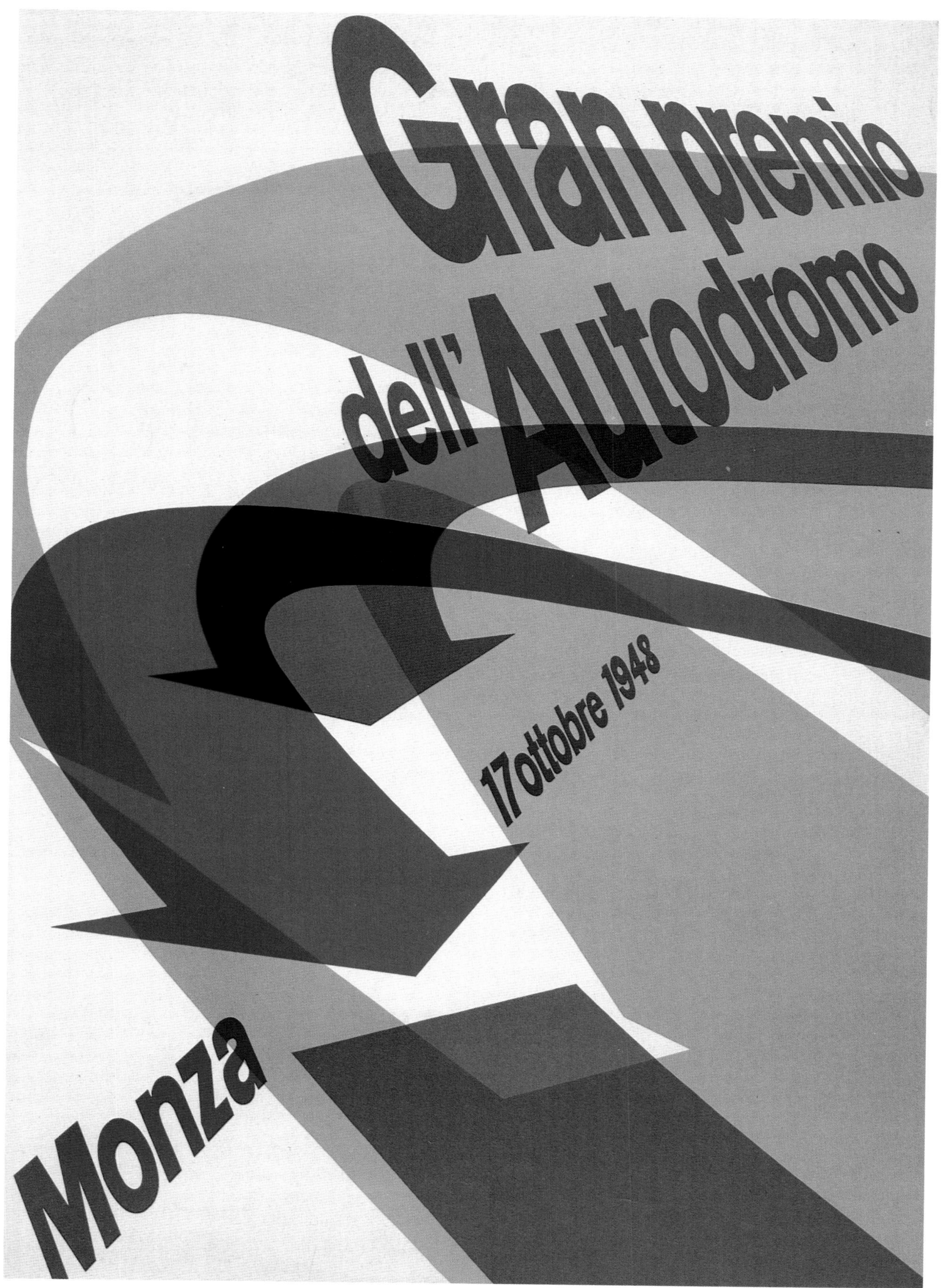
Gran premio
dell' Autodromo
17 ottobre 1948
Monza

would have to in order to survive in front of the reader. Legibility, clarity and elegance were apparent throughout. Tschichold worked on more than five hundred books before returning to Switzerland in December 1949, and long after he left many of his rules continued to be applied by his successor Hans Schmoller.

Tschichold's rejection of his earlier principles and embracing of traditional forms earned him a severe attack from the pen of the Swiss designer Max Bill in 1946, following the report of a lecture Tschichold had given. Bill's comments attacked the "threadbare" and "reactionary" quality of Tschichold's arguments, which prompted the victim to hit back with a long reply[1] outlining his position on Modernism versus classicism and showing that, if anything, the threadbare and reactionary labels were more appropriate for his critic's arguments. In his impasssioned defence Tschichold positioned traditional typefaces and layouts as representative of a rich, organic process understood and appreciated by many and contrasting with the arcane and absolute new rules of the Modernist typography. The celebration of mechanisation was attacked as a dehumanising and essentially pointless concern. He also criticised the obsession with sans serif faces, saying they were fine for some display work but not suitable for text, and he praised the functional stripping away of superfluous elements advocated by the new typography, celebrating its contribution of increased awareness of compositional quality. But, with a sense of irony, he pointed out that many of the new typography rules obeyed by Bill were set down by him, Tschichold, and he had not rejected those points in his apparently "reactionary" move.

In passing, Tschichold acknowledged the debt he felt was owed to Stanley Morison and his colleagues at Monotype for the rebirth and development of so many classic types, an undertaking which had "brought with it a typographic revival the world over that is as important as the cleaning-up process of the new typography was for Germany". In 1946, the principles of that rebirth were crystallised in a slim volume written by the man who was instrumental in advising the choice of Tschichold for the Penguin job, Oliver Simon. In the 1920s Simon had been the editor of the first four issues of *The Fleuron*, preceding those edited by Morison, and in the 1930s he had run another typographic magazine, *Signature*, while also working as director and typographer of the fine book printer The Curwen Press. Now, in his *Introduction To Typography*, Simon set down the principles of good practice in book typography of the kind Tschichold and Morison admired, and good printers knew by heart. It was written for the young printers, publishers and other interested parties who were to be involved in the rapid growth of post-war printing. The volume went into a number of editions, and can be seen as a further propagator of the orthodox standing firm against the Modernists. It did not even mention their new typography or those designers associated with it.

Opposite: book covers from 1943 onwards designed by Jan Tschichold after his rejection of the new typography and his revival of traditional values. Above are two covers he designed for Birkhäuser in Basel with (below) three covers that resulted from his reshaping of Penguin typography from the sober styling and colour-coding of The Penguin Classics and The Buildings of England series to the less heavily branded Puffin books for children. Inside, the text typography obeyed strict composition rules that demanded close word-spacing, letterspacing of words in capitals, indents of one em for paragraphs, and so on. Tschichold's masterplans of typographic detail were followed by Penguin throughout the 1950s, and were implemented by his successor as art director, Hans Schmoller.

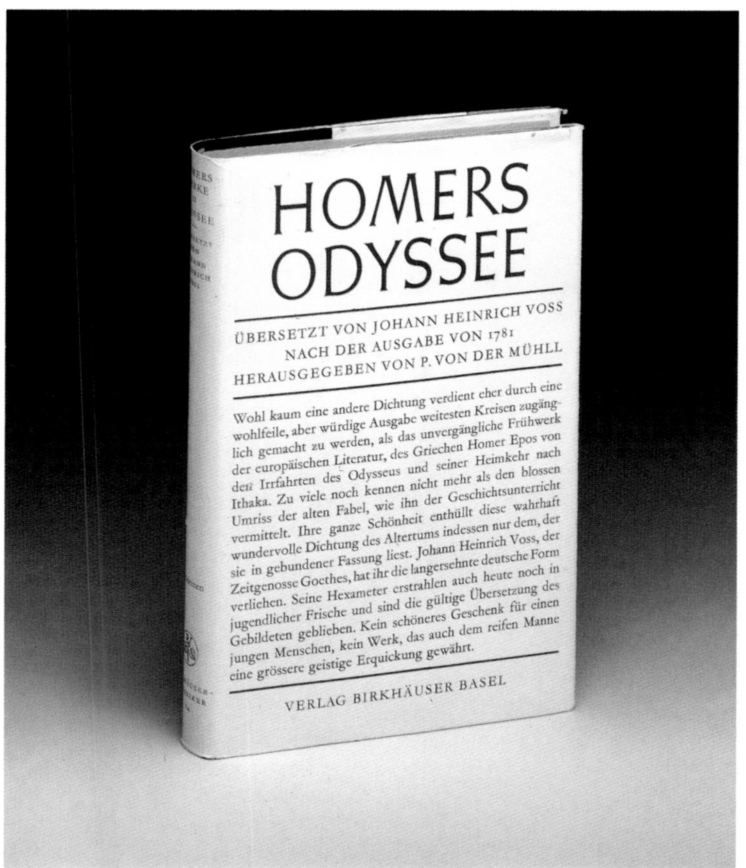
HOMERS
ODYSSEE
ÜBERSETZT VON JOHANN HEINRICH VOSS
NACH DER AUSGABE VON 1781
HERAUSGEGEBEN VON P. VON DER MÜHLL
Wohl kaum eine andere Dichtung verdient eher durch eine wohlfeile, aber würdige Ausgabe weitesten Kreisen zugänglich gemacht zu werden, als das unvergängliche Frühwerk der europäischen Literatur, des Griechen Homer Epos von den Irrfahrten des Odysseus und seiner Heimkehr nach Ithaka. Zu viele noch kennen nicht mehr als den blossen Umriss der alten Fabel, wie ihn der Geschichtsunterricht vermittelt. Ihre ganze Schönheit enthüllt diese wahrhaft wundervolle Dichtung des Altertums indessen nur dem, der sie in gebundener Fassung liest. Johann Heinrich Voss, der Zeitgenosse Goethes, hat ihr die langersehnte deutsche Form verliehen. Seine Hexameter erstrahlen auch heute noch in jugendlicher Frische und sind die gültige Übersetzung des Gebildeten geblieben. Kein schöneres Geschenk für einen jungen Menschen, kein Werk, das auch dem reifen Manne eine grössere geistige Erquickung gewährt.
VERLAG BIRKHÄUSER BASEL

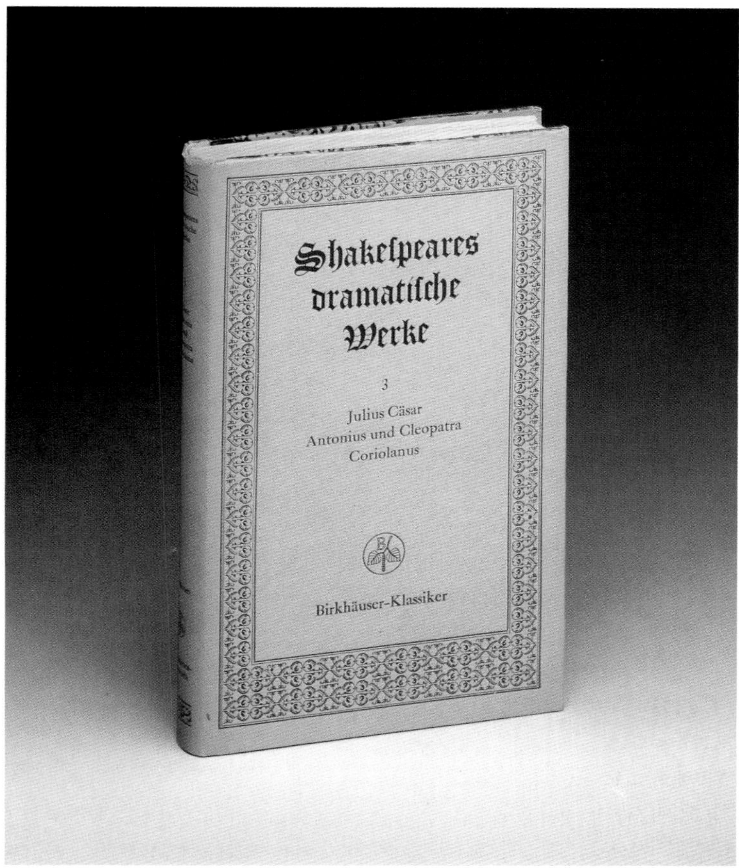
Shakespeares
dramatische
Werke
3
Julius Cäsar
Antonius und Cleopatra
Coriolanus
Birkhäuser-Klassiker

YOUNG
WALTER SCOTT
E. J. GRAY

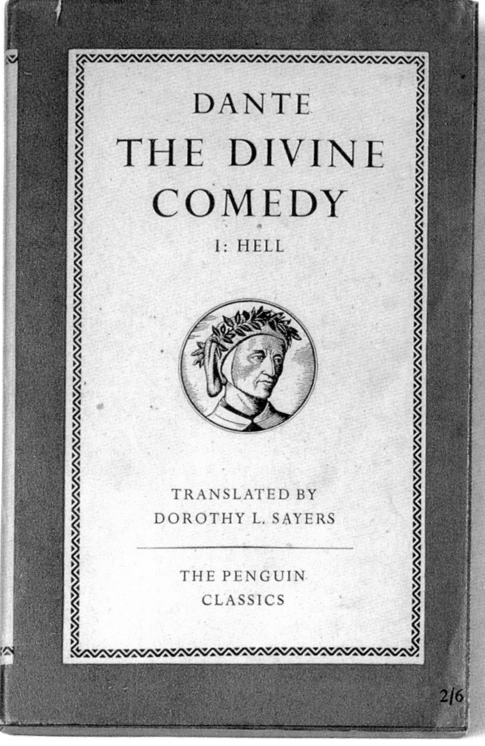
DANTE
THE DIVINE
COMEDY
1: HELL
TRANSLATED BY
DOROTHY L. SAYERS
THE PENGUIN
CLASSICS
2/6

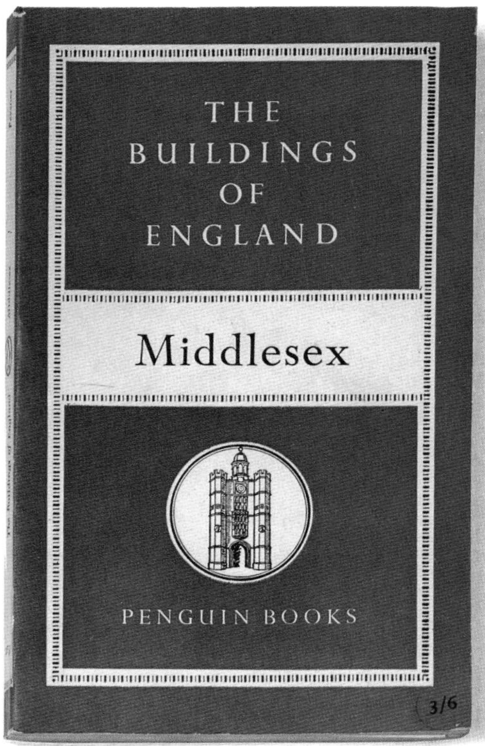
THE
BUILDINGS
OF
ENGLAND
Middlesex
PENGUIN BOOKS
3/6

HelveticaHelveticaHelvetic
HelveticaHelveticaHelvetica
HelveticaHelvetica

# 1950...

More new technology and new ideas: Swiss-style rationalism in the perspective games of the advertising for Helvetica and Adrian Frutiger's innovative descriptive system for Univers (the title "1950" is set in four weights ranging from the light of Univers 45, through 55, 65 and 75). Right are details of the three faces that made Hermann Zapf's reputation: Melior, 1952 (top); Optima, 1958 (centre); Palatino, 1950 (bottom). "Le Roi" is set in Choc, 1953, one of several highly popular French faces used for advertising.

Far right: two early photosetting systems. On the left is the intertype Fotosetter, reputed to be the first machine that could cope with commercial operation; in many ways, it was imitative of the operation of a hot-metal setter except that the individual letter matrix was on film and, rather than metal, light was poured into it to expose the film. On the right, a Monophoto Filmsetter from Monotype, featuring a film matrix case containing a character set that moved into position under the light source on instruction from the keyboard.

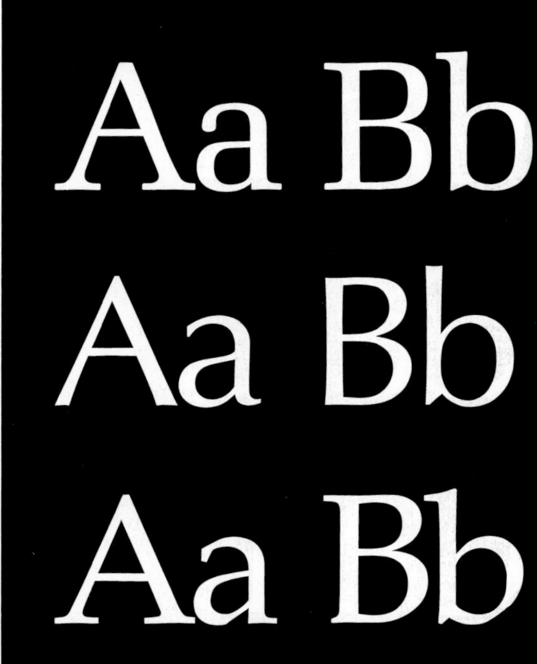

As industry recovered from the Second World War, so the demand for printed material rose to new heights. The multiplying mass of business communications and packaging added to the growth in consumer publishing. Such developing markets for the type designer and the typographer, coupled with the changing technologies of printing machines and the materials on to which their work could be applied, called for the practical application and refinement of the fairly theoretical ideas originating in the 1920s and tried out thereafter. This applied both to the development of new faces and their implementation.

"Typography is fundamentally two-dimensional architecture", wrote the distinguished type designer Hermann Zapf (born 1918) in his 1954 book of typographic quotes and exercises, *Manuale Typographicum*, in which he collected and displayed a range of quotes on type and typography in a variety of visual explorations. In doing so he illustrated the attitude underlying the book, which was produced on the cusp of a further explosion in the quantity and diversity of typographic communication. For any questioning of the need for yet more new faces and the reason that typography should not be contained statically by a set of rigid rules as to good practice (in the way that language teachers might seek to simplify the rules for spoken grammar), Zapf had a measured response:

***The letters in-dwelling wealth of form is a fresh, unending astonishment. As there are many splendid types of earlier centuries that we still gladly use in printing, it may perhaps be asked why new types are designed. Our time, however, sets the designer other tasks than did the past. A new type must, along with beauty and legibility, be adapted to the technical requirements of today, when***

Cc Dd
Cc Dd
Cc Dd

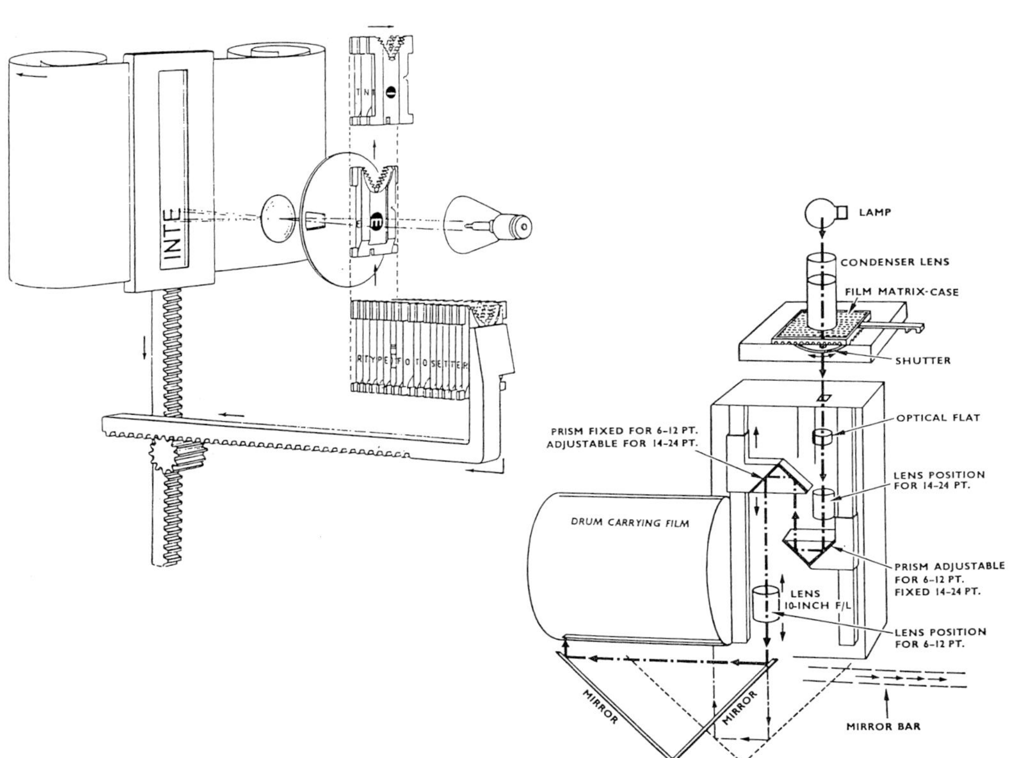

***high-speed presses and rotary presses have replaced the hand press, and machine-made paper supplanted the handmade sheet. Just as musicians and artists seek to create some new expression of our time and link it to a rich past, so too must the work of type designers and type founders remain bound to the great tradition of the alphabet.***

While emphasising the vital importance of tradition in its building of a perception of acceptable letterform, Zapf also noted the inevitable requirements for change wrought by new audiences, new media and new technology. And such novelty was infringing on type design and typographic practice from all these areas, once the restricted resources and opportunities of the immediate post-war era ceased (paper rationing, for example, was not lifted in Britain until 1951).

This period also saw the further growth of cinematic and, particularly, television audiences which generated new challenges for the application of type and lettering. The development of moving typographic imagery called for labours similar to those involved in a paint-and-trace animation, an elaborate frame-by-frame drawing. While the movement and flexibility associated with film and broadcast images drew on twentieth-century breakthroughs in scientific understanding, however, the process of creating type was still dependent on materials and processes that were more in keeping with nineteenth-century knowledge.



Below and below right: from Westvaco Inspirations 180, about 1950, designed by Bradbury Thompson. Thompson's constant typographic invention in the corporate booklets from the West Virginia Pulp and Paper Company reached a peak with his "alphabet 26" proposal. Thompson merged the upper and lower cases of Baskerville by selecting only one form of each letter; capitals are simply set larger.
Right: the McDonald's hamburger chain corporate logo "M", in use as concrete arches, 1952. The use of oversized typographic forms in architecture became increasingly prevalent after the war with the growth of the corporate image.

Above: the CBS "eye" logo by Robert Golden, 1951, containing a statement of the company's name and business, became a classic corporate logo. Its simplicity, combined with its widespread dissemination through broadcasting and print, made for an instantly recognisable symbol in which the typographic message is one with the overall image. The positioning of the type reinforces the message that CBS is directly communicating with its audience.

aLPHaBeT 26

THROUGHOUT THIS ISSUE, ONLY ONE SYMBOL FOR EACH OF THE 26 CHARACTERS OF THE ALPHABET IS USED. ORDINARILY, 19 OF THESE CHARACTERS ARE REPRESENTED BY TWO SYMBOLS QUITE UNLIKE IN APPEARANCE. THE OTHER SEVEN CHARACTERS ARE ESSENTIALLY IDENTICAL IN BOTH UPPER- AND LOWER-CASE DESIGN. THIS EXPERIMENT IS BASED ON THE LOGIC, REPRESENTED BY THESE SEVEN LETTERS AND BY THE ILLUSTRATION AT RIGHT, THAT A SYMBOL OR TRADE-MARK OF ANY KIND, TO BE EFFICIENT, SHOULD BE CONSTANT.

IN OBSERVING THE EARLIEST READING EFFORTS OF CHILDREN TODAY WHO ARE TAUGHT TO RECOGNIZE WORDS EVEN BEFORE MEMORIZING INDIVIDUAL LETTERS OF THE ALPHABET, ONE MAY SEE A FALLACY IN SINGLE CHARACTERS HAVING TWO DESIGNS. [SEE BELOW.]

A PREVIOUS EXPERIMENT IN ISSUE 152 ENTITLED THE "MONALPHABET" SUGGESTED THE EXCLUSIVE USE OF THE LOWER-CASE DESIGN FOR ALL CHARACTERS. TO PROVIDE LARGE LETTERS PERFORMING THE FUNCTION OF CAPITALS, THAT PLAN REQUIRES THE REDESIGN OF TRADITIONAL LETTERS WITH ASCENDERS OR DESCENDERS TO ENABLE THEM TO FIT ON THE CUSTOMARY TYPE BODY. WITH "ALPHABET 26," AS THIS PRESENT EXPERIMENT IS CALLED, THE PROBLEM IS AVOIDED BY ELIMINATING DESIGNS HAVING ASCENDERS OR DESCENDERS. THE ALPHABET AT LOWER RIGHT EMPLOYS SOME UPPER-CASE AND SOME LOWER-CASE VERSIONS.

OF IMPORTANT CONSIDERATION ARE THE LETTERS "a, e, m AND n." THE LOWER-CASE DESIGNS ARE SELECTED BECAUSE THEY DO NOT

CONTINUED ON FOLLOWING PAGE

DESIGN AND TYPOGRAPHY OF THIS ISSUE: BRADBURY THOMPSON

A SPADE IS ALWAYS A SPADE

RED CROSS TRADE-MARK IS CONSTANT

a = A

ALL SYMBOLS SHOULD BE UNIFORM

Run Pal.
See him run.
Go Pal.
See him go.

FROM THE ABOVE PAGE OF A FIRST READER, A CHILD LEARNS TO RECOGNIZE THE WORDS "RUN" AND "GO" ONLY TO BE CONFUSED IN THE LINES BELOW BECAUSE THE SAME WORDS ARE DIFFERENT IN APPEARANCE, AS UPPER- AND LOWER-CASE "Rs" AND "Gs" ARE UNLIKE.

aBCDe
FGHIJK
LmnOP
QRSTU
VWXYZ

UPPER-CASE DESIGN IS USED FOR THESE CHARACTERS
LOWER-CASE DESIGN IS USED FOR THESE FOUR CHARACTERS
ONLY ONE DESIGN EXISTS FOR THESE SEVEN CHARACTERS

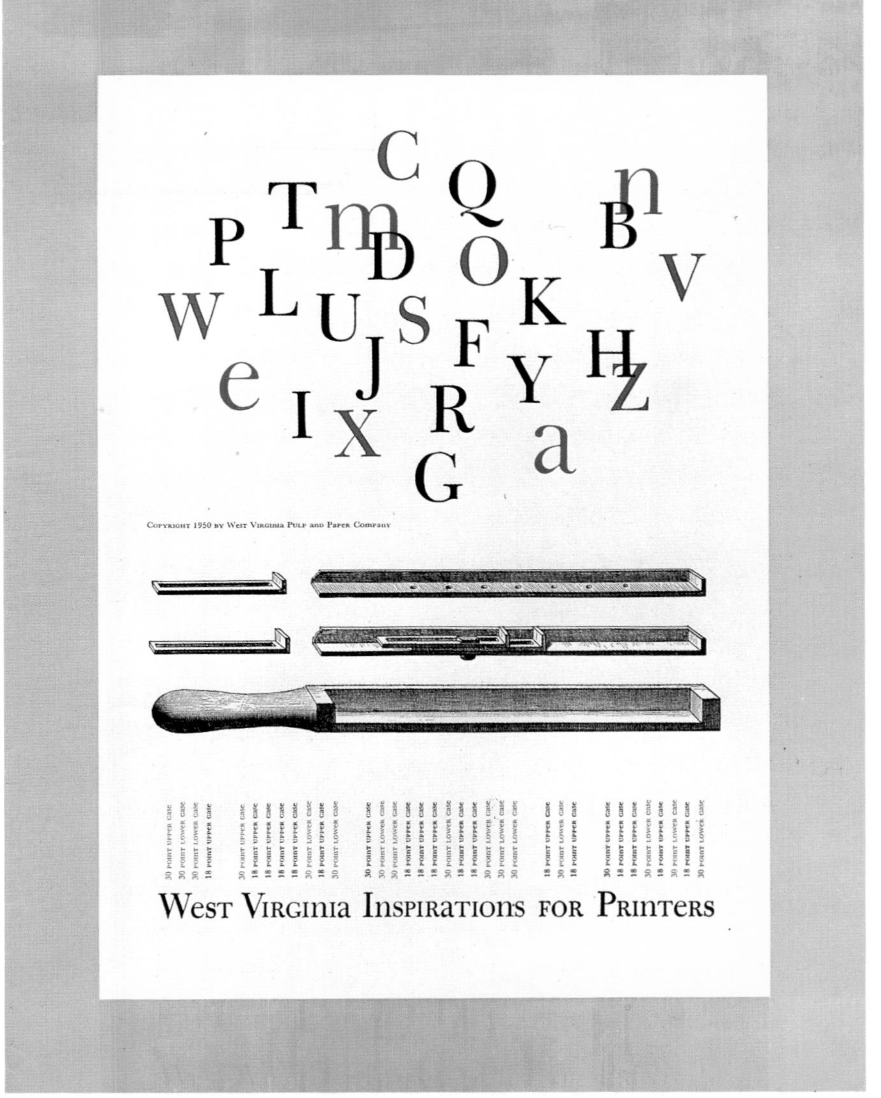


IBM

IBM

IBM

IBM

IBM

IBM

Above: IBM logo, 1956, by Paul Rand: a cluster of square serif capitals which quickly became distinctively IBM. The computer company came early to the realisation that control, rather than quirkiness, was the key to making a corporate identity work through all its applications. At this stage there is no clever symbolism (as came later with the "eye-bee-M" visual pun): instead, the image is a grey-suited one, in which a simple typographic statement is consistently underpinned by strong guidelines on its usage.

Lettering for titles and other screen imagery was as easily created by hand; the alternative of setting the type was an elaborate exercise for the production of a single proof that could be photographed and transferred to film. There was no more efficient way of developing typographic forms – although photosetting would soon clearly offer an alternative based on the processes of film technology. By the 1960s photosetting had clearly gone beyond the experimental and was promising radical change in the process of generating type.

Meanwhile, the 1950s were the final decade of hot metal's unchallenged leadership in typographic communication. Zapf, whose direction straddles tradition and change, produced his most memorable work during these years. In the late 1940s as design director of the Stempel foundry in Germany he drew Palatino, an old-style face that quickly proved a highly popular Italianate cut, displaying the classical sense of proportion and a lightness of form, combined with faint traces of calligraphic flourishes. The strong serifs, distinctively placed on the outside only of the final strokes as if with a lifting pen, couple this sense of penmanship with a strength of line that stands up under indifferent printing or on coarser paper. Palatino is a widely used and elegant face, suitable for finer printing, but soon after producing this design Zapf went on to design Melior, more an outright newspaper face and moving on from old-face Italian characteristics to more modern, contrasting forms, with shorter ascenders and descenders, and some more square letters. The face was specifically produced in 1952 to be suitable for the range of printing processes then current (letterpress and offset) at different qualities. Comparison of the lower case "c" in Melior and Palatino show the breadth of difference in Zapf's approach to the two different romans: the boxy, heavily seriffed, upright stress of the Melior character contrasts with a fluid, obliquely stressed Palatino letter that displays the angle of the pen, making no allowances for the deficiencies of mass printing.

Characteristics of both faces can be found lurking in Zapf's most original face, and the third in this highly active few years, Optima, which first appeared in 1958. Various names exist for this style of face – humanist roman, stressed sans serif, serif-less roman, modified sans serif, calligraphic roman – but it can be seen as a distinct contribution to the search for a face that combined the purity of line of the sans serifs with the flow, and hence readability, of serifs. Not originally intended as a book face, it did acquire popularity as a text face that had some of the overall visual qualities of sans serifs while forming word groupings in the coherent way more readily achieved with seriffed faces. In all three of his notable faces of this period, Zapf displayed the importance of his calligraphic interests (drawing on a long admiration for the work of Rudolf Koch) aligned with a commitment to solving modern technical problems and printing tasks. Optima emerged as a face highly representative of its time in that it threw off the traditions of the text face, yet was also a definite modification of the sans serif movement, softening the principle of the geometric letterform to take in more of the great tradition of the alphabet and its handwritten origins. It draws particularly on Italian inscriptional lettering – Zapf was one of the many typographers to have derived inspiration from the lettering carved on the marble floor tombs at Sante Croce in Florence and on the Arch of Constantine in Rome. There are many examples of Italian inscriptional lettering of the fifteenth century that show this stressed, flexed stroke without serifs: it was the work of Renaissance craftsmen looking for a more dynamic script to suit a time of changing sensibilities.

Right: combined catalogue and poster for a Dada exhibition, designed by Marcel Duchamp, 1953. In contrast to the elusive games played in his own Dadaist art, Duchamp (1887–1968) here produces a striking essay in complex and rigorously functional typography. With two-colour printing on one side of a 20×30 inch sheet Duchamp presents the list of the exhibits, four features on the exhibition, plus a clear announcement readable from across the street. It shows a masterly awareness of creating colour and pattern with type, and also a sensitive handling of the detailed typography that ensures that individual parts are readable. From close up, different fonts distinguish the articles from each other, while the alternate strips of light and bold effectively create "white space" as a contrasting shadow around the particular article that is being read.

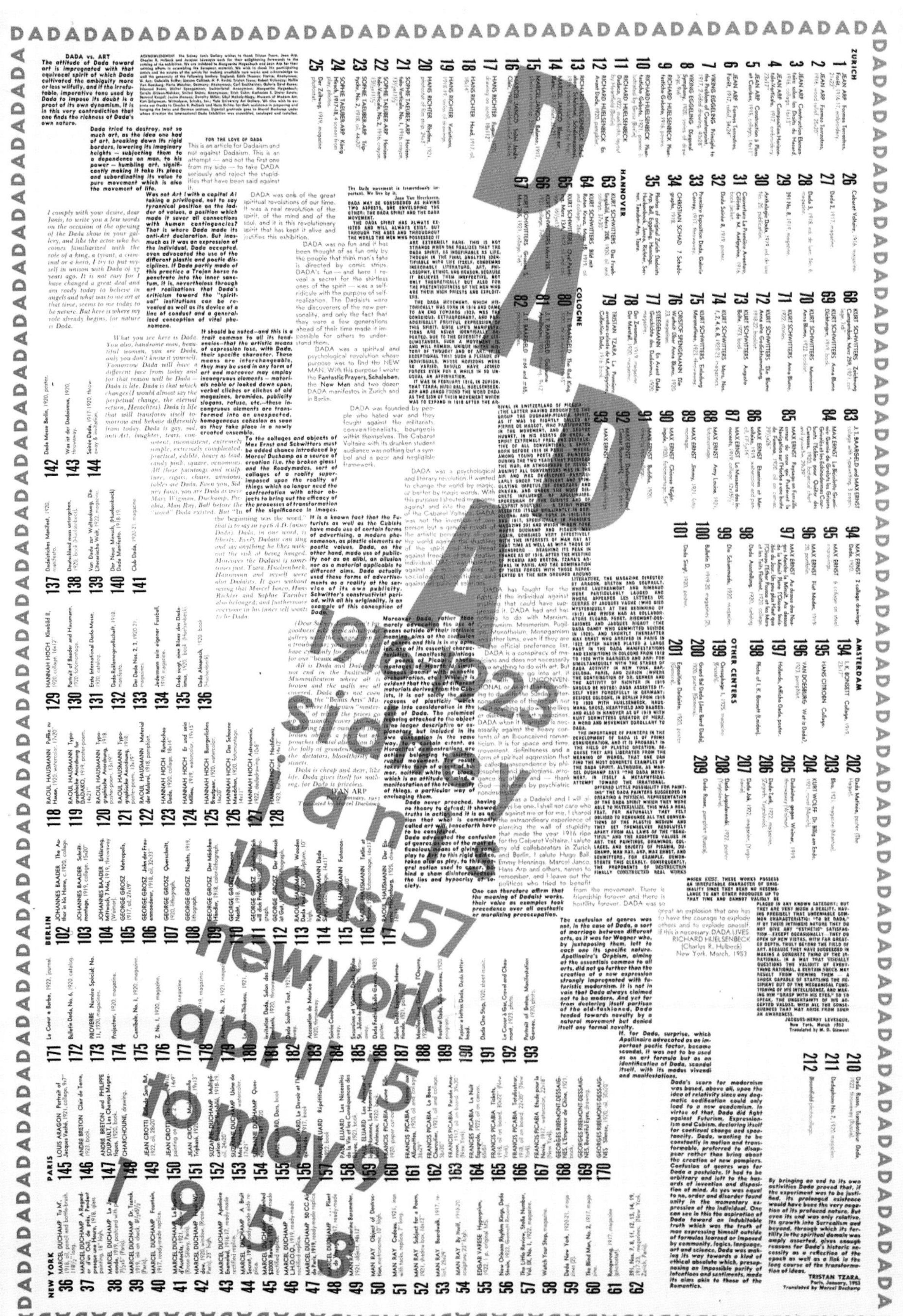
DADA
1916 1923
sidney janis
15 east 57
new york
april 15
to may 9
1953

Not that Optima, or indeed any of Zapf's faces, were commonplace during this period. But there was a definite interest once again in the potential of the handwritten form to give a fresh character to communication, particularly in the commercial sphere with advertising. Unlike the rather crazy and gimmicky faces of the period between the wars in the US where a whole host of bizarre and almost unusable theme alphabets were created, these scripts were more serious attempts to find a fresh, more expressive voice. The output of the French designer Roger Excoffon (1910–83), with his work for the Fonderie Olive and his design-studio implementation of his type ideas, is a fine demonstration of the interest in such faces. In Excoffon's 1950s designs of the faces Banco, Choc, Mistral and Diane can be seen a coverage of the options in Script forms, from a heavy stroke laid down as if with a paintbrush for Banco and Choc, to the lightest and most contrasting of strokes in Diane. But it is Mistral that is perhaps the most interesting, being a serious attempt to produce a script that would join up as with handwriting in all its various letter combinations and yet display the irregularities of the living hand, while remaining highly legible. This face had to be cut on to punches for hot-metal setting, which called for an appreciation of the need to contain the letter on its shank as far as possible to avoid damage. What is most distinctive about Mistral is that Excoffon met these requirements with a face that has no clear baseline – the letters sit on different points of the line, with the vagary of handwriting itself. There are even alternate versions of some letters, reflecting the characteristics of writing and also meeting the need for different conjunctions between letters.

Excoffon's designs, distributed by the small Fonderie Olive, were rarely seen outside France, but have been highly popular there and still contribute to the graphic character of French commercial communication. His most serious face, Antique Olive, a sans serif released in the early 1960s, was presaged by the heavy yet elegant lettering for the Air France logo that he created in the late fifties and whose basic design remains part of the company's corporate identity.

The distinct character of Zapf's and Excoffon's work was very distant from that of the school that came to dominate any subsequent view of the major graphic design of the period: the Swiss International Style. The work of the designers in this group had a massive impact, projecting theories of typographic

Type specimen brochures designed by Roger Excoffon to show his faces for Fonderie Olive: Banco, 1951 (below); Mistral, 1953 (right); Choc, 1953 (far right and below right). These brush scripts, along with others by Excoffon such as Chambord and Calypso, were designed primarily for advertising and quickly gained popularity in the late 1950s and 1960s, giving a distinctive character to much French promotional material. Although apparently exuberant, stylised and freehand, these designs required great skill and perseverance in the drawing so that they could be practical as well as characterful. Mistral manages the feat of joining up the lower-case characters as if they were informally handwritten, despite their being separate pieces of type. This required extensive exploration of the likely combinations and rhythms of stroke that could be set up when whole words were created. Letters have alternate versions, unusual ligatures, and (just like handwriting) do not all sit precisely on the baseline. Yet each letter is cleanly located within the rectangle of type so that there is no overhang (unlike with some ornate faces) which would cause the face to wear badly. Indeed, the roughness of the script means that it wears extremely well.

A B C D E F G
H I J K L M N O P
BANCO
Q R S T U V W
X Y Z Æ Œ Ç É È Ê Ë
«:?,&.!;»
1234567890

«-,:?(")!';.»

A B C D E F G H I J K L M N O

P Q R S T U V W X Y Z Æ Œ

1 2 3 4 5 6 7 8 9 0

a b c d e f g h i j k l m

n o p q r s t u v

w x y z æ œ

TOURISME c. 12 32 A — distinguée 76 a 3 k 500

TOURISME c. 14 30 A — distinguée 92 a 4 k 600

TOURISME c. 16 24 A — distinguée 60 a 5 k 100

TOURISME c. 20 22 A — distinguée 50 a 6 k 900

TOURISME c. 24 16 A — distinguée 32 a 7 k 500

TOURISME c. 30 12 A — distinguée 24 a 8 k 500

TOURISME c. 36 10 A — distinguée 20 a 10 k 300

TOURISME c. 48 6 A — distinguée 14 a 12 k 500

TOURISME c. 60 5 A — distinguée 10 a 14 k 200

TOURISME c. 72 4 A — distinguée 9 a 14 k 800

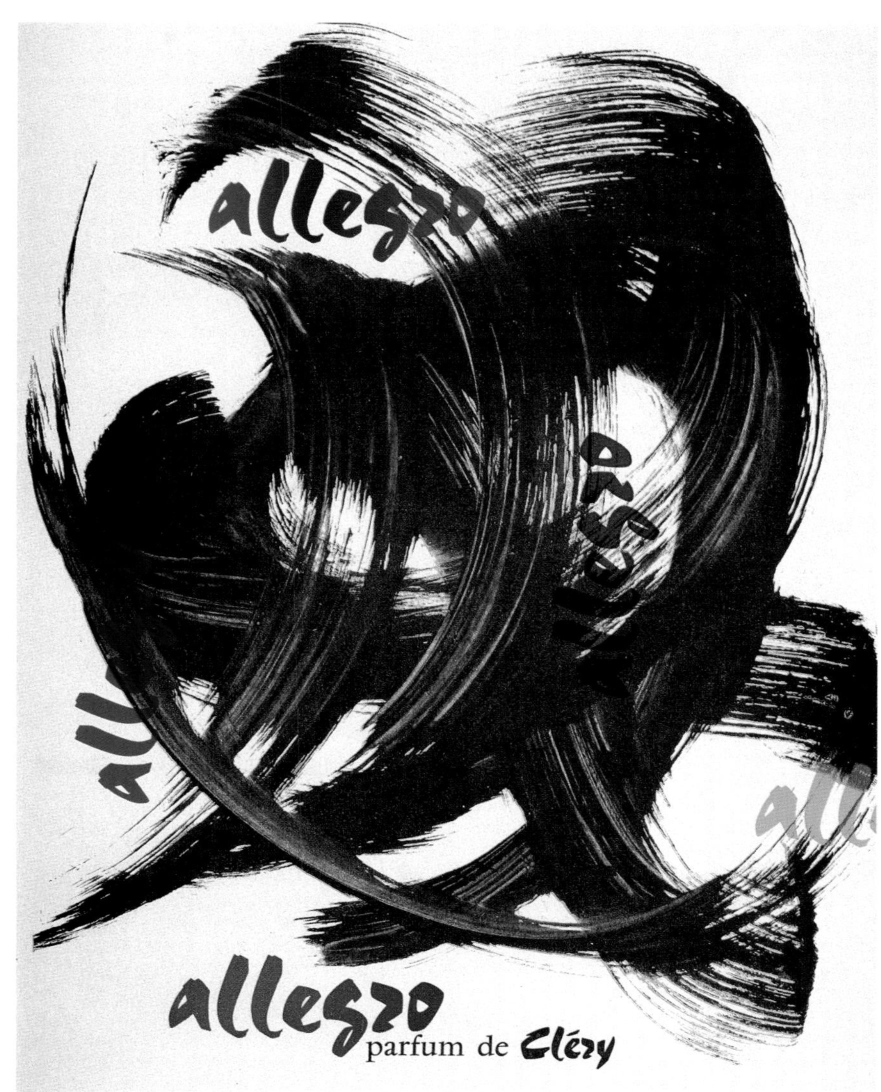


La terreur et l'épouvante
sont souvent sorties de ce palais; qu'elles y rentrent
aujourd'hui au nom de la loi!
Que tous ceux qui l'habitent sachent que le Roi
seul est inviolable, que la loi y atteindra sans distinction
tous les coupables et qu'il n'y a pas une tête qui,
convaincue d'être criminelle,
puisse échapper à son glaive!

Vergniaud (1792)

form that still underpin much that is taught and practised despite many years of reaction to the approach. At heart the International Style is seen as being based on the creation of a grid for all purposes, with a concentration on sans serif faces and asymmetric layouts. Its roots can be seen in the work of Theo Ballmer in the late twenties, but it is clearly also a derivation and pursuit of the ideals espoused by the Bauhaus and Tschichold at that time, as well as having links with the De Stijl artists' reduction of form to rectangular blocks and lines. One non-Bauhaus teacher in particular would be seen later to have had a major influence: from 1918 until 1956 Ernst Keller (1891–1968) taught at the Kunstgewerbeschule (applied art school) in Zürich. Among his early pupils was Ballmer; later both Adrian Frutiger (born 1928) and Edouard Hoffman (who were, respectively, behind the seminal 1950s faces Univers and Helvetica), were taught his ideas of clarity and simplicity, restricted styles and close letter-fit. For the Swiss designers whose work gave birth to the International Style, this stern reduction of graphic design and typographic content to simple, and repeated, elements was seen as a way of arriving at a clarity in communication divorced from the baggage of tradition and the clutter of unnecessary associations. A concept, put across with the minimum of fuss, was necessarily the clearest and most precise form of expression, they thought.

The idea of some form of a grid underpinning layout was not new, either in the 1950s or even in the 1920s, with the grid displayed deliberately in Ballmer's posters. Newspaper layouts, after all, were quite clearly fiercely governed by the vertical stressed structure of their columns. But it is the introduction of the squared grid, vertical and horizontal, and the idea of drawing up a grid in relation to the contents – determining the number of fields within the grid on a page to reflect the amount and variety of those contents – that transpired from the output of the German and Swiss designers. Ballmer's rather crude work and Max Bill's strikingly reductive layouts of the early 1930s were the most overt early representations of this approach. By splitting the page or poster into a

Right: press advertisements for Avery weighing scales, designed by Paul Peter Piech at the W. S. Crawford agency, London, 1950s. A remarkable absence of type distinguishes them: usually such communications were overburdened with explanatory words, but here a single word sums up and expresses the image, with each different advertisement embodying a single concept at the heart of the products. The type, loosely spaced and minuscule, makes a dynamic contrast with the illustration. This work displays a growing awareness of the power of an emotional charge in the combination of image and word; advertising training books laid down a more orthodox arrangement of picture, headline and body copy.

abcdefffffiflghijklmnopqrstuvwxyz
ABCDEFGHIJKLMNOPQRSTUVWXYZ
1234567890

abcdefghijklmnopqrstuvwxyz
ABCDEFGHIJKLMNOPQRSTUVWXYZ
1234567890

abcdefghijklmnopqrstuvwxyz
ABCDEFGHIJKLMNOPQRSTUVWXYZ
1234567890 1234567890

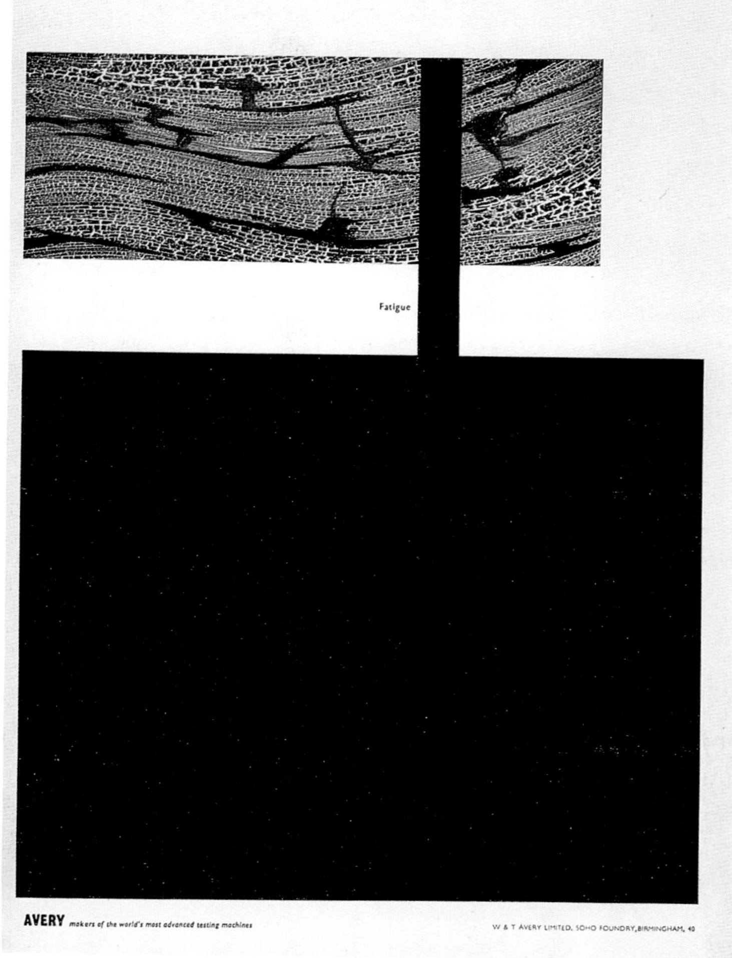


Left and right: three faces by Hermann Zapf: Melior, 1952 (top); Optima, 1958 (centre); Palatino, 1949–50 (bottom). Strong, inclined serifs and short descenders distinguish Palatino from other old-face designs; its underlying elegance in continuous book text has made it one of the most popular faces designed since the war. In contrast to this delicacy, Melior was designed to stand up to rougher uses, such as in newspapers; its heavy letterforms have an overall design based on the rectangle. Optima is an innovative attempt to design a face between a roman and the modern sans serif, being a stressed sans serif that displays clear calligraphic qualities. It caused a stir on its release, challenging the notion that sans serif faces were inherently less readable than roman. It is a truly original design – merging Venetian forms, geometric modern sans serif ideas and calligraphic skills.

Ncogrn

Ncogrn

Ncogrn

grid, a series of modules were arrived at that could be used to articulate clearly the proportion, balance and perspective relating to the different elements.

In 1950 Bill began teaching at the Hochschule für Gestaltung in Ulm, Germany, developing a curriculum that incorporated his ideas, uniting the lessons learnt from his early Bauhaus background with an attempt at a more universal statement about typography. His search for a rigorous mathematical logic to graphic design was similar to that of Emil Ruder (1914–70) who was teaching in Basel around the same time, seeking to pare down the thinking of his students to an appreciation of the value of white space and formal rhythms in relation to the type. He stressed that the empty space was as crucial a part of the design as the printed areas, and encouraged a highly limited selection of faces, weights and styles. But he was not a cold functionalist: he appreciated the need for novelty, and for dynamic qualities in layout. This was not seen as an excuse for unaccountable idiosyncrasy, however.

Ruder advocated concern at the distribution of space between lines, words, letters and within letters. Unlike certain other Swiss theorists, he was not opposed to justified setting, seeing it as perhaps preferable to ragged right as it balances the block of text and also opens it up from being a dense, even mass.

Joseph Müller-Brockmann (born 1914), a Swiss designer whose poster work and books were striking representations of the principles behind the International Style, was stricter than Ruder and Bill in laying down the law. Believing in



Below and right: from *Neue Grafik*, 1958–66. The philosophy underlying the more extreme rationalism of Swiss style, which was to be projected into International Style, was most clearly expressed in this magazine which was launched in 1958 and edited by Zürich-based designers Josef Müller-Brockmann, Richard Lohse, Hans Neuberg and Carlo Vivarelli. A severe application of the organisational grid emphasises the scientific approach being taken to design. Helvetica is the only typeface used in a range of sizes to denote headline, text and caption. This was not so much a magazine as a primer in the principles of Swiss school design. The founders had been developing their grid system since the 1930s and the compelling

Systematische Grafikerausbildung
A Training System for the Graphic Designer
Formation méthodique des graphistes

33

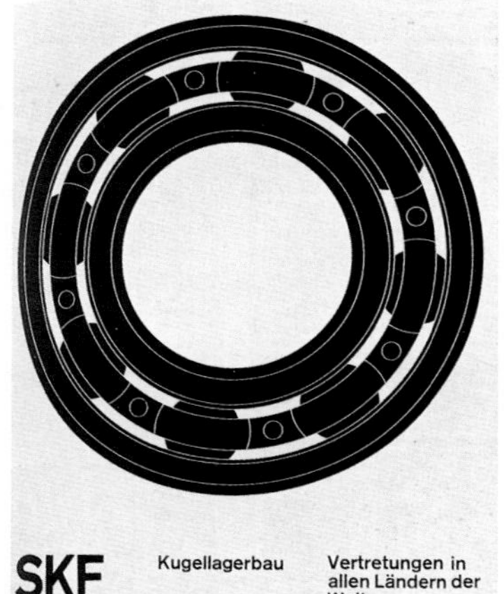

SKF

Kugellagerbau

Zürich
Falkenstrasse 24

Vertretungen in allen Ländern der Welt.
Hauptgeschäft in Göteborg.

la pratique et prennent conscience de leur futur métier. Les exemples représentés sont des travaux caractéristiques exécutés durant les quatre ans d'apprentissage. Leur présentation n'emprunte rien à la chronologie, mais elle est divisée selon les différentes disciplines. Le premier essai important confié à l'élève qui entre dans la classe de graphisme ne constitue nullement un travail très attrayant et qui exige néanmoins une attention soutenue: il consiste en la définition des propositions de formes et de volume afin d'en trouver une application pratique. Telle qu'elle se présente, à l'aide de dessins et de photos de modèles, la tâche comprend les problèmes essentiels suivants:

1. Huit surfaces en forme de cercle doivent être trouvées dans des grandeurs différentes, mais ayant une proportion réciproque entre elles. Ces proportions doivent répondre à un principe logique et satisfaire l'esthétique.
2. Ces huit cercles sont posés chacun sur une surface carrée. Les huit surfaces carrées ainsi obtenues sont disposées sur la feuille de dessin de telle façon que les espaces, les carrés et les marges constituent également une proportion bien définie.
3. Avec les huit cercles, il convient de créer une composition. Cette composition ne doit pas choquer la logique, c'est-à-dire qu'elle devra se conformer à la forme et à l'esthétique. Les distances qui séparent les cercles seront conformes à des proportions définies.
4. La composition avec les huit cercles est assujettie à une projection de plan. Parmi les huit corps à trois dimensions, il convient de définir la forme et la grandeur. Chaque dimension doit donner une mesure logique de proportion.
5. La composition des trois dimensions est exécutée dans une matière que l'élève choisira lui-même si possible (bois ou métal, matière plastique, etc.).

M.
Rein zeichnerische Versuchsarbeiten
167
Eduard Müller
Diese als Werkzeichnung ausgeführte Arbeit symbolisiert die Präzision des SKF-Kugellagers. Die Typografie ist organisch dazu in Beziehung gebracht
168
Alois Märchy
Zeichnerische Formulierung einer Hallenkonstruktion
169
Gianfranco Verna
Konstruktionszeichnung, grafisch überarbeitet

M.
Work consisting of pure drawing
167
Eduard Müller
This drawing symbolises the precision of SKF ball bearings. The typography is organically related to the drawing.
168
Alois Märchy
Drawing for the construction of a hall
169
Gianfranco Verna
Drawing for a construction retouched

M.
Travaux résolus par le dessin
167
Eduard Müller
Ce dessin d'usine symbolise la précision des roulements à billes SKF. La typographie est en rapport direct avec le dessin
168
Alois Märchy
Construction d'une halle figurée par le dessin
169
Gianfranco Verna
Dessin de construction travaillé par le graphisme

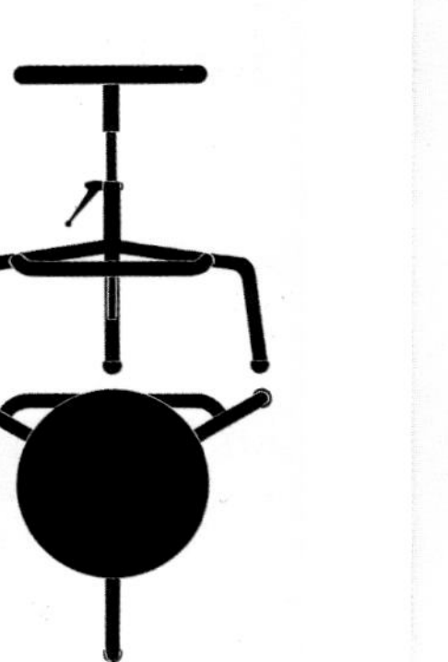

54

Verantwortliche Formgebung
Design and Responsibility
Sens de responsabilité
dans le dessin industriel

eine Form angenommen haben, die einem Gesetz unterliegt.
Bei den erwähnten klassischen Schönheiten der Technik hegen wir keine Zweifel über die Echtheit ihres Gestaltcharakters, denn die Gesetzmäßigkeit ihrer Form ist offensichtlich. Wie aber sind diese Dinge gleichzeitig zu ihrem hohen Grad von Zweckmäßigkeit und zu ihrer formalen Gesetzlichkeit gekommen, ohne daß jemand mit formkünstlerischen Interessen oder Absichten am Werk gewesen ist? Woher diese gleichsam zwangsläufige Schönheit? Es fällt auf, daß alle diese als Beispiele aufgezählten Schönheiten der Energieumsetzung dienen. Das Gesetz, das hier regiert, ist vielleicht ein optisch transparent gewordenes Naturgesetz.
In der Tat: Bei diesen der Energieübertragung dienenden Konstruktionen können wir durch Messung des Wirkungsgrades gleichsam ermitteln, wie nahe wir mit der Konstruktion an die naturgesetzliche Ideallösung herangekommen sind. Analoges ließe sich zeigen, wo es um die Sichtbarwerdung von statischer Festigkeit geht.
Was sich von solchen naturgesetzlich bedingten Gestalten sagen läßt, ist indessen nicht auf alle technischen Konstruktionen übertragbar, beispielsweise weil der optisch wirksame Einfluß des Fertigungsprozesses denjenigen der statischen oder dynamischen Gestaltungsfaktoren in den Hintergrund drängen kann. Wir kommen also zum Schluß, daß die Beweiskraft dieser Klasse von Konstruktionen begrenzt bleibt und nicht ausreicht, um der Zweckschönheitsthese allgemeine Gültigkeit zu sichern.
Damit könnten wir mit unseren Untersuchungen weiterschreiten zur Gruppe der nichtprominenten Zeugen für die Richtigkeit der Zweckschönheitsthese, zu den Legionen von mehr oder weniger einfachen, weniger oder mehr komplizierten technischen Dingen, deren Gestalt nicht so spürbar von statischen, dynamischen oder energetischen Gesetzen erzwungen wird.
Wenn wir uns die Ansicht zu eigen machen, daß es meist gar nicht darum geht, die vielen technischen Dinge ihrer formalen Zurückhaltung zu berauben, so bleibt zu prüfen, worauf es denn beruht, daß den Dingen eine im gesamten wohltuende Neutralität eignet, während andere durch ihre Häßlichkeit Anstoß erregen. Vielleicht läßt sich hier ein nützlicher Einblick gewinnen, wenn wir den Verlauf des Gestaltungsprozesses selber einmal näher anzusehen versuchen, weil anzunehmen ist, daß ein Zusammenhang zwischen der Arbeitsweise des Konstrukteurs und dem formalen Gehaben seines Erzeugnisses besteht. Dem Konstrukteur ist mit der Aufgabenstellung vielleicht ein festes Bedingungsprogramm gegeben, eine Aufreihung aller physikalischen, technischen und praktischen Eigenschaften, eine Aufzählung der den Gebrauchswert bestimmenden Merkmale, die das zu schaffende Ding aufweisen soll.

In der Bewältigung dieses Bedingungsprogrammes, das heißt bei der Auseinandersetzung mit Kategorien wie Funktion, Baustoff, Herstellung und Gestalt, finden wir unseren Konstrukteur scheinbar hoffnungslos verstrickt in einem kaum übersehbaren Geflecht von Relationen seiner Anliegen mit etwa folgenden Faktoren, die einzeln oder gruppenweise eine Vielzahl von Teilproblemen hervorrufen: Seine Rücksichten gelten Vorschriften, Schutzrechten, den Gestehungskosten, dem Energieverbrauch, den Betriebskosten, der Betriebssicherheit, der Lärmfreiheit, der Gebrauchsdauer, örtlichen mechanisierten Bedingungen, klimatischen Verhältnissen, der Verwendung vorhandener Teile, Baustoffnormen, offiziellen und werkinternen Konstruktionsnormen, den verfügbaren Arbeitskräften, dem vorhandenen Maschinenpark, der Materialbeschaffungslage, der Abfallverwertung, den Hilfsvorrichtungen, Lehren und Prüfmitteln, der Einzelteilfertigung, der Oberflächenbehandlung, der Montage, der Größe, dem Gewicht, der Instruktion für Gebrauch und Wartung usw.
Nach allen diesen Richtungen hin hat er Verantwortung zu tragen, denn er ist zu nichts Geringerem befugt als dazu, dem Ding Gestalt zu geben. Eine Vielzahl dieser Faktoren finden wir wiederum in einer wichtigen Beziehung zur Auflage stehen, das heißt zur Stückzahl, die in der Fabrikation als Serie aufgelegt werden will.
Am Ende soll ein Erzeugnis die Fabrik verlassen, das vom Kunden begehrt und mit Genugtuung erworben wird. Und wir möchten wissen, wie solch Ergebnis unter diesen schwierigen Umständen zustande kommt.
Wenn der Mensch ganz auf das angewiesen wäre, was wir gemeinhin als Verstand bezeichnen, dann wäre die Lage dieses gestaltenden Ingenieurs, wie wir sie bis jetzt kennengelernt haben, ganz einfach hoffnungslos. Glücklicherweise sind in tieferen, unterhalb der Sphäre des Bewußten liegenden Schichten Funktionen lokalisiert, die am Vorgang des Gestaltens entscheidenden Anteil haben.
Lassen Sie mich aus persönlicher Sicht einiges zum Ablauf dieses Vorganges sagen:
Die eigentliche schöpferische Arbeit kann nicht beginnen, bevor der Gestalter das ganze Programm von Funktionen und Bedingungen, die das Werk unter Berücksichtigung aller angedeuteten Faktoren erfüllen soll, vollinhaltlich in sich aufgenommen hat; einerlei, ob das Programm niedergeschrieben wurde, als Pflichtenheft vorliegt oder nicht. In der Regel ereignet sich kaum etwas Sichtbares, ehe er dieses Bedingungsgefüge nicht eine der Aufgabe und seiner Veranlagung angemessene Zeit lang im Geiste mit sich herumgetragen hat; abgesehen von Vorstudien und allfälligen Vorversuchen.
Im Unterbewußten muß ein intensives Assoziieren und Dissoziieren im Gange sein, ohne daß wir es wahrnehmen, bis in irgendeinem Augenblick die Vor-

stellung eines Lösungsansatzes, eines funktionell dienenden Strukturprinzips, die Schwelle des Bewußtseins überschreitet.
Jetzt bemächtigt sich der Intellekt dieses durch Intuition zutage geförderten Ansatzes und prüft schrittweise, ob der Ansatz sich bis zur Erfüllung aller Bedingungen des Funktionsprogrammes im Rahmen einer strukturellen Gesetzlichkeit entwickeln läßt. Das ist – vor allem bei komplizierten Programmen – selten auf Anhieb der Fall.
Es ist ein Merkmal von formal ungepflegter Technik, daß sie sich ohne weiteres mit einem oder auch mehreren strukturell fremden, neuen Ansätzen behilft, die die Aufgabe haben, die verbliebenen Bedingungen noch zu erfüllen. Wenn es eine industrielle Formgebung als Disziplin gibt, dann setzt sie hier an diesem Punkte ein. Die ‹Karten› werden niedergeschlagen, und das Unterbewußtsein wird um einen neuen, weiterreichenden Lösungsansatz gebeten.
Ist ein neuer Ansatz da, so wird er wiederum derselben Prüfung unterzogen und gleichfalls verworfen, wenn er nicht durch das ganze Programm von Bedingungen hindurch hält. Es besteht da eine gewisse Verwandtschaft zwischen der stilvollen Lösung einer Gestaltungsaufgabe und der Auflösung einer Differentialgleichung. Auch dort taugt ein Lösungsansatz nur, wenn die Lösung sämtliche Randbedingungen erfüllt. Dieser fundamentale Prozeß kann ein langes, mühsames, ja nahezu entmutigendes Hin und Her, eine Art von anhaltendem, gleichsam über die Bewußtseinsschwelle rückgekoppeltem geistigem Vorgang absetzen, um ein Wort des Elektronikers zu gebrauchen.
Wenn es bei aller Geduld einfach nicht gelingen will, dann führt mich die Ansicht, daß es kein gutes Bedingungsprogramm gibt, das sich nicht stilvoll erfüllen läßt, zur Überprüfung des Programmes selber. Vielleicht haben wir etwas gewollt, das nicht in Ordnung ist. Vielleicht stimmt etwas in der Hierarchie der Werte nicht; möglicherweise sind Gewichte verschoben, indem wir einem Faktor zuviel, einem anderen zuwenig Bedeutung beigemessen haben. So geht das Ringen auch auf dieser Ebene weiter. Nicht selten transformiert sich dabei das Programm der Bedingungen unter dem Einfluß des Gestaltungsprozesses, ganz abgesehen davon, daß es in der Regel ohnehin in dessen Verlauf umfänglicher und differenzierter wird, in dem Maße, wie die Vorstellungen an Relief gewinnen.
Damit ist nun auch gesagt, daß eine verantwortliche Formgebung oder Gestaltung nicht bestehen kann, ohne daß dem Gestalter die Möglichkeit gegeben ist, das Programm der Funktionen mitzugestalten. Hat er aber diese Befugnis, dann ist die Beurteilung des Stils, der Haltung des so gewonnenen Gebildes ein letzter Test für die Qualität nicht nur der Ausführung, nicht nur der Lösung, sondern auch des Bedingungsprogrammes. Haben diese Bemühungen

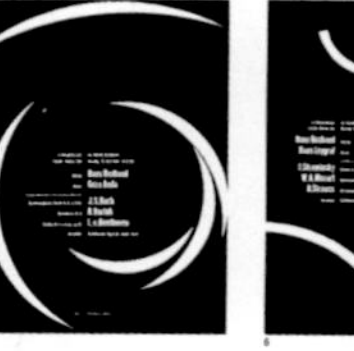

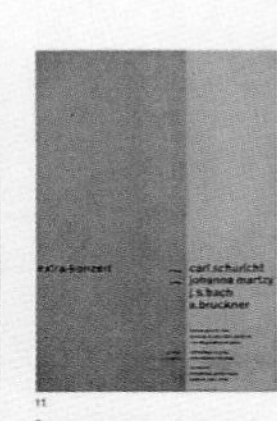

logic of their graphic design led rapidly to an international following. The spread (left) includes music posters from a series designed by Müller-Brockmann in the 1950s. Simple, stark contrasts – such as curved abstracts against the rigour of the underlying grid, white reversed out of black or the whole type grid shifted to the diagonal – are used to give dynamic properties to a pared-down, functional message.

Below: "You too are liberal", poster by Karl Gerstner, 1956. This is Swiss style at its most reductive – even the typeface seems cut down in size, in keeping with the brevity of the statement. The suggestion – that the viewer, rather than the man pointing, is the object in focus – is reinforced by the upper-case "D" drawing attention to "you".

Verantwortliche Formgebung
Design and Responsibility
Sens de responsabilité
dans le dessin industriel

## Design and Responsibility

Hans Hilfiker, Delegate of the Executive Board of Therma AG, Schwanden GL.

Responsibility inevitably involves a certain degree of authority. The one conception conditions the other and indeed they are so directly related that in all practical matters we combine the two ideas without conscious effort.
It is necessary to bear this in mind before we even begin to consider what kind of responsibility we take upon ourselves in designing the objects which make up our environment and what we are in fact to understand by design in relation to responsibility.
Man alone among all living creatures is distinguished by the power of expressive speech and by the ability to invent things which do not occur and never have occured in nature. His mind is so marvellously constituted that he can rise in thought above the level of existing phenomena, explore the realm of mere possibility and go even farther. His senses and the nervous system controlling his muscles are so sensitive and can be disciplined to such an extent that he is able to translate his thoughts into concrete reality. If we do not wish to deny him the right to exercise these potentialities this means that man is given authority in order to play his part in the unending creative process. To do justice to the overwhelming nature of this situation, it is essential, according to the statement made at the beginning of this lecture, to acknowledge the great importance of the responsibility which is the necessary corollary of this privileged authority.
All creative activity is ethically based on the recognition of this responsibility. To make use of this distinguishing authority without acknowledgement of the corresponding responsibility is incompatible with our innate conception of duty and justice.
For some years now thoughtful discussions of this subject have been going on both nationally and internationally, not only among engineers but in culturally interested circles of the utmost variety.
You know the various reasons which have given rise to such debates in the past and will continue to do so. The fact that technology has given individuals the power to decide whether man shall continue to exist or not is only one of those reasons.
This present meeting has been preceded by others concerned with the problem of industrial design, largely occasioned by the fact that industrial technology has been reproached for its deleterious influence on man's natural environment which—regarded as his proper sphere—is destined to affect the development and character of all those who live in it.
It was difficult to get discussions of the above subject and there is still a good deal of constraint in dealing with it because with so fundamental a question there is no way of bridging the gulf between the opposing points of view. In one camp we find the majority of constructional engineers and technologists, in the other a minority of these

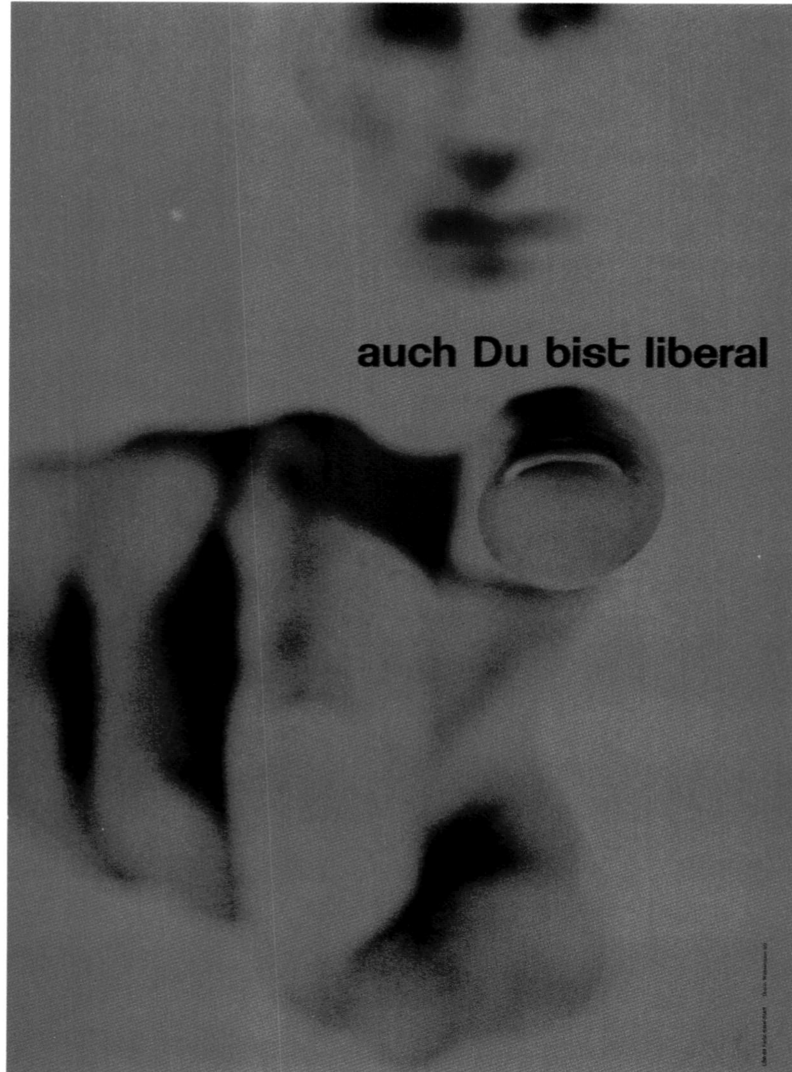

the notion of a kind of "objective design" that was freed from a designer's subjective expressions and quirks of taste, he proposed a purely functional communication, opposing the combination of different type families, or even the use of different forms of the same family, within one design. Different sizes were also to be avoided, and the type area was to be contained as compactly as possible. Line spacing should not allow any line to be seen as isolated and interword spacing was to be uniform. He preferred sans serif faces for their avoidance of the "decorative" notions of contrasting weight of strokes and the "ornament" of the serif, believing that they functioned as well as romans for most reading tasks.

These views, building on those of Ballmer, Bill, Ruder and Keller, were promoted during the 1950s and through the 1960s; and from being essentially Swiss-based they became known to a much wider public, not only through the movement of respected designers around Europe and the United States (Herbert Bayer, Herbert Matter, Piet Zwart and Max Huber were among those who influenced or were influenced by the development of grid theory and the search for a reductive typographic philosophy), but also by the clear projection of these principles through the launch of *Neue Grafik* magazine in 1959. Edited by Müller-Brockmann, Richard Lohse, Hans Neuberg and Carlo Vivarelli, *Neue Grafik* was published in German, English and French and promoted the party line in a highly effective way, illustrating the principles with the best of the current Swiss typography.

The argument for sans serif faces projected by the Swiss typographers built on the earlier influence of the Bauhaus which had led all the major foundries to turn out copies of Futura in the late 1920s and 1930s. By the 1950s Futura and these close copies (for example, ATF's Spartan in the US) had become a leading choice for advertising designers. Contemporary reviews of typeface usage and change of fashion in advertising noted that whereas in the UK in 1929, Cheltenham, Goudy and an unspecified sans serif grouping were first, second and third in popularity, by 1953 the figures had been transposed so that contemporary sans serif cuts were the first choice, followed by revived sans serifs, and then Monotype's Plantin.[1] In the US, Garamond, Caslon and Bodoni were the top three in 1929, but Bodoni, Century and Futura were leading in 1952.[2] Now they were being advocated for even wider use, despite the traditional opposition to the readability qualities of sans serif in text.

This demand fed the creation of two major sans serif type families, Helvetica and Univers. While designers were interested in working with sans serifs, there were signs of dissatisfaction with the geometric sans serifs available. It was neither Futura nor one of the post-Bauhaus faces that the Swiss typographers favoured above all – instead the 1896 Berthold face Akzidenz Grotesk (or Standard, as it was often called) was the constant choice of Max Bill and others. While being a "modern gothic" rather than one with squared, contrasting stroke style associated with earlier sans serifs (such as Benton's ever-popular Franklin Gothic or Goudy's 1901 Copperplate Gothic), Akzidenz Grotesk was favoured over the geometrics for its ability to provide a more comfortable close fit of letters. It has a rhythm and character missing in the geometric faces (there is a slight contrast of stroke, and tails to letters such as "a", "j", "t" and "u").

Edouard Hoffman at the Haas foundry noted the popularity of Akzidenz Grotesk and commissioned Max Miedinger to refine it and provide Haas with a version to sell; this resulted in Neue Haas Grotesk (1951–3), later renamed

Right: four pages that unfold in a brochure/wrapper for sending out samples of the *National Zeitung* newspaper, designed by Karl Gerstner, 1959, at the fledgling advertising agency GGK (Gerstner, Gredinger and Kuttner). The basic unit of language grows as the pages are opened out to express visually and verbally the message about the paper's coverage. Gerstner emphasised the logic underlying art, and took up painting full time in 1970.

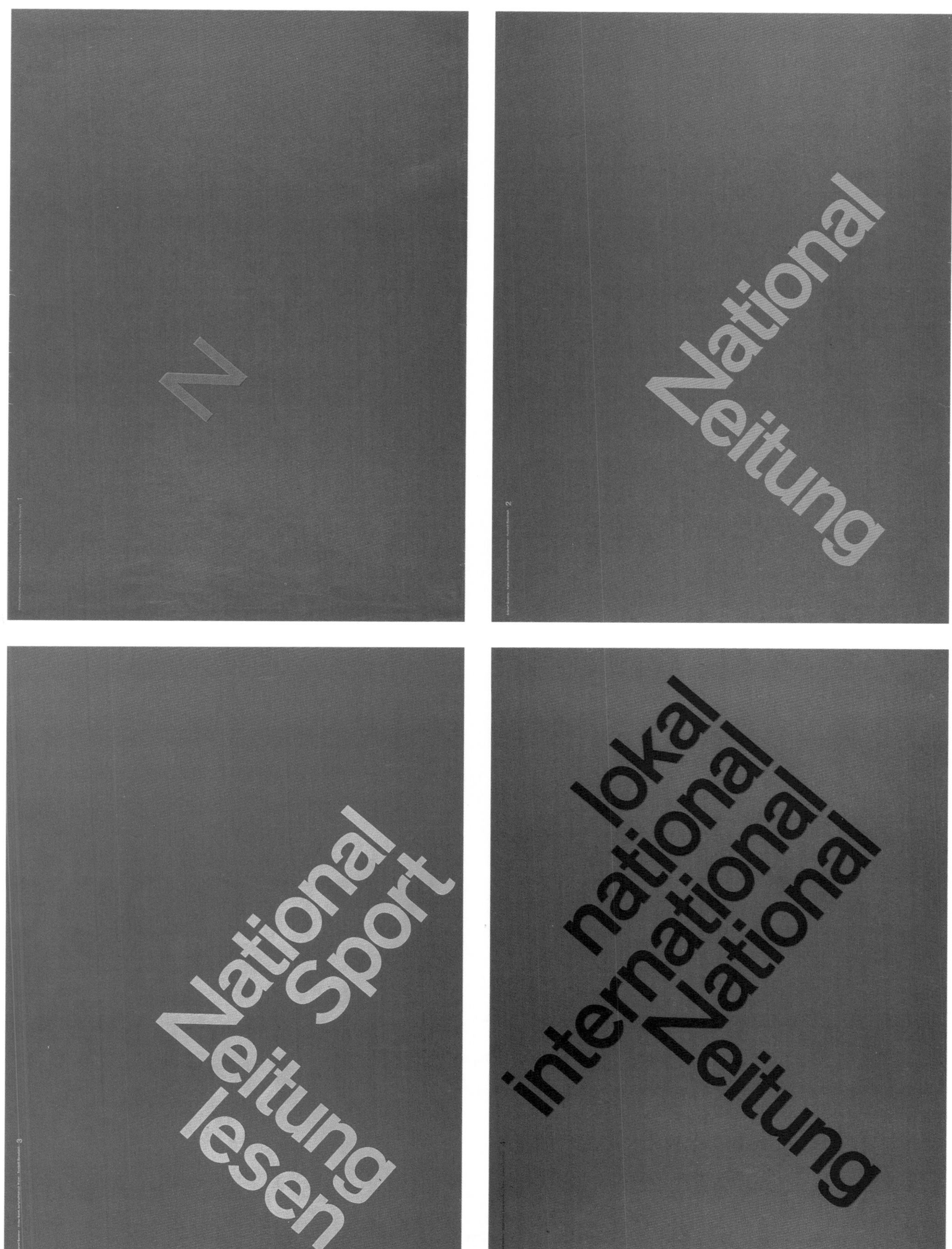
N
National
eitung
National
Sport
eitung
lesen
lokal
national
international
National
eitung

Promotional material for Neue Haas Grotesk (1958) and Helvetica (early 1960s). The popularity of Akzidenz Grotesk with the Swiss typographers of the 1950s prompted Eduard Hoffman of the Haas foundry to ask his in-house designer Max Miedinger to develop a more modern version of the fifty-year-old face. Neue Haas Grotesk not only had a larger x-height than its late nineteenth-century inspiration but took in some influence from the twentieth-century geometric sans serifs, such as the more consistent forms and a more monotone line. Designed by Miedinger and Hoffman in 1951–3, it was licensed by Haas to Stempel and to Linotype who renamed it Helvetica (Latin for Switzerland). Compact and expressing modernity, as well as having the branding that suggested the Swiss style, Helvetica (below) soon became the most popular sans serif, a position it looks likely to hold at least for the remainder of the twentieth century. It has been suggested that both Helvetica and Univers (see pages 148–9) owe a debt to the teachings of Ernst Keller, who taught both Hoffman and Adrian Frutiger.

abcdefghijklmnopqr

ABCDEFGHIJKLMN

1234567890

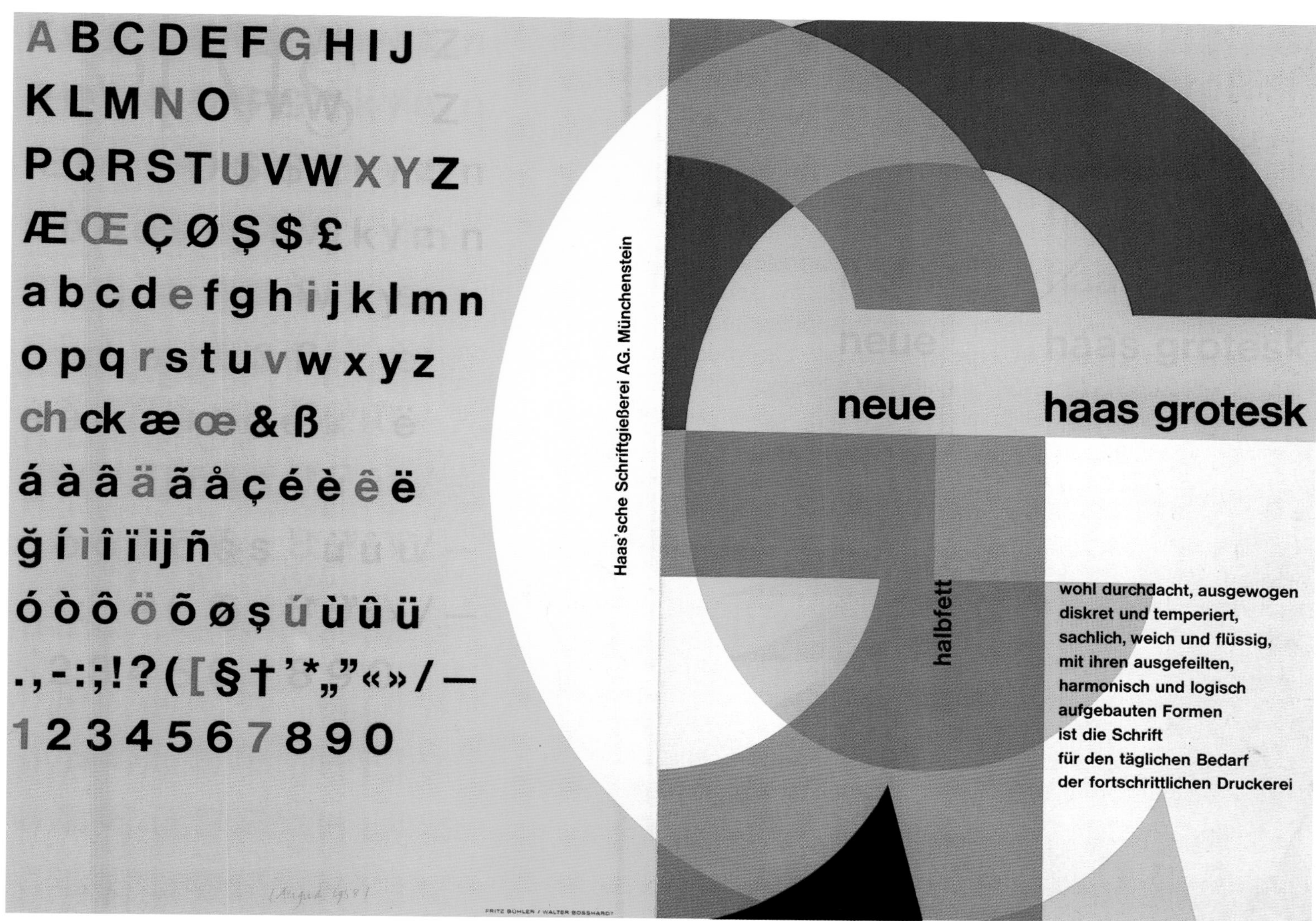
ABCDEFGHIJ
KLMNO
PQRSTUVWXYZ
ÆŒÇØŞ$£
abcdefghijklmn
opqrstuvwxyz
ch ck æ œ & ß
áàâäãåçéèêë
ğíìîïijñ
óòôöõøşúùûü
.,-:;!?([§†'*„"«»/—
1234567890
Haas'sche Schriftgießerei AG. Münchenstein
neue
haas grotesk
halbfett
wohl durchdacht, ausgewogen
diskret und temperiert,
sachlich, weich und flüssig,
mit ihren ausgefeilten,
harmonisch und logisch
aufgebauten Formen
ist die Schrift
für den täglichen Bedarf
der fortschrittlichen Druckerei

stuvwxyz

OPQRSTUVWXYZ

&.,:;!?[]*

Helvetica when sold to Stempel (1957) and then Linotype, and produced in a full family of variants. This face was distinctive in being developed not as an experiment, nor as a punt into the marketplace, nor as a sport, but rather as a clear response to overwhelming demand. It quickly proved immensely popular, and is now the most commonly used face for many advertising typographers, while retaining an occasional role in text settings. Several typographers have found this disconcerting, and rude quips can be heard about the ubiquity of Helvetica and the dead hand of its applications.

Helvetica's success lay in offering a fairly comprehensive family that fitted the taste of the time and also had a raw functional quality that would endure beyond simple shifts in taste. The same qualities provide the clue to the immense impact of the other great sans serif of the period, Univers. In name and deed, Univers attempted and delivered an integrated family that took the basic desire for a modern, lightly stressed sans serif and produced it in a comprehensive range of twenty-one variants, presented in a nomenclature that attempted a revolution in type description. Designed by Adrian Frutiger, Univers was launched in 1954 by Deberny & Peignot with a distinctive specimen sheet that presented weight and width in a logical palette, with reference numbers rather than imprecise names such as "extra bold". The idea was not a great success (printers were not to be shifted from their traditional view of type simply in order to accommodate the new method, however modern and logical), but it was entirely in keeping with the grid theory application for which the face was intended; the relationship of different weights and perspective shifts (from expanded to italic to condensed) was even expressed on the specimen sheet through a grid display.

Univers was also distinctive in being produced in both a photosetting and a metal version. It was originally begun as an experimental unified series by the twenty-five-year-old Frutiger, before he was invited by Deberny & Peignot to help select typefaces suitable for transfer to photosetting. This led to the Univers project and its availability in photocomposition and metal versions.

Univers, designed by Adrian Frutiger for Deberny & Peignot, 1954–7. As the name suggests, it was intended to be a universal face, being drawn with 21 variations as shown in Frutiger's explanatory diagram: first presented in 1954, it was a revolutionary conception of how typefaces and families could be described. Frutiger was proposing to abandon such terms as "condensed", "extended", "light", "bold", "roman" and "italic", and use instead a numbering system that establishes the relationships between the variations. At the centre of the scheme is Univers 55, the equivalent of standard book setting, shown in the sample font below. The vertical axis expresses different weights: any variation that begins with the same number is of the same weight. The horizontal axis notes perspective shifts, from extended to condensed and with italic variations; anything ending with an even number is italic.

abcdefghijklmnopqr

ABCDEFGHIJKLMN

1234567890

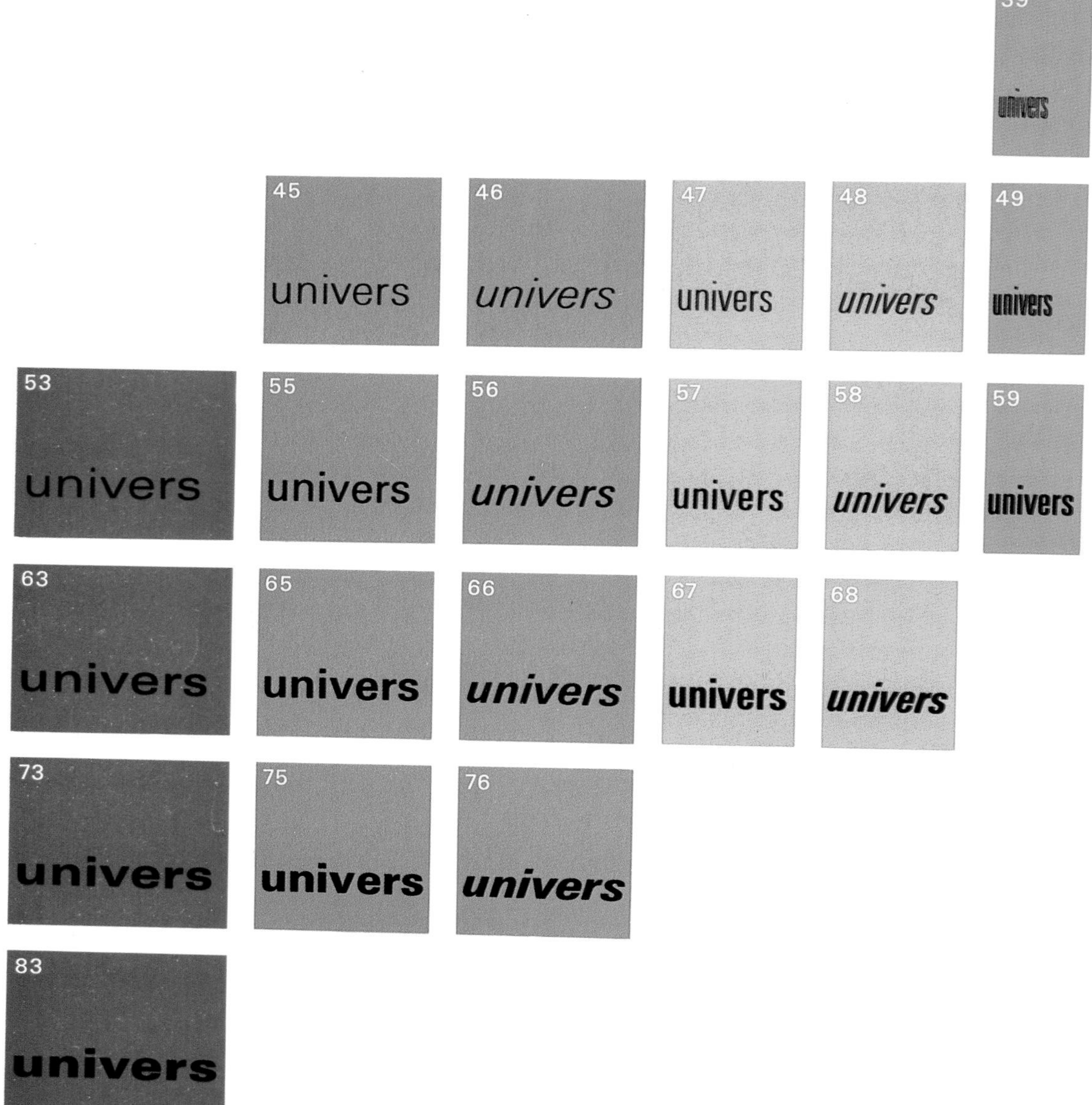


stuvwxyz

OPQRSTUVWXYZ

&.,:;!?[]*

The booming demand, a fresh phase of type design and the conceptual typographic debate of the 1950s took place in the context of a new round of radical change in the means of production of typeset letterforms. Although there had been experimentation with photosetting ever since the turn of the century, particularly in the 1930s, photocomposition was not seen as a reality until the 1950s. Then a wave of machines with slightly differing methods but all based around the same key process came into being, though not on a commercial scale. At their core was a means of exposing a master negative of the characters on to photographic film in the required size. Focus, alignment, consistency of exposure and spacing had been problems but these were tackled until a range of competitive machines came on to the market. Among them were the Rotofoto, the Monophoto from Monotype, the manually operated Varityper headline setter, the Photon machines based on the Higonnet and Meyroud system of using a spinning disk to carry the type master, Berthold's backing of the Diatype, and the Linofilm. Different methods of storing the type information were used, sometimes disks, sometimes grids. From experimental usage at the beginning of the decade, the systems had advanced to real commercial application by the end – for example, in 1959 *National Geographic* magazine installed the first full production model of a Linofilm. The Linofilm had had an unusual developmental background: the manufacturers, Mergenthaler Linotype, had been encouraged to develop a machine that had the potential of converting computer data into type, in order to cope with the requirements of the American Space Programme where there was an urgent need for an alternative to the unmanageable volumes of almost illegible teleprinter output.

At this stage, the benefits and problems of mass adoption of photocomposition were still to be seen. Clearly it held out immense benefits in the means of production, being a cheaper, cleaner and faster way of typesetting and easily applicable to the advancement in film science as applied to offset lithography. But in typography the benefits proved less certain: while the flexibility of type positioning had been improved (kerning was easier), the problems of enlarging type to different sizes from a master, rather than holding different cuts in different sizes, led to the degrading of qualities in the individual letterforms that made up the easier-to-set typography. Early computer-setting was being pioneered at the same time, and this too had disadvantages as well as advantages. While it held out the prospect of saving the labours of justifying type, it also began the degradation of line-setting quality still common and associated with computers (particularly in newspapers) where the program either crudely expands the line to produce gaping word spaces, or else displays inadequate or insensitive hyphenation.

And there is a final note as to technological revolution. Much less sophisticated, but nevertheless highly significant, the process of Letraset instant wet-transfer lettering was made into a viable commercial proposition during the 1950s, with the company being properly set up to exploit its potential in 1959. This was to be a vital contributor to the spirit of eclectic adventure that, in the 1960s, shook out the rather staid, craftsman-like associations of graphic design, bringing typographic experimentation into the hands of anyone who could afford a sheet of rub-down letters.



Right and far right: cover of *Rassegna Grafica*, 1955, and an advertisement for printers Alfieri & Lacroix, 1960, both by Franco Grignani, Milan. Grignani (born 1908) explored self-consciousness in typography; the methods of manipulation undertaken in printing are partly revealed or punned with – such as the switch from a printed character to a photographic one for the magazine cover, or the distortion that suggests the rotary press by which the type is finally produced.
Below: *Revue Cenpa*, 1953, designed by Jean Carlu and Jacques Nathan. This magazine for the French paper industry merged a knowledge of new typography with an appreciation of the finest qualities of traditional typography and printing. Carlu, a leading poster artist of the 1920s and 1930s, displayed a subtle mastery of white space that does not neatly fit any movement.

la vente, utilisent la publicité écrite — ont depuis longtemps compris la vertu de la lettre et l'importance de son choix, et ils n'hésitent pas à s'adresser à des artistes de valeur pour la composition de leurs annonces ou de leurs affiches. Je crains, par contre, qu'ils n'accordent trop souvent qu'une attention distraite à l'emballage considéré à tort comme un support négligeable de publicité, surtout lorsqu'il s'agit d'un produit vulgaire ou de consommation courante. Ils oublient qu'un habile couturier peut conférer de l'élégance à la femme la plus insignifiante. C'est par ailleurs mal connaître la psychologie de l'acheteur et celle du promeneur constamment en quête d'une distraction ou d'un spectacle, si minime soit-il, serait-ce la simple vue d'une marque sur un paquet. Ceci vaut encore plus pour les hommes que pour les femmes. Dans la rue, la femme est infiniment moins distraite que l'homme. Les vitrines ou les propos futiles échangés avec une amie la captivent tout

entière. Par ailleurs, inexplicable en ceci
pour le reste, elle éprouve un plaisir
à porter des paquets. L'homme par contre
survivance peut-être du temps où le
ne régnait pas encore sur le monde —
à porter le moindre objet. Là où une
sera ravie d'exhiber ses emplettes, un
éprouvera une sorte de gêne, sauf
si le paquet qu'il porte est le signe d'une
taine élégance qui satisfait sa propre
Il convient donc de tenir compte de
psychologie de l'acheteur et de ne pas
que l'emballage, s'il a pour fonction de
muler un objet, doit en même temps
la nature et la provenance de cet objet avec
maximum de discrétion, mais aussi sous
aspects les plus propres à attirer et à
les regards. On utilisera donc un papier ou
carton qui s'adapte à la nature de l'objet,
en choisira avec soin la couleur, et en
de ces deux éléments, on déterminera le
du caractère destiné à composer le nom

Rassegna Grafica
31
maggio-giugno 1955
grignani
la rivista bimestrale per le arti grafiche e cartotecniche
RASSEGNA GRAFICA

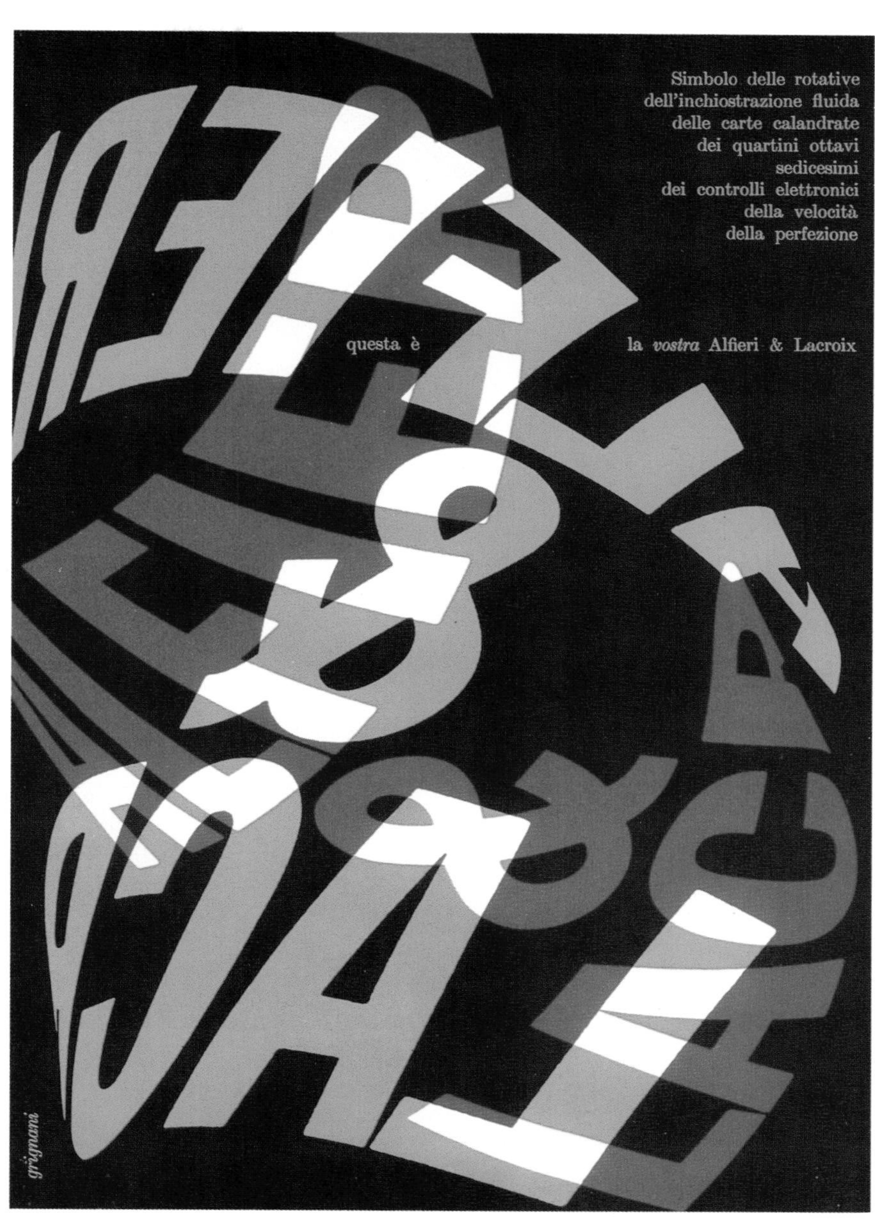
Simbolo delle rotative
dell'inchiostrazione fluida
delle carte calandrate
dei quartini ottavi
sedicesimi
dei controlli elettronici
della velocità
della perfezione
questa è
la *vostra* Alfieri & Lacroix
grignani

industrie
b
antiques et égyptiennes
acier
béton
ACTUALITÉ 53
31

AVANT GARDE

Visual puns abounded in this period, such as Herb Lubalin's ligatures on the Avant Garde logo. Computer developments called for new standardizations for machine-readable codes – such as the

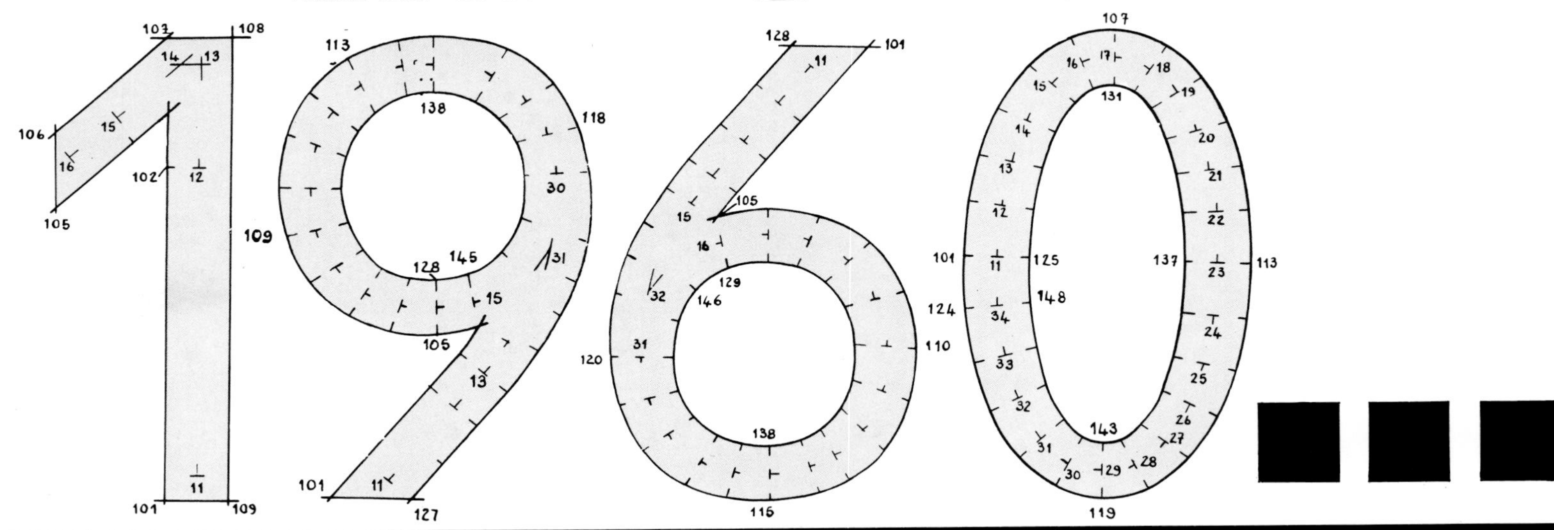

European Computer Manufacturers' Association alphanumeric character set instructions of 1965, details for which are shown in "1960". This spawned the faces OCR-A and OCR-B. Meanwhile, Jan Tschichold was working on Sabon, a face that was designed to work – and look the same – across all typesetting technologies. Roger Excoffon's Antique Olive was an attempt to create a more refined sans serif than that offered by the increasingly ubiquitous Helvetica and Univers.

*Sabon*

**Antique Olive**

OCR-A

In 1960 the London *Times Literary Supplement* referred to a new technology of "cold type", marking the presence of the photosetting process as something of relevance to the printing establishment, to business and to broader culture; it had a name, it had arrived. From the late 1950s onward, there was a rush to market numerous photocomposition machines: some were successful and fostered the emergence of new companies that supported type design programmes (such as Compugraphic and Hell), some displayed a crucial failure to pick up on the significance of the changes – notably American Type Founders, which emerged triumphant at the end of the nineteenth century from its wholesale espousal of hot metal, but which disappeared fifty years later under a takeover from Lanston Monotype after a failed investment in its own photocomposition machine.

Such activity and unpredictable changes of direction within the business of creating typefaces and developing typesetting technology reflected the imponderable questions underlying the use of the new forms of type: just how much and where would the demand be? The uncertainty was furthered by the practices of the type consumer: publishers and designers, who were subject to these new influences and were interested in forcing the new technology to achieve effects that were virtually impossible with metal, were also often prepared to accept the loss of some of the finer qualities of metal-setting, be it for price or other practical and non-aesthetic reasons. That photosetting brought about a drop in quality among many traditional facets of typographic skill was often lamented. Suddenly type was becoming a flexible right-reading image that could easily be photographically manipulated, instead of being a rigid, wrong-reading relief letterform. Characters could be enlarged or shrunk, kerned or spaced almost at will, overlapped and positioned in a few moments in ways that would have taken hours of skilful setting and subsequent construction on the printer's stone.

All this was encouraging for those seeking novelty, and dispiriting for those concerned with the traditional details. Poor fit of letters and ugly letterforms began to appear, fed by foundries and printers who expected to generate a whole range of point sizes out of a single matrix, inevitably distorting the face. It was also fed by the ignorance of the user: with hot metal, much skill resided with the compositor, skill that a typographic designer could rely on and even, to some extent, take for granted. Niceties such as ligatures disappeared, partly because the ease of kerning should have overcome some of their need, but it was a point that fine typographers missed.

The new systems began to chip away at the knowledge base of the compositor, gradually reducing specific skills to those of a glorified typist. Initially cold composition worked in a similar way to a Monotype machine, in that it produced a tape that drove the setting machine (the subsequent setting, however, was not as easily corrected: a new piece of film bromide being required, rather than the insertion of a single letter). During the 1960s, though, computers began to have an impact upon this operation, offering systems programmed to assist with the justification of setting, and using memories that could summon an image on a CRT (cathode ray tube) screen as reference. But this reliance on early computer programs brought problems, too, with the programmers and their systems often being unable to offer the qualities of spacing and word-break control that a good compositor would have supplied previously. Nevertheless, hot metal was increasingly ousted by the effects of lower costs and the convenience of cold type, matched by a further move from letterpress printing to offset lithography, which was better suited to meet the growth in quality and demand for colour printing.

Other new methods of satisfying the growing demand for print and business communication constituted a further threat to the print establishment. In 1961 the IBM Selectric golfball typewriter was launched, offering an office machine with the capability of changing its characters to a different face and size – an early indication of the transfer of finer-quality output into the hands of the office worker and a step towards today's desktop publishing systems. Of more creative impact was another development launched in 1961: Letraset's instant dry transfer lettering. As already mentioned, the company had marketed wet transfer lettering from 1959, but had failed to impress the American market. The dry method was much cleaner and simpler to use and did break through in the US: graphic designers soon realised that it gave them the power to produce the artwork for their own headlines and other display elements, avoiding the problems of instructing the printers and also bringing down costs, indeed making fancy display setting available for many who had not had access to it. Early Letraset advertising presented the system as something for everyone to use to brush up their communications, suggesting that typography was open to anybody – one over-enthusiastic piece of copywriting even stated that there was "no talent needed" to achieve fine results (a remarkable prefiguring of contemporary claims sometimes made for desktop publishing).

Letraset's library of faces grew quickly, not just with copies of existing faces (which were often good cuts, taken under licence from the original foundry

Right: four Penguin covers from the 1960s. *Killer's wedge* was designed by Romek Marber and Alan Spain, 1964; *Girls in their Married Bliss* by Alan Aldridge, 1964; *London Dossier* by the author Len Deighton, 1967; *Credos and Curios* by Bentley, Farrell and Burnett, 1969. Penguin's move away from strongly typographic covers reflects the variety and deliberate rule-breaking of 1960s design. It also reflects the pressure on books to compete as popular entertainments, hence the more boldly illustrative or photographic imagery taken from television and film. Alan Aldridge, appointed Fiction Art Director in 1963 aged 23, was either a pioneer or a philistine; he resigned in 1967 with the reassertion of typographic control.

Right: mixed media sculptures by Robert Indiana, 1960–2. Found materials, primarily weathered wood, are combined with "found" graphics – the stencilled letters of vernacular signage. Indiana (born 1928) was an American Pop artist who took the techniques and language of commercial and sign graphics and made them fine art. Far right: cover of promotional brochure for Ad Lib, designed by Freeman Craw for American Type Founders, 1961. This display typeface suggests both nineteenth-century wood-letter and a modern rhythm in its chunky cut-out letters. Craw (born 1917) cut variations of letters in the upper case ("E", "N", "O", "R", "S" and "T") and numerous variations in the lower case. He even designed some of the lower-case alternatives so that they could be turned upside down without losing alignment, thus adding to the list of variations, and suggesting the effect of hand-drawing. This was a reaction against the smooth neutrality of modern sans serif faces. The rectangular nature of type is declared in the cut, with circles and curves squared off.

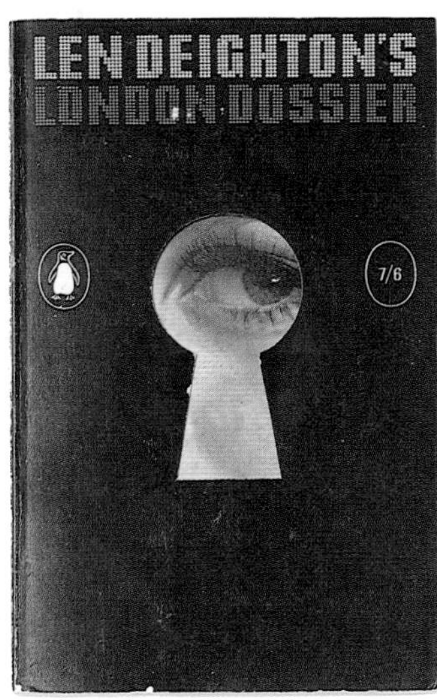

FGHIJKL
MNOPQR
STUVWX
YZABCD
ZABCDE
FGHIJKL
MNOPQR
STUVWX
KLMNOP
FGHIJKL
MNOPQR
ZABCDE
FGHIJKL

Right: phototypesetting and transfer lettering were developments that came through in the 1960s to have a major effect on display type design and typography (text phototypesetting was not widespread until the 1970s). Letraset launched dry transfer lettering to quick success in the early 1960s, and revived the sense of fun in typeface design. Besides creating a large library of familiar and established faces so that designers could directly create artwork for film, Letraset also commissioned work from many famous designers and had a strong creative direction, for many years under Colin Brignall. The faces shown here include Milton Glaser's Baby Teeth (top) and Brignall's own Countdown (bottom), a sci-fi period piece and the first Letraset original design.
Far right: two advertisements from the mid-1960s made possible with ease only with phototypesetting. They were set on the Photo Typositor, launched in 1961, which enabled display setting effects such as distortions of type to be easily controlled. While the effects of cutting and tearing, as with the words "Arthritis" or "Alaska", could have been done traditionally, the distortion and exposure trickery of "Mental Illness" and "Narcotic" were entirely photographic.

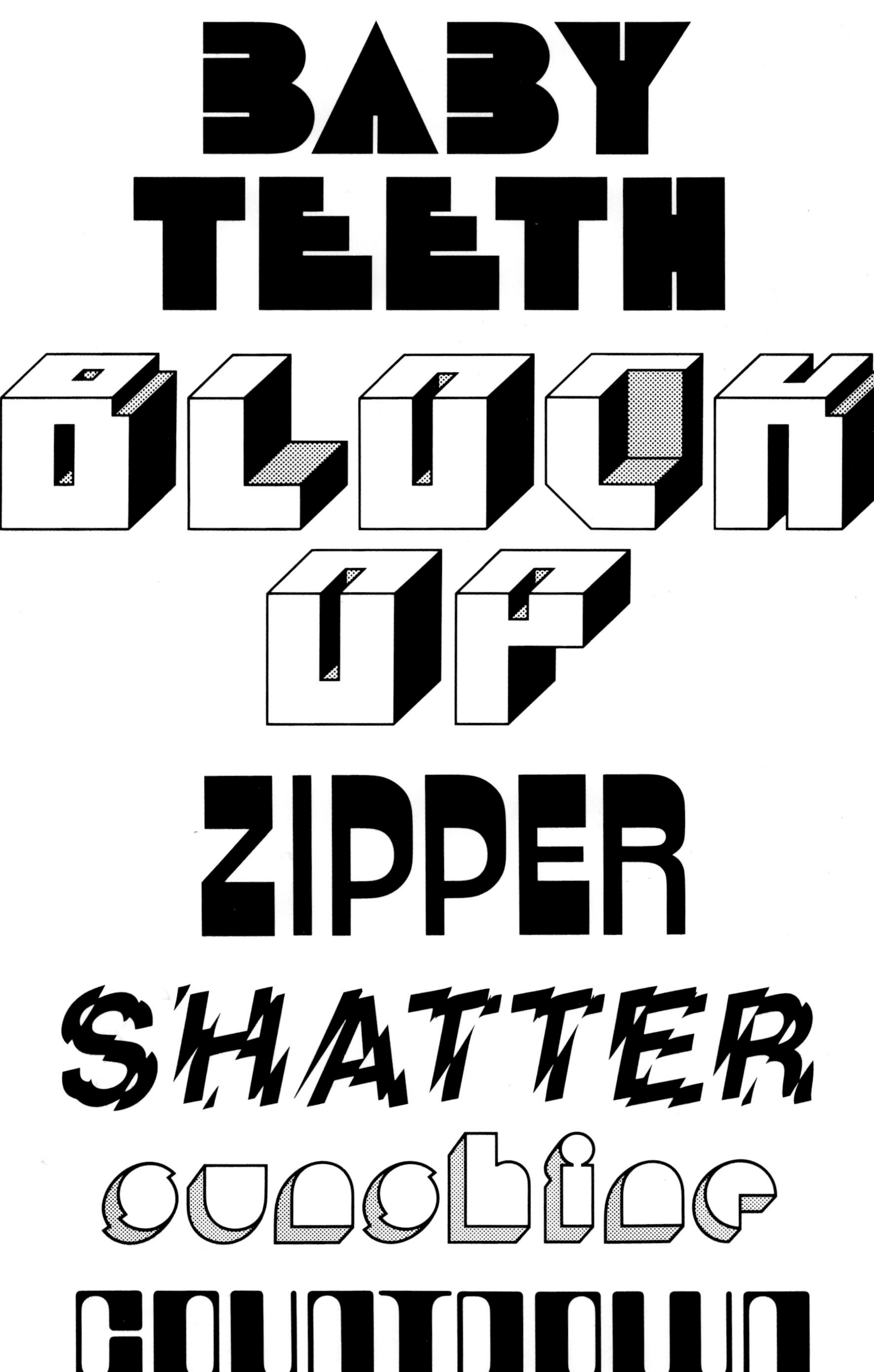

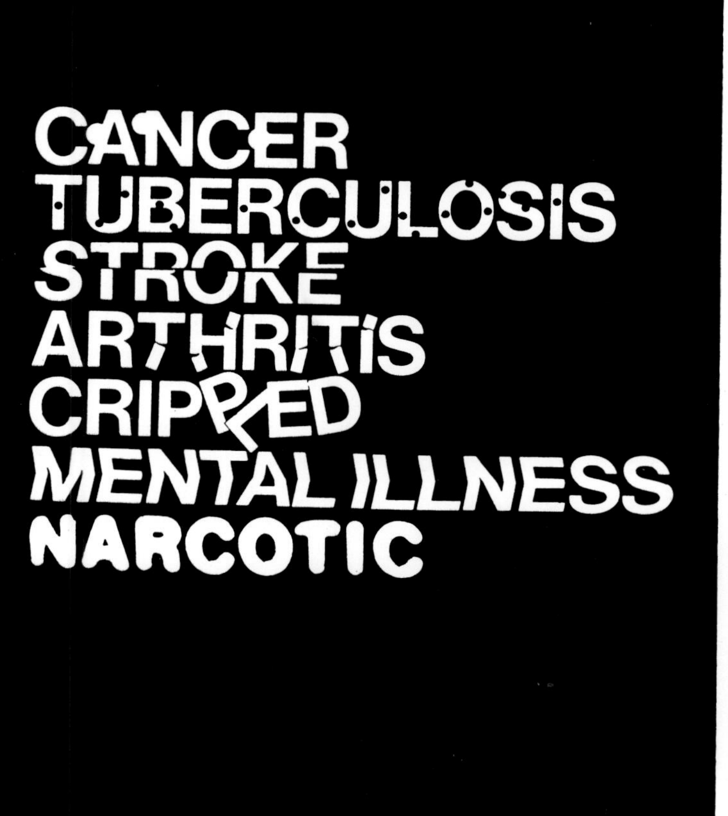
CANCER
TUBERCULOSIS
STROKE
ARTHRITIS
CRIPPLED
MENTAL ILLNESS
NARCOTIC

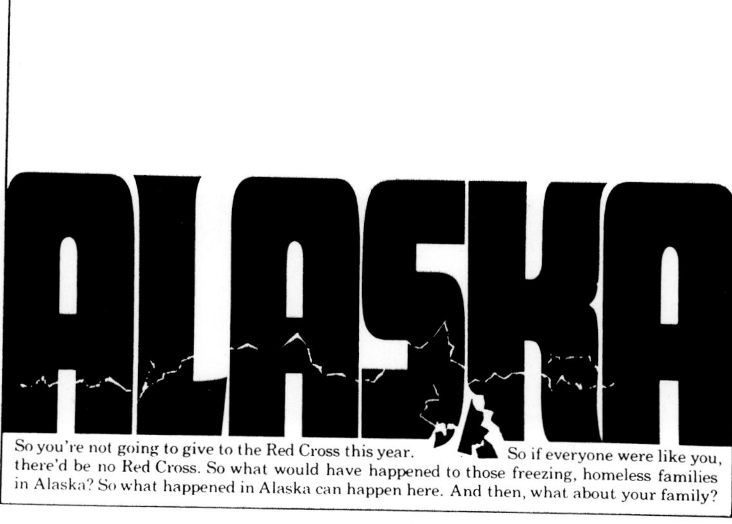
ALASKA
So you're not going to give to the Red Cross this year. So if everyone were like you, there'd be no Red Cross. So what would have happened to those freezing, homeless families in Alaska? So what happened in Alaska can happen here. And then, what about your family?

drawings), but also under its own type design programme. The first, and one of the most distinctive period pieces, was Countdown. Designed by Colin Brignall, who became design director at the company, the face conjures up images of 1960s science fiction and also inspired many shop signs (particularly for boutiques) that wanted to shout their futuristic modernity. Other bizarre or eccentric faces were also produced that may seem just ephemeral gimmicks in one way, but are notable in that they caught the spirit of the age. Quick, convenient and expressively modern: such was Letraset, with an impact on everything from magazines to posters, mass advertising to local newsletters. The company was able to create specially commissioned artwork for companies that required their logo and other artwork in rubdown form, and there was also potential for television graphics, the lettering being ideal for producing titles, information graphics or as the basis for set design lettering. While the type design was inventive and the system's widespread relevance made it a vital constituent for many a design studio, the poor quality of much that resulted undermined Letraset's place in any history of typography. However, it was a crucial contributor to the enfranchisement of a wider body of users involved in the process of making decisions about type. The British graphic designer Rodney Mylius, who helped mount an exhibition of Letraset at the London Design Museum in 1990, summarised the character of the company's contribution to typography in the 1960s: "Looking back at early photographs of the company at work, there is a real sense of frontiers being reached and crossed. Look, for example, at the extraordinary 'modern' design of their retail outlets: huge graphic hands working with giant letters across a designer chess board. You could hardly miss such dynamic design, clean cut and graphic, amidst its dusty retailing neighbours. The early Habitat must have looked tame in comparison. With such a successful product and such a bold image it is easy to understand why Letraset became a household name generic for graphic design."[1]

All this technological change, from major systems to typewriters and rubdown lettering, supported a more open, questioning climate for design, now completely freed from post-war austerity in Britain and other parts of Europe, and reacting, in the US, to the brasher consumerism of the 1950s. The major art movement of the period, Pop Art, was built out of, or against, the prevailing dominance of abstract art and many of the artists who came to be grouped under the label included elements of vernacular typographic and popular graphics in their work: in Britain Eduardo Paolozzi and Richard Hamilton in montage, later processed into a painted form; Andy Warhol, Roy Lichtenstein and Robert Indiana in the US. The ironies, the mixture of visual and verbal wit and the deliberate throw-away, consumer-culture exploration of much of this work can be seen to relate to the punning and ironies introduced into much graphic design in the 1960s, which had implications for type choices as well as layout. The changed climate, the break with ideas of pure, functional design and the realisation that a serious message could be expressed with humour deeply affected the content of innovative commercial communication. Spearheading this change was the work of the American advertising agency Doyle Dane Bernbach. Their Volkswagen Beetle advertising campaign, which began in the late 1950s and ran through the 1960s, not only inverted advertising assumptions by its self-effacing pitch, but also impressed its audience with fresh but restrained typography, the use of a form of Futura suggesting the modern German origins of the car and the sense of good engineering. Type was being

Opposite: two campaigns from Doyle Dane Bernbach, New York, 1960s. Under the leadership of Bill Bernbach (1911–82) – one-time copywriter to Paul Rand – this agency during the late 1950s and 1960s led a creative revolution in advertising, the effects of which were seen around the world. Rules about the relationship of type and image were challenged, conventions about using or not using certain kinds of typeface or setting were abandoned: the concept was everything. For Volkswagen, DDB had a campaign that stressed functional, simple, cheap and reliable qualities – contrary to emphasis on speed, style and glamour. The typographic identity (which still essentially survives) reinforced this: a version of Futura semi-bold connoting Germanic technical know-how. The simplicity of the layout also undercut the pretensions of rival advertising. The campaign for Levy's says everything through picture and headline; the qualities of the concept lie in the linking of typographic and photographic detail. The much-maligned Cooper Black (designed by Oswald B. Cooper, 1921) is resurrected for its generous, rich forms which echo the sandwich in the picture.

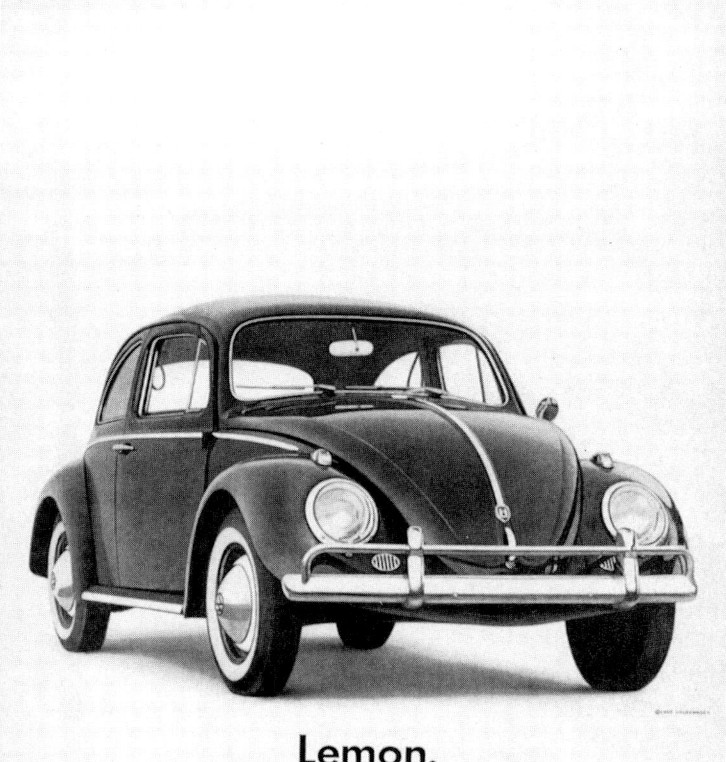
Lemon.
This Volkswagen missed the boat.
The chrome strip on the glove compartment is blemished and must be replaced. Chances are you wouldn't have noticed it; Inspector Kurt Kroner did.
There are 3,389 men at our Wolfsburg factory with only one job: to inspect Volkswagens at each stage of production. (3000 Volkswagens are produced daily; there are more inspectors than cars.)
Every shock absorber is tested (spot checking won't do), every windshield is scanned. VWs have been rejected for surface scratches barely visible to the eye.
Final inspection is really something! VW inspectors run each car off the line onto the Funktionsprüfstand (car test stand), tote up 189 check points, gun ahead to the automatic brake stand, and say "no" to one VW out of fifty.
This preoccupation with detail means the VW lasts longer and requires less maintenance, by and large, than other cars. (It also means a used VW depreciates less than any other car.)
We pluck the lemons; you get the plums.

All good things must come to an end.
Volkswagens die. Like everything else.
Only some people don't believe it.
Take Mrs. Carson Brooks of Oxford, Alabama. So far her '59 has gone over 600,000 miles. And that's with only two engine transplants.
Try telling her the end is near and she'll laugh you right off the farm.
That kind of owner loyalty begins at the VW factory where 100% of production time is spent making our little bug work better and 0% is spent making it look better (see ugly picture above).
It's the only car that's put through 15,397 inspections before it's put up for sale.
It won't give you radiator problems because we never gave it a radiator.
It comes fully equipped with 35 pounds of paint to protect its top and a protective steel bottom to protect its bottom.
So when you see one that looks on its last legs, feel no pity.
It's probably led a healthier life than you have.

You don't have to be Jewish
to love Levy's
real Jewish Rye

You don't have to be Jewish
to love Levy's
real Jewish Rye

You don't have to be Jewish
to love Levy's
real Jewish Rye

used for its wider associations, not its inherent graphic or legibility qualities. Similarly, in DDB's advertisements for Levy's rye bread, the thick, soft but strong contours of Cooper Black are so overtly in sympathy with the basic concept of the wholesome product as to be readable as some form of typographic pun. "Allusive typography" was to become one of the mainstays of the decade. In such work, concept was all important: once the communication had been reduced to the key point and the simplest, most entertaining message had been put across, everything else was made to follow suit.

It was an approach also apparent in the work of many of the leading graphic designers of the era. Reid Miles's art direction of expressive record covers for the Blue Note label from the mid-fifties through the sixties developed an increasingly strong relationship of type and layout to photography, with sympathetic play between the elements, often chopping up type or photography, and frequently merging the two; these techniques were startlingly advanced compared with many other record sleeves. Not only did the communicative power of the apparently simple elements of name, title and picture of the artist(s) provide Miles with new potential, but the consistent strength of his work reinforced the whole label's identity. Herb Lubalin, who moved from an advertising background in the fifties to a type design career in the seventies, produced some of his most memorable work during the sixties, often through relying on typographic tricks to reinforce a strong concept: one famous proposed magazine logo, "Mother & Child", in which the child was an ampersand sitting in the bowl – or womb – of the "o" in mother, was almost trite, but saved by the perfect matching of the visual forms. Indeed, much of the visual punning of the period can seem laboured, but the best work explores the double meanings, the ironies possible when presenting imagery to an audience that was becoming increasingly sophisticated – and jaded – in its consumption of mass communication.

American advertising and its art directors also explored the visual and conceptual potential of typography, and their work found echoes across the Atlantic in the influential designs in Britain of Alan Fletcher, Colin Forbes and Bob Gill, the 1962–5 partnership from which the international design group Pentagram subsequently emerged in 1972. They displayed a similar ability to reduce the statement of a piece of commercial art to a key point that was boldly presented, often through a typographic pun.

The reductive, conceptualising approach is not essentially visual in its initiation, but is broader-based in its search for stimulation for the senses of the target audience. This was a new concern, overlaid on those of the still advancing Swiss School and the International Style. For ordering a mass of information and sorting out a typographic hierarchy, the commandments of Müller-Brockmann and his Swiss School colleagues on *Neue Grafik* offered a truly modern solution, suggesting a method of containing the given material in the most appropriate form, communicating its content in the clearest way. But the rules of International Style did not allow for a display of fun ideas, and were hardly the basis for exciting advertising. By contrast, the conceptual, expressive approach drew on the associations around the subject matter to arrive at a solution that is more than the sum of its parts. As a general rule today, it is this conceptual, associative approach that is used for display work such as posters and press advertising, magazine and brochure design, while the teachings of International Style are more often applied inside publications where there is a mass of information.

Three record sleeves designed by Reid Miles for Blue Note records, 1964–5. From 1954–69 Reid Miles designed an extraordinarily inventive range of sleeves for this specialist jazz record label, exploring the potential of traditional and new technology in capturing the excitement of the subject matter (ironic as he was not a jazz fan). From the photographic methods that enabled the enlarged typewriter face of *right now!* to the redrawing of type for the *In 'n Out* pun, Miles consistently found new ways of developing the expressiveness of sleeve typography. The cover copy was handled as a theme for exploration, akin to a jazz musician working around a tune. Many of his sleeves give motion to the type through repetition, unexpected contrasts, changes of setting and relationship to any underlying grid or baseline.

right
now!
Jackie
McLean
STEREO
THE FINEST IN JAZZ SINCE 1939
Larry Willis/Bob Cranshaw/Clifford Jarvis
84215 BLUE NOTE


CHARLES TOLLIVER HERBIE HANCOCK CECIL MCBEE ROY HAYNES
STEREO
84179 BLUE NOTE
JACKIE McLEAN
"it's time!"...!!!!!!!!

JOE HENDERSON
Kenny Dorham Richard Davis Elvin Jones etc.
STEREO
84166 BLUE NOTE
in'n
OUT

Right: Herb Lubalin was in the forefront of the trend for expressive typography, as seen in the "Spasm" advertisement for a pharmaceutical company and the *Families* magazine logo. His art direction of *Avant Garde* magazine led to the design of the geometric sans serif logotype. This was developed into a complete typeface, whose geometric properties and enlarged ligatures,

coupled with Lubalin's penchant for tight letterspacing, created immensely strong blocks of type, which, thanks to the careful distinction of forms, were surprisingly legible.

Above: *Twen*, December 1965, art directed (and sometimes edited) by Willy Fleckhaus. The typography of this magazine rigorously separated out the components of editorial design and depended on strong photography as the visual treat. Fleckhaus presented a style of art direction in the magazine from 1959–70 that came to be highly influential on magazines and colour supplements.

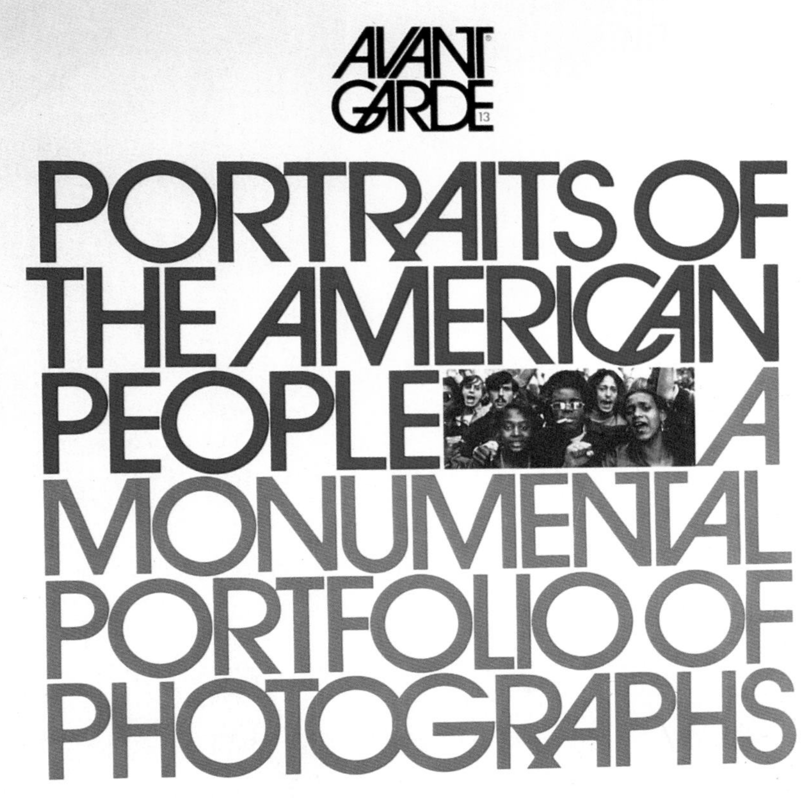

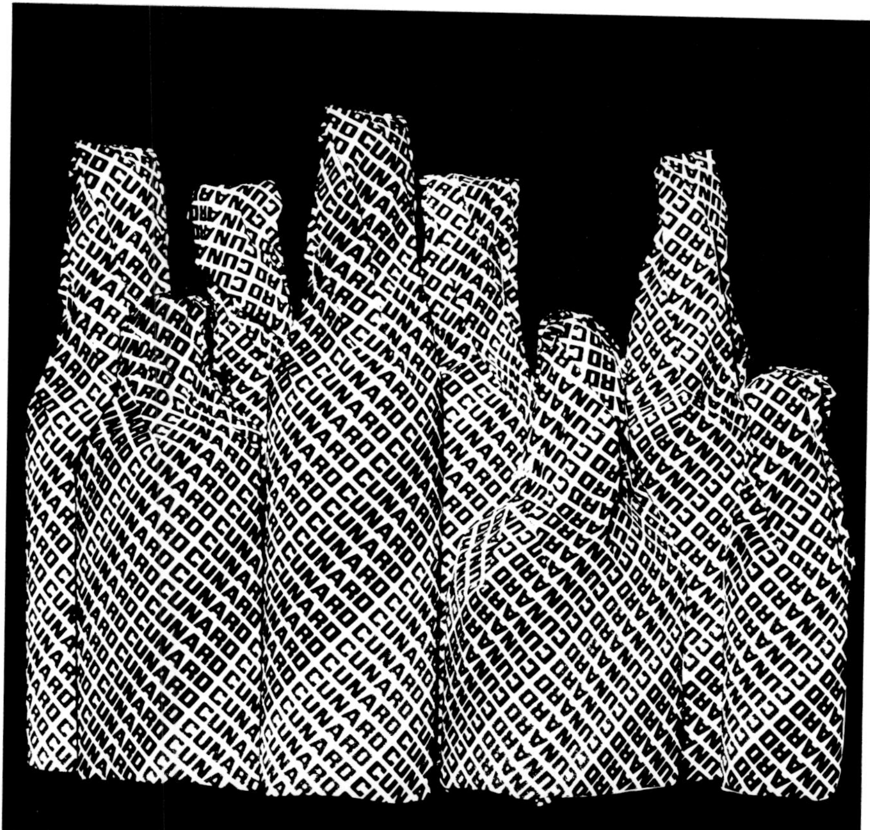

Above, top and above right: three examples of the 1960s output of the Fletcher, Forbes and Gill partnership that later became Pentagram. The expressive typography and the corporate identity development being promoted by American designers found a strong echo in the work of Alan Fletcher, Colin Forbes and Bob Gill whose graphic work ranged from advertising (such as the Pirelli slippers advertisement which uses a typographic pun for a bus poster) to corporate identity (alphabet for Cunard with packaging application shown) to retail design (supermarket poster for Shredded Wheat).

Above: logo for the 1968 Olympic Games in Mexico, designed by Lance Wyman. The rigour of International Style and the discipline of corporate identity combined here with an attempt to reflect the character of the location. Wyman (born 1937) abstracted the stripe pattern from Mexican imagery, refining it into a logo that also suggests sporting metaphors.

Other stylistic associations of the sixties are much more melodramatic in their period quality, responding to the sense of release expressed around youth culture, music and fashion and new attitudes that challenged establishment ideas. In the field of magazine design one of the most influential practitioners, whose work continues to have resonance twenty years later, was Willi Fleckhaus (1925–83). His work on the German magazine *Twen* through the sixties showed the art director in the ascendant (Fleckhaus had trained as a journalist and his input to the magazine included the origination of ideas and treatments). His pioneering approach involved ferociously cropping photography for dramatic effect, clearing body copy off visual spreads and on to solid pages of text, and using blocks of type like building blocks to construct the page, suggest the grid or challenge the order. Often, dramatic contrasts in the scale of type added tension to the page, with Fleckhaus elaborately cutting and adjusting type to fit his intentions and the space allotted. Echoes of this work can be seen in the fresh look of *Nova* magazine in Britain in the sixties, also targeted at the younger set and containing provocative features that devoted opening spreads to dramatic photography, often paring down the text and playing with different typefaces to convey a more emotive kick to the beginning of an article and merge more fluidly with the illustrative content.

Fleckhaus designed the covers of many titles for the publisher Suhrkamp, which were exclusively typographic, with the type on or out of a deliberately restricted palette of background colours. Despite the simplicity of the elements he produced highly expressive and varied covers which reinforced an overall identity for the publisher. There were, of course, precedents for such an approach, with the work of Morison for Gollancz and Mardersteig for Albatross in the 1930s, and Tschichold's Penguin books up to the 1950s.

However, in the 1960s Penguin started to break with its heritage of overwhelming identity, reinforced by classical good taste, and instead – noticeably through the covers designed by Alan Aldridge – joined the bandwagon of Pop culture, seeking to impart to the new Penguin titles a little of the spirit of the age. Penguin's founder and chairman Allen Lane took a dislike to this, and demanded a halt to "vulgar covers" in 1967. But the agenda of the "permissive generation" could not be avoided, and there was a typographic implication. In the mid- and late sixties record sleeves branched out into a whole range of eclectic type design, often snatching old designs and redrawing letters. "Underground" magazines and other expressions of protest broke the rules wilfully: articles in the magazine *Oz*, for example, could and did appear with excessively long lines, ranged right with a ragged left stepping out, and all reversed from a sludgy photograph. The point was not necessarily readability or even legibility: the protest was evident in its appearance. Typewriter text was popular not only because it was cheap, but also because it embodied the right associations of rejecting business processes and being the product of a counter-culture. Poster art for rock concerts and festivals produced some of the most striking examples of unreadable but highly communicative calligraphy, with elaborately hand-drawn or photographically stretched words suggestive of the tricks of distortion that computers and photocopiers would make much easier a few years later. Victor Moscoso's psychedelic posters in the US were the most polished examples of this work, although it was a style widely copied, with different variations – in Britain, the revival of Art Nouveau ideas propelled the florid lettering of that period into more psychedelic forms.

Opposite: the 1960s counter culture, and particularly the rock music industry, developed its own forms of graphic communications. Underground magazines, notably *Oz*, challenged legibility in their illustrative collages of text, photography and striking uses of process colour. But it was the posters of the San Francisco music scene that set the pace and took the psychedelic expressiveness furthest, as shown by the four here which distort lettering and its meaning to the point of no return. Top left: concert poster for Procol Harum at the Fillmore, designed by Lee Conklin, 1967. Top right: concert poster for The Grateful Dead, The Doors and others at the Fillmore, designed by Wes Wilson, 1966. Bottom left: concert poster for The Doors and others at the Avalon Ballroom, designed by Victor Moscoso, 1967. Bottom right: concert poster for The Yardbirds, The Doors and others, designed by B. McLean, 1967. Tied in with the styling of these posters is a rejection of the straitjacket, establishment values of type. However, there are traditional bases for the designers' work – Moscoso repeatedly used Playbill as the face to distort, while Art Nouveau is a clear influence on other artists. Typewriter faces would sometimes appear as a suitably unrefined method of adding extensive credits and other non-display text.

BILL GRAHAM PRESENTS IN SAN FRANCISCO
TICKETS

BILL GRAHAM PRESENTS IN SAN FRANCISCO
GRATEFUL DEAD
CHICAGO BLUES BAND
TICKETS

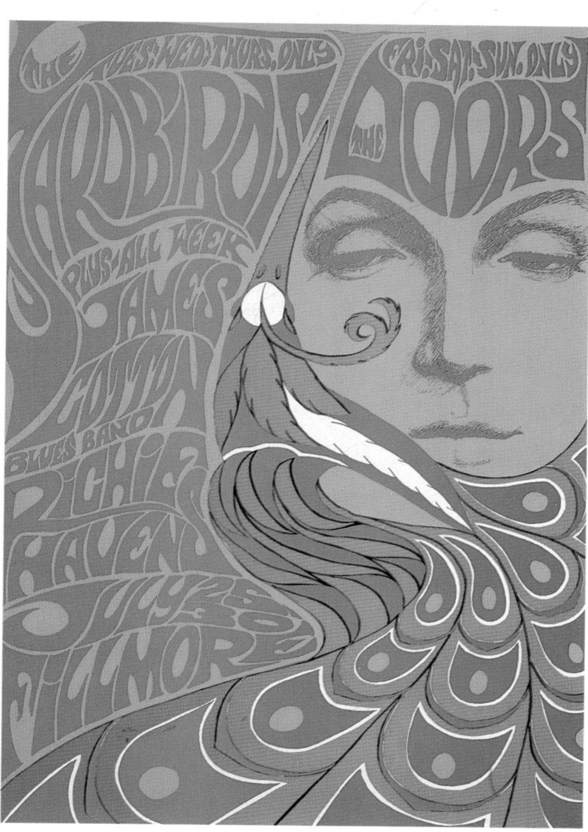
TUES·WED·THURS, ONLY
FRI·SAT·SUN. ONLY
THE DOORS
PLUS·ALL WEEK
BLUES BAND

This comparative frivolity did nothing to divert the research behind one of the more seminal achievements of the period: optical character recognition (OCR) and the creation of the early faces that could be read by computers. OCR-A was issued in 1966 and is an extremely coarse design, with characters produced on a 4 by 7 grid. OCR-B, issued in 1968 and with Adrian Frutiger as a consultant on its design, works to a much finer grid of 18 by 25 enabling a more sophisticated design. OCR-A and its forerunner, E13B, could be seen to influence the stylised sixties "robot" faces such as Letraset's Countdown, as well as the elegantly squared-off designs of Aldo Novarese's Eurostile, extended from his earlier Microgramma.

At the same time research was proceeding into faces that could work for screen display as well as input. Here simplicity was of the essence in order to create distinctions that the machine could comprehend, as well as create clear forms that the human eye could swiftly assimilate. The Dutch designer Wim Crouwel, for one, was committed to the idea that the screen would be the pre-eminent source of typographic communication, and was concerned that more effort should go into developing appropriate designs. He devised a simplified alphabet that used only horizontal and vertical elements, having no diagonals or curves. All the characters are the same width and to form "m" and "w" he had to underline the "n" and "v", respectively. There was only one alphabet, not an upper and lower case.

Such experimentation has mercifully, for human readers at least, been largely bypassed by rapid development of the ability of machines to read, display and output high-quality fonts with enough information to satisfy the designs of more familiar and legible faces. But it still has some relevance to dot matrix displays and other public information systems.

Below: the need for computerised machinery to read the alphabet led engineers and designers to develop a range of faces. At the same time the excitement attached to technological advance, epitomised by the space race between the US and the USSR, led to the fashion for apparently machine-readable or machine-generated lettering on signs, advertising and other display applications. OCR-A (below) and OCR-B (bottom) came as a result of standards laid down by the European Computer Manufacturers' Association (ECMA) in 1965 for computer-readable faces. OCR-A was designed by ECMA engineers in 1966. OCR-B was produced two years later with Adrian Frutiger as design advisor in collaboration with ECMA; its design is nearly four times finer than the earlier version, and it therefore requires much greater processing power for it to be read by machine.

ABCDEFGHIJKLM
NOPQRSTUVWXYZ
1234567890

a b c d e f g h i j k l m n o p q r s t u v w x y z
A B C D E F G H I J K L M N O P Q R S T U V W X Y Z
1 2 3 4 5 6 7 8 9 0

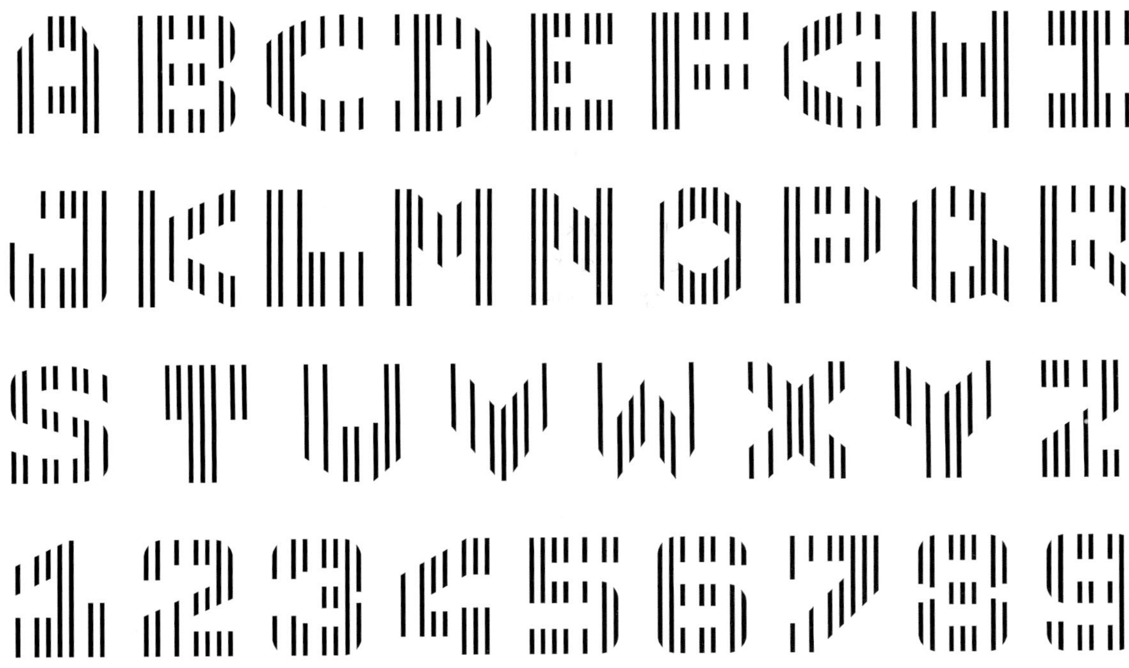

Left: CMC7, a face developed for use with magnetic inks in the early 1960s (designers unknown). It found very little demand since its crude methods of creating character recognition were so soon superseded.
Below left: E13B, developed by unknown designers for the American Bankers' Association and widely adopted for machine-recognisable numerals; it can still be seen on cheque books today. No alphabet exists, but the creation of distinctive characters with the minimal grid has similarities with the simplified letter structure in Wim Crouwel's poster and in Crouwel's New Alphabet project of 1967 (below) as well as in Letraset's Countdown (see page 156), where the rectangular, ill-balanced look is now taken simply as a modern styling.

Left: exhibition poster by Wim Crouwel, 1968. Crouwel (born 1924) was the designer of a minimal, single alphabet experimental typeface in 1967 (above), and his interest in reducing letterforms to their essential components is further explored in this poster. The visible grid plots the construction of the characters, but the result (albeit intentionally) is more easily read by computers than by humans.

This period of rapid technological change and Swingin' Sixties libertarian attitudes did not enthral the traditionalists. Stanley Morison, responsible for reviving so many classic faces while at Monotype, could be relied upon to present a sober argument for meticulous respect for the orthodox. In a new edition of 1967 of his classic 1930 essay "First Principles of Typography", he wrote in a postscript his rejoinder to the pressure of International Style and the new wave of sans serif faces:

***. . . claims are made that the style appropriate for the time consists not only in the choice of sans serif type but that it be composed in asymmetrical form, without recourse to italics. Paragraphs are to be closely set without indentation, and the whole appearance of the page must depart wherever possible from age-old custom. The twentieth century would thus mark itself off by its distinctive typography as the great period of revaluation . . . Tradition itself is not well understood at the present day in some quarters. If it were a reflection of the stagnation or prejudice of past ages of printers, little attention need be given to it by historians and none by practitioners of the arts and crafts. But tradition is more than the embalming of forms customary in states that have been long since cast aside. The sum of experience accumulated in more than one man's lifetime, and unified by succeeding generations, is not to be safely discarded. Tradition, therefore, is another name for unanimity about fundamentals which has been brought into being by the trials, errors and corrections of many centuries. Experientia docet.***

Appropriately perhaps, Morison ended on a note that, with the decline of classical education, would be savoured by few of the new generation of typographers. As for those ignoring his fundamentals, they made the sixties a period of typographic exuberance, shoddiness, research and invention, some of which bore fruit soon after.

Right: Sabon, designed by Jan Tschichold, 1964–7; the last major work by a typographer who had managed to lead both the new typography and the traditional revival. In receiving the commission for this face he was effectively being asked to span the two sides of his career. A group of German printers had the idea of developing a face that would look the same whether it was produced from hand-composed foundry type, Monotype matrices or linecast by a Linotype; as the project developed, it came to take in photosetting as well. This technologically driven requirement was to be manifested through a design akin to a slightly condensed form of Monotype Garamond, with Linotype, Monotype and Stempel all to manufacture the result. In many ways, Tschichold's design matches Stanley Morison's dictum that good type design is invisible: in producing Sabon, he had to cope with three sets of body widths for the three different systems which, in particular, meant a problem since on Linotype kerning cannot be done – the lower-case italic "f" was chopped at the bottom instead.

Below right: Antique Olive, designed by Roger Excoffon for the Olive type foundry, 1962–6, a sans serif to follow the success of the Swiss-designed Helvetica and Univers. It is modern, with a tendency towards the geometric, and compact, with a high x-height and very short ascenders and descenders, but has a distinctive flair that takes it away from the coldness sometimes found in its two contemporaries. Points of sharp contrast where the curves meet the stems, belying the otherwise squared, monotone line, give it a sparkle that recommends it – at least to the French. Excoffon was aiming for maximum legibility; although its sans serif form perhaps inhibits a widespread use in text. Its use in French advertising is firmly established. That it is not more internationally used is strange, since its high x-height gives it a fairly uniform effect in different languages; for example, it tends to absorb differences such as the high number of capitals in German. Antique Olive lacks the neutrality of both Helvetica and Univers, for which they have been criticised, but which is also their strength.

Sabon &

SABON 123

& *Sabon*

abcdefghijklmnopqrstuvwxyz
ABDCEFGHIJKLMNOPQRSTUVWXYZ
ABDCEFGHIJKLMNOPQRSTUVWXYZ
1234567890 1234567890 .;:‘’ß&!?

**Antique Olive**

**abdcefghijklmnopqrstuvwxyz**
**ABCDEFGHIJKLMNOPQRSTUVWXYZ**
**1234567890**

"1970" is set in American Typewriter, by Joel Kaden and Tony Stan, an early face from the International Typeface Corporation, an important advocate of the rights of the type designer. Below right is part of a page from Wolfgang Weingart's 1976 graphic essay for *Typografische Monatsblätter*, one of his influential projections of a typography that broke with the

1970...

Himmelblau
Blau
Beige

hingestreuter
hingetupfter
weisser Punkt
weisse Kapelle

z

reductive Swiss style. Matthew Carter's Galliard "G" and its distinctive "g" are shown top, a 1978 digital revival of the style of face associated with the sixteenth-century French punchcutter Robert Granjon. The details right are elements highly enlarged from six point of Carter's Bell Centennial of 1978; the highly distorted lines and curves show Carter's carefully designed compensations for ink spread and impaired legibility when the face endured usage in telephone directories, where a combination of six point size under high-speed printing on poor quality paper demanded a resilient type. The "z" is from Hermann Zapf's Chancery of 1979, a highly calligraphic face in which the roman slopes as well as the italic. The "f" set shows the different weights available in Frutiger, designed by Adrian Frutiger and released in 1976.

fffff

Kaktus
Steinödendistel
Steinöde
langsames Drehen
Windmühlensegel
Windmühlenkegel
weisse Treppe
sanfter Anstieg


A successful new toy will be tested to destruction – and phototypesetting in the late 1960s and early 1970s suffered the same treatment. The wonders of easier letterspacing and kerning and of mixing sizes and faces were there for the taking and were taken – at a cost. Many typographers gave in to the temptation to devise innovative distortions around the potential of a particular face, often in ways that lessened the legibility and aesthetic qualities of the original design. Creative exuberance was sometimes to blame, but the more common reason was pressure to be more economical with space. Newspapers were among the worst transgressors: the potential for getting headlines to fit at the expense of a balanced layout was all too evident.

But even among those whose work is of the highest quality, such as Herb Lubalin or Willi Fleckhaus, the tendency to use letterspacing so tight that words became blocks of ligatures was clearly in part due to the opportunity of at last being able to play with type in this way with relative ease. Positive spacing – positioning the letters more widely apart than normal setting – was only a small inconvenience in hot metal, requiring the insertion of a space, but the process of negative letterspacing required the filing down of a metal letter, and kerned letters had to be specially cut with the character projecting beyond the shank of the type. With phototypesetting, however, the typographer needed only to specify that the copy should be set minus one or two units, and there was no need for letter-by-letter adjustment, as before. Phototypesetting not only changed the way type could be generated and manipulated, but also changed the degree to which this could be done. Until the late nineteenth century, by long-standing tradition, typographic spacing had been measured by the point: one-twelfth of an em, 72 to the inch. The advent of the Monotype system in the late 1890s brought a new level of sophistication: Monotype worked to a unit-based system, founded on the principle of units relative to an em, where the em measurement was the width of the "m" of the typeface. Monotype used 18 units to one em. The extra advantage of photosetting was the increased number of units possible to the em once the physical limitations of metal were dispensed with. The Maxphoto system, for instance, uses 96 units to one em.

With the new systems, type could be spaced so tightly that letters overlapped and words became squeezed and only semi-legible. At one point this became quite fashionable, lending itself best to sans serif faces: after all, it transformed the appearance of the design into something that was uniquely modern. Only experimental or art work, such as Werkman's typographic constructions, had previously explored this merging of letterforms.

There was more to the notion of tight letterspacing than a simple whim of fashion. Underlying some of the experimentation was a further development of the hitherto unanswered search for archetypal word- and letterforms. It seemed to some that, at last, the support for sans serif faces as being the most functional letterforms was to be reinforced by a technology that increased their legibility. The long-standing argument that serifs help guide the eye along the line, joining letters into words, could be balanced by photocomposition's ability to close up sans serif faces into tight "word images", suggesting that a more functionally precise typography had found a different solution to the same problem. Other evidence, however, still holds that long measures of text are more comfortably read when set in certain serif faces. In this debate, based both on theoretical and empirical data, finite answers are unlikely to emerge. It is an area in which there is still an absence of hard fact – and impressions fall between statistics and subjectivity, legibility and readability.

Modernism's love of geometric forms could not supply a definitive specification for the communication of text, for such geometry bears no inherent relationship to the nature of the alphabet. Adrian Frutiger demonstrated in the 1970s that if characters from some of the most widely read typefaces were overlaid on to each other (Garamond, Baskerville, Bodoni, Times, Palatino, Optima and Helvetica), the skeletal forms that emerged from the superimpositions corresponded closely to faces used in the mass market of newspaper type (Excelsior, Caledonia). The sans serifs Helvetica and Univers matched the basic outline exactly, but deviated, of course, in having no serifs and a more constant stroke thickness. For Frutiger, this illustrated that:

***the foundations of legibility are like a crystallisation, formed by hundreds of years of use of selected, distinctive typefaces. The usable forms that have stood the test of time are perhaps permanently accepted by humankind as standards conforming to aesthetic laws . . . where there are excessive innovations of form or designs of poor quality, the typeface encounters a certain resistance in the reader and the reading process is hindered.***[1]

The concern about "designs of poor quality" was well founded. As with the change to hot metal, the rush of manufacturers to offer an impressive variety of faces on their phototypesetting systems, increased by a good range of anything innovative, prompted the supply of many poorly drawn faces. Distortions inevitably resulted from the magnification of one master size to give different sizes, instead of supplying masters in the different sizes themselves – ignoring, in this corner-cutting process, the need for the slight changes of balance, in cuts at different sizes, that would preserve the same visual character. There was also a failure in many instances to see equivalent standards of setting observed by photocompositors as were practised under the more restrictive terms of hot metal. And the alleged decline in typographic quality was not restricted only to the methods of generating the type, but spread to methods of printing: the transfer of most printing from letterpress to offset lithography, plus the advent



Right: "Basics" packaging from Sainsbury supermarkets, UK, early 1970s, an example of how far the International Style spread. Own-brand products were colour-coded in rational, minimal packs on which sans serif type simply named the product clearly, with the minimum of supporting detail. The sales pitch was that there was no sales pitch: with styling to match a rational presentation, the message was that nothing was wasted on packaging and that therefore the product must be good value.

Below and below right: Mobil signage and newsletter advising on corporate identity application, designed by Chermayeff & Geismar Associates. The new Mobil logo has a red "o" which is both a pun on wheels and also, at least initially, a link back to the earlier red flying horse logo. A comprehensive identity was established and extended, requiring the designers to pass on their ideas of typographic and other visual control to all staff involved in its implementation, through such means as the newsletter.

Above: pictograms by Otl Aicher for the Munich Olympics, 1972. The clarity and expressiveness of these symbols advanced an area of growing importance and relevance to type designers and typographers, namely how best to communicate quickly in situations of multi-lingual demand. Later developed for wider use, these signs clearly depict different sports from the basis of a 20×20 grid, with an overall identity that makes them stand out easily among other signage.

## Mobil Graphics 9

### Editor's Note

The Mobil Graphics series was initiated to establish good two-way communications to achieve Mobil's graphics design goals.

Articles in the series are tailored to meet the need for guidance in graphics problem areas as they are identified by Mobil people around the world. In previous issues, there have been articles on the use of alphabets, general arrangement of type, line spacing and obtaining reproduction copy.

This issue features a detailed description and visual illustrations of the Mobil Alphabet's letter spacing, which was generated by numerous requests received worldwide.

**Graphic Design Advisory Group Expanded**
The Mobil Graphic Design Advisory Group, the central graphic coordinating body at New York Headquarters has, with the addition of the Exploration and Producing Division in 1976, been expanded to ten members. The Group now represents:

1 U.S. Marketing and Refining Division
2 International Division
3 Exploration & Producing Division
4 Mobil Chemical
5 Mobil Sales and Supply
6 Corporate Purchasing
7 Trademark Counsel
8 Corporate Controllers
9 Corporate Research, Engineering, Products and Packaging
10 Corporate Relations

The members of this group represent the principal graphics areas of Mobil's worldwide operations.

**Mobil 1 Packages**
The Mobil 1 brand name and package design is now being marketed worldwide in a variety of sizes, three of which are shown here. The graphics, which had to be adjusted for each container size and configuration, were developed by Mobil's graphics consultants and coordinated by the Corporate Design and Graphics Development department.

## Mobil Graphics 10

### Editor's Note

One of the most frequently asked graphics questions is when is it appropriate and permissible to use the concentric "o" version of the Mobil Trademark. Actually the question is more pertinent today than it was in the early stages of the program when its use was limited simply to technical and economical considerations. This issue covers all aspects of this important subject.

### Specialty Packages Now International

The new specialty package design, originally developed for Mobil Oil Française, is now being used in English language versions throughout much of the International Division. The photo below shows part of the Australian product range.

The bold new package shapes, colors, and graphics were specifically designed for maximum display impact and customer convenience. Products are grouped by color coding: white packages for Service Group; yellow packages for Home/Do-it-yourself Group; red packages for Additive Group; green packages for Windshield Service Group; blue packages for Appearance Group.

The packages are a mixture of pigmented plastic containers and printed metal cans. All are tall and slim, with a full width plastic cap in contrasting white or black. The product designation, essentially a clear generic description of the contents, is printed in Mobil Alphabet lettering in black or white to match the cap color. Because of the strong emphasis on color coding, the concentric "o" version of the Mobil trademark has been used on all colored packages.

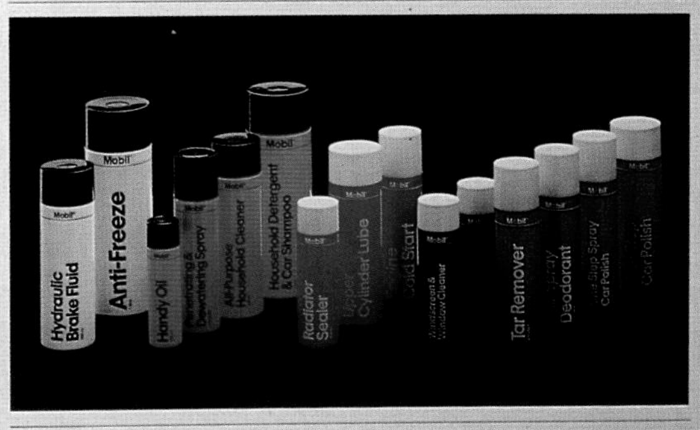

of inkjet and laser printing technology, unleashed all sorts of problems in which new forms of control were seen as desirable. The type historian and writer Fernand Baudin saw the changes as "shattering" and thought they had "overturned typographic discipline".[2] The series of rapid changes in the nature of typographic composition, including the IBM typewriter and Letraset as well as computer-driven setting, had all arrived in swift succession, throwing up new opportunities and making new demands on skills, but Baudin shrewdly observed an underlying lack of any direction. To counteract this he called for the instigation of a code of copy preparation as a basic part of education, a modern equivalent to the training of fine handwriting in previous years:

***workshops bulge with a surplus of modern machinery, conscripted technicians and engineers and experts who more-or-less know what they are doing. It cannot be said that everyone is happy . . . the composition and preparation of any text is a material as well as an intellectual exercise, a hard, painstaking task requiring drafts and successive recopying . . .***

An international and interdisciplinary approach to the integration of this concern about copy and layout status into education was vital to improving print standards, said Baudin. A retrospective glance at twenty years of photocomposition and other print developments reveals his cry as acutely sensitive to the implications inherent in the new-found freedom of many designers, office workers and others persuaded by "desktop publishing" technology.

Despite Baudin's lament, certain moves were being made in the 1970s to devise a profession of type design and typography to match the modernity of the means. There was, of course, a clear need to understand the workings of the new technology, and colleges sought to answer this while major manufacturers gave some support. But there was also a changing attitude within the profession of graphic design, expressed by a significant new arrival on the scene of type producers that expressed both the changing needs of the type specifier and the potential of the technology: this was the International Typeface Corporation, ITC.

Below: Trinité by Bram de Does, issued by BobstGraphic/Autologic. Trinité was issued with three lengths of ascender and descender – short, medium and long. In the long form it appears to be an older, transitional face; in the short form it takes on the compact, high x-height character of ITC faces and is more in keeping with its period.
Right: Bell Centennial, commissioned by AT&T from Linotype and designed by Matthew Carter, 1975–8. The telephone company wanted a more "efficient" typeface than its existing Bell Gothic (designed in 1938 by Chauncey Griffith of Mergenthaler Linotype), to be legible with the least space consumption for use in directories. Carter designed letters and numbers that retained wide distinctions even when their forms became degraded, allowing for deformations and ink spread by substantial cut-aways on the characters. He also created a range of fonts for the different aspects of the listings: the name and number was in bold, with slightly wider and taller letters, while the address was in a lighter, more condensed form.

1 In former days the shape a new book was

2 In former days the shape a new book was

3 In former days the shape a new book was

Tddyyy

NNN

ABCDEFGHIJKLM
NOPQRSTUVWXYZ
1234567890

Auctoritas in his regionibus maxima erat. Iam admodum mitigati raptarum animi erant sed earum parentes tum maxime sordida veste lacrimisque et querelis civitates concitabant undique legationes mittebantur ad Titum Tatium regem Sabinorum cuius auctoritas in his regionibus maxima erat.

Auctoritas in his regionibus maxima erat. Iam admodum mitigati raptarum animi erant sed earum parentes tum maxime sordida veste lacrimisque et querelis civitates concitabant undique legationes mittebantur ad Titum Tatium regem Sabinorum cuius

**Auctoritas in his regionibus maxima erat. Iam admodum mitigati raptarum animi erant sed earum parentes tum maxime sordida veste lacrimisque et querelis civitates concitabant undique legationes mittebantur ad Titum**

**AUCTORITAS IN HIS REGIONIBUS MAXIMA ERAT. IAM ADMODUM MITIGATI RAPTARUM ANIMI ERANT SED EARUM PARENTES TUM MAXIME SORDIDA VESTE LACRIMISQUE ET QUERELIS CIVITATES**

Right: Frutiger, designed by Adrian Frutiger, 1973–6. Originally created for signage at Charles de Gaulle Airport, Paris, which opened in 1975, it was issued by Linotype in 1976 and was quickly taken up by many other type manufacturers. A descendant of Frutiger's Univers in its basic choice of forms, it is much more open – the "c" and "e" scarcely begin to close in, the "j" and "g" do not hook round. Capitals are smaller than in Univers, and ascenders and descenders longer. Frutiger looked back to Roman inscriptional capitals for these forms, notably less geometric than Univers, and moving away from the earlier Swiss-style neutral forms.

Frutiger

abcdefghijklmnopqrstuvwxyz

ABCDEFGHIJKLMNOPQRSTUVWXYZ

1234567890

ITC was formed in 1970 by designers Herb Lubalin and Aaron Burns joining forces with Ed Rondthaler of Photo-Lettering Inc., to set up a company that would market new typeface designs as artwork supplied to other type and typesetting equipment manufacturers. In effect, ITC was a type design agency, building on the expertise and archive that the Lubalin and Burns partnership had already created, but bringing in new designers and designs to license across manufacturers. Royalties would be paid on the usage of the face, and the success of the design would directly benefit its creator. This was not just a vaguely good-spirited punt at offering a service, but a reaction to the prevailing trend of typeface piracy. If one supplier had a design that another did not have, photo-technology made it extremely easy simply to duplicate the master matrix characters and present a design under a new name, without any royalties going to the originators of that face. It was not in the interests of good typeface designers or manufacturers for such a situation to continue, but neither was it desirable or practical to expect good designs to be tied to one system only.

ITC launched its type library in 1971 with Lubalin's Avant Garde Gothic, drawn from his work for *Avant Garde* magazine in the sixties. Next was a recut extended family by Ed Benguiat of a turn-of-the-century design, Souvenir, originally carried by American Type Founders, at that point effectively defunct. New faces, recut faces and extended families poured forth. ITC was, and is, effectively a publisher – a new face being a new title and needing to perform through different retailers (or type manufacturers) for ITC to be profitable. Achieving this, and propagating information about new typographic practice, was done through *U&lc* magazine, first published in 1973 and now said to have a worldwide readership of around one million. While it is at one level a sophisticated piece of direct mail, it also represents, and has helped to create, the idea of a world typographic community who share a need for information on new faces and new techniques.

In the first edition *U&lc* took up as a campaigning issue the subject that had helped spawn the company – type piracy. An article by Rondthaler admitted that the copying of faces was as old as typefounding itself (and was certainly very much a part of the hot-metal era), but insisted that it was only the arrival of

**1970...**

Examples of the early output and impact of the International Typeface Corporation (ITC) and its founders are shown here and on pages 178–9. Right: Tiffany, designed by Ed Benguiat in 1974, drew its inspiration from the late nineteenth-century Ronaldson and the early twentieth-century Caxton Old Face from ATF. American Typewriter, designed by Joel Kaden and Tony Stan in 1974, set out to create the flavour of early typewriter faces — unlike those, however, it has different letter widths and has been developed into a large family. ITC Fat Face, designed by Bonder and Tom Carnase, was released in 1970, one of the company's first display faces. Serif Gothic, designed by Herb Lubalin and Tony DiSpagna in 1972–4, takes the geometric simplicity of modern sans serif faces by having a monotone line, then adds small serifs; the designers were aiming for a face that worked well in display and text. Below: strong designs carried on the promotional brochures used to launch ITC faces.

# Tiffany

## American Typewriter

I am admidum mitigati raptarun animi erant sed earum tum maxime sordida veste misque et querelis civitates con citabant undique legationes mit tebantur ad Titum Tatium regem Sabino om cuius auctoritas in his regionibus ima erat. Iam admodum mitigati raptarum animi erant sed earum parentes tum ime sordida veste lacrimisque et querelis vitates concitabant undique legationes mit ad Titum Tatium regem Sabinorum.

## Fat Face

## Serif Gothic

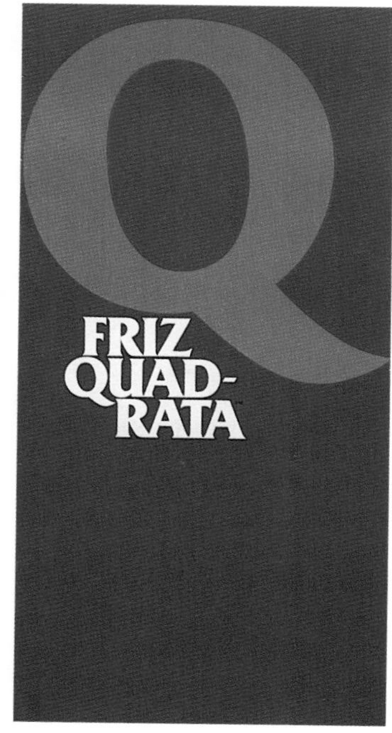

Right: the first issue of ITC's magazine *U&lc*, 1973, designed by Herb Lubalin, which contained a blistering attack on type piracy. Below: Avant Garde, designed by Herb Lubalin and Tom Carnase and based on the lettering created by Lubalin for *Avant Garde* magazine. Offering an unusually high number of ligatures and alternative letters in its display sizes, it was intended to be highly flexible and allow wide creative expression by art directors and designers. Lubalin, who used it set tight, was appalled at some of the uses it was put to; when the Audi campaign ran in the early 1970s using Avant Garde for headline and body copy so tight that letters even join together (opposite page), he wrote an article praising Helmut Krone, the DDB art director who created it.

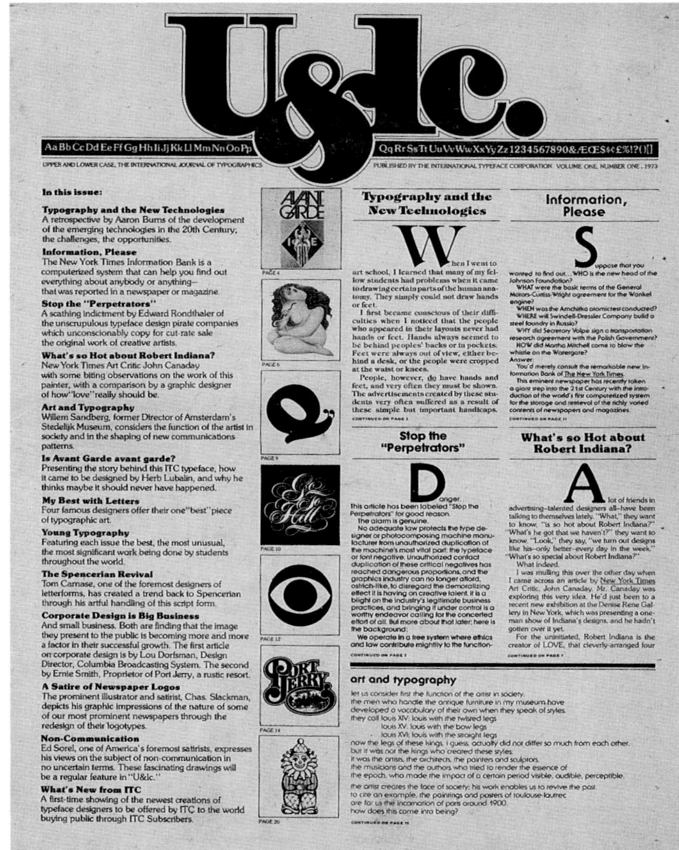

U&lc.

Aa Bb Cc Dd Ee Ff Gg Hh Ii Jj Kk Ll Mm Nn Oo Pp Qq Rr Ss Tt Uu Vv Ww Xx Yy Zz 1234567890&ÆŒ$¢£%!?()[]

UPPER AND LOWER CASE, THE INTERNATIONAL JOURNAL OF TYPOGRAPHICS

PUBLISHED BY THE INTERNATIONAL TYPEFACE CORPORATION. VOLUME ONE, NUMBER ONE, 1973

**In this issue:**

**Typography and the New Technologies**
A retrospective by Aaron Burns of the development of the emerging technologies in the 20th Century; the challenges, the opportunities.

**Information, Please**
The New York Times Information Bank is a computerized system that can help you find out everything about anybody or anything— that was reported in a newspaper or magazine.

**Stop the "Perpetrators"**
A scathing indictment by Edward Rondthaler of the unscrupulous typeface design pirate companies which unconscionably copy for cut-rate sale the original work of creative artists.

**What's so Hot about Robert Indiana?**
New York Times Art Critic John Canaday with some biting observations on the work of this painter, with a comparison by a graphic designer of how "love" really should be.

**Art and Typography**
Willem Sandberg, former Director of Amsterdam's Stedelijk Museum, considers the function of the artist in society and in the shaping of new communications patterns.

**Is Avant Garde avant garde?**
Presenting the story behind this ITC typeface, how it came to be designed by Herb Lubalin, and why he thinks maybe it should never have happened.

**My Best with Letters**
Four famous designers offer their one "best" piece of typographic art.

**Young Typography**
Featuring each issue the best, the most unusual, the most significant work being done by students throughout the world.

**The Spencerian Revival**
Tom Carnase, one of the foremost designers of letterforms, has created a trend back to Spencerian through his artful handling of this script form.

**Corporate Design is Big Business**
And small business. Both are finding that the image they present to the public is becoming more and more a factor in their successful growth. The first article on corporate design is by Lou Dorfsman, Design Director, Columbia Broadcasting System. The second by Ernie Smith, Proprietor of Port Jerry, a rustic resort.

**A Satire of Newspaper Logos**
The prominent illustrator and satirist, Chas. Slackman, depicts his graphic impressions of the nature of some of our most prominent newspapers through the redesign of their logotypes.

**Non-Communication**
Ed Sorel, one of America's foremost satirists, expresses his views on the subject of non-communication in no uncertain terms. These fascinating drawings will be a regular feature in "U&lc."

**What's New from ITC**
A first-time showing of the newest creations of typeface designers to be offered by ITC to the world buying public through ITC Subscribers.



**Typography and the New Technologies**

When I went to art school, I learned that many of my fellow students had problems when it came to drawing certain parts of the human anatomy. They simply could not draw hands or feet.

I first became conscious of their difficulties when I noticed that the people who appeared in their layouts never had hands or feet. Hands always seemed to be behind peoples' backs or in pockets. Feet were always out of view, either behind a desk, or the people were cropped at the waist or knees.

People, however, do have hands and feet, and very often they must be shown. The advertisements created by these students very often suffered as a result of these simple but important handicaps.

CONTINUED ON PAGE 3

**Information, Please**

Suppose that you wanted to find out... WHO is the new head of the Johnson Foundation?

WHAT were the basic terms of the General Motors-Curtiss-Wright agreement for the Wankel engine?

WHEN was the Amchitka atomic test conducted?

WHERE will Swindell-Dressler Company build a steel foundry in Russia?

WHY did Secretary Volpe sign a transportation research agreement with the Polish Government?

HOW did Martha Mitchell come to blow the whistle on the Watergate?

Answer:

You'd merely consult the remarkable new Information Bank of The New York Times.

This eminent newspaper has recently taken a giant step into the 21st Century with the introduction of the world's first computerized system for the storage and retrieval of the richly varied contents of newspapers and magazines.

CONTINUED ON PAGE 11

**Stop the "Perpetrators"**

Danger.

This article has been labeled "Stop the Perpetrators" for good reason.

The alarm is genuine.

No adequate law protects the type designer or photocomposing machine manufacturer from unauthorized duplication of the machine's most vital part: the typeface or font negative. Unauthorized contact duplication of these critical negatives has reached dangerous proportions, and the graphics industry can no longer afford, ostrich-like, to disregard the demoralizing effect it is having on creative talent. It is a blight on the industry's legitimate business practices, and bringing it under control is a worthy endeavor calling for the concerted effort of all. But more about that later; here is the background:

We operate in a free system where ethics and law contribute mightily to the function-

CONTINUED ON PAGE 2

**What's so Hot about Robert Indiana?**

A lot of friends in advertising—talented designers all—have been talking to themselves lately. "What," they want to know, "is so hot about Robert Indiana?" "What's he got that we haven't?" they want to know. "Look," they say, "we turn out designs like his—only better—every day in the week." "What's so special about Robert Indiana?"

What indeed.

I was mulling this over the other day when I came across an article by New York Times Art Critic, John Canaday. Mr. Canaday was exploring this very idea. He'd just been to a recent new exhibition at the Denise Rene Gallery in New York, which was presenting a one-man show of Indiana's designs, and he hadn't gotten over it yet.

For the uninitiated, Robert Indiana is the creator of LOVE, that cleverly-arranged four

CONTINUED ON PAGE 7

**art and typography**

let us consider first the function of the artist in society.
the men who handle the antique furniture in my museum have
developed a vocabulary of their own when they speak of styles.
they call louis XIV: louis with the twisted legs
louis XV: louis with the bow legs
louis XVI: louis with the straight legs
now the legs of these kings, i guess, actually did not differ so much from each other.
but it was not the kings who created these styles:
it was the artists, the architects, the painters and sculptors,
the musicians and the authors who tried to render the essence of
the epoch, who made the impact of a certain period visible, audible, perceptible.

the artist creates the face of society; his work enables us to revive the past.
to cite an example, the paintings and posters of toulouse-lautrec
are for us the incarnation of paris around 1900.
how does this come into being?

CONTINUED ON PAGE 15

abcdefghijklmnopqrstuvwxyz ABCDEFGHIJKLMNOPQRSTUVWXYZ 1234567890

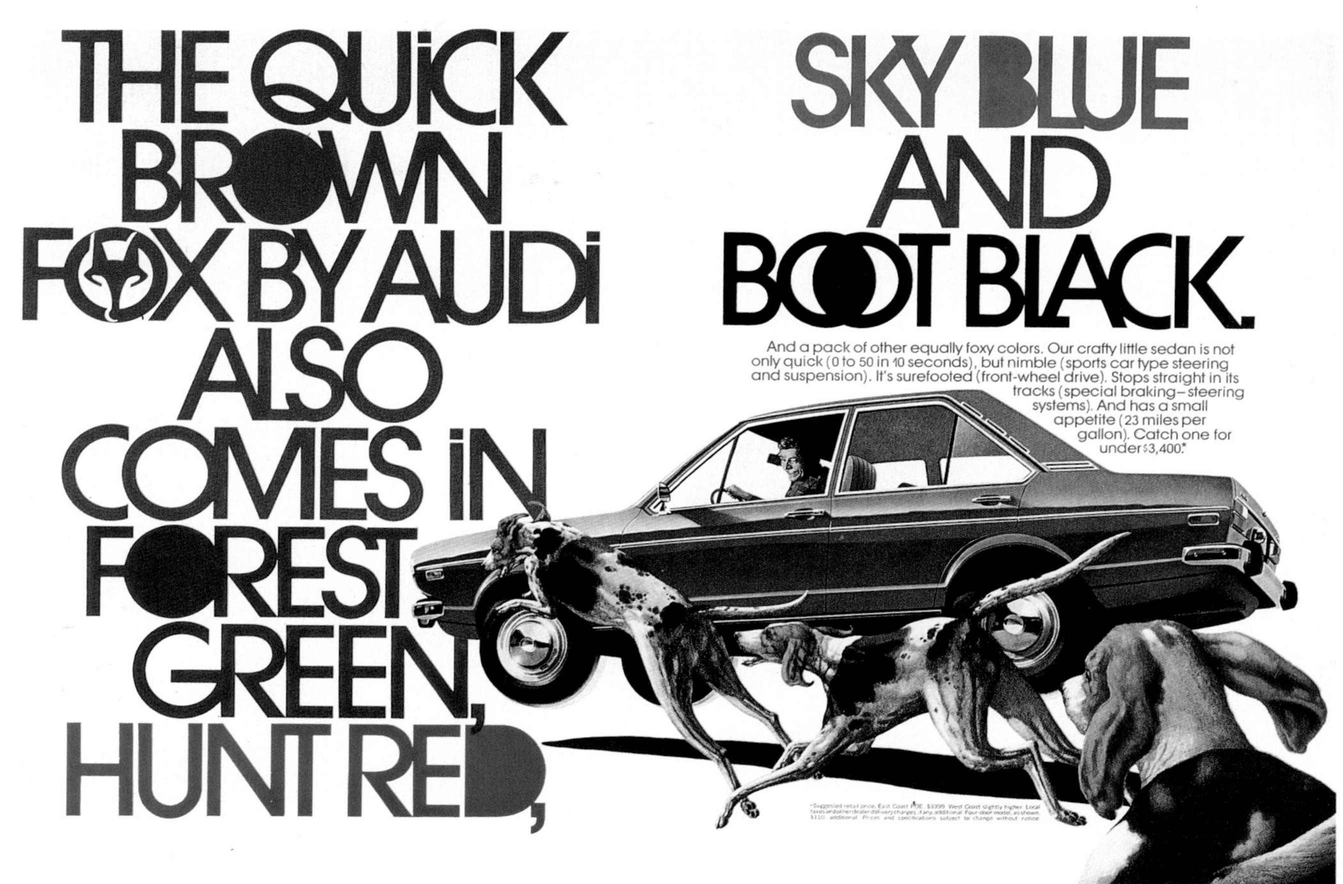
THE QUICK BROWN FOX BY AUDI ALSO COMES IN FOREST GREEN, HUNT RED,
SKY BLUE AND BOOT BLACK.
And a pack of other equally foxy colors. Our crafty little sedan is not only quick (0 to 50 in 10 seconds), but nimble (sports car type steering and suspension). It's surefooted (front-wheel drive). Stops straight in its tracks (special braking–steering systems). And has a small appetite (23 miles per gallon). Catch one for under $3,400.*

A Fox is quick (0 to 50 in 10 seconds). It's surefooted (front-wheel drive). This sly, cunning sedan can take the sharpest turns nimbly (sports car type steering and suspension). It can stop practically in its tracks (power front disc brakes). And it doesn't eat much (23 miles per gallon). Best of all, for under $3,200* you can catch the Fox.
YOUR HUNT IS OVER. THE QUICK, SLY, CRAFTY,
CUNNING FOX BY AUDI IS HERE.

"phototypography" that had reduced the time and costs involved to the point at which it had made the pirating of type a real threat to the origination of new work. He commented:

***photography has been the technological salvation of the typesetting business, but when used unethically it can rob the type designer of his livelihood. It can do worse than that. It is now threatening to throw the creative arm of the industry into chaos.*** [3]

He called for designers to boycott suppliers who did not use properly licensed designs and compared the use of anything else as being akin to passing off counterfeit money. Without strong action, warned Rondthaler, there was no reason why designers, foundries or manufacturers should consider investing in the design of new typefaces. The 1970s would mark either the demise of type design or the beginning of a renaissance, he concluded.

As it turned out, the latter was the case. Moves were made in international copyright law to clamp down on such piracy, and there were also followers of ITC's initiative – other type licensing enterprises and new manufacturers such as Hell and Compugraphic who invested in new designs. ITC's leadership was not uncritically received, however; the ubiquity of its faces meant that if it marketed a bad design, this could be widely adopted at the cost of a better, earlier precedent. The American graphic designer Paula Scher commented later, for example: "ITC had an enormous impact in this country because it was a national type business. It sold to all the small suppliers, but it destroyed the face of Garamond and it destroyed the face of Bookman." ITC designs generally have a large x-height and a close character fit, modern characteristics that may be functional but erode the finer qualities of these classic designs – a comparison of ITC's Garamond of 1975 by Tony Stan with that of Berthold's of 1972 by Gunter Gerhard Lange shows precisely these differences, with Lange's looking a great deal more elegant for its faithfulness. Lange's work at Berthold (where he began in 1950, and became artistic director in 1961) encompasses the creation of perhaps the most admired library of classic faces transferred first to photosetting and latterly to digital form. Its "diatronic" system of photosetting, using a glass negative image of the font, was remarkable for a very high quality of output that further enhanced the company's reputation. (However, to avoid a biased notion of the relative strengths of ITC and Berthold designs, a glance at the four-volume Berthold typeface specimen catalogue reveals many ITC faces, including its version of Garamond. Whatever the questions of taste, the demand for different qualities in a font for different jobs dictates that it makes sense for Berthold to offer the choice.)

The whole process of drawing a typeface also began to undergo significant change during the 1970s with the arrival of the idea of designing directly on-screen and utilising a computer program to remove the more tiresome parts of the procedure. Instrumental in this process was the Ikarus system developed by Peter Karow in Hamburg. Launched in 1974, it was quickly taken up by Berthold and Linotype, and soon found users across Europe, the US and in Japan. It offered a way of converting screen-designed images to line drawings; converting drawings to digitised information for screen working; and a way of automatically developing variants around the key design, so giving an option of removing some of the hard work from creating the different weights, slants, extensions and other alterations required for a comprehensive type family. Other systems have since been launched with comparable facilities, but updated forms of

## 1970...

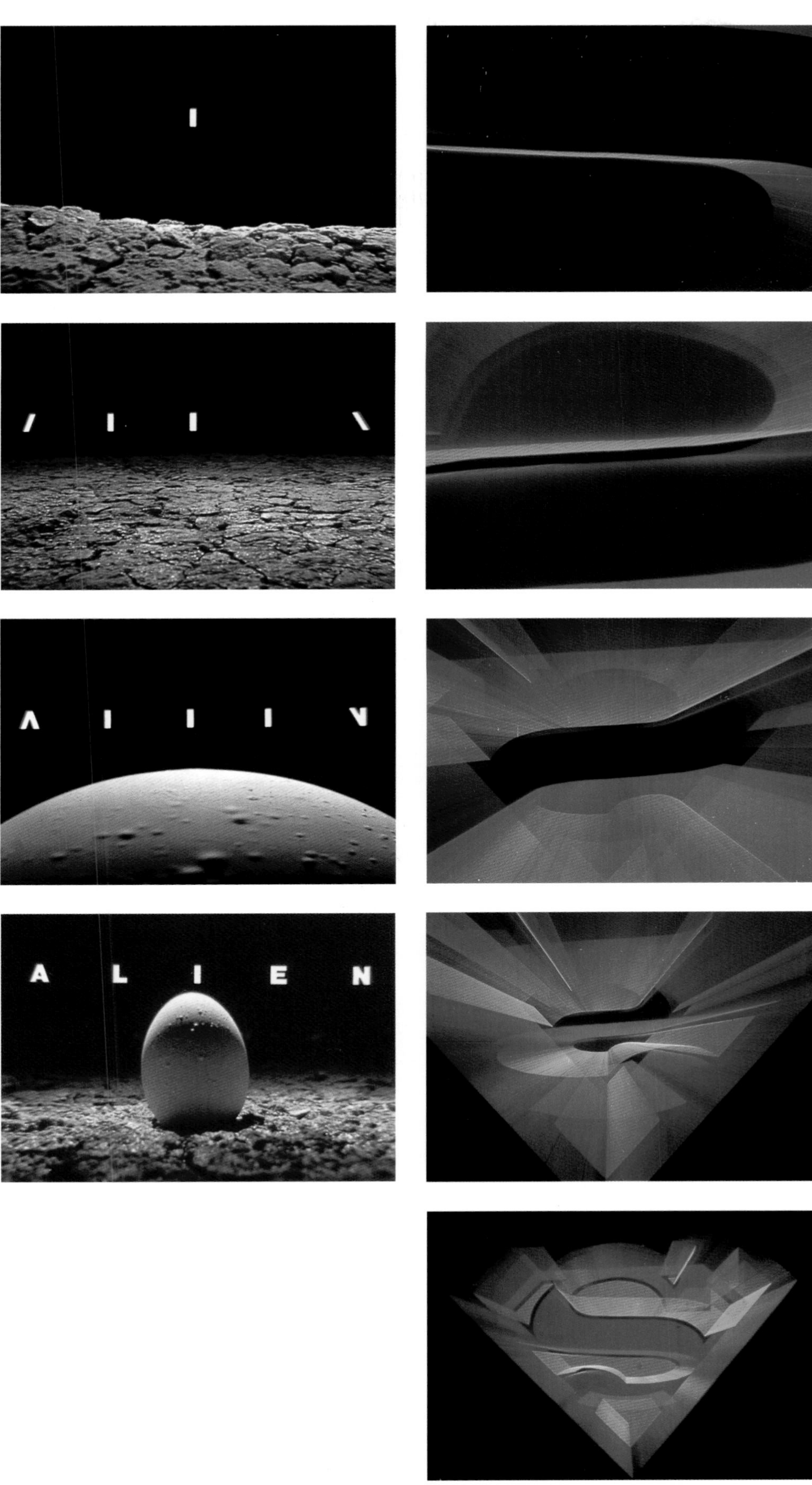


Left: titles for the films *Alien* and *Superman*, designed by R/Greenberg Associates, late 1970s, the first prominent use of high-powered computer graphics in film title sequences. The streaks of light speeding from the letterforms in the *Superman* titles could only have been produced by the innovative software developed around this project. In the *Alien* sequence, a mystery is built up that unfolds the title of the film at the same time as the origins of the plot to come: letters forming from mysterious points of white light lead to a cracking egg that also emits light. Computer graphics were used to achieve otherwise impossible effects; where type was required, it could be integrated, moved and lit as an active part of the whole sequence. The huge costs involved, however, meant that only research projects, high-budget films and advertising were suitable users of this approach.

Ikarus have remained the most widely employed for the more sophisticated type design programs, although much ground was taken in the 1980s by less powerful programs that could be used with desktop systems.

As regards development in typography, the implications inherent in the massive shift from hot-metal setting to photosetting and the possibilities of wider typographic application demanded greater flexibility of typographic material. After almost two decades of International Style proliferation, there were signs of insurrection, and they started in its homeland. This reaction was to become known as the New Wave, and its key instigator was the Swiss designer Wolfgang Weingart.

In 1968 Weingart, then twenty-seven, began teaching at the Basel School of Design, whose philosophy he had spurned when a student there, opposing the dogmatic approach identified with the Swiss typography of Emil Ruder and Armin Hofmann, both teachers at the school. But their recognition of his talents led to an invitation to come back and present an alternative voice. This he accepted, placing himself at the centre of a new orthodoxy and circle of influence that stretches across Europe to the West Coast of the US, April Greiman being perhaps his most noted pupil.

Weingart rejected the reductive approach that had taken Swiss typography to its position of pre-eminent intellectual credibility in typography: where Josef Müller-Brockmann managed to reduce the number of typefaces to one face in two sizes (text and headline), positioned in a clear relationship organised around the right angle and placed on a grid, Weingart asked his class to find principles of typographic composition that did not rely on any systemic approach, but drew

**1970...**

Pages from a special edition of *Typografische Monatsblätter*, December 1976, designed by and featuring the personal work and observations of Wolfgang Weingart. Throughout the early and mid-1970s Weingart argued for a break with the hard line of Swiss style and a more experimental approach to typography. This issue of the journal of Swiss typographers showed how far he was prepared to go in breaking away from the rules of legibility as he presented a more complex interpretation of readability. Broken and cut grids, reversed and stepped blocks, different ranging areas of text – all manner of devices were presented as a post-rational method of injecting a dynamic expressive quality to a page and its content. Weingart's work spawned the New Wave typography.

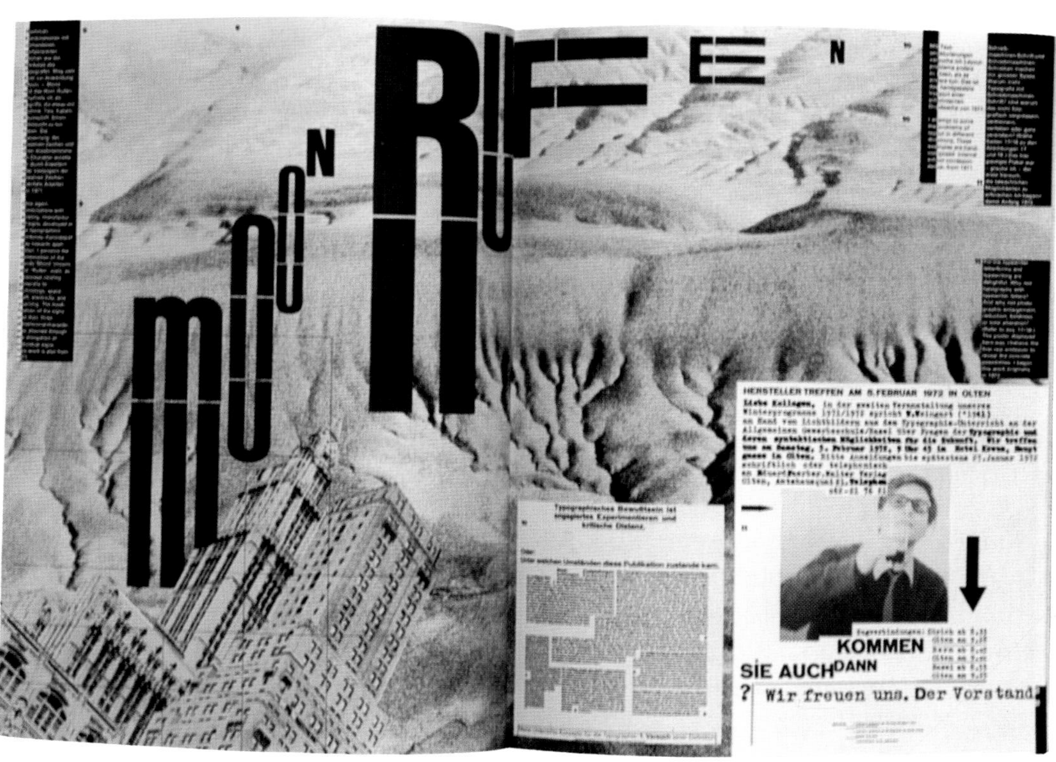

2 reden von ihr lebhaft als Kommunikations-, sprich: ‹Verständigungs›-Mittel. Selbstzweifel breiten sich aus: wir haben jedes tiefe Interesse an der Typografie verloren, betrachten aber interessiert die von Weingart.

ATHEN

POiNT

iTALY

STO?

FLYiNG

Interpretation of a poem by the Zurich poetess Elsbeth Bornoz, 1972–73.

At one time, I was intrigued with the combinations of existing printing type, into novel, legible signs and words. These are a few of the results.

At the same time, 1971–72, the "Semantic Interpretations" were created. Visualizations, and their conceptual meanings, are pictorially expressed, and associations solicited.

Interessiert, jedoch kaum begeistert. Denn das ist ein weiterer Vorzug dieses Typografen: er sitzt zwischen allen Stühlen. Er ist kein Praktiker, schon gar kein Theoretiker, für einen Handwerker zu unbekümmert, für einen Grafiker zu kreativ, beharrlich bis zur Ignoranz, ein Idealist, wie er im Buche steht.

Er sitzt zwischen allen Stühlen und fühlt sich dabei offensichtlich auch noch ganz wohl. Er kultiviert das. Er macht das vor allem für sich produktiv. So wie er seine eigenen Widersprüchlichkeiten und die seiner Typografie für sich produktiv macht. Natürlich, wie er sagen würde: ‹unbewusst›.

‹Wir leben in einer destruktiven, geschmacklosen Zeit, und ich versuche dagegenzuarbeiten mit dieser Art von Typografie›, sagt Weingart. Aber er zerstört dafür die klassische ‹Schweizer› Typografie: Weingart verzerrt, zerschneidet, sperrt, durchstreicht, verquatscht!

Er verschreibt sich dafür dem Experiment, dem fortwährenden Suchen und Probieren. Aber kaum etwas ist auffälliger in diesen Arbeiten als die durchgehende Linie, die Kontinuität des Stils.

Er hat auch als Lehrer eine genaue und in sich schlüssige Lehre entwickelt, deren Schwerpunkt in seinem typografischen Denken und Handeln liegt. Und er predigt, typografiert, vertreibt sie mit missionarischem Eifer.

| 12 1976 | Typografische Monatsblätter | Schweizer Grafische Mitteilungen | Revue suisse de l'Imprimerie Edition spéciale Décembre 1976 |
|---|---|---|---|
| | TM | SGM | RSI |

Eine Auswahl bestimmter Arbeiten Weingarts von 1969 bis 1976. Gedanken und Beobachtungen eines Freundes. Und persönliche Bemerkungen von ihm.

# Ist diese Typografie noch zu retten?

**Oder leben wir auf dem Mond? Is This Typography Worth Supporting, Or Do We Live On The Moon?** A special selection from the works of Weingart, from 1969–1976. Thoughts and observations of a friend. And personal comments from the author.

0001 **Die Typografie ist noch nicht tot! Sie wirkt zwar heute ein bisschen**
0094 Typography is not dead, yet! But its effect is undoubtedly
**blutarm und unentschlossen. Doch im grossen und ganzen ist sie in Ordnung.**
anemic and vague. But by and large, it is intact. It is definitely less than ever
0002 **Sie ist zwar weniger denn je eine Gebrauchskunst. Dafür aber steht ihr**
0095 a practical skill. Instead, it endures as an intrinsic necessity.
**Gebrauchswert hoch im Kurs.**
Typography lives! It is not regarded today with the primacy of
**Die Typografie lebt! Sie nimmt sich heute vielleicht nicht mehr so**
perhaps 10 or 20 years ago, and is comprehended less as a "picture", but
0003 **wichtig wie vor 10 oder 20 Jahren, versteht sich weniger als Bild, tritt**
0096 rather, more as a "text". Nevertheless, it remains a prominent element of "visual
**hinter den Text zurück. Trotzdem ist sie noch immer ein wichtiger Teil ‹visueller**
communication": indispensable, and occasionally fresh, even original.
**Kommunikation›: überall gefördert, ansehnlich und mitunter sogar noch**
Currently: typography is still typography, although less
**überraschend originell.**
0097 complacent, conceited, and self-confident, than in the late fifties. And,
0004 **Kurzum: die Typografie heute ist noch immer Typografie. Weniger**
correspondingly, more functional, in that it has become completely adjusted
**selbstgefällig, selbstbewusst und selbstsicher zwar als noch Ende der**
to the rapid methods of mass communication.
**fünfziger Jahre. Dafür aber ‹funktionaler›: in den schnellen Verwertungsprozess**
0098 This connotes "adapted": adapted to the developments
0005 **der Massenkommunikation voll eingepasst.**
within the composing and print technologies; to the stipulations of an unstable
**Das heisst: angepasst. Angepasst an die Erfordernisse neuerer Satz-**
market; to the supposedly effective usage by the design profession; and
**und Drucktechniken. An die Bedingungen schnell sich verändernder**
0099 also adapted to a particularly unpleasant phenomenon of our profession: to design

Fortsetzung des Textes: Seite 4/Innenteil
Continuation of text: inside/page 14

Sondernummer Dezember 1976 Special Edition December 1976

from the structures suggested to some degree by the processes themselves. He wanted typographic design mixed in as part of a range of tools within the graphic designer's control. His students also studied other areas such as photography, drawing, colour theory and packaging. When he started they only had hot-metal and letterpress machines to work with, but a deep knowledge of these processes, including substantial experience of hand-setting their own work, was seen as crucial to gaining an understanding of the principles by which graphic design is achieved, principles which, today, embrace computer technology, particularly Apple Macintosh-related programs.

What Weingart was making his students experience was not wholly new, but the rigour of the approach and its presentation as a thrusting away of the rules established in the previous twenty years were remarkable. From this dedication to the potential of the tools and their expressive qualities emerged a self-conscious kind of design, in keeping with the mood of an era of self-conscious forms characterising the post-modern culture of the decade: literature, films, music, three-dimensional design and architecture that question basic assumptions of structure.

However, such radicalism quickly became rather formulaic. Weingart has admitted that the experimentation he sought to foster, apparent in his own work, was inspired by the potential of pushing hot-metal processes to the limit and standing them on their head. Stylised features became associated with New Wave typography – stepped blocks, bold reversal out of type, different spacing of letters with some wide, some close, and underlining, to name but a few. One common visual emphasis was heavily screened photography where the halftone dot size is quite visible and the picture is read clearly as a graphic element, not consumed as a piece of realism.

For all the radicalism, however, the Swiss origins are still evident. Weingart did not throw caution to the wind to the extent of wildly mixing type of different sizes, weights, styles or fonts. Instead he preferred certain families and tended to stick with them, with a penchant for Akzidenz Grotesk/Helvetica and Univers for the sans serifs, most popularly used for all the poster and other display work emanating from his class and studio, and Times and Garamond for text. Weingart's aim was to break out of a "stiff and boring" orthodox quality that he felt constrained typographic forms. Although his direct influence has been to create the New Wave style, the underlying thrust of his teaching has encouraged a more questioning, rule-breaking attitude. His was not the only influence on young typographers in the period: there was also a growing interest in a more vernacular approach to typography. This was related to the spirit of cheap and inventive publishing of posters and magazines in the later 1960s, partly made possible by the wonders of golfball typewriters and transfer lettering, whose "fanzine" (music fan magazine) mentality continued through the mid- to late seventies, particularly evident in the punk graphics of the UK. There is a direct connection here to the character of the graphically stimulating magazines in the 1980s that were to help put typographic invention close to the heart of the expression of the style-conscious "youth culture".



Right: *Never Mind The Bollocks* record sleeve for the Sex Pistols, designed by Jamie Reid, 1977. Powerful typography did not need to be immaculately composed or to use innovative faces – Reid's appropriation of typographic materials and lurid colours was a mode of communication in keeping with the anarchistic statement of punk. His work found many imitators as it pushed the same point as Weingart, that readability did not mean "easy reading".
Far right: poster for CBS Records to show "The Best Of . . ." range of jazz records, designed by Paula Scher, 1979. References to past graphic styles abound in the work of Scher, then art director of CBS Records and since a consultant designer and, from 1991, a partner in Pentagram. Wood type is arranged with angles and tangents in a manner alluding to Russian Constructivism, a point reinforced by the colour choice; it was initially rejected by design awards juries before being enthusiastically recognised, then copied. Far from being a copy itself, the poster is an example of a growing practice of making reference to other graphics as a valid way of adding ironic meaning, and an awareness that this meaning could be found by readers.
Right: *Pyramids*, poster for Benson & Hedges cigarettes, UK, created by Collett Dickenson and Pearce (art director Neil Godfrey; photographer Jimmy Wormser), 1979. Faced with tighter restrictions on cigarette advertising, CDP began a long-running campaign of surreal associations, based on visual tricks with the cigarettes' gold pack, with no words at all. But the advertisement depends considerably for its effect on an understanding of how the consumer perceives the health warning that has to run underneath. The message is so familiar as to be automatically ignored and yet, as a regular device, it serves to remind the viewer that this is a Benson & Hedges cigarette advertisement. Thus the campaign partly depended for its success on the insistently dull typography of H.M. Government Health Department.

bodies
holidays in The Sun
no feelings
OVED 136
NEW YORK
SuB·Mission
SEVENTEEN
GOD Save THE QUEEN
ANARCHY IN THE U.K.
EMI Unlimited Edition
problems
liar
pretty vacant
SEX PISTOLS ℗ 1977
VIRGIN RECORDS LTD.

HUMPHREY
HUBERT LAWS
MAHAVISHNU ORCHESTRA
FERGUSON
STEVE KHAN
HUBBARD
RETURN TO FOREVER
COBHAM
THE BEST OF
STAN GETZ
ERIC GALE
WILLIAMS
TOM SCOTT
GORDON

MIDDLE TAR As defined by H.M. Government
H.M. Government Health Departments' WARNING:
CIGARETTES CAN SERIOUSLY DAMAGE YOUR HEALTH

THE FACE

As digital typography and the desktop publishing revolution took off, the 1980s became marked by experiments with new faces that could work with lower-resolution output – whether the radical low-information bitmap "1980" from Emigre Graphics, designed to cope

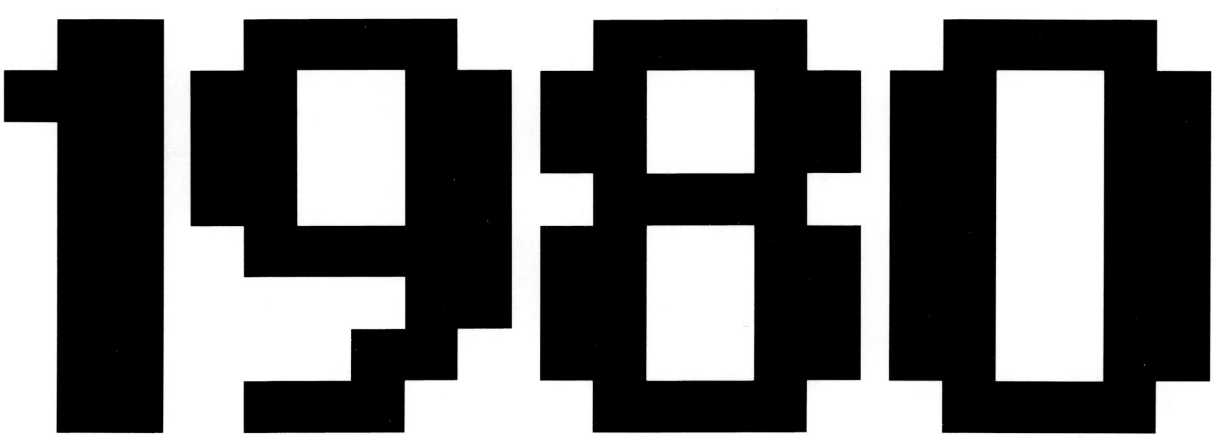

with a screen resolution of 72 dots per inch, or the smoother outline of Sumner Stone's Stone family (far right), workable across a range of resolutions. Stone was designed for Adobe in 1984–7; 18 variants were created for low-cost display advertising work, to signage, through to long text in books. Stubby short serifs on flared strokes that can degrade into a suggestion of humanistic sans serif at low resolution; open forms, and an absence of sharp contrasts of stroke all work to maintain legibility and character at different resolutions. Magazine designers such as Rudy VanderLans at *Emigre* and Neville Brody at *The Face* made the new potential of typography a fashionable subject, while the Cranbrook School gave it a new intellectual direction into Deconstruction theory, as shown by the detail from a work by Edward Fella (below).

EMIGRE

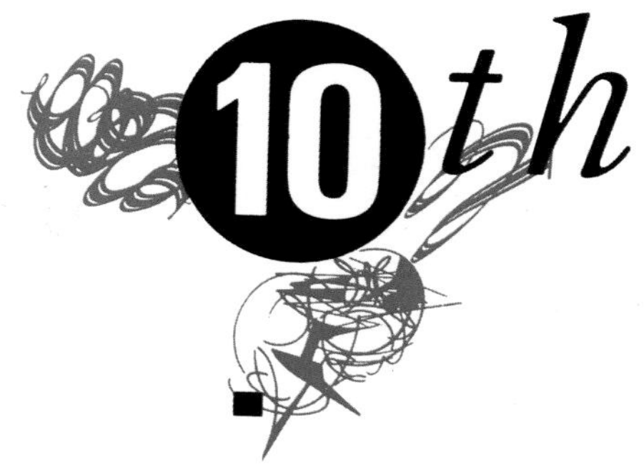

ITC Stone serif
*ITC Stone serif*
**ITC Stone serif**
***ITC Stone serif***
**ITC Stone serif**
***ITC Stone serif***
ITC Stone informal
*ITC Stone informal*
**ITC Stone informal**
***ITC Stone informal***
**ITC Stone informal**
***ITC Stone informal***
ITC Stone sans
*ITC Stone sans*
**ITC Stone sans**
***ITC Stone sans***
**ITC Stone sans**
***ITC Stone sans***

"Most of my life," recalls Matthew Carter, "I dreaded situations like dinner parties where people ask you what you do for a living. People had no idea what a type designer actually did. Nowadays, I'll be in a restaurant and a waiter will come up to me and ask, 'Did I hear you talking about fonts?' "[1] An exceptional waiter, perhaps, but such was the radical shift in the access to typographic decision-making in the 1980s. From being an arcane area of initiation (and interest) of which even some graphic designers had only an elementary knowledge, typography is now something that is practised in many millions of homes and offices. Where once only specialist bookshops and libraries contained information on type design and typography, now (and since the mid-eighties) information on directly handling type is widely available through magazine and many other reference publications. And these are not aimed specifically at the print industry or even necessarily at designers, but are computer magazines – by the end of the decade computing was by far the largest category of advertising in business magazines, supporting hundreds of titles.

Two parallel developments in computing had dramatic effects on typesetting and the context for typographic and type design. One was in the sophistication of high-end systems; the other in the creation of a whole new area of personal, desktop machines with typographic functions that were sold at a price affordable by small companies and individuals.

During the 1970s advances in phototypesetting and digital setting had been aided by the rapid development of much more powerful and compact computer technology. The typesetter's terminal became advanced in its editing controls, with greater display on screen of the text as it was set (instead of the previous near "blind" setting). At first these systems, both phototypesetting and digital, were reproducing the model of hot-metal days – a typesetter carrying out the production of the typographic material for the designer or art director. However, the development of powerful computer systems capable of showing a whole page on screen presented the basis for a different, electronic, way of working, one in which the creative person could work directly with the input of the typographic instructions. Initially, electronic page composition came in the province of the typesetter in the old order of job functions, but the potential for huge cost savings and production benefits soon forced change. There were notable confrontations in the newspaper industry, with great resistance to job losses in traditional typographic production trades. Type creation was increasingly being derived from digital information that could both represent the setting on screen and help lay down instructions to drive a typesetter, either directly as part of the same device (direct entry typesetters such as the Linotype CRTronics) or as coded information passed on from the front-end setting terminal to a slave typesetter that would output the setting on bromide (such as those developed by Atex and popular in newspapers). Instead of the mechanical world of hot metal or earlier photosetters, typographic information was now becoming electronic, both in the existence of the typeface and in the manner in which it was composed.

But it was the arrival of the personal computer that released a massive potential for a new order in type production and typographic design practice. It both fulfilled the promise of new communication technology and laid the base for a new approach to the techniques of creating communication. In 1981 there was the first true PC, an expensive IBM machine that was subsequently available in much cheaper copies. With the launch of the Apple Macintosh in 1984, distinguished by the "user-friendly" approach of its "graphical user interface" display, the small computer became a device capable of revolutionising the design and production of graphics. Apple concealed the complexities of a computer's operating language, instead presenting the user with a screen based on a metaphor of the desktop and an attempt at "what you see is what you get" ("wysiwyg") presentation. Wysiwyg presentation had been developing in the large typesetting systems, but when made available at this level it had the potential to mean a whole lot more. It did not simply make easier and quicker the work of existing typesetting practice; rather, it revolutionised the practices possible in design and the manner in which type could be created. Unlike computers that required complex series of instructions to be embedded in the document being worked upon, here a piece of work appeared on screen in a simulation of how it would appear when printed. Thus the small computer could be used by designers as an instrument for creating layouts and inserting type on screen. Even if the final product was intended to be output on a more powerful, higher-resolution system, typography could be taken to a more complete stage of visualisation during the creative process, before outside suppliers were brought in, direct control was lost and costs mounted.

This shift of the typesetting function into the design studio (which is still continuing) calls for complete typographic knowledge by the designer, rather than a sharing of it with the typesetter. A designer working on an Apple Mac, or latterly on other systems that have a wysiwyg graphical user interface, needs access to the training and concern for typographic detail that is held by a typesetter but is often lacking in a design education. As a result, some of the worst aspects of crude typographic functions and low-resolution outputs were all too apparent in early desktop publishing: poor tracking, crude type designs or typefaces distorted by crude styling tools of italicisation and weight, bad breaks, widows, orphans and all the other unfortunates that a good typesetter had taken care of as second nature, but that the designer was too blind, too lazy or too pushed for time to cope with.

Initially fairly primitive, by the end of the eighties hardware and software had been repeatedly revised to match demand, and the graphics industry had been wooed by the potential of control, speed and economy possible through having

Opposite page: spreads from *i-D* magazine in July 1986 (top) and December–January 1988–9 (below). Under the art direction and editorship of Terry Jones, *i-D* (founded in 1980) challenged the conventions of what was "good" photography, layout and typography. Cut-up images and text, laid down seemingly without recourse to any underlying grid, typewriter fonts, handwriting and "found" setting from cut-up print were among the techniques that stood out for their contrast to magazine design orthodoxy. Photographs might be Super 8, photocopied or occasionally immacutely polished fashion portraiture; unpredictability was the formula. Surprise and the deliberate display of technique both drew on graphic traditions (a rag-bag of ideas taken from magazine designers of various times and also from fine art), but also reflected a sensibility built out of the confrontational and ironic treatment of clothing and music displayed by punk and its later developments in street fashion.

Right: from *Arena* magazine, art directed by Neville Brody, designed by Brody, Ian Swift and Robin Derrick, 1987. Despite expressing a deep loathing of the widespread use of Helvetica, Brody has often used it – deliberately for its neutrality, or pushing it into unexpected, expressive modes. Here it carries a headline and standfirst that take over the page without having any overbearing characteristics. In contrast to the quest for a communicative anarchy seen in the typography of *i-D*, Brody's highly influential magazine work of the 1980s expressed a new sense of order and design, often extending through into specially designed fonts.

**an englishman abroad**

with an international reputation as a designer of quintessentially

british men's wear, *paul smith*'s first lov

es remain retailing and shops.

his new manhattan store is his latest flame

ARENA 24 SUMMER ARENA 25 SUMMER

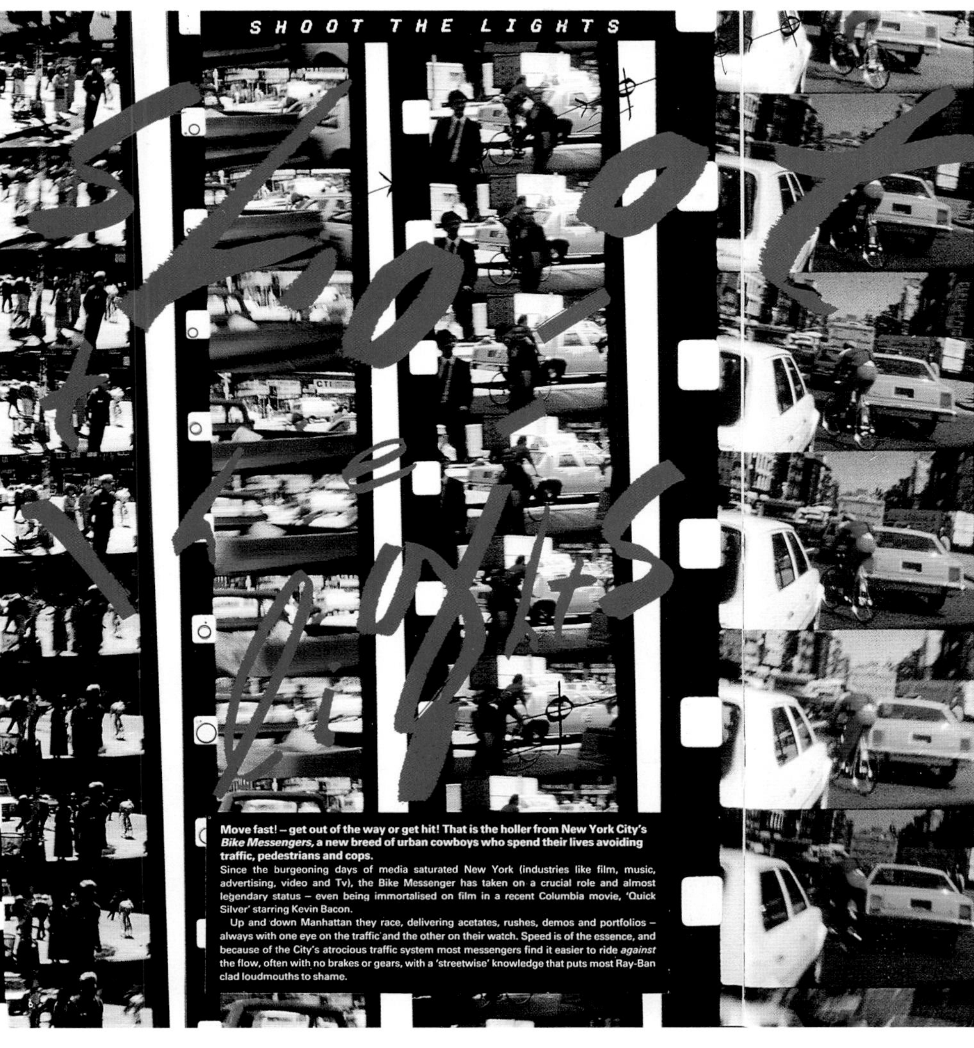



Move fast! – get out of the way or get hit! That is the holler from New York City's *Bike Messengers,* a new breed of urban cowboys who spend their lives avoiding traffic, pedestrians and cops.

Since the burgeoning days of media saturated New York (industries like film, music, advertising, video and Tv), the Bike Messenger has taken on a crucial role and almost legendary status – even being immortalised on film in a recent Columbia movie, 'Quick Silver' starring Kevin Bacon.

Up and down Manhattan they race, delivering acetates, rushes, demos and portfolios – always with one eye on the traffic and the other on their watch. Speed is of the essence, and because of the City's atrocious traffic system most messengers find it easier to ride *against* the flow, often with no brakes or gears, with a 'streetwise' knowledge that puts most Ray-Ban clad loudmouths to shame.

SUPER 8 AND PHOTO REPORT BY SIMON FLEURY

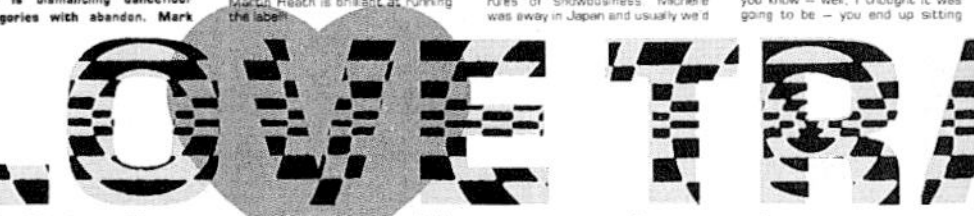

# LOVE TRAIN

**of all the dj acts to emerge this year, mark moore's s-express has been the most successful. but the story of s-express isn't just about success — it's the story of a how a dj turned into a pop star during the summer of love.** Interview by **John Godfrey**

**As far as the dancefloor is concerned, '88 will be remembered for two reasons – acid house and the DJ record. Both revolutionised club culture and spawned a host of British dance acts that dominated the charts, the most successful of which was Mark Moore's S-Express. One of the first London DJs to play acid house music and a regular guest DJ at the early Shoom nights, Mark was instrumental in the spread of a music that he specifically kept S-Express away from. But it wasn't just a decision designed to steer clear of tabloid hysteria because S-Express are one of a growing number of club-based acts who are redefining, not only dance music, but the business of making records. S-Express is a platform for whoever Mark Moore bumps into in a nightclub, a pool of club talent that is dismantling dancefloor categories with abandon. Mark Moore is breaking all the rules, and it might have something to do with the fact that he's turning into a hippy.**

**The first time I met you you'd only just discovered what a slip mat was**

Nooo yeah no er, yeah you're right. That was when I'd just started to mix records. Well, you've got to start somewhere haven't you?

**And now you refuse to answer the phone**

Only to you John.

**But hasn't the past year totally changed your life?**

Basically this year started off as a good laugh. We did this record purely for a laugh and it got to number one. And then the second one 'Superfly Guy' got to number five. And then suddenly it all started to get serious. Rhythm King became this very big record company and it all became work. It became, oh you've got to go on tour, you've got to do this... I went through an odd phase thinking this isn't what I want to be doing. I just wanted to make records and didn't want to be this public figure, to be public property. It got to the point where I was working all the time and not seeing my friends and not going out as much. I found that I wasn't enjoying myself, 'cos what I enjoy are my friends and going out. So I stopped doing anything to *promote* records and just concentrated on *making* them. Which was what the idea of Rhythm King was all about in the first place – it wasn't to conform to all this. Of course, and make sure you print this, Rhythm King is the only label who'd put up with a band like S-Express, and Martin Heath is brilliant at running the label!

> **"When we got our second (hit) nobody said a word – it was as if to say 'you bastard'"**

**One of the labels that's dogged you this year has been acid house**

I was looking through some of my old interviews the other day and someone from the NME was asking me why house wasn't taking off in London. He actually said he didn't think it ever would. I remember saying then that every b-side I did would be an acid house b-side 'cos then only a handful of people were into it. That's when I was a guest DJ at Shoom, but Shoom was never about acid house – it was about an attitude and freedom. Consequently I've always tried to avoid being labelled an acid house band, simply 'cos the media has never really understood what it was all about. Since then it's all got out of hand. It was obvious the tabloids were after a story when they kept asking me about drugs – but now the media hysteria is just ridiculous. Anyway, the whole point behind S-Express music is to make it unclassifiable – it's not house, disco or funk; it's all of those things.

**Do you still enjoy deejaying at clubs?**

Yes, although I don't think it's vital to still DJ to make dance records. The only thing that's important is going to nightclubs and staying in touch – you never know who you're going to bump into. Take Billy Martin who sings on the new single – I bumped into her under the strobe lights at Shoom. Now she's got her own band called Electribe signed to Phonogram. E-Mix used to sing/rap at the Soul II Soul and RIP clubs, and I'd always thought he had a brilliant voice, so I got him to sing on 'Special & Golden' and 'Can You Feel Me' for the album. That's the thing about S-Express – we decided we didn't want to follow the rules of showbusiness. Michelle was away in Japan and usually we'd wait 'til she came back and let her do the vocals, but, er, this time we didn't. Michelle beat me up when she got back. But the point is, every other band, when they get to number one, have got everything mapped out for them, everything is under control. With S-Express it's so chaotic. Basically there are no official members – some people will appear on one record, others won't, but they'll always be there for future things. Hopefully anyway. It was always my idea to have S-Express as a showcase for clubland talent, to ignore the rules of pop songs and bands. It's a whole new concept.

**Hasn't that caused problems?**

Sometimes. When S-Express went to Japan I didn't go with them 'cos I had to work on the album and then I fell ill. The truth is that all this was fun at first – going on Breakfast TV and buying all the magazines and papers I was in, it was all quite a laugh. But then it got extremely boring. When I was considering just making records and not doing Top Of The Pops, I also didn't want to do any interviews – which I'm still not doing, this is one of the only ones – because I wanted to remain anonymous, I didn't want to get any more famous. At the moment I can walk down the street and some people may stop me, but it's not like I'm getting mobbed. It might sound like I'm moaning now – things aren't dreadful but I think Rhythm King are slightly pissed off with me 'cos they think I don't want to cooperate. I think they wanted to make us like their priority act, the act that would get in all the glossy magazines and stuff like that. But now they're concentrating on Bomb The Bass as the main act. I went in the other day and the office was covered with Bomb The Bass T-shirts, slip mats, badges, you name it. I suppose they're just playing me at my own game.

**So you're getting tired of the business?**

I've been promoting records all over Holland, France and it gets a bit boring, it's not like having a holiday you know – well, I thought it was going to be – you end up sitting around TV studios. Although they loved us in Harlem – it was the only place in the States that I liked, and it was the only place our US record company (Capitol) tried to keep us away from. They were scared we wouldn't come out of it alive.

**Mark, are you or are you not a hippy?**

Very much. Basically there's been so little trouble in clubs compared to a year ago when I was going to loads of hip hop clubs. Attitudes have definitely changed and it's not just down to drugs. People are getting rid of their inhibitions, they're a lot more loving – it's not peace and love, but *peace and loving.* Also people are thinking beyond slogans and getting into philosophy. Philip Salon and me came back from the Mud one night and we saw this guy who looked slightly Shoomy in the 7-11 and Philip says, "Oh, come back to ours and have a cup of tea", no hanky panky, he just genuinely invited him back. And this guy was saying that if we'd spoken to him six months ago he'd have hit us. It becomes more obvious when you meet people who never go to clubs. I was at the Trip once when I came across this bloke in a wheelchair. He was looking pretty glum and nobody was talking to him so I went up to him and started talking to him. It turned out he was a Pop Will Eat Itself fan who had got left behind after the gig had finished. He had to wait 'til everybody had left the building before he could get out. By that time his friends had [illegible] out and there was nobody to carry him up the stairs. So [illegible] to sit through four hours of screaming clubbers and wait for the club to clear. I bought him a drink but I couldn't cheer him up. No, don't laugh, he hated acid house.

**So you still talk to people when you go out?**

Well, I try. It was great being known as a cult DJ, 'cos you'd go out and get all the freebies and people would come up and talk to you. But now I've gone one step further and people are too scared or they're afraid it looks like they're ligging. Sometimes it feels like I go to clubs in this plastic bubble, and if I go to talk to people I freak them out. I say 'How are you?' to people, and it's like 'Why is the guy from S-Express saying how are you?' They're either too cool to be seen ligging or too scared. Suddenly it's become a lot harder to meet people, which is one thing I enjoyed about going to clubs – meeting all these wonderful people.

**What about other DJs? Have they treated you any differently?**

When we got our first hit everyone said "well done" and "congragulations". When we got our second nobody said a word – it was as if to say "you bastard". It's alright to get one hit, but nobody likes you getting another. There is definitely a lot of jealousy – and I'm not the only one to say this – other DJs who've made records have said the same things. People don't want to play a record by another DJ in London.

**What about your new single 'Hey Music Lover'?**

It will be interesting to see what people will make of the single. It's based on an old Sly & The Family Stone song and is basically a happy happy acid pop record – [illegible] overtly commercial [illegible] the others. But the last two singles weren't playlisted until they got to number three and six anyway. All the records have got there through club support and nothing else.

The b-side is called 'What Is This Thing Called Love?' and we've called it a New Beat track. When Matthew Collin went on holiday to Belgium and wrote about New Beat (i-D no. 62) he wrote about a scene that didn't really exist. But since then everybody's gone mad on New Beat so we did it as a laugh.

**What about the album?**

The album's called 'Original Soundtrack' and I'm 99% happy with it – a cowbell should have been louder on one of the tracks. But I think the people who bought the singles are going to be surprised. We've gone one step further than all the DJ collage sampling business. Basically all the previous records by DJs [illegible]

**Where are you going to spend Xmas Day?**

On Xmas Day I'm going to be at my mother's in Wembley. I don't think she realises what's going on. I never told her that I'd made a record until a week before we were on Top Of The Pops. The next week she said to me, 'Mark, if I give you a hundred pounds will you go out and make another record?' She'd read somewhere that that was how much the first one cost.

**What's made it all worthwhile?**

This tiny cute girl came up to me at a club once and said frantically, 'Excuse me, are you Mark Moore, are you Mark Moore?' and I thought, oh no another fan, so I said, 'Thankyou, thankyou very much – what's your name?' She said, 'I'm Gillian from New Order, this is Barney.' And he said, 'You're a genius.' I thought, oh my God, New Order, my idols – probably one of the few bands I'd want a compliment from, telling me I'm a genius. I had to sit down for the rest of the evening.

> **"I had to sit down for the rest of the evening"**

*S-Express single 'Hey Music Lover' is out now. The album 'Original Soundtrack' is released in January/February.*

32 i-D THE LOVE ISSUE

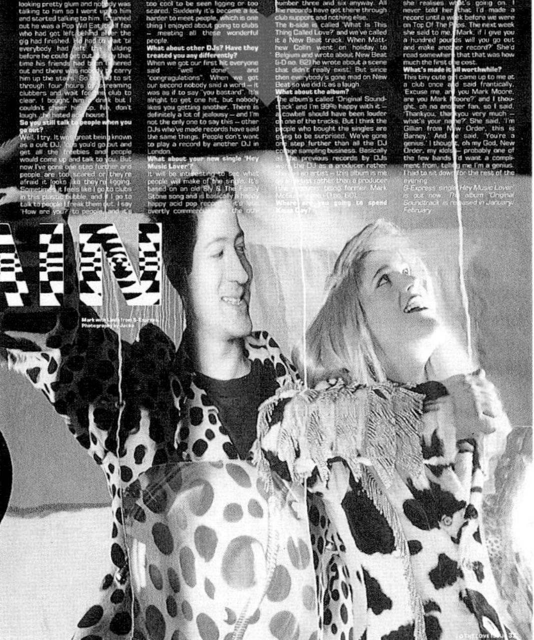

some degree of computer involvement. Increasingly, software for handling the input of words and pictures into the on-screen layout was also made available. Lower-cost scanners and easier links with other programs provided the means for inputting into the computer a mass of print, photographic and film information. At the same time developments in software for related areas of activity, notably word-processing, allowed material on disk to be presented directly to typographers involved in the new technology. From the traditional basis of an art-directed layout where type, pictures and other components were originated and handled separately and then dropped into position, the potential for working practice now suggested a seamless production in which all the material could be generated in the same format – digitally – and carried through production processes without having to be drawn afresh.

This did not happen overnight, of course, and the majority of print production still takes place with a greater or lesser reliance on traditional practices (this book itself involves a hybrid mix – Apple Macintosh-based data storage and word processing, with traditional methods for layout, art production and proofing). But the rapid adoption and development of the technology happened at a pace much faster than the move to previous technologies in print and communications. Where hot metal took decades to become established and gain the support of a wide variety of typefaces, and phototypesetting took twenty years to turn around from initial take-up to dominance, the digital revolution happened much more quickly. The move from metal to film bromide to electronic storage of the crucial type and typographic information happened so swiftly that all three technologies were in use at the same time, although hot metal declined fast. Significantly, the adoption of digital technology does not apply only to print: the generation and application of type in the computer era is equally apposite for televisual communication; it can also meet the requirements of numerous other areas of signage and display.

This phase of extraordinarily rapid development is still continuing and is fuelled by the options provided by new technology. At the beginning of the 1980s designers did not have access to affordable computer systems for use in the studio, but had the option of putting out their type requirements to suppliers. Such computer facilities as there were existed mostly in large generators and consumers of text and design, such as printers and newspapers, and phototypesetting was the principle form of type. By the end of the decade it



Below: three major faces that mark a decade of rapidly developing type technology. Nimrod (top), designed by Robin Nicholas for Monotype in 1980, was drawn with concern for maximising legibility, particularly bearing in mind the conditions of small type on newsprint and yet with characteristics that would work at headline size: there is a large x-height, open counters, thin strokes that remain firm, and heavy serifs. Charter (bottom), designed by Matthew Carter for Bitstream in 1987 (the company's first original face), was a pioneering product of the electronic age, designed on computer after the preliminary sketches were digitised. Its qualities are similar in many respects to those of Nimrod, despite the intention to design a face to work on computer-driven devices. Lucida (below right), designed by Charles Bigelow and Kris Holmes for Adobe in 1985, was the first original face designed for laser printers; its approach extended across a family of faces, serif (top) and sans serif (bottom), with exact alignment and harmony of proportions between the different members of the family.
Right: two faces by Neville Brody, designed for use in *The Face* magazine. Typeface Two, 1984 (near right) sought geometric qualities coupled with the "authoritarian" overtones Brody was interested in questioning: he was

abcdefghijklmnopqrstuvwxyz
ABCDEFGHIJKLMNOPQRSTUVWXYZ
1234567890

abcdefghijklmnopqrstuvwxyz
ABCDEFGHIJKLMNOPQRSTUVWXYZ
1234567890

ABCDEFGHIJKLMN
OPQRSTUVWXYZ !+
abcdefghijklmn
opqrstuvwxyz!

A B C
D E F
G H I
J K L
M N O
P Q R
S T U
V W X
Y Z ?
[!]

abcdefghijklmnopqrstuvwxyz
ABCDEFGHIJKLMNOPQRSTUVWXYZ
1234567890

abcdefghijklmnopqrstuvwxyz
ABCDEFGHIJKLMNOPQRSTUVWXYZ
1234567890

looking particularly for a resonance between the politics and design of the 1930s, and of 1980s Britain. This design allowed for curious, dynamic and subversive usage: for example, the axis of certain characters can be changed, providing alternative forms that contradict the rhythm of words, such as moving an "O" from its vertical stress to a horizontal. Typeface Six, 1986 (above) exists only in upper case; designed to replace Futura, it uses the same geometric basis of the square and the circle. It bears the Brody stamp most notably in the severity of the geometry which is taken beyond Bauhaus concerns about functional minimalism and becomes instead a stylistic device.

Examples of the work of Neville Brody, from his first coming to prominence as the art director of *The Face* (right and below far right), to his later work as a consultant, here for the advertising agency Weiden & Kennedy, as in the Nike advertisement (far right).

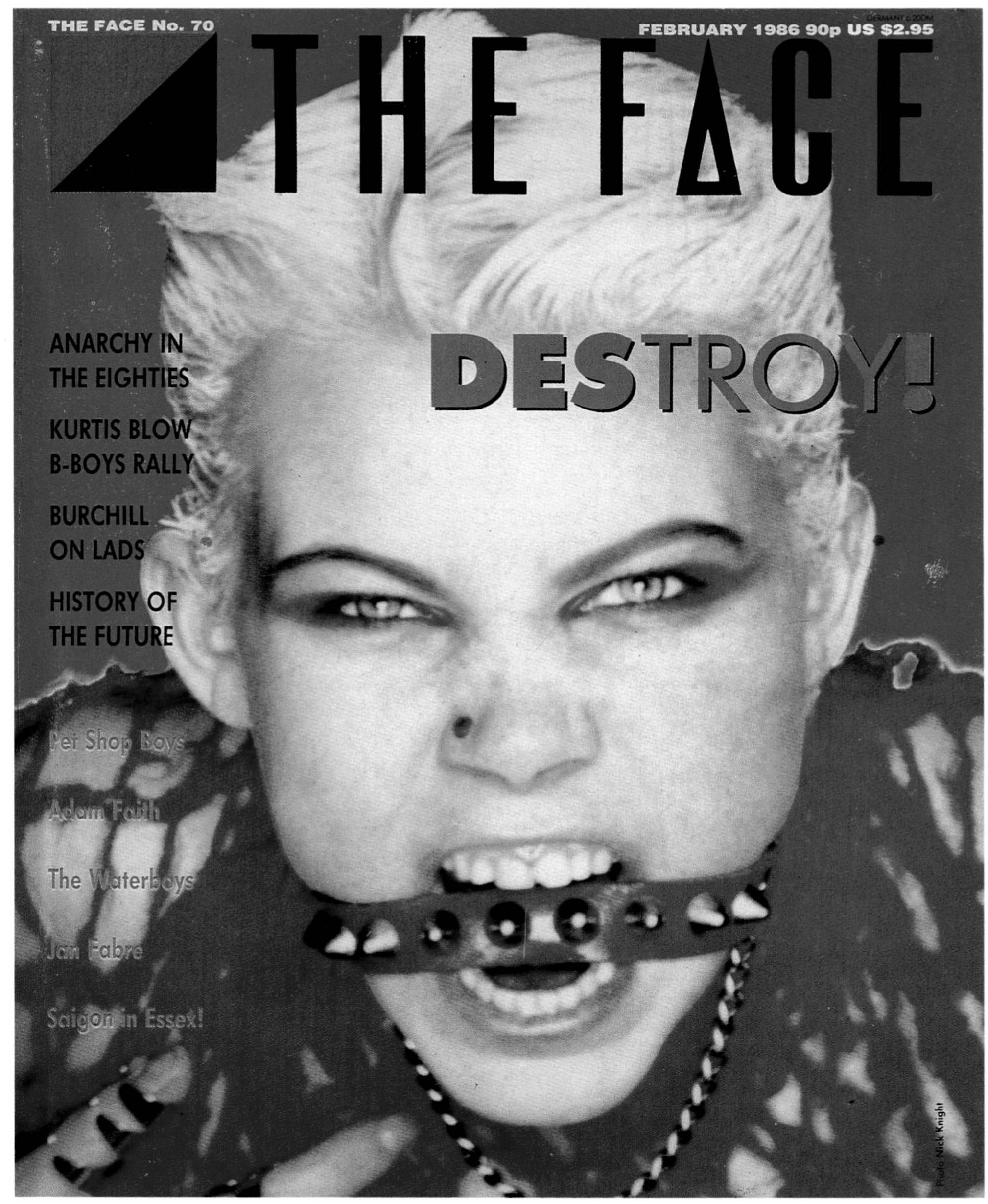

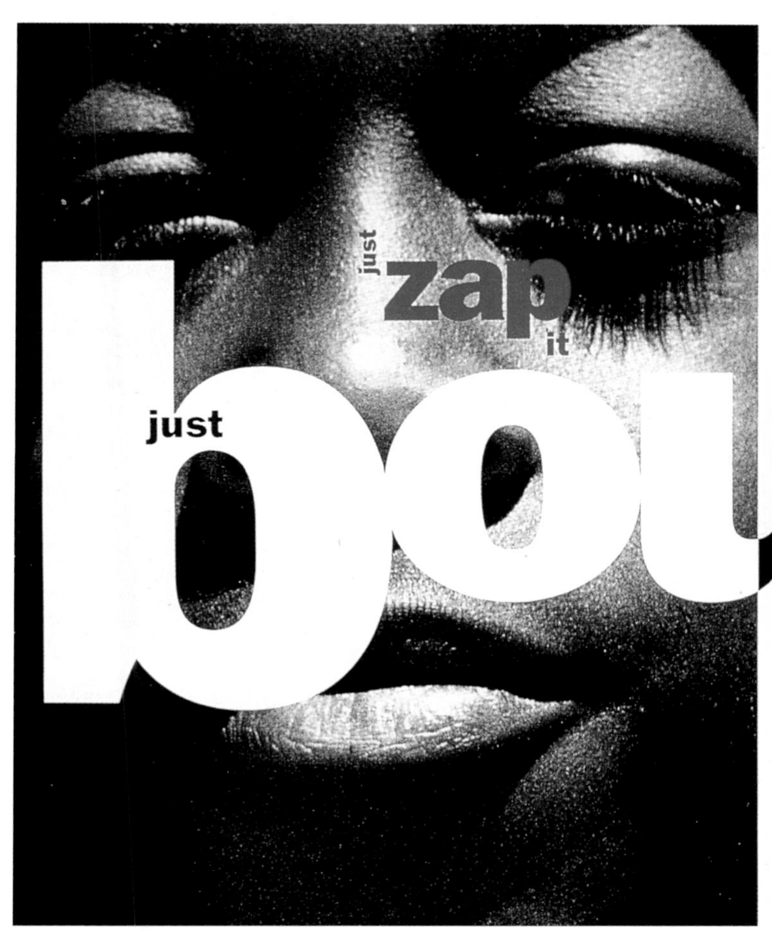
just zap it
just bou

NIKE
just slam it
nce
just smash it
just it
just do it

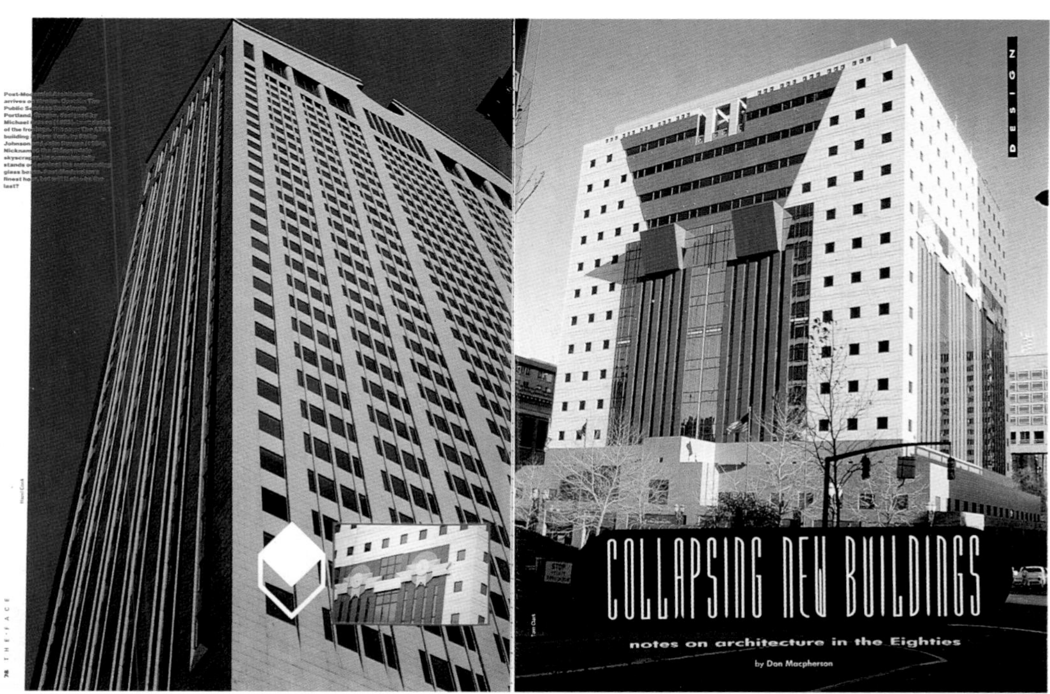
DESIGN
COLLAPSING NEW BUILDINGS
notes on architecture in the Eighties
by Don Macpherson

could be claimed that *millions* of people had gained the power to specify and output type through cheaper computing and the wide choice of software applied to creative tasks. A survey in the US in 1990 reported that 68 per cent of graphic designers used computers and a further 26 per cent were in the process of buying a system.[2] Meanwhile, the majority of office printers, which have a typographic potential way beyond that of the typewriter, are used by non-design professionals.

"Within my experience, the time taken to conceptualise and produce a real letter [character] has gone from a year to a day," commented Matthew Carter in contrasting the beginnings of his type design career (learning punchcutting at the venerable Dutch printing firm Enschedé in the 1950s) with the power that off-the-shelf font design programs gave designers by the mid- to late eighties.[3] Carter's career neatly encapsulates the changes, as well as being an important contribution to typographic history. After working for Crosfield and then Linotype as a designer who adapted and developed types for photocomposition, Carter formed Bitstream in 1981, with colleagues from Linotype. In some ways it followed the route mapped out by ITC, that of a system-independent type supplier. Bitstream's *raison d'être*, though, was to sell digitised typefaces to the new companies that were launching electronic imaging equipment and needed the support of good type libraries to make their systems viable. Bitstream rapidly set in motion a policy of digital face development and licensed the faces so that individual manufacturers did not need to develop their own libraries. Clearly, many of the classic faces had to be adapted to offer a useful library, and so the great majority of Bitstream faces are those whose basic forms are in the public domain, or are in turn licensed from others, such as ITC. Over the decade the library has grown to more than 1,000 faces and these are licensed to around 300 manufacturers, which gives some indication of the explosion of options available for outputting type, when compared to the small group of manufacturers able to invest seriously in hot-metal and then photocomposition technology.



Opposite page: titles for the television programme *Opinions*, 1988, by English Markell Pockett. The flexibility of working for screen display and on videotape enabled the designers to animate type as an illustrative medium. Streams of type suggestive of a range of opinions and subject matter become more complex until they begin to create forms that build up to make the main title. EMP was one of the main independent television design companies in the UK (Robinson Lambie-Nairn was perhaps the most notable) which advanced television graphics during the 1980s as a result of developments in production technology and computer graphics, along with greater competition between television stations.
Below: from *Amore Baciami*, a short film by Oliver Harrison, 1987. First created as a graduation film when Harrison was a student at St Martin's College of Art and Design, London, and subsequently re-edited for use in a Valentine's Day commercial for the Post Office, this meticulously animated piece pioneered the idea that fine typography could be used in film and video and its qualities augmented by animation.

IRA
reviewed

officials?
new policy of keepin

soffer
Jewish
civilian to
five

reported
the Labour

Opinions

The library includes important new designs, beginning with Carter's own Charter (1987). This is one of a number of faces designed in recent years that tackles the problem of variable printer quality and how this can seriously degrade a face. With a high-resolution typesetter of 1,200 dots per inch (dpi) or more, the finer points of a design will be reproduced. But with the popular 300 dpi laser and inkjet printers (and some with even lower resolution) many faces can be degraded. This is particularly noticeable in smaller sizes where the number of dots drawing the design of, say, an eight-point character will be too few to render fine serifs. Charter responds to these conditions by offering a limited family (regular, bold, black and italic) that has robust, open letterforms, which do not lose definition or fill in when produced on standard low-resolution printers. Bitstream Amerigo (also 1987) by Gerard Unger is another original design commissioned by the company and aimed at coping with modern output conditions. It is described by Bitstream as an elegant "flared serif", akin to Wolpe's classic Albertus and Zapf's Optima, where the serif is part of the main stroke rather than being a separate tick. Again, the design was produced in response to a brief for a laser printer output that would print more accurately than a face such as Optima, which is too subtle for such reproduction.

Unger is a Dutch designer whose work with the pioneering German digital typesetting manufacturer Dr.-Ing. Rudolf Hell GmbH deserves note. His family of faces, Demos, Praxis and Flora, released between 1976 and 1980, laid down some of the ground rules for coping with low-resolution output. The three faces – serif, sans serif and italic – demonstrate the large x-height, openness and sturdiness of form seen in the later Amerigo, Charter and other digital faces

Right: two posters by Uwe Loesch (born 1943), Düsseldorf, 1989. "That's your problem" confronts and interrogates the viewer figuratively (through the pointing hand), verbally (through the statement) and graphically, through a range of devices such as the deliberately awkward breaking of the words, the surprise use of the bright colours to pick out abstract forms rather than the image or words, and the clear layering of a message (title, group name, individuals, designer credit). "Survival during war" shows Loesch's distinctive flair for finding a key graphic device that can be made into a resonant pun or symbol: here, the text is disrupted to communicate the violent disruption of people's lives by war.

Near right: "Photography and the Soviet Union", poster by Bruno Monguzzi for the Kunsthaus, Zürich, 1989. Monguzzi (born 1941) is a Swiss-Italian designer who couples a late modernist exploration of ideas that go back to the 1920s with a strong sense of national culture. His posters often tend towards solutions which are either boldly typographic or photographic – here the latter, where the type is crunched in an arrangement suggestive of Russian Constructivism, while the pictures say a thousand words about the changes and perspectives recorded by the exhibits.

Far right: *Le Mystère des Voix Bulgares*, record sleeve designed by Vaughan Oliver for 4AD, 1988. The last years of the vinyl format for music provided an unrivalled opportunity for dramatic display type and information design. Oliver's selection of often florid type and his incorporation of type into image showed an appreciation of the opportunity for closer sympathies between the verbal and visual message; his designs often involved working closely with photography. Such an approach was assisted by advances in type generation and image-manipulation technology.

DAS KOM M ÖDCHEN Leitung: Kay Lorentz
DAS IST IHR PROBLEM!
Thomas Freitag, Jutta Hahn, Harald Schmidt
Texte: Matthias Deutschmann, Wolfgang Franke,
Michail Krausnick, Harald Schmidt
Keyboards: Matthias Bröde Bass: Thomas Giesler
Drums: Peter Baumgärtner
Bühne: Pit Fischer
Regie: Kay Lorentz

1939 bis 1945
im Ruhrgebiet
1989 bis 4. März 1990
10 bis 18 Uhr

4AD CAD 801
5 014436 801013
A 1 Kaval Sviri arr. Peter Lioudev Ensemble TRAKIA 2 Stani Mi, Maytcho comp. Krasimir Kyurkdjiyski Choeur RTB Solo: Nadejda Chwoineva 3 Di-Li-Do arr. Kyrill Stefanov Ensemble PIRIN 4 More Zajeni Se Ghiouro arr. K. Kyurkdjiyski Choeur RTB 5 Tche Da Ti Kupim Bela Seitsa arr. K. Kyurkdjiyski Choeur RTB 6 Ovdoviala Lissitchkata Orchestra Yvan Kirev solo: Verka Siderova / Tinka Pescheva 7 Messetchinko Lio arr. trad. Choeur RTB Solo: Nadejda Chwoineva 8 Ei Mori Roujke arr. Krasimir Kyurkdjiyski Ensemble PIRIN Solo: Vasilka Karadalieva 9 Dragana I Slavei arr. Kyrill Stefanov Choeur Philip Koutev Solo: N. Karadjova / St. Petkova / Y. Taneva / S. Nikolova arr. Philip Koutev
B 1 Atmadja Duma Strachilu Choeur RTB Solo: Kalinka Valcheva arr. Krasimir Kyurkdjiyski 2 Dve Tourlaski Pesen Quatuor vocal: Kalinka Valcheva / Vasilka Andonova / Paulina Gortscheva / Stoyanka Boneva arr. Nik. Kaufman 3 Trenke, Todorke Choeur RTB arr. K. Kyurkdjiyski 4 Besrodna Nevesta Choeur RTB Solo: Radka Aleksova arr. Nik. Kaufman 5 Izpoved Choeur RTB arr. K. Kyurkdjiyski 6 Ghiore Dos Choeur RTB arr. Stefan Moutafchiev 7 Spis Li, Milke Le Choeur RTB (extrait de "Starobulgarski Chroniky" Oratorio) comp. Gueorgui Mintchev
Volume 2

LE MYSTÈRE DES VOIX BULGARES

intended for wide-ranging application. While Unger was undoubtedly a pioneer of digital type, he noted that the requirements of such work are not dissimilar from the basic parameters of effective, straightforward typeface design of the last four hundred years – an acknowledgement that for all the advances in technology, the basics of a letterform remain unchanged.

Kris Holmes and Charles Bigelow's Lucida family (created in 1985 for the font publisher Adobe) took this idea seriously, calling on research into legibility and readability to develop a deliberately simplified sans serif and serif that would reproduce the preferred characteristics of classic typefaces but through the terms of the new low-resolution technology. As Holmes explained:

***The basic Lucida letterforms are purposely free of complexity and fussiness so that the underlying letter shapes can emerge legibly from "noise" of the printer-marking techniques. Certain traditionally complex details, such as swelling stems, brackets and serifs, are rendered diagrammatically as polygonal shapes rather than as subtle curves. In small sizes and low resolutions, these produce clear forms; in larger sizes and higher resolutions, they reveal interesting modulations.***

Rationalising of weight and spacing were other factors included in the design of the letters so that the effect of one cut being used in different sizes would be minimised by being "averaged". What was striking about the family was the way in which it was aimed firmly below the level of the professional graphic arts typesetting output. It acknowledged the existence of a newly enfranchised majority of typographic decision-makers – and the market they offered. As with Unger's series of faces for Hell, Lucida was a face that offered compatible serif and sans serif forms, a development that had only occasionally been ventured (but became more common with the speed of design possible with computer font-creation programs).

Holmes and Bigelow also created a comparable range of bitmapped screen fonts called Pellucida, conceived to express best the different qualities of the family with the very poor resolution of the monitor screen (72 dpi equivalent on a typical display). Since the introduction of the wysiwyg concept, all faces for digital setting have needed a screen font version, but the inaccuracy of many makes them difficult to work with, as "what you see" is not "what you get" at all. Pellucida was an early attempt to overcome some of the worst aspects of this. One problem with screen fonts, besides their low resolution, is that they are often partly drawn by the computer from knowledge of the nearest sizes that are properly designed: this can lead to highly unattractive renditions of the face on screen as the computer may "refine" the wrong elements of the design. Adobe, the company producing Lucida, at first pioneered a sometimes controversial method of overcoming this drawback called "hinting": a process built into the type information that automatically adjusts the face in small sizes to overcome low-resolution problems, but does so at the cost of some of the original character of the design. The introduction of the Adobe Type Manager program enabled more accurate information to be drawn from the printer font and used to upgrade the screen image.

While the established manufacturers moved rapidly to take up the new technology, and young companies such as Bitstream took advantage of the more open conditions of the market to offer type design services, other demands were created by the technology itself. Fundamental among these was

Right: "Summer theatre", poster by Rosemarie Tissi, 1981. The Zürich studio of Siegfried Odermatt and Rosemarie Tissi forged a distinctive style of typographic expression involving the creation of arresting, figurative shapes from blocks of colour and type, retaining at the same time traces of the Swiss style in the limited palette of sans serif type. They humanised the hardline Swiss style, keeping its purity but discovering the opportunity for humour and using colour as a bold, associative device.

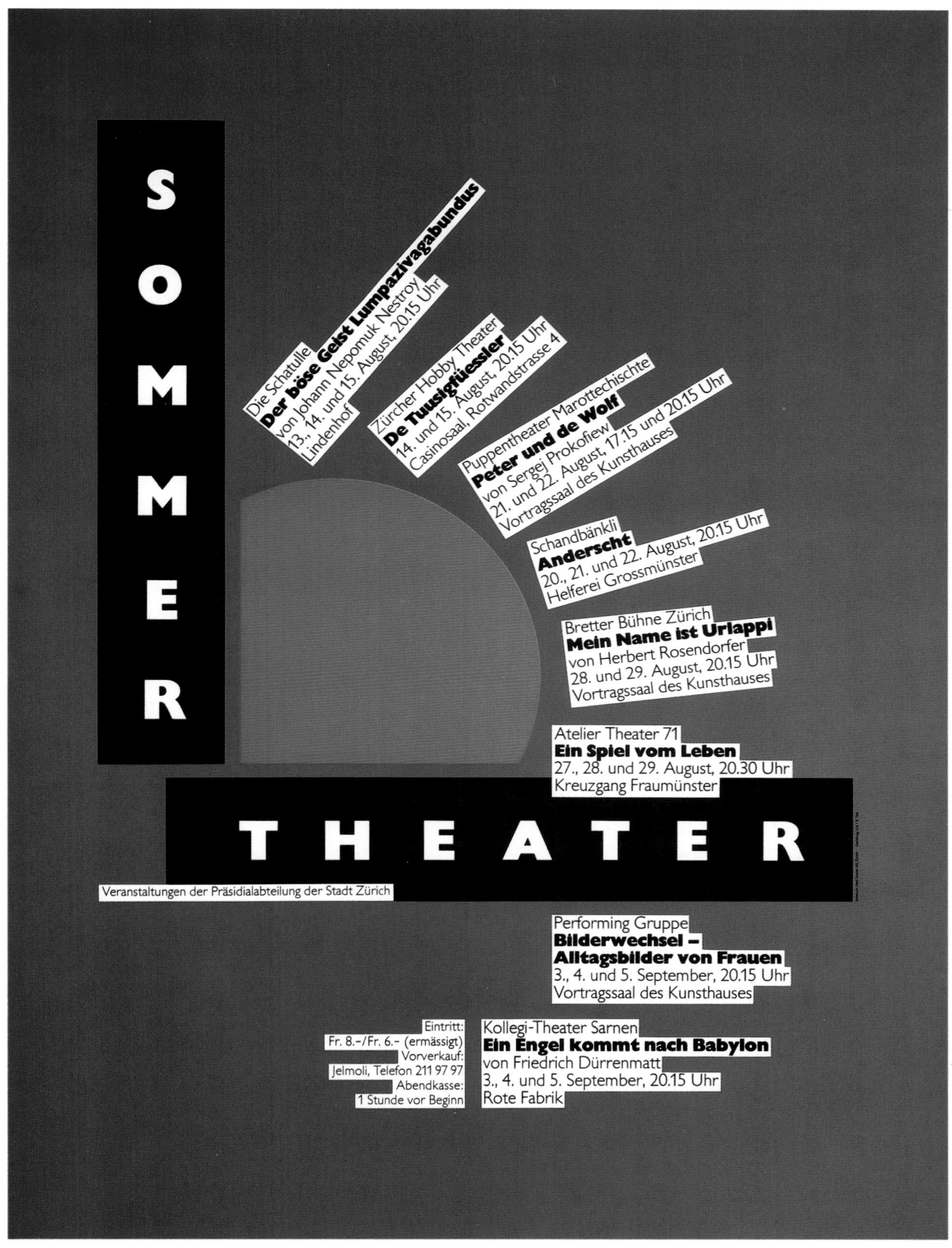

SOMMER
Die Schatulle
Der böse Geist Lumpazivagabundus
von Johann Nepomuk Nestroy
13., 14. und 15. August, 20.15 Uhr
Lindenhof
Zürcher Hobby Theater
De Tuusigfüessler
14. und 15. August, 20.15 Uhr
Casinosaal, Rotwandstrasse 4
Puppentheater Marottechischte
Peter und de Wolf
von Sergej Prokofiew
21. und 22. August, 17.15 und 20.15 Uhr
Vortragssaal des Kunsthauses
Schandbänkli
Anderscht
20., 21. und 22. August, 20.15 Uhr
Helferei Grossmünster
Bretter Bühne Zürich
Mein Name ist Urlappi
von Herbert Rosendorfer
28. und 29. August, 20.15 Uhr
Vortragssaal des Kunsthauses
Atelier Theater 71
Ein Spiel vom Leben
27., 28. und 29. August, 20.30 Uhr
Kreuzgang Fraumünster
THEATER
Veranstaltungen der Präsidialabteilung der Stadt Zürich
Performing Gruppe
Bilderwechsel –
Alltagsbilder von Frauen
3., 4. und 5. September, 20.15 Uhr
Vortragssaal des Kunsthauses
Eintritt:
Fr. 8.–/Fr. 6.– (ermässigt)
Vorverkauf:
Jelmoli, Telefon 211 97 97
Abendkasse:
1 Stunde vor Beginn
Kollegi-Theater Sarnen
Ein Engel kommt nach Babylon
von Friedrich Dürrenmatt
3., 4. und 5. September, 20.15 Uhr
Rote Fabrik

the notion of a common language for converting computer files carrying type information into a form that could be handled by desktop printers. With so many different manufacturers of composing, design and output devices, there was a need for a way in which a system comprising different elements could communicate between its constituent parts. Different "languages" were developed, but by far the most successful was – and is at the time of writing – Adobe's PostScript, launched in 1983. PostScript is a language that describes the material of an electronic page – the text, images, other graphics and layout information. It uses codes based on descriptions of the various coordinates of the page that determine the shapes contained therein; this information is device-independent, driving printers to fill in outlines dot by dot to the extent of their resolution. PostScript-encrypted fonts contain not only the printer font, but a screen font resolution for display on the computer while it is being worked with. One area of concern relating to PostScript, or indeed any device-independent form of type information, is that the typeface exists in an abstracted, non-visual form: it is only manifested in reproductions derived from that information which are not necessarily the same. For example, a 300-dots-per-inch rendition is not going to have the same qualities as a 1,200-dots-per-inch printer will deliver, and this can substantially affect the appearance of fine serifs and other delicate features of a design. Are both faces the same? They are – and they are not; it is a problem not dissimilar to the effects on a typeface of printing on different papers with different inkspread. Improvements in printer resolution are gradually removing this problem of dramatically different qualities of image.

With a whole digital type industry coming into being in the space of perhaps five or six years, and literally thousands of faces being re-drawn, based on pre-digital precedents, or being originated, the practice and output of the typographer has been radically questioned. While many designers could – and did – go on producing work that looked as if it might have been done from photosetting or even hot metal, there was also a new generation of designers who thrived on the freedom with which typographical form could now be exploited, aided and abetted by other media technology advances in photographic and film form.

Among these was Neville Brody, whose high-profile name was associated with a school of New Wave magazine design, carried forth by other designers working with him at *The Face* in the early 1980s, such as Robin Derrick and later Ian Swift, whose magazine work made an impact across Europe. This was apparent initially in the exploitation of letterforms as graphic devices, in the design of new display forms, and in the reliance on typographic elements as expressive features of the page. In its manipulation of the language of digital typography as something to exploit and express, there were connections with the New Wave approach of expressionist typography taught by Weingart. Brody's early to mid-1980s work was influential on young designers in its playful handling of typographic elements, but was often quite rough and ready – an almost unavoidable implication of the low-cost, music-business and style-magazine world in which he worked. His later work as a freelance designer and director of his own digital type foundry, FontWorks, has seen a refinement of his approach into something more indebted to Modernist and International Style ideas of grid and simplicity. Brody's fame, though, is not to be assessed so much for his work as for the disproportionately large interest taken in his career when compared to previous typographers: while still in his twenties he earned

Right: exploration of ways to express multi-tiered information on screen, developed at the Visible Language Workshop at Massachusetts Institute of Technology with designs by Muriel Cooper and tools by Suguru Ishizaki, 1989. The work of Cooper (born 1925) and others at MIT aims at providing a bridge between printing and electronic media. Here, text and images are layered in different ways, with Cooper showing how the different arrangements, foregrounding and backgrounding of the four images and three text segments can be worked. As a reader browses through a particular part of the screen display, other elements are knocked back and re-ordered, with different colours, leading and measures to differentiate the type.

Far right: Spectacolor sign above Piccadilly Circus, London, 1988, by Jenny Holzer (born 1950), from a project commissioned by Artangel and the Institute of Contemporary Arts. Holzer is one of many conceptual artists who have drawn from typographic conventions to subvert and question the language of mass communication, linking to Pop and also to Dada. In turn, the potential for irony in such communications increasingly found resonance in commercial graphics, where designers and typographers can play with the distance of the reader from the message and the different viewpoints that may exist and can be acknowledged. Here, instead of the expected brutal selling message, is a victim's cry for help. Holzer has applied her messages to a range of new technology, including giant Sony Jumbotron screens at sports stadia with bitmap-style display. Other conceptual artists working with words and exploring typographic issues include Barbara Kruger, Louise Lawler, Thomas Locher and Joseph Kosuth.

DESIGN
NEW ELEMENT
REMOVE ELEMENT
SHOW ATTRIBUTES
MOVE
SCALE
COLOR PALETTE
PROGRAM
MOVE SPACE
RESIZE SPACE
SET SPACE COLOR
SET PEN TRANS
SET PEN COLOR
SET PEN WIDTH
NEW SKETCH
DELETE STROKE
CLEAR ALL LINE
CLOSE SKETCH
PHASE2
Three phases of the graphic
computer will evolve:
-Traditional Tools that emulate
production tools of old media
with greater speed, economy,
flexibility and interaction and
place professional tools in the
hands of non-professionals
will change traditional
profesional practices and
patterns of design and
production
Phase 2
Phase 3
Computers and Design

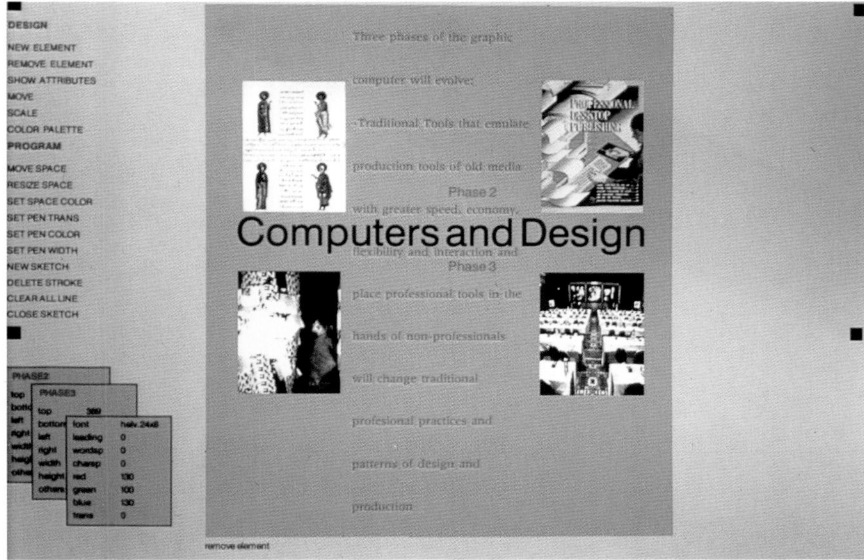
DESIGN
NEW ELEMENT
REMOVE ELEMENT
SHOW ATTRIBUTES
MOVE
SCALE
COLOR PALETTE
PROGRAM
MOVE SPACE
RESIZE SPACE
SET SPACE COLOR
SET PEN TRANS
SET PEN COLOR
SET PEN WIDTH
NEW SKETCH
DELETE STROKE
CLEAR ALL LINE
CLOSE SKETCH
PHASE2
PHASE3
Three phases of the graphic
computer will evolve:
-Traditional Tools that emulate
production tools of old media
with greater speed, economy,
flexibility and interaction and
place professional tools in the
hands of non-professionals
will change traditional
profesional practices and
patterns of design and
production
Phase 2
Phase 3
Computers and Design
remove element

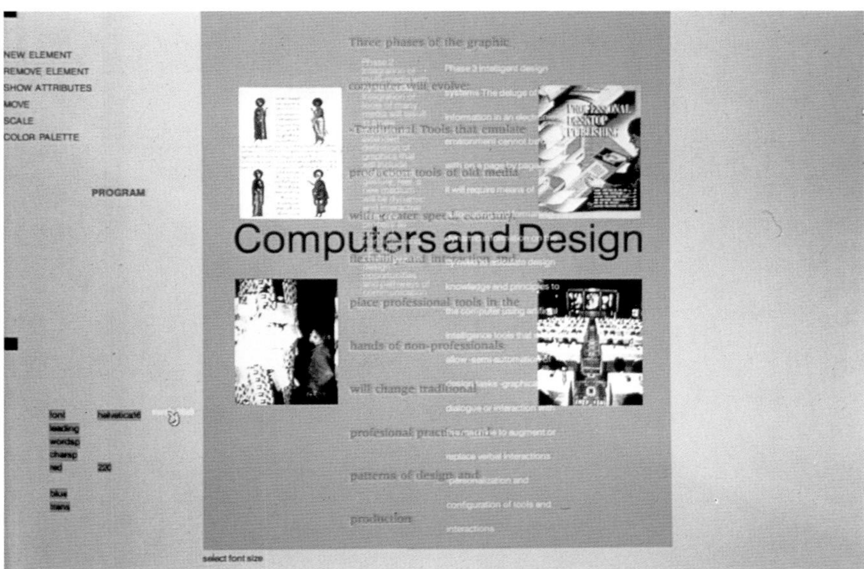
NEW ELEMENT
REMOVE ELEMENT
SHOW ATTRIBUTES
MOVE
SCALE
COLOR PALETTE
PROGRAM
Three phases of the graphic
computer will evolve:
-Traditional Tools that emulate
production tools of old media
with greater speed, economy,
flexibility and interaction and
place professional tools in the
hands of non-professionals
will change traditional
profesional practices and
patterns of design and
production
Computers and Design
select font size

MAIDEN
PROTECT ME
FROM WHAT
I WANT
CARPETS CURTAINS UPHOLSTERY
Sketchley
CONTRACT CLEANING SERVICES

an exhibition at the Victoria & Albert Museum in London, which then went on a world tour; profiles of him were published around the world, an expression of how fashionable a little know-how about type had become. Brody's skills as a designer are not questioned, but they are in a way secondary to his significance as a type phenomenon in the 1980s.

Another magazine designer involved in the influential batch of British "style magazines" of the 1980s was Terry Jones, who launched and still runs *i-D* magazine. Here legibility was severely questioned in a manner akin to the psychedelia of the late sixties, with the basic meaning of the words subverted by garish overprinting and crude typewriter text, copy reversed out from four colours, photocopier distortions and many more graphic experiments. All this "noise" was part of the message, with typographic quality for the audience of *i-D* involving viewability as much as legibility in order to create readability. Jones came from a fashion background (he was at one time art director on British *Vogue*) and his ideas related clearly to the demands of fashion. In typographic terms, his work is a kind of terrorism against fine type – abusing all the rules to produce something that is quite unacceptable outside its own parameters, but brilliant within those, doing whatever is necessary to capture the attention of a reader who is less interested in reading, but more into viewing and taking part as a style wearer. Style magazines such as *i-D*, *The Face* and *Blitz* in the UK, or related magazines such as *Actuel* in France or *Wiener* in Germany, were partly badges of affiliation, to be worn as well as read.

*Emigre* magazine, designed and produced in Berkeley, California by Rudy VanderLans, was and is an innovative variation on the potential of new type technology and the youth-culture magazine: it is a magazine of and about experimental type and typography. Prior to this decade, such a magazine would have had a very academic circulation. But *Emigre* sells internationally through outlets such as record stores (albeit still a comparatively small circulation of

Examples of the output of Emigre Graphics, the company run by Rudy VanderLans, editor and designer of *Emigre* magazine, which he began in 1984. Concepts of readability and legibility are explored by these faces (principally designed by Zuzana Licko), especially in the context of the low- and medium-resolution printer output common in most publishing systems. *Emigre* celebrates such conditions rather than being in conflict with them. Thus early Emigre fonts such as Oakland Six (far right) and Emperor (below right) were designed to maximise the expressiveness of the screen bitmap and its low-resolution output; they continued to be sold and developed after the arrival of PostScript, which converted the bitmap into an outline for higher-resolution output. The bitmap appearance was seen by VanderLans as expressing the very conditions of production of digital design, but the *Starting From Zero* issue of 1991 (right and pages 204–5) suggested that experimentation in design may always lead back to simplicity.

MATRIX TALL

Matrix

Wide & Narrow

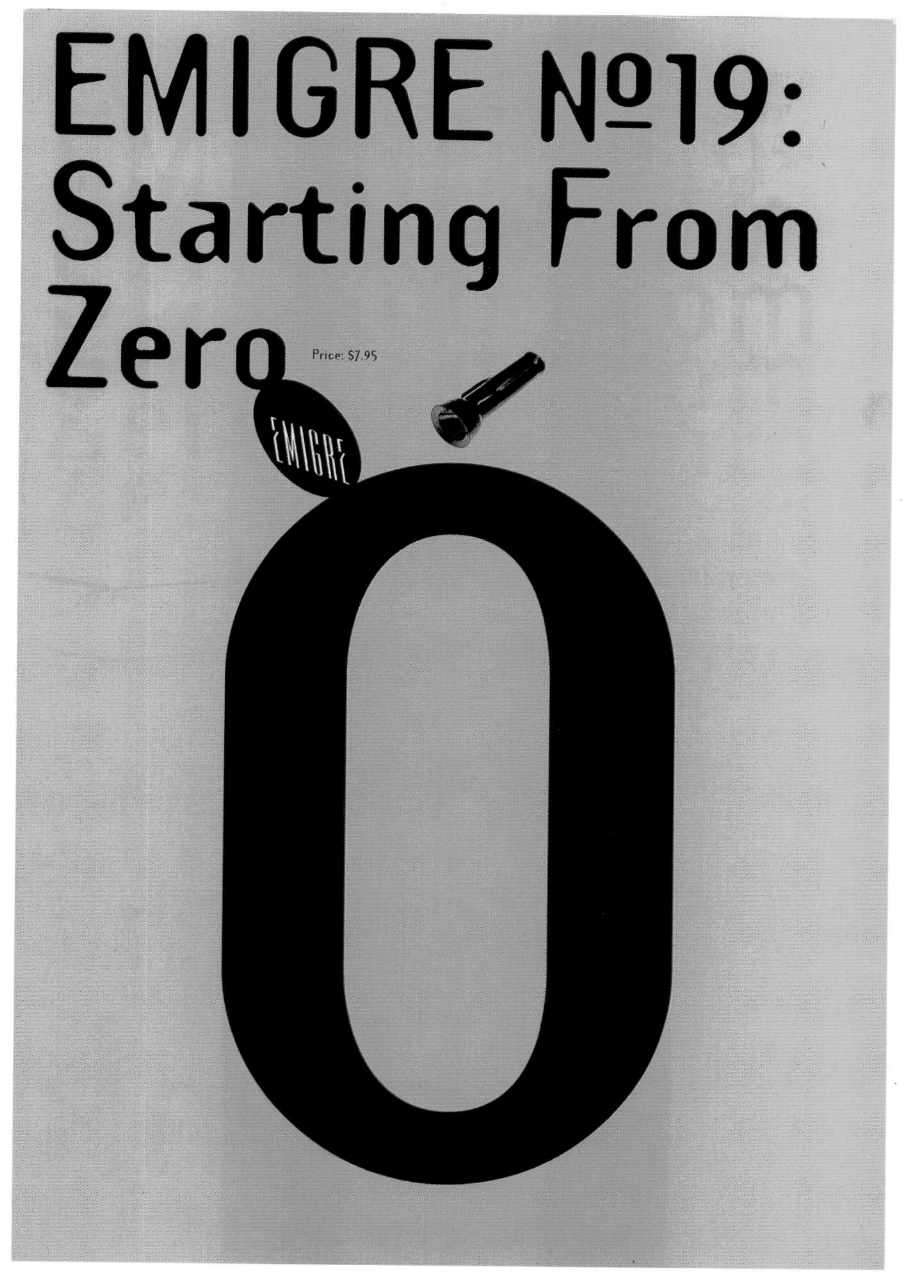


ABCXYZ

Emperor

around 6,000 copies by the end of the decade). It is a typophile's "fanzine", aimed at the new order of interest stimulated by Apple Macintosh technology. It is also a kind of type library promotion: the magazine is produced using Apple Macintosh technology and features Emigre Graphics' own faces, designed by Zuzana Licko (born 1961) on the Fontographer program and others in PostScript format, and marketed by the company through the magazine. But this does not undermine the seriousness or quality of its subject matter, which principally revolves around interviewing leading type designers and showing and commissioning new work. Through the eighties the magazine fostered the sense of an international community of those interested in exploiting the implications of bitmapped fonts; of a link between "punk graphics" and the earlier revolutionary impact of Modernism, of a case for art typography. It is now broadening its scope, so that Emigre Graphics offers related products such as music and posters.

The taking-apart and re-assembly of digital type and typography, as displayed to a greater or lesser extent in the above magazines, was further promoted by the students at the Cranbrook Academy of Art, which for twenty years has been a source of innovative design in the US. The teaching and work of Katherine McCoy in the graphic design area had the support of key students such as Jeffery Keedy, Edward Fella, David Frej and Allen Hori. An early project, the design of an issue of the academic communication theory magazine *Visible Language* in 1978, set the tone: the text was re-presented by a variety of

Below: *Starting From Zero, Emigre* 19, set in Template Gothic and designed by Barry Deck, suggests a return to simplicity, instead of the earlier layering and baroque qualities of *Emigre*'s type and layouts.
Right and below right: *Emigre* 6, a less focused magazine, in which non-typographic and graphic design subjects were likely to be explored through the deliberately coarse net of bitmapped faces (by Zuzana Licko) and layers of text.

Henk Elenga is one of the founding members of the Dutch design group Hard Werken. He moved to California in 1981 to open the "L.A. Desk" of Hard Werken in Hollywo
Although his business card states that he specializes in graphic and furniture design, Elenga has been involved in music, video, performance art and photography. His furniture designs and photographs have been exhibited around the world. Among the many clients that he works for are Esprit and Warner Brothers Records, for whom has designed numerous album covers. Currently he is working on the design of the new mannequins for Esprit. He remains one of the most inspirational influences to th magazine's designer.

"Creativity at its deepest, i
a return to a primary process rather than a respons
to external stimuli. My choice of using photography, in the artistic process, is only for formalization and sty zation."

Henk
Elenga

# Tuxedomoon's Princ

always said that our music is very "soundtracky." Many people have made visuals to our music.

Also in Holland and Belgium there are many so called "art movies" being made. Lots of them are sponsored or subsidized by the government. So there is always some money to begin with, and that's the key to it. In America you have less of that. That's back to that whole thing I was saying about culture in Europe. The government gives money to these filmmakers, but who goes to see their movies? Not the regular people in the street. So the movies don't make any money. It's not really that you are getting anywhere because the government gives you the money, but at least they give you the money. Here, if you can really get people's attention they flock in the millions, but in Europe they won't come anyway. Maybe for a week. It is a strange thing to be doing, trying to battle entertainment and success and still keep your artistic integrity and remember what you are doing and at the same time earn a living. It's all pretty fascinating and actually a great challenge.

EMIGRE: *It's interesting to see an American band moving to Europe. Certainly the trend is for most European bands to come to the U.S. to make it big.*

PETER: We sort of did this intuitively on purpose for those reasons. We're often trying to swim against the current, test our muscles, as it were. We've always managed to avoid being pegged by the media as a punk or post-punk or new wave or electronic or experimental or whatever the hell and we would like to keep one step ahead of it all, so we don't become a package to hang on the wall that's been finished. We are an ongoing project. I don't think we will ever perfect our thing because it is always too far ahead of us. But not so far ahead, I hope, that the audience just gets annoyed because we are pretentious.

I DON'T THINK WE WILL EVER PERFECT OUR THING BECAUSE IT IS ALWAYS TOO FAR AHEAD OF US. BUT NOT SO FAR AHEAD, I HOPE, THAT THE AUDIENCE JUST GETS ANNOYED BECAUSE WE ARE PRETENTIOUS.

EMIGRE: *Is it to your advantage being an American band in Belgium? Does it add to your "differentness" and does it give you an edge over local bands?*

PETER: Yes I am sure about that. I am sorry to say, but it is true.

EMIGRE: *Were you aware of that when you left for Europe, that you could use that in your search for fame and fortune?*

PETER: So, not exactly, actually we thought when we first went to Europe that we would have an international lifestyle. I expected by now to have apartments in Japan and New York. I don't mean expensive apartments, I mean places to stay with keys I could give to friends when I wasn't there. But in fact it didn't work out because the money is just too tight. But I would like to have been that successful. A few things happened to mess that up. Immediately after we moved to Holland, Blaine Reininger, our violinist, was hit by a car in Amsterdam, broke his fingers and his leg. We couldn't do anything for a year, although we were doing shows with him in a wheelchair where we carried him on and off the stage. We were living in Utopia (the former municipal waterworks building which is now occupied by artists) in Rotterdam, and they said, "We can't have a wheelchair victim in Utopia." So we had to move out of there, and we went to Brussels. That was a quick escape. In Brussels we met some people who had a record company and then slowly but surely we got connected with Crammed discs and that has been the most lucrative thing that has happened for us in Europe, because a lot of European companies are kinda screwy. So are a lot of American companies of course. It has nothing to do with the country. It is difficult being independent. Tuxedomoon has been in business longer than many record companies we do business with.

I MISS AMERICA FOR SOME THINGS, NOT FOR OTHERS. TV FOR INSTANCE. TV IN EUROPE IS HORRENDOUS, IT'S "DALLAS" IN SIX LANGUAGES.

EMIGRE: *If you look into the future, what will Tuxedomoon be doing?*

PETER: Hopefully, more movie soundtracks. And I hope that the next time we come to America, we'll be able to rally more energy to tour more and go to places with bigger stages, etc. In Europe, we are used to bigger stages and more lights so we can do shows that are much more visual than we can here. Although tonight was not as bad as some on the American tour, little dives with a two sector square stage that is elevated one inch. At any rate, I know that I will continue to work, because I can't for the life of me think of any other reasons to stand here on this planet and breathe this air – wherever that takes me. I hope it will take me to places like Bombay and Japan.

Which reminds me of another reason why I like Europe, and this is a major reason. Here in America, when you are of a foreign culture everybody tries to forget it, you try to spell your name like Smith or Jones and you try to wear brown shoes and look like a regular person, but in Europe every culture is really militant. They are all throwing bombs at the people next door shouting, "We want separatism, we want our own isolated little place where we can speak our own language spoken by 10,000 people." That's really exciting in a way. When you are in America, you have no idea how small Europe is and how much struggle it took to keep the French language separate from the German language and how much the concepts and philosophies of these peoples differ. They fought millions of wars and killed lots of people and expended a lot of good real estate for the purpose of staying individual. Whereas here in America, they all try to build McDonald's everywhere and hide everything. You turn on the radio in Europe and you hear African, Arabic, Yiddish, French, and Dutch music and all this unusual stuff. Whereas here in America you basically have five different kinds of disco, five different kinds of rock, some easy listening and a lot of other white music, but that's it.

EMIGRE: *Have you been influenced by any European music?*

PETER: Actually more by Arabic, Indian and African music than by the European. That's for myself. But I know Steven is a fan of the Italian romantic singers. I love Marconi, Nino Rota etc., but I already knew about them before I went to Europe because they are big stars here. But a lot of European music has gone in one ear and out the other, usually because they are imitating American or British music.

EMIGRE: *How about England, is Tuxedomoon doing well there?*

PETER: Tuxedomoon has never gone over well in England. They always hated us for being too "arty" or they didn't understand what we were doing. We toured England a few times, we were on Charisma Records, but the whole thing bombed out. Now we don't even go there anymore. I've got to admit that I liked the English music more a few years ago, but they are still great and they have the best studios. They got a great sound over there, that's for sure. We did one album in London that was during our first European trip and that was also motivated by the European thing. We wanted to get out of America because we couldn't find any engineers that knew how to record rhythm machines, etc. Here in America I actually had a conversation in a Boston club with a guy who was asking "Why should the PA be in stereo? Is the singer in stereo?" That's the kind of mentality we tried to get away from. We knew John Fox, because he was trying to sign us to his label years ago, we wrote to him and we got him to introduce us to his engineer, Gareth Jones, who is now kind of a megastar. We did "Desire" together, which was a great experience for us.

EMIGRE: *How has Tuxedomoon managed to stay together for so long as a non-commercial band?*

PETER: (Jokingly) We are a military organization and we run guns on the side.

EMIGRE: *Who's the boss?*

PETER: Me. No, there is no boss, we are a very loosely organized collective. It's anarchy which has run us very well because we are always dealing with the laws of chance and have been lucky.

EMIGRE: *Lucky in terms of staying together?*

PETER: Yes, lucky in terms of being able to work out all our things, and sometimes we don't see each other for four months. We are always having a baby, like another project that Gary hires us for so we go to Spain to do TV or whatever. There is always something good coming up.

10

11

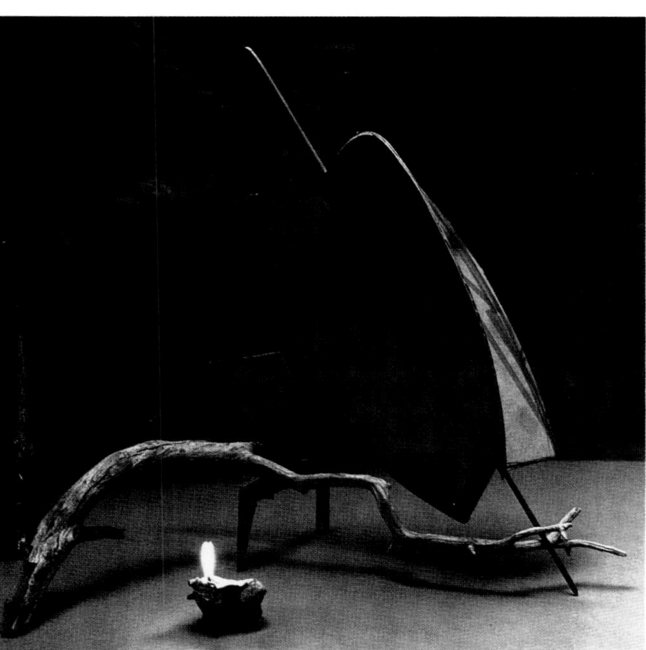

Henk Elenga, Prototype for light fixture, 1988

(Source of inspiration)

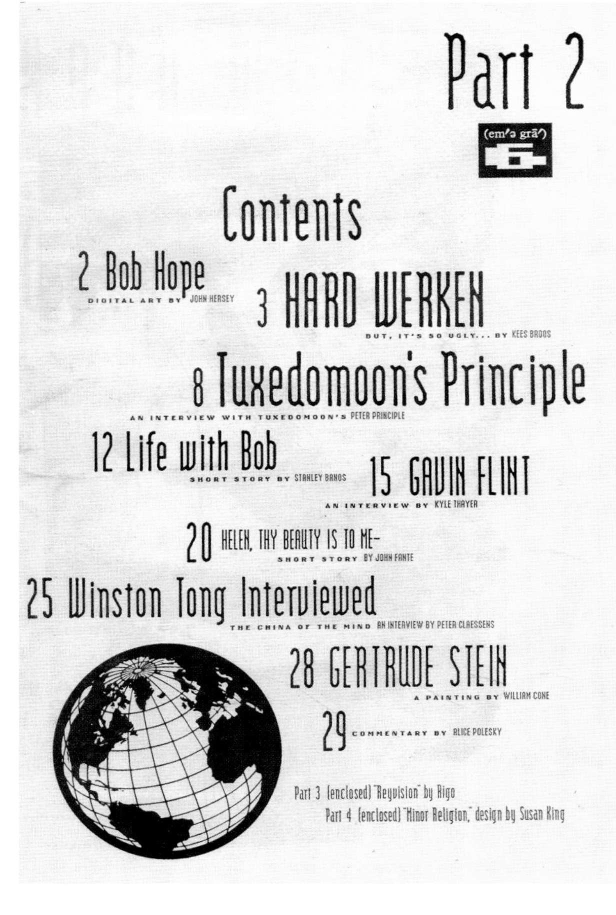

Part 2

(em'ə grā) 6

Contents


2 Bob Hope DIGITAL ART BY JOHN HERSEY

3 HARD WERKEN BUT, IT'S SO UGLY... BY KEES BROOS

8 Tuxedomoon's Principle AN INTERVIEW WITH TUXEDOMOON'S PETER PRINCIPLE

12 Life with Bob SHORT STORY BY STANLEY BANOS

15 GAVIN FLINT AN INTERVIEW BY KYLE THAYER

20 HELEN, THY BEAUTY IS TO ME– SHORT STORY BY JOHN FANTE

25 Winston Tong Interviewed THE CHINA OF THE MIND AN INTERVIEW BY PETER CLAESSENS

28 GERTRUDE STEIN A PAINTING BY WILLIAM CONE

29 COMMENTARY BY ALICE POLESKY

Part 3 (enclosed) "Requision" by Rigo

Part 4 (enclosed) "Minor Religion," design by Susan King

devices at work on the typography (reversals, hugely exaggerated word spacing, ragged margins and much more) to the point of being almost unreadable. McCoy projected this approach as part of an exercise exploring the "linguistics" of typography: she was seeking to express in the work those aspects of typography which are "hardware" – the basic structure of the communication – and those which are "software" – the meaning in the work. The dislocation caused by the deconstructed layouts was a way of trying to prise loose an awareness of the signified from the signifier, to use the terminology of a Cranbrook influence, the earlier writings of pioneering language theoretician Ferdinand de Saussure.

The work of the Cranbrook group of designers is not the stuff of widespread commercial acceptance. But it does provide a body of work that is a highly inquisitive response to the relationship between designed and vernacular communications, between typographic and calligraphic forms, between type and art.

Edward Fella is one Cranbrook graduate whose work draws together different strands of the typographic debate, from printer's vernacular to punk, merging illustration with type. Fella was a mature student at Cranbrook, having worked for many years as a commercial illustrator before gradually becoming more "art-design" orientated. In his typographic compositions, which include some commercial commissions as well as entirely experimental works, he has developed a range of techniques that contradict the notion of "slick design", the world of corporate and other high-quality image-making, where everything is extremely "neat". As an antidote, he presents an aesthetic which is anti-aesthetic, where type is variably spaced and aligned, or chopped up, where rough calligraphy mixes with degraded, found letterforms. The irregular and the inconsistent are familiar modes for Fella, his work being the stimulation of a blast of sand in the eye, the evidence of a strong wind. In an interview with Keedy, he pointed out that his

Different directions in American typography during the decade. Right, top and below: two posters by Edward Fella for CalArts school of art, California, late 1980s. Fella, who plays with the "loaded messages and hidden ones", produces works with typographic arrangements that constantly ask questions of the viewer – how to decode the message, how to interpret the signs of the designer's involvement, how to assess the possible different meanings within a construction. He challenges notions of legibility, deliberately slowing the consumption of a message so that readers have to appreciate their involvement in the process.

Right: *WigWag* magazine, November 1989; art directed by Paul Davis, *WigWag* had a highly conventional, retro appearance, reminiscent of the *New Yorker*. However, lurking within the pages were ironic comments in the choice of typographic elements; curious, unexplained illustrations, and other devices that undermined and questioned the user-friendly aspects of the pages. The traditionalism of the typography was mocking rather than affectionate – and it assumed the reader could spot such sophisticated layering. The short life of the magazine perhaps suggests they did not.

Before leaving Chelsea, we went to look at one more apartment, just a block away. Reminding me of the criteria I had originally given him, the broker extolled the safety of the block as we traversed it. We stopped at a cheery-looking Art Deco building. A burly doorman admitted us and made us sign our names in a book. We took the elevator to a high floor, opened the door of an apartment, and found ourselves looking at a very agreeable view: the Empire State Building, the Chrysler Building, lots of sky, and a billboard showing an enormous bottle of Miche-

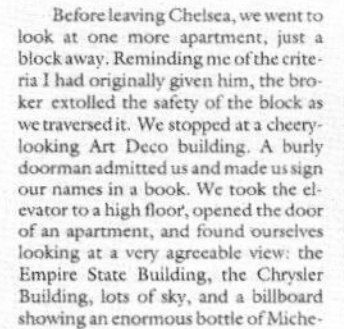

lob being poured into an enormous glass. We admired it in silence; nothing could be heard through the thick, prewar walls, and we were too high above the street for its sounds to reach us. There was nothing in the apartment but clean white appliances in the bathroom and kitchen, and there was nothing on the walls but fresh white paint. I told the broker I would take it. Then he told me how much it would cost. The figure he named was my salary. When I got back to Hell's Kitchen that night, I looked out my window and saw a young woman who lived on the second floor being carried out of the building on a stretcher. After the ambulance pulled away, I noticed that someone had put an accent on the "E" in "RISQUE."

—Lindsley Cameron

**Saturday morning at rodeo practice.**

The more civilized a little town gets, the less interesting its newspapers are to read, or at least that's what's happening here. Lately, the *Dispatch* has been full of nothing but civic-interest stuff—articles on bond elections, zoning feuds, the latest in the wastewater disposal debate. For the more eye-opening stories, the kind you rush home to tell your wife, we depend on more traditional small-town sources. Bambi Murchison, for instance, who waits tables at Mr. Mike's Cafe, is well informed, but she's young yet and her knowledge of human nature is not as seasoned as the ladies' over at the Clip 'n' Curl. And Alex Applewhite, our town barber, also knows the score, but Alex punctuates his words with his scissors, and you have to watch him when he gets excited in mid-yarn. A less perilous but equally reliable source are the old ranchers sitting on George Fry's roping-pen rail. It was there one Saturday a while back that I first heard about the strange change in Billy Rippy.

A couple of weekends a month, George runs a kind of informal roping practice, and the morning my sons and I stopped by to borrow a piece of farm equipment, his place was the sort of scene a boy dreams of. Cowboys and horses were everywhere, calves were bawling in the chute, and lariats whistled through the air. I admit it excited me, too, and while the boys ran off to help shag strays, I went over to join the collection of old coots and horseflesh critics sitting like a flock of birds on the roping-pen rail, where you could get a view of the action from above the dust. There were many good local ropers in attendance, but I automatically looked for Billy Rippy first.

Tall, lean, and always Stetsoned, Billy is one of eight brothers of the Rippys of Rippy's Feeds. Among them, Curtis Rippy does his share of ranching, and brother Pug taught the Western Arts classes in our high school before becoming our county commissioner, but it's Billy who's the family cowboy. He's the one who trained and rode the big white-stockinged sorrel quarter horse named Santa Claus that was widely regarded as the finest calf-roping horse in the nation for many years. The walls of the office at Rippy's are covered with photos of Billy and Santa sliding to a stop while the calf

POSTCARD COURTESY D.J. STOUT

42 WIGWAG NOVEMBER 1989

runs out of slack. Santa Claus died in 1982. A few years later, Billy was up roping in Oklahoma and came across a horse identical in color and markings. He bought him on the spot. Although Santa Two never fully lived up to his name, he was a steady roping horse, good enough that he and Billy were top contenders at the VFW Rodeo in Wimberley every year. But they weren't among the contestants at George Fry's that Saturday, which was odd. As our town's prize cowboy-cowhorse team, they've become the standard against which other ropers measure themselves, as well as the role model for the roping kids.

Number of Taxis

**Tucson: About 165**
**Manhattan: 11,787**
**(all five boroughs)**
**Dripping Springs: None**
**Cambridge: 248**
**Washington: 6,253**

And at a roping practice like this it's the kids who do most of the work. They herd the calves up the trap and into the chute one by one. Then, when the roper in the starting box nods his head, they pull the spring-loaded chute gate and out bursts the calf, sprinting for safety at the far end of the arena, with a horse and cowboy in hot pursuit. If all goes well and the calf is roped, thrown, and tied, the kids run out whooping from the sidelines to untie him and hand the cowboy back his pigging string.

That is, if all goes well, which it wasn't that morning. George Fry had had these calves for over six weeks, and after six weeks of being chased from a chute they'd become as nimble as acrobats. They were popping out of the gate going every which way, each calf with his own personal style and repertoire of tricks. It looked like a total victory for the calves.

The old rancher I climbed up next to grunted as he watched a long-necked cowboy throw well wide of a calf. "Shoot, that's Smitty for you." He shook his head and took a look at me. "Say, aren't you the fellow who rides English with his wife, and jumps?"

"Yes, sir, I am." I always find it best to admit to this right away. "But I roped as a kid, on my granddad's ranch."

"Oh, well," the old fellow said. "That's all right." He looked back at the arena, where the next roper was backing his horse up into the starting box. "I bet you can still rope better than this banker fella can."

The banker fella was actually a new neighbor of Sally's and mine. He just bought a ranchette not too far from ours, and makes the long commute daily to his downtown Austin bank. He's a genial, roly-poly man, and from the way he was dressed that morning, complete with new hat and chaps, I could see that he had many of the same cowboy fantasies as my kids.

Weekend cowboys aren't terribly unusual out here—in fact, the countryside depends on them. This is hilly, rocky country, and while it's very picturesque, it's not what agricultural people call strong land. That is, it's pretty to look at but hard to make a living on. About thirty years ago, oil barons looking for loopholes began buying up these big, unprofitable Angora goat ranches. They built huge, rustic-looking "ranch houses," put up massive stone entry gates, sold the goats, and hired a foreman to raise a herd of those antique, colorful Texas longhorns that look much prettier on a hillside than on a dinner plate. Then they went away, returning only for weekends during deer season, when they could ride around in their jeeps wearing safari jackets.

The number of Texas oil barons has dwindled lately, but up until a few years ago the price of land continued to climb. The result was that when Grandpa passed away, his heirs had a hard time finding a buyer for an unprofitable multimillion-dollar place. Naturally, real estate agents appeared and chopped up the old ranchstead into ranchettes, where people like me and my neighbor could experience Ponderosa life.

Anyway, this Saturday morning my neighbor, the suburban cowboy, was experiencing both problems and pleasures on his borrowed horse. It was a big horse, a sorrel, and though I didn't recognize him immediately, it was obvious that he was much more talented than the banker on his back. When each

calf burst out of the chute, he tracked well and set his rider up, but time and again kids and cowboys on the sidelines had to hit the dirt to avoid getting caught in the banker's loop.

After each miss, the horse would look back over his shoulder, as if to say, Hey, I'm doing *my* job, what about you? My neighbor seemed thick-skinned

43

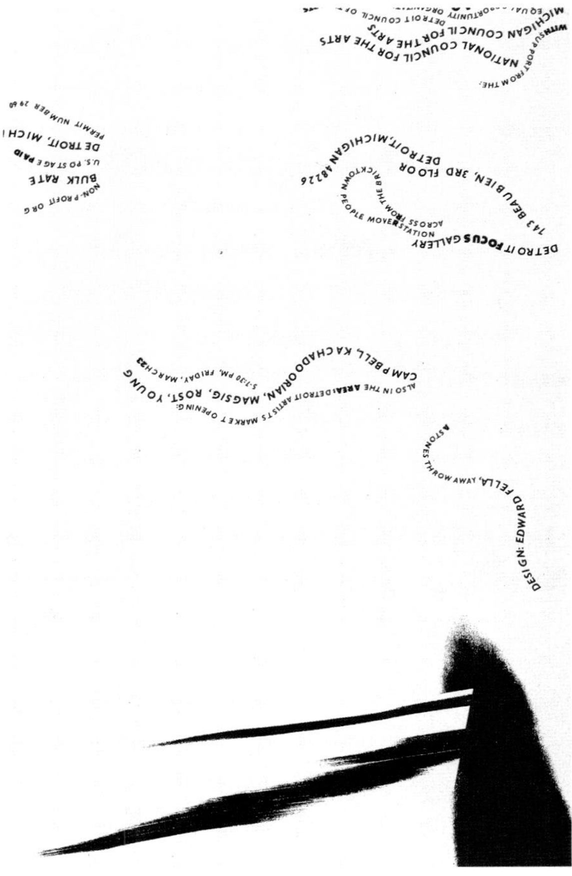


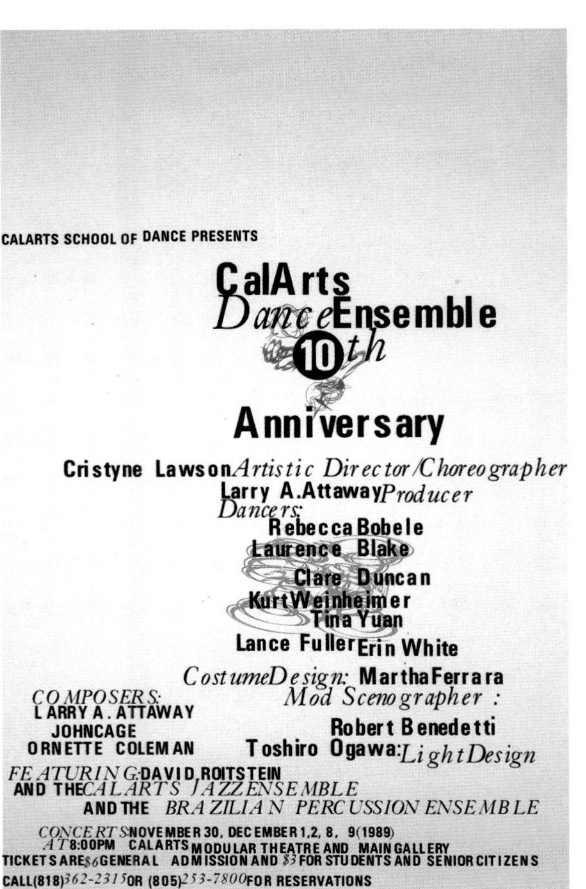

CALARTS SCHOOL OF DANCE PRESENTS
CalArts Dance Ensemble
10th
Anniversary
Cristyne Lawson Artistic Director/Choreographer
Larry A. Attaway Producer
Dancers:
Rebecca Bobele
Laurence Blake
Clare Duncan
Kurt Weinheimer
Tina Yuan
Lance Fuller Erin White
Costume Design: Martha Ferrara
Mod Scenographer:
Robert Benedetti
COMPOSERS:
LARRY A. ATTAWAY
JOHN CAGE
ORNETTE COLEMAN
Toshiro Ogawa: Light Design
FEATURING: DAVID ROITSTEIN
AND THE CALARTS JAZZ ENSEMBLE
AND THE BRAZILIAN PERCUSSION ENSEMBLE
CONCERTS: NOVEMBER 30, DECEMBER 1, 2, 8, 9 (1989)
AT 8:00PM CALARTS MODULAR THEATRE AND MAIN GALLERY
TICKETS ARE $6 GENERAL ADMISSION AND $3 FOR STUDENTS AND SENIOR CITIZENS
CALL (818) 362-2315 OR (805) 253-7800 FOR RESERVATIONS


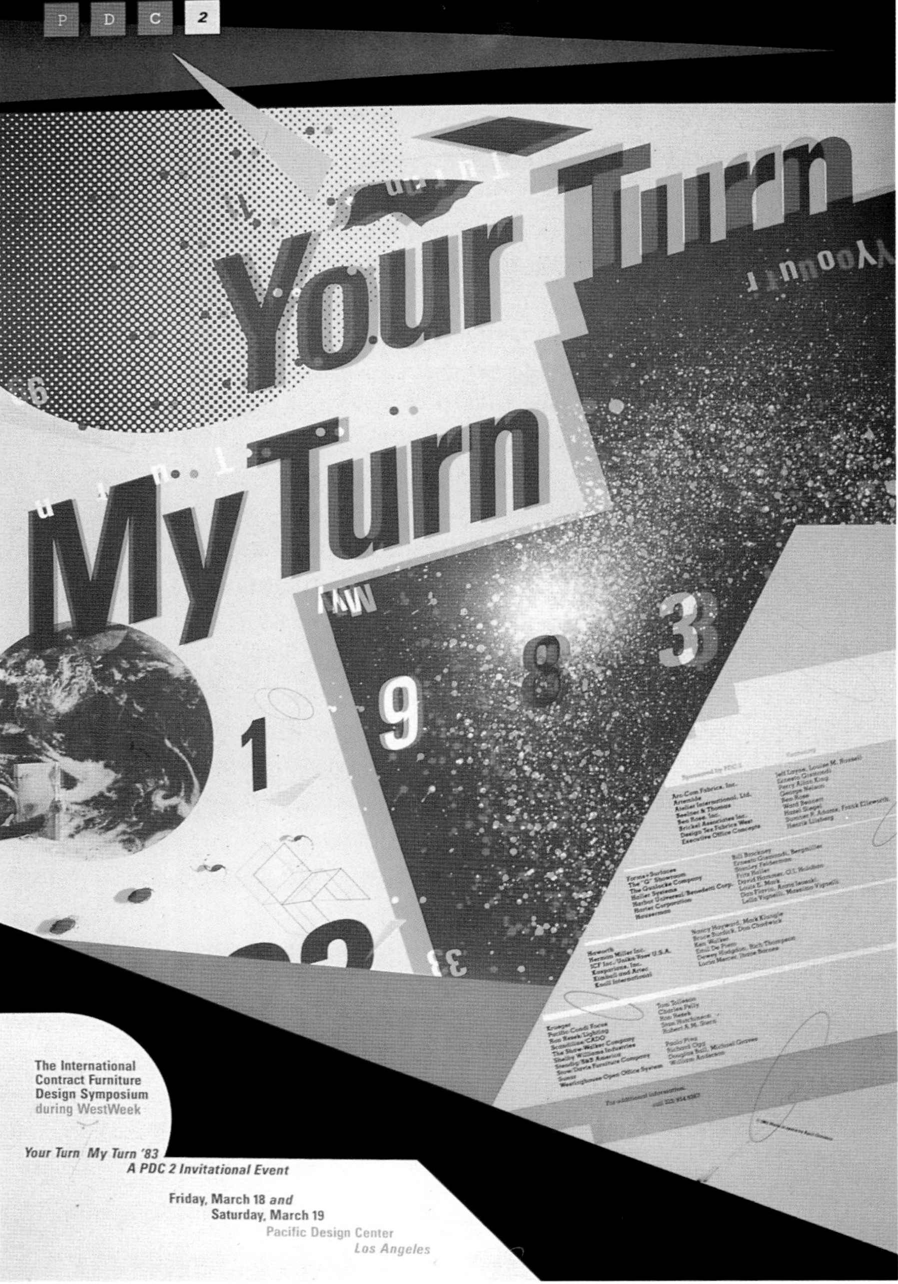


Above: *Your Turn My Turn*, poster by April Greiman for the Pacific Design Center, 1983, showing her development of New Wave graphics from the basis of studies under Wolfgang Weingart in Basel in the early 1970s. From the stepped blocks and reversals of Weingart, Greiman (born 1948) developed a graphic style that she named "Hybrid Imagery", an anything-goes environment that draws on computer and video culture to arrive at often highly colourful, typographically obscured results. Here, colour suggests a depth or out-of-register element related to television screen images, with perspective shifts encouraged by the reversals (as with "1983"). This expressiveness does not ignore, but rather supports, the ordering and layering of the information.

***irregularity is rigorously thought out, based loosely on deconstruction. If deconstruction is a way of exposing the glue that holds together western culture, I thought "what is it that holds together typography? It's space." . . . So the idea was simply to play with that little bit of space and see if you had a bit of room to manœuvre with that glue that holds it all together.***[4]

Fella suggests that the quest for perfect letter-, word- and line-spacing had led to some stifling of expression. He also said the element of time, of the duration taken to read parts of a message, deserved more consideration and flexibility.

Such experiments have resonance beyond this growing world of "art typography" bandied around in magazines. Besides commenting on conditions pertaining to print communication, they also have a clear bearing on the dominant communication culture of moving images – of television, in particular. Here, the degraded quality of broadcast imagery poses a different challenge to typographers. As the majority of programme titles and credits continue to reveal, there is much to be done often to achieve basic legibility, let alone the interest level sought for readability. Fella's concern about duration and the ability to take in degraded letterforms has a clear, if unintended, relevance here. However, the development of more advanced computer graphics systems during the eighties did foster new techniques and qualities in television graphics. The image manipulation and retouching systems pioneered by Quantel, Paintbox and later Harry, offered a method of achieving sophisticated effects relatively easily through electronic trickery. When used with restraint by those skilled in design and animation, appealing new integrations of graphics with photographic and film imagery became possible. But there was still virtually no special effort applied to generating new faces for the particular conditions of television, despite this being the prime medium of communication. For the most part, titles and other typographic information would either be in a simply drawn bold face with crudely spaced and leaded lines ("TV spacing", as it is commonly specified) or there would be an attempt at something more adventurous that would fall foul of the unsuitable nature of most print faces, whose use on-screen displayed all the shortcomings of degraded imagery identified with low-quality printers, only much worse. Fine weights and serif forms do not survive the 625-line-or-less rolling scan of televison image-construction.

Graphics by M & Co, New York. For Tibor Kalman (born 1949), an art director and designer who trained as a journalist, questioning, or at least tweaking, the conventions of commercial communication along with disrespect for highly crafted graphic design traditions and a respect for the vernacular of roadside Americana, produces work that often contains fresh typographic ideas. Below: in *(Nothing but) Flowers*, video for Talking Heads designed by Tibor Kalman and Emily Oberman, 1988, lyrics were superimposed or screened on to the group, sometimes in figuratively suggestive patterns ("waterfall", for example, was a fall of type); however, between lyrics other words and disturbing facts were superimposed in typography that suggested different messages. Right and far right: for Restaurant Florent, a menu board advertisement (by Kalman and Bethany Johns) and a postcard (by Marlene McCarthy and Kalman). The canteen-style, movable-noticeboard lettering carries associations that are disrupted by their extra content in this usage. Below right: logo for Knoll Orchestra by Dean Lubensky and Kalman.

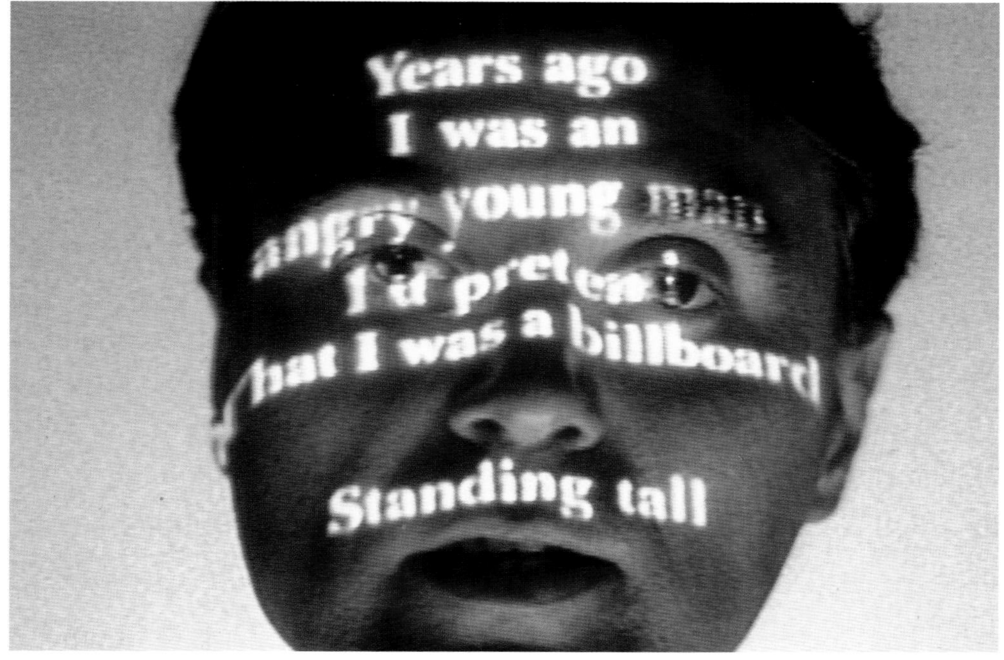

NOVEMBER

SOUP BOUDIN & WARM TARTS

GUSTY WINDS

HIGH S UPPER 40S TO MID 50S

LOWS UPPER 30S TO MID 40S

FLORENT

OPEN 24 HOURS 989 5779

WATCH FOR HEAVY RAINS

WEAR YOUR GALOSHES

MNCO

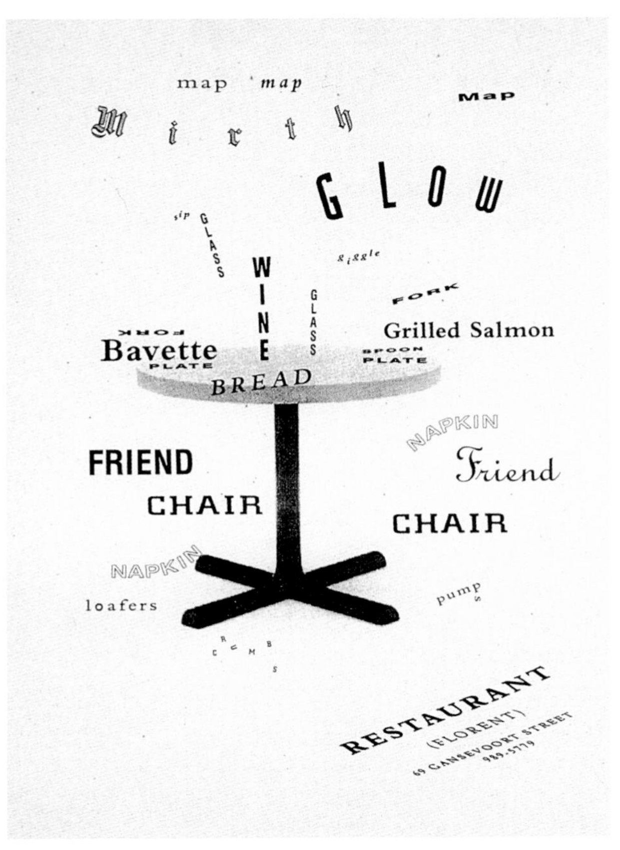

map map
Map
Mirth
GLOW
GLASS
WINE
GLASS
giggle
FORK
FORK
Bayette
Grilled Salmon
PLATE
SPOON
PLATE
BREAD
NAPKIN
FRIEND
Friend
CHAIR
CHAIR
NAPKIN
loafers
pump
RESTAURANT
(FLORENT)
69 GANSEVOORT STREET
989-5779


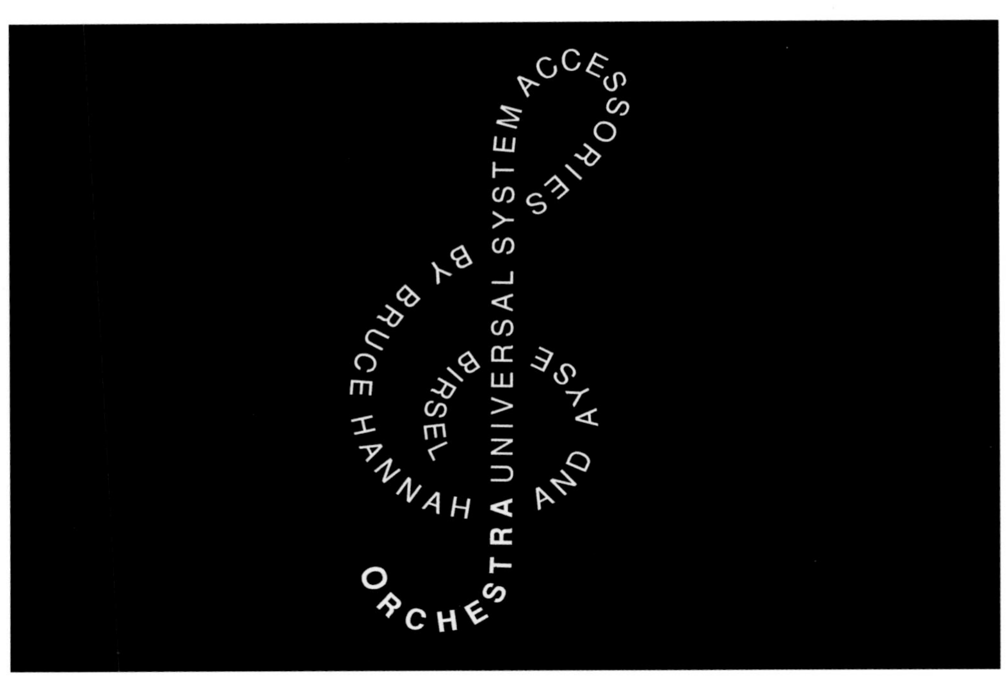

Besides the innovation in technology and the work of those designers attuned to it, the 1980s was also a time for eclectic revivals and widely sourced graphic imagery, snatched from the vernacular and from other cultures. This was aided by the ease with which scanning technology made it possible to work with found imagery on a computer layout. For typographers this proved a great advantage: classic old faces that might exist only in a specimen book or a piece of print could be scanned in and reworked, then used as the basic lettering in a new design.

Ironically, two of the most influential revivalist designers of the 1980s in the US did not use the Apple Macintosh at all for the work that brought them to wide attention, but relied on old-fashioned illustrative and lettering skills. Joe Duffy and Charles Spencer Anderson of the Duffy Design Group of Minneapolis won numerous awards, before splitting up in 1988, for a range of packaging and other commercial print design work that drew heavily on the display forms of the between-the-wars era, on Art Deco imagery and on the tradition of humorous illustrative branding. In England, the boom in graphic design also generated numerous opportunities for revival work in tweaking established identities and brands, or launching new, pseudo-traditional products and services. Typography served the cause of the client by wearing whatever fashion was most suitable. For example, lavish annual reports and other corporate literature for some time seemed to require not highly readable documents, but highly finished work in which the words were given serious status, as opposed to looking interesting. Slabs of dull text amid acres of white space, with expensive photography or illustration, encased in a double wrap cover with full colour throughout – such was the typical big company report.



Right and below: work by Studio Dumbar, The Hague. The *Nina Wiener* poster for the Holland Festival, 1987, is one of a series in which the key statement – Holland Festival – is three-dimensional and unchanging, while different type is laid over for the events. The ANWB manual coolly dramatises the dry matter of corporate identity. Both projects show the influential approach of Gert Dumbar (born 1941), building on the Dutch Modernists, such as Piet Zwart. Considerable emotive charge is given to the typographic communication, with the text integrated or central to the whole.

Below right: A dot matrix indicator board as seen on transport systems or, in slightly different form, in public offices, canteens and elsewhere. In such displays characters are reduced to the minimum number of distinguishing units for quick relay through computerised update systems. Although crude, the signage is effective and rapidly became established as a vernacular form during the 1980s. The signs can attract attention by having lettering moving through the display, which allows them also to show more information than would fit at any one time on the light panel.

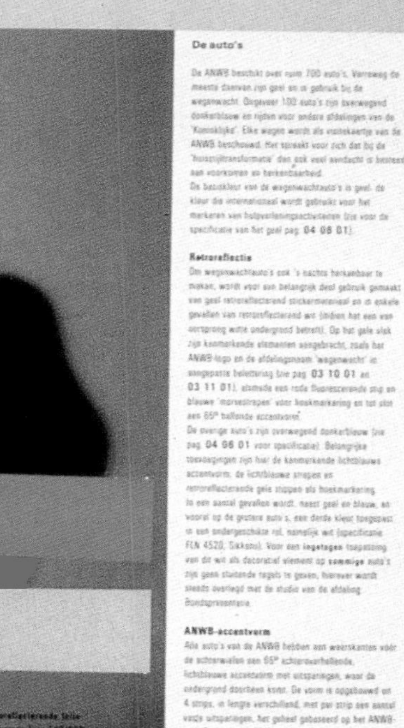

**De auto's**

**Retroreflectie**

**ANWB-accentvorm**

# 1990...

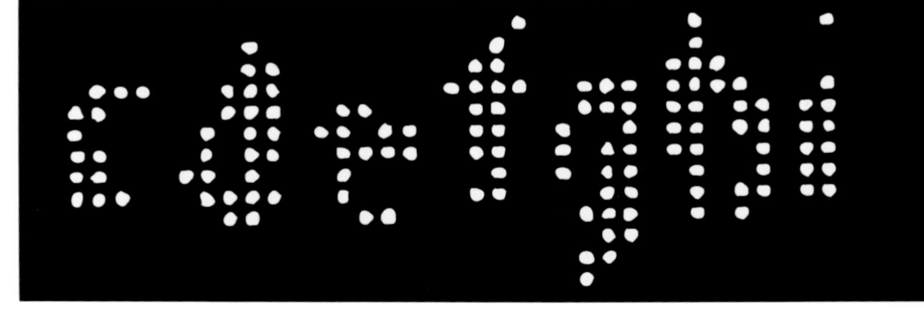

The beginning of the 1990s is already almost sated with the plethora of activity concerning any and every aspect of computerised typography. Thousands of typefaces are available in exchange for a credit card number. Multimedia, "virtual reality" and sundry other concepts that would until recently have belonged solely to science fiction are now the familiar subjects of "futurology" games at numerous conferences and exhibitions, promoting new typographical advances and confirming the widespread effect of new communication methods. Information abounds on the new methods of communication and their accessibility.

Faced with this wave of commercial and cultural enthusiasm, it would be easy to presume that the concluding decade of the century will see a technology-driven advance of typographic form. In the leading countries of typographic demand (those with the most advanced consumer cultures) designers are fast buying desktop publishing technology for their studios, almost inevitably also procuring digital typesetting if they output through bureaux.[1] Yet for all such gung-ho adoption of computers, this is driven essentially by time and cost savings, not by a mass movement of designers eager to grapple with the intricacies of digital design. Instead, digital design is having to grapple with meeting more effectively some of the traditional demands of graphic designers and art directors. Niceties such as kerning, optical scaling and small capital letters are now being asked for and supplied. Typographers, after the rapid revolutions of both photosetting and digital processes, are increasingly making clear their appreciation of some of the qualities of metal-setting. The precision, the detail, the quality of some of the letterforms and of the page furniture that sometimes went with them are all in demand. In some cases this is manifested in retro-design, reviving the look as well as the standard. In others, it is less obvious: certain typographers, for example, go to the lengths of setting in hot metal even though the finished execution will be carried out by a screened, lithographic process. The benefits of a "hands-on" approach outweigh the clear efficiency of the digital design process.

Which way now: from the subtle reworking of traditions in "1990" (Times Millenium) for a different age, audience and technology, to "and beyond" in a radical face of today, Variex Bold by Zuzana Licko. Will the digital revolution continue to celebrate and explore its means of production (as the detail, left, from Just van Rossum's *Fuse* poster suggests) or will it progress – or retreat – to a reiteration of traditional type design and typography?

Such attitudes indicate a growing concern with the qualities of the "typographic engine" as well as its technical abilities; in other words, with the software that makes the type work. The detail admired in hot-metal printing, or in the practices that went into it, is partly acknowledged by this emphasis on creating software that is more sympathetic to such output. And it is not only the professional who will be affected by the advance of typographic controls in computers. With desktop publishing and word-processing equipment making amateur typographers of many office- and home-workers, there is a need to assist the generation of good typography from such systems. Some designers now create corporate identity programmes that feature coded software written to ensure that workers can only use house style when laying out a document. But handcuffing the user is clearly not as desirable as building-in a better typographic education or a method of immediate ad hoc instruction. Systems that integrate a typesetting and layout function within word-processing capabilities are often so complex that even professional designers leave the actual working to a dedicated operator.

This shuffling of skills is also connected to the loss of many of the craft values associated with traditionally trained typesetters. There is a desperate need for a more organised approach to the typographic education of anyone now involved in typesetting, be they secretaries in the office, journalists carrying out direct inputting, or the many graphic designers and art directors who find themselves embroiled in the detailed typographic problems that an invisible typesetter used to resolve. As with the coming of earlier technologies, the age of electronic graphics has also encouraged the destruction or neglect of certain standards of design, which are now, it is hoped, being reappraised and restored.

The effect of these technology-related issues on the aesthetic of typographic form can only be sketched in. After a decade in which self-conscious digital forms have often been used, exploring both the type generation and that of the photographic image, it would seem that the process may be absorbed and a more political statement may emerge in the way type is used. A period of eclecticism from the mid- and the late 1980s has had no overwhelmingly strong directions and would seem to be open to a more principled direction. The marketing of popular music in recent decades is a case in point. Can a distinctive graphic character emerge that will sell rap music in the way that psychedelia or punk graphics gave an image to earlier musical movements? It is overdue if it is coming, but rap and hip-hop would seem to be musical forms that, in their information-excess and self-consciousness, could be strongly related to typographic exploration, for everything from CD sleeves to clothing logos, magazines and video graphics.

In newspaper typography, photosetting and the widespread adoption of on-screen page make-up both allow changes in styling that dramatically improve legibility and readability. Many newspapers, now clearly marginalised to a supporting role in mass communication, use the values of traditional typography to reinforce a sense of authority, and suggest modernity through layout and the introduction of colour print. *The Independent* was an award-winning and influential launch in London in the late 1980s, whose classical styling was both adopted and parodied by the *Modern Review* in 1991. More modern systems of presentation, featuring sans serif display type and the use of white space to

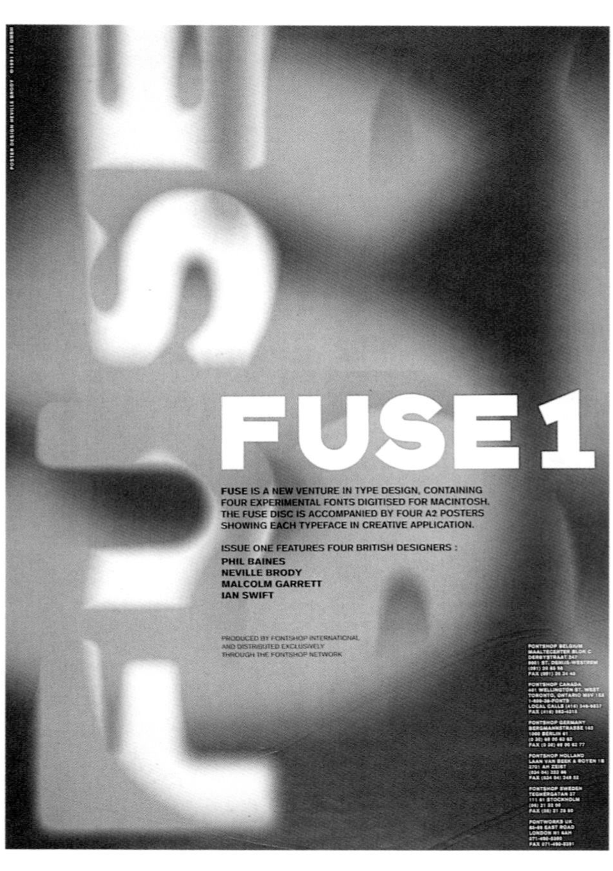
FUSE 1
FUSE IS A NEW VENTURE IN TYPE DESIGN, CONTAINING FOUR EXPERIMENTAL FONTS DIGITISED FOR MACINTOSH. THE FUSE DISC IS ACCOMPANIED BY FOUR A2 POSTERS SHOWING EACH TYPEFACE IN CREATIVE APPLICATION.
ISSUE ONE FEATURES FOUR BRITISH DESIGNERS :
PHIL BAINES
NEVILLE BRODY
MALCOLM GARRETT
IAN SWIFT
PRODUCED BY FONTSHOP INTERNATIONAL AND DISTRIBUTED EXCLUSIVELY THROUGH THE FONTSHOP NETWORK

2
FUSE2
FUSE : THE NEW VENTURE IN TYPE DESIGN. IT CONTAINS FOUR EXPERIMENTAL FONTS DIGITISED FOR MACINTOSH. THE FUSE DISC IS ACCOMPANIED BY FOUR A2 POSTERS SHOWING EACH TYPEFACE IN CREATIVE APPLICATION.
FUSE TWO, RUNES, FEATURES FOUR DUTCH DESIGNERS :
MAX KISMAN
GERARD UNGER
ERIK VAN BLOKLAND
JUST VAN ROSSUM
PRODUCED BY FONTSHOP INTERNATIONAL AND DISTRIBUTED EXCLUSIVELY THROUGH THE FONTSHOP NETWORK
FONTSHOP BELGIUM
MAALTECENTER BLOK C
DERBYSTRAAT 247
9051 ST. DENIJS-WESTREM
(GENT), BELGIUM
TEL: (32) 91 202620
FAX: (32) 91 203445
FONTSHOP CANADA
401 WELLINGTON ST. WEST
TORONTO,
ONTARIO M5V 1E8
CANADA
TEL: (1) 416 348 9837
FAX: (1) 416 593 4318
FONTSHOP GERMANY
BERGMANSTRASSE 102
D-1000 BERLIN 61
TEL : (49) 30 69 00 62 57
FAX : (49) 30 69 00 62 77
FONTSHOP HOLLAND
LAAN VAN BEEK
& ROYEN 1D
3701 AH ZEIST, HOLLAND
TEL: (31) 3404 32366
FAX: (31) 3404 24952
FONTSHOP ITALY
C/O ROGER BLACK INC.
VIA MASOTTO 21
20159 MILANO, ITALY
TEL: (39) 2 7000 1176
FAX: (39) 2 7010 4199
FONTSHOP SWEDEN
TEGNÉRGATAN 37
111 61 STOCKHOLM,
SWEDEN
TEL: (46) 8 21 52 00
FAX: (46) 8 21 28 80
FONTWORKS UK
65-69 EAST ROAD
LONDON N1 6AH,
UNITED KINGDOM
TEL: (44) 71 490 5390
FAX: (44) 71 490 5391


Three posters produced by *Fuse* magazine from 1991 onwards. Opposite page, left: Nevile Brody's State, an experimental typeface that tries "to get inside the structure of the alphabet and to accentuate the shapes that are inherent in written language. The negative shapes are given equal prominence to the positive in an attempt to diffuse the power of language and the hierarchy imposed by typographical rules. Perhaps for this reason, the typeface is not practical for day-to-day use. Readability is a conditioned state. I wanted to take the role of typography away from a purely subservient, practical role towards one that is potentially more expressive and visually dynamic . . ." Left and far left: two other posters by Brody that promote the first and second issues of the magazine.

add emphasis (lessons drawn from the 1920s) are still comparatively rare in the more serious newspapers. And whereas excessive choice of type style and font is less common, colour is now often the device used freely to add expression to the newspaper page.

The area that has the highest need of improved typography is that connected with televisual information, now the main method of mass communication, yet still crude in terms of its ability to carry written information within programmes. Although there have been substantial creative advances in the handling of type on-screen in recent years, embracing ideas both from print and from new film and post-production technology, greater sophistication is prevented by the poor resolution of a standard television screen (625 lines in the UK, for instance, and only 525 in the US). Small sizes and fine strokes simply break up when subjected to the blurring effect of such resolution. High-definition television monitors, possibly with twice as many lines on-screen and with a slightly more landscape-format screen, could revolutionise the potential for sophisticated television typography. The technology is currently available, but the difficulty of establishing a common standard between European, American and Japanese systems has held back its implementation. By the end of the decade, this problem is likely to have been long buried. There may also be a development of more comfortable forms of lighting to avoid the present eye-straining halos around type on conventional cathode ray tubes, especially as better research into the effect of prolonged exposure to screen images becomes available.

Recent advances in titling reveal a growing interest in stretching the potential for type on-screen. Futura as a face has become popular again, since its simple geometric forms do not break down at even comparatively small sizes on-screen. Research into readability and legibility on-screen is continuing, along with the creation of new faces for screen display. The efforts of units such as the

Right and below: consecutive spreads from *Beach Culture* magazine, 1990, designed by David Carson. The headline on the right reads "laird hamilton", but has been stretched by copier to the very edge of illegibility, as has the accompanying article in which type has been set in different fonts and sizes, cut and pasted over each other with varying line lengths and with disruptive breaks in words. The following spread (below) takes a very different tack – just as expressive, but as tight as could be in contrast to the anarchy preceding. Both are profiles of surfers for a magazine that centred on surf culture. The contrast of tight forms and chaotic moments; the speeding up and slowing down of the time taken to pass through parts of the text; the sudden, unexplained, seemingly random elements – these features are part of a synthesis of the reading experience with the surfing one.

Far right: cover of *Domus* magazine, September 1991, art directed by Italo Lupi. The use of OCR-A as the headline face is an interesting twist, exploiting the suggestions of computer print-out and urgency. At the same time, the graphic regularity of the characters makes them work well as blocks of text against the illustrative covers. The distinctive qualities of the face, coupled with the use of contrasting colours, enable the cover lines to stand apart, despite being numerous and set relatively small.

**h a**

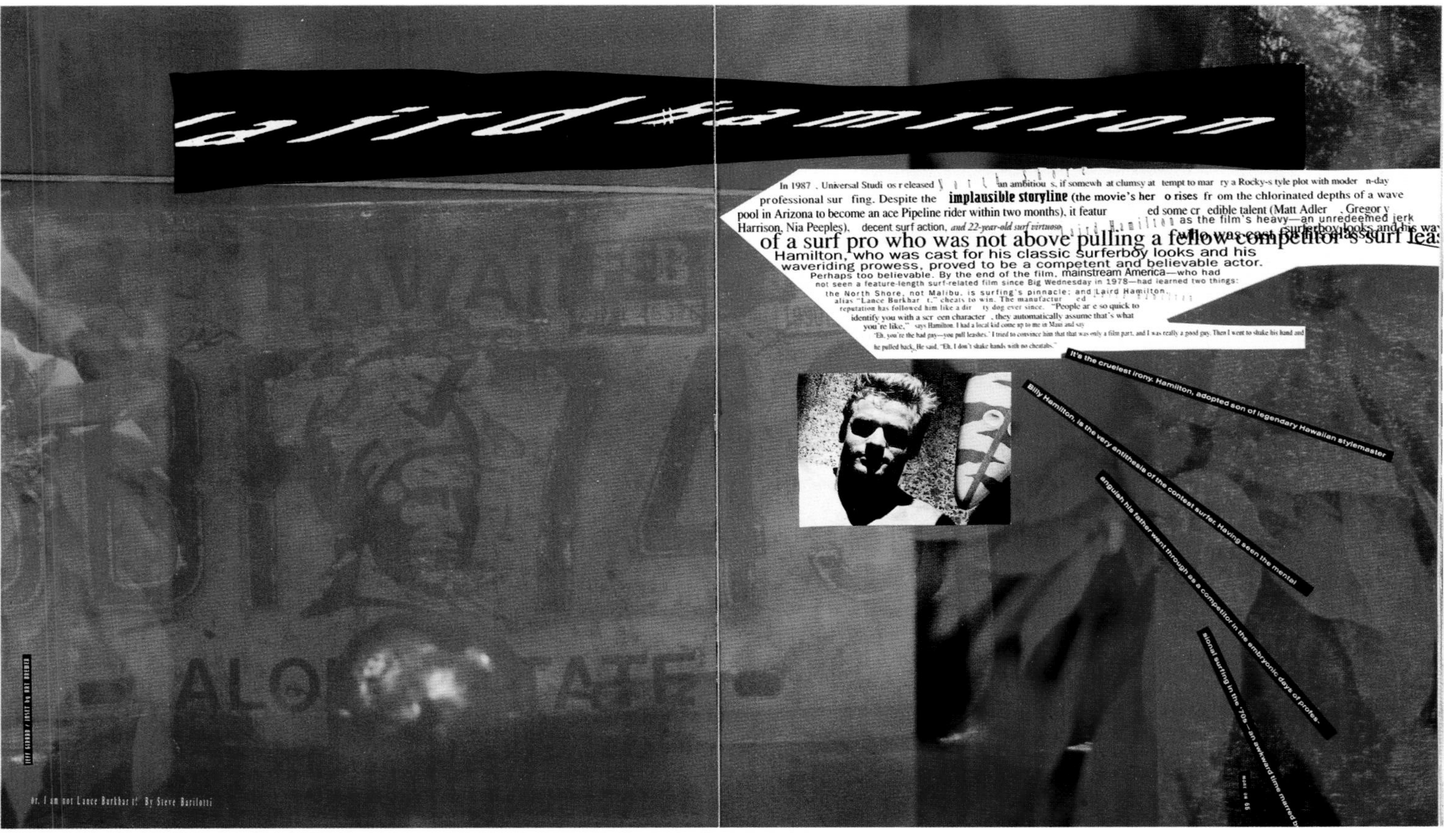

laird hamilton

In 1987 , Universal Studi os r eleased an ambitiou s, if somewh at clumsy at tempt to mar ry a Rocky-s tyle plot with moder n-day professional sur fing. Despite the **implausible storyline** (the movie's her o rises fr om the chlorinated depths of a wave pool in Arizona to become an ace Pipeline rider within two months), it featur ed some cr edible talent (Matt Adler , Gregor y Harrison, Nia Peeples), decent surf action, *and 22-year-old surf virtuoso* Laird Hamilton as the film's heavy—an unredeemed jerk of a surf pro who was not above pulling a fellow competitor's surf lea

Hamilton, who was cast for his classic surferboy looks and his waveriding prowess, proved to be a competent and believable actor. Perhaps too believable. By the end of the film, mainstream America—who had not seen a feature-length surf-related film since Big Wednesday in 1978—had learned two things: the North Shore, not Malibu, is surfing's pinnacle; and Laird Hamilton, alias "Lance Burkhar t," cheats to win. The manufactur ed reputation has followed him like a dir ty dog ever since. "People ar e so quick to identify you with a scr een character , they automatically assume that's what you're like," says Hamilton. I had a local kid come up to me in Maui and say "Eh, you're the bad guy—you pull leashes." I tried to convince him that that was only a film part, and I was really a good guy. Then I went to shake his hand and he pulled back. He said, "Eh, I don't shake hands with no cheatahs."

It's the cruelest irony. Hamilton, adopted son of legendary Hawaiian stylemaster Billy Hamilton, is the very antithesis of the contest surfer. Having seen the mental anguish his father went through as a competitor in the embryonic days of professional surfing in the '70s—an awkward time marred b

more on 66

or, I am not Lance Burkhart! By Steve Barilotti

Jeff Girard / Inset by Art Brewer

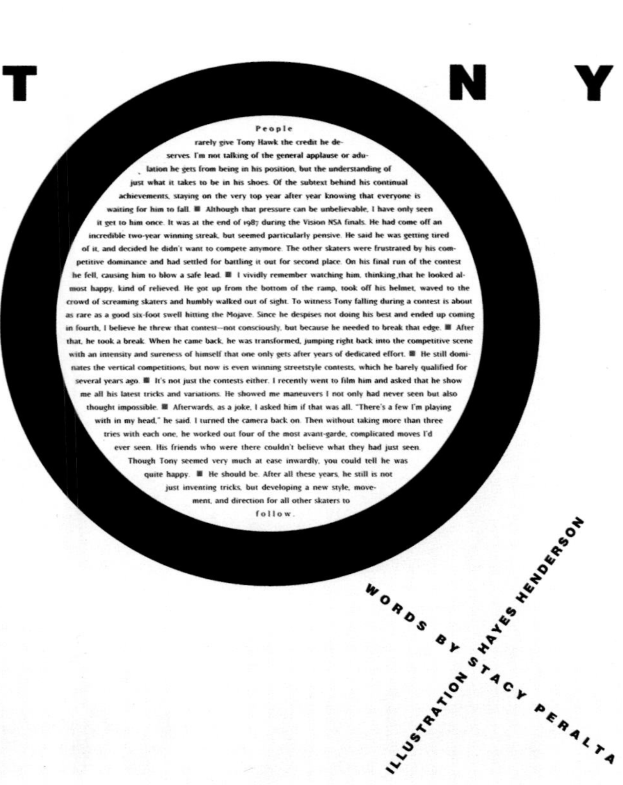

T N Y

People rarely give Tony Hawk the credit he deserves. I'm not talking of the general applause or adulation he gets from being in his position, but the understanding of just what it takes to be in his shoes. Of the subtext behind his continual achievements, staying on the very top year after year knowing that everyone is waiting for him to fall. ■ Although that pressure can be unbelievable, I have only seen it get to him once. It was at the end of 1987 during the Vision NSA finals. He had come off an incredible two-year winning streak, but seemed particularly pensive. He said he was getting tired of it, and decided he didn't want to compete anymore. The other skaters were frustrated by his competitive dominance and had settled for battling it out for second place. On his final run of the contest he fell, causing him to blow a safe lead. ■ I vividly remember watching him, thinking that he looked almost happy, kind of relieved. He got up from the bottom of the ramp, took off his helmet, waved to the crowd of screaming skaters and humbly walked out of sight. To witness Tony falling during a contest is about as rare as a good six-foot swell hitting the Mojave. Since he despises not doing his best and ended up coming in fourth, I believe he threw that contest—not consciously, but because he needed to break that edge. ■ After that, he took a break. When he came back, he was transformed, jumping right back into the competitive scene with an intensity and sureness of himself that one only gets after years of dedicated effort. ■ He still dominates the vertical competitions, but now is even winning streetstyle contests, which he barely qualified for several years ago. ■ It's not just the contests either. I recently went to film him and asked that he show me all his latest tricks and variations. He showed me maneuvers I not only had never seen but also thought impossible. ■ Afterwards, as a joke, I asked him if that was all. "There's a few I'm playing with in my head," he said. I turned the camera back on. Then without taking more than three tries with each one, he worked out four of the most avant-garde, complicated moves I'd ever seen. His friends who were there couldn't believe what they had just seen. Though Tony seemed very much at ease inwardly, you could tell he was quite happy. ■ He should be. After all these years, he still is not just inventing tricks, but developing a new style, movement, and direction for all other skaters to follow.

WORDS BY HAYES HENDERSON

ILLUSTRATION BY STACY PERALTA

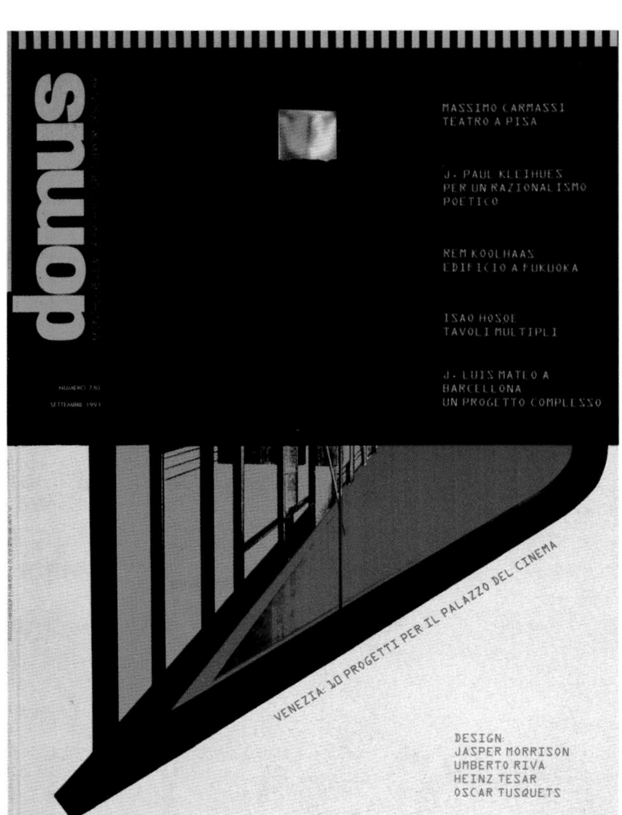

domus
NUMERO 730
SETTEMBRE 1991
MASSIMO CARMASSI
TEATRO A PISA
J. PAUL KLEIHUES
PER UN RAZIONALISMO
POETICO
REM KOOLHAAS
EDIFICIO A FUKUOKA
ISAO HOSOE
TAVOLI MULTIPLI
J. LUIS MATEO A
BARCELLONA
UN PROGETTO COMPLESSO
VENEZIA: 10 PROGETTI PER IL PALAZZO DEL CINEMA
DESIGN:
JASPER MORRISON
UMBERTO RIVA
HEINZ TESAR
OSCAR TUSQUETS

Media Lab and Visible Language Workshop at Massachusetts Institute of Technology, alongside experimental deconstructivist typography, indicate a reassessment – perhaps a revolution – in the way typographic messages can work sequentially as a narrative, and in relation to image.

For traditional typographers and lovers of print the notion that the screen will carry the main area of activity for future typographic development may seem highly undesirable. But it is not just a probability – for many it is already the reality. People in developed countries the world over will spend on average more than a decade of their life watching a television screen. There is plenty of work to be done to make that decade an exciting period of efficient and inspiring communication.

Cutting a new typeface is now scarcely a physical task and can take little time – anybody can produce one, it seems, with the aid of the right software.[2] But drawing an attractive and useful face still relies on a detailed understanding of the function or functions it is supposed to serve, and an aesthetic concern for what it may express. The "new typography" of today, such as that practised by the designers associated with *Emigre* magazine and the Cranbrook School in the United States, questions the notion that legibility is paramount, detecting within such an assumption a glib political agenda requiring conformity to a narrow range of meaning, a single route, a rejection of the potential of a text to have many levels of meaning and ways of expression. This debate is not merely a chic game, played with the sometime fashionable deconstructionist philosophy. Such designers, and many others involved in type design, manufacture and use, are attempting to find a way through the mass of information that civilisation surrounds us with today and to communicate, question and represent the values of such a culture. The legacy of tradition in printing and design is being constantly reassessed; developing technology may improve the methods by which a typeface is designed and used, but human analysis and judgement are still vital necessities; questions of form and function, aesthetics and practicality, continue to exert their own pressures, as they have done for many centuries. Indeed, anything that does not take from the past in some degree will be incomprehensible to the reader's experience. The challenge of the years ahead lies in the appropriate integration of conventional values with the opportunities and demands of the new media.

New Times Millenium by Aurobind Patel, a design development of Times New Roman for use in *The Times* newspaper, London, 1991. This subtle evolution of the most popular Latin typeface in the world reveals the effect that technological and cultural changes have had on type over a sixty-year period. Right: article by the editor in the issue that launched the new design, explaining some of the detailed differences. Below: the face, which can be compared with Times New Roman by Stanley Morison (page 115). The change of type cost the newspaper around £200,000; in comparison, £29,000 was spent on Morison's work in 1932, equivalent to more than £700,000 at today's values, showing how much more expensive it was to change hot-metal typesetting. As with Times New Roman, the exercise here was to restore characteristics which were felt to have been lost in the evolution of the paper, in this case with the change from letterpress to photoset offset. The changing nature of newspaper information and of readers was also significant; as Patel comments, in 1932 "the paper was predominantly typographic. All headlines were set in capitals across a single column and the page conveyed a restful, dignified feel."

**NEW TIMES MILLENNIUM**

# THE TIMES

MONDAY NOVEMBER 25 1991

**Simon Jenkins**, editor of *The Times*, introduces the change to Times Millennium

## New types, new faces

'Reading *The Times* used to be an act of heroic endeavour, a Spartan trudge for the eye, obliged to plough endless unbroken furrows of dense print." So declared this newspaper in introducing its famous Times New Roman in 1932, designed by Stanley Morison and carved by the Monotype Corporation. That face has dominated world typography ever since. It would, said Morison, "lose no scintilla of that legibility which rests upon fundamental ocular laws, or of that readability which rests upon age-long customs of the eyes".

Half a century on comes Times Millennium. Designed by the typographer Aurobind Patel, the new face is firmly based on Morison's principles of clarity and familiarity. Morison's type itself went back to William Caslon's earliest fonts for *The Daily Universal Register* in the 1780s; they in turn referred back to the Latin faces of Garamond and Aldus in the Middle Ages. Typography is one of the great trace elements of Western culture.

Whereas from Aldus to Caslon and Morison new types had to be carved, Times Millennium has used modern computer graphics, taking typography straight from the age of hot metal to that of digital typesetting and laser printing. Our aim is to give readers a typeface that looks clear and elegant. In the place of the old roman and black are three strengths of colour — roman, demi and bold — all of which can be used for text, headlines, advertisements and City prices. Look at the wonderful teardrop described by the lower case "a" above.

a a

**Altered images: Times past (left) and Times present**

The most noticeable characteristic of the face is a more flowing line to the letters and less prominence to lower-case ascenders and descenders (h, g, d, p, etc). The serifs are angular rather than horizontal, the font width is more elongated, less chunky. This has given us more words in the same text space and more white round them, with wider gutters between columns. There should be a more open feel to the pages of the paper. While clarity is as much a matter of printing quality as typography, the typographer can at least help.

The change is intended to be subtle rather than drastic. Times New Roman was a superb work of industrial art, but one designed for hot metal setting and the banging pressure of rotary letterpress. It had come to look insipid and often spidery when set by computer printed offset. Aurobind Patel, who recently redesigned the typeface of *The Economist*, has sought to restore some of the robustness of Morison's original.

Patel has been "eating and sleeping" the project for the past year, working with David Driver, *The Times*'s head of design, and the Icelandic typographer Gunnlaugur Briem. "When Times Roman was introduced the paper was predominantly typographic," says Patel. "All headlines were set in capitals across a single column and the page conveyed a restful, dignified feel. Today's paper is a mix of headlines, pictures, captions, graphics, reflecting the more urgent nature of world news."

The jump from aesthetics to the high technology of digitised faces indicates the excitement typography still holds for industrial designers. Mr Patel's work is no less that of an artist for being the product of a team of workers stooping over Apple Mac computers, "mouse" in hand.

The Times Millennium family has been arranged in 14 groups, including differing weights of headline and new faces for italics, advertising and tabulated statistics. This has meant the on-screen drawing of some 5,000 characters. A program called Fontstudio has enabled the designer to maintain a family likeness across groups of characters more precisely than if they had been drawn by hand (let alone carved in wood). The output of each design is not a picture of a letter but a mathematical formula for feeding into a computer typesetter. The new faces will be marketed worldwide and will, we hope, attain the same distinction as Times New Roman.

Improvements in typography are arcane, like the improvements sound technicians claim to be able to make in old music recordings. Such changes are often barely perceptible. Yet over time we do notice and appreciate them. They employ technology to push out the frontiers of what is feasible in art. To the journalist, as to the musician, they help us talk to each other. If you have noticed Times Millennium today, we hope you like it.

abcdefghijklmnopqrs
tuvwxyzABCDEFGH
IJKLMNOPQRSTU
VWXYZ1234567890

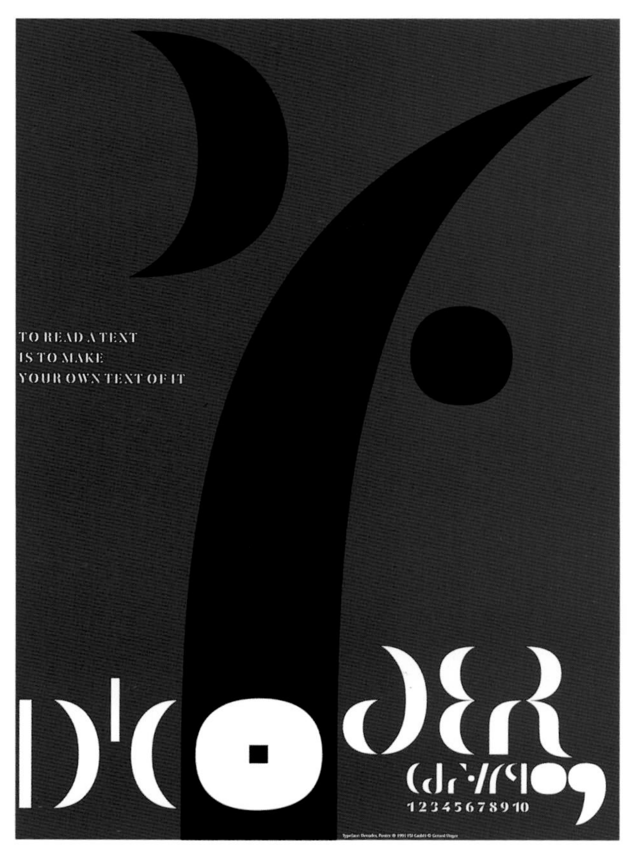
TO READ A TEXT
IS TO MAKE
YOUR OWN TEXT OF IT
DECODER
1 2 3 4 5 6 7 8 9 10

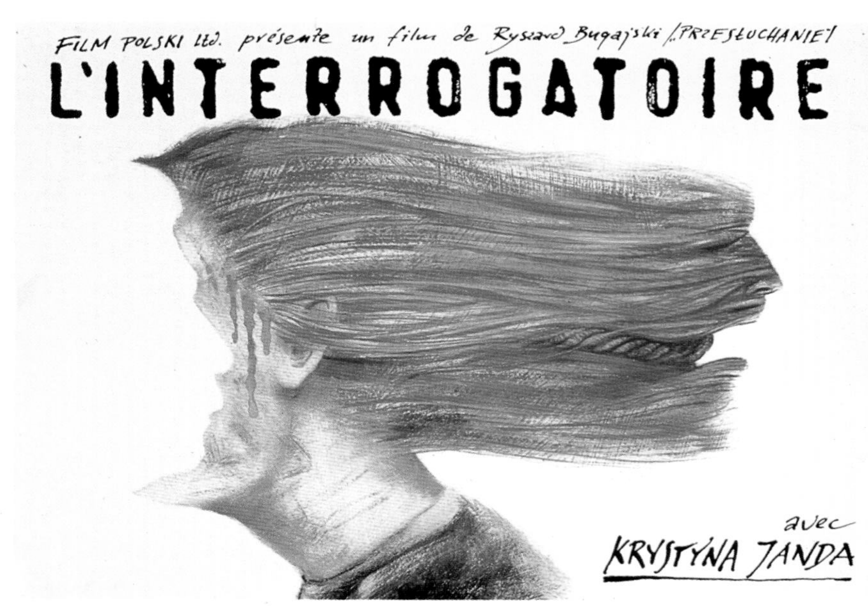
FILM POLSKI Ltd. présente un film de Ryszard Bugajski „PRZESŁUCHANIE"
L'INTERROGATOIRE
avec
KRYSTYNA JANDA

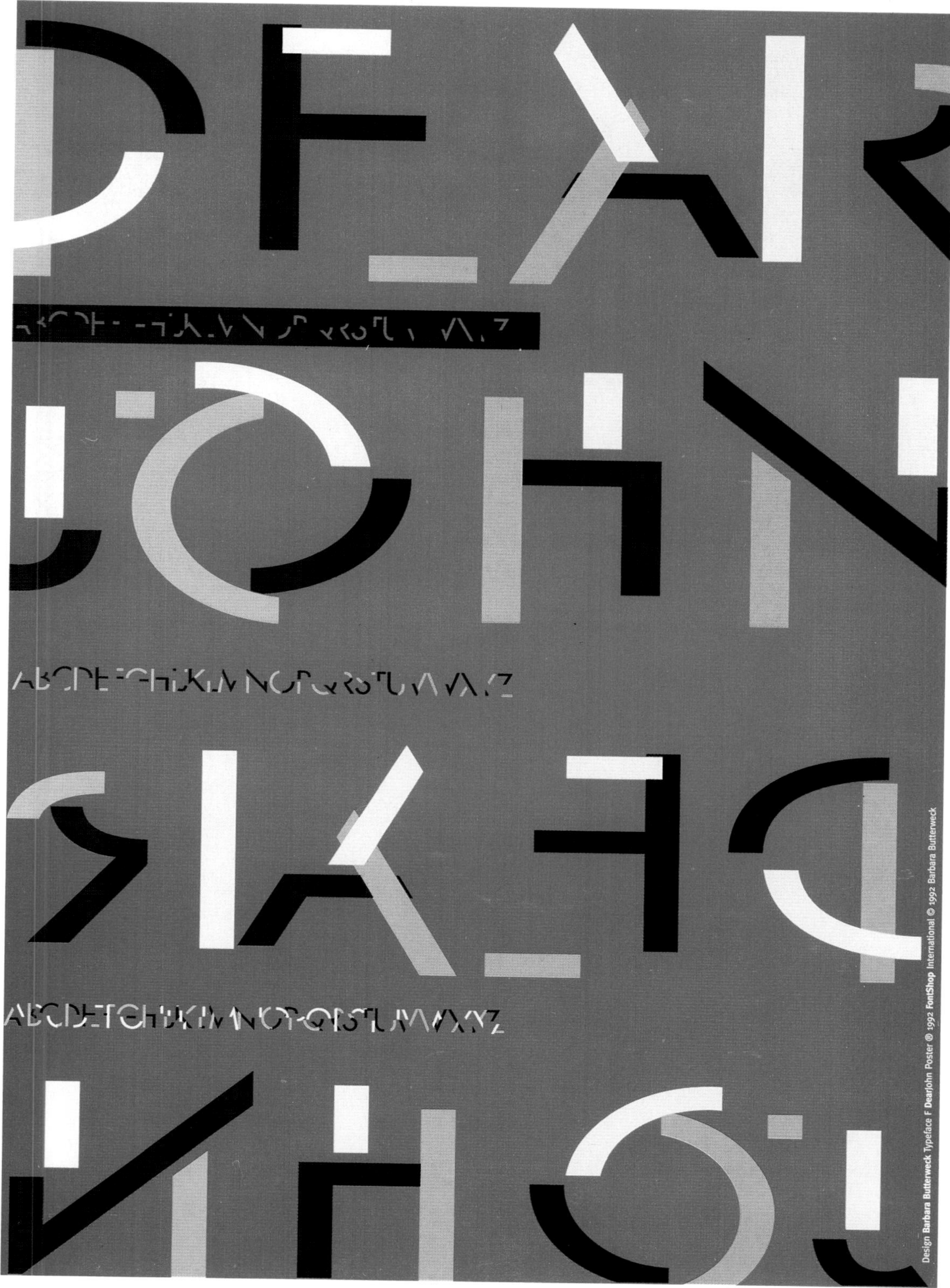


Left and opposite page, top: three experimental faces published by *Fuse* magazine. From the left: Decoder, by Gerard Unger (born 1942) is scarcely a face at all, rather the "raw material", the most basic ingredients of letters – arcs and straight lines. Unger proposed that typographers should take these elements into their computers and assemble them to see "how little you need to make yourself understood". Flixel, 1991, by Just van Rossum, explores the significance and potential of bitmap imagery. Typeface F, Dearjohn, 1992, by Barbara Butterweck. The elements that make up a character – upright and vertical strokes, curves, diagonals – are deconstructed, as are the options for delivering the sign – black, tone, or white out of colour. Different characters have different elemental parts (often defined simply by the particular union of two strokes and their angle of conjuction). Butterweck takes these to the edge of legibility and, by reversing them, shows how each character's essential difference is quite clear in relation to the others. This is one of many examples of how designers today are exploring the essence of characters; "familiarity" and coherence is seen as a key factor in determining the functionality of the font.

Far left: Film poster by Andrzej Pagowski, Poland, 1990s, from a country where summary visual metaphor excels, probably both because of its graphic brevity and for its ability to say more than words. Shortage of materials and a slow take-up of new type and printing technology froze some of the development of Eastern European graphic arts. However, strong traditional craft skills (particularly illustrative and modelmaking) are now becoming allied to computerised graphic tools, a combination which is likely to lead to a different inflection than seen in the West.

**athol** fugard **gives** the impression that **doing** the **right** thing is **easy,** **that** doing **the** right thing **makes** you **feel** **alive,** that **it** is as **easy** as breathing to **know** the **right** **way** from the **wrong** way.

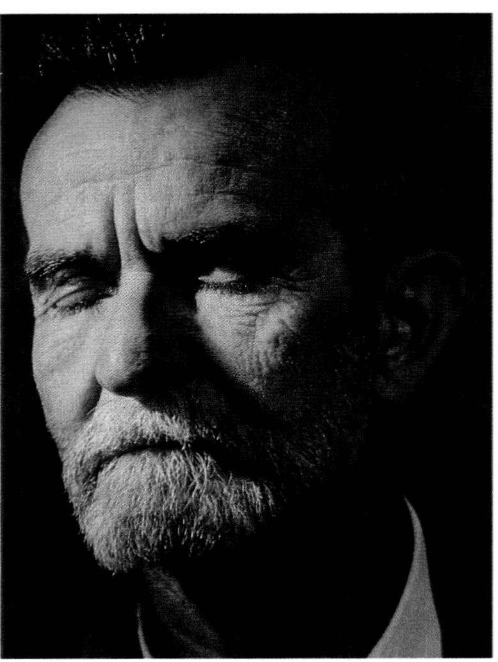

Left: from *Interview*, art directed by Tibor Kalman, New York, 1990. Variety, colour and visual puns were introduced into the typography of this magazine after Kalman took over. While main texts obeyed standard rules of legibility (except for being set in sans serif), headlines, introductions, quotations and other extra type matter were used in an illustrative manner rather than being coldly neutral. Strongly different treatments would be found for each article; although the main type choices remained consistent, other faces could be introduced for dramatic highlights and to express the character of an article or image.

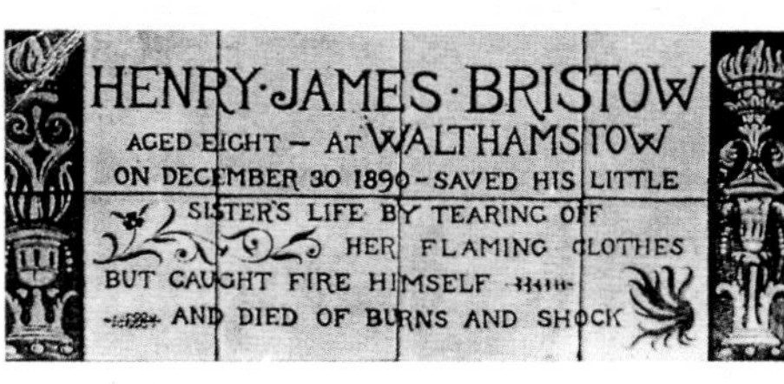


*Monument*, 1981-1988
**Susan Hiller** (b. 1942), American
39 C-type photographs, audiotape, park bench
*Courtesy of Pat Hearn Gallery*

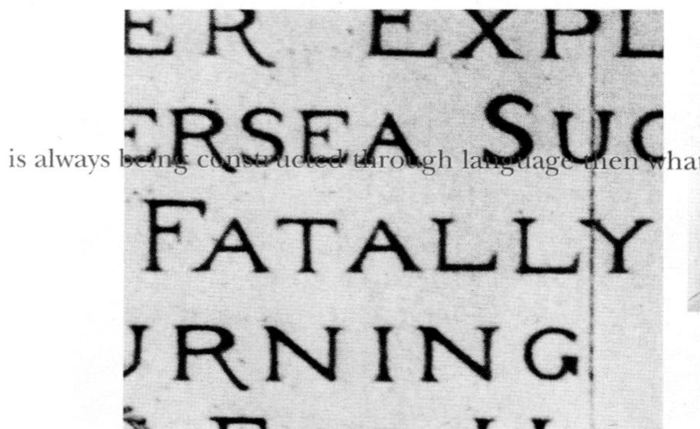


is always being constructed through language then what is 'out

TABLE *of* CONTENTS

Participating Artists 6
Acknowledgments 8
Introduction 10 By Anita Contini
The New Urban Landscape: Spectators in a Visionary City 18 By Richard Martin
The New Urban Landscape: Public Art for Private Eyes? 24 By Nancy Princenthal
A Photographic Essay 26 By David McGlynn
CITY TAKES: TEN ESSAYS ON THE NEW URBAN LANDSCAPE 35
Douglas Blau 36 Rosetta Brooks 48
Bruce Ferguson 40 Adam Gopnik 42
Elizabeth Hardwick 44 Dave Hickey 45
Sanford Kwinter 46 Herbert Muschamp 48
Mark J. Plotkin 50 Mark Richard 52
THE EXHIBITION: TWENTY-EIGHT WORKS ABOUT THE NEW URBAN LANDSCAPE 55
Vito Acconci 56 Dennis Adams/Andrea Blum 58 Kim Adams 60 Judith Barry 62
Alan Belcher 64 Dan Graham 66 Susan Hiller 68 Hodgetts + Fung 70 Henry Jesionka 72 Kristin Jones and Andrew Ginzel 74 Michael Kalil 76 Kawamata 78
Jon Kessler 80 Kunst Brothers 82
Justen Ladda 84 Morphosis 86 Matt Mullican 88 Jean Nouvel 90
Joel Otterson 92 Nam June Paik 94
Liz Phillips 96 Robert Price 98 Martha Schwartz 100 Haim Steinbach 102
Mierle Laderman Ukeles 104 Jacques Vieille 106 Richard Wentworth 108
Stephen Willats 110 MICA-TV 112
Explanatory Notes 114 By Philip Yenawine
Seven Photographs 118 By Elizabeth Zeschin
Contributors Biographies 124

*Olympia & York Arts & Events Program*
Anita Contini, Director
Melissa Coley, Manager
Andrzej Drews, Design Consultant

*Exhibition/Education Committee*
Gary Garrels
Barbara Jakobson
Peter Nagy
Lisa Phillips
Valerie Smith
Philip Yenawine

*Exhibition and Catalogue Coordination*
Livet Reichard Company, Inc.
Ann Philbin, Coordinator
Anne Blair Wrinkle, Research

*Board of Advisors*
David Childs
Mildred Friedman
Frank Gehry
Richard Koshalek
Richard Martin
Cesar Pelli
Andrée Putman

*Catalogue Concept, Design, and Editorial Consultation*
Drenttel Doyle Partners

*Catalogue Editor*
Richard Martin

*Installation Design Concept*
David Childs
Frank Gehry
Audrey Matlock

*This catalogue documents the exhibition* The New Urban Landscape *held at The World Financial Center, Battery Park City, New York, from October 14 through December 31, 1988, sponsored by Olympia & York Companies (U.S.A.).*

*This exhibition was a part of the program to celebrate the opening of the the public spaces at The World Financial Center.*

*Printed in the United States of America.*
*Published 1990 by Olympia & York Companies (U.S.A.) and Drenttel Doyle Partners.*
*Library of Congress Catalogue Card Number: 89-063218*
*ISBN: 0-9624916-0-8*
*Distributed by Rizzoli International Publications, Inc.*
*300 Park Avenue South, New York, New York 10010*

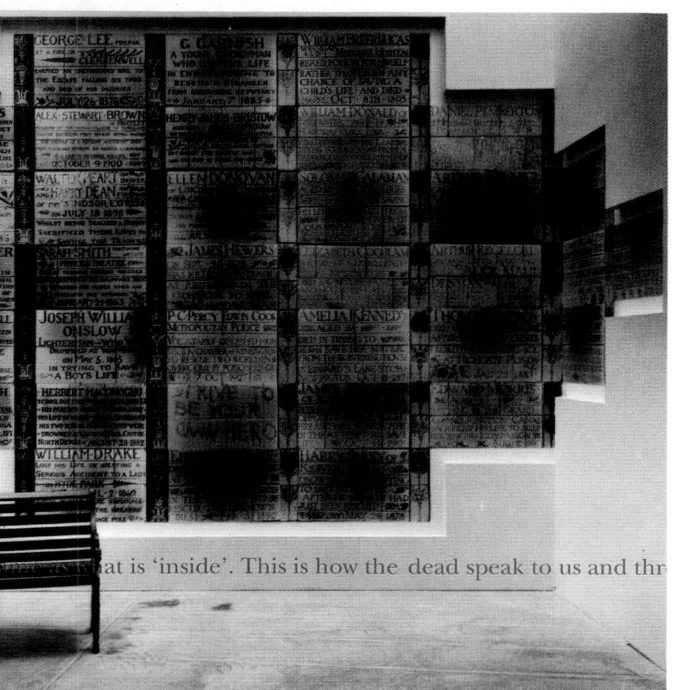

at is 'inside'. This is how the dead speak to us and thr
69

Above and left: *The New Urban Landscape*, exhibition catalogue, 1990, designed by Drenttel Doyle Partners, New York. Contrasts of font, size, colour, line length, ranging and measure are all used to layer the information. The many different areas of communication contained on the contents spread do not have a clear hierarchy in terms of the order in which they should be read but clear emphasis is given to the list of artists and exhibitors by means of the size and weight of type used for their names. The spread from inside the catalogue shows how the layering of information over the picture of an exhibit is akin to a televisual experience – the image is maintained as the typeset commentary carries on over it, rather as with a voiceover.

This page and opposite below: frames from three commercials directed by Tony Kaye, London, 1991, that went into uncharted areas for type in advertising film or even television. For Tag Heuer watches, the words "Don't Crack Under Pressure" are presented sequentially as cut-out images upon images of sporting excellence. For Barclays Bank, a series of words are superimposed sequentially at various depths during the main film, which shows moody shots of individuals. The words are released slowly, both in actual time and in the typography which is always clear and simple yet has enough character to hold the viewer's eye. The typographer Phil Baines (born 1958) worked with Kaye on both Tag and Barclays, while Jon Barnbrook was advisor for the commercial for the Tower of London. A more explosive sequence of animated typography concludes a commercial which sets up a sense of mystery leading to the striking typographic end sting; Barnbrook derived such devices from a study of old religious texts.
Far right: *The Terminator Line* by Jake Tilson, 1991. This book was a flowering of the ideas explored by Tilson (born 1958) in his art magazine *Atlas* during the 1980s. A mass of printed and visual ephemera is drawn into the net of this novel about a cartographer. Hand-positioned type, copier art, low-resolution computer-generated characters, typewritten copy, found objects – all this and more are combined by Tilson in a work that questions how texts can be assimilated by readers in an age dominated by television. Print as a medium of multiple linearities is explored and the typography reflects this complexity and confusion.

He is caught at sea,
a wet mass around him,
before the swamps had
encroached.
His head clears the frothy
Brontosaurus
on a background
Civil War
20 million frenzied,
scrawled planes.
the fridge was empty
He walked
across
worn, green lino,
down stone
green
12 flights
WESTERN
the
TERMINATOR
LINE
by JAKE TILSON
01 09 10 04
Toxic dollar
Watchtower policies
International oversight
Cubatao
Dollar mechanics
Their souls
Slaughterhouse government
Spit
Incontinent medicatio
fee wafts
eggs
Try the back
table is free way
below the cracked,
brown ceiling.
p and cake eater.
Fate on a plate.

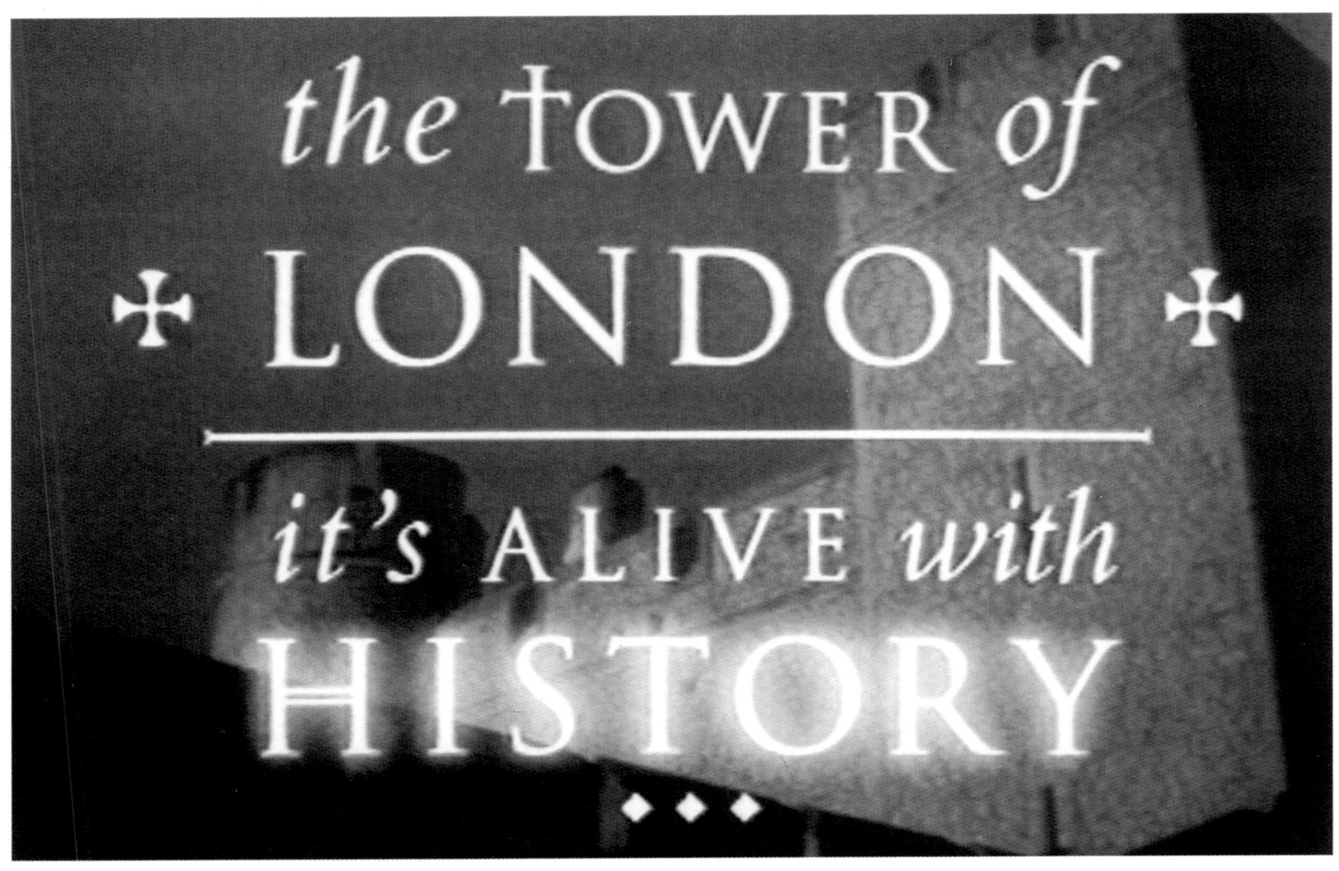
the TOWER of
LONDON
it's ALIVE with
HISTORY

Opposing directions in American graphics. Right and below: two spreads from *Rolling Stone*, 1990, art directed by Fred Woodward, under whom the magazine has refined its pillaging of the American graphic heritage to a state of lavish detail, involving much hand-lettering for introductory spreads and often utilising research into old wood-letter faces. The mass of typographic detail such as coloured borders and linking symbols through the issue proves immensely successful at giving coherence to a magazine in which advertising often dominates a turn-spread. Opposite page, far right: pages from the Southern California Institute of Architecture student workbook *from the edge*, 1991, designed by April Greiman. In contrast to *Rolling Stone*, Greiman continues to strive for modernity – often suggestive of screen-based information media – and plays with the immediacy and translucency of differing effects on the page, holding back type or foregrounding it through reversals, changes of size, partial obscuring and running colours across sections of a page.



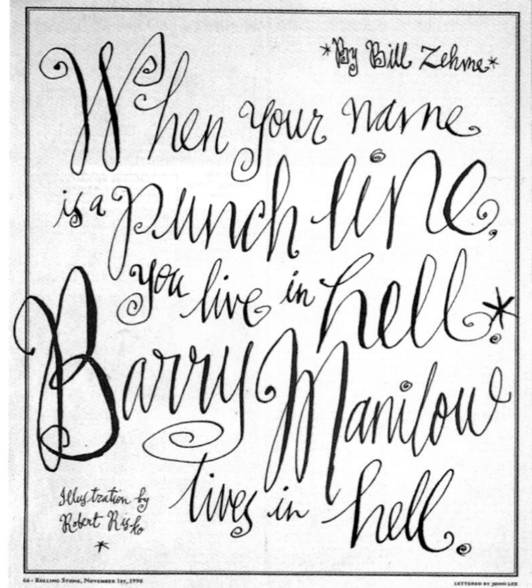

Degree Programs

Robert Mangurian Director

The **Grad 1, 2, and 3** programs, designed for differing abilities of the entering graduate student, lead to a first professional degree, the Master of Architecture. The program is an intensive period of study intended to allow the student to acquire proficiency in architectural design, knowledge of some sophistication about the discipline of architecture and its history, and an attitudinal structure concerning the role of architecture within the evolving culture. The program balances a concern for skills and pragmatic knowledge with a concern for theoretical and historical knowledge.

The core program consists of an intense and integrated set of courses that stress the fundamentals of the discipline. The four core studios are complemented by three visual studies skills courses, three history seminars, a three-course construction and structures sequence and certain electives.

GA

Intro

Two views of the future for type and typography, as recorded in *Emigre* magazine. Right: an opinion of the Californian designer Jeffery Keedy, set in Keedy (formerly called Bondage), released through Cipher/Emigre Graphics. Keedy challenges regularity and clarity, arguing that these are not the same as readability. He sees new technology releasing the potential for typefaces to become much more idiosyncratic and personal, a point that ties in with the changing nature of information (for example, notebook computers capable of recording handwriting and subsequently generating this as a calligraphic face).
Below right: Variex by Zuzana Licko, a radical face of today.
Opposite page: Totally Gothic, by Zuzana Licko, with a statement from an interview with her. Licko worked from a bitmapped black-letter face, imported into a font design program (Fontographer), and held in the background on screen as a guide for the character of letter she was looking for, albeit in a modern idiom. The enlarged characters above the statement show an intermediate stage of design, after the bitmapped black-letter face was traced. The result is surprisingly readable and illustrates her statement: legible type and typography require distinction of characters in order to have meaning, but beyond that there is not necessarily any such thing as "good typography" – only what holds meaning in relation to our aesthetic senses, our previous reading. These things change . . .

There will never be a font that is as pervasive as *Helvetica* again, because there are going to be just too many typefaces out there, too many designers wanting to do things that are specific.

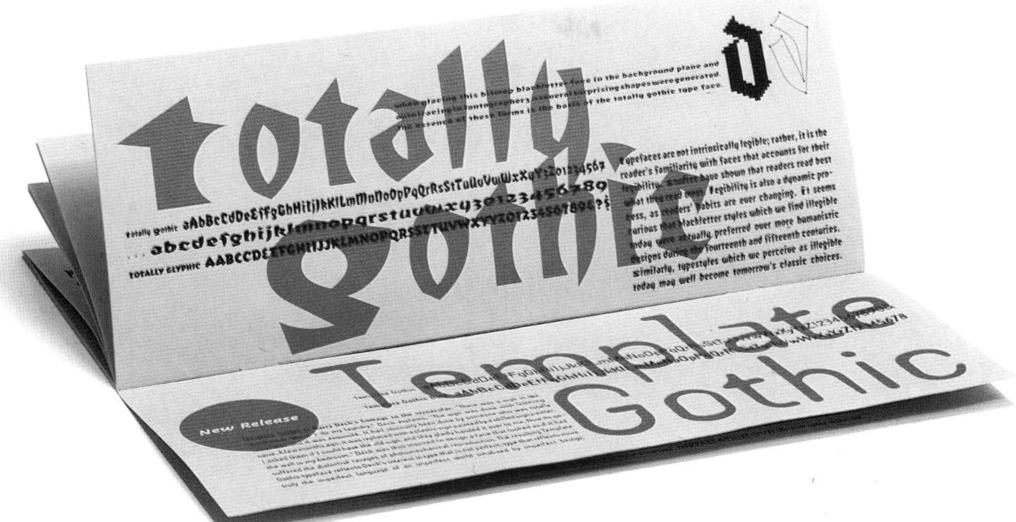


"typefaces are not intrinsically legible. rather, it is the reader's familiarity with faces that accounts for their legibility. studies have shown that readers read best what they read most. legibility is also a dynamic process, as readers' habits are everchanging. it seems curious that blackletter typestyles, which we find illegible today, were actually preferred over more humanistic designs during the eleventh and fifteenth centuries. similarly, typestyles that we perceive as illegible today may well become tomorrow's classic choices."

# Analysis of characters and measurements

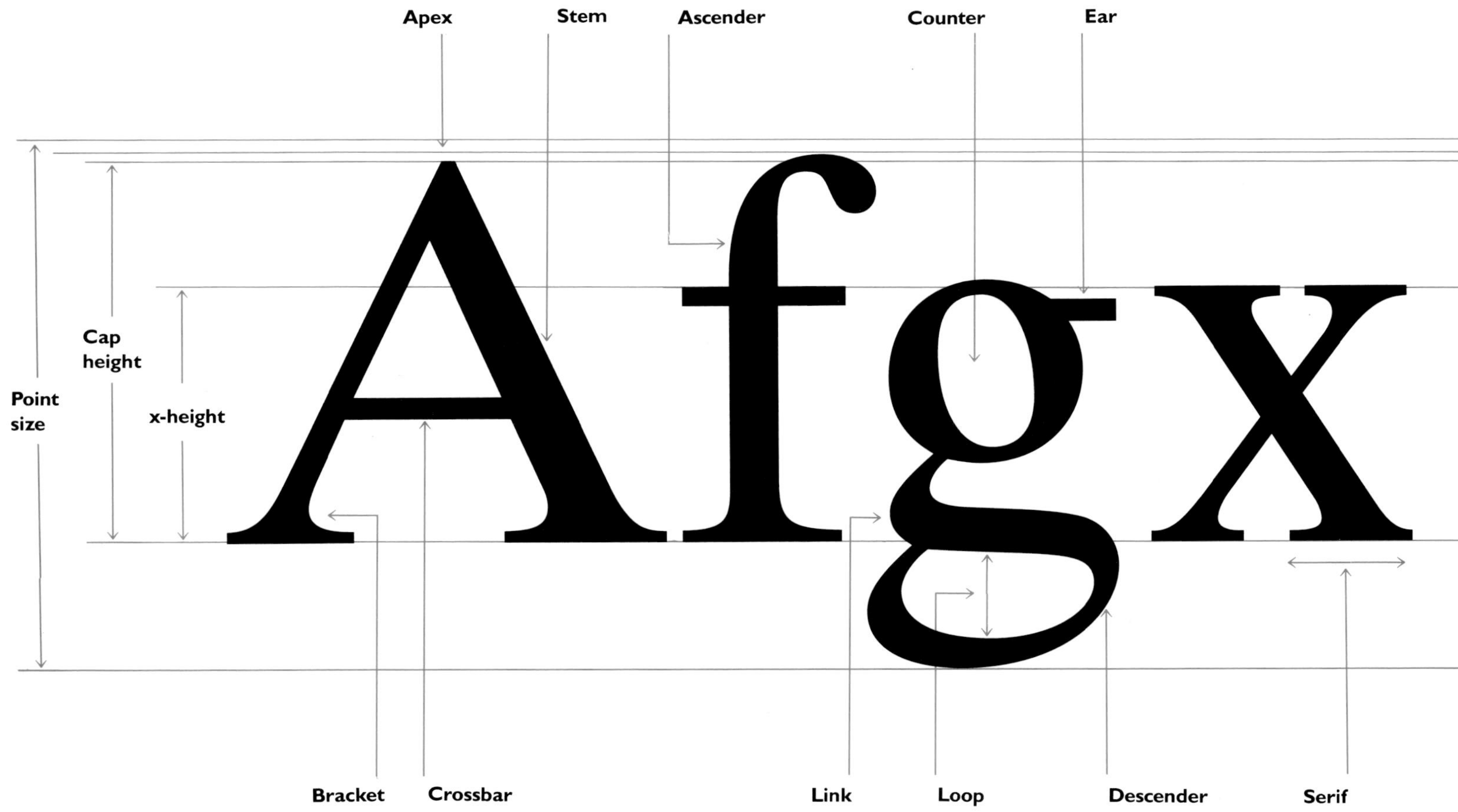


**Apex**
The outside point at which two strokes meet, as at the top of an *A* or *M*, or at the bottom of *M*.

**Arm**
The projecting horizontal or upward stroke not enclosed within a character, as in *E*, *K* or *L*.

**Ascender**
The lower-case letter *stem* that rises above the *x-height*, as in *b*, *d* or *k*.

**Baseline**
The line on which the *x-height* rests.

**Body clearance**
The space between the character and the edge of the unit.

**Body size**
The unit height on which the character is mounted. See also *Point size*.

**Bowl**
The oval stroke that encloses the *counter*, as in *b*, *p* or *O*.

**Bracket**
A curving joint between the *serif* and the *stem*.

**Cap height**
The height of the upper case in a font, taken from the *baseline* to the top of the character.

**Cicero**
European unit of typographical measurement, equal to 12 *corps*. This is slightly smaller than the UK and US equivalent of one *pica* or 12 points, at 4.155mm.

**Corps**
European measurement of *point* or *body size*, but slightly smaller than the UK and US equivalents.

**Counter**
The white space within a *bowl*.

**Crossbar**
The horizontal stroke in *A*, *H*, *f* or *t*; also known as a bar or a cross-stroke.

**Descender**
The lower-case letter *stem* or lower part that falls below the *baseline*, as in *p* or *g*.

**Ear**
A small projecting stroke sometimes attached to the *bowl* of the *g* or the *stem* of the *r*.

**Leg**
The downwards oblique stroke of the *R* and *K*; can also be called the *tail*.

**Link**
A connecting stroke when the *g* has a *bowl* and *loop*.

**Loop**
The portion of the *g* that falls below the *baseline* when it is entirely closed.

**Pica**
Unit of typographical measurement equal to 12 *points*, $\frac{1}{6}$ or 0.166 of an inch or 4.218mm.

**Point**
The basic unit of typographical measurement, approximately $\frac{1}{72}$ or 0.0138 of an inch or 0.351mm.

**Point size**
Equivalent to the body size, the height of body on which the type is cast (even if, with today's technology, it is rarely "cast").

**Serif**
The small stroke drawn across and out of a *stem*, *arm* or *tail*.

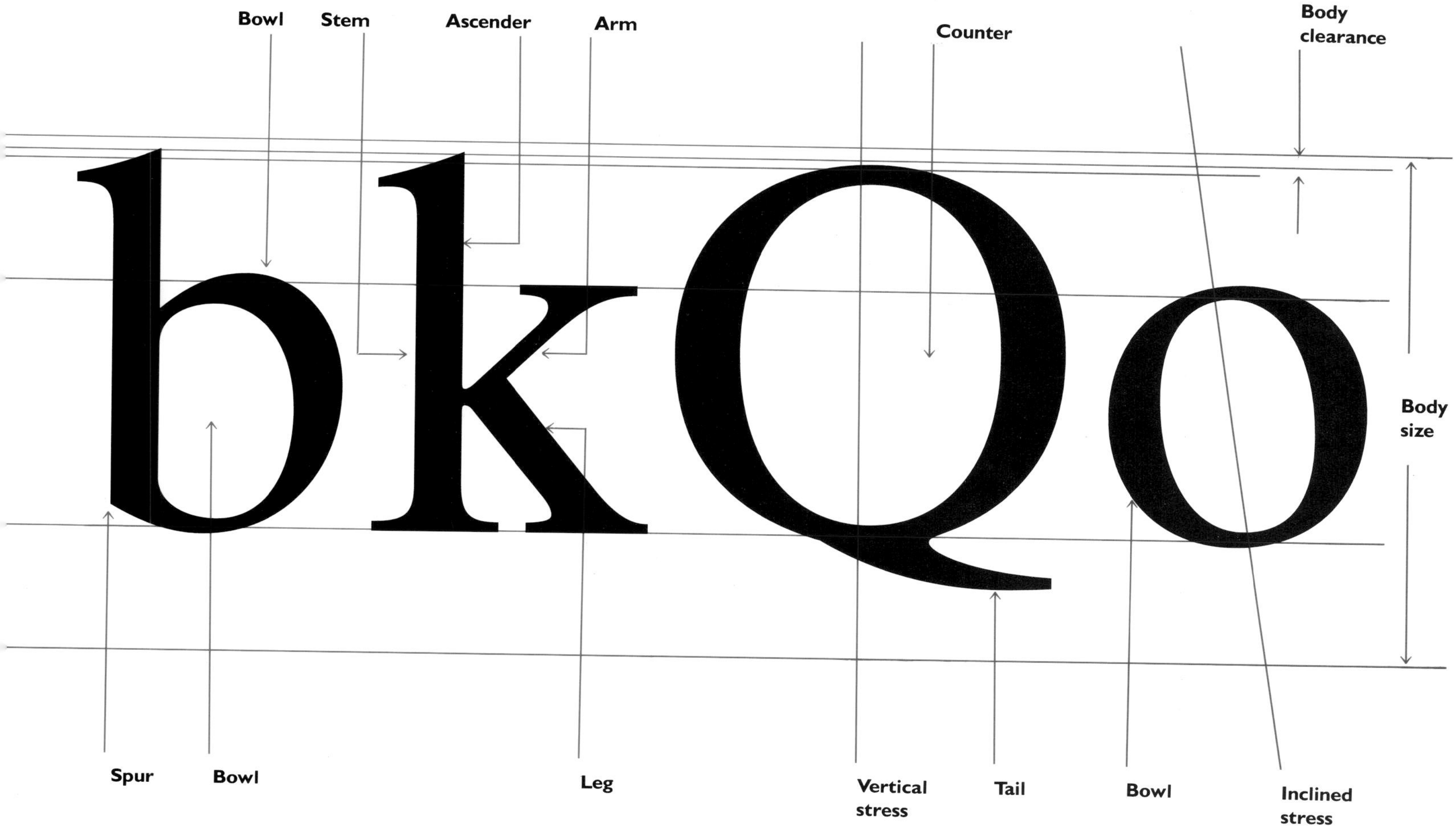

Bowl
Stem
Ascender
Arm
Counter
Body clearance

bkQo

Body size

Spur
Bowl
Leg
Vertical stress
Tail
Bowl
Inclined stress

**Spine**
The main curved stroke of an *S* or *s*.

**Spur**
The projection seen sometimes on the bottom of a *b* or *G*.

**Stem**
The principal vertical or oblique stroke in a letter, as in *L*, *B*, *V* or *A*.

**Stress**
The inclination suggested by the relationship of thick and thin strokes in a letter. Characters can have an inclined or a vertical stress.

**Stroke**
The principal line within a character.

**Tail**
The short stroke that rests on the *baseline* in *R* and *K*, or below it in *Q*. In *R* and *K* it can also be called the *leg*.

**x-height**
The lower-case character height when *ascenders* and *descenders* are excluded.

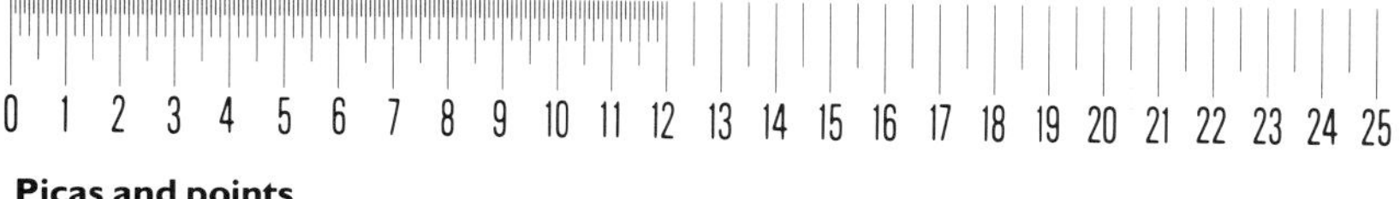

**Picas and points**

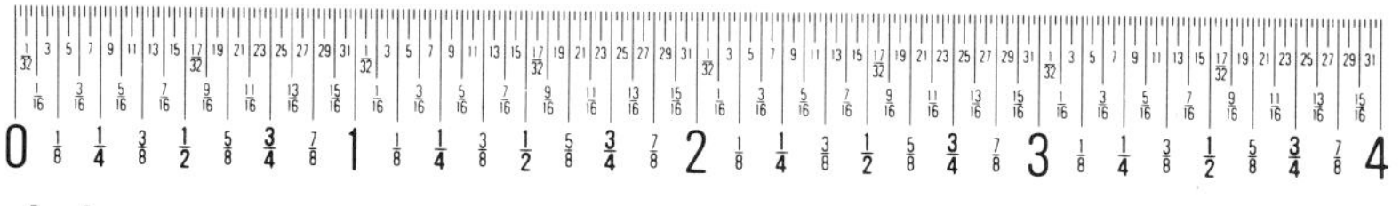

**Inches**

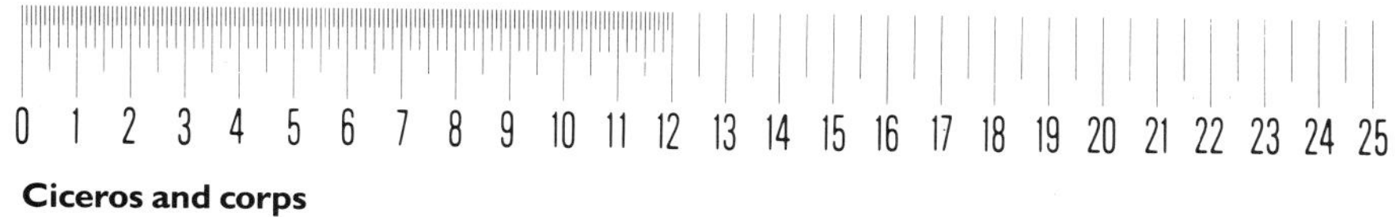

**Ciceros and corps**

**Millimetres and centimetres**

# Type description and classification

Certain methods of analysis are used to identify the various attributes of individual type characters, the fonts to which they belong, the families of fonts, and the contrasting and comparative groupings that can be made between them. While these methods try to explain matters, they can also be confusing. This is because various terms, tables and systems of measurement have been devised over centuries of typographic evolution. As new ideas and new technologies have changed the nature of type, so new forms of typographic practice have emerged to challenge the classification systems. With a subject such as measurement, the issue is by its nature fairly precisely defined and different systems can be readily compared. The description of character attributes – stem, serif, bowl and so on – is also comparatively straightforward, although there are points at which verbal definitions of visual forms run into problems (for example, where does a serif simply become the flared termination of a stroke?).

The larger descriptive problem arises when typefaces are assigned to different categories. This is important for an appreciation of the relationship between different designs and can also be of practical assistance when an art director needs to choose substitute or contrasting faces, or in order to simplify the task of finding a way around the many thousands of faces that exist. Typeface categories have emerged by evolution, one form developing from another and a range of faces being produced as a result, but their relationship is not explained by describing them only along historical lines. Even the revised categories devised by the typographic historian Maximilien Vox as recently as the 1950s and widely adopted thereafter in various guises now prove inadequate for explaining the huge number of new typeface designs since. A digital black-letter face, for instance, such as can be seen in the 1990s, looks in a number of directions, while some modern re-drawings of earlier faces make changes (such as increasing the x-height) that effectively convert them into a different kind of face from the one the name would suggest. Even the apparently simple split between serif and sans serif is complicated by designs such as Copperplate Gothic, in which the minuscule terminus strokes are intended to assert the squared ends of the stroke rather than act as clear serifs. In the near future, as Adobe's multiple master-fonts push out designs that can be altered by the user, classifiers will be challenged to find new methods of describing typefaces that are not defined visually but by a range of oppositional axes with increasingly numerous permissible variations. Are such typefaces an area of meaning between assigned poles (serif/sans serif, condensed/extended, light/bold, and so on) rather than a precise visual representation? Or should each variation be seen as an individual face – albeit a variation on essentially the same basic character description software? (The structural relationships suggest parallels with linguistic analysis, which is a subject thorny enough to have filled many books of philosophical debate.) For here, we are concerned to present a practical guide to typeface categories. Our system draws on the Vox classification of historical groups, while adding in sub-divisions and extensions to cover less conventional forms and contemporary design. The categories are guidelines, explanatory but never definitive.

All faces are presented here in 20 point, output from twentieth-century designs that have been digitised. Most are those carried in the Linotype library of faces. They are indications of the faces, rather than definitive cuts – different technologies, different printing surfaces, make different impressions. For a true idea of, say, the work of Manutius or Garamond, nothing matches seeing an original (such as those presented in the King's Library at the British Museum in London); in this context it is possible to see why certain letterforms were designed – to cope with inkspread, to work in certain sizes and so on – in the same way that contemporary designs are made to cope with or take advantage of screen displays and other new media technology. These classifications cover the principal areas of typeface design discussed in the book, so do not include black-letter, italic faces, or non-Latin typefaces.

# Neor

A group of faces that take their inspiration from the early roman style, in particular the work of Nicolas Jenson (1420–80), a French printer whose most notable work was produced in the last decade of his life during which he lived in Venice. The face is based upon humanist writing seen in fifteenth-century manuscripts, as opposed to the black-letter hand that Gutenberg used for the first printing with movable type in the 1450s. Humanist writing was rounder and broader, and was produced with a broad-nibbed pen that helped give certain inflections. (The angle of stress in these faces matches the diagonal stress that would be given to, say, an "O" if it were drawn with a broad-nibbed pen held at an angle to the page.) The features that distinguish humanist faces from later romans are: a sloping bar on the "e", a marked inclination of stress backwards to the left, and little contrast between thick and thin strokes. Several founders have produced revivals of the face seen in Jenson's books. Cloister Old Style, by Morris Fuller Benton for American Type Founders in 1897, was the first revival of the mechanical composition era; William Morris's Golden drew on Jenson's face, as did Doves, but these were more loosely derived. Frederic Goudy's Kennerley of 1911 and Bruce Rogers' Centaur of 1914/1929 are based on Jenson, while having several differences: for example, Kennerley has noticeably shorter descenders and Centaur is generally lighter. The distinctive sloping bar characteristic of the group is displayed in Horley Old Style, a compact and robust face produced by Monotype in 1925, which in other respects is closer to a later garalde roman.

abcdefghijklmnopqrstuvwxyz
ABCDEFGHIJKLMNOPQRSTUVWXYZ
1234567890

Centaur

abcdefghijklmnopqrstuvwxyz
ABCDEFGHIJKLMNOPQRSTUVWXYZ
1234567890

Cloister

abcdefghijklmnopqrstuvwxyz
ABCDEFGHIJKLMNOPQRSTUVWXYZ
1234567890

Horley Old Style

abcdefghijklmnopqrstuvwxyz
ABCDEFGHIJKLMNOPQRSTUVWXYZ
1234567890

Jenson

abcdefghijklmnopqrstuvwxyz
ABCDEFGHIJKLMNOPQRSTUVWXYZ
1234567890

Kennerley

These faces, formerly called Old Face or Old Style, have a horizontal bar to the "e" but in other respects share features with the humanist grouping. Pen-influenced characteristics such as the oblique stroke on lower-case ascender serifs are still present and the characters tend to have a backwards slope (although not always as pronounced as in humanist). Contrasts between thick and thin strokes are more marked. The first models for garalde faces are those of the Venetian printer Aldus Manutius (1450–1515) and the punchcutter Francesco Griffo, used in books from the late 1490s onwards. The twentieth-century revival form Bembo (Monotype, 1929, and later other founders) takes its name from Cardinal Bembo's *De Aetna* of 1495, the book in which the Manutius/Griffo face was first seen. However, it was the sixteenth-century French typecutter and designer Claude Garamond (1500–61) who was the first to produce a notable reworking of the Aldine Press faces, creating a face seen from the 1530s onwards that has been redrawn by most foundries in the twentieth century for their own Garamonds. Granjon, based on the face associated with the sixteenth-century French type designer Robert Granjon, is close to Garamond, and the characteristics are still there in the eighteenth-century Caslon, itself modelled on seventeenth-century Dutch designs, such as those associated with Christophe Plantin. Stanley Morison's Times Roman of 1932, while having the short ascenders and descenders of newspaper type, in other respects takes its idea of stress and contrast from the Plantin-Caslon tradition.

abcdefghijklmnopqrstuvwxyz
ABCDEFGHIJKLMNOPQRSTUVWXYZ
1234567890

Bembo

abcdefghijklmnopqrstuvwxyz
ABCDEFGHIJKLMNOPQRSTUVWXYZ
1234567890

Caslon Old Face

abcdefghijklmnopqrstuvwxyz
ABCDEFGHIJKLMNOPQRSTUVWXYZ
1234567890

Garamond

abcdefghijklmnopqrstuvwxyz
ABCDEFGHIJKLMNOPQRSTUVWXYZ
1234567890

Goudy Old Style

abcdefghijklmnopqrstuvwxyz
ABCDEFGHIJKLMNOPQRSTUVWXYZ
1234567890

Granjon

abcdefghijklmnopqrstuvwxyz
ABCDEFGHIJKLMNOPQRSTUVWXYZ
1234567890

Palatino

Hermann Zapf's Palatino of 1950, named after a sixteenth-century Italian calligrapher, drew on Italian Renaissance lettering along with Roman inscriptions, which helps explain its generous counters and unorthodox serifs on the outside only of certain letters. Jan Tschichold's Sabon is a garalde that was designed to work across the different technologies of composition (being hand, hot metal and photocomposition at the time of design in the 1960s).

abcdefghijklmnopqrstuvwxyz
ABCDEFGHIJKLMNOPQRSTUVWXYZ
1234567890

Plantin

abcdefghijklmnopqrstuvwxyz
ABCDEFGHIJKLMNOPQRSTUVWXYZ
1234567890

Sabon

abcdefghijklmnopqrstuvwxyz
ABCDEFGHIJKLMNOPQRSTUVWXYZ
1234567890

Times Roman

abcdefghijklmnopqrstuvwxyz
ABCDEFGHIJKLMNOPQRSTUVWXYZ
1234567890

Weiss Roman

# Neor

Transitional faces are so called because they have characters that show the transition from the "old style" garalde to the "modern" didone faces that first emerged in the late eighteenth century. Transitional typefaces tend to be more upright than garaldes, with either a vertical or only slightly inclined stress. They may also have more contrast. Serifs may be bracketed and oblique as before, or horizontal and tending towards the starkness of the didone serif. The faces of the English typographer John Baskerville (1706–75) and the French founder Pierre Fournier (1712–68) are central to this grouping, while its links with what came before are suggested by the inclusion in the category of certain twentieth-century reworkings of Caslon and Garamond. W. A. Dwiggins' Caledonia of 1938 is a transitional that incorporates aspects of the didone style: horizontal serifs are lightly bracketed and shade into an unbracketed "t".

abcdefghijklmnopqrstuvwxyz
ABCDEFGHIJKLMNOPQRSTUVWXYZ
1234567890

Baskerville

abcdefghijklmnopqrstuvwxyz
ABCDEFGHIJKLMNOPQRSTUVWXYZ
1234567890

Caledonia

abcdefghijklmnopqrstuvwxyz
ABCDEFGHIJKLMNOPQRSTUVWXYZ
1234567890

Caslon

abcdefghijklmnopqrstuvwxyz
ABCDEFGHIJKLMNOPQRSTUVWXYZ
1234567890

Fournier

abcdefghijklmnopqrstuvwxyz
ABCDEFGHIJKLMNOPQRSTUVWXYZ
1234567890

Perpetua

abcdefghijklmnopqrstuvwxyz
ABCDEFGHIJKLMNOPQRSTUVWXYZ
1234567890

Stempel Garamond

# Neor

Here the contrast between thick and thin strokes is extreme; lower-case serifs are horizontal and often unbracketed; the stress is vertical. These characteristics were exemplified in the work of Giambattista Bodoni (1740–1813) of Parma, who took the French types of Fournier and the Didots and refined them to the characteristics outlined above. Firmin Didot had produced the first didone (hence the name for the group) in the 1780s, its thin serifs and abrupt contrasts featuring hairline strokes which took advantage of improved paper and printing. Bodoni's typography made the most of this approach to typeface design, generous use of white space being in keeping with the sparkling, high-contrast qualities of the face. Several twentieth-century revivals of his face attempt to retain these qualities while making it more efficient in its demands on space (for example, while the ATF cutting was the first and most commonly followed, the Bauer Bodoni is a more refined but less robust version). Torino is an early twentieth-century revival from the Nebiolo foundry with exaggerated serifs and other terminal flourishes, while Didi ITC is an exaggerated form of didone created for display purposes by Bonder and Carnase in 1970. Walbaum, a wider and less rounded didone, is based on designs by the German punchcutter Justus Erich Walbaum (1768–1839) who followed Didot rather then Bodoni.

abcdefghijklmnopqrstuvwxyz
ABCDEFGHIJKLMNOPQRSTUVWXYZ
1234567890

Bauer Bodoni

abcdefghijklmnopqrstuvwxyz
ABCDEFGHIJKLMNOPQRSTUVWXYZ
1234567890

Bodoni

abcdefghijklmnopqrstuvwxyz
ABCDEFGHIJKLMNOPQRSTUVWXYZ
1234567890

Didi ITC

abcdefghijklmnopqrstuvwxyz
ABCDEFGHIJKLMNOPQRSTUVWXYZ
1234567890

Torino

abcdefghijklmnopqrstuvwxyz
ABCDEFGHIJKLMNOPQRSTUVWXYZ
1234567890

Walbaum

# Neor

This group covers those serif faces that display a complex, hybrid mix of features that do not feature in the previous historical evolution of form. They are sturdier faces than the thin didones, often originally cut in the nineteenth century to overcome problems of reproduction as larger print runs, poorer-quality papers and the demand for more compact faces put the typefaces of finer printing under stresses they were not capable of meeting. Bookman was originally a mid-nineteenth-century face, revived again in the 1920s; originally called Antique Old Style, it boasted a composite of features rather than being a straightforward garalde. Century Schoolbook, designed by Morris Fuller Benton and released in 1915, was – as the name suggests – intended for schoolbooks and is based on Century, the slightly condensed face designed by Linn Boyd Benton in the 1890s for the *Century* magazine. Upright stress, short ascenders and descenders and heavy serifs are all elements that make for its compact but legible letters. Excelsior, a newspaper face of 1931, has similar features since it strives for maximum legibility under stressful printing conditions. The massive popularity of the Cheltenham family, originally begun in the 1890s, was based upon its robustness and maintenance of character across many weights, widths, sizes and other variations.

abcdefghijklmnopqrstuvwxyz
ABCDEFGHIJKLMNOPQRSTUVWXYZ
1234567890

Bookman

abcdefghijklmnopqrstuvwxyz
ABCDEFGHIJKLMNOPQRSTUVWXYZ
1234567890

Century Schoolbook

abcdefghijklmnopqrstuvwxyz
ABCDEFGHIJKLMNOPQRSTUVWXYZ
1234567890

Cheltenham

abcdefghijklmnopqrstuvwxyz
ABCDEFGHIJKLMNOPQRSTUVWXYZ
1234567890

Excelsior

# Neor

This group is simply defined by name: those typefaces with heavy, square-ended serifs, with or without brackets. Clarendon, released by R. Besley & Co. in 1845, was the prototype slab-serif which gave its name to a wide grouping of faces. Its clarity and sturdiness made it suitable for emphasis in text setting as well as for widespread use in display forms, such as posters. Robert Harling's Playbill of 1938 was an extreme form that made the serifs heavier than the main strokes in an imitation of Victorian playbill style. The late 1920s and early 1930s saw a major revival of slab-serif forms, of which some examples are given here: Memphis by Rudolf Weiss (1929); Beton by Heinrich Jost (1931); Rockwell for Monotype (1934). Serifa is a slab-serif version made in 1967 by Adrian Frutiger of his earlier sans serif Univers.

abcdefghijklmnopqrstuvwxyz
ABCDEFGHIJKLMNOPQRSTUVWXYZ
1234567890

Beton

abcdefghijklmnopqrstuvwxyz
ABCDEFGHIJKLMNOPQRSTUVWXYZ
1234567890

Clarendon

abcdefghijklmnopqrstuvwxyz
ABCDEFGHIJKLMNOPQRSTUVWXYZ
1234567890

Memphis

abcdefghijklmnopqrstuvwxyz
ABCDEFGHIJKLMNOPQRSTUVWXYZ
1234567890

Playbill

abcdefghijklmnopqrstuvwxyz
ABCDEFGHIJKLMNOPQRSTUVWXYZ
1234567890

Rockwell

abcdefghijklmnopqrstuvwxyz
ABCDEFGHIJKLMNOPQRSTUVWXYZ
1234567890

Serifa

# Neor

The first lineales, or sans serifs, can be found in catalogues at the beginning of the nineteenth century; they were bulky and tended to exist only in the upper case. Wood-letter forms existed, but were restricted to large-scale display use. At the beginning of the twentieth century there was interest in the form with the growth of display print needs, and Morris Fuller Benton was quick to cover the market for ATF with Alternate Gothic (1903), Franklin Gothic (1904) and News Gothic (1908). The strokes have contrast and there is a squared-off crudeness to the curves. The later Trade Gothic, by Jackson Burke (1948) is altogether smoother; however, Franklin Gothic has more than stood the test of time to remain immensely popular.

abcdefghijklmnopqrstuvwxyz
ABCDEFGHIJKLMNOPQRSTUVWXYZ
1234567890

Alternate Gothic

**abcdefghijklmnopqrstuvwxyz**
**ABCDEFGHIJKLMNOPQRSTUVWXYZ**
**1234567890**

Franklin Gothic

abcdefghijklmnopqrstuvwxyz
ABCDEFGHIJKLMNOPQRSTUVWXYZ
1234567890

News Gothic

abcdefghijklmnopqrstuvwxyz
ABCDEFGHIJKLMNOPQRSTUVWXYZ
1234567890

Trade Gothic

Lineale
b Neo-grotesque

These are similar to the grotesque grouping of lineales, but the stroke width contrasts are less marked – in effect, the characters show more signs of being designed than of retaining any pen-drawn characteristics. The jaws of letters such as "C" tend to be more open than with the grotesques. The most marked distinction between the two groups is that the neo-grotesques do not have a lower bowl to the "g", but an open stroke. Akzidenz Grotesk, released by Berthold in 1896 and also known as Standard, became popular with the Swiss Style typographers; in the 1950s it underlay the design of Neue Haas Grotesk/Helvetica by Max Miedinger and Edouard Hoffman and also of Univers by Adrian Frutiger. Folio, by Konrad Bauer and Walter Baum of 1957, follows the same pattern. Venus, a Wagner & Schmidt design for Bauer of 1907, had some popularity with the Modern Movement and exists in a wide range of variations.

abcdefghijklmnopqrstuvwxyz
ABCDEFGHIJKLMNOPQRSTUVWXYZ
1234567890

Akzidenz Grotesk

**abcdefghijklmnopqrstuvwxyz**
**ABCDEFGHIJKLMNOPQRSTUVWXYZ**
**1234567890**

Folio

abcdefghijklmnopqrstuvwxyz
ABCDEFGHIJKLMNOPQRSTUVWXYZ
1234567890

Helvetica

abcdefghijklmnopqrstuvwxyz
ABCDEFGHIJKLMNOPQRSTUVWXYZ
1234567890

Univers

**abcdefghijklmnopqrstuvwxyz**
**ABCDEFGHIJKLMNOPQRSTUVWXYZ**
**1234567890**

Venus

# Neor

Sans serif faces that follow the rules of minimalist geometric shapes – the circle and square – and obey the rule of "form follows function" make up this group. Stroke widths tend to the constant. Chief among them is Futura of 1927, by Paul Renner, a face that quickly grew and kept popularity as it expressed both Modernist ideas and a sense of classic proportions within and between letters. It was widely copied. Erbar (1922), by Jakob Erbar, slightly predates Futura and is similar. Kabel (1927), by Rudolf Koch, is a more individual design that departs at times from the minimalism of its contemporary geometrics. Eurostile (1962), by Aldo Novarese, is sometimes grouped with neo-grotesques, but is essentially geometric in its interpretation of letterforms in relation to the square. Avant-Garde Gothic, by Herb Lubalin and Tom Carnase of 1970, developed the geometric model for a face that would have a high degree of legibility in different uses, the numerous upper-case ligatures giving the opportunity for a distinctive character in display applications. The Metro family of faces by W. A. Dwiggins (1929) had versions No. 1 and No. 2, which contrasted splayed and pointed letters (a splayed "M" and a pointed "N", "W" and "V" coming in the No. 2 series); of the four distinct weights, Metromedium is shown here.

abcdefghijklmnopqrstuvwxyz
ABCDEFGHIJKLMNOPQRSTUVWXYZ
1234567890

Avant Garde Gothic

**abcdefghijklmnopqrstuvwxyz**
**ABCDEFGHIJKLMNOPQRSTUVWXYZ**
**1234567890**

Erbar

abcdefghijklmnopqrstuvwxyz
ABCDEFGHIJKLMNOPQRSTUVWXYZ
1234567890

Eurostile

abcdefghijklmnopqrstuvwxyz
ABCDEFGHIJKLMNOPQRSTUVWXYZ
1234567890

Futura

abcdefghijklmnopqrstuvwxyz
ABCDEFGHIJKLMNOPQRSTUVWXYZ
1234567890

Kabel

**abcdefghijklmnopqrstuvwxyz**
**ABCDEFGHIJKLMNOPQRSTUVWXYZ**
**1234567890**

Metro

# Neor

These faces do not so much follow nineteenth-century sans serif precedents, but rather go right back to Roman inscriptions for their roots as well as drawing inspiration from the lower-case hand of humanist writing, which is apparent also in the seriffed humanist and garalde faces. They have some contrast of stroke width. Gill Sans of 1928, by Eric Gill, drew on Edward Johnston's type for the London Underground as well as Gill's signwriting and stone carving that brought him instinctively close to the inscriptional base of the roman forms. Optima, by Hermann Zapf (1958), and Pascal by José Mendoza y Almeida (1960) have notable variations in stroke width that break with the more monotonous line of the geometric and neo-grotesques that were prevailing at the time. Goudy Sans, by Frederic Goudy (1925), is something of a sport, offering variant letterforms and with a pronounced tendency to the inscriptional in the "chiselled" junctions, placing it closer to the glyphic group of faces.

abcdefghijklmnopqrstuvwxyz
ABCDEFGHIJKLMNOPQRSTUVWXYZ
1234567890

Gills Sans

abcdefghijklmnopqrstuvwxyz
ABCDEFGHIJKLMNOPQRSTUVWXYZ
1234567890

Goudy Sans ITC

abcdefghijklmnopqrstuvwxyz
ABCDEFGHIJKLMNOPQRSTUVWXYZ
1234567890

Optima

abcdefghijklmnopqrstuvwxyz
ABCDEFGHIJKLMNOPQRSTUVWXYZ
1234567890

Pascal

Neor

Instead of the calligraphic base, these faces suggest more that they are chiselled than written. They look more to the expression of inscriptions rather than the effect of the pen on paper, often taking their inspiration from Roman stonework. The characters tend to be comparatively uniform in width, as if measured out on the page – or stone – before being inscribed. Sharply cut, large, triangular serifs are often used. In Augustea, by Aldo Novarese and Alessandro Butti for Nebiolo (1951), there are heavily pronounced serifs (note the "T" and "L") and also distinctive touches such as the serifs on the bar of the "f" and "t", the triangular dots over the "i" and "j", and the enclosed "2". Albertus, by Berthold Wolpe for Monotype (1932), takes a different approach in that the serifs are more thickened terminals than separate strokes, tending towards the look of a humanist lineale, but the effect is still to suggest the stone-carved inscription rather than writing. Latin is a curious hybrid offered by several type founders in various forms, distinguished by the triangular serifs that suggest the chisel cut while in other respects it has features in common with a Clarendon-style slab-serif.

abcdeffiflffghijklmnopqrstuvwxyz
ABCDEFGHIJJKLMNOPQQRSTUVWXYZ
122345678900
Albertus

abcdefffghijklmnopqrstuvwxyz
ABCDEFGHIJKLMNOPQRSTUVWXYZ
1234567890
Augustea

abcdefffffiffififlghijklmnopqrstuvwxyz
ABCDEFGHIJKLMNOPQRSTUVWXYZ
1234567890
Latin

A wide-ranging group that is drawn together around the idea that the typeface is an imitation of handwriting. The florid twirls of Robert Hunter Middleton's Coronet (1937) can be seen to ape a fine hand, but Roger Excoffon's Choc (1955) and Mistral (1953) are more painterly, Mistral being remarkable for the manner in which the lower-case joins up. Matthew Carter's Snell Roundhand (1966) also manages some effective junctions and takes as its basis the work of the seventeenth-century writing master Charles Snell (his rules for consistency in writing help the product to be imitated in type). Hermann Zapf's Chancery for ITC (1979) is an altogether more restrained and readable face, while still displaying many pen-drawn inflections.

abcdefghijklmnopqrstuvwxyz
ABCDEFGHIJKLMNOPQRSTUVWXYZ
1234567890

Choc

abcdefghijklmnopqrstuvwxyz
ABCDEFGHIJKLMNOPQRSTUVWXYZ
1234567890

Coronet

abcdefghijklmnopqrstuvwxyz
ABCDEFGHIJKLMNOPQRSTUVWXYZ
1234567890

Mistral

abcdefghijklmnopqrstuvwxyz
ABCDEFGHIJKLMNOPQRSTUVWXYZ
1234567890

Snell Roundhand

abcdefghijklmnopqrstuvwxyz
ABCDEFGHIJKLMNOPQRSTUVWXYZ
1234567890

Zapf Chancery ITC

## Stylised

Many faces have characteristics that are not easily grouped with other faces or that have strong references which overlay all other features. Rather than forcing them to conform to groupings they essentially reject, we will loosely categorise them here as "stylised". A number imitate typewriter characters, of which American Typewriter, by Joel Kaden and Tony Stan for ITC of 1974, is one (various styles of open lettering are associated with typewriters, but it is the inter-character consistency of spacing that is perhaps its most distinguishing aspect). Broadway, by Morris Fuller Benton (1929), is a curious hybrid of heavy and light sans serif, as is his Parisian (1928), both picking up on Art Deco style. Cooper Black, by Oswald B. Cooper of 1921, is an exaggerated heavy version of his Cooper Old Style that takes on a distinct character with its blurred serifs and small counters. Copperplate Gothic, by Frederic Goudy of 1901, is sometimes seen as a lineale but does have tiny serifs that work optically to give a crisp definition to the terminals; this face proved popular for titling and cards and has been imitated. Eckmann, by Otto Eckmann of 1900, reflects the Art Nouveau aesthetic; Matrix Printer is a face that takes its aesthetic

abcdefghijklmnopqrstuvwxyz
ABCDEFGHIJKLMNOPQRSTUVWXYZ
1234567890

American Typewriter ITC

abcdefghijklmnopqrstuvwxyz
ABCDEFGHIJKLMNOPQRSTUVWXYZ
1234567890

Broadway

abcdefghijklmnopqrstuvwxyz
ABCDEFGHIJKLMNOPQRSTUVWXYZ
1234567890

Cooper Black

ABCDEFGHIJKLMNOPQRSTUVWXYZ
ABCDEFGHIJKLMNOPQRSTUVWXYZ
1234567890

Copperplate Gothic

abcdefghijklmnopqrstuvwxyz
ABCDEFGHIJKLMNOPQRSTUVWXYZ
1234567890

Eckmann

a b c d e f g h i j k l m n o p q r s t u v w x y z
A B C D E F G H I J K L M N O P Q R S T U V W X Y Z
1 2 3 4 5 6 7 8 9 0

Matrix Printer

from the terms of production in dot-matrix printing and signage. OCR-A of 1967 also takes its reference from the need for machine-readable type, while Stop by Aldo Novarese of 1970 draws upon computer print and neon sign technology to develop its letterforms. Tea Chest, one of many stencil faces, was designed for Stephenson Blake in 1939 and based itself on the slab-serif form. Cassandre's Peignot of 1937 is in some ways a humanist lineale, but with the overriding stylistic trait that the lower-case letters take the upper-case form except for "b", "d" and "f". Many other faces could be added to this group of miscellaneous styles . . . the numerous recent faces that display the nature of digital, bitmap forms being perhaps a sub-section of their own.

ABCDEFGHIJKLMNOPQRSTUVWXYZ
1234567890

OCR-A

abcdefghijklmnopqrstuvwxyz
ABCDEFGHIJKLMNOPQRSTUVWXYZ
1234567890

Parisian

abcdefghijklmnopqrstuvwxyz
ABCDEFGHIJKLMNOPQRSTUVWXYZ
1234567890

Peignot

ABCDEFGHIJKLMNOPQRSTUVWXYZ
1234567890

Stop

ABCDEFGHIJKLMNOPQRSTUVWXYZ
1234567890

Tea Chest

# Glossary

Note: some terms relating to characters and type groups are already explained on pages 230–1.

**Baseline**
The line (not printed) on which letters tend to sit and align. Descenders fall below this line.

**Bezier curves**
Curves created by drawing lines in relation to a series of coordinates. At the heart of the *PostScript* page description language.

**Bitmap**
The dots that make up a *digital* image. Digital typefaces have a bitmap image for screen display, each size having a separate cluster of bitmap information. This screen bitmap is low-resolution, and an accompanying printer font in high-resolution information, encoded in a form such as *PostScript*, enables the generation of a high-quality output.

**Black-letter**
Typefaces that are based on the medieval script, the gothic minuscule. Textura, Fraktura, Old English, Rotunda and Schwabacher are groups of black-letter faces.

**Body type**
The type used for a main text, as opposed to headline or display usage; also known as text type. It is most often seen in sizes between 6 and 14 point.

**CD-ROM**
Compact disc, read-only memory. In the 1990s type libraries are being transferred complete on to CDs capable of being read by computers with CD drives. More than 2000 faces may be in a library and accessible to view, but users only have to buy faces as and when they need them; this is possible through the use of codes that unlock just those faces on the disc that a user wants to pay for.

**Chase**
The metal frame in which the *galleys* of metal type were locked as pages ready for printing or for a *stereotype* plate to be taken.

**Cold type**
Printing which is not produced by the *hot-metal* process, but involves the use of *founders' type*, *photosetting* or electronic processes.

**Colour**
In typography this can apply to purely monochrome pages, as it refers to the density of black/grey/white generated by the mass of type on the page. Choice of type, line length, leading, tracking – all these factors and others can affect the colour of the type.

**Composition**
The process of assembling individual characters of type into set matter of words, sentences, pages. This can be done by hand, *hot-metal* machine, *photosetting* or electronically through *digital* information.

**Condensed**
A typeface is condensed when the character form is compressed to a narrower width than is normal; the opposite is extended (or expanded). New technology of the *photosetting* and computer era enables characters to be condensed or extended by machine rather than specially *cut* as was required with metal setting.

**CRT**
Cathode ray tube, the technology central to television projection which also has an important part in the development of image-setting systems for type. Initial digital typesetting systems used a CRT to generate the type image as a series of pixels (picture elements) that were exposed on to a light-sensitive film, as with *photosetting*. *Laser setting* has now superseded CRT as the prime technology behind typesetting/image-setting.

**Cut**
Often used to define a particular font; a term dating from the days when a design was cut into a punch that was then used to form the matrices from which individual pieces of type were struck.

**Digital**
The term for the electronic technology that has taken over print and image manipulation systems since the 1980s. At the root of all the computer systems is the notion of sorting information digitally, as a mass of binary data.

**DPI**
Dots per inch, usually applied to output devices, such as printers and image-setters, to define the resolution of the image that is available. Dot matrix printers have a low dpi, hence the visibility of the dots and the crudeness of the resulting characters and graphics. Rapid developments in printer technology mean that most now offer at least 300 dpi. High-end systems for quality reproduction, as in book printing, are in excess of 2000 dpi.

**Dry transfer**
Process behind the development of companies such as Letraset and Mecanorma, where sheets of lettering are sold as transfers to be rubbed down and transferred as ready-made artwork, replacing the need for some setting. Originally the system was wet transfer, a messier and more awkward process.

**DTP**
Desktop publishing, the computerized design and production of print that was made possible by the introduction of small, low-cost computer systems offering a *wysiwyg* screen image that enabled designers to work on screen effectively. It has been available from the early 1980s.

**Electrotype**
A printing plate formed by the electrolytic deposition of copper on a wax mould of the original printing plate. See also *stereotype*.

**Em**
A unit of measurement that is normally the square of a given point size of type. It is based on the letter "m", which tends to form a square piece of type, its width the same as the height of the face.

**En**
A unit of measurement half the width of an *em*.

**Extended/expanded**
Terms to describe the stretching of a typeface to a larger width than the normal dimensions of characters; the opposite is *condensed*.

**Family**
In type, a term given to a range of typeface designs that are all variations on one central design. Principal variations are roman, italic, bold, light, condensed and extended/expanded.

**Font/fount**
The meaning has changed over time; the current usage defines the complete character set of a particular typeface in a particular size and style.

**Founders'/foundry type**
Setting based on the use of pre-cast metal characters of type composed by hand from a tray of type.

**Foundry**
The place of manufacture for type, dating from the days when a type foundry was a place for serious metalwork.

**Furniture**
As in "page furniture", those regular elements of a layout that are not type, but are part of the typographic arrangement, such as rules and bars, fleurons and the like.

**Galley**
Strip of set type, either in hot metal when arranged on the *stone* or as a bromide strip output from *photosetting* or image-setting.

**Half-tone**
Blocks or pieces of film converted from images into a form ready for printing. They consist of a greater or lesser number of dots that depict light and dark areas.

**Hardware**
The physical machinery in computer systems, as opposed to the *software*, which is the particular operating system and other *programs* carried on the equipment. The CPU (central processing unit) is at the heart of any system, with the screen and printer being described as peripherals.

**Hot metal**
Term for type and the printing process that involves casting type from hot metal in order to print.

**Inline/outline**
Characters are inlined when part of the character stroke is cut away to create a white area within the letter other than a bowl. They are outlined when a line is put on the outside edge to create an open aspect to the form. This is different from adding a shadow effect, although they may be combined.

**Justification**
The ranging of type on both left and right sides;

see also *ranged left* and *ranged right*.

**Kerning**
The spacing of letters closer than is standard, usually in order to create the optical effect of consistency of space between characters; see also *tracking*.

**Laser setting**
Lasers fire flashes of light according to the information of the character outline (which could be *PostScript* encoded, or some other page description, or *bitmap*). This light either records an image on a light-sensitive surface (laser typesetters/image-setters), or generates an electrostatically charged image that is put directly on to paper (laser printers). The former have high resolution, the latter lower resolution.

**Leading**
The space between lines. Prior to photocomposition, this was created by physically inserting a strip of metal called a lead into the page make-up in order to give more white space between the lines of type.

**Legibility**
In typography, legibility and readability are two terms that have precise and separate meanings. Legibility is usually taken to mean the quality of distinction between characters—the clarity of the individual letters. Readability is the quality of reading provided by a piece of typography, in which kerning, leading and other factors will have a bearing on the function of the type.

**Letterspacing**
The insertion of greater than normal spacing between characters.

**Ligature**
The joining of two or more letters for optical purposes (as with æ, fl or fi,), a feature common in metal setting but less so with *photosetting*, where the enlarged character set thus required is undesirable for the manufacturers. There are signs, however, that ligatures are returning with digital typography.

**Linotype**
Describes a company, machine, system and type library. Linotype was the original hot-metal system, launched in 1886 and involving the setting of a line of type in hot metal by an operator working a keyboard directly attached to the setting machine. In contrast the *Monotype* machine set one character at a time.

**Lithography**
Printing process that works on the principle of having an image on metal (or, originally, stone), parts of which will take ink, and parts (which are not to print) which reject ink; the surface to be printed is placed against this lithographic image. Water can be used to create the process of the attraction and repelling of ink. Offset lithography is where the image is first offset on to another surface (the "blanket") and this then transfers on to the surface to be printed.

**Matrix**
In metal setting, the mould from which the type is cast; it carries an impression of the type character which has been struck from the *punch*; it is made from copper or brass. In *photosetting*, the term used for the grid of characters that often carries the character set of a face.

**Mechanical composition**
The process of selecting and arranging type by machine rather than by hand. Prior to the *Linotype* and *Monotype* machines at the end of the nineteenth century, there was no commercially viable method of mechanical setting that could select, cast and re-sort (or melt down) type.

**Monotype**
A company, machine, system and type library developed in the 1890s shortly after the *Linotype*. It offered a system based on setting individual pieces of type in hot metal, following instructions punched into a spool of tape by a keyboard operator. Monotype has been associated with the development of a fine type library, along with later type and print technology.

**Multiple masters**
Technology developed by Adobe Systems that allows the generation of a wide variety of fonts from one typeface – condensed and extended, or light and bold, even serif to sans serif. The software takes up a comparatively small amount of computer memory, providing a sophisticated range of options on relatively small systems at much lower costs than buying all the fonts. The first faces, Myriad and Minion, were launched early in 1992.

**OCR**
Optical character recognition; OCR devices can scan, or read, type so that it can be processed by computer. From the late 1950s onwards the issue of machine-readable faces has been important; this led to specially designed faces, as well as being related to the development of scanning technology.

**Offset lithography**
See *lithography*.

**Outline**
See *inline/outline*.

**Pantograph**
An instrument capable of transferring a design by tracing the master drawing. Linn Boyd Benton's pantographic *punchcutter* made it easier to convert a design for type on to the *punch* and made possible the development of *mechanical composition*.

**Photosetting/phototypesetting**
The setting of type by exposing the image of a type character on to light-sensitive film, with the photosetter outputting a bromide that is then used for paste-up on a page. The resulting artwork, when proofed and combined with other graphics, goes through a further film process to generate plates for offset *lithography*.

**Pica**
Typographical measurement comprising 12 points and thus amounting to roughly $\frac{1}{6}$ of an inch; also formerly the term applied to 12 point type.

**Point**
Typographical measurement; in the US and UK it is 0.0138 of an inch or 0.351mm; in Continental Europe it is 0.346mm.

**PostScript**
The digitial page description language developed by Adobe Systems and widely adopted as a standard for digital page software. It is device- and resolution-independent, requiring only a PostScript-compatible system, and is thus able to work on a wide range of equipment. Type is described in a series of mathematical formulae that generate *Bezier curves* which are then filled in with dots to the output-system resolution.

**Press**
The printing machine, so-called because it traditionally works by pressing a piece of paper against the surface carrying the image, whether a relief image of metal type or a rubber blanket carrying an offset lithographic image. For each colour a separate plate exists and a separate impression is made. A flatbed press carries the image on a flat surface at the base and moves the paper against it, while a rotary press wraps the image as a plate round a rotating drum under which is passed the surface to be printed.

**Program**
The computer software carrying the instructions and operating methods of a particular system. A typesetting program has to be loaded on to the hardware – the computerized equipment – before it can work as a typesetter.

**Punch**
Metal bar containing the master design of a type character used for striking a *matrix* for casting the type for printing.

**Punchcutter**
The highly skilled craftsman who physically inscribed the design of a typeface on to the metal bars of the *punch*. Prior to the *pantograph* this was a job of such individual skill that the punchcutter was often the same as the type designer, or was regarded as contributing to the design.

**Ranged left**
Ranging of type at the left side, leaving the right side ragged; also called unjustified. See *justification*.

**Ranged right**
Ranging of type at the right side, leaving the left side ragged; such a setting is unjustified. See *justification*.

**Readability**
See *legibility*.

**Reversed out**
Type which is the unprinted area, standing out of black or a coloured background.

**RIP**
Raster image processor. Device for converting ("rastering") the information from, say, a *PostScript* encryption into a series of dots, produced to a density determined by the output device.

**Software**
Programs in computer systems carrying typefaces and other typographic information. They work on the system hardware such as the screen, printer and, at the core, the central processing unit.

**Stereotype**
A duplicate metal plate made from a relief printing plate by taking an impression in a soft material (such as a papier-mâché plate) and then casting the duplicate from this mould. This was often the process for converting a page of set matter into a plate suitable for printing.

**Stone**
The flat surface on which metal type was imposed (laid out) before being tightened up in the *chase* ready for printing or plating.

**Stress**
The angle of thickening across a curved letter. For example, modern faces are distinguished by a pronounced vertical stress, whereas humanist faces have an inclined backward-sloping stress, imitative of a pen-drawn character.

**Swash**
The flourish that may extend a stroke or replace a serif on a letter; characters with fancy flourishes are known as swash letters.

**Tracking**
The spacing standard set between characters in a text. *Photosetting* and digital setting has made it much easier to play with tracking, either "negative" tracking where characters have closer *kerning*, or "positive" tracking whereby a word, line or text is given *letterspacing*.

**Wysiwyg**
What you see is what you get; computer systems that reproduce on screen a working simulation of the graphic information that could be output by the system.

# Notes

**1910**

1 Filippo Marinetti, translated in *Futurismo and Futurismi*, Bompiani, 1986.
2 Filippo Marinetti, translated in *Marinetti: Selected Writings*, edited by R. W. Flint, Secker and Warburg, 1972.
3 For a fuller description of the Russian Futurists, see Susan P. Compton, *The World Backwards: Russian Futurist Books 1912–16*, The British Library, 1978.

**1920**

1 László Moholy-Nagy, in *Staatliches Bauhaus, Weimar, 1919–23*, translated in *Bauhaus 1919–28*, catalogue edited by Herbert Bayer, Walter Gropius and Ise Gropius, The Museum of Modern Art, 1938.
2 Letter to the journalist Antal Nemeth answering a questionnaire: "Until the 1920s my works were experimentations under the influence of the *MA*." Translated in Krisztina Passuth, *Moholy-Nagy*, Thames and Hudson, 1985.
3 "Zeitgemasse Typographie – Ziele, Praxis, Kritik", *Gutenberg Festschrift*, translated in Krisztina Passuth, *Moholy-Nagy*, Thames and Hudson, 1985.
4 From an essay on Cassandre by Henri Mouron, *Baseline*, issue 10.

**1940**

1 Jan Tschichold, "Glaube und Wirklichkeit", *Schweizer Graphische Mitteilungen*, June 1946, translated as "Belief and Reality" in Ruari McLean, *Jan Tschichold: Typographer*, Lund Humphries, 1975.

**1950**

1 Information from *Advertiser's Weekly*, quoted in Kenneth Day, *The Typography of Press Advertisement*, Ernest Benn, 1956.
2 Information from *Printer's Ink*, November 1952, quoted in Kenneth Day, ibid.

**1960**

1 Rodney Mylius, quoted in *Creative Review*, July 1990.

**1970**

1 Adrian Frutiger, *Der Mensch und seine Zeichen*, Weiss Verlag, 1978, translated as *Signs and Symbols: their Design and Meaning*, Studio Editions, 1989.
2 Fernand Baudin, in *Penrose 1978–79, International Review of the Graphic Arts*, volume 71.
3 Ed Rondthaler, quoted in Hugh Aldersey-Williams, *New American Design*, Rizzoli, 1988.

**1980**

1 Matthew Carter, *PC Computing*, January 1989.
2 Grafix National Conference survey, reported in *U&lc*, summer 1991.
3 Matthew Carter, *Communication Arts*, January-February 1989.
4 Edward Fella interview, *Emigre*, number 17.

**1990 . . . and beyond**

1 The survey "Design with Technology", *Communication Arts*, May–June 1991, reported that only 10 per cent of the designers in its sample did not have computers; of these, 90 per cent were about to buy them. Of the users, 75 per cent had Macintosh systems, and the majority used more than twenty different typefaces.
2 This is a dramatic change, confirmed by René Kerfante, managing director of Monotype Typography, at a launch of the corporation's Desktop Solutions, a product aimed at the newly enfranchised hordes of typographers. His company's potential market, he claimed, had gone from a few hundred to "1 to 2 million", and was heading towards "50 to 60 million". He based his expectations partly on the estimates of Microsoft, the powerful software company whose programs are helping to bring graphics and personal computing together; the figures are probably on the conservative side.

# Further reading


Aldersey-Williams, Hugh, *New American Design*, Rizzoli, New York, 1988.

Aldersey-Williams, Hugh, and others, *The New Cranbrook Design Discourse*, Rizzoli, New York, 1991.

Anikst, Mikhail, *Soviet Commercial Design of the Twenties*, Thames & Hudson, London, 1987.

Bartram, Alan, *The English Lettering Tradition*, Lund Humphries, London, 1986.

Baudin, Fernand, *How Typography Works*, Lund Humphries, London, 1989.

Bauhaus Archive and Magdalena Droste, *Bauhaus*, Benedikt Taschen, Cologne, 1990.

Bayer, Herbert, Walter Gropius and Ise Gropius, *Bauhaus*, The Museum of Modern Art, New York, 1938.

Bigelow, Charles, and others, *Fine Print On Type*, Lund Humphries, London, 1988.

Bruckner, D. J. R., *Frederick Goudy*, Harry N. Abrams, New York, 1990.

Carter, Sebastian, *Twentieth Century Type Designers*, Trefoil, London, 1987.

Carter, Sebastian, and others, *Eric Gill: The Continuing Tradition*, The Monotype Recorder, Monotype Corporation, Salfords, 1990.

Compton, Susan P., *The World Backwards: Russian Futurist Books 1912–16*, The British Library, London, 1978.

Day, Kenneth, and others, *Book Typography 1815–1965*, Ernest Benn, London, 1966.

Eason, Ron, and Sarah Rookledge, *Rookledge's International Handbook of Type Designers*, Sarema Press, London, 1991.

Edge, Kevin, *The Art Of Selling Songs*, Futures Publications, London, 1991.

Fenton, Erfert, *The Macintosh Font Book*, Peachpit Press (second edition), Berkeley, California, 1991.

Friedman, Mildred, and others, *De Stijl: 1917–1931 Visions of Utopia*, Walker Arts Center, Minneapolis and Abbeville Press, New York, 1982.

Gaskell, Philip, *A New Introduction to Bibliography*, Oxford University Press, Oxford, 1972.

Gill, Eric, *An Essay on Typography*, Lund Humphries, London, 1988 (facsimile reissue of 1936 edition).

Goudy, Frederic W., *The Alphabet* and *Elements of Lettering*, Bracken Books, London, 1989 (joint edition; originally 1918 and 1942).

Grundberg, Andy, *Brodovitch*, Harry N. Abrams, New York, 1989.

Frutiger, Adrian, *Type, Sign, Symbol*, ABC Verlag, Zürich, 1980.

Frutiger, Adrian, *Signs and Symbols*, Studio Editions, London, 1989.

Heller, Steven, and Seymour Chwast, *Graphic Style: from Victorian to Post-Modern*, Harry N. Abrams, New York, 1988.

Hightower, Caroline, and others, *Graphic Design in America*, Walker Arts Center, Minneapolis, 1989.

Hulton, Pontus, and others, *Futurismo and Futurismi*, Palazzo Grassi/Bompiani, Venice/Milan, 1986.

Hutt, Allen, *The Changing Newspaper*, Gordon Fraser, London, 1973.

Kallir, Jane, *Viennese Design and the Wiener Werkstätte*, Thames & Hudson, London, 1986.

Kelly, Rob Roy, *American Wood Type 1828–1900*, Van Nostrand Reinhold, New York, 1969.

Kery, Patricia Frantz, *Art Deco Graphics*, Thames & Hudson, London, 1986.

Lawson, Alexander, *Anatomy of a Typeface*, Hamish Hamilton, London, 1990.

Lissitzky, El, *About 2 Squares*, Artists Bookworks, Forest Row, East Sussex, 1990 (facsimile reprint with translation of the original Scythian Press edition of 1922).

Lissitzky, El, and Hans Arp, *The Isms Of Art*, Eugen Rentsch Verlag, Zürich, 1925 (reprinted Verlag Lars Müller CH, Baden, 1990).

Lloyd Jones, Linda, and Jeremy Aynsley, *Fifty Penguin Years*, Penguin Books, London, 1985.

McDermott, Catherine, *Street Style: British Design in the 80s*, The Design Council, London, 1987.

McLean, Ruari, *Jan Tschichold: typographer*, Lund Humphries, London, 1975.

McLean, Ruari, *Typography*, Thames & Hudson, 1980.

Meggs, Philip B., *A History of Graphic Design*, Van Nostrand Reinhold, New York, 1983.

Moran, James, *Printing in The Twentieth Century: A Penrose Anthology*, Northwood Publications, London, 1974 (and any of *The Penrose Annual*, published from 1895 for more than 80 years).

Morison, Stanley, *First Principles of Typography*, Cambridge University Press, Cambridge, 1957 (edition of 1930 essay).

Mouron, Henri, *Cassandre*, Rizzoli, New York, 1985.

Müller Brockmann, Josef, *The Graphic Designer and his Design Problems*, Arthur Niggli, Teufen AR, Switzerland, 1983.

Musatti, Riccardo, and others, *Olivetti*, Olivetti, Ivrea, 1958.

Olins, Wally, *Corporate Identity*, Thames & Hudson, London, 1989.

Passuth, Krisztina, *Moholy-Nagy*, Thames & Hudson, London, 1985.

Perfect, Christopher, and Gordon Rookledge, *Rookledge's International Typefinder*, Sarema Press (second edition), London, 1990.

Pincus Jaspert, W., W. Turner Berry and A. F. Johnson, *The Encyclopedia of Typefaces*, Blandford (fourth edition), London, 1970.

Rand, Paul, *A Designer's Art*, Yale University Press, New Haven and London, 1985.

Ruder, Emil, *Typography: a manual of design*, Arthur Niggli, Teufen AR, Switzerland, 1967.

Schweiger, Werner J., *Wiener Werkstätte: Design in Vienna 1903–1932*, Thames & Hudson/Abbeville Press, London and New York, 1984.

Spencer, Herbert, *Pioneers of Modern Typography*, Lund Humphries (second edition), London, 1982.

Spencer, Herbert, *The Liberated Page*, Lund Humphries, London, 1987.

Spiekermann, Erik, *Rhyme & Reason*, H. Berthold AG, Berlin, 1987.

Steinberg, S. H., *Five Hundred Years of Printing*, Penguin Books, London, 1955.

Stone, Sumner, *Typography on the Personal Computer*, Lund Humphries, London, 1991.

Swann, Cal, *Language & Typography*, Lund Humphries, London, 1991.

Thompson, Bradbury, *The Art of Graphic Design*, Yale University Press, New Haven, 1988.

Tisdall, Caroline and Bozzolla, *Futurism*, Thames & Hudson, London, 1977.

Tracy, Walter, *The typographic scene*, Gordon Fraser, London, 1988.

Updike, D. B., *Printing Types*, Harvard University Press, Cambridge, Massachusetts (second edition), 1937.

Wallis, Lawrence W., *Modern Encyclopedia of Typefaces 1960–90*, Lund Humphries, London, 1990.

Wallis, Lawrence W., *A Concise Chronology of Typesetting Developments 1886–1986*, Wynkyn De Worde Society/Lund Humphries, London, 1988.

Wildbur, Peter, *Information Graphics*, Trefoil, London, 1989.

Wozencroft, Jon, *The Graphic Language of Neville Brody*, Thames & Hudson, London, 1988.

Wrede, Stuart, *The Modern Poster*, The Museum of Modern Art, New York, 1988.

Zapf, Hermann, *About Alphabets*, MIT Press, Cambridge, Massachusetts, 1970.

Zapf, Hermann, *Manuale Typographicum: 100 Typographic Pages with Quotations. . .*, MIT Press, Cambridge, Massachusetts, 1970.


## Magazines

*Baseline*, Esselte Letraset, 195-203 Waterloo Road, London SE1, UK.

*Creative Review*, 50 Poland Street, London W1, UK.

*Emigre*, 48 Shattuck Square, no 175, Berkeley, CA 94704-1140, USA.

*Fuse*, 65–69 East Road, London N1, UK.

*Graphis*, 141 Lexington Avenue, New York, NY 10016, USA.

*Idea*, Seibundo-Shinkosha, 1-13-7 Yayoicho, Nakanoku, Tokyo 164, Japan.

*Print*, 104 Fifth Avenue, New York, NY 10011, USA.

*U&lc*, International Typeface Corporation, 2 Hammarskjold Plaza, New York, NY 10017, USA.

## Type catalogues and other information from type manufacturers/distributors

Adobe Systems Inc., 1585 Charleston Road, PO Box 7900, Mountain View, CA 94039-7900, USA.

Berthold, H., AG, Teltowkanalstrasse 1–4, D-1000, Berlin 46, Germany.

Emigre Graphics, 48 Shattuck Square, no 175, Berkeley, CA 94704-1140, USA.

Fontshop, Bergmanstrasse 102, 1000 Berlin 61, Germany; also offices in Belgium, Canada, Germany, Holland, Sweden, UK.

International Typeface Corporation, 2 Hammarskjold Plaza, New York, NY 10017, USA.

Letraset, Esselte Letraset, 195–203 Waterloo Road, London SE1, UK.

Linotype Ltd (Mergenthaler Type Library), Bath Road, Cheltenham, Glos GL53 7LR, UK.

Monotype Typography, Salfords, Redhill, Surrey RH1 5JP, UK.

# Picture credits

The St Bride Printing Library, off Fleet Street, London, generously allowed many items from its vast and important collection to be photographed expressly for this publication. The St Bride Printing Library has been abbreviated to SBPL in the following list.

**12** "1980": SBPL. **14 left** SBPL. **14 right** L. A. Legros & J. C. Grant, *Typographical printing-surfaces*, London, 1916, p. 196. SBPL. **15, 16 and 17** SBPL. **18 left and above right** The Coca-Cola Company, Atlanta, Georgia. **18 below right** The Trustees of the Victoria & Albert Museum, London/© DACS 1992. **20** SBPL.
**22** Courtesy of Jonathan Stephenson, The Rocket Press, Blewbury. **23 above left** American Type Founders Company, *American Specimen Book of Type Styles*, 1912, p. 179. SBPL. **23 above right** *op. cit.*, p. 233. SBPL. **23 below** Robert Besley & Co., *A General Specimen of Printing Types*, circa 1850. SBPL. **25 below** SBPL. **27 above left** Will Bradley, *Springfield Bicycle Club Tournament*, 1895. Poster 20.87 × 14.17 in/53 × 36 cm. Library of Congress, Washington DC. Collection of Miss F. B. Johnston. **27 above right** Will Bradley, *The Chap Book*, 1895. Line block 21.25 × 14 in/54 × 35.6 cm. The Museum of Modern Art, New York. Acquired by exchange. **27 below** Deberny & Peignot, *Spécimen Général*, volume I, 1926. SBPL. **29 above left** Rowntree Mackintosh/© Société des Produits, Nestlé SA, Vevey, Switzerland. **29 above right** Designer unknown, *Victor Cycles*, 1898. Lithograph 28.5 × 19.53 in/72.4 × 49.6 cm. The Museum of Modern Art, New York. Gift of the Lauder Foundation. **29 below left** Deberny & Peignot, *Spécimen Général des Fonderies Deberny et Peignot*, volume 2, undated, p. 116. SBPL. **29 below right** H. Berthold, *Register-Probe*, volume 2, circa 1922, p. N180b. SBPL. **30 below** Österreichisches Museum für Angewandte Kunst, Vienna. **32 left** P. B. Shelley, *A letter from Percy B. Shelley to T. Peacock, July MDCCCXVI*, Essex House Press, London, 1901, p. 8. SBPL. **32 right** Österreichisches Museum für Angewandte Kunst, Vienna. **33** *Doves Press Bible*, I Samuel 13, 1903. SBPL. **34 above** Österreichisches Museum für Angewandte Kunst, Vienna. **35** Österreichisches Museum für Angewandte Kunst, Vienna. **36** Rudhard'fche Giekerei in Offenbach-am-Main, *Behrens Schriften-Initialen und Schmuck nach Zeichnungen von Professor Behrens*, 1902–3, p. 20. SBPL. **37** AEG Archives, Frankfurt-am-Main. **38** *ATF Specimen Book*, *op. cit.*, p. 739. SBPL. **39 above** *op. cit.*, pp. 700–1. SBPL. **39 below left** *op. cit.*, p. 739. SBPL. **39 below right** *op. cit.*, p. 683. SBPL. **41 above left and right** Arxiu Historic de la Ciutat, Barcelona. **41 below** Retrograph Archive, London.
**42** "1910": London Transport Museum/I. M. Imprimit, London. **44** © DACS 1992. **45** Mattioli Collection, Milan/Scala, Florence/© DACS 1992. 15 × 11.8 in/38 × 30 cm. **47 below** Arxiu Historic de la Ciutat, Barcelona. **50 right** Stedelijk Museum, Amsterdam. **51 above left** Lucian Bernhard, *Das ist der Weg sum Frieden*, 1915. Lithograph 33.85 × 22.44 in/86 × 57 cm. Museum für Gestaltung, Zürich. **51 below left** Louis Oppenheim, *Kriesgefangenenheimkehr Auskunft Rat Hilfe*, 1919. Lithograph 34.6 × 22.8 in/88 × 58 cm. Museum für Gestaltung, Zürich. **51 right** Heartfield Archiv, Akademie der Künste zu Berlin/© DACS 1992. **53** Arxiu Historic de la Ciutat, Barcelona. **55 above left** *Typographica*, Summer 1927, number 5 (*A specimen of the Village and other Types cast at the Village Letter Foundery, Marlboro-on-Hudson N.Y. by Fred & Bertha Goudy*), p. 6. SBPL. **55 above right** House of Naylor, London. **55 below** Wm. Atkins (ed.), *The Art and Practice of Printing*, volume I, London, 1932, p. 122. SBPL. **56 above and centre** Courtesy of Jonathan Stephenson, The Rocket Press, Blewbury. **56 below** House of Naylor, London. **57 above left** Oxford University Press. **57 above right** By Permission of The Houghton Library, Harvard University, Cambridge, Massachusetts. **57 below** SBPL **58** *Lead Soldiers on Parade* (Klingspor promotional booklet), undated. SBPL. **60** The Trustees of the Victoria & Albert Museum, London [# E47-1936]. **61 above and below** London Transport Museum.
**64** *Offset Buch und Werbekunst*, number 7, Leipzig, July 1926, p. 381. SBPL/© DACS 1992. **65** *op. cit.* cover. SBPL/© DACS 1992. **66 above** *op. cit.*, p. 399. SBPL/© DACS 1992. **66 below** Bauhaus Archiv, Berlin/Atelier Schneider/© DACS 1992. **67 above and below** *op. cit.*, pp. 397 and 400. SBPL/© DACS 1992. **68** SBPL. **70 left** Mikhail Anikst, *Soviet Commercial Design of the Twenties*, London, 1987, p. 55/Calmann & King Archives, London. **70 right** BFI Stills, Posters and Designs, London/© DACS 1992. **71** BFI Stills, Posters and Designs, London. **73** all Annely Juda Fine Art, London. **77 above** Haags Gemeentemuseum, The Hague/© DACS 1992. **77 below** The Trustees of the Victoria & Albert Museum, London (Library II. RC. M. 11)/© DACS 1992.
**78–79** The Trustees of the Victoria & Albert Museum, London (Library 95.JJ.96)/© DACS 1992. **79 above** Theo van Doesburg and Kurt Schwitters, *Kleine Dada Soirée* [Small Dada Evening], 1922. Lithograph 11.9 × 11.25 in/30.2 × 28.6 cm. The Museum of Modern Art, New York. Gift of Philip Johnson, Jan Tschichold Collection/© DACS 1992. **80** Stedelijk Museum, Amsterdam. **81 above** Haags Gemeentemuseum, The Hague/© DACS 1992. **81 below** Stedelijk Museum, Amsterdam. **83** *Futura* (promotional pamphlet), circa 1930, inside **and front and back cover. SBPL. 85 both** *op. cit.*, SBPL. **86 above** © DACS 1992. **86 below** SBPL. **87 above** *Memphis* (promotional pamphlet), circa 1935, cover back and front. SBPL. **87 below** *Grobe Kabel* (Klingspor Offenbach promotional pamphlet), circa 1928, p. 13. SBPL. **88** Courtesy of Jonathan Stephenson, The Rocket Press, Blewbury. **89 below** SBPL. **90 left** Theo H. Ballmer, *Norm*, 1928. Lithograph 49.9 × 35.6 in/126.7 × 90.5 cm. The Museum of Modern Art, New York. Estée and Joseph Lauder Design Fund. **91** Fortunato Depero Museum, Rovereto/© DACS 1992. **92 left** Ludlow Typefaces, *A specimen book of Matrix Fonts*, circa 1930, p. 156. SBPL. **92 right** *The New Yorker*, 21 February 1925. Cover drawing by Rea Irvin © 1925, 1953 The New Yorker Magazine, Inc. **93 above and below** *The Broadway Series* (American Type Founders promotional pamphlet), 1929. SBPL. pages 94 and 95 House of Naylor, London. **97 above and below left** *Words* (Deberny & Peignot brochure advertising Bifur), circa 1930. SBPL. **97 below right** A. M. Cassandre, *Nord Express*, poster for French Railways, 1927. Lithograph 41.33 × 29.13 in/105 × 74 cm. Museum für Gestaltung, Zürich/© ADAGP, Paris and DACS, London 1992. **99** Collections/Brian Shuel, London.
**100** Retrograph Archive, London/© DACS 1992. **101 above left** Retrograph Archive, London/© DACS 1992. **101 right** *Stahl* (Klingspor Offenbach promotional pamphlet), circa 1939. SBPL. **102 above** *Transito* (Amsterdam Type Foundry promotional booklet), circa 1935. SBPL. **102 below right** SBPL. **105 above** Herbert Matter, *Für schöne Autofahrten die Schweiz, En route pour la Suisse, All roads lead to Switzerland*, 1935. Gravure 39.76 × 25.2 in/101 × 64 cm. Museum für Gestaltung, Zürich. **105 below left** Xanti Schawinksy, *Olivetti*, 1934. Lithograph 21 × 13.75 in/53.3 × 34.9 cm. The Museum of Modern Art, New York. Purchase fund and gift of Mrs Schawinsky. **105 below right** Max Ernst, *Kunsthaus Zürich*, 1934. Letterpress 39.37 × 27.55 in/100 × 70 cm. Museum für Gestaltung, Zürich/© SPADEM/ADAGP, Paris and DACS, London 1992. **107 above left and right** *De Onafhankelijke* (Amsterdam Type Foundry promotional pamphlet), circa 1930, cover and inside page. SBPL. **107 below** *Playbill* (Stephenson Blake & Co. Ltd, Sheffield, promotional pamphlet), 1938, cover. SBPL. **108** *Libra medium and light* (Amsterdam Type Foundry promotional pamphlet), circa 1938. SBPL. **109 above** SBPL. **109 below** *Beton: Anwedungen* (promotional pamphlet), circa 1931. SBPL.
**112–113** *The Peignot: A New Type Drawn by A. M. Cassandre* (Deberny & Peignot promotional booklet), circa 1938. SBPL. **115** House of Naylor, London.
**116–117** The British Library, London. **118** Victor Gollancz Ltd, London. **119 above** Reproduced by permission of Penguin Books Ltd. **119 below left** Royal Institute of British Architects, London. **119 below centre** *The Picture of Dorian Gray by Oscar Wilde*, Tauchnitz Edition, Leipzig, 1908. Private collection, London. **119 below right** *The Albatross Book of Living Prose*, 1947. Private collection, London. **120 right and 121** SBPL. **124** Herbert Bayer, *Our Allies Need Eggs*, 1944. Print 20 × 29.9 in/51 × 76 cm. Museum für Gestaltung, Zürich/© DACS 1992. **125 above left** Ben Shahn, *This is Nazi Brutaility*, 1942. Offset lithograph 37.8 × 28.35 in/96 × 72 cm. Museum für Gestaltung, Zürich © Ben Shahn/DACS, London/VAGA, New York 1992. **125 right and below** © The Upjohn Company & Lester Beall. **126–127** Courtesy Paul Rand, Weston, Connecticut. **129** Max Huber, *Gran premio dell'Autodromo Monza 17 Ottobre 1948*, Offset lithograph 27.56 × 19.29 in/70 × 49 cm. Museum für Gestaltung, Zürich. **131 above left** *Homers Odyssee*, 1953. Verlag Birkhäuser, Basel. **131 above right** *Shakespeares dramatische werke*, 1943. Verlag Birkhäuser, Basel. **131 below** *Young Walter Scott*, 1948; *Dante: The Divine Comedy*, 1949; *The Buildings of England*, 1951. Reproduced by permission of Penguin Books Ltd.
**133** Arthur Phillips, *Computer Peripherals and Typesetting*, H.M.S.O., London, 1968, pp. 452 and 464. SBPL. **134 right and 135 below left** Westvaco, New York. **136** Courtesy Sidney Janis Gallery, New York City/© ADAGP, Paris and DACS, London 1992.
**138** *Banco* (Fonderie Olive, Marseille promotional pamphlet), circa 1955. SBPL. **139 above left** *Mistral* (Fonderie Olive, Marseille promotional pamphlet), circa 1955. SBPL. **139 above right** *Choc* (Fonderie Olive, Marseille promotional pamphlet), circa 1955. SBPL. **139 below** *3 Scriptes* (Fonderie Olive, Marseille promotional pamphlet), 1956. SBPL. **140 centre and below** Courtesy of Jonathan Stephenson, The Rocket Press, Blewbury. **141 above** Paul P. Piech, Porthcawl. **142 left** *Neue Grafik*, 7th issue, September 1966, p. 33. SBPL. **142–3** *Neue Grafik*, 15th issue, March 1963, pp. 54–55. SBPL. **143 above** *Neue Grafik*, 4th issue, December 1959, pp. 22–23. SBPL. **143 below right** Karl Gerstner, *auch Du bist liberal*, 1956. Offset lithograph 50.4 × 35.6 in/128 × 90.5 cm. Museum für Gestaltung, Zürich. **145** Karl Gerstner, *Lokal National International Nationalzeitung*, 1960. Print 50.4 × 35.6 in/128 × 90.5 cm. Museum für Gestaltung, Zürich. **146 above** *Helvetica* (Haas Typefoundry promotional book), undated. SBPL. **147 above** *Neue Haas Grotesk* (Haas Typefoundry promotional booklet), August 1958, front and back cover. SBPL. **149 above** *Univers* (Deberny & Peignot promotional booklet), 1954. SBPL. **150 below left** Retrograph Archive, London. **151 above left and right** Courtesy Franco Grignani, Milan. **152** "1960": ECMA (European Computer Manufacturer Association), *ECMA Standard for the Alphanumeric Character set OCR-B for Optical Recognition*, November 1965. SBPL.
**154–5** Salama-Caro Gallery, London. **155 above** Reproduced by permission of Penguin Books Ltd. **155 below right** *Ad Lib* (American Type Founders Company brochure), circa 1961, cover. SBPL.
**156** Letraset UK Ltd. **157** James Moran (ed.), *Printing in The Twentieth Century: A Penrose Anthology*, London, 1974, pp. 293 and 292. **159 below** DDB Needham Worldwide, New York. **161** *right now Jackie McLean*, 1965; *Jackie McLean "it's time!"*, 1964; *Joe Henderson in 'n out*, 1964. **162 left** The Vintage Magazine Company Ltd, London. **162 right** The Herb Lubalin Study Center of Design and Typography, New York. **163 above and below left** Pentagram Design Ltd, London. **165 above left & 152 detail** Lee Conklin, concert poster for Procol Harum at the Fillmore, 1967. Offset lithograph 21.26 × 14.17 in/54 × 36 cm. Museum für Gestaltung, Zürich. **165 above right** Wes Wilson, concert poster for The Grateful Dead, The Doors and others at the Fillmore, 1966. Offset lithograph 22.5 × 14.7 in/57 × 36

cm. Museum für Gestaltung, Zürich. **165 below left** Victor Moscoso, concert poster for The Doors and others at the Avalon Ballroom, 1967. Offset lithograph 20.5 × 14.17 in/52 × 36 cm. Museum für Gestaltung, Zürich. **165 below right** B. McLean, concert poster for The Yardbirds, The Doors and others, 1967. Offset lithograph 21.26 × 14.17 in/54 × 36 cm. Museum für Gestaltung, Zürich. **167 below left** Total Design, Amsterdam. pages 172 and 173 below Chermayeff & Geismar Inc., New York. **173 above left** The Robert Opie Collection, London. **176–7** Covers of ITC typeface specimen booklets © International Typeface Corporation, New York. Reprinted by permission. **178 above** Cover of *U&lc*® volume 1, number 1 © International Typeface Corporation, New York. Reprinted by permission. **179** DDB Needham Worldwide, New York. **181** Greenberg Associates Inc., New York. **182 and 183** SBPL. **185 above right** Courtesy Pentagram Design Ltd, London. **185 below** Collett Dickinson Pearce, London. **186** "1980": Emigre Graphics, Berkeley, California. **188** © *Arena* (London), July–August 1987, pp. 24–25. © Wagadon Ltd. Reproduced by permission. **189 above** © *i–D* (London), July 1986, pp. 6–7. Reproduced by permission. **189 below** © *i–D* (London), December 1988—January 1989, pp. 32–33. Reproduced by permission. **190 above** The Monotype Corporation plc. **191 above left** Jon Wozencroft, *The Graphic Language of Neville Brody*, London, 1988, p. 26. **191 above right** FontWorks UK, London. **192** © *The Face* (London), February 1986, cover. Reproduced by permission. **193 above** Courtesy Neville Brody, London. **193 below** © *The Face* (London), May 1985, pp. 78–79. Reproduced by permission. **195** English Markell Pockett, London. **196** Bruno Monguzzi, *Photography & the Soviet Union*, for the Kunsthaus, Zürich, 1989. Museum für Gestaltung, Zürich. **197 above left** Uwe Loesch, *That's your problem! Das Kom(m)ödchen*, Düsseldorf, 1989. 33 × 46.85 in/84 × 119 cm. Courtesy Uwe Loesch. **197 above right** Uwe Loesch, *Survival during War*, for Ruhrlandmuseum, Essen, 1990. 33 × 46.85 in/84 × 119 cm. Courtesy Uwe Loesch. **197 below** Vaughan Oliver, London. **199** Studio Odermatt & Tissi, Zürich. **201 left** © MIT Media Lab. **201 right** Institute of Contemporary Arts, London/Steve White. pages 202 to 205 Courtesy Emigre Graphics, Berkeley, California. **206** *Wigwag*, November 1989, pp. 42–43. © The Wigwag Magazine Company, Inc., New York. **207 left above and below** Courtesy Edward Fella, Calarts School of Art, Valencia, California. **207 right** Courtesy April Greiman Inc., Los Angeles, California. *Your Turn My Turn* 3d poster 1983, by April Greiman for the Pacific Design Center, 24 × 36 in/61 × 91.5 cm. **208 and 209** M & Co., New York. **210 and 211 above** Studio Dumbar, The Hague. **211 below** London Transport Museum. **212** "1990": News International, London. **212** "cdefghi": Fontshop International, Berlin. **213** "and beyond": Emigre Graphics, Berkeley, California. **214 and 215** Fontshop and Neville Brody, London. **216 and 217 above** *Beachculture*, April–May 1990, pp. 46–47, 44–45. © *Beach Culture* Magazine, Surfer Publications Inc., San Juan Capistrano, California. **217 below right** © *Domus* (Milan), number 730, September 1991. **219 below** Aurobind Patel and Gunnlaugur S E Briem/News International, London. **220 above left** Gerard Unger, *Typeface Decoder*, Poster for *Fuse 2*, London, 1991. Fontshop International, Berlin. **220 above right** Just Van Rossum, Poster for *Fuse 2*, London, 1991. Fontshop International, Berlin. **221** Design Barbara Butterweck, *Typeface F. DearJohn Poster*®, 1992. Fontshop International, Berlin © 1992 Barbara Butterweck. **222 below and 223** Richard Martin (ed.), *The New Urban Landscape*, Olympia & York Companies (USA), pp. 68–69, Contents. **225 above** Jake Tilson, *Atlas*, London. **226 above** *Rolling Stone*, 6 September 1990, pp. 58–59. **226 below** *Rolling Stone*, 1 November 1990, p. 66–67. **227 above right** Courtesy April Greiman Inc., Los Angeles, California. *Sci-Arc Summer Programs*, 1991, by April Greiman & Sean Adams, for Southern California Institute of Architecture, 7.5 × 11 in/19.1 × 27.9 cm, 160 pages. **227 below** Courtesy April Greiman Inc., Los Angeles, California. *From the edge: Sci-Arc Student Workbook*, 1991, by April Greiman & Sean Adams, for Southern California Institute of Architecture, 7.5 × 11 in/19.1 × 27.9 cm, 160 pages. **228 and 229** Emigre Graphics, Berkeley, California.

# Index

Numbers in *italics* refer to captions


Abstract art 158
Adobe Systems Inc. *186*, *190*, 198, 232, 251
Adobe Type Manager 198
Advertising *24*, 26, 106, *111*, 123, *138*, 148, 158, 163, *178*, *184*, *192*, *224*
AEG 38
Agha, Mehemed Fehmy 104
Aicher, Otl *173*
Albatross editions *119*
Albers, Josef *67*
Albion Press *16*
Aldridge, Alan *154*, 164
*Alien* *181*
Allusive typography 160
American Bankers' Association *167*
American Type Founders 22, 24, 38, 153, *154*, 176
*Amore Baciami* *194*
Anderson, Charles Spencer 210
Animated typography *194*, *224*
Animation 134
Annual reports 210
Apollinaire, Guillaume *46*, 52
Apple Macintosh 184, 188, 202
Architecture, typography as 133
*Arena* *188*
Art Deco *90*, 94, 210
Art directors, emergence of 10
Art Nouveau *24*, 26, 164
Arts and Crafts Movement 18, 31
Asymmetry 72, 82
AT&T *174*
Atex system 187
Audi *178*
Authoritarian type *190*
*Avant Garde* *162*, 176

Baines, Phil *224*
Ballmer, Theo *90*, 102, 140
Barclays Bank *224*
Barnbrook Jon *224*
Basel School of Design 182
Baseline 248
Basic packaging *172*
Baudin, Fernand 174
Bauhaus 63, 74, 99, 102, 140
Bayer, Herbert *65*, 72, 74, *100*, 104, 123
*Beach Culture* *216*
Beall, Lester 123, *125*, 126
Beggarstaff Brothers (William Nicholson and James Pryde) *28*
Behrens, Peter 36
Benguiat, Ed 176
Benson & Hedges *184*
Bentley, Farrell and Burnett *154*
Benton, Linn Boyd 16, *22*, 24
Benton, Morris Fuller 24, 38, *92*
Berlewi, Henryk 84
Bernbach, Bill 123, 158
Bernhard, Lucien *51*
Berthold foundry *28*, 180, 251
Bezier curves 248
*BIF & ZF + 18* *42*, *46*
Bigelow, Charles *190*, 198
Bill, Max 102, 130, 140, 144
Binder, Joseph 123
Bitmap *186*, *198*, *202*, *228*, 248
Bitstream *190*, 194
Black-letter 58, *101*, *228*, 248
*Blast* *58*
Blue Note records 160
Bobstraphic/Autologic *174*
Body type 248
Boggeri, Antonio, and Studio Boggeri 106, *128*
Book typography 88, 114, 128, 164
Bradley, Will *26*, 28
Brignall, Colin *156*
Brodovitch, Alexey 104, 112
Brody, Neville *186*, *188*, *190*, *192*, 200, *214*
Burliuk, Vladimir and David 46, 48, *49*
Burne-Jones, Edward *20*
Burns, Aaron 176
Butterweck, Barbara *221*

Calligraphy 164, *228*
Calligrams *46*, 52
Carlu, Jean 123, *150*
Carnase, Tom *176*
Carra, Carlo 44
Carson, David *216*
Carter, Matthew *170*, *174*, 187, *190*, 194
Cassandre, A. M. (Adolphe Jean-Marie Mouron) *62*, 94, 104, *106*, 112
Cathode ray tube, generating type with use of 248
CBS *134*, *184*
CD-ROM 248
Characters, analysis of constituent parts 230
Charles de Gaulle Airport *175*
Chase 248
Chéret, Jules *18*, 26
Cigarette advertising *184*
Cinema and typography 44, 70, 82, 134
Classical typography 84, 99, 214
Classification of type 10, 232
Cobden-Sanderson, Thomas 31
Coca-Cola 18
Collage 164, *188*
Cold-metal setting 14, *20*, 153, 248
Collett Dickenson Pearce *184*
Colour, type and *136*, 184, 248
Commercials *224*
Composition 13, 14, *15*, 248
Composing stick *20*
Compugraphic 153, 180
Computer graphics *181*
Computers, survey into graphic designers' use of 194
Conceptual art *200*
Condensed type 248
Conklin, Lee *164*
Constructivism 46, *71*, *184*, *196*
Consumerism 158
Container Corporation of America 123
Cooper, Muriel *200*
Cooper, Oswald B. *158*
Copy preparation 174
Copyright in type design 176
Corporate identity 134, *163*, *172*, 210
Cranbrook Academy of Art *186*, 204, 218
Craw, Freeman *154*
Crosfield 194
Crouwel, Wim 166
Cubism 43
Cunard *163*
Cut, description of typeface as 248
Czechoslovakia 84

Dada 48, 76, *78*, *104*, *136*
Davis, Paul *206*
Deberny & Peignot 94, 112, 148
Deck, Barry 204
Deconstruction *186*, *206*, 218, *221*
Defamiliarisation 76, *221*
Deighton, Len *154*
Depero, Fortunato *90*
Derrick, Robin *188*
Desktop publishing 154, 174, 188, 213, 248
Design studios 160, 188, 210, 213
De Stijl 50, 68, 76, 140
Devetsil 84
Didone group of typefaces 237
Digital revolution 190, 213, 248
Digital type *170*, 180, *186*, 198
Direct entry typesetting 187
DiSpagna, Tony *176*
Does, Bram de *174*
Doesburg, Theo van *42*, 50, 68, 76
*Domus* *216*
Dots per inch, output in 248
Dot matrix display 166, *211*
Doves Press 20, 31
Doyle Dane Bernbach 158, *178*
Drawing type, changes in 180
Drenttel Doyle Partners *223*
Druksels *80*
Dry transfer (see also transfer lettering and Letraset) 248
Duchamp, Marcel *136*
Duffy, Joe 210
Dumbar, Gert *210*

Eastern European graphics *221*
Eckersley, Tom 128
Eclecticism in design 214
Egyptian: see slab serif
Electronic imaging equipment 194
Electrotype 24, 248
Em (unit of typographic measurement) 248
Emigration of designers *100*, 123
Emigre Graphics and *Emigre* magazine *186*, 200, 218, *228*, 251
English Markell Pockett *194*
Enschedé en Zonen 194
Ephemera, printed *224*
Ernst, Max *104*
European Computer Manufacturers' Association 166
Excoffon, Roger 138, *168*
Explosion of typographic interest 187
Expressive typography *162*, 200
Extended/expanded type 248

*Face, The* *186*, *192*, 200
Families of type 24, 148, *190*, 248
Fanzines 184
Fashion in typography 200
Fella, Edward *186*, 204
Fillmore posters *164*
Fleckhaus, Willi *162*, 164
Fletcher, Alan 160, *163*
*Fleuron, The* 84, *89*
Fonderie Olive 138
Font/fount 248
Fontographer program 204, *228*
Fontshop 251
Forbes, Colin 160, *163*
*For Reading Out Loud* *75*
Founders'/foundry type 246
Foundry 248
Fournier, Pierre Simon *89*
Fraktur *101*
Frej, David 204
*from the edge* *226*
Frutiger, Adrian *132*, 140, 148, 166, *170*, 172, *175*
Furniture (page elements) 248
*Fuse* *213*, *214*
Futurism 43, *90*; Russian Futurism 46 *49*

Galley 248
Games, Abram 128
Garalde group of typefaces 234
Garamond, Claude 232
Geometric type *67*, *101*, *162*, 172, 216
Gerstner, Karl *143*, *144*
Gill, Bob 160, *163*
Gill, Eric *92*, 94, *120*
Glaser, Milton *154*
Glyphic faces 40, 244
Godfrey, Neil *184*
Golden, Robert *134*
Golfball typewriter 154
Gollancz, publishers *118*
Goodhue, Bertram *22*, 26
Goudy, Frederic *30*, 40, 54
Granjon, Robert *170*
Graphical user interface 188
Grasset, Eugène *24*, 28
Grateful Dead *164*
Great Depression 99, 104
Greiman, April 182, *207*, *226*
Grid theory *90*, 102, 140, *142*, 148, *167*, *173*, *182*
Griffith, Chauncey *174*
Grignani, Franco *150*
Grotesque, lineale (sans serif) group of typefaces 240
Gropius, Walter 63, 104
Gutenberg, Johannes 9, 13, *15*, 233

Haas foundry 144
Half-tones in printing 248
Hamilton, Richard 158
Hand lettering *226*
Hand press *16*
Handsetting 13, *102*, 118, 184
Handwriting 174, *228*
*Harper's Bazaar* 104
Hardware (computer) 248
Harrison, Oliver *194*
Heartfield, John 48, *87*
Hell typesetting company 153, 180, 198
Henrion, F.H.K. 128
High-resolution output 188, 196, 202
High-resolution television 216
Hinting, adjustment in type drawing by 198
Hitler, Adolf *101*
Hofmann, Armin 182
Hoffman, Edouard 140, 144
Holmes, Kris *190*, 198
Holzer, Jenny *200*
Hori, Allen 204
Hot-metal setting 14, 40, 136, 184, 248
Huber, Max *128*
Humanist group of typefaces 22, 233
Humour with type 158
Huszár, Vilmos 50, *80*

IBM 123, *135*, 154, 188
*I-d* *188*, 200
Ikarus type drawing system 180
*Independent, The* *214*
*Indiana, Robert* *154*
Industrial Revolution 13
Information design 160
Inkjet printing 174
Inkspread *170*, *174*
Inline/outline 248

Inscription lettering 136, *175*
International Typeface Corporation (ITC) *170*, 176, 194, 251
International Style (see also Swiss Style) 138, *172*
Intertype machine 52
*Interview 222*
*Isms of Art, The (Die Kunstismen) 72*
Irony in design *188*, *206*
Italy 106
Itten, Johannes 63

Jenson, Nicolas 22, 24, 233
Johns, Bethany *208*
Johnston, Edward 54, 58
Jones, Terry *188*, 200
Jost, Heinrich *98*
*Jugend* magazine *40*
Junoy, J. M. *46*
Justification 248

Kaden, Joel *170*, *176*
Kalman, Tibor *208*, *222*
Karow, Peter 180
Kaye, Tony *224*
Keedy, Jeffery 204, *228*
Kelmscott Press *17*
Keller, Ernst 102, 140
Kerning *168*, 170, 249
Koch, Rudolf 58, *87*, *101*, 136
Krone, Helmut *178*

Lane, Allen 164
Lange, Gunter Gerhard 180
Lanston, Tolbert *14*
Lardent, Victor 114
Laser printing 174, *190*, 196, 249
Layered typography *200*, *223*
Leading between lines 249
Legibility 10, 26, *89*, 99, 106, 118, 124, 164, *170*, 171, 200, 216, *221*, *228*, 249
Leonni, Leo 123
Letraset 150, 154, *156*, 251
Letterpress printing 184
Letterspacing 171, 249
Licensing type design 176, 194
Lichtenstein, Roy 158
Licko, Zuzana *202*, 204, *213*, *228*
Ligatures *152*, *178*, 249
Lineale (also called sans serif) groups of typefaces 240–3
Linofilm 150
Linotype 118, 150, *168*, *174*, *175*, 187, 194, 232, 249, 251
Linotype linecaster 13, *15*, 16, 52, 54
Lissitsky, El 46, *62*, *72*, 74
Lithography 26, 249
Loesch, Uwe *196*
Logotypes *18*, *134*, *163*
London & North Eastern Railway *120*
London Underground 58
Low-resolution output *186*, 196, 198, *202*, *224*
Lubalin, Herb *152*, 160, *162*, *176*
Lubensky, Dean *208*
Ludlow machine 52
Lupi, Italo *216*

M & Co. *208*
Machine-readable characters 166
Macintosh computer, see Apple Macintosh
Magazines 14, *162*, 164, 184, 200, *216*, *228*
Magnetic inks *167*
Malevich, Kasimir 46, 72
Manutius, Aldus *88*, 232
Mardersteig, Giovanni *88*, *119*, 128
Marinetti, Filippo Tommaso 43
Marber, Romek *154*
Mass communication 118
Masters, type drawings as 172
Matrix/matrices 14, *16*, 52, 249
Matter, Herbert 102, 123
Maxphoto 171
Mayakovsky, Vladimir 46, 48, *49*, *62*, *71*, *75*
McCarthy, Marlene *208*
McCoy, Katherine 204
McDonald's hamburger chain *134*
McLean, B. *164*
Measurements in typography, comparison of systems of 230
Mechano Faktur 84
Media Lab, The, at Massachusetts Institute of Technology 218
Mergenthaler, Ottmar 16, 18
*Merz 76*
Metaphor *163*, 188, *221*
Middleton, Robert Hunter *106*
Miedinger, Max 144
Miles, Reid 160
Minimalism in type and typography *167*, 172
Ministry of Information 128
*Mise en Page* by A. Tolmer 96, *111*
Mixed media sculpture 154
Mobil *172*
Modernism *52*, *98*, 104, 123, 130, 172, *196*
Modernisme *40*, 50
*Modern Review* 214
Moholy-Nagy, László 63, 68, 104
Monguzzi, Bruno *196*
Monotype character caster 13, *14*, *16*, 18, 54
Monotype Corporation 92, 114, 130, *132*, 150, 168, 171, *190*, 249, 251
Morison, Stanley 84, *89*, 114, 130, 168
Morris, William 11, *12*, 18, *20*
Moscoso, Victor 164
Moser, Koloman *30*, 32
Müller-Brockmann, Joseph 142, 182
Multimedia *200*, 213
Multiple masters 232, 249
Mylius, Rodney 158

National Socialism 99
*Neue Grafik 142*, 144
Neutrality in type *188*
Neue Sachlichkeit 31
Newspapers 14, 114, 118, 136, 187, 214, 216, *218*

New Transitional Serif group of typefaces 238
*New Typography, The (Die Neue Typographie) 68*, 82, 99
*New Urban Landscape, The 223*
New Wave typography 182
New York as design centre 123
*New York Tribune* 16
*New Yorker, The 92*
Nicholas, Robin *190*
Nike *192*
Notebook computers *228*
Noucentisme 50, *52*
*Nova* 164
Novarese, Aldo 166

Oberman, Emily *208*
Objective design 144
Odermatt, Siegfried *198*
*Offset Buch und Werbekunst 65*
*Of Two Squares 72*
Office of War Information 123
Offset lithography 172
Oliver, Vaughan *196*
Olivetti 104
Olympic Games *163*, *173*
Oppenheim, Louis *51*, *87*
Optical character recognition (OCR) 166, 249
Own-brand products 172
*Oz* 164

Packaging *172*
Page description languages for computer typography 200
Pagowski, Andrzej *221*
Pantographic punchcutter 13, *14*, 16, 249
Paolozzi, Eduardo 158
Patel, Aurobind *218*
Penguin Books *119*, 128, *154*, 164
Pentagram 160, *163*, *184*
Personal computers 187
Perspective *128*, *132*
Photocomposition *102*, 118, 120, *132*, 148, 150, 153, 170, 174, 214, 249
Photocopiers 164, *216*
Photography 160, 164, 178, 214
Photogravure 26
Photo Lettering Inc. 176
Photomontage *51*, 68, *87*
Photo Typositor *156*
Pica (unit of typographic measurement) 249
Picabia, Francis 50
Pictograms *173*
Piech, Paul Peter *140*
Pierpont, Frank Hinman *56*
Piracy of type 176
Pirelli *163*
Plakatstijl *51*, 82, *102*
Plantin, Christophe 114
Points system of measurement 40, 171, 249
Poland 84, *221*
Pop Art *154*, 158
Posters 26, 94, 123, 127, 184, *221*

Post-production in film and video 216
PostScript, page description language 200, *202*, 249
Press, definition of 249
Prince, Edward 20, 31
Private press movement 18
Procol Harum *164*
Program (computer) 249
Propaganda 99, 123
Protest typography 164
Psychedelia 164
Public domain type design 196
Public information systems 166
Punch 14, 249
Punk graphics 184
Puns in typography *49*, 108, *152*, *221*

R/Greenberg Associates *181*
Rand, Paul 123, *126*, *135*
Random elements in design *216*
Rap music 214
Raster image processor (RIP) 250
Readability 10, *89*, 164, 171, *182*, 200, *214*, 216, *228*, 249
Reading research 171, 216
Record sleeves 160
Reid, Jamie *184*
Renner, Paul 82
Resolution, see screen resolution
Revival typefaces 60, *98*, 114
Rhythm 127
Robinson Lambie-Nairn *194*
Rock concerts, tyopgraphy for 164
Rodchenko, Aleksandr 46, 68, *71*, 76
Rogers, Bruce 56
*Rolling Stone 226*
Rondthaler Ed 176
Rossum, Just van *213*, *221*
Ruder, Emil 142, 182

Sainsbury supermarkets *172*
Sampling type by scanning 210
Sans serif 38, 82, 99, 108, 112, 136, 144, 240–3
Scale in typography 164
Scanners (for computer input) 190, 210
Schawinsky, Xanti 104
Scher, Paula 180, *184*
Schmidt, Joost 74, 106
Schmoller, Hans 130
Schwitters, Kurt 48, 76
*Scope 125*
Screen display 166, 187, *208*, 216, *226*
Screen resolution *186*, *202*, 208
Script group of typefaces *138*, 245
Secession movement 31
Second World War 123
Self-conscious typography 68, *150*, 184
Serifs *186*, 196
Sex Pistols *184*
Shadow *123*
Shahn, Ben *124*

Shredded Wheat *163*
Signage *172*, *175*, *211*
Simon, Oliver 130
Single alphabet experiments *67*, *68*, 72, *79*, 82, *108*, 112, 124, 166
Slab serif *87*, 108, 239
Soffici, Ardengo 43, *46*
Software for type design and setting 213, 250
Southern California Institute of Architecture *226*
Soviet Union 74
Spain, Alan *154*
Stan, Tony *168*
Stempel foundry 136, *168*
Stenberg, Vladimir and Georgy *71*
Stencil faces *102*, *106*
Stereotype 13, 250
Stephenson Blake foundry *106*
Stone (printer's term) 250
Stone, Sumner *186*
Stress (angle of accent) 250
Studio Dumbar *210*
Stylised group of typefaces 246
Suhrkamp 164
*Superman 181*
Surrealism 104
Sutnar, Ladislav 84
Symmetry 99
Swash letters 24, 99, 250
Swift, Ian *188*
Swiss Style *90*, 128, 138, *175*, 182

Tag Heuer *224*
Talking Heads *208*
Tauchnitz editions *119*
Technology and tradition 213
Teige, Karel 84
Television, typographic implications of 134, *194*, 208, 216, *224*
Television, viewing trends for 218
Telingater, Solomon *102*
*Terminator Line, The 224*
*Times, The* 14, 114, *218*
Thompson, Bradbury 123, 124, *134*
Tilson, Jake *224*
Time (as a constituent of typographic communication) 208, *216*
Tissi, Rosemarie *198*
Titles, film and television *181*, *194*
Tolmer, Albert 96, *111*
Tower of London commercial *224*
Tracking (inter-letter spacing) 250
Traditionalism 168, 190, *206*
Transfer lettering 150, 154
Transitional group of typefaces 236
Transport systems *211*
Tschichold, Jan *68*, 82, 99, *102*, *106*, 120, 128, 130, *152*, *168*
*Twen 162*, 164
Typefaces
Akzidenz Grotesk/Standard *12*, *28*, 144, 184, 241

Albertus 196, 244
Alphabet 26, 124
Alternate Gothic 240
American Typewriter *170*, *176*, 246
Amerigo 196
Antique Olive 138, *152*, *168*
Antique Number Seven *12*
Augustea 244
Auriol *28*
Avant Garde *152*, 176, *178*, 242
Baby Teeth *156*
Banco 138
Baskerville *88*, 99, 126, 172, 236
Bayer type *100*
Bell 99
Bell Centennial *170*, *174*
Bell Gothic *174*
Bembo *88*, 234
Beton *98*, *108*, 239
Bifur 94
Bodoni 20, *88*, 144, 172, 237
Bookman/Antique Old Style 92, 180, 238
Broadway *92*, 96, 246
Caledonia 172, 236
Calypso *138*
Caslon 144, 236
Caslon Old Face 234
Caxton Old Face *176*
Centaur *42*, 56, 233
Century *12*, *22*, 144, 238
Chambord *138*
Chancery *170*
Charter *190*
Chaucer *16*, *20*
Cheltenham *12*, *22*, 24, 144, 238
Choc *132*, *138*, 245
Clarendon *12*, *22*, 239
Clearface *38*
Cloister Old Style 24, 233
CMC7 *167*
Cooper Black *158*, 246
Copperplate Gothic *30*, *40*, 232, 246
Corona 118
Coronet 245
Countdown *156*
Dearjohn *221*
Decoder *221*
Demos 198
Diane 138
Didi 237
Doves 31
Dynamo *108*
*E13B 166*
*Eckmann 30*, *34*, 246
ECMA *152*
Emperor *202*
Endeavour *32*
Erbar 82, 242
Eurostile 166, 242
Excelsior 118, 172, 238
Felicity 94
Flixel *221*
Flora 198
Folio 241
Fournier *89*, 236
Franklin Gothic 38, 240
Frutiger *170*, *175*
Futura 82, 108, 124, 144, 216, 242
Galliard *170*
Garamond 99, 144, *168*, 172, 180, 234, 236
Gill Sans 92, *94*, 243
Golden *16*
Goudy Sans 243
Goudy Old Style *42*, 56, *56*, 234
Granjon 234
Grasset *26*
Helvetica 28, *132*, *142*, 172, 184, 241
Horley Old Style 233
Imprint *42*, 54, *56*
Independent *106*
Ionic 118
Irvin *92*
ITC Fat Face *176*
Janson 99
Jenson 22, 54, 233
Kabel *87*, 242
Keedy *228*
Kennerley 54, 233
Latin 244
Libra *108*
Lucida 198
Matrix Printer 246
Maximilian Antiqua *58*
Melior *132*, 136, *141*
Memphis *87*, 239
Metro 242
Mistral 138, 245
Motor *108*
Neue Haas Grotesk (see Helvetica)
New Alphabet *167*
New Johnston 60
News Gothic *30*, *38*, 240
Nimrod *190*
Oakland Six *202*
OCR-A/B *152*, 166, *216*, 247
Opticon 118
Optima *132*, 136, *141*, 172, 196, 243
Palatino *132*, 136, *141*, 172, 234
Paragon 118
Pascal 243
Parisian 247
Peignot *98*, 112, 247
Pellucida 198
Perpetua 94, 236
Plantin *56*, 144, 234
Playbill *106*, *164*, 239
Poliphilus *88*
Praxis 198
Profil *123*
Rockwell 239
Ronaldson *176*
Sabon *152*, *168*, 234
Serifa 239
Serif Gothic *176*
Snell Roundhand 245
Souvenir 176
Spartan 144
State *214*
Steel *101*
Stencil *106*
Stone *186*
Stop 247
Tea Chest 247
Template Gothic 204
Times Millenium *213*, *218*
Times New Roman 114, 172, 234
Tiffany *176*
Torino 237
Totally Gothic *228*
Trade Gothic 240
Transito *102*
Trinité *174*
Troy *16*, *20*
Typeface Two *190*
Typeface Six *191*
Underground *60*, 92
Univers *132*, 148, 184, 241
Variex *213*, *228*
Venus *82*, 241
Walbaum 237
Weiss 234
Zapf Chancery 245
Typesetting bureaux 213
Typewriter 13, 106, 126, 154, 164
*Typografische Monatsblätter 170*, *182*
Typographer, concept of the 54, 188
Typographical revolution 43
*Typographische Gestaltung*, 99
Typography, definition of 9, 31

*U&lc* 176, *178*
Uher, Edmund *102*, 118
Uhertype *102*
Ulm school 142
Uncial script *108*
Underground publishing 164
Unger, Gerard 196, 198, *221*

VanderLans, Rudy *186*
Vernacular *104*, 184, *211*
Virtual reality 213
*Visible Language* 206
Visible Language Workshop, Massachusetts Institute of Technology *200*, 218
Visualisation 188
*Vogue* 104
Volkswagen advertising 158
Vorticism 46
Vox, Maximilien 10, 232

Walker, Emery 20, 31
Warhol, Andy 158
Weiden & Kennedy *192*
Weight *114*
Weingart, Wolfgang *170*, 182, 200
Weiss, Rudolf *87*
Werkman, Hendrik 78, *80*, 171
*Westvaco Inspirations* 124, *134*
Wiener Werkstäte *30*, 31, *34*
*WigWag 206*
Wilson, Wes *164*
Wood letter 26, *106*, *154*, *184*, *226*
Woodward, Fred *226*
Word image 171
Words-in-freedom 43
*Works of Geoffrey Chaucer, The 12*, *20*
Wormser, Jimmy *184*
Wyman, Lance *163*
Wyndham Lewis, Percy 46
Wysiwyg (what you see is what you get) 250

X-height 118, 146

*Zang Tumb Tumb* 43
Zapf, Hermann *132*, 136, *141*, *170*
Zaum 49
Zdanevitch, Ilya 48, *49*
Zwart, Piet *76*, 78, *80*, *210*